D0933760

First Canadian Edition

entrepreneurship

A PROCESS PERSPECTIVE

ROBERT A. BARON

Wellington Professor of
Management

Lally School of Management
& Technology

Rensselaer Polytechnic
Institute

Troy, NY

SCOTT A. SHANE

Professor of Economics and
Entrepreneurship

Weatherhead School of
Management

Case Western Reserve
University

Cleveland, OH

A. REBECCA REUBER

Associate Professor of
Strategic Management and
Entrepreneurship

Rotman School of
Management

University of Toronto

Toronto, ON

THOMSON

NELSON

Australia   Canada   Mexico   Singapore   Spain   United Kingdom   United States

THOMSON

NELSON

Entrepreneurship, First Canadian Edition

by Robert A. Baron, Scott A. Shane, and A. Rebecca Reuber

Associate Vice President, Editorial Director:
Evelyn Veitch

Editor-in-Chief, Higher Education:
Anne Williams

Publisher:
Veronica Visentin

Marketing Manager:
Ann Byford

Developmental Editor:
Joanne Sutherland

Photo Researcher:
Indu Ghuman

Permissions Coordinator:
Indu Ghuman

Content Production Manager:
Jaime Smith

Production Service:
GEX Publishing Services

Copy Editor:
Mariko Obokata

Proofreader:
GEX Publishing Services

Indexer:
GEX Publishing Services

Manufacturing Coordinator:
Joanne McNeil

Design Director:
Ken Phipps

Interior Design:
Word and Image

Cover Design:
Johana Liburd

Cover Image:
Romilly Lockyer/Getty Images, William Sallaz/Getty Images, and Brand X Pictures/Fotosearch

Compositor:
GEX Publishing Services

Printer:
Courier Kendallville

COPYRIGHT © 2008, by Nelson, a division of Thomson Canada Limited.

Adapted from Entrepreneurship, First Edition by Robert Baron & Scott Shane, published by South-Western, part of the Thomson Corporation. Copyright ©2005 by South-Western

Printed and bound in the United States of America
1   2   3   4   09   08   07

For more information contact Nelson, 1120 Birchmount Road, Toronto, Ontario, M1K 5G4. Or you can visit our Internet site at http://www.nelson.com

Statistics Canada information is used with the permission of Statistics Canada. Users are forbidden to copy this material and/or redisseminate the data, in an original or modified form, for commercial purposes, without the expressed permissions of Statistics Canada. Information on the availability of the wide range of data from Statistics Canada can be obtained from Statistics Canada's Regional Offices, its World Wide Web site at <http://www.statcan.ca>, and its toll-free access number 1-800-263-1136.

ALL RIGHTS RESERVED. No part of this work covered by the copyright herein may be reproduced, transcribed, or used in any form or by any means—graphic, electronic, or mechanical, including photocopying, recording, taping, Web distribution, or information storage and retrieval systems—without the written permission of the publisher.

For permission to use material from this text or product, submit a request online at www.thomsonrights.com

Every effort has been made to trace ownership of all copyrighted material and to secure permission from copyright holders. In the event of any question arising as to the use of any material, we will be pleased to make the necessary corrections in future printings.

Library and Archives Canada Cataloguing in Publication

Baron, Robert A
  Entrepreneurship / Robert A. Baron, Scott A. Shane, A. Rebecca Reuber. -- 1st Canadian ed.

Includes index.
ISBN-13: 978-0-17-610334-7
ISBN-10: 0-17-610334-1

  1. Entrepreneurship. 2. New business enterprises. I. Shane, Scott Andrew, 1964- II. Reuber, Allison Rebecca, 1956- III. Title.

HB615.B37 2007   338'.04   C2006-905024-4

To Rebecca, Randy, Paul, Jessica, and Ted—the people who make my life what, almost always, it is—a journey through warm, golden sunshine; and to Richard, who, when he was needed, showed the strength I always knew he had
(RAB)

And

To Lynne for supporting me in writing this book, as well as everything else I do; and to Hannah for giving my life a central purpose
(SAS)

And

To my daughters, Julia, Allison, and Fiona Macleod, and my parents, Grant and Peggy Reuber, with love and thanks
(ARR)

BRIEF CONTENTS

CONTENTS

PREFACE

IN SEARCH OF THE IDEAL BALANCE

It almost never fails: at a cocktail party or other social gathering, someone we have just met asks, "What do you do for a living?" When we tell them that we are professors, their next question is usually something like "What do you teach?" When we reply "entrepreneurship," many seem truly fascinated, and they soon make it clear *why* they find this information so intriguing: in their eyes, entrepreneurs are a truly remarkable group—modern-day versions of the mythical character who could spin straw into gold. Instead of starting with straw, though, our new acquaintances assume that entrepreneurs begin with dreams and ideas and spin these into gold—new companies that quickly make them fabulously wealthy. In short, many people we meet are convinced that teaching courses about entrepreneurship, and doing research on it, is a very exciting career.

We are certainly not going to argue with that conclusion! We all ardently believe that entrepreneurship is a fascinating topic. In fact, it is our personal commitment to the field of entrepreneurship that led us to write this book. More specifically, we believe that in recent years, the field has made rapid progress toward the goal of understanding entrepreneurship as a process, and that this progress, in turn, has yielded important implications for assisting entrepreneurs in their efforts to create new ventures. It was only a small step from these beliefs to asking ourselves the following question: "Could we write a new text that would accurately reflect these changes—a text that would emphasize the growing sophistication and usefulness of our field?" Being optimists by nature (!), we concluded that it was worth a try, and the result is the text you are about to read.

Once we decided to write this book, we immediately realized that we needed a clear strategy for reaching our goals—for preparing a text that would represent the field of entrepreneurship in an accurate, comprehensive, and up-to-date manner. We'll describe this strategy, and the specific steps we took to implement it, here. Before doing so, however, we feel that it is important to comment briefly on several basic principles that have guided our thinking throughout this project.

I. OUR GUIDING PRINCIPLES

Here is an overview of the principles that have guided our efforts in writing this book:

A. Entrepreneurship is a process. We believe that recently the field has come to view entrepreneurship as an ongoing *process* rather than as a single event (e.g., founding of a company or recognition of an opportunity). We reflect this growing consensus by focusing on the entrepreneurial process as it unfolds through several distinct phases:

- **Generation of an Idea for a New Business and/or Recognition of an Opportunity**

- **Assembly of Resources (Financial, Human, Information) Needed to Develop the Opportunity**

- ◼ **Launching the New Venture**
  - • Managing Growth
  - • Harvesting the Rewards

While the divisions between these phases are frequently far from distinct, sometimes occur simultaneously, and the cycle often repeats itself even within specific companies, we also believe that entrepreneurs' efforts to start new ventures generally follow this basic process. Thus, this book, too, adopts this sequence and consistently presents a process view of entrepreneurship.

B. At each phase of the process, *individual-level* variables, group or *interpersonal-level* variables, and *societal-level* variables all play a role. Until recently, the field of entrepreneurship was marked by a continuing debate over the following question: In studying the entrepreneurial process, should we focus on the entrepreneur (e.g., this person's skills, abilities, talents, motives, traits, etc.), group-level variables (e.g., information provided by other persons; relations with cofounders, customers, venture capitalists, etc.), or on the societal context in which the entrepreneur operates (e.g., government policies, technology, economic conditions)? We view this question as largely unnecessary because during each phase of the entrepreneurial process, all three types of variables play a role.

For instance, consider the question of opportunity recognition. Certainly, this process occurs in the minds of specific persons and reflects the impact of individual-level variables such as a person's existing knowledge and unique life history. But recognition of opportunities cannot occur unless something that is potentially profitable emerges from ever-changing technological, societal, and economic conditions—societal-level factors. Further, other people with whom the entrepreneur has contact—friends, associates, or even figures in the mass media—are often important sources of information and may play a key role in opportunity recognition (group-level factors). In short, all three levels of analysis (individual, group, societal) are relevant and must be considered in order to fully understand opportunity recognition. **We suggest that the same is true for every other phase of the entrepreneurial process**; in other words, individual-level, group-level, and societal-level factors interact to influence every action and every decision taken by entrepreneurs. Consequently, all three levels of analysis will be represented throughout the book.

C. There is no split or tension between theory and practise; on the contrary, they are two sides of the same coin. The field of entrepreneurship has a dual nature: on the one hand, it seeks greater understanding of the process—how it unfolds and the many factors that shape it and determine entrepreneurs' success. On the other hand, it is concerned with providing entrepreneurs with the practical information and skills they need in order to reach their goals. Is there any "disconnect" between these two goals? In our view, absolutely not! It is a well-established principle that in almost all fields, systematic knowledge and increased understanding are necessary for successful practise. In other words, we must first understand the basic nature of entrepreneurship as a process before we can proceed with the task of providing entrepreneurs with the practical help they seek. For this reason, we have worked hard throughout the text to attain a good balance between theory and research, on the one hand, and practical advice and application on the other. In each chapter, we summarize "state of the art" knowledge about specific aspects of the entrepreneurial process—and then indicate how this information can be applied to solving practical problems faced by entrepreneurs. This is the **ideal balance** mentioned in the title of this preface, and attaining it has been a major goal of the book.

D. Many perspectives can contribute to our understanding of entrepreneurship. The field of entrepreneurship is eclectic by nature: it has important roots in many older and more well-established disciplines, such as economics, psychology, management, and sociology. Each of these fields offers a different perspective, and each can contribute significantly to our understanding of entrepreneurship as a process. Thus, fully representing all of them in this book is yet another guiding principle we have adopted. The fact that together, our training and experience covers virtually all of these fields helped assure that we would adopt an eclectic, inclusive approach. But since this is much too important a goal to take for granted, we have also made including these different perspectives one of our guiding principles.

II. SPECIFIC FEATURES DESIGNED TO MAKE THE BOOK MORE USEFUL

Agreeing on guiding principles is one thing; implementing them consistently is quite another. How, then, have we sought to incorporate these principles throughout this book? Here are some specific steps we have taken.

A. Breadth of coverage. First, we have attempted to provide very broad coverage of the field of entrepreneurship. Consistent with this goal, we have included many topics not covered in other texts. Here is a small sample:

- **Cognitive bases of creativity and opportunity recognition**

- **Choosing cofounders wisely**

- **Indirect techniques for gathering marketing information**

- **Potential pitfalls faced by decision-making groups**

- **The legal environment of business (e.g., business contracts)**

- **The marketing process in a new company**

- **Complementary assets as a strategy for new firm performance**

- **Essential people skills for entrepreneurs: creating trust, exerting influence, managing stress**

- **Recruiting, selecting, and motivating high-performing employees**

- **The impact of entrepreneurs' personal lives (e.g., their families) on their success**

- **The role of negotiating skills in exit strategies**

- **Developing and protecting intellectual property**

- **How to make an effective business plan presentation**

B. Balance between theory and practise. To attain this balance, we have included coverage of the most recent findings and information available in every chapter. The result: The research we draw upon is quite recent, with many citations coming from 2000 or later. To assure that practise is fully represented, we have included two special features:

1. **Danger! Pitfall Ahead!** These sections highlight potential snares and hazards of which entrepreneurs should be aware—ones that can prove fatal to their new ventures, and their dreams! More importantly, these sections provide practical examples of the key concepts outlined in each chapter.

DANGER! PITFALL AHEAD!

How to Create an Affective Conflict When There Is None

Back in the mid-1990s, Delta Air Lines, like many other large carriers, was going through hard times, and for the first time in its history had to cut a number of jobs throughout the company. When asked by reporters to comment on the extent to which this had upset employees, Delta CEO Ronald W. Allen remarked, "So be it." This callous remark proved very costly. Delta's employees were furious, and let everyone—the media, passengers, and government officials—know about it. In fact, within a few days of Allen's remark, thousands of Delta employees donned "So Be It" buttons, and wore them proudly as a sign of their anger and contempt for Allen. Morale plunged, and the heat was truly on for Allen. In fact, the board of directors declined to renew his contract so that soon he, too, was out of a job.

What was going on here? A textbook illustration of affective conflict—a conflict that may have started with divergent interests, but which quickly escalated into a bitter dispute in which basic issues were quickly submerged in a tide of angry emotion. Consider the situation in the cold light of reason: Both Allen and Delta's employees wanted to save the company from a mounting sea of red ink. Yet, although some of their major interests coincided, Allen managed to drive a wedge between top management and Delta's employees—one that could only be healed by his departure.

There is an important message in these events for entrepreneurs: If affective conflict can prove so costly for a huge company like Delta Air Lines, imagine how devastating it can be when it occurs between members of the founding team or between this team and key employees. For this reason, being familiar with techniques for avoiding and defusing affective conflict is an important skill that entrepreneurs should definitely acquire—and practise!

THE VOICE OF EXPERIENCE

Business Planning Is More Important
Than the Business Plan

Since writing their first business plan in 2002, Amy Ballon and Danielle Botterell have been growing Admiral Road for the past four years. Recently, they talked with me about the process of writing that first business plan and the role that business planning plays in their company. Their first business plan is shown in the Appendix to this chapter.

Reuber: "How did you come to found a blanket manufacturing business?"

Admiral Road: "We had a burning desire not to work on Bay Street and gave ourselves three months to find an alternative. We started with a list of criteria for a start-up: it had to have low

capital-intensity, it had to be low-tech and we had to be able to balance the business with children." (In the four years since starting Admiral Road, Ballon and Botterell have each had two children, as you can see from the photo.) "We spent days and days making lists of possible businesses, and matching them against our skill sets, our interests, and what we thought market demands were. We have a regular Sunday night dinner group, and each week we would throw out ideas and find out what people thought of them. This feedback was valuable—for example, no one could see us being calm enough to run a spa! Within a month, we'd narrowed it down to a couple of choices. Amy had been a customer of the blanket business we ended up

continued

A few examples:

- Exploiting an Incremental Innovation by Starting a Firm (Chapter 2)
- "Too Much Invested to Quit": The Potentially Devastating Effect of Sunk Costs (Chapter 3)
- The Seven Deadly Sins for New Venture Business Plans (Chapter 8)
- Stymied by the Dominant Design: The Story of Electric Vehicles (Chapter 10)
- The Costs of Negotiating to Win: Watch Out for the "Ankle-Biters" (Chapter 13)

2. **The Voice of Experience.** Several chapters contain interviews with highly successful entrepreneurs. The entrepreneurs share their views about various aspects of the entrepreneurial process, thus providing concrete examples of how principles covered in a given chapter can be applied. A few examples:

- Some Thoughts on Avoiding False Alarms (Chapter 3)
- Why People Skills Really Matter (Chapter 4)
- Business Planning is More Important that the Business Plan (Chapter 8)

III. FEATURES DESIGNED TO MAKE THIS BOOK MORE APPEALING TO READERS

LEARNING OBJECTIVES

After reading this chapter, you should be able to:

1 Define an entrepreneurial opportunity and explain why such opportunities exist.

2 Describe how technological, political/regulatory, and social/demographic changes generate entrepreneurial opportunities.

3 List the different forms that entrepreneurial opportunities can take, and explain why some forms are better for new firms than others.

4 Explain why new firms are more successful in some industries than in others, and identify the four major types of industry differences that influence the relative success of new firms.

5 Identify the three different dimensions of knowledge conditions, and explain how they influence an industry's supportiveness of new firms.

6 Identify the three different dimensions of demand conditions, and explain how they influence an industry's supportiveness of new firms.

7 Identify the two different dimensions of industry life cycles, and explain how they influence an industry's supportiveness of new firms.

8 Identify the four different dimensions of industry structure, and explain how they influence an industry's supportiveness of new firms.

9 Explain why established firms are usually better than new firms at exploiting entrepreneurial opportunities.

10 Identify the types of opportunities that new firms are better at exploiting, and explain why new firms are advantaged at the exploitation of those opportunities.

Our own teaching experience (more than 50 years combined), tells us that if students find a textbook difficult or boring to read, its value is sharply reduced. With this thought in mind, we have included several features to make this book more interesting to read, and more convenient to use. First, it is written in what we believe to be a clear and direct style—one that will communicate with readers rather than bore or irritate them. Second, we have included a number of features designed to help students with their studying. All chapters begin with a **Chapter Outline** and **Learning Objectives**. Brief reviews of **Key Points** appear at the end of major sections of the text within chapters. All charts and graphs have been specially prepared for this text, and contain special captions to help readers with correct interpretation (see p. xiv for an example). Each chapter ends with a **Summary and Review of Key Points.**

All **Key Terms** are printed in **boldface** within the body of the text, and are defined in a **Glossary** section at the end of the chapter. End-of-chapter materials for each chapter include **Discussion Questions**, which are designed to stimulate in-class discussion of major points, and several **Getting Down to Business** exercises designed to give readers practice with the principles presented and to help students to write a feasibility study or business plan for their own venture idea. **InfoTrac** exercises are also included at the end of each chapter, and students can find additional InfoTrac exercises on the book support Web site. These exercises are designed to direct readers to relevant articles from established academic journals to illustrate the chapter concepts, as well as to spark further interest in them. Finally, we have included an abundance of case resources. Cases illustrating concepts for each chapter can be found in the **Case Studies Appendix**. Teaching notes for the cases are included in the instructor's manual.

We believe that together, these features will make this a book that students will actually read—and that, of course, is the first, crucial step toward learning.

IV. ANCILLARIES

This text is supported by a complement of excellent ancillary materials for instructors; these are all available on an Instructor Resource CD-ROM (ISBN 0-17-644264-2). Included on the IRCD are an **Instructor's Manual**, **Test Bank**, **PowerPoint slides**, and **ExamView testing software**. A **VHS video** is available with video segments from the Small Business School (ISBN 0-324-28821-2). Last, the book support Web site, **www.entrepreneurship.nelson.com**, is an excellent resource for instructors and students, including access to the PowerPoint slides for instructors and students, and full access to instructor ancillaries for registered instructors.

V. ACKNOWLEDGMENTS

Many of our colleagues graciously offered comments and suggestions during the writing and development of this text. We are grateful for their time and conscientious feedback.

Robert B. Anderson,
University of Regina

Thomas Astebro,
University of Toronto

John Chamard,
Saint Mary's University

Eileen Fischer,
York University

Walter Isenor,
Acadia University

Wayne King,
Memorial University of Newfoundland

Sandra Malach,
University of Calgary

Geoffery Malleck,
University of Waterloo

Tom McKaig,
Ryerson University

Dr. Teresa V. Menzies,
Brock University

Pramodita Sharma,
Wilfrid Laurier University

A NOTE TO STUDENTS

This Book: A Useful Tool for Studying...and for Starting Your Own Company

When we think back over our own years in college, both of us can remember using texts that were, to be perfectly honest, *mind-numbing*. Not only were they boring and hard to understand, but they offered absolutely no help when we tried to study from them, often late at night. And because they were so painful to read, it was difficult to remember any useful information they might have contained; we just wanted to forget about them as quickly as possible!

Consequently, when we decided to write this text, we took a personal pledge that this would not be the kind of book we would produce. On the contrary, we would do our best to prepare a text that would be easy to read and useful, both now when you study for exams, and later, when you start your own company. What steps have we taken to reach these ambitious goals? Here is an overview:

- **Chapter Outlines:** Research findings indicate strongly that information that is organized is easier to understand and remember than information that is not. For this reason, we start each chapter with an outline of the major sections. If you take a moment to read through these outlines, they will help you to see how each chapter "flows" and how its various parts fit together; that, in turn, will help you to understand—and remember—the information presented.

- **Review of Key Points at the End of Each Major Section:** Often, it is easy to "lose the forest for the trees"—to get so bogged down in details that the main points are lost from view. To avoid this possibility, each major section of text is followed by a review of the key points made. If you consider this carefully, it will help you to remember the most central points and information, and that, in turn, will make your studying more efficient.

- **Boldface of Key Terms:** Our own students often ask us: "What are the most important points or concepts?" To help you recognize these, they are printed in **bold type** like this.

- **Glossary:** In addition, these key terms are clearly defined at the end of each chapter in a separate Glossary. Having these definitions in one place, as well as in the text, is not only convenient—it will help you remember the meaning of these terms both now, when you study for exams, and later, when you use the information in this book to start your own company.

- **Special Labelling of All Charts and Graphs:** Instead of merely copying charts and graphs that appear in other sources, we have specially designed *all* of them so that they are easy to understand. And to help you grasp the main points they illustrate, all charts and graphs contain special labels that call your attention to these points and explain why they are important.

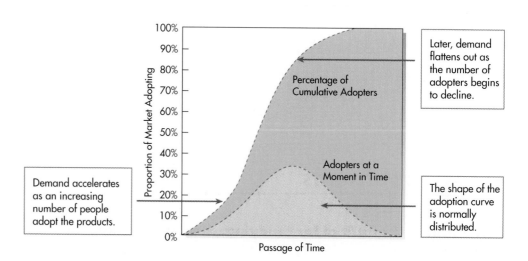

- **End-of-Chapter Summary and Review of Key Points:** All key points are summarized once again at the end of the chapter; this will make it easier for you to review them—and to see how they are related to each other.

- **InfoTrac Exercises:** These are research exercises closely linked to the content of each chapter, designed to illustrate and highlight key points and concepts.

- **End-of-Chapter "Getting Down to Business" Exercises:** These exercises will give you actual practice in using the key principles presented in each chapter. Together, they will help you prepare to write an actual feasibility study or business plan for your new venture.

- **Special Sections Designed to Help You Become a Successful Entrepreneur:** We have included two different kinds of sections that we believe you will find both interesting and useful:

  - *Danger! Pitfall Ahead!* These sections are designed to emphasize potential dangers that lie in wait to trap unwary entrepreneurs. Recognizing them may help you avoid lots of painful experiences in the future!

  - *The Voice of Experience.* Several chapters contain interviews with highly successful entrepreneurs. The entrepreneurs share their views about various aspects of the entrepreneurial process, thus providing concrete examples of how principles covered in a given chapter can actually be applied.

THE VOICE OF EXPERIENCE

Some Thoughts on Avoiding False Alarms

- **Case Studies Appendix (Appendix 1):** The Case Studies Appendix includes case studies for 13 chapters of the text, illustrating with real-world detail the concepts you've learned in each chapter.

We sincerely believe that together, these features make the book more interesting to read, more useful as a tool for studying, and—perhaps most important of all—a good source of practical information you can use when you start your own company. We hope you will agree, and that you will find this book to be one you consult over and over again in the years ahead. Good luck both in your course and in the exciting years ahead when *you* will start the companies that strongly shape the future.

ABOUT THE AUTHORS

Robert A. Baron is Dean R. Wellington Professor of Management and Professor of Psychology; Ph.D., University of Iowa. He recently completed terms of office as Interim Dean and Interim Director of the Severino Center for Technological Entrepreneurship (2001–2002). Professor Baron has held faculty appointments at Purdue University, the University of Minnesota, University of Texas, University of South Carolina, University of Washington, and Princeton University. In 1982 he was a Visiting Fellow at Oxford University. From 1979 to 1981 he served as a Program Director at the National Science Foundation (Washington, D.C.). In 2001 the French Ministry of Research appointed him as a Visiting Senior Research Fellow; he held this post at the Universite des Sciences Sociales, Toulouse. He has been a Fellow of the American Psychological Association since 1978, and is also a Charter Fellow of the American Psychological Society.

Professor Baron has published more than 100 articles in professional journals and 30 chapters in edited volumes. He is the author or co-author of more than 40 books in the fields of management and psychology, including Behavior in Organizations (8th ed.) and Social Psychology (10th ed.).

Professor Baron served as a member of the board of directors of the Albany Symphony Orchestra (1993–1996). He holds three U.S. patents and was founder, president, and CEO of Innovative Environmental Products, Inc. (1993–2000).

Professor Baron's research and consulting activities focus primarily on the following topics: (1) social and cognitive factors in entrepreneurship, (2) workplace aggression and violence, and (3) impact of the physical environment (e.g., lighting, air quality, temperature) on productivity.

Scott A. Shane is Professor of Economics and Entrepreneurship at the Weatherhead School of Management at the Case Western Reserve University and Academic Director of the Center for Regional Economic Issues; Ph.D., University of Pennsylvania. Dr. Shane has held faculty appointments at the University of Maryland, Massachusetts Institute of Technology, and Georgia Institute of Technology. The author of over 50 scholarly articles on entrepreneurship and innovation management, Dr. Shane's work has appeared in *Management Science, Academy of Management Journal, Academy of Management Review, Strategic Management Journal, Decision Science, Journal of Economic Behavior and Organization, Journal of Management, Journal of Business Venturing, Journal of International Business Studies*, and *Entrepreneurship Theory and Practice*, among other journals. He is currently departmental editor of the R&D, Innovation, Entrepreneurship, and Product Development Division of Management Science. His current research examines how entrepreneurs discover and evaluate opportunities, assemble resources, and design organizations. Dr. Shane has consulted to numerous large and small organizations and has taught in executive education programs in Norway, Poland, New Zealand, and the United States. His research has been quoted in *The Wall Street Journal*, Inc., and *Entrepreneur Magazine*.

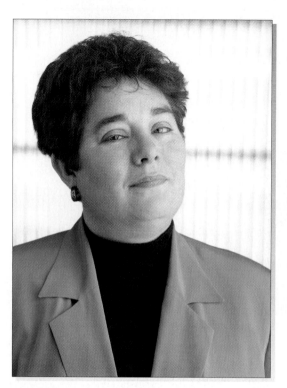

A. Rebecca Reuber is a professor of entrepreneurship at the Rotman School of Management, University of Toronto; Ph.D., Queen's University.   Dr. Reuber has held visiting faculty appointments at Dartmouth College, the Australian National University and the University of Victoria, and has been a Research Fellow of the Asia Pacific Foundation of Canada.   Her research has won awards from the World Conference of the International Council for Small Business, the Academy of Management, the Administrative Sciences Association of Canada and the Canadian Council of Small Business & Entrepreneurship, and has been published in journals such as *Journal of Business Venturing, Entrepreneurship Theory & Practice, Journal of International Business Studies, Journal of Small Business Economics, Decision Support Systems* and *Canadian Woman Studies.* She is a member of several journal editorial boards and entrepreneurship award selection committees, and has consulted to a number of private and public sector organizations. Dr. Reuber's perspectives on entrepreneurs and entrepreneurship have been widely quoted in media outlets such as CBC Radio, TVO, the *Globe & Mail*, the *Financial Post*, the *Toronto Star*, and the *Hamilton Spectator.*

PART 1

ENTREPRENEURSHIP: WHO, WHAT, WHY?

What precisely is entrepreneurship, both as an activity and a field of study? How does it unfold over time as a process? How can we gather systematic and valid information about entrepreneurship? What are opportunities and how do they emerge? What cognitive factors play a role in creativity and in the generation of ideas for new products or services? What qualities do successful entrepreneurs possess? Because understanding the roots of entrepreneurship is essential for following the discussion in subsequent sections of this book—a comprehensive examination of the entire entrepreneurial process—we focus on these basic issues in this initial section of the text.

ALL PHOTOS THIS PAGE ©
PHOTODISC, INC.

CHAPTER 1

ENTREPRENEURSHIP: A FIELD—AND AN ACTIVITY

LEARNING OBJECTIVES

After reading this chapter, you should be able to:

1 Define "entrepreneurship" as a field of business.

2 Explain why the activities of entrepreneurs are so important to the economies of their countries, and why entrepreneurship is an increasingly popular career choice.

3 Describe the process perspective on entrepreneurship, and list the major phases of this process.

4 Explain why entrepreneurship can be viewed as arising out of the intersection of people and opportunities.

5 Explain why certain sources of knowledge about entrepreneurship are more reliable and useful than others.

6 Describe the basic nature of systematic observation, experimentation, and reflection (i.e., the case method and other qualitative methods).

7 Explain the role of theory in the field of entrepreneurship.

All photos this page © PhotoDisc, Inc.

> "A pessimist sees the difficulty in every opportunity; an optimist sees the opportunity in every difficulty." (Sir Winston Churchill)

In the spring of 1990, I (Robert Baron) discovered that entrepreneurs are optimists as described in these words from Sir Winston Churchill. The situation went something like this. My daughter was in second year of university. She loved her school, but complained incessantly about the dormitory: "It's so noisy that I can't study," she told me, "and the air is terrible—dusty, stale, and it smells bad, too!" Then she said something that, in a sense, changed my life: "Dad, you're an expert on how the physical environment affects people, so can't you come up with an invention that would help?" (She was referring to the fact that for more than 15 years, I had conducted research on the impact of environmental factors, such as temperature, air quality, and lighting, on human performance.) I had been a consultant to many companies on such matters, but until that point, I had never really thought about inventing a product to help deal with such problems as excess noise and stale, dusty air in small spaces, such as offices or dorm rooms. After my daughter's comment, though, wheels began to turn inside my head: Couldn't I actually design a device that would address the problems she mentioned? If I could, wouldn't it be both useful and eminently marketable? I am not an engineer, so I began to search for a partner who could help me convert this idea into an actual product. I soon found one (although, as I'll note later in this chapter, perhaps not the right one!), and together we came up with a working prototype: a device that filtered the air, contained a separate system for reducing noise and yet another system for releasing pleasant fragrances. Each system could be operated independently by users. At that point, we felt we had something, so we applied for a U.S. patent. We received it, and two others on related products, in the next two years. Now, though, we faced another challenge: how to bring the product to market. We checked carefully and learned that to produce it ourselves would require several million dollars'

worth of equipment, so we decided to seek a corporate partner. That search, too, was successful, and within a year, our product—which we called the PPS (for Personal Privacy System)—was being sold in stores and on TV by our large corporate partner (see Figure 1.1). My own company (IEP, Inc.) handled direct sales through an Internet site and ads in magazines. Our product continued to sell for several years and IEP was modestly—but not wildly—profitable. We ceased operations in 2000, mainly because I had reached a point where I had to choose between my career as a professor and running the company full-time, and also because of my growing realization that I had fallen into several of the major pitfalls that lie in wait for unwary entrepreneurs (e.g., choosing partners unwisely and losing control over the quality of one's products). For seven years, though, I was truly an entrepreneur in every sense of the word; when I feel the itch to do it again (which I do with increasing frequency!), I can only conclude that I may be one again in the future.

Figure 1.1 The Author as Entrepreneur

The device shown here—a combination air cleaner, sound-reduction, and fragrance release system—was patented by one of the authors (Baron), manufactured by a corporate partner of the author's company, and sold nationally.

Source: Photo courtesy of R.A. Baron.

Why do we begin with this bit of personal history? Primarily because it illustrates the fact that entrepreneurship is a process—a chain of events and activities that takes place over time—sometimes, considerable periods of time. It begins with an idea for something new—often, a new product or service. But that is only the start: Unless the process continues so that the idea is converted into reality (actually brought to market through a new business venture, licensing to existing companies, etc.), it is not entrepreneurship. Rather, it is just an exercise in creativity or idea generation.

Second, this brief personal history illustrates that direct, personal experience with being an entrepreneur underlies this book. As a result, when we write about the processes involved in entrepreneurship—processes such as recognizing an opportunity and developing the means to exploit it—we understand these events and activities from the inside, not simply as observers. As we will note in later discussions, we feel this is very important from the point of view of making this book not only accurate and up-to-date, but also useful to anyone who is now, or wants to become, an entrepreneur.

Having clarified these important points, we will now turn to several tasks that we want to accomplish in this initial chapter. Briefly, these are as follows. First, we will present a definition of entrepreneurship both as an activity and as a field of study. Next, we'll offer a framework for understanding entrepreneurship as a process—one that unfolds over time. This process is affected by a multitude of factors, some relating to individuals (i.e., to entrepreneurs), some to their relations with other people (e.g., partners, customers, venture capitalists), and some to society as a whole (e.g., government regulations, market conditions). A major theme of this book will be that all three categories of factors (individual, group, societal) play an important role in every phase of the entrepreneurial process. As part of this discussion, we will emphasize yet another key theme: At the heart of the entrepreneurial process is the intersection of opportunities generated by changing economic, technological, and social conditions and enterprising people capable of distinguishing potentially valuable opportunities from less valuable ones and of actively exploiting them. This theme will be examined in more detail in Chapter 2, which focuses on the emergence of opportunities, and in Chapter 3, which focuses on the role of cognition in this process.

Third, we will consider the question of how we know what we currently know about entrepreneurship—in other words, how the information presented in this book was obtained. We think this is important because, in general, it is dangerous to accept any information as accurate without knowing something about its source. Finally, we will provide you with an overview of the contents of this book and a description of its special features.

Why do we begin with these preliminary tasks instead of just jumping right into a discussion of various aspects of entrepreneurship? Mainly for this reason: Research findings in the field of cognitive science strongly suggest that people have a much better chance of understanding, remembering, and using new information if they are first provided with a framework for organizing it. We believe that this text contains much new information about entrepreneurship—information you probably have not already encountered. The topics discussed in this introductory chapter will provide you with a framework for making this knowledge your own and for using it in your future life and career. So please read carefully: This will be effort well spent, and it will definitely help you to understand the information presented in later chapters.

THE FIELD OF ENTREPRENEURSHIP: ITS NATURE AND ROOTS

LEARNING OBJECTIVE

1 Define "entrepreneurship" as a field of business.

Definitions are always tricky, and for a field as new as entrepreneurship, the task is even more complex. It is not surprising, then, that currently there is no single agreed-upon definition of entrepreneurship, either as a field of study in business or as an activity in which people engage. Having said that, we should note that a definition offered recently by Shane and Venkataraman[1] has received increasing acceptance. Broadly paraphrased, their definition suggests the following: Entrepreneurship, as a field of business, seeks to understand how opportunities to create something new (e.g., new products or services, new markets, new production processes or raw materials, new ways of organizing existing technologies) *arise* and are *discovered* or created by *specific persons*, who then use various means to *exploit* or *develop* them, thus producing a wide range of *effects*. (Italics added by the current authors.) By implication, this definition suggests that entrepreneurship, as an activity carried out by specific persons, involves the key actions we mentioned earlier: identifying an opportunity—one that is potentially valuable in the sense that it can be exploited in practical business terms (i.e., one that can potentially yield sustainable profits)—and identifying the activities involved in actually exploiting or developing this opportunity. In addition, as we will note in a later section of this chapter, the process does not end with the launching of a new venture; it also involves being able to run a new business successfully after it has come into existence.

We believe that this definition is a clear and useful one, and does indeed capture the essential nature of entrepreneurship. Although it helps to clarify many important questions, perhaps the most central of these is: "Just what makes someone an entrepreneur?" Obviously, if we can't agree on that issue, there is little hope of developing systematic knowledge about what entrepreneurship involves. To see how the definition offered by Shane and Venkataraman helps significantly in this respect, consider the following individuals. For each, ask yourself this question: "Is this person truly an entrepreneur?"

- A student who enjoys making his own peanut butter, which his family and friends love, decides to start a company to make and sell nut spreads.

- A university scientist engaged in basic research on the biochemistry of life makes important discoveries that advance the frontiers of his field; however, he has no interest in identifying practical uses of his discoveries and does not attempt to do so.

- After being downsized from his management-level job, a middle-aged man hits upon the idea of processing old tires in a special way to make edging for gardens.

- A retired Canadian Armed Forces officer develops the idea of purchasing obsolete amphibious vehicles from the government and using them to start a company that specializes in tours of remote wilderness areas.

- A young computer scientist develops new software that is far better than anything now on the market; she seeks capital to start a company to develop and sell this product.

Which of these individuals are entrepreneurs? At first glance, you might be tempted to conclude that only the last two are really entrepreneurs—that only *they* are creating something truly new. We suggest, however, that *all* of these persons with the exception of the university scientist are entrepreneurs. Why? Recall our definition: Entrepreneurship involves recognizing an opportunity to create something new— and that something does not have to be a new product or service. On the contrary, it can involve recognizing an opportunity to develop a new market, to use a new raw material, or to develop a new means of production, to mention just a few possibilities. According to this definition, the peanut butter–making student is acting as an entrepreneur because he has recognized a new market—one that will pay a premium price for healthy snacks. In fact, this is just what Jason Dorland did when he started Skeet & Ike's, a Vancouver company that manufactures and distributes natural and organic snacks.[2] Similarly, the downsized executive is using a new raw material—old tires—in a new way. This, too, qualifies as entrepreneurship. The retired Canadian Armed Forces officer and the computer scientist are also entrepreneurs: Both have identified opportunities for new products or services, and both have taken active steps to convert these ideas into going business concerns.

In contrast, the university scientist is not an entrepreneur, according to our definition. Although his research does add appreciably to human knowledge, the fact that he makes no effort to apply his discoveries to the development of new products, services, markets, or means of production suggests that he is not an entrepreneur. Certainly, he is playing a valuable role in society, but he is not an entrepreneur.

In essence, then, entrepreneurship requires creating or recognizing a commercial application for something new. The new commercial application can take many different forms, but simply inventing a new technology, product, or service, or generating a new idea is not, in itself, enough. As shown in Figure 1.2, many inventions never result in actual products for the simple reason that they offer no commercial benefits (or, alternatively, no one can think of a marketable use for them), and so they cannot

Figure 1.2 Newness Is Not Enough!

The fact that a product is new is not sufficient to assure that it will be developed and brought to market.

Close To Home © 2001 John Mcpherson. Reprinted By Permission Of Universal Press Syndicate. All Rights Reserved.

Barry's new Executive Power Stilts™ gave him an air of superiority over co-workers who once intimidated him.

really serve as the basis for a profitable new business. Indeed, after surveying more than 1,000 inventors who received support from the Inventor's Assistance Program at the Canadian Industrial Innovation Centre in Waterloo, Ontario, Professor Thomas Astebro concluded that fewer than 7 percent of the inventions of independent inventors reach the market.[3] In sum, we agree with Shane and Venkataraman that entrepreneurship emerges out of the intersection of what might be termed "the inspired" and "the mundane," recognizing opportunities for something new that people will want to own or use and taking vigorous steps to convert these opportunities into viable, profitable businesses.

A Note on Intrapreneurship

Before turning to other topics, we should note, briefly, that recognizing opportunities for creating or developing something new can occur within existing organizations as well as outside them. In fact, many successful companies are deeply concerned with encouraging innovations and take active steps to provide an environment in which they can flourish.[4] York University professor Thomas Keil argues that this approach allows companies to adapt to changing conditions in the business environment.[5] It involves such steps as developing a corporate culture receptive to new ideas rather than one that routinely rejects them and providing concrete rewards for innovation.[6] For instance, employees at General Electric (GE) who come up with innovative ideas receive a share of the resulting profits. The upshot? GE has obtained more U.S. patents during recent decades than any other U.S. company and now holds more than 51,000 in total! Individuals who act like entrepreneurs inside a company are often described as being **intrapreneurs**—persons who create something new, but inside an existing company rather than through the route of founding a new venture. Although our focus will be firmly on entrepreneurs throughout this book, we do want to note that individuals can act entrepreneurially in several different contexts, including large, existing companies.

A Note on Social Entrepreneurship

Social entrepreneurship is gaining increased recognition in Canada and around the world. Social entrepreneurs innovate to benefit humanity. Their ventures may be for-profit or not-for-profit, but their most important goals are social, such as economic development, environmental sustainability, and disaster relief. One example of Canadian social entrepreneurship is the First Nations Bank of Canada, which was created in 1996 as a partnership between the Toronto-Dominion Bank and the Federation of Saskatchewan Indian Nations. Professor Bob Anderson, of the University of Regina, has studied such partnerships between Canadian corporations and Canada's First Nations and found the results encouraging. While there are economic, as well as social, motivations behind corporate behaviour, there are positive economic and social benefits for all parties.[7] Not all social entrepreneurship involves an established corporation. For example, Markets Initiative is a coalition of three environmental organizations: Friends of Clayoquot Sound, Greenpeace Canada, and Sierra Club of Canada, BC Chapter.[8] Markets Initiative was started in

1999 to safeguard forests through the development of practical alternatives to wood and paper products, and can boast of some notable achievements. There are now nine Ancient Forest Friendly book papers available in Canada. In 2004, the publishers of 34 Canadian magazines, including *Canadian Geographic* and *OWL Magazine,* pledged to shift away from papers containing tree fibre. Furthermore, in 2005, the Canadian edition of *Harry Potter and the Order of the Phoenix,* published by Vancouver's Raincoast Books, was the world's only edition that is ancient forest friendly. While we emphasize markets and profit-seeking in this book, the concepts we discuss are relevant to social entrepreneurs who are recognizing and developing new opportunities.

Entrepreneurship: An Engine of Economic Growth

When one of us (Robert Baron) began his career as a university professor (in 1968), courses such as the one you are now taking simply did not exist. Now, in contrast, they are offered by virtually every school of management or business and have shown a pattern of rapidly growing enrollments in recent years. Why? One reason is that such courses reflect parallel growth in the number of persons choosing to become entrepreneurs—or at least to start their own businesses. Each year, more than 125,000 new businesses are launched in Canada.[9] Although not all of these would meet our definition for involving entrepreneurship, all—to the extent they are successful—contribute to economic growth. Consider the following facts:

> **LEARNING OBJECTIVE**
>
> 2   Explain why the activities of entrepreneurs are so important to the economies of their countries, and why entrepreneurship is an increasingly popular career choice.

- Currently, more than 2.5 million individuals are self-employed in Canada (Industry Canada, 2005)—about 15 percent of all working Canadians!

- Over the past decade, the number of self-employed women has grown by 23 percent and the number of self-employed men has grown by 20 percent (Industry Canada, 2005).

- Entrepreneurial activity is highest for Canadian men and women in the 25- to 34-year-old age category.[10]

- More than 40 percent of the private sector Gross Domestic Product (GDP) in Canada is produced by small or medium-sized enterprises, which have fewer than 500 employees (Industry Canada, 2005).

- Eighty-five percent of Canadian exporters are small businesses, with fewer than 100 employees (Industry Canada, 2005).

These statistics suggest that the activities of entrepreneurs have a truly major impact on the Canadian economy.

Even a casual glance at history suggests that entrepreneurs have always existed and have always made waves in their societies: Vast fortunes were certainly amassed by entrepreneurs of the past, such as Roy Thomson, Timothy Eaton, and John Molson. However, considerable evidence suggests that more people than ever are pursuing, or considering, this role. What factors are responsible for this trend? Many appear to be playing a role. First, the media are filled with glowing accounts of successful entrepreneurs, such as Heather Reisman of Indigo Books & Music, Jim Balsillie of Research In Motion, and Jeffrey Skoll of eBay (see Figure 1.3). As a result, the role of entrepreneur has taken on a very positive and attractive aura. In an age when political heroes are few and far between, entrepreneurs have, in a sense, become the new heroes and heroines, so it is far from surprising that a growing number of persons are choosing to pursue this kind of career.

Second, there has been a fundamental change in what has often been termed "the employment contract"—the implicit understanding between employers and employees.[11] In the past, this implicit agreement suggested that as long as individuals performed their jobs well, they would be retained as employees. Now, in an era of downsizing and right-sizing, this agreement has been broken, with the result that

CP PHOTO/Toronto Star(Keith Beaty)

Figure 1.3 The Romance of Entrepreneurship

In a sense, entrepreneurs are the new heroes and heroines: They are often presented in very flattering terms by the media. As a result, the appeal of becoming an entrepreneur has increased greatly in recent years. (Shown here: Jeffrey Skoll of eBay.)

many individuals feel little loyalty to their current employers. It is just one small step from such feelings to the conclusion, "I'd be better off working for myself!"

A third factor is a change in basic values. In the past, security was a dominant theme for many people: They wanted a secure job with steady increments in salary. Now, surveys indicate that young people, especially, prefer a more independent lifestyle—one that offers choice in place of certainty or predictability.[12] Together, these and many other factors have combined to bolster the allure of becoming an entrepreneur, and as noted earlier, this focus has translated into the creation of hundreds of thousands of new businesses employing millions of persons. This trend is strong in Canada: the Global Entrepreneurship Monitor estimates that the total entrepreneurial activity here is second only to that of the United States among G7 nations.[13] Entrepreneurship seems to be picking up steam around the world, as government leaders in many countries recognize that, in fact, entrepreneurs do matter—and matter greatly.

Entrepreneurship: Foundations in Other Disciplines

Nothing, it has often been said, emerges out of a vacuum. Where the field of entrepreneurship is concerned, this is certainly true. Entrepreneurship, as a branch of business, has important roots in several older and more established fields—and with good reason. Consider, again, our definition of entrepreneurship—a field of study that seeks to understand how opportunities arise to create new products or services, new markets, production processes, ways of organizing existing technologies, or raw materials and are discovered by specific persons, who then use various means to exploit or develop these opportunities. This definition implies that in order to understand entrepreneurship as a process—and as an activity in which entrepreneurs engage—it is essential to consider (1) the economic, technological, and social conditions from which opportunities rise; (2) the people who recognize these opportunities (entrepreneurs); (3) the business techniques and legal structures they use to develop them; and (4) the economic and social effects produced by such development. All of these elements play a role in entrepreneurship, and all must be taken into account if we are ever to fully understand this complex process. This definition, in turn, implies that the field of entrepreneurship is closely linked to older and more established disciplines, such as economics, behavioural science (psychology, cognitive science), and sociology. The findings and principles of these fields can shed much light on many aspects of entrepreneurship and provide valuable frameworks for understanding key questions addressed by the field: "How do opportunities arise?" (see Chapter 2); "Why do some persons but not others recognize these opportunities?" (see Chapter 3); and "What factors influence the success of new ventures after they are launched?" (see Chapters 10, 11, and 12).

Admittedly, all of this is somewhat abstract, so perhaps a concrete example will be helpful. Consider the rapid growth of one successful high-tech company: Expedia.ca. Expedia, founded in 1995, is an online travel service that allows users to book flights, hotel rooms, and rental cars from any computer with access to the Internet. The company's growth has been swift, so it seems clear that its founders recognized an excellent opportunity and have gone on to exploit it well. But consider the following question: Could Expedia.ca have been launched prior to 1990? The answer is "Almost certainly no." The reason is straightforward: Technological, economic, and social forces had not yet generated the opportunity that the founders of Expedia.ca recognized. From a technological point of view, an online travel service could not exist until many millions of persons had access to the Internet and until software capable of integrating the schedules of dozens of airlines and the rates of thousands of hotels existed. From an economic point of view, such a service could not be viable until a safe and reliable way of making payments over the Internet existed and unless airlines and hotels were willing to pay commissions to an Internet company instead of (or in addition to) traditional travel agents. Finally, from a social perspective, an online travel service could not exist and prosper until large numbers of persons had enough confidence in online information to entrust their travel plans to it and until large numbers of persons became aware of the fact that travellers on the same flights often paid hugely different fares (see Figure 1.4). In sum, the opportunity for founding Expedia.ca did not always exist; rather, it emerged—and became available for discovery by specific persons—out of a combination of many factors—economic, technological, and social.

In a similar manner, the disciplines of economics, behavioural science, and sociology can help to provide answers to other basic questions addressed by the field of entrepreneurship: "Why do some persons but not others recognize opportunities?" "Why are some entrepreneurs so much more successful than others?" and "Why are some means for developing opportunities more effective than others?" Clearly, the field of entrepreneurship does not exist in an intellectual vacuum; rather, its roots rest firmly in several older disciplines that, together, provide it with a firm foundation for understanding one of the most complex—and important—business processes in existence.

One final comment: Are some of these disciplines more useful than others in our efforts to understand entrepreneurship as a process? In other words, should we focus primarily on economic factors, on factors relating to entrepreneurs, or on factors relating to society as a whole in our efforts to understand the entrepreneurial process? This issue has sometimes been debated in the context of a distinction found in several other branches of management: **macro** versus **micro** approaches.[14] Macro approaches take a top-down perspective, seeking to understand how and why new ventures are founded and why they succeed or fail, by focusing largely on what are often termed "environmental factors"—economic, financial, and political variables. Presumably, these factors, which are largely beyond the direct control of individuals, shape the behaviour and decisions of individual entrepreneurs, so understanding

Figure 1.4 A Opportunity in the Making

In recent years, increasing numbers of persons have become aware of the fact that people on the same flights or staying in the same hotels often paid very different rates. This awareness was one factor that created the opportunity Expedia.ca and similar companies exploited.

Copyright 2006 Expedia, Inc. All rights reserved.

their impact is crucial. In contrast, micro approaches take a bottom-up perspective, seeking to understand the entrepreneurial process by focusing primarily on the behaviour and thoughts of individuals or groups of individuals (e.g., founding partners). Presumably, the way in which individuals behave is the key to understanding the entrepreneurial process. Is either view more accurate or more useful than the other? We strongly doubt it. On the contrary, we believe that full understanding of entrepreneurship can only be gained through careful consideration of both perspectives. In fact, we view them as complementary rather than competing. Thus, both will be represented throughout this book.

KEY POINTS

- Entrepreneurship, as a field of business, seeks to understand how opportunities arise to create something new (new products or services, new markets, new production processes or raw materials, new ways of organizing existing technologies) and are discovered or created by specific persons, who then use various means to exploit or develop these opportunities, thus producing a wide range of effects.
- In recent years, the allure of entrepreneurship has increased, with the result that more people than ever are choosing this activity as a career.
- Entrepreneurship, as a branch of business, has important roots in economics, behavioural science, and sociology.
- The field of entrepreneurship recognizes that both the micro perspective (which focuses on the behaviour and thoughts of individuals) and the macro perspective (which focuses primarily on environmental factors) are important for obtaining a full understanding of the entrepreneurial process.

ENTREPRENEURSHIP: A PROCESS PERSPECTIVE

LEARNING OBJECTIVE

3 Describe the process perspective on entrepreneurship, and list the major phases of this process.

Now that we have offered a working definition of entrepreneurship, highlighted its importance, and briefly described its intellectual roots in related disciplines, we will turn to another key task: suggesting a framework for understanding entrepreneurship as a process. This will be a guiding theme of the remainder of this book, so it is important that we present it clearly and that you—our readers—understand what it implies.

The view that entrepreneurship is a process rather than a single event is certainly not new or unique to this text. On the contrary, there is a growing consensus in the field that viewing entrepreneurship as a process that unfolds over time and moves through distinct but closely interrelated phases is both useful and accurate.[15] Further, there is general agreement that this process follows key phases:

- *Recognition of an opportunity.* The entrepreneurial process begins when one or more persons recognize an **opportunity**—the potential to create something new (new products or services, new markets, new production processes, new raw materials, new ways of organizing existing technologies, etc.) that has emerged from a complex pattern of changing conditions—shifts in knowledge, technology, or in the economic, political, social, and demographic climate.[16] Opportunities have the potential to generate economic value (i.e., profit) and are viewed as desirable in the society in which they occur (i.e., development of the opportunity is consistent with existing legal and moral standards and would, therefore, not be blocked or constrained by these standards).

We will examine the emergence of opportunities in Chapter 2 and the cognitive roots of entrepreneurship in Chapter 3, but for the moment, we want to emphasize just one point: In a sense, there really is nothing entirely new under the sun. Ideas do not emerge out of a void; on the contrary, they almost always consist of a novel combination of elements that already exist. What is new is the combination—not the components of which it consists. To take a striking example from history, Alexander Graham Bell did not invent the telephone out of sheer creative genius. Rather, he combined component ideas that already existed and had been generated by other persons (e.g., electric batteries, basic research on the nature of sound, etc.) in a new way—and hence invented a product that revolutionized human communication.

A similar argument holds for recognizing opportunities. The opportunities themselves are generated by economic, technological, and social factors—factors that are in a constant state of change. What is new is the act of noticing a pattern in these changes—connecting the dots, so to speak, so that the idea for something new emerges in the minds of one or more persons. For instance, consider David Martin and Nancy Knowlton, the co-founders, in 1987, of SMART Technologies, Inc. They originally founded the Calgary-based company to be a distributor for a U.S. projector company, but had a vision of an interactive whiteboard that let groups interact with people in the same room—or around the world. After having shifted revenue from projector sales to research and development on a computer-controlled whiteboard, they launched their first product in 1991. Sales were slow at first, since people weren't sure what an interactive whiteboard was or why they would use one. From this shaky beginning, though, SMART Technologies has prospered and won numerous awards, such as being named Canada's Exporter of the Year, one of Canada's Fastest Growing Companies, and, for six straight years, one of Canada's Best Managed Private Companies.[17] A variety of factors contributed to the richness of this opportunity (see Figure 1.5). Why did Martin and Knowlton and no one else recognize it? (Like many good opportunities, it seems so obvious in retrospect!) We will consider this question in detail in Chapter 3. Here, we simply want to note that the entrepreneurial process does indeed begin with the recognition of the potential for something new in the minds of one or more persons who—if they choose to develop these opportunities—become entrepreneurs.

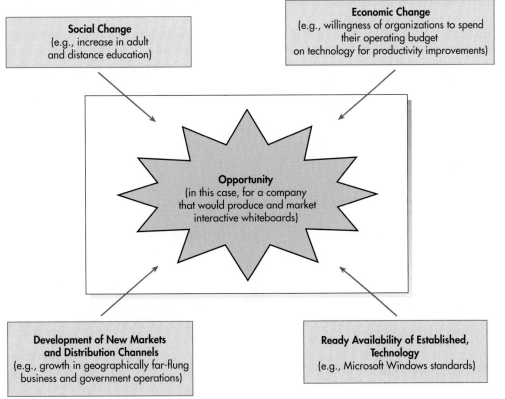

Figure 1.5 Opportunities Emerge out of a Confluence of Factors

Opportunities—the potential to create something new (new products or services, new markets, new production processes, new raw materials, new ways of organizing existing technologies, etc.)—emerge from a complex pattern of changing conditions (shifts in knowledge, technology, or in the economic, political, social, and demographic conditions). This was certainly true for David Martin and Nancy Knowlton, who based their highly successful company (SMART Technologies, Inc.) on a convergence of the factors shown here.

- *Deciding to proceed and assembling the essential resources.* Having an idea for a new product or service or recognizing an opportunity is only, of course, the first step in the process. At that point, an initial decision to proceed—to do something active about the idea or opportunity—is required. As Shane, Locke, and Collins[18] suggest, the entrepreneurial process occurs because specific persons make this decision and act upon it. In their view, understanding entrepreneurs' motives is crucial to comprehending the entire process. Deciding to start a business is one thing; actually doing so is quite another. Would-be entrepreneurs quickly discover that they must assemble a wide array of required resources: basic information (about markets, environmental and legal issues), human resources (partners, initial employees), and financial resources. Gathering these resources is one of the most crucial phases of the entrepreneurial process, and unless it is completed successfully, opportunities—no matter how attractive—or ideas for new products and services—no matter how good—come to naught. It is at this stage, and especially when seeking financial backing, that entrepreneurs typically prepare a formal **business plan**—a detailed description of how they plan to develop their new venture. (Assembly of required resources will be covered in Chapters 5 through 8, and 12.)

- *Launching a new venture.* Once the required resources are assembled, the new venture can actually be launched. Doing so involves a wide range of actions and decisions: choosing the legal form of the new venture, developing the new product or service, establishing the roles of the top management team, etc. Sadly, many new entrepreneurs do not fully grasp the complexities of starting a new venture, and as we will note in later chapters, this lack of preparedness can burden them with problems that could, in fact, have been avoided. (The issues involved in actually launching a new venture will be covered in Chapters 7 through 11.)

- *Building success.* Although moving from an idea to an actual, going concern represents major progress, it is just the start of another key phase in the entrepreneurial process: running the new venture and building it into a growing, profitable business. Many entrepreneurs recognize that this phase requires additional financial resources. However, in our experience, a smaller proportion fully recognizes the importance of human resources in this process. No business can grow without talented, motivated employees, so at this phase of the process, issues such as how to attract such persons, motivate them, and prevent them from leaving (often with vital information that may be shared with competitors!) become crucial. Devising a strong business strategy is yet another aspect of the process during this phase. Finally, we should note that as a new venture grows, entrepreneurs find themselves having to deal with issues such as conflicts within the top management team and negotiating with others outside the company over a wide range of issues. (These aspects of the entrepreneurial process will be covered in Chapters 4 and 12.)

- *Harvesting the rewards.* In this final phase, founders choose an exit strategy that allows them to harvest the rewards they have earned through their time, effort, and talents. There are many ways of reaping the benefits of successful entrepreneurship (see Chapter 13), and individual entrepreneurs must choose carefully among them so as to maximize the benefits they gain from what, in many cases, have been years of sacrifice and commitment.

One additional comment: We do not mean to imply that entrepreneurship can be readily divided into neat and easily distinguishable phases. In fact, the process is far too complex for that to be true. But the activities described here do tend to unfold over time in an orderly sequence, with idea generation or opportunity recognition occurring first; an active decision to proceed, next; and so on. We believe that viewing entrepreneurship in this manner offers several benefits. First, it helps avoid a static view of entrepreneurship—one that sees entrepreneurship as a specific act (launching of a new venture) that occurs and is then complete. Such a view ignores the fact that entrepreneurs face an ever-changing array of tasks and challenges, and that they often think and feel differently about these tasks and challenges as they change and unfold. Second, viewing entrepreneurship as an ongoing process draws attention to the key activities entrepreneurs must perform as they proceed with their efforts to convert ideas for new products or services into successful businesses. It has long been recognized that how well entrepreneurs perform these activities is often more central to their success than their personal characteristics or background.[19] Attention to entrepreneurs' tasks, in turn, gives us a good handle on identifying the skills, knowledge, and characteristics they need to function effectively in this role. From this angle, too, a process perspective is useful. (An overview of the major phases is shown in Figure 1.6. Please examine it carefully, because it provides a basic framework for understanding much of what follows in later chapters. As we noted earlier, having such mental frameworks is often very useful.)

Levels of Analysis: Micro Versus Macro Revisited

Until recently, the field of entrepreneurship was marked by a controversy over the following question: In studying the entrepreneurial process, should we focus primarily on the entrepreneur (e.g., this person's skills, abilities, talents, motives, and traits) or primarily on the economic, technological, and societal context in which the entrepreneur operates (economic and market conditions, government policy, etc.)? As you can guess from our earlier comments on the macro/micro issue, we view this question as largely irrelevant. On the contrary, we believe that at every stage of the entrepreneurial process, individual-level (micro) variables, group, or interpersonal-level variables, and societal-level (macro) **variables** all play a role (please refer to Figure 1.6).

For instance, consider the question of opportunity recognition. Certainly, this crucial process occurs in the minds of specific persons and must, therefore, reflect the impact of individual-level variables, such as the existing knowledge structures and the unique life histories of these persons. But nothing having to do with people—not even basic aspects of cognition—occurs in a social vacuum. On the contrary, the kinds of ideas people generate reflect the times in which they live, the current state of technological knowledge, and many other aspects of their contemporary societies. Further, other people with whom the entrepreneur has contact—friends, associates, or even figures in the mass media—often suggest the germ of an idea for a new product or service. In short, all three levels of analysis (individual, group, societal) are relevant and must be considered in order to understand idea generation fully.

Here's another example: Why do some persons, but not others, choose to become entrepreneurs? Again, all three categories of variables play a role. With respect to

Figure 1.6 Entrepreneurship as a Process: Some Key Phases

The entrepreneurial process unfolds over time and moves through a number of different phases. Events and outcomes during each phase are affected by many individual-level, group-level, and societal-level factors.

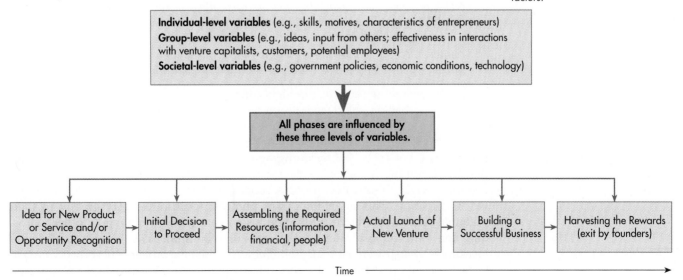

Individual-level variables (e.g., skills, motives, characteristics of entrepreneurs)
Group-level variables (e.g., ideas, input from others; effectiveness in interactions with venture capitalists, customers, potential employees)
Societal-level variables (e.g., government policies, economic conditions, technology)

All phases are influenced by these three levels of variables.

| Idea for New Product or Service and/or Opportunity Recognition | Initial Decision to Proceed | Assembling the Required Resources (information, financial, people) | Actual Launch of New Venture | Building a Successful Business | Harvesting the Rewards (exit by founders) |

Time

individual factors, some persons have higher energy, are more willing to accept risk, and have greater self-confidence (self-efficacy) than others; those high on these dimensions are probably more likely to choose the entrepreneurial role.[20]

Turning to group-level factors, it seems possible that persons who receive encouragement from friends or family members and those who have been exposed to entrepreneurs in their own lives are more likely to proceed than ones who do not receive encouragement and have not been exposed to models of entrepreneurs. For instance, being raised in a family that owns a business is likely to influence a person's attitudes towards business ownership, for better or worse. There may even be pressure to join the family firm rather than starting a new business, given that succession is the most pressing issue for Canadian family firms.[21]

Societal-level factors, too, are important: Persons who come from certain social and economic backgrounds, or who live in countries where government policies are favourable to starting new ventures, are more likely to choose this role than persons from other backgrounds or who live in other countries. Indeed, a group of researchers from the University of Victoria and the University of Western Ontario has found that there are significant differences across countries in people's beliefs about the resources necessary for start-up; their receptiveness to entrepreneurship; and the knowledge, skills and abilities required to start a business.[22] We could continue with other examples, but by now, the main point should be clear: Individual-level, group-level, and societal-level factors influence *every action and every decision taken by entrepreneurs during all phases of the entrepreneurial process*. Taking note of this fact, we will employ all three levels of analysis throughout the text. This approach will, indeed, add complexity to our discussions of many topics. But it will also, we firmly believe, offer a more complete, accurate, and useful picture of what we know about the process of entrepreneurship today. If that is not the ultimate goal of any text, then we, as authors, researchers, and entrepreneurs, have no idea as to what it should be!

Entrepreneurship: The Intersection of Valuable Opportunities and Enterprising Individuals

LEARNING OBJECTIVE

4 Explain why entrepreneurship can be viewed as arising out of the intersection of people and opportunities.

About a year ago, one of us (Robert Baron) had the honor of introducing a highly successful entrepreneur, Mukesh Chatter, at a banquet held in his honor. (Chatter was receiving the Entrepreneur of the Year award given annually by the university and had just sold his company to Lucent Technologies for almost $1 billion.) During his acceptance speech, Chatter made the following remarks:

Success comes from many sources. Yes, you have to recognize an opportunity.... But to recognize it, it has to be there in the first place—something must have changed so as to generate the opportunity. After that, you have to recognize it and be able to tell that it is a good one—something you can turn into a successful business. Luck definitely plays a role; you have to be in the right place at the right time and know the right people who can help you. But after that, it's largely a matter of hard, mind-bending work; if you are not willing to put in the hours and give up lots of other things in your life, you won't succeed—you won't make it happen.

We believe these remarks are highly insightful. In just a few sentences, Chatter captured another key theme in entrepreneurship—and this book. Briefly stated, this theme suggests that it is the intersection of valuable opportunities and enterprising individuals that is the essence of entrepreneurship. Opportunities, as Chatter pointed out, are generated by changing economic, technological, and social conditions; but nothing happens with respect to these opportunities until one or more energetic, highly motivated persons recognizes them, and the fact that they are worth pursuing. This is an important point: Opportunities vary greatly in their potential value, with the result that only some are worth pursuing. In other words, only for some opportunities is the ratio of risk-to-potential benefits sufficiently favourable to justify efforts to exploit them. As you have probably observed yourself, some business opportunities are superior to others. They occur in industries that are faster growing or more profitable, or ones in which customer needs are easier to identify or satisfy. Further, some opportunities are easier to protect against competition. In Chapter 2, we will carefully examine the specific characteristics that make some opportunities more viable or promising than others. The key point we wish to make here, however, should be obvious: At the very heart of entrepreneurship is a nexus (connection) between opportunities and people. It is this connection or intersection that starts the process—and sometimes changes the world!

KEY POINTS

- Entrepreneurship is a process that unfolds over time and that moves through distinct but closely interrelated phases.
- The entrepreneurial process cannot be divided into neat and easily distinguished stages, but in general, it involves generation of an idea for a new product or service and/or recognition of an opportunity; assembling the resources needed to launch a new venture; launching the venture; running and growing the business; and harvesting the rewards.
- Individual, group, and societal factors influence all phases of the entrepreneurial process. Thus, there is no reason to choose between a micro and a macro approach to entrepreneurship; both perspectives are necessary.
- It is the nexus of valuable opportunities and enterprising individuals that is the essence of entrepreneurship.

SOURCES OF KNOWLEDGE ABOUT ENTREPRENEURSHIP: HOW WE KNOW WHAT WE KNOW

Throughout this book, we will discuss many aspects of entrepreneurship—how opportunities arise, how some people recognize them, why some means of developing opportunities are better than others (at least in some contexts), why some entrepreneurs are successful while others fail, and so on. As we discuss each of these issues, we will present the most accurate and up-to-date information currently available. This approach, in turn, raises an important question: How do we know which information fits this description—which information is the most accurate and useful? As any visit to a local bookstore will suggest, many potential sources of information about entrepreneurship exist, and there is no shortage of self-proclaimed experts on this topic. So how have we chosen the information to include in this book? The answer is straightforward: Insofar as possible, we have selected information that has been gathered in accordance with a set of rules or methods for acquiring reliable knowledge—methods that have proven extremely helpful in many other fields ranging from the physical sciences, on one hand, through various branches of management on the other. What are these methods, and can they really be applied to the study of entrepreneurship? The methods themselves are quite complex and far beyond the scope of this brief discussion; however, their essential nature was stated concisely by the French philosopher Diderot (1753) more than 250 years ago. Diderot suggested that "There are three principal means of acquiring knowledge: observation, reflection, and experimentation. Observation collects facts; reflection combines them; experimentation verifies the result of that combination...."

That these methods can be used to study entrepreneurship is strongly suggested by the fact that they are currently being employed in a large volume of entrepreneurship research. Because this is the case, and because much of the information presented in this text has been gathered through these methods, it seems useful to describe them briefly here. Our goal is certainly not that of turning you into an entrepreneurship researcher; on the contrary, it is simply to provide you with a basic understanding of

LEARNING OBJECTIVE

5 Explain why certain sources of knowledge about entrepreneurship are more reliable and useful than others.

these methods so that you can become a more informed consumer of knowledge about entrepreneurship, deciding for yourself whether, and to what extent, alleged facts about it are really accurate.

Observation, Reflection, and Experimentation: Alternative Routes to Knowledge

Because it is the method most frequently used to study entrepreneurship, we will start with **systematic observation**. The basic idea is straightforward: We observe certain aspects of the world systematically, keeping careful records of what we notice. Then, we use this information as a basis for reaching conclusions about the topics we wish to study—and understand. For example, suppose that a researcher had reason to believe that the number of persons leaving secure jobs to become entrepreneurs is influenced by economic conditions. Further, the researcher reasons as follows: When the economy is strong, and many jobs are available, more people are willing to take the risk of becoming an entrepreneur because they know that if their new ventures fail, they can always find another job. When the economy is weak, in contrast, fewer people are willing to take the plunge and become entrepreneurs because they fear that if they give up their jobs, they may not get another one. To study this idea— which would be termed a **hypothesis**—an as yet untested prediction or explanation for a set of facts—the researcher would gather information on economic conditions (e.g., unemployment rate, growth in GDP) and also on the number of persons leaving secure jobs to become entrepreneurs. If the hypothesis were correct, these two variables—aspects of the world that can take different values—would be observed to change together: As economic conditions improve, the number of entrepreneurs increases, and vice versa. In other words, the variables would be correlated—changes in one are accompanied by changes in another. Knowing that two variables are correlated can be very useful because to the extent they are correlated, it is then possible to predict one from the other. (Correlations can range from 0.00 to +1.00 or –1.00. The greater the departure from zero, the stronger the relationship between two or more variables). In this case, for instance, knowing that economic conditions have declined (e.g., that growth in the GDP has declined or that the unemployment rate has increased) would allow us to predict that there would soon be a drop in the number of new ventures started.

So far, so good. But now, imagine that research on this question yielded precisely the opposite finding: As economic conditions decline, the number of persons who start new ventures *increases*, and as economic conditions improve, this number drops—precisely the opposite of the researcher's initial hypothesis. Would this finding still be useful even though it contradicts the researcher's expectations? Absolutely. In fact, if data gathered in systematic observation contradict a hypothesis, this finding can be extremely informative. In this particular case, the unexpected pattern of results suggests that although economic conditions and entrepreneurship are indeed related, the explanation for this relationship is different from the one initially proposed; in other words, an alternative hypothesis is more accurate. Here is one explanation that has been suggested by economists to explain this finding: When economic conditions are poor and many people are unemployed, the opportunity costs for engaging in entrepreneurship are reduced relative to times when economic conditions are good. An opportunity cost is any cost associated with giving up one activity in order to engage in another. If people are unemployed, their opportunity costs for becoming entrepreneurs are lower than if they were employed; they give up less by choosing to become entrepreneurs.

Although all this may seem a bit confusing, it provides a clear illustration of the value of systematic observation from the point of view of increasing our understanding of entrepreneurship. On the face of it, both explanations seem reasonable, and it is only through systematic observation (gathering appropriate data in a careful and systematic manner) that we can choose between them. In fact, there is simply no substitute for such research if we really want to understand how the entrepreneurial process unfolds and what factors influence it. All the educated guesses offered by self-proclaimed experts on entrepreneurship are not, in our view, nearly as informative as the findings of careful research. (By the way, actual research on this issue supports this alternative hypothesis rather than the original one.)[23, 24]

Having made that important point, we should quickly add that although systematic observation and the correlations it yields are invaluable tools, they leave one important point unresolved: causation. We don't know whether changes in one variable cause changes in the other, or vice versa—or whether they are not causally linked at all (i.e., both are affected by some other factor). In the research described earlier, for instance, we don't know whether changes in the economy cause changes in the number of people deciding to become entrepreneurs or whether the number of people becoming entrepreneurs affects the economy. On the face of it, the first interpretation makes more sense; but, if the best people leave their companies to start new ventures, their departures might adversely affect the performance of the companies they leave and start the economy on a downward spiral. So, in fact, if large numbers of people decide to become entrepreneurs, their career changes could, conceivably, result in negative economic ripples. Again, it seems much more reasonable to suggest that economic conditions make it easier, or harder, for individuals to become entrepreneurs rather than vice versa, but on the basis of a correlation between these variables, we cannot tell for certain.

In order to deal with the issue of causality, researchers in many fields turn to another technique known as **experimentation**. In essence, experimentation involves systematically changing one variable in order to see whether such changes affect one or more other variables. Note that this approach involves active interventions by the researcher; in systematic observation, in contrast, the researcher merely observes the variables of interest and does not attempt to change one. When conducted carefully, experimentation is a very powerful tool. The reasoning behind it is impeccable: If we change one variable while holding everything else constant, and these changes affect another variable, we can conclude that changes in the first do indeed cause changes in the second.

Can this method be used to study entrepreneurship? In many cases, not very readily. Continuing with this example, it would certainly be impossible to change economic conditions in a society in order to determine whether more or fewer persons choose to become entrepreneurs! But in some instances—especially research relating to the behaviour of individual entrepreneurs—it *is* possible to use experimentation. For example, consider the hypothesis that entrepreneurs' appearance influences their success—the more attractive they are, the more successful they tend to be. (This finding would not be at all surprising: Research in human resource management and organizational behaviour has frequently reported that attractiveness is related to success in many fields.)[25] Systematic observation could be readily used to study this question. For instance, photos of a large number of entrepreneurs could be rated for attractiveness (low to high) by many persons, and then these ratings could be correlated with measures of the entrepreneurs' success (e.g., growth rates of their companies, personal income, etc.). Suppose such research found that the higher the entrepreneurs' attractiveness, the greater their success (e.g., the more rapid the growth of the companies they found, or the greater the companies' profitability). This finding is interesting, but it does not indicate whether attractiveness *causes* success or whether, alternatively, success boosts attractiveness. For instance, it is possible that successful people have more money to spend on their appearance and so become more attractive.

Experimentation could help to solve this puzzle. One approach would involve obtaining a large number of photos of entrepreneurs and then choosing ones that show entrepreneurs who are rated either high, moderate, or low in their level of attractiveness. These photos would next be presented to a large number of people (ones holding a wide variety of jobs). Their task would be that of rating the entrepreneurs in the photos on various dimensions—the entrepreneurs' future success, the extent to which they would be able to convince potential customers to use their new products or services, and so on. If the entrepreneurs who were rated high in their level of attractiveness received higher ratings than the entrepreneurs who were rated moderate in attractiveness, who, in turn, received higher ratings than those who were rated as being low in attractiveness, this finding would provide evidence that entrepreneurs' appearance does influence other people's perceptions of them and so, perhaps, their success (see Figure 1.7).

Going further, the photos could be attached to summaries of ideas for new products or services, and participants in the research could then rate the quality of these ideas on several dimensions (creativity, market appeal, potential to generate profits). The ideas would be identical, but for some persons, the photos accompanying them would show attractive entrepreneurs; for others, the photos would show unattractive entrepreneurs. If the ideas received higher ratings when paired with the attractive photos, this finding would suggest that entrepreneurs' appearance influences not only ratings of them, but also reactions to their ideas. (In fact, this is just what recent research has found: Ideas linked to attractive entrepreneurs are indeed rated more favourably than ideas linked to unattractive entrepreneurs).[26]

Because of practical constraints (e.g., it is difficult to vary the factors of interest systematically), experimentation is not used very often in the study of entrepreneurship. Instead, researchers employ a wide range of statistical techniques to help determine causality on the basis of other methods, such as systematic observation. One way to do this is to determine whether one variable or change occurs before another. Something that occurs later in time cannot reasonably be the cause of something that occurred earlier. This concept, called Granger Causality, can be used to establish the direction of causality in systematic observation. Returning to the previous example, suppose that photos of entrepreneurs appearing in their high school yearbooks were rated for attractiveness by a large number of persons. Because these photos were taken *before* the entrepreneurs started new ventures, differences in their level of attractiveness were there first, before they became entrepreneurs. If these ratings were found to be correlated with their later success as an entrepreneur, this finding would provide some evidence that attractiveness is a cause of entrepreneurs' success rather than vice versa.

Now, let's turn to the third method of acquiring knowledge mentioned by Diderot—reflection. Does this, too, play a role? Absolutely. Combining facts in a careful and systematic way is central to the **case method** and other qualitative methods of research, methods that are used very frequently in entrepreneurship research.[27] The case method involves gathering large amounts of data about one organization or specific persons and then using this information to reach conclusions about which factors have influenced important outcomes, such as economic success. For example, consider a case study of the French information systems and services company Steria, carried out by Pier Abetti.[28] This company was founded on the principle that it would gradually be owned by employees of all ranks. Initially, 51 percent of its shares were owned by the seven founding entrepreneurs and one employee. Thirty years later, 1,000 active or retired employees of the company owned 57 percent of the shares; thus, the plan to gradually transfer ownership to employees had succeeded. But how did this process

LEARNING OBJECTIVE

6   Describe the basic nature of systematic observation, experimentation, and reflection (i.e., the case method and other qualitative methods).

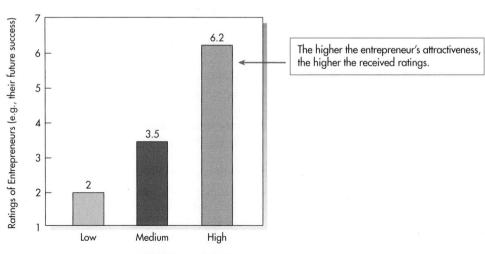

Figure 1.7 Experimentation in Entrepreneurship Research: An Example

In the study illustrated here, photos of entrepreneurs rated as low, medium, and high in attractiveness were shown to a large number of persons working in a wide variety of jobs. These persons rated the entrepreneurs on various dimensions (e.g., likelihood of future success, ability to "sell" their products or services). Results indicate that the more attractive the entrepreneurs, the higher the ratings they received. These findings suggest that entrepreneurs' appearance may play a role in their success.

unfold? Careful study of Steria indicated that it passed through several distinct phases en route to this goal—an initial revolt by dissatisfied employees; managed, gradual growth; a severe drop in profitability; and later, exponential growth coupled with a 400 percent increase in share value. By studying this company in detail, the researcher was able to obtain insight into factors that played a major role in the company's ultimate success; and as the basic theme of this book suggests, these factors involved the behaviour and characteristics of the founding entrepreneurs, relations between the founders and their employees, and the economic and technological climate in which the company operated.

Here's another example of qualitative methods of research. In 1984, villagers in Sri Lanka were given one hectare of land plus food, financial aid, and technical training. Although all villagers received equal treatment, 10 years later, more than half had lost their land and were in debt, while others had prospered greatly. Researchers[29] used a wide variety of sources—in-depth longitudinal case studies, surveys, government reports, commercial documents, and contracts—to identify factors that played a role in these contrasting outcomes. Results indicated that failure was due primarily to villagers' poor skills at negotiating good prices for their crops and their spending of profits on consumer goods rather than needed equipment. Success, in contrast, seemed to stem from the ability to negotiate good prices, and to both recognize and manage opportunities over time. The basic idea behind qualitative methods is that they permit us to capture the tremendous complexity of the entrepreneurial process—complexity that can, occasionally, be missed if we attempt to quantify all factors that play a role.

In sum, there are several different methods for gathering useful—and accurate—information about various aspects of entrepreneurship. None is perfect, but it is our strong conviction that all three are very useful and are greatly superior to the kind of informal, shoot-from-the-hip approaches taken in many popular books on entrepreneurship. Don't misunderstand: We do not mean to imply that the persons writing such books are ill-intentioned or totally lacking in useful insights about the entrepreneurial process. Rather, we only wish to note that the information they communicate is based almost entirely on their own experience and other informal sources. Although these publications can sometimes provide important insights, they rest on less certain (i.e., reliable) foundations than information gathered through the use of systematic observation, experimentation, or the case method. For that reason, we will emphasize information gathered through those methods throughout this book.

Theory: Answering the Questions "Why" and "How"

There is one more aspect of the quest for knowledge about entrepreneurship that we should mention briefly before concluding: the role of **theory** in this endeavour. The term "theory" has a special meaning in the realm of science. It refers to efforts to go beyond merely describing various phenomena to the point at which we can explain them—understanding why and how they happen or take place as they do. For instance, with respect to opportunity recognition, we don't want merely to be able to state that some people are better at recognizing opportunities than others or to report the percent of people who are highly skilled at this task. We want to be able to explain *why* this is so and *how* they go about recognizing these opportunities. In other words, we want to know just what it is about certain people that allows them to be so good at recognizing opportunities that other people miss. Theories are frameworks for explaining various events or processes. Given the fact that the field of entrepreneurship has been in existence for only a relatively short period of time, it is not surprising to learn that this discipline has few well-developed theories of its own; in fact, it has sometimes been criticized for lacking such frameworks.[30] Up to this point in time, entrepreneurship has largely borrowed theories from other fields, such as economics, psychology, and cognitive science. For instance, efforts have recently been made to apply prospect theory, a well-developed theory of decision making,[31] to several important issues relating to entrepreneurship (e.g., the question of how entrepreneurs perceive risk)[32] to answer the previous question.

LEARNING OBJECTIVE

7 Explain the role of theory in the field of entrepreneurship.

Again, we should emphasize that theories are extremely useful because they help explain why certain events or processes occur as they do. But how are they derived in the first place? Briefly, the process goes something like this:

1. On the basis of existing evidence or observations, a theory reflecting this evidence is proposed.

2. This theory, which consists of basic concepts and statements about how these concepts are related, helps to organize existing information and makes predictions about observable events. For instance, the theory might predict the conditions under which individuals recognize or do not recognize opportunities.

3. These predictions, known as *hypotheses*, are then tested by actual research.

4. If results are consistent with the theory, confidence in its accuracy is increased. If they are not, the theory is modified and further tests are conducted.

5. Ultimately, the theory is either accepted as accurate or rejected as inaccurate. Even if it is accepted as accurate, however, the theory remains open to further refinement as improved methods of research are developed and additional evidence relevant to the theory's predictions is obtained. (See Figure 1.8 for a summary of these steps.)

Our discussion so far has been quite abstract, so perhaps a concrete example will help. Suppose that, on the basis of careful observations, an entrepreneurship researcher formulates the following theory: Individuals who choose to become entrepreneurs think differently, in various ways, from people who do not choose this role.[33] Specifically, individuals who choose to become entrepreneurs (1) are more likely than other persons to be susceptible to several kinds of cognitive errors or biases (e.g., they are more likely to be overoptimistic, to suffer from the illusion of control—overestimates of their ability to control the outcomes they experience, etc.) and (2) are more likely than other persons to think about situations in terms of the gains they will give up if they do not launch a new venture; which, in turn, causes them to be more accepting of risk. These predictions are then formulated as specific hypotheses and tested in actual research. For instance, actual or would-be entrepreneurs could be compared with persons who have no interest in starting new ventures in terms of their susceptibility to cognitive errors and their tendency to think about various situations in terms of losses. Measures of all these variables already exist and have been used in previous studies, so designing research to test these hypotheses is

Figure 1.8 The Role of Theory in Entrepreneurship Research

Theories both organize existing knowledge and make predictions about how various events or processes will occur. Once theories are formulated, hypotheses derived logically from them are tested through careful research. If results agree with predictions, confidence in the theory is increased. If results disagree with such predictions, the theory may be modified or—ultimately—rejected as false.

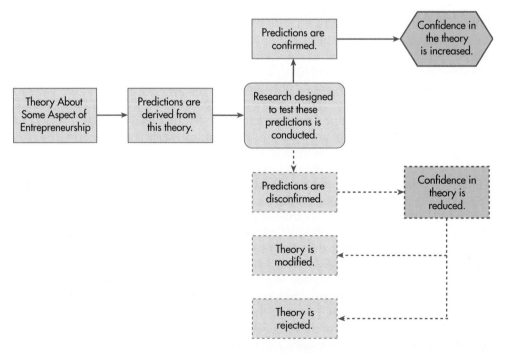

quite feasible. If results are consistent with predictions derived from the theory, confidence in it would be increased: There would be increased basis for accepting the theory's premise that entrepreneurs do indeed think differently from other persons. On the other hand, if results were not consistent with predictions derived from the theory, confidence in it would be reduced.

Why should the field of entrepreneurship, which is eminently practical in orientation, be interested in theory? Because, as one social scientist remarked many years ago, "There is nothing as practical as a good theory."[34] He meant that having a good theory—a clear understanding of why or how a process occurs as it does—is very useful from the point of view of intervening in beneficial ways. In other words, if we have good and well-verified theories about entrepreneurship, we will understand this process in ways that enhance our ability to assist entrepreneurs in their efforts to start new ventures. That, of course, would be a very positive outcome. In short, developing good theories is more than an exercise in basic science: It is an important step toward attaining valuable, practical results.

Two final points: First, theories are never proven in any final, ultimate sense. Rather, they are always open to test and are accepted with more or less confidence depending on the weight of available evidence relating to them. Second, research should never be undertaken to prove or verify a theory; it is performed to gather evidence relating to the theory. If researchers set out to prove a pet theory, this intention is a serious violation of the methods that should be followed to gather accurate information about any topic. Why? Because in setting out to prove a theory, the researchers may lose objectivity and either subconsciously (or even consciously) design the research so that it tips the balance in favour of the theory. Clearly, any results obtained under these conditions are on shaky ground.

KEY POINTS

- Many potential sources of knowledge about entrepreneurship exist, but the most accurate and reliable knowledge is provided by methods found to be useful in other fields: systematic observation, experimentation, and reflection.
- Systematic observation involves careful measurement of variables of interest in order to determine whether they are related (correlated) in any orderly manner. To the extent they are, one can be predicted from the other.
- Experimentation involves direct interventions: One variable is changed systematically in order to determine whether such changes affect one or more additional variables.
- In the case method, large amounts of information are gathered about one organization or specific persons, and this information is then used to reach conclusions about which factors have influenced important outcomes, such as economic success.
- Theory involves efforts to explain rather than merely describe various phenomena—to understand why and how they occur. Research is conducted to obtain data relevant to theories—not to prove them.

A USER'S GUIDE TO THIS TEXT

Although it has been many years since we were students, we both remember the following fact well: Not all textbooks are equally useful or equally easy to read. For this reason, we have taken many active steps to make this book one of the good ones. Here is an overview of the steps we have taken to reach this goal.

First, we have included many reader aids. Each chapter beings with an outline of the topics covered and a list of key learning objectives: what you should know after you have finished reading the chapter. These objectives are numbered and also appear next to specific sections of the text relating to them. Within the text itself, important terms are printed in **bold type like this** and are followed by a definition.

These terms are also defined in a glossary at the end of each chapter. To help you retain what you have read, each major section is followed by a list of Key Points—a brief summary of major points covered in that section. All figures and tables are clear and simple, and most include special labels and notes designed to help you understand them (see Figure 1.7 for an example). Finally, each chapter ends with a Summary and Review of Key Points. Reviewing this section can help you retain more of the information presented and help you to benefit more from this text.

Second, two special features are included to make the text more useful—and interesting. One—titled The Voice of Experience—reports interviews that we have conducted with experienced entrepreneurs. In these interviews, which are presented at the end of various chapters, entrepreneurs give their perspective on the topics covered in that chapter, discussing factors that contributed to their success—and to their failures. We think you will be amazed by the degree of overlap between what their practical experience has told them and what you find reported on the pages of this book.

The second feature is titled Danger! Pitfall Ahead! These sections, which appear within each chapter rather than at the end, highlight potential snares and hazards that entrepreneurs should be aware of—threats that can prove fatal to entrepreneurs' new ventures and their dreams. Having been there ourselves, we are only too aware of these pitfalls; it is crucial that we call them to your attention.

Third, each chapter is followed by experiential exercises titled Getting Down to Business. As this title suggests, these exercises are designed to provide you with practice in using the information presented in the chapter. Finally, it is important to note that the chapters follow the time line presented earlier in this chapter (refer to Figure 1.6). Thus, Part 1 (Chapters 1 through 4) examines the field of entrepreneurship, the emergence and recognition of opportunities, and the personal qualities that have been found to be important to entrepreneurs. Part 2 (Chapters 5 through 8) focuses on assembly of the resources needed to launch a new venture—people financial, intellectual, and planning resources. Part 3 (Chapters 9 through 12) examines the actual launch of new ventures, considering such topics as the legal form of such ventures, marketing, strategic planning, and developing human resources. Finally, Part 4 (Chapter 13) focuses on the logical conclusion to the entrepreneurial process: alternative ways in which entrepreneurs can harvest the rewards of their efforts.

One last word. As authors and teachers, we promise faithfully that we will not lose sight of our major goals in writing this book: providing you with an accurate and up-to-date overview of what we currently know about entrepreneurship as a process. In closing, we wish to add that we agree with Lady Mary Montagu (an English author) who, in writing about personal wealth, once remarked: "Tis a sort of duty to be rich, that it may be in one's power to do good.... " We believe that successful entrepreneurs do indeed "do good." True, they add to their own wealth but, in addition, they do much more. The products and services they bring into being improve the lives of countless millions of persons; on top of this, they are often extremely generous in donating substantial portions of their wealth to eminently worthy causes. For instance, Michael Lee-Chin, CEO of AIC Limited, generously supports education, health, and arts organizations in Canada and his native Jamaica (see Figure 1.9). Under his leadership, the AIC-owned National Commercial Bank in Jamaica contributed more than $11 million (Jamaican) to assist flood victims in May 2002 and $212 million (Jamaican) to assist victims of the 2004 hurricane disaster in the Caribbean. All of the authors work in schools of management that are named for the entrepreneurs who made generous donations to support the schools and the universities in which they are located. If this book helps you, as an emerging entrepreneur, to succeed in attaining your dreams—and therefore enhances your ability to do good with the wealth you acquire—we will feel that as authors, we too have done our part.

Figure 1.9 Entrepreneurs: Key Contributors to Society

Entrepreneurs do not merely add to their own personal fortunes; in addition, they improve the lives of millions of persons through the new products and services they bring to market. Moreover, they often make generous donations to worthy causes; for instance, in 2003 Canadian entrepreneur Michael Lee-Chin donated $30 million to the Royal Ontario Museum in Toronto. Shown here is a preview of the Michael Lee-Chin Crystal at the ROM.

Image: Miller Hare © ROM 2005. All rights reserved.

Summary and Review of Key Points

- Entrepreneurship, as a field of business, seeks to understand how opportunities to create new products or services arise, and are discovered or created by specific persons; these persons then use various means to exploit or develop them, thus producing a wide range of effects.
- In recent years, the allure of entrepreneurship has increased, with the result that more people than ever before are choosing this activity as a career.
- Entrepreneurship, as a branch of business, has important roots in economics, behavioural science, and sociology.
- The field of entrepreneurship recognizes that both the micro perspective (which focuses on the behaviour and thoughts of individuals) and the macro perspective (which focuses primarily on environmental factors) are important for obtaining a full understanding of the entrepreneurial process.
- Entrepreneurship is a process that unfolds over time and moves through distinct but closely interrelated phases.
- The entrepreneurial process cannot be divided into neat and easily distinguished phases but, in general, it involves generation of an idea for a new product or service and/or recognition of an opportunity; assembling the resources needed to launch a new venture; launching the venture; running and growing the business; and harvesting the rewards.
- Individual, group, and societal factors influence all phases of the entrepreneurial process. Thus, there is no reason to choose between a micro and a macro approach to entrepreneurship; both perspectives are necessary.
- It is the nexus of valuable opportunities and enterprising individuals that is the essence of entrepreneurship.
- Many potential sources of knowledge about entrepreneurship exist, but the most accurate and reliable knowledge is provided by methods found to be useful for in other fields: systematic observation, experimentation, and reflection.
- Systematic observation involves careful measurement of variables of interest in order to determine whether they are related (correlated) in any orderly manner. To the extent they are, one can be predicted from the other.
- Experimentation involves direct interventions: One variable is changed systematically in order to determine whether such changes affect one or more additional variables.
- In the case method, large amounts of information are gathered about one organization or specific persons, and this information is then used to reach conclusions about which factors have influenced important outcomes, such as economic success.
- Theory involves efforts to explain rather than merely describe various phenomena—why and how they occur. Research is conducted to obtain data relevant to theories—not to prove them.

Glossary

Business Plan: A written expression of the entrepreneur's vision for converting ideas into a profitable, going business.

Case Method: A research method in which large amounts of data about one organization or specific persons are gathered and then used to reach conclusions about which factors have influenced important outcomes, such as economic success.

Experimentation: A research method in which one variable is systematically changed in order to determine whether such changes affect one or more other variables.

Hypothesis: An as yet untested prediction or explanation for a set of facts.

Intrapreneurs: Persons who create something new, but inside an existing company rather than through founding a new venture.

Macro (Perspective): A top-down perspective that seeks to understand the entrepreneurial process by focusing largely on environmental factors (i.e., economic, financial, political factors) that are largely beyond the direct control of an individual.

Micro (Perspective): A bottom-up perspective that seeks to understand the entrepreneurial process by focusing on the behaviour and thought of individuals or groups of individuals (e.g., founding partners).

Opportunity: The potential to create something new (new products or services, new markets, new production processes, new raw materials, new ways of organizing existing technologies, etc.) that has emerged from a complex pattern of changing conditions—shifts in knowledge, technology, or in the economic, political, social, and demographic climate.

Systematic Observation: A research method in which certain aspects of the world are observed systematically, keeping careful records of what is detected. This information is then used as a basis for reaching conclusions about the topics under investigation.

Theory: Refers to efforts to go beyond merely describing various phenomena and, instead, to explain them.

Variables: Aspects of the world that can take different values.

Discussion Questions

1. Is there any difference between an inventor and an entrepreneur? If so, describe it.

2. Suppose that the government passed a series of laws that made it much more difficult to start a new business. What effect(s) do you think this new legislation would have on the economy?

3. One basic question in the field of entrepreneurship is "Why do some persons leave secure jobs and lives to become entrepreneurs?" How would you study this question from the micro perspective? From the macro perspective?

4. In this chapter, we suggested that entrepreneurs are the new heroes and heroines in many cultures. Do you agree? If so, why do so many people see entrepreneurs as being heroic? If you do not think it is accurate, why not?

5. Suppose you came across an article in a magazine with the title, "First-Borns Make the Best Entrepreneurs." The article contends that entrepreneurs who are the oldest child in their family are more successful than entrepreneurs who are second- or third–born children. What questions should you ask yourself about how this information was obtained in order to decide whether to view it as accurate or valid?

InfoTrac Exercises

1. **The Role of Self-employment in U.S. and Canadian Job Growth** (in the 1990s) *Marilyn E. Manser; Garnett Picot.*

   Monthly Labor Review, April 1999 v122 i4 p10(16)

   Record: A55010245

   Abstract: Self-employment rates have been higher in Canada than in the United States for some time, and this tendency became more pronounced during the 1990s.

   1. According to the article, self-employment rates were higher in Canada than in the United States during the 1990s. List the reasons cited by the authors for this trend.

   2. According to the article, what role does self-employment play in the Canadian economy?

   3. What steps can government take to encourage economic growth via entrepreneurship? Consider ideas from the article, then add your own.

2. **Competition Opens the Door for New-Age Entrepreneurs** (includes related article on management expert Peter Drucker's definition of entrepreneurship) *John E. Gnuschke; Coy A. Jones*

   Business Perspectives, July 1997 v10 i1 p2(5)

   Record: A57445160

   Abstract: Entrepreneurs are unquestionably important to economic growth. Statistics indicate that new and small companies have contributed 95 percent of all radical innovations and roughly 50 percent of all innovations since World War I. Entrepreneurs have bridged the gap from science to the consumer market with innumerable, useful products. Even if less than 50 percent of all new businesses survive more than four years, the creation of value and addition of it to the distribution chain have been remarkably critical to economic expansion.

   1. According to the text, how is entrepreneurship defined?

   2. According to the related article by Peter Drucker, how is entrepreneurship defined?

   3. Compare and contract these two definitions. Then develop your own definition for entrepreneurship.

GETTING DOWN
TO BUSINESS

Becoming an Entrepreneur: Is It Right for You?

A key theme of this chapter has been that the entrepreneurial process begins when enterprising individuals identify potentially valuable opportunities. Clearly, this perspective implies that not everyone is suited to becoming an entrepreneur. Just being able to spot potentially profitable opportunities is not, in itself, enough. In addition, entrepreneurs must be willing, ready, and able to run with the ball—to take the vigorous and continuing steps necessary to launch a new venture. Are you such a person? Are you capable of not only developing a vision of where you want to get but of arriving there? If not, you should reconsider, because entrepreneurship definitely lives up to Edison's suggestion that "Success is 2 percent inspiration and 98 percent perspiration."

Although there is no single test of entrepreneurial potential,[35] there is general agreement that becoming a successful entrepreneur requires several key characteristics. Rate yourself on each of these dimensions—and then ask several people who know you well to also rate you. The results may give you valuable insight into whether you are cut out to be an entrepreneur.

1. **Can You Handle Uncertainty?** Is security (e.g., a regular paycheque) important to you, or are you willing to live with uncertainty—economic and otherwise?

2. **Are You Energetic?** Do you have the vigour and good health required to work very long hours for long periods of time in order to reach goals that are important to you?

3. **Do You Believe in Yourself and Your Abilities?** Do you believe that you can accomplish whatever you set out to accomplish, learning what you need along the way?

4. **Can You Handle Reversals and Failures Well?** How do you react to negative outcomes—with discouragement or with renewed commitment to succeeding the next time around and learning from your mistakes?

5. **Are You Passionate About Your Goals or Vision?** Once you establish a goal or a vision of where you want to be, are you willing to sacrifice almost everything else to get there, because you are truly passionate about it?

6. **Are You Good with Other People?** Can you persuade others to see the world the way you do? Can you get along with other people well (e.g., handle conflicts, build trust)?

7. **Are You Adaptable?** Can you make mid-course corrections easily? For instance, can you admit that you made a mistake and reverse course to correct it?

8. **Are You Willing to Take Risks or Leaps of Faith?** Once you establish a goal, are you willing to take reasonable risks to reach it? In other words, are you willing to do what you can to minimize the risks, but then, once you have done so, proceed?

Current evidence suggests that successful entrepreneurs are high on all of these dimensions—higher than other persons.[36] Successful entrepreneurs can handle uncertainty, are energetic, believe in themselves, react well and flexibly to reversals, are passionate about their beliefs, get along with other people, are highly adaptable, and are willing to accept reasonable levels of risk. To the extent you possess these characteristics—or a least most of them—you may be well-suited for the role of entrepreneur. We suspect that if you are reading this book, you fit this description— otherwise, you would not be in this course! If you find that you are relatively low on several of these characteristics, however, you might want to reconsider; perhaps becoming an entrepreneur is not really your particular cup of tea.

Answering Questions about Entrepreneurship: Practice in Thinking like a Researcher

In this chapter, we discussed various methods for answering questions about entrepreneurship in ways that yield information that is both reliable and accurate. Although we certainly don't expect you to become an expert in using these methods (that takes years of study and practice), we think it is important to understand how these research methods work; you will become an informed consumer of knowledge about entrepreneurship. In other words, you will be able to tell what information is useful to you and what is purely conjecture—or worse!

To gain practice in using these methods, try the following exercise. Consider the following questions and, for each, describe how you might go about answering it through use of (1) systematic observation, (2) experimentation, or (3) qualitative methods, such as the case method. For each, try to specify clearly the variables you would study and the ways in which you would gather information about these variables. Also try to formulate specific hypotheses about how your results will turn out. Finally, consider the implications for entrepreneurs if your findings confirm, or do not confirm, your initial hypothesis.

1. Do companies that are first to market with a new product have a competitive edge over companies that enter the same market later?

2. Do repeat entrepreneurs (people who found one successful company after another) search for opportunities differently from entrepreneurs who found only one company?

3. What factors lead individuals to give up secure and well-paid jobs to become entrepreneurs? Are these factors the same for women and men?

Enhanced Learning

You may select any combination of the resources below to enhance your understanding of the chapter material.

- **Appendix: Case Studies** — Twelve cases provide opportunities to apply chapter concepts to realistic entrepreneurial situations. These brief cases call for careful analysis of real business problems and ask you to think about potential solutions.

- **Video Case Library** — Nine cases are tied directly to video segments from the popular PBS television series Small Business School. These cases and video segments (available on the Entrepreneurship website at http://www. entrepreneurship.nelson.com) give you unparalleled access to today's entrepreneurs, with expert advice and insights on how to start, run, and grow a business.

- **Management Interview Series Video Database** — This video interview series contains a wealth of tips on how to manage effectively. Access to the database and practical exercises are available on the book support website at http://www.entrepreneurship.nelson.com.

Notes

1 Shane, S., & Venkataraman, S. 2000. The promise of entrepreneurship as a field of research. *Academy of Management Review* 25(1): 217–226.

2 Our history. http://www.skeetike.com/history.html.

3 Astebro, T. 1998. Basic statistics on the success rate and profits for independent inventors. *Entrepreneurship Theory and Practice* 23(2): 41–48.

4 Ricchiuto, J. 1997. *Collaborative creativity.* New York: Oakhill.

5 Keil, T. 2004. Building external corporate venturing capability. *Journal of Management Studies* 41(5): 799–825.

6 Koen, P.A., & Baron, R.A. 2003. *Predictors of resource attainment among corporate entrepreneurs: Executive champion versus team commitment.* Paper presented at the Babson-Kauffman Entrepreneurship Research Conference, Babson Park, MA, June, 2003.

7 Anderson, R.B. 1997. Corporate/indigenous partnerships in economic development: The First Nations in Canada. *World Development* 25: 1483–1503.

8 About us. http://www.marketinitiatives.org/about.

9 Industry Canada. 2005. *Key Small Business Statistics, July 2005.* Ottawa: Industry Canada.

10 Riverin, N., Filion, L-J., Muzyka, D.F., Vertinsky, I., Pe'er, A., Comeau, J., Li, A., & Branzei, O. *Canadian National Report 2003, Global Entrepreneurship Monitor.* http://www.gemconsortium.org.

11 O'Reilly, B. 1994. The new deal: What companies and employees owe each other. *Fortune* 129(12): 44–52.

12 Bedeian, A.G., Ferris, G.R., & Kacmar, K.M. 1992. Age, tenure, and job satisfaction: A tale of two perspectives. *Journal of Vocational Behavior* 40(1): 33–48.

13 Riverin, N., Filion, L-J., Muzyka, D.F., Vertinsky, I., Pe'er, A., Comeau, J., Li, A. & Branzei, O. Canadian National Report 2003, *Global Entrepreneurship Monitor.* http://www.gemconsortium.org.

14 Greenberg, J., & Baron, R.A. 2003. *Behavior in organizations.* 8th ed. Upper Saddle River, NJ: Prentice-Hall.

15 Baron, R.A. (2002). OB and entrepreneurship: The reciprocal benefits of closer conceptual links. In B.M. Staw & R. Kramer (eds.). *Research in organizational behavior* (pp. 225–269). Greenwich, CT: JAI Press.

16 Ardichvili, A., Cardozo, R., & Ray, S. 2003. A theory of entrepreneurial opportunity identification and development. *Journal of Business Venturing* 18(1): 105–124.

17 Company info. http://www.smarttech.com/company/aboutus/index.asp.

18 Shane, S., Locke, E.A., & Collins, C.J. 2002. Entrepreneurial motivation. *Human Resource Management Review* 13(2): 257–280.

19 Gartner, W.B. 1990. What are we talking about when we talk about entrepreneurship? *Journal of Business Venturing* 5(1): 15–28.

20 Markman, G.D., Balkin, D.B., & Baron R.A. 2002. Inventors and new venture formation: The effects of general self-efficacy and regretful thinking. *Entrepreneurship Theory and Practice* 27(2): 149–165.

21 Chua, J.J, Chrisman, J.H., & Sharma, P. 2003. Succession and nonsuccession concerns of family firms and agency relationship with nonfamily managers. *Family Business Review* 16(2): 89–107.

22 Mitchell, R.K., Smith, J.B., Morse, E.A., Seawright, K.W., Peredo, A.M., & McKenzie, B. 2002. Are entrepreneurial cognitions universal? Assessing entrepreneurial cognitions across cultures. *Entrepreneurship Theory and Practice* 26(4): 9–32.

23 Evans, D., & Leighton, L. 1989. Some empirical aspects of entrepreneurship. *American Economic Review* 79(3): 519–535.

24 Alba-Ramirez, A. 1994. Self-employment in the midst of unemployment: The case of Spain and the United States. *Applied Economics* 26(3): 189–204.

25 Langlois, J.H., Kalakanis, L., Rubenstein, A.J., Larson, A., Hallam, M., & Smoot, M. 2000. Maxims or myths of beauty? A meta-analytic and theoretical review. *Psychological Bulletin* 126(3): 390–432.

26 Baron, R.A., Markman, G.D., & Bollinger, M. 2006. Exporting social psychology: Effects of attractiveness on perceptions of entrepreneurs, their ideas for new products, and their financial success. *Journal of Applied Social Psychology* 36(2): 467–492.

27 Gartner, W.B., & Birley, S. 2002. Introduction to the special issue on qualitative methods in entrepreneurship research. *Journal of Business Venturing* 17(5): 387–395.

28 Abetti, P.A. 2003. The entrepreneurial control imperative: A case history of Steria (1969–2000). *Journal of Business Venturing* 18(1): 125–143.

29 Kodithuwakku, S.S., & Rosa, P. 2002. The entrepreneurial process and economic success in a constrained environment. *Journal of Business Venturing* 17(5): 431–455.

30 Shane, S., & Venkataraman, S. 2000. The promise of entrepreneurship as a field of research. *Academy of Management Review* 25(1): 217–226.

31 Plous, S. 1993. *The psychology of judgment and decision making.* New York: McGraw-Hill.

32 Stewart, W.H., Jr., & Roth, P.L. 2001. Risk propensity differences between entrepreneurs and managers: A meta-analytic review. *Journal of Applied Psychology* 86(1): 145–153.

33 Krueger, N.F., Jr. 2003. The cognitive psychology of entrepreneurship. In Z. Acs & D.B. Audretsch (eds.). *Handbook of entrepreneurial research* (pp. 105–140). London: Kluwer Law International.

34 Lewin, K. 1951. *Field theory in social science.* New York: Harper & Row.

35 Chen, C.C., Green, P.G., & Crick, A. 1998. Does entrepreneurial self-efficacy distinguish entrepreneurs from managers? *Journal of Business Venturing* 13(4): 295–316.

36 Stewart, W.H., Jr., Watson, W.E., Carland, J.C., & Carland, J.W. 1999. A proclivity for entrepreneurship: A comparison of entrepreneurs, small business owners, and corporate managers. *Journal of Business Venturing* 14(2): 189–214.

CHAPTER 2

UNCOVERING OPPORTUNITIES: UNDERSTANDING ENTREPRENEURIAL OPPORTUNITIES AND INDUSTRY ANALYSIS

LEARNING OBJECTIVES

After reading this chapter, you should be able to:

1 Define an entrepreneurial opportunity and explain why such opportunities exist.

2 Describe how technological, political/regulatory, and social/demographic changes generate entrepreneurial opportunities.

3 List the different forms that entrepreneurial opportunities can take, and explain why some forms are better for new firms than others.

4 Explain why new firms are more successful in some industries than in others, and identify the four major types of industry differences that influence the relative success of new firms.

5 Identify the three different dimensions of knowledge conditions, and explain how they influence an industry's supportiveness of new firms.

6 Identify the three different dimensions of demand conditions, and explain how they influence an industry's supportiveness of new firms.

7 Identify the two different dimensions of industry life cycles, and explain how they influence an industry's supportiveness of new firms.

8 Identify the four different dimensions of industry structure, and explain how they influence an industry's supportiveness of new firms.

9 Explain why established firms are usually better than new firms at exploiting entrepreneurial opportunities.

10 Identify the types of opportunities that new firms are better at exploiting, and explain why new firms are advantaged at the exploitation of those opportunities.

Sources of Opportunities: The Origins of New Ventures
> Technological Change
> Political and Regulatory Change
> Social and Demographic Change

Forms of Opportunity: Beyond New Products and Services

Industries That Favour New Firms: Fertile Grounds for New Ventures
> Knowledge Conditions
> Demand Conditions
> Industry Life Cycles
> Industry Structure

Opportunities and New Firms
> Why Most Opportunities Favour Established Firms
> Opportunities That Favour New Firms

All photos this page © PhotoDisc, Inc.

28

NEL

"In great affairs we ought to apply ourselves less to creating chances than to profiting from those that offer." (La Rouchefoucauld, *Maxims*, 1665)

In Chapter 1, we explained that entrepreneurs recognize opportunities to create new products or services, to use new means of production, to exploit new ways of organizing, to use new raw materials, and to tap new markets that are made possible by technological, political, regulatory, demographic, or social change. For example, some entrepreneurs have developed new products, such as DVD players, which people can use to watch movies. Other entrepreneurs have come up with new ways of organizing, such as using retail superstores to make goods less expensive. Others have figured out how to use new materials, for example, using oil to make gasoline. Still other entrepreneurs have developed new production processes, such as computer-aided drug discovery, which allows people to come up with new drugs to cure diseases. One more group worth mentioning has identified new markets for products, for example, crackers made from seaweed, which are popular in Japan.

Not only do entrepreneurial opportunities have different sources and take different forms, but they also differ in value. For example, the potential profits from establishing a new pizza restaurant on the corner of a university campus are not as large as the potential profits that one can make from developing a new biotechnology company that has formulated a cure for breast cancer. In fact, research has shown that some industries consistently produce more valuable opportunities for new businesses than others. Jon Eckhardt, a Ph.D. student of mine (Scott Shane), now teaching at the University of Wisconsin, looked at the industries in which the Inc. 500 companies were found. The Inc. 500 is a list put together by Inc. magazine that identifies the fastest growing young private companies in the United States. Over an 18-year period (1982–2000), Jon found that some industries had a consistently

higher percentage of start-up companies listed on the Inc. 500 than other industries (see Table 2.1).[1] He also found that many of these same industries had a higher percentage of start-up companies that had gone public. These data show that if a random entrepreneur started a business in certain industries and not in others, that person would be much more likely to have a very rapidly growing public company. Unless the entrepreneurs who enter certain industries are more talented than the entrepreneurs who enter other industries, Jon's data mean that some industries must have better opportunities for founding new companies than others.

What makes some opportunities better than others for starting new companies? Existing evidence suggests that some industries and opportunities are more favourable to new firms than others—a favourability that helps new firms grow and become profitable.

Table 2.1 Some Industries Produce More High-Growth Companies Than Others

The industries in the top half of the chart are more attractive to entrepreneurs than those at the bottom of the chart because they had a higher ratio of Inc. 500 companies to new firms from 1989–1997.

SIC	INDUSTRY	NUMBER OF Inc. 500 FIRMS	NUMBER OF FIRM STARTS	Inc. 500 FIRMS AS A PERCENT OF STARTS
261	Pulp mills	6	33	0.181818
357	Computer and office equipment	99	2,359	0.041967
376	Guided missiles, space vehicles, parts	2	60	0.033333
335	Nonferrous rolling and drawing	14	581	0.024096
474	Railroad car rental	3	136	0.022059
382	Measuring and controlling devices	49	2,482	0.019742
262	Paper mills	3	152	0.019737
381	Search and navigation equipment	6	310	0.019355
366	Communications equipment	29	1,543	0.018795
283	Drugs	20	1,092	0.018315
384	Medical instruments and supplies	55	3,025	0.018182
316	Luggage	3	172	0.017442
314	Footwear, except rubber	4	271	0.014760
623	Security and commodity exchanges	2	141	0.014184
496	Steam and air-conditioning supply	1	83	0.012048
356	General industrial machinery	26	2,173	0.011965
386	Photographic equipment and supplies	7	646	0.010836
276	Manifold business forms	3	281	0.010676
363	Household appliances	4	390	0.010256
362	Electrical industrial apparatus	11	1,080	0.010185
811	Legal services	10	129,207	0.000077
581	Eating and drinking places	34	494,731	0.000069
175	Carpentry and floor work contractors	4	66,383	0.000060
651	Real estate operators	5	90,042	0.000056
701	Hotels and motels	2	39,177	0.000051
172	Painting and paper hanging contractors	2	43,987	0.000046
546	Retail bakeries	1	22,165	0.000045
541	Grocery stores	5	112,473	0.000045
593	Used-merchandise stores	1	24,442	0.000041
753	Automotive repair shops	5	124,725	0.000040
723	Beauty shops	3	79,081	0.000038
836	Residential care	1	27,710	0.000036
784	Videotape rental	1	27,793	0.000036

Source: Adapted from Eckhardt, J. 2003. When the weak acquire wealth: An examination of the distribution of high growth startups in the U.S. economy. Ph.D. Dissertation, University of Maryland.

The remainder of this chapter will expand on the role of opportunities in entrepreneurship. In the first section, we will discuss where new opportunities come from. Three major sources of change—new technology, political and regulatory shifts, and social and demographic changes—make it possible for people to start firms to exploit opportunities to make new products, to develop new production processes, to organize in new ways, to open up new markets, and to use new raw materials.

In the second section, we will explain why opportunities are sometimes exploited through one of these forms and why they are exploited through other forms at other times. For instance, why did the development of the Internet, a new technology, lead to a new way of organizing, e-tailing, but fail to change the types of products sold? In contrast, why did the invention of the internal combustion engine, also a new technology, lead to the development of a new product, the automobile, but not produce changes in the way businesses were organized?

In the third section, we will return to the discussion that we started in the beginning of this chapter about the industry differences that make some industries more attractive than others for the founding of new businesses. We will explain the characteristics of different industries that researchers have shown make some of them more fertile environments than others for founding new firms.

In the final section of the chapter, we will focus on differences across opportunities, and will explain why some opportunities are better for new firms than for established firms. Although established firms are better than new firms at exploiting opportunities most of the time, new firms sometimes have distinct advantages in exploiting entrepreneurial opportunities. We want you to learn how to exploit those advantages.

SOURCES OF OPPORTUNITIES: THE ORIGINS OF NEW VENTURES

LEARNING OBJECTIVE

1 Define an entrepreneurial opportunity and explain why such opportunities exist.

As we explained in Chapter 1, an entrepreneurial opportunity is a situation in which shifts in technology or in the economic, political, social, and demographic climate generate the potential to create something new.[2] As we mentioned earlier, an entrepreneurial opportunity can be exploited through the creation of a new product or service, the opening of a new market, the development of a new way of organizing, the use of a new material, or the introduction of a new production process. But where do these opportunities come from? Why do they make it possible for people to come up with new business ideas that have the potential to generate a profit?

Researchers have provided two explanations for the existence of entrepreneurial opportunities. Israel Kirzner, an economist at New York University, explains that entrepreneurial opportunities exist because people have different information.[3] Some people know about a new technological discovery, while others know about a storefront in a strip mall lying vacant. The different information that people have makes some people better than others at making decisions about a particular business idea. Because people with inferior information make worse decisions, there are always shortages, surpluses, and errors that allow people with better information to make more accurate decisions. For example, you might have better information than a local businessperson about what the people in your dorm would like to do on a Saturday night. As a result, the local businessperson might have put a pizza place on the street just outside the edge of campus. However, you might be able to make a greater profit than the owner of the pizzeria by taking over the spot and putting in a nightclub. Your greater information about what the people in your dorm want to do (go to a club) allows you to take advantage of a prior decision-making error (creating a pizza place) that generates a new business opportunity.

In contrast, Josef Schumpeter, an Austrian economist, argued that truly valuable entrepreneurial opportunities come from an external change that either makes it possible to do things that had not been done before or makes it possible to do something in a more valuable way.[4] For example, the invention of the laser made it possible to develop a new product, the supermarket scanner, that electronically scans the bar codes on food. In the absence of the external change—the invention of the laser—this opportunity would not have existed. Researchers who have followed in the tradition of Josef Schumpeter have identified three major sources of opportunity: technological change, political and regulatory change, and social and demographic change.

These changes really do drive the creation of opportunities for new businesses. Amar Bhide, an entrepreneurship professor at Columbia University, has shown that the founders of half of the Inc. 500 companies started their businesses in response to a specific change in technology, regulation, fashion, or other source of opportunity.[5]

Technological Change

Researchers have shown that technological change is the most important source of valuable entrepreneurial opportunities that make it possible for people to start new businesses.[6] Technological changes are a source of entrepreneurial opportunities because they make it possible for people to do things in new and more productive ways (see Figure 2.1). For example, although people communicated with each other before the invention of e-mail by using faxes, letters, the telephone, and face-to-face meetings, when the Internet was invented, several entrepreneurs discovered that people could use electronic mail to communicate. Although e-mail did not replace these other modes of communication completely, savvy entrepreneurs realized that e-mail was better than these other modes of communication for certain things. That is, the invention of a new technology made it possible to develop a more productive form of communication, e-mail, and so was a valuable source of opportunity.

Researchers explain that larger technological changes are a greater source of entrepreneurial opportunity than smaller technological changes because larger technological changes make possible bigger changes in productivity from exploiting the new technology. For example, a new material that is 50 percent stronger than steel would be a lesser source of entrepreneurial opportunity than a new material that is 10 times stronger than steel because there would be many more ways that a material that is 10 times stronger than steel could be used. In fact, in a study of the efforts to commercialize inventions belonging to the Massachusetts Institute of Technology, I (Scott Shane) found that the more important the technological

> ### LEARNING OBJECTIVE
> **2** Describe how technological, political/regulatory, and social/demographic changes generate entrepreneurial opportunities.

Figure 2.1 Technological Change Is an Important Source of Entrepreneurial Opportunities

The BlackBerry, developed by Waterloo-based Research In Motion has revolutionized wireless communication and yielded entrepreneurial opportunities for a diverse group of third-party developers and manufacturers. Technological advances in 3-D computer graphics chips provide video game makers like Edmonton-based BioWare with opportunities to develop ever-sophisticated games.

© Steven May/Alamy

Courtesy of BioWare Corp.

advance represented by an invention, the more likely someone was to found a new firm to exploit it.[7]

Political and Regulatory Change

Other important sources of opportunity are political and regulatory changes. These changes make it possible to develop business ideas to use resources in new ways that are either more productive or that redistribute wealth from one person to another. For example, deregulation in telecommunications, utilities, and health care make it more difficult for established organizations to deter the entry of new competitors and allow entrepreneurs to introduce more productive business ideas into these industries.[8]

Researchers have shown that certain types of regulatory and political change are particularly valuable sources of entrepreneurial opportunities (see Figure 2.2). First, as we mentioned earlier, deregulation is a valuable source of opportunity by making it easier for people to enter industries with their new ideas. Second, regulations that support particular types of business activity encourage entrepreneurs to undertake those activities. For example, researchers have shown that government regulation to certify daycare centres in Toronto led to an increase in the formation of new daycare centres.[9] Third, regulations provide a source of opportunity by providing resources that either increase demand for particular activities or subsidize firms that undertake them. For example, municipal pesticide bylaws, such as the one in Halifax, have led firms to offer eco-friendly solutions to lawn care.

Indeed, in Canada and many other countries, governments have become increasingly aware of the importance, for economic health, of encouraging innovation. There are a host of innovation assistance programs sponsored by federal and provincial governments. The National Research Council's Industrial Research Assistance Program (NRC-IRAP) is Canada's premier innovation assistance program for small and medium-sized Canadian enterprises. The program provides customized innovation assistance to 12,000 firms each year, sharing the financial risk with more than 3,000 R&D projects and pre-commercialization activities. For example, NRC-IRAP support enabled METOCEAN, a company that designs and manufactures oceanographic equipment in Dartmouth, Nova Scotia, to carry out R&D on a new kind of float that measures the temperature and salinity of oceans for climate research. With NRC-IRAP assistance, the R&D was completed in time to meet market demand and so METOCEAN could become a major supplier on the world market.[10]

Social and Demographic Change

Social and demographic changes are also an important source of entrepreneurial opportunities. Think about the clothes that you wear and the music that you listen to. They are probably different from the clothes and music that your parents favoured when they were your age. Changes in people's preferences make it possible for alert entrepreneurs to provide products and services that people demand.

Suppose you knew that next year there was going to be a change in fashion among university students. Instead of jeans, t-shirts, and baseball caps, people were going to start wearing suits to class. You could take advantage of this social change to begin a company to manufacture and sell suits to university students. Does this sound preposterous? Maybe it is. But the reverse shift certainly happened. In the 1950s, university students wore ties and jackets to class, but stopped doing so in the 1960s. The result? Entrepreneurs who started making jeans and t-shirts to sell to university students in

Figure 2.2 Political and Regulatory Changes Are Sources of Entrepreneurial Opportunities

Many of the regulations passed by the federal and provincial governments are sources of opportunity for alert entrepreneurs. Deregulation of the Canadian airline industry provided opportunities for the entry of new airlines, such as Calgary-based WestJet.

CP Photo/Adrian Wyld

the 1960s took advantage of a social trend to exploit an opportunity to sell different clothing to university students than had been sold in the past.

In addition to social trends, demographic changes are also an important source of entrepreneurial opportunities. The demographics of the Canadian population change all the time. Over the past 20 years, the population has become older, generating opportunities for entrepreneurs to make products for the elderly, such as assisted living facilities. The population has become more spread out from major cities, creating opportunities for entrepreneurs to build malls further from the centre of cities and to provide products, such as books on CD, to entertain people during lengthy commutes. Similarly, as people have immigrated to Canada from a wider variety of countries, opportunities have grown to provide food, clothing, and entertainment to meet new consumer preferences.

Why are social and demographic changes a source of entrepreneurial opportunity? We think there are two reasons. First, social and demographic changes alter demand for products and services. Because entrepreneurs make money by selling products and services that customers want, changes in demand create opportunities to produce different things. Second, social and demographic changes make it possible to generate solutions to customer needs that are more productive than those currently available.[11] For example, the demographic shift of women entering the workforce in large numbers created a need for a more efficient way to prepare food for dinner. This opportunity for more efficient food preparation led to the introduction of frozen dinners, a more efficient solution to food preparation than what had previously existed.

Social and demographic trends certainly created opportunities for Chip Wilson. He started Westbeach Clothing in Calgary to create cool, comfortable clothes for the increasing numbers of snow and skateboarders. After growing the company to eight stores and sales offices in the United States and Austria, Wilson sold it 1987 and started taking yoga classes. Quickly noticing there were mostly women in the room, he also realized that women were 56 percent of university grads, and there was a strong correlation between education level and athletics, health, and longevity. He predicted that yoga was going to be as big as surfing, skating, or snowboarding, and there would be a large market demand for high-quality yoga clothing. As a result, he founded Lululemon Athletica in Vancouver in 1998 to sell yoga-inspired athletic apparel, and to promote female participation in athletics, yoga, and a healthy, balanced, fun-filled way of life. By mid-2005, Lululemon Athletica had grown into a $44-million business with 500 employees and stores throughout Canada and in the United States, Australia, and Japan.[12]

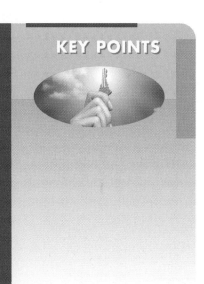

KEY POINTS

- An entrepreneurial opportunity is a situation in which a person can exploit a new business idea that has the potential to generate a profit.
- Entrepreneurial opportunities exist because people differ in their information. These differences influence the accuracy of their decision making, and creates shortages and surpluses—and the potential for better ways of doing things.
- Entrepreneurial opportunities also exist because of external sources of change, particularly technological change, regulatory and political change, and social and demographic change.
- Technological changes are sources of entrepreneurial opportunity because they make it possible for people to do things in new and more productive ways.
- Political and regulatory changes are sources of opportunity because they make it possible to develop business ideas to use resources in new ways that are either more productive or that redistribute wealth from one person to another.
- Social and demographic changes are sources of opportunity because they alter demand for products and services, as well as make it possible to generate solutions to customer needs that are more productive than those currently available.

FORMS OF OPPORTUNITY: BEYOND NEW PRODUCTS AND SERVICES

LEARNING OBJECTIVE

3 List the different forms that entrepreneurial opportunities can take, and explain why some forms are better for new firms than others.

Most people tend to think of the sources of opportunities as leading entrepreneurs to develop new products and services. Although this view is certainly true, these sources also generate a much wider range of things that entrepreneurs can do. As we explained in Chapter 1, entrepreneurs can develop business ideas to take advantage of five different types of opportunity that result from technological, political/regulatory, and social/demographic change: new products and services, new methods of production, new markets, new ways of organizing, and new raw materials.[13]

New types of accounting software and new surgical devices are examples of business ideas that entrepreneurs use to take advantage of new product opportunities. Amazon.com is an example of a business idea that an entrepreneur, Jeff Bezos, used to take advantage of a new way of organizing—selling books without using physical bookstores. The introduction of seaweed-flavoured snack crackers into the North American market is an example of an effort to take advantage of a new market because this business idea had existed earlier in Japan, but not in North America. Mississauga-based environmental company Knowaste, which processes used disposal diapers into wood pulp and plastic pellets, is an example of an effort to take advantage of an opportunity to use a new raw material. Finally, biotechnology start-ups that come up with new cancer drugs through computer-aided drug discovery are examples of business ideas that come from opportunities to use new modes of production.

Though opportunities exist for all five forms, entrepreneurs who create new businesses focus primarily on the first and second forms. Most of the time, entrepreneurs introduce new products or services or enter new markets, rather than exploit new materials, come up with new ways of organizing, or establish new methods of production.[14] In fact, Jim Utterback, a professor at the Sloan School of Management at MIT, has shown that, in a wide range of industries, entrepreneurs founding new firms are usually the ones to introduce new products and services, and established firms are the ones that introduce new production processes and ways of organizing. Why? Because new production processes and ways of organizing usually demand experience operating in an industry.[15]

However, founding a new business with a form of opportunity that is most commonly used by entrepreneurs might not always be the best approach. As we will describe in more detail in Chapter 11, success at entrepreneurial activity requires the entrepreneur to develop a business idea that he or she can defend against competition. Researchers have shown that entering a new market is a particularly risky form of opportunity exploitation because it is virtually impossible for an entrepreneur to defend this form of exploitation against competition. Moreover, business ideas to exploit new methods of production are often better forms of opportunity exploitation than business ideas to exploit new products, because new methods of production can be kept secret. Because entrepreneurs sell new products to customers, all of the attributes of their new products are available for others to see. Competitors can buy one of the entrepreneur's new products and take it apart to see how it works. Then the competitor can copy the product. In contrast, an entrepreneur does not have to show anyone else the production process that he or she uses. Therefore, it takes much longer, is much more difficult, and costs much more for competitors to imitate business ideas that take the form of new production processes than take the form of new products and services.[16]

Take Toronto-based Tira Wireless as an example of a company that is successfully exploiting an opportunity to create something other than a new product. Tira Wireless has developed a technology that will enable the deployment of mobile Java applications across a broad range of handsets, languages, and mobile operator requirements. With the proliferation of mobile devices, such as cellphones,

FORM OF THE OPPORTUNITY	TECHNOLOGICAL CHANGE	EXAMPLE OF A BUSINESS IDEA IN RESPONSE TO THE OPPORTUNITY	REASONING
New product or service	Internal combustion engine	Automobile	The internal combustion engine is used to power automobiles.
New way of organizing	Internet	Online book sales	The Internet allows people to sell products without retail outlets.
New market	Refrigeration	Refrigerated ship	The refrigerated ship allows ranchers in one country to sell their meat in another country.
New method of production	Computer	Computer-aided design	The computer allows designers to make products without building physical prototypes.
New raw material	Oil	Producing gasoline	Oil is refined into gasoline to power vehicles.

Table 2.2 Examples of Different Forms of Entrepreneurial Opportunities That Result from Technological Change

A single source of opportunity, such as technological change, can generate all five forms of opportunity.

there is a huge variety of displays. Even two cellphones from the same manufacturer could have quite different displays. This variety of displays poses a problem for developers of content, such as games, because they cannot possibly develop a version of the game for each device on which it could potentially play. The Tira Wireless technology can perform a translation process, which content providers use to adapt and deploy their mobile content for multiple devices and operator networks.[17]

To help clarify the relationship between the source of opportunity and the form that the opportunity takes, we show examples of all five different forms of opportunities for a single source of opportunity—technological change—in Table 2.2.

KEY POINTS

- Entrepreneurial opportunities do not only take the form of new products and services; they also take the form of new methods of production, new raw materials, new ways of organizing, and new markets.
- Entrepreneurs' business ideas typically involve the introduction of new products and services or entry into new markets.
- The most common form of opportunity exploitation by entrepreneurs is not necessarily the best. Researchers have shown that new businesses that enter new markets or introduce new products and services tend to perform worse than those that develop new production processes.

INDUSTRIES THAT FAVOUR NEW FIRMS: FERTILE GROUNDS FOR NEW VENTURES

One of the most interesting observations that researchers have made about entrepreneurship is that the ability of people to found successful new firms varies dramatically across industries. For instance, if you take two entrepreneurs with exactly the same skills and abilities and you place one in an industry favourable to new firm formation and place another in an industry unfavourable to new firm formation, the probability that the new firm will survive, the likelihood that the new firm will go public, the amount of sales growth it will have, and the level of profits it will earn have been shown to be as much as 10 times higher in the favourable industry than in the unfavourable one.[18]

LEARNING OBJECTIVE

4 Explain why new firms are more successful in some industries than in others, and identify the four major types of industry differences that influence the relative success of new firms.

One of the most important things that a budding entrepreneur can learn is to identify industries that are favourable to new firms. After all, if you are going to go through the trouble of starting a new business, you might as well increase your odds that it will be successful. Four different dimensions of industry differences influence the relative success of new firms: knowledge conditions, demand conditions, industry life cycles, and industry structure. In the following sections, we will describe these dimensions of industry differences so that you can learn what industry characteristics to look for as you think about starting your own company.

Knowledge Conditions

LEARNING OBJECTIVE

5 Identify the three different dimensions of knowledge conditions, and explain how they influence an industry's supportiveness of new firms.

"Knowledge conditions" is a term that economists use to refer to the type of information that underlies the production of products and services in an industry. It includes such factors as the degree of complexity of the production process, the level of new knowledge creation in the industry, the size of the innovating entities, and the degree of uncertainty. Take, for example, a comparison of the pharmaceutical industry and the retail clothing industry. The production of drugs is much more complex, requires much greater investment to produce new knowledge, requires larger entities to undertake innovation, and is much more uncertain than the production of clothing.

So what does this have to do with starting new firms? You probably guessed it already. Three dimensions of an industry's knowledge conditions are favourable to new firms. First, industries that have greater **R&D intensity** are more favourable to new firms than industries that have lesser R&D intensity.[19] R&D intensity is a measure of how much research and development expense firms incur for every dollar of sales. This measure captures how heavily firms invest in the creation of new knowledge. Researchers have found that R&D-intensive industries have more new firms because the invention of new technologies is a source of opportunity for new business ideas. The more R&D there is, the more new technology is invented. The more new technology that is invented, the more opportunities there are for new businesses (see Figure 2.3).

But, you might ask, why don't the companies that invested in the R&D capture these opportunities? Established firms take advantage of many of them. However, they cannot take advantage of all of them because of a concept called **knowledge spillovers**. Knowledge spillovers occur when information about how to develop new technology leaks out to other people.

Fortunately for entrepreneurs, these spillovers occur all of the time. Take, for example, an engineer from ATI Technologies who goes out for lunch with a friend who just graduated from university. The two talk about their work and the engineer starts to describe how ATI is developing a new type of computer graphics chip. Unbeknownst to the ATI engineer, the new graduate had been thinking of starting a business to produce a new generation of computer chip. However, his undergraduate thesis showed that he

Figure 2.3 The R&D Intensity of an Industry Influences New Firm Formation

New knowledge is created in every industry, making it possible for people to take advantage of it to found new firms, but some industries are more knowledge intensive than others. Compare, for example, the R&D required for Vancouver-based Lululemon Athletica to design a new piece of clothing and for Markham, Ontario-based ATI Technologies to design a new 3-D computer graphics chip.

Photo: Indu Ghuman

AP Photo/ATI

was missing a key piece of the puzzle about how to do it. The engineers at ATI had figured out the missing piece. Over lunch, this knowledge spilled over from the ATI engineer to the recent university graduate, who then uses it to start a new business.

Another aspect of knowledge conditions that enhance new firm formation is the **locus of innovation**. This term refers to who produces the technology that is a source of opportunity. In some industries, such as automobile manufacturing, private sector firms produce most of this knowledge; in other industries, such as pharmaceuticals, public organizations—including universities and government research labs—are the sources of much knowledge creation. Researchers have shown that industries in which public sector organizations produce most of the new technology have more new firm formation.[20] The reason is simple. As you probably suspected, senior management at ATI and other companies are not very big fans of knowledge spillovers. Spillovers allow other firms to exploit opportunities that their companies otherwise would have exploited. As a result, they take great pains to minimize the amount of knowledge that spills over to others through research publications, presentations, and loose-lipped engineers trying to impress their friends. In contrast, universities and research labs have a very different mission. The goal of universities is to put knowledge into the public domain so that society can benefit from it. When electrical engineering professors and students invent new computer chips, they tend to publish their research. This effort of people in the public sector to put knowledge in the public domain makes it easier for people to found new firms using public sector knowledge.

A third dimension of knowledge conditions that makes new firm formation more likely is the nature of the innovation process. In some industries, such as automobile manufacturing, innovation and new technology development require a very large scale of operations and lots of capital, leading most of the innovation to be done by large, established companies, such as General Motors and Ford. In other industries, for example, computer software manufacturers, innovation and technology development require flexible and nimble organizations, leading most of the innovation to be undertaken by new and small firms. Because new firms tend to start small, they do better at coming up with new products and services in industries in which small firms are the better innovators. Therefore, industries in which innovation demands smaller organizations tend to have more new firm formation than industries in which innovation demands larger organizations.[21]

Demand Conditions

"Demand conditions" is a term that researchers use to explain the attributes of customer preferences for products and services in an industry. Customers can express light demand or heavy demand for products. That demand can be growing or shrinking; it can be stable or changing; or it can be homogenous or heterogeneous.

Three attributes of demand conditions enhance new firm formation: market size, market growth, and market segmentation. Researchers have shown that new firms perform better in larger markets than in smaller ones because larger markets are more profitable for new firms.[22] Entrepreneurs face a fixed cost to found new firms. This fixed cost can be **amortized**, or spread out, over more sales in a larger market than in a smaller market. As a result, the expected returns to founding a firm are greater in a larger market than in a smaller market.

Market size is a particularly important issue for new firms in Canada, because the domestic market in many industries is small. To achieve the same level of sales as American companies, which typically have a much larger domestic market, Canadian companies need to sell in foreign markets. In many sectors, particularly technology-based sectors, Canadian firms cannot survive by relying on sales solely from their domestic market. **Export intensity** is the percentage of sales that come from foreign markets, or, in other words, foreign sales divided by total sales. Because Canadian domestic markets are smaller, it is not surprising that many Canadian industries have a higher export intensity than American industries. For example, Canadian companies selling Geographic Information Systems (GIS) obtain 20 percent of their revenue from foreign markets, while their American counterparts obtain 12 percent of revenues from

LEARNING OBJECTIVE

6   Identify the three different dimensions of demand conditions, and explain how they influence an industry's supportiveness of new firms.

foreign markets.[23] There is an even larger difference for food and drink manufacturers, with Canadian firms receiving roughly 22 percent of sales from exports and American firms receiving roughly 6 percent of sales from exports.[24] These figures mean that good opportunities for Canadian businesses frequently require considering foreign markets at start-up.

The second aspect of demand that affects new firm formation is market growth. New firms perform better in more rapidly growing markets than in less rapidly growing, or shrinking, markets because new firms can enter rapidly growing markets to serve customers that established firms are unable to serve.[25] Not only does this growing market allow new firms to gain customers who are relatively easy to persuade—they have excess demand—but it also allows new firms to avoid trying to take customers away from existing firms as a way to make sales.

Finally, new firm formation is more common in markets that are more heavily segmented. Industries differ in their degree of market segmentation. For example, there are many more types of cars targeted at different types of buyers than there are types of frozen corn targeted at different types of buyers (see Figure 2.4). The reason is that people have more varied preferences for automobiles than they do for frozen corn. Market segmentation enhances new firm formation[26] because niche markets require organizations that can exploit them without producing at a high volume. New firms are better than the average established firm at small-scale production. In addition, the exploitation of niches requires quick and agile firms that can take advantage of market segments that other firms have left unsatisfied. New firms tend to be quicker and more agile than other firms. Furthermore, market segmentation allows a new firm to enter a market and obtain a foothold without going after the mainstream customers of an established firm. As a result, new firms can enter segmented markets without the level of retaliation that they face in entering unsegmented markets where they must attack the customer base of established firms directly.

Industry Life Cycles

LEARNING OBJECTIVE

7 Identify the two different dimensions of industry life cycles, and explain how they influence an industry's supportiveness of new firms.

Like people, industries are born, mature, and die. Most of you are aware of the birth of electronic commerce as an industry. But you are probably less aware of the death of the Pony Express, unless you watch a lot of late-night Westerns on television. The birth, maturation, and death of industries, what researchers call the industry life cycle, is important to entrepreneurs because the life cycle has a powerful impact on the ability of entrepreneurs to found successful new firms.

First, researchers have shown that new firms do much better when industries are young than when they are older.[27] As your marketing professor will tell you, the adoption of new products is normally distributed. A small number of people are lead users; a moderately large number of people are early adopters. Most people adopt products in the middle of the curve. A moderately small number of people are late adopters, and a small number of people are laggards. As you may remember from your first course in

Figure 2.4 New Firm Formation Is Easier in More Segmented Markets Than in Less Segmented Ones

The automobile industry is highly segmented because people have very different preferences for the cars that they drive.

Source: Adapted from Rogers, E. 1983. *Diffusion of innovations.* New York: Free Press, p. 243.

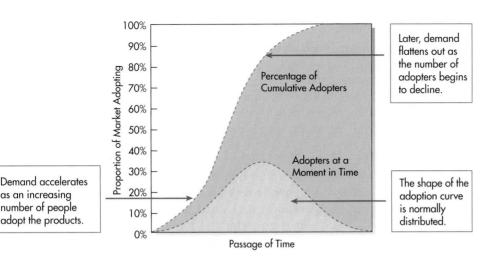

Figure 2.5 New Firm Formation Is Easier in Younger Industries Than in Older Ones

A normal distribution of adopters generates an S-shaped pattern of market growth.

calculus, a normal distribution of adopters will yield an S-shaped curve of market growth (see Figure 2.5). So if most products are normally distributed, most markets experience S-shaped growth patterns in which demand will first accelerate and then decelerate. Because we said earlier that it is easier for new firms to enter markets during periods of demand growth, new firms do better in younger markets than in older ones.

Moreover, when industries are new, no existing firms are available to meet changes in demand. Without existing firms present to compete with the entrepreneurs to meet demand, new firms do better than when they have to compete with existing firms to serve customers.

Furthermore, firms get better at meeting the needs of customers through experience. Because firms have to operate in an industry to gain experience, new firms are at a disadvantage when compared to established firms. Early in the life of an industry, this disadvantage is very small because even the oldest firms have very little experience. However, when the industry becomes mature, the level of experience that older firms have is much greater than that of new firms, making it very hard for new firms to perform well.

Second, when industries mature, they tend to converge on a **dominant design**. A dominant design is a common approach or standard used to make a product. For example, the internal combustion engine is a dominant design. None of the major auto companies use engines based on steam power anymore. However, this was not always the case. Early in the life of the auto industry, many firms used engines based on steam power rather than the internal combustion engine.

The concept of a dominant design is important to entrepreneurship because new firms tend to do much better before a dominant design emerges in an industry than after it has been established. Before a dominant design is established in an industry, entrepreneurs can adopt any design that they want for the new venture's product or service. However, the establishment of a dominant design limits the approaches that entrepreneurs can take to those designs that fit the standards that established firms are already using. Not only does the new firm have to use a design for its products that the established firms already have greater experience with, but once a dominant design has been established, the basis of competition in an industry changes. Instead of competing to see who has the design that fits the preferences of customers the best, firms compete on who can make a standard design most efficiently. Because established firms are larger and have more experience, they can produce more efficiently and so have distinct advantages once a dominant design has emerged in an industry.

Take VHS tapes for example. Once the video recording industry converged on the VHS standard as the dominant design, it became almost impossible for new companies to introduce other tape formats. The major Japanese companies that produced VHS tapes, such as Matsushita, were able to produce the tapes more efficiently than anyone else and were able to out-compete everyone else.

Industry Structure

LEARNING OBJECTIVE

8 Identify the four different dimensions of industry structure, and explain how they influence an industry's supportiveness of new firms.

Industries also differ in their structure, making some of them more hospitable to new firms than others. Researchers have identified four aspects of the structure of an industry that make it easier for a person to found a successful new firm. First, some industries are more **capital intensive** than others. Capital intensity refers to the degree to which the production process in an industry relies on capital rather than on labour. New firms perform relatively poorly in capital-intensive industries.[28] When firms are initially created, entrepreneurs must spend capital to obtain equipment, establish production facilities, set up distribution, and otherwise organize. This expenditure of capital occurs before the new business can sell its products or services and so generate revenue. Because new firms do not generate cash from their existing operations, they must obtain this capital from investors. For reasons we will describe in more detail in Chapter 6, investors charge more for capital than it costs to use internally generated capital. For now, let it suffice to say that entrepreneurs know much more about their business ideas and venture opportunities than the investors who back them, and so the investors demand a risk premium to compensate for those entrepreneurs who might try to take advantage of the investors' relative ignorance. Because existing firms can use capital from their current operations to finance new business ideas, this premium puts new firms at a disadvantage. This disadvantage grows as the capital intensity of the business increases.

Second, new firms perform worse in advertising-intensive industries, such as consumer products, than they do in industries that do not rely heavily on advertising, such as industrial chemicals. Brand reputations are developed over time through repeated advertising efforts. As a result, it takes considerable time for new firms to develop the same level of brand name recognition as established firms. Moreover, advertising is subject to **economies of scale**. "Economies of scale" is a term that economists use to explain that the cost of each unit of a product goes down as the volume of production increases. Scale economies exist anytime that there is a much larger cost to producing the first unit of something than there is to producing additional units. Because the cost of developing a television or radio advertisement is the same regardless of the number of units of the product that you sell, the cost per unit of advertising is significantly lower as you produce and sell more units of your product. Therefore, the small size of new ventures makes it hard for them to keep their per-unit advertising costs as low as those facing established firms (see Figure 2.6).[29]

Third, new firms perform worse in concentrated industries than they do in fragmented industries.[30] **Concentration** refers to how much market share lies in the

Figure 2.6 New Firm Formation Is More Difficult in Advertising-Intensive Industries

Economies of scale in advertising mean that the per-unit cost to advertise a product or service goes down with the volume of units produced. Because new firms tend to start small, they face significant disadvantages in advertising intensive industries.

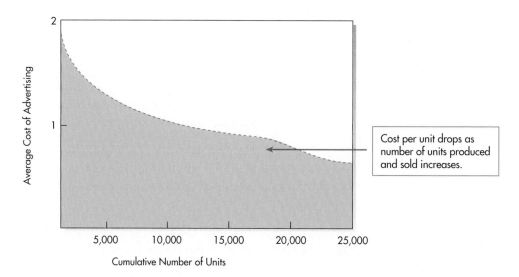

Cost per unit drops as number of units produced and sold increases.

Cumulative Number of Units

hands of the largest firms in the industry. When industries are concentrated, new firms have to challenge the customer base of established firms with the power and resources to drive them out of business. In contrast, when industries are fragmented, new firms can enter by challenging small and weak established firms whose customers are more vulnerable.

Fourth, new firms perform better in industries that are composed of firms of smaller average size.[31] Most new firms are started small because starting small allows entrepreneurs to minimize the cost and risk of establishing their new ventures. Because entrepreneurs are often wrong about their business opportunities, they like to minimize the cost of being wrong, which they accomplish by starting on a small scale and testing whether their business ideas work.

In industries composed mostly of small firms, starting small does not put a new firm at much of a disadvantage relative to established competitors. However, in industries composed mostly of large firms, starting small greatly disadvantages new firms whose established firm competitors can purchase in greater volume, produce at a lower average manufacturing cost, and spread their costs of advertising and distribution over more units. Therefore, new firms do relatively more poorly in industries made up of relatively large firms.

KEY POINTS

- New firms perform better in R&D-intensive industries because the invention of new technologies is a source of opportunity for new business ideas.
- Industries in which public sector organizations are the locus of innovation have more new firm formation because public sector organizations do not try as hard as private sector firms to minimize knowledge spillovers.
- New firms perform better in industries in which most of the innovation is conducted by small firms because innovation in these industries requires agile and flexible organizations, and new firms are agile and flexible.
- New firms perform better in larger markets than in smaller ones because larger markets allow the fixed cost of firm formation to be amortized over more sales.
- New firms perform better in more rapidly growing markets because new firms can enter rapidly growing markets to serve customers that established firms are unable to serve.
- Market segmentation enhances new firm formation because niche markets require organizations that can exploit opportunities on a smaller scale; because the exploitation of niches requires quick and agile firms; and because market segmentation allows a new firm to enter a market and obtain a foothold without going after the mainstream customers of an established firm.
- Young industries are more supportive of new firms because demand grows more rapidly in young industries than in mature ones; because no existing firms are available to meet demand in young industries; and because firms gain experience operating in industries as they mature.
- Industries are less supportive of new firms after a dominant design has been established because a dominant design means that new firms have to use a design for its products that the established firms already have greater experience with, and because the basis of competition in an industry changes to favour efficiency, which established firms are better at achieving.
- Capital-intensive industries are more hostile to new firms because external capital, on which new firms must rely, is more costly than internally generated capital.
- Advertising-intensive industries are more hostile to new firms because advertising has effects that cumulate over time and because advertising faces strong economies of scale.
- Concentrated industries are more hostile to new firms because concentration means that new firms must try to take customers from large, established firms that have the power to drive them out of business.
- Industries with larger average firm size are more hostile to new firms because new firms, which are established on a small scale so that entrepreneurs can minimize cost and risk, are at a much greater disadvantage in industries with large average firm size than with small average firm size.

OPPORTUNITIES AND NEW FIRMS

One of the difficulties that people face in founding successful new businesses is that the individuals who run established firms would also like to profit from the exploitation of opportunities. So not only does an entrepreneur have to identify and exploit a valuable opportunity to start a new company, but the entrepreneur also has to do so despite competition from established companies. Researchers have shown that the major reason that entrepreneurs are able to identify and exploit opportunities despite the desire of the founders and managers of established businesses to profit from opportunities is that certain opportunities favour established businesses, while other opportunities favour new businesses. By focusing on those opportunities that favour new businesses, an entrepreneur can increase the likelihood of success. In this section, we will review the opportunities that favour established firms and the opportunities that favour new firms.

Why Most Opportunities Favour Established Firms

LEARNING OBJECTIVE

9   Explain why established firms are usually better than new firms at exploiting entrepreneurial opportunities.

Most of the time, established companies will do a better job than a new company at exploiting an opportunity. When companies are in business for awhile, they develop several advantages over new companies. First, companies face a **learning curve** when they develop any product or service. A learning curve is a graphical depiction of how well someone does at something as a function of the number of times that they have done it (see Figure 2.7). For example, think about how long it took the first time you made your favourite recipe and how much easier and efficient it is each time you make it. The same is true for companies. Initially, they find it difficult to manufacture products efficiently because they have not worked out the kinks in their production processes. Moreover, they haven't yet figured out the best way to sell products to customers. However, just like you and your recipe, as companies produce more of something, they get better at doing it. Because new companies have not yet moved down the learning curve, they are worse at manufacturing and marketing products than established companies.

Second, business depends a great deal on reputation. Research has shown that people are much more likely to buy products from suppliers that they know and trust.[32] Experience interacting with a particular supplier gives a customer confidence in the products and services that it supplies. Think about going out to dinner. If you've eaten at a restaurant before, you know whether or not you like it. Although you might have a better meal at a new restaurant, you don't know if the

Figure 2.7 The Manufacturing Learning Curve

Because a new company has not manufactured as many products as an established company, it will manufacture those products much less efficiently.

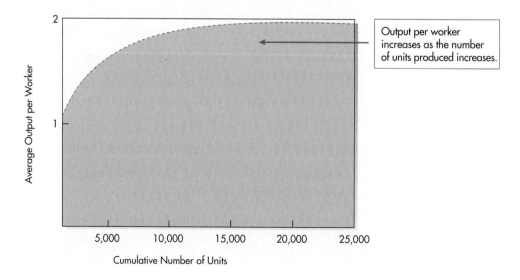

Output per worker increases as the number of units produced increases.

meal will be any good. The reputation that the established restaurant has developed with you keeps you coming back and makes it harder for the new restaurant to get you in the door.

Third, if businesses are successful, they develop positive **cash flow**. That is, they bring in more cash than they spend to produce and distribute their products and services. This cash flow is useful for developing new products and services. If an established business has positive cash flow, it can use that cash to invest in producing new products and services that meet the needs of customers. For example, Dell invested the cash it had earned from selling computers into making and selling printers. Because new companies haven't yet sold any products to customers, they do not have positive cash flow and have to borrow money or issue stock to raise money. Raising money costs more than using internal cash and puts new companies at a disadvantage relative to established companies in terms of producing new products.

Fourth, many businesses face economies of scale. For example, think about the cost of producing a computer game. To write the software code for the first copy of the game is very expensive. A computer programmer will have to spend several hundred hours writing the code. However, once the game has been written, a person can burn CDs of the game for only pennies. Economies of scale benefit established companies over new companies because the established companies are already producing products and services. When buying raw materials or advertising or doing anything else that requires economies of scale, the established company faces lower costs than the new company because the established company produces more units of the product or service.

Fifth, new companies often find it difficult to compete with established companies because they lack **complementary assets**. Complementary assets are things that are used along with the entrepreneur's new product to produce or distribute that product. For example, suppose you have developed a new golf club that can be used to drive a golf ball twice as far as the standard driver. There would probably be a decent market for that driver. But to sell the driver, you would first have to manufacture it, and then you would have to distribute it to customers. After all, most golfers don't want to buy blueprints for making their own drivers. To get into the driver business, you would need a manufacturing plant, and you would need access to sporting goods stores. The manufacturing plant and the sporting goods stores are complementary assets for the driver you developed. An established golf club manufacturer, say Callaway, already has manufacturing plants and contracts with sporting goods stores. Therefore, its control over these complementary assets would give it an advantage over your new firm in introducing a new driver.

Opportunities That Favour New Firms

For entrepreneurs to found successful new companies, they need to exploit opportunities that new companies would be better at exploiting than established companies. Moreover, this advantage has to be large enough to offset the established company advantages that we just described. What kinds of advantages do new companies have in exploiting opportunities?

One major advantage that new companies have is that they are better at exploiting **competence-destroying** change. Earlier in the chapter, we explained that one of the major sources of opportunity is technological change. Technological change makes it possible to introduce a new product or service, open up a new market, use a new raw material, develop a new way of organizing, or introduce a new production process. Researchers have explained that technological change can be competence enhancing or competence destroying. Competence-enhancing technological change is a change that makes people better at what they are already doing; competence-destroying technological change is a change that makes people worse at what they are doing.[33]

LEARNING OBJECTIVE

10 Identify the types of opportunities that new firms are better at exploiting, and explain why new firms are advantaged at the exploitation of those opportunities.

Most change is competence enhancing. For instance, companies that have been exploiting a technology for awhile are better at doing things that make use of further advances of the technology because of the learning curve that we described earlier. As long as the effort to produce a new product, develop a new production process, exploit a new product, use a new raw material, or organize in a new way takes advantage of something that had been learned before, the established firm, which has moved further up the learning curve, has an advantage. But sometimes change is competence destroying. In those cases, having done something in the past doesn't make you any better at exploiting a business idea than someone who hasn't done that thing—in fact, it makes you worse. Why? Because, as we explained earlier, people get locked into old ways of thinking and doing things, and they find it harder to do new things than people with no experience at all.

For example, when the Internet first came into existence, experience with bricks-and-mortar retailing didn't help established clothing companies very much as e-tailers. In fact, it made the established companies worse. Their managers kept trying to use the experience that they gathered from their retail stores in their online sites without realizing that people cannot try on or touch clothes online the way that they can in a retail store. The managers' experience got in the way of approaching the online sales of clothing in a new way—a way that new companies with no experience in retailing were able to figure out because the Internet was a competence-destroying technological change.

Not only does a competence-destroying technological change, such as the Internet, undermine the learning curve advantages of established companies, but established companies face several other disadvantages in exploiting competence-destroying changes. To invest in a competence-destroying technological change, an existing company has to **cannibalize** its existing business. Cannibalization occurs whenever a company launches a new product or service that replaces its existing products or services. For example, Internet book sales cannibalized the existing business of Indigo Books & Music. By introducing chapters.indigo.ca, Indigo ended up serving many customers who would have bought books in its stores, but at an additional cost—the cost of setting up the online business. This was not the case for Amazon.ca because Amazon did not have stores. New companies have an advantage over existing companies when a technological change requires the existing company to make investments that cannibalize its existing products and services because established companies do not like to make these types of investments (see Figure 2.8).[34]

Moreover, companies develop routines for doing business efficiently. These routines allow companies to do things without having to evaluate whether those activities are worthwhile every time they do them. For example, companies might have procedures for manufacturing a CD player that focus the company on using a certain technology to make the player. Although these routines are useful for manufacturing the CD player efficiently, they hinder efforts to explore new technologies, such as the technology behind MP3 players. New companies often have an advantage in doing things that are new, for example, investigating the MP3 technology, because they are not constrained by existing routines for doing something else. It is not surprising that in the revolution from 2-D to 3-D computer graphics chips, it was newcomer 3Dfx that produced a 3-D chip with no 2-D functionality at all and defined what the new generation of technology would look like.

Established companies also seek to satisfy their existing customers. As your marketing professor will tell you, satisfying customers is important if a company is going to sell its products. But keeping your customers happy has a downside. When companies develop new products, they often ask their customers what they think of those products. Much of the time, customers reject new products either because those products aren't useful to them, because they simply cannot envision

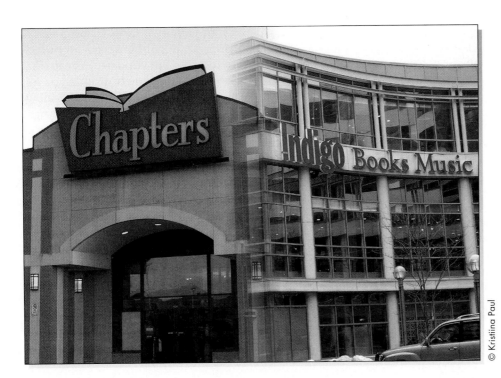

Figure 2.8 Established Companies Do Not Like to Make Investments That Cannibalize Their Existing Assets

After building a national network of bookstores, Indigo Books & Music has spent millions developing an online shopping site to compete against Amazon.ca.[35]

© Kristiina Paul

changing to something new, or because changing requires effort. Because established companies run the risk of losing their existing customers by pursuing products that these people do not want, they often avoid pursuing those products.[36] For example, when IBM developed the laser, its lawyers weren't sure that the company should patent it because IBM's customers couldn't find any use for the technology. But as we know, there is a huge market for lasers in everything from supermarket scanners to making CDs. Another example is healthy fast food. Existing customers of established fast-food companies were not particularly interested in healthy items, and so these companies were followers, rather than pioneers, in developing healthy menus. The lesson is that new companies are often better than established companies at developing new products or services because established companies are constrained by their existing customers. If their existing customers tell them that they don't like a new product, the company risks losing customers by pursuing it. A new company, in contrast, has no customers to lose by pursuing new products.

New companies are also more successful when they develop products and services that are **discrete**. An example of a discrete product is a BlackBerry device. Research In Motion can sell the BlackBerry without embedding it in other devices. In contrast, a windshield wiper is not discrete, but is part of a system. When a windshield wiper is disconnected from the rest of a car, bus, or other vehicle, it is pretty much useless. The reason that discrete products are better for new companies is that they can be developed without the cost and difficulty of trying to replicate existing companies' systems.[37] Think about how difficult it would be to produce an entire car if all you wanted to do was sell windshield wipers. As hard as it was to develop the BlackBerry, at least it can be used independently.

New companies are also more successful when their business ideas are embedded in **human capital**. Human capital is value invested in people, and it is different from physical capital, such as machines and equipment. New businesses do better with business ideas that are embedded in human capital rather than physical capital because human beings can move relatively easily from an existing organization to pursue an entrepreneurial opportunity; physical assets are much less mobile. For example, if you developed an idea for how to better fit customers to snowboards while working at a ski shop, you could quit and start your own shop. If you are right about how to fit the customers to the snowboards, you could attract a lot of customers away from your old employer and do pretty well. But suppose, instead, that your employer had a great machine for fitting customers to snowboards. If you left and took that machine with you to start your own ski shop, you would be stealing. The ability to fit customers is better than a machine to fit customers for starting a company because the first lies in human capital and is mobile, but the second lies in physical capital, and is not.

This is only a small sample of the many differences in the types of opportunities that favour new and established firms that have been uncovered in careful research. Some others are summarized in Table 2.3. The main point of the current discussion is simply this: Because new firms are different from established firms, new firms are better at pursuing some opportunities, while established firms are better at pursuing others. Differentiating between these different types of opportunities is crucial for entrepreneurs, so we focus on it in our discussion of opportunities. (For a discussion of one type of opportunity that can be problematic for entrepreneurs founding new firms, please see the **Danger! Pitfall Ahead!** section.)

DANGER! PITFALL AHEAD!

Exploiting an Incremental Innovation by Starting a Firm

You have spent a lot of time thinking about a business idea for your new venture, and you have come up with what you think is a good one—to produce a waterproof CD/DVD player. You think that this is a really great idea. All of your friends think that it would be really cool to have a waterproof CD/DVD player so they can play music and movies when they're camping without worrying that the system will be ruined. So why is your entrepreneurship professor telling you that this isn't a very good idea for founding a new firm?

Your business idea is an incremental improvement on a product that existing firms already produce. Sure it is a good idea, and people would buy the player if it were made. The problem is that your new company is not the right company to make it. When existing firms produce a product, for example, CD/DVD players, they develop skills and capabilities that make them better at producing and selling a product, the more of the product that they produce and sell. This is the idea behind the learning curve that we described here. The companies that already make CD/DVD players know a whole lot more than you do about how to make and sell them. Your idea for making the player waterproof is only a small improvement over their existing models. If Sony or Toshiba

wanted to compete with you, all they would have to do would be to figure out how best to make their players waterproof. On the other hand, to compete with them, you would have to figure out how to make a CD/DVD player. What you would have to do would be a lot harder to do than what they have to do, and they have more resources (money, knowledge, people) than you to do it. The fact that their innovation is incremental, combined with the experience that they have developed, puts you at a disadvantage.

But, what if your business idea was to put a device under people's skin so that they could download music from the Internet and then listen to it wherever they went? Okay, this idea might be a little too science fiction for today, but suppose you could do it. Because no one else has figured out how to do this yet, the new technology would not just be an incremental improvement on an existing product or service. It would be a radical change. No one in the business of making devices for downloading and listening to music, or making computers, has any experience with the type of device that you are thinking of making. So no one else is ahead of you on a learning curve. As a result, you would stand a chance of creating a valuable company to exploit this type of business idea.

The moral of the story: Don't waste your time trying to develop incremental innovations—there is too much against you.

DIMENSION OF THE OPPPORTUNITY	WHO IT FAVOURS	REASONS WHY	EXAMPLE
Relies heavily on reputation	Established firm	People are more likely to buy from those whom they know and trust.	Jewellery store
Has a strong learning curve	Established firm	Established firms can move up the learning curve to get better at producing and distributing products.	Automobile manufacturer
Takes a lot of capital	Established firm	Established firms have existing cash flow that they can use to produce a new product or service.	Jet aircraft manufacturer
Demands economies of scale	Established firm	The average cost of producing a product or service goes down with the volume produced when economies of scale exist.	Steel plant
Requires complementary assets in marketing and distribution	Established firm	The ability to meet customer needs often requires access to retail distribution.	Maker of running shoes
Relies on an incremental product improvement	Established firm	The established firm can add the incremental improvement to its products more easily and cheaply than the new firm can imitate its product or service.	Manufacturer of DVD players
Employs a competence-destroying innovation	New firm	The established firm's experience, assets, and routines are undermined.	3-D computer graphics chip
Does not satisfy the needs of existing firms' mainstream customers	New firm	Established firms focus on serving their mainstream customers and will not pursue products or services that do not meet the needs of those customers.	Healthy fast food
Is based on a discrete innovation	New firm	New firms can exploit discrete innovations without replicating the entire system belonging to established firms.	BlackBerry
Lies in human capital	New firm	Whoever has the knowledge can produce a product or service that meets customer needs.	Character animator

Table 2.3 Some Opportunities Are Better for New Firms Than Others

Some opportunities favour new firms, while others favour established firms.

KEY POINTS

- The managers of established companies would like to exploit many of the same opportunities as entrepreneurs.
- Established firms are better than new firms at exploiting most opportunities.
- Established firms have the advantage of the learning curve, which improves their ability to introduce a new product or service, tap a new market, use a new material, take advantage of a new production process, or organize in a new way.
- Established firms have reputations, which encourage customers and suppliers to do business with them.
- Established firms have cash flow from existing operations, which they can invest in the exploitation of new opportunities at a lower cost than new firms can tap external capital.
- Established firms have access to complementary assets in manufacturing, marketing, and distribution, which are necessary to exploit opportunities.
- To found successful new firms, entrepreneurs must exploit opportunities that favour new firms.
- Competence-destroying technology favours new firms because competence-destroying change undermines the capabilities of existing firms and forces established firms to cannibalize their existing assets.
- Opportunities that an established firm's mainstream customers reject are good for new firms because established firms focus on activities to serve those mainstream customers.
- Opportunities that are discrete are good for new firms because entrepreneurs can exploit them without having to replicate the established firms' entire system of assets.
- Opportunities that are embedded in human capital are better for new firms because entrepreneurs can leave their employers to found firms that exploit the knowledge in their heads, but they cannot take their employer's physical assets with them.

Summary and Review of Key Points

- An entrepreneurial opportunity is a situation in which a person can exploit a new business idea that has the potential to generate a profit.
- Entrepreneurial opportunities exist because people differ in their information. These differences influence the accuracy of their decision making, the potential for better ways of doing things, and create shortages and surpluses.
- Entrepreneurial opportunities also exist because of external sources of change, particularly technological change, regulatory and political change, and social and demographic change.
- Technological changes are sources of entrepreneurial opportunity because they make it possible for people to do things in new and more productive ways.
- Political and regulatory changes are sources of opportunity because they make it possible to develop business ideas to use resources in new ways that are either more productive or that redistribute wealth from one person to another.
- Social and demographic changes are sources of opportunity because they alter demand for products and services, as well as make it possible to generate solutions to customer needs that are more productive than those currently available.
- Entrepreneurial opportunities do not only take the form of new products and services; they also take the form of new methods of production, new raw materials, new ways of organizing, and new markets.
- Entrepreneurs' business ideas typically involve the introduction of new products and services or entry into new markets.
- The most common form of opportunity exploitation by entrepreneurs is not necessarily the best. Researchers have shown that new businesses that enter new markets or introduce new products and services tend to perform worse than those that develop new production processes.
- The likelihood of founding a successful new firm varies dramatically across industries, making it important for entrepreneurs to assess how supportive an industry is to new firms.
- Researchers have identified four different dimensions of industry differences that influence the relative success of new firms: knowledge conditions, demand conditions, industry life cycles, and industry structure.
- Three different dimensions of knowledge conditions influence the industry's supportiveness of new firms: R&D intensity, the locus of innovation, and the nature of innovation.

- New firms perform better in R&D-intensive industries because the invention of new technologies is a source of opportunity for new business ideas.
- Industries in which public sector organizations are the locus of innovation have more new firm formation because public sector organizations do not try as hard as private sector firms to minimize knowledge spillovers.
- New firms perform better in industries in which most of the innovation is conducted by small firms because innovation in these industries requires agile and flexible organizations, and new firms are agile and flexible.
- Three different dimensions of demand conditions influence the industry's supportiveness of new firms: large markets, growing markets, and segmented markets.
- New firms perform better in larger markets than in smaller ones because larger markets allow the fixed cost of firm formation to be amortized over more sales.
- New firms perform better in more rapidly growing markets because new firms can enter rapidly growing markets to serve customers that established firms are unable to serve.
- Market segmentation enhances new firm formation because niche markets require organizations that can exploit opportunities on a small scale, because the exploitation of niches requires quick and agile firms, and because market segmentation allows a new firm to enter a market and obtain a foothold without going after the mainstream customers of an established firm.
- Two aspects of industry life cycles influence the benevolence of an industry toward new firms: industry age and the presence of a dominant design.
- Young industries are more supportive of new firms because demand grows more rapidly in young industries than in mature ones, because no existing firms are available to meet demand in young industries, and because firms gain experience operating in industries as they mature.
- Industries are less supportive of new firms after a dominant design has been established because a dominant design means that new firms have to use a design for their products that the established firms already have greater experience with, and because the basis of competition in an industry changes to favour efficiency, which established firms are better at achieving.
- Four aspects of industry structure make industries more supportive of new firms: capital intensity, advertising intensity, concentration, and average firm size.

- Capital-intensive industries are more hostile to new firms because external capital, on which new firms must rely, is more costly than internally generated capital.
- Advertising-intensive industries are more hostile to new firms because advertising has effects that cumulate over time, and because advertising faces strong economies of scale.
- Concentrated industries are more hostile to new firms because concentration means that new firms must try to take customers from large, established firms that have the power to drive them out of business.
- Industries with larger average firm size are more hostile to new firms because new firms, which are established on a small scale so that entrepreneurs can minimize cost and risk, are at a much greater disadvantage in industries with large average firm size than with small average firm size.
- The managers of established companies would like to exploit many of the same opportunities as entrepreneurs.
- Established firms are better than new firms at exploiting most opportunities.
- Established firms have the advantage of the learning curve, which improves their ability to introduce a new product or service, tap a new market, use a new material, take advantage of a new production process, or organize in a new way.

- Established firms have reputations, which encourage customers and suppliers to do business with them.
- Established firms have cash flow from existing operations, which they can invest in the exploitation of new opportunities at a lower cost than new firms can tap external capital.
- Established firms have access to complementary assets in manufacturing, marketing, and distribution, which are necessary to exploit opportunities.
- To found *successful* new firms, entrepreneurs must exploit opportunities that favour new firms.
- Competence-destroying technology favours new firms because competence-destroying change undermines the capabilities of existing firms and forces established firms to cannibalize their existing assets.
- Opportunities that an established firm's mainstream customers reject are good for new firms because established firms focus on activities to serve those mainstream customers.
- Opportunities that are discrete are good for new firms because an entrepreneur can exploit them without having to replicate the established firm's entire system of assets.
- Opportunities that are embedded in human capital are better for new firms because entrepreneurs can leave their employers to found firms that exploit the knowledge in their heads, but they cannot take their employer's physical assets with them.

Glossary

Amortized: A method of distributing the cost of an investment over the number of units produced or sold.

Cannibalize: An effort to produce and sell a product or service that replaces a product or service that one already produces and sells.

Capital Intensive: The degree to which the production process in a firm or industry relies on capital rather than on labour.

Cash Flow: The internally generated funds available to a firm after costs and depreciation are subtracted from revenues.

Competence-Destroying: A form of change that undermines the skills and capabilities of people who are already doing something. It is contrasted with competence-enhancing change, which enhances the skills and capabilities of people who are already doing something.

Complementary Assets: Assets that must be used along with an innovation to provide a new product or service to customers, typically including manufacturing equipment and marketing and distribution facilities.

Concentration: The proportion of market share that lies in the hands of the largest firms in an industry. This concept is commonly measured by the four-firm concentration ratio, a government measure of the market share that lies in the hands of the four largest firms in an industry.

Discrete: A characteristic of a new product or service that makes it independent of a system of other assets necessary to use the product or service.

Dominant Design: A common approach or standard to making a product on which firms in an industry have converged; for example, many software companies design their products to operate with Microsoft Windows.

Economies of Scale: A reduction in the cost of each unit produced as the volume of production increases.

Export Intensity: The percentage of a firm's revenue that comes from foreign markets, or, foreign revenue divided by total revenue.

Human Capital: Investment or value in human resources rather than physical assets.

Knowledge Spillovers: The accidental transfer of information about how to create new products, production processes, ways of marketing, or ways of organizing, from one firm to another.

Learning Curve: A relationship that measures the per-unit performance at production as a function of the cumulative number of units produced.

Locus of Innovation: The location, both within the value chain and between the public and private sector, in which efforts to apply new knowledge to the creation of new products, production processes, and ways of organizing occur.

R&D Intensity: The proportion of a firm's sales that are devoted to creating new scientific knowledge and applying that knowledge to the creation of new products and production processes.

Discussion Questions

1. Say you discovered a cure for lung cancer. Is that an entrepreneurial opportunity? What about if you invented a perpetual motion machine?

2. What do you think are the major sources of entrepreneurial opportunities over the next five years? Why are these things sources of opportunity?

3. Think of five entrepreneurial opportunities. What forms do these entrepreneurial opportunities take? Are some of these forms of opportunities better for entrepreneurs founding new firms? Why or why not?

4. Pick three industries you know well. What dimensions of these industries make them favourable or unfavourable to new firm formation? Why or why not?

5. Go back to the five entrepreneurial opportunities that you thought of in response to question 3. Would established firms have an advantage over new firms in exploiting those opportunities? Why or why not?

InfoTrac Exercises

1. **23-Year-Old Princeton Dropout and Entrepreneur Creates Product Completely Out of Garbage; Wal-Mart Canada Puts Product in Every Store.**

   PR Newswire, Feb 15, 2005

   Article A128650600

   After reading this article, supplement your understanding of TerraCycle by visiting the company's website: http://www.terracycle.org.

   1. What type of external change made it possible for Tom Szaky and Jon Beyer to start this new business?

   2. What is the locus of innovation for this new business venture? How is it an advantage to them?

   3. How would you assess Szaky and Beyer's new business opportunity in light of your reading in Chapter 2? Are conditions favourable for their success? Why or why not?

   4. Is this venture an example of social entrepreneurship? Why or why not?

2. **Midlife Crisis? Bring It On! How Women of This Generation Are Seizing That Stressful, Pivotal Moment in Their Lives to Reinvent Themselves.** (Society)(Cover Story)

   Nancy Gibbs.

   Time, May 16, 2005 v165 i20 p52

   Full Text: COPYRIGHT 2005 Time, Inc .

   1. According to the article, what types of demographic characteristics are related to entrepreneurial opportunities?

   2. According to the article, what changes in demographics are creating new entrepreneurial opportunities?

   3. Research a young Canadian venture that is leveraging these demographic changes to develop and sell a new business or service. Explain how the company is able to compete against established firms.

3. **Tomorrow's Entrepreneur: Graying Boomers, Booming Teens** (brief article)

   Inc., May 29, 2001 p86

   Record: A75318268

   Full Text: COPYRIGHT 2001 Goldhirsh Group, Inc. Graying Boomers, Booming Teens

   1. From the article, identify characteristics of senior or teen markets.

   2. Research new ventures in senior or teen markets. Pick one new Canadian company and analyze how it is leveraging demographic change to develop and sell a new product or service.

GETTING DOWN
TO BUSINESS

The Hunt for Opportunities: Building Your Skills

We defined an opportunity as the potential to create something new and desirable (new products or services, new markets, new production processes, new raw materials, new ways of organizing existing technologies, etc.) that has emerged from a complex pattern of changing conditions. You will need to identify an entrepreneurial opportunity to start your business. We believe that you can use some of the topics that we discussed in this chapter to identify an entrepreneurial opportunity. Follow these steps:

Step 1: Construct a list of recent changes in (1) technology, (2) demographics (changes in the makeup of the population), (3) lifestyle and other social changes, (4) markets, and (5) government policies.

Changes You Observe

Technology:

1.

2.

3.

Demographics (changes in the makeup of the population):

1.

2.

3.

Lifestyle and other social changes:

1.

2.

3.

Markets:

1.

2.

3.

Government policies:

1.

2.

3.

Step 2: Once you have constructed this list, try to identify the following: (1) new products or services that these changes make possible, (2) new markets that they open up, (3) new production processes that they allow firms to use, (4) new raw materials that they make possible, and (5) new ways of organizing that these changes would lead to. Remember to identify the source of the opportunity that you identified along with the new products or services, new markets, new production processes, new raw materials, and new ways of organizing that result from these changes.

Example: The invention of the Internet (a technological change) creates an opportunity to sell books without having a freestanding bookstore (a new way of organizing).

1.

2.

3.

4.

5.

If you succeed, congratulations! You have accomplished the first, crucial stage in the entrepreneurial process: identifying a bona fide entrepreneurial opportunity.

Industry Analysis

We discussed the importance of analyzing the industry that your new business will enter to make sure that it is a favourable sector for new firms. We believe that you can use some of the topics that we discussed in this chapter to analyze the industry that your new business will enter. Follow these steps:

Step 1: For each of the five business opportunities that you listed in exercise 1, identify the industry where that opportunity would be found. Define the industry in which the business will operate. Then match that business description to the Canadian government's list of national industrial codes at http://strategis.ic.gc.ca/sc_ecnmy/sio/about_naics_eng.html.

Step 2: Once you have a definition of the industry in which your five business opportunities will operate and the national industrial codes that correspond to the industry, evaluate the favourability of the those industries to new firm formation across the three main dimensions we described earlier in the chapter: knowledge conditions, industry life cycles, and industry structure. Consider all the aspects of each of these dimensions of industry. For each of your five opportunities, provide evidence for why the industry is favourable or not favourable for a new firm.

1.

2.

3.

4.

5.

Should a New Firm Pursue the Opportunity? Comparing the Opportunity Fit with Established Firms

We discussed the advantages that established firms have in exploiting entrepreneurial opportunities. Consider the possibility that a large, established firm has also identified each of the five business opportunities you identified in Step 2 of The Hunt for Opportunities: Building Your Skills. Explain why an established company would be better or worse than your new venture at exploiting each of the opportunities. Consider all of the advantages that large, established firms have in pursuing opportunities that we discussed in this chapter: learning curves, reputation, positive cash flow, economies of scale, complementary assets, greater ease in managing systemic innovations, and advantages in exploiting incremental change.

Enhanced Learning

You may select any combination of the resources below to enhance your understanding of the chapter material.

- **Appendix: Case Studies** – Twelve cases provide opportunities to apply chapter concepts to realistic entrepreneurial situations. These brief cases call for careful analysis of real business problems and ask you to think about potential solutions.

- **Video Case Library** – Nine cases are tied directly to video segments from the popular PBS television series Small Business School. These cases and video segments (available on the Entrepreneurship website at http://www. entrepreneurship.nelson.com) give you unparalleled access to today's entrepreneurs, with expert advice and insights on how to start, run, and grow a business.

- **Management Interview Series Video Database** – This video interview series contains a wealth of tips on how to manage effectively. Access to the database and practical exercises are available on the book support website at http://www.entrepreneurship.nelson.com.

Notes

1. Eckhardt, J. 2003. *When the weak acquire wealth: An examination of the distribution of high growth startups in the U.S. economy*, Ph.D. dissertation, University of Maryland.

2. Ardichvili, A., Cardozo, R., & Ray, S. 2003. A theory of entrepreneurial opportunity identification and development. *Journal of Business Venturing* 18(1): 105–124.

3. Kirzner, I. 1997. Entrepreneurial discovery and the competitive market process: An Austrian approach. *The Journal of Economic Literature* 35(1): 60–85.

4. Schumpeter, J.A. 1934. *The theory of economic development: An inquiry into profits, capital credit, interest, and the business cycle.* Cambridge, MA: Harvard University Press.

5. Bhide, A. 2000. *The origin and evolution of new businesses.* New York: Oxford University Press.

6. Shane, S. 1996. Explaining variation in rates of entrepreneurship in the United States: 1899–1988. *Journal of Management* 22(5): 747–781.

7. Shane, S. 2001. Technology opportunities and new firm creation. *Management Science* 47(2): 205–220.

8. Holmes, T., & Schmitz, J. 2001. A gain from trade: From unproductive to productive entrepreneurship. *Journal of Monetary Economics* 47(2): 417–446.

9. Baum, J., & Oliver, C. 1992. Institutional embeddedness and the dynamics of organizational populations. *American Sociological Review* 57(4): 540–559.

10. National Research Council, Industrial Research Assistance Program. *Fostering Canadian Technological Innovation: Sink or Swim—New Device Does Both While Monitoring the Oceans.* http://irap-pari.nrc-cnrc.gc.ca/success/metocean_e.pdf.

11. Eckhardt, J., & Shane, S. 2003. The individual-opportunity nexus: A new perspective on entrepreneurship. In Z. Acs & D. Audretsch (eds.) *Handbook of entrepreneurship* (pp. 161–191).

12. Kennedy, P. 2005. From the yoga mat to the lumber yard, here are some of the faces of B.C.'s future. *GlobeandMail.com*, March 2; Company history. http://www.lululemon.com/about/.

13. Schumpeter, J.A. 1934. The *theory of economic development: An inquiry into profits, capital credit, interest, and the business cycle.* Cambridge, MA: Harvard University Press.

14. Ruef, M. 2002. Strong ties, weak ties, and islands: Structural and cultural predictors of organizational innovation. *Industrial and Corporate Change* 11(3): 427–450.

15. Utterback, J. 1994. *Mastering the dynamics of innovation.* Boston, MA: Harvard Business School Press.

16. Mansfield, E. 1985. How rapidly does technology leak out? *Journal of Industrial Economics* 34(2): 217–223.

17. About us. http://www.tirawireless.com.

18. Shane, S. 2003. *A general theory of entrepreneurship: The individual–opportunity nexus.* London: Edward Elgar.

19. Dean, T., Brown, R., & Bamford, C. 1998. Differences in large and small firm responses to environmental context: Strategic implications from a comparative analysis of business formations. *Strategic Management Journal* 19(8): 709–728.

20. Audretsch, D., & Acs, Z. 1994. New firm startups, technology, and macroeconomic fluctuations. *Small Business Economics* 6(6): 439–449.

21. Acs, Z., & Audretsch, D. 1989. Small firm entry in U.S. manufacturing. *Economica* 56(2): 255–266.

22. Eisenhardt, K., & Schoonhoven, K. 1990. Organizational growth: Linking founding team, strategy, environment, and growth among U.S. semiconductor ventures, 1978–1988. *Administrative Science Quarterly* 35(3): 504–529.

23. MacPherson, A., & Hartung, V. 2001. A comparison of the industrial and market characteristics of Canadian and U.S. firms in the commercial Geographic Information Systems (GIS) sector. *Canadian Journal of Regional Science* 24(2): 249–264.

24. *The economic position of the agri-food sector: Productivity analysis.* Food and Drink Branch, APFCE Division, Department for Environment, Food & Rural Affairs, United Kingdom, July 2004.

25 Mata, J., & Portugal, P. 1994. Life duration of new firms. *The Journal of Industrial Economics* 42(3): 227–243.

26 Shane, S. 2001. Technology regimes and new firm formation. *Management Science* 47(9): 1173–1181.

27 Barnett, W. 1997. The dynamics of competitive intensity. *Administrative Science Quarterly* 42(1): 128–160.

28 Audretsch, D. 1991. New firm survival and the technological regime. *Review of Economics and Statistics* 73(3): 441–450.

29 Shane, S. 2003. *A general theory of entrepreneurship: The individual–opportunity nexus.* London: Edward Elgar.

30 Eisenhardt, K., & Schoonhoven, K. 1990. Organizational growth: Linking founding team, strategy, environment, and growth among U.S. semiconductor ventures, 1978–1988. *Administrative Science Quarterly* 35(3): 504–529.

31 Audretsch, D., & Mahmood, T. 1991. The hazard rate of new establishments. *Economic Letters* 36(2): 409–412.

32 Aldrich, H. 1999. *Organizations evolving.* London: Sage.

33 Tushman, M. & Anderson, P. 1986. Technological discontinuities and organizational environments. *Administrative Science Quarterly* 31(3): 439–465.

34 Arrow, K. 1962. Economic welfare and the allocation of resources for inventions. In R. Nelson (ed.). *The rate and direction of inventive activity.* Princeton, NJ: Princeton University Press.

35 Strauss, M. 2004. Indigo set to launch revamped website. *Globe and Mail,* October 28: B7.

36 Christensen, C., & Bower, J. 1996. Customer power, strategic investment, and the failure of leading firms. *Strategic Management Journal* 17(3): 197–218.

37 Winter, S. 1984. Schumpeterian competition in alternative technological regimes. *Journal of Economic Behavior and Organization* 5(3–4): 287–320.

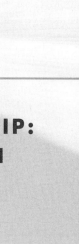

COGNITIVE FOUNDATIONS OF ENTREPRENEURSHIP: CREATIVITY AND OPPORTUNITY RECOGNITION

LEARNING OBJECTIVES

After reading this chapter, you should be able to:

1 Explain why cognitive processes provide an important foundation for understanding creativity and opportunity recognition.

2 Describe working memory, long-term memory, and procedural memory, and explain the roles they play in creativity and opportunity recognition.

3 Explain why we tend to use heuristics and other mental shortcuts, and how these shortcuts can influence entrepreneurs.

4 Define creativity and explain the role that concepts play in it.

5 Distinguish between analytical, creative, and practical intelligence, and explain how all three are combined in successful intelligence.

6 List several factors that influence creativity, as described by the confluence approach.

7 Explain the role of access to information and utilization of information in opportunity recognition.

8 Describe signal detection theory and distinguish between hits, false alarms, and misses.

9 Explain the difference between a promotion focus and a prevention focus, and describe the effects these contrasting perspectives may have on entrepreneurs' efforts to discover valuable opportunities.

10 List several steps you can take as an individual to increase your skill at recognizing potentially valuable opportunities.

The Raw Materials for Creativity and Opportunity Recognition: Mental Structures That Allow Us to Store—and Use—Information
 Cognitive Systems for Storing—and Using—Information: Memory, Schemas, and Prototypes
 Limited Capacity to Process Information: Why Total Rationality Is Rarer Than You Think

Creativity: Escaping from Mental Ruts
 Creativity: Generating the Extraordinary
 Concepts: Building Blocks of Creativity
 Creativity and Human Intelligence
 Encouraging Creativity: The Confluence Approach

Opportunity Recognition: A Key Step in the Entrepreneurial Process
 Access to Information and Its Effective Use: The Core of Opportunity Recognition
 Opportunity Recognition: Additional Insights from Cognitive Science
 Practical Techniques for Increasing Opportunity Recognition

All photos this page © PhotoDisc, Inc.

"When written in Chinese the word *crisis* is composed of two characters. One represents danger and the other represents opportunity." (John F. Kennedy, 1959)

In Chapter 1, we suggested that the entrepreneurial process begins when one or more persons either formulate an idea for something new (a new product or service, a new means of production, a new raw material, etc.) or recognize an opportunity that has emerged out of economic, technological, and social factors. To the extent this theory is true, an intriguing question arises: Why do some persons, but not others, create new ideas for products, services, or markets or recognize emerging opportunities that can be developed into successful new ventures? The answer is certainly complex, but as already noted in Chapters 1 and 2, we believe that, in essence, a successful new venture involves a convergence between opportunities and specific individuals. In other words, some people, but not others, come up with useful ideas or recognize promising opportunities because they are, in a sense, the right person, at the right place, at the right time. What makes specific persons right in these respects? Existing evidence suggests that the answer involves two key factors: (1) such persons have better access to crucial information—information helpful in recognizing opportunities or formulating new ideas and (2) they are better able to utilize—to combine or interpret it in ways that reveal the opportunities other persons overlook.[1]

That was certainly true for Marianne Bertrand, a graduate in business administration from Acadia University, who created a business making and selling high-quality boots for dogs. Like many entrepreneurs, Bertrand started her business in her home. Her crisis came during the winter of 1994. Her basset hounds had been suffering from cold and salty roads and so she had made boots for them. When she walked her dogs, other dog walkers asked where they could get similar boots. At the same time, she needed to find $500 to pay her mortgage, and realized that the weather forecast was calling for another two weeks of extreme cold. Taking a risk, she bought fabric with the mortgage money she *did* have, made dog boots at her dining room table, and took them to local Toronto pet stores. Within a week, when all 130 sets had sold out, she paid her mortgage and started exploring dog boot designs. Muttluks Inc. was born. Clearly Bertrand's knowledge of dog owners and dog needs, her business savvy and her innovativeness made her the right person to recognize this particular opportunity and to move forward with it.[2, 3]

The remainder of this chapter will expand upon these basic ideas about access to, and utilization of, information. It focuses on three key, and closely related, processes in entrepreneurship: **idea generation**—the production of ideas for something new, **creativity**—the generation of ideas that are both new and potentially useful, and **opportunity recognition**—the process through which individuals conclude that they have identified the potential to create something new that has the capacity to generate economic value (i.e., potential future profits).[4] In a sense, these processes fall along a continuum of increasing relevance to the process of founding new ventures—a dimension that moves from sheer production of new ideas (idea generation), to ideas that are also potentially useful (creativity), and finally to ideas that can also potentially serve as the basis for a profitable new venture—bona fide opportunities (see Figure 3.1).

Although many approaches to understanding these processes exist, we believe that among them, a cognitive perspective is especially helpful. Because new ideas and the recognition of emerging opportunities must, ultimately, occur inside the skulls of particular persons, important insights into these processes can be gained by focusing on basic aspects of **human cognition**—the mental processes through which we acquire information, enter it into storage, transform it, and use it to accomplish a wide range of tasks (e.g., making decisions, solving problems).[5] Indeed, we believe that trying to understand idea generation, creativity, and opportunity recognition

Figure 3.1 Idea Generation, Creativity, and Opportunity Recognition

These three processes—which all play a role in entrepreneurship—can be viewed as falling along a dimension moving from origination of ideas that may or may not be useful (idea generation), to ideas that are not only new but also potentially useful (creativity), and finally to ideas that are not only new and useful but also have the potential to generate economic value (opportunity recognition).

Idea Generation	**Creativity**	**Opportunity Recognition**
Production of ideas for something new.	Production of ideas for something new that is also potentially *useful*.	Recognition that ideas are not only new and potentially useful, but also have the potential to generate economic value.

⟶ **Increasing Relevance to Founding New Ventures** ⟶

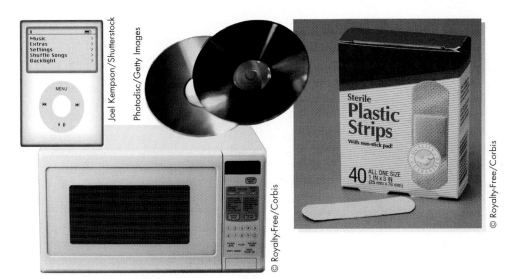

Figure 3.2 Creativity: Ideas for What's New—and Useful

New products that survive and gain widespread use are not only novel, they are also useful to large numbers of people.

without careful attention to their cognitive origins is like to trying to solve complex mathematical problems without a basic knowledge of algebra and calculus: In both cases, essential tools are lacking. In the discussion that follows, therefore, we will focus on the cognitive foundations of these crucial, initial steps in the entrepreneurial process.

Ideas, including those for new products or services, do not emerge from nowhere; on the contrary, they occur when individuals use existing knowledge they have gained (and retained) from their experience to generate something new—thoughts they did not have before. Often, this process is stimulated by some external event or occurrence, for instance, a new experience, information provided by other people, or simply by observing changes in the world around us. But no matter how or why the process begins, it depends heavily on the raw materials individuals already possess—their unique store of knowledge. For this reason, we will begin with a brief overview of the cognitive systems and structures that allow us to store knowledge and transform it in various ways—including changing it into something new. Following this discussion, we will turn to creativity—the act of coming up with something that is both novel and useful. As shown in Figure 3.2, just being new is not enough; in order to be viewed as creative, ideas must also have the potential to be useful. If they are not, then they are better viewed as mere flights of fantasy than as the potential basis for new venture. As part of this discussion, we will consider ways in which you can enhance your own creativity. Finally, we will turn to opportunity recognition. Here, we will focus on the basic nature of this process and the question of why some persons are better than others at identifying opportunities that have emerged from changes in technology, markets, economic conditions, government policies, demographics, and other factors. Several theories of human cognition are relevant to this issue, so we will briefly examine them here. Finally, we will conclude with a discussion of steps that you—as nascent entrepreneurs—can take to enhance your own ability to recognize valuable opportunities.

THE RAW MATERIALS FOR CREATIVITY AND OPPORTUNITY RECOGNITION: MENTAL STRUCTURES THAT ALLOW US TO STORE—AND USE—INFORMATION

LEARNING OBJECTIVE

1 Explain why cognitive processes provide an important foundation for understanding creativity and opportunity recognition.

In an ultimate sense, everything we think, say, or do is influenced by, and reflects, cognitive processes occurring inside our brains. Are you reading and understanding these words? Can you conjure an image of what you ate for dinner last night, the house where you grew up, the face of the person you love most dearly? Can you play a musical instrument? Ride a bicycle? Speak more than one language? Do you have plans for the future? Memories of events that occurred many years ago? Goals? Intentions? All these activities, and countless others, reflect complex neurochemical events occurring within your brain. Indeed, recent advances in neuroscience now permit us to observe these activities that occur within our brains as we think, reason, and make decisions.[6]

It is clear that cognitive processes are the basis for generating new ideas, for creativity, and for opportunity recognition. But why do some persons generate ideas for new products or services or identify opportunities for profitable new ventures overlooked by others? To take one concrete example, why, in 1990, did Debra Boyle, founder of Pro Organics, come up with the idea of purchasing fresh organic produce from local farmers in British Columbia and selling it to natural food retailers? That this was a good idea is indicated by the fact that, by 2003, Pro Organics was the leading distributor of certified organic fresh foods in Canada, with three distribution facilities and roughly $35 million in revenue.[7, 8, 9] The answer, we suggest, is that Boyle had just the right combination of past experience—and just the right store of information at her disposal—to permit her to formulate and execute this excellent business strategy. Indeed, as an ex-hippie, vegetarian mother who raised children and organic produce on Gabriola Island and later worked in Vancouver natural food cooperatives, Boyle understood her business concept from the perspective of a supplier, a distribution channel, and an end consumer. To repeat: We are suggesting that the raw materials for new ideas and for recognizing opportunities are present in the cognitive systems of specific persons as a result of their life experience. For each of us, our experience is unique, and the information we have at our disposal, too, is unique, which is a key reason why specific ideas occur to some of us but not others. To the extent that this reasoning is correct, two basic questions arise: (1) What are these cognitive systems for retaining and processing information like? (2) Can they be stretched or augmented in ways that enhance creativity and the ability to recognize viable opportunities? We will consider the second question in detail as part of our discussion of opportunity recognition. Here, though, we think it is important to pave the way for our later discussions of creativity and opportunity recognition by briefly describing the nature of our cognitive systems for storing and processing information.

Cognitive Systems for Storing—and Using—Information: Memory, Schemas, and Prototypes

LEARNING OBJECTIVE

2 Describe working memory, long-term memory, and procedural memory, and explain the roles they play in creativity and opportunity recognition.

A basic finding in entrepreneurship research is that the more experience people have in a given field, the more likely they are to identify opportunities in it.[10] Similarly, the more experience venture capitalists have—at least to a point—the better they are at spotting good opportunities.[11] Why should this be so? In part, because such experience provides a wealth of useful information people can store and later use in various ways to create or recognize something new. The most basic cognitive system for storing information is known as **memory**, and life without it would be unthinkable. Without memory, we would be unable to recall the past, retain new information, solve problems, or plan for the future. So clearly, memory is a very central aspect of our cognitive systems.

Actually, memory consists of several closely related systems. One, known as *working memory*, holds a limited amount of information for brief periods of time— perhaps up to a few seconds. If you look up a phone number and then try to remember it just long enough to dial it, you are using working memory. Another is known as *long-term memory*. This system allows us to retain truly vast amounts of information for long periods of time. In fact, research findings indicate that there may be no limits to how much long-term memory can hold or how long it can retain information stored in it. So, you can, indeed, go on learning throughout life: There is no apparent limit to the amount of information you can retain or the number of skills you can acquire.

As you already know from your own experience, memory can hold several different kinds of information. Some involve *factual information* that you can readily put into words (e.g., How far is it from Montreal to St. John's? Who was the first prime minister of Canada?). Some involve more personal knowledge about events we have experienced as individuals (e.g., memories of a trip to the dentist, your first love, the first time you had an idea for a new venture).

Still other information we retain in memory is much harder to put into words than the preceding two types. For instance, skilled athletes can't readily explain to other persons why they perform so well. Similarly, musicians can't state how they remember a long piece of music—they just do. In fact, trying to express this kind of information in words can interfere with these activities (see Figure 3.3). Such information is stored in *procedural memory*.

What does procedural memory have to do with entrepreneurship? More than you might guess. For instance, suppose you asked highly successful venture capitalists to explain how they go about choosing new ventures in which to invest. Could they do so? Research findings provide the following answer: not very well. Yes, the venture capitalists can offer explanations about how they reach their decisions. But, in fact, these explanations are not closely aligned with what they actually do—how they really seem to make their decisions, as assessed by data relating to their choices.[12] In short, successful venture capitalists have indeed learned how to recognize good opportunities and have stored information and strategies useful in making such decisions in memory. But after years of practice, this information has become mainly automatic (i.e., it is now a part of procedural memory) so they can't readily describe it in words. The same is true for entrepreneurs: If asked how they go about recognizing opportunities, most can provide some sort of answer. But, in fact, this process seems to involve a large component of information that cannot be readily put into words, so it, too, is related to procedural memory.

© Getty Images/PhotoDisc

Figure 3.3 Procedural Memory in Action

Information stored in procedural memory allows us to perform skilled actions such as the one shown here. Such information, while present in memory, cannot readily be described verbally. In fact, trying to do so can have negative effects. If the person shown here tried to think about what she was doing while doing it, her performance might well suffer. Research findings indicate that venture capitalists cannot explain clearly how they choose the new ventures they wish to support; this is another example of procedural memory in action.

Using and Transforming Information: Schemas and Prototypes

Retaining information we acquire from experience is important, but it is only part of the total picture. In addition, we must also be able to interpret new information as we encounter it and to integrate it with the information already present in memory. This process is essential for creativity and for recognizing opportunities, because these activities involve generating or recognizing something *new*—something that is not already present in memory.

Research in the field of cognitive science suggests that we accomplish these tasks by creating mental frameworks—mental scaffolds that help us to understand new information and to integrate it (often in original ways)—with information we already possess. Several kinds exist, but among the most important are **schemas**—cognitive frameworks representing our knowledge and assumptions about specific aspects of the world. Here is one example: You undoubtedly have a well-developed schema for eating in a restaurant. A host seats you, a waiter asks for your drink order and later returns for your food order, and so on. (Schemas of this type that provide us with an outline for a series of events are known as *scripts*.) Another important kind of mental framework we possess are **prototypes**—abstract, idealized mental representations that capture the essence of a category of objects (e.g., a prototype of a gym: a room filled with exercise equipment, sweating people, a locker room, and so on).

As we will note in our later discussion of creativity and opportunity recognition, schemas and prototypes are important because they can facilitate or hinder both processes. For instance, continuing with our restaurant example, what's your idea of a menu? Probably, a list of set dishes: Customers choose the one they like from what

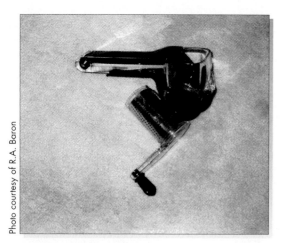

Figure 3.4 Prototypes and Creativity

The cheese grater shown here is far superior to others currently on the market because the cutting blades are based on tools used in fine woodworking. These tools have existed for centuries, so why didn't anyone incorporate them into cheese graters before now? Perhaps because the prototype for such graters did not include this kind of blade and that prevented people from seeing that it could be used in this kind of product.

is offered. Does it have to be this way? Your schema for eating in a restaurant would lead you to expect that it does; it would, in a sense, restrict your creativity. But think again: John Sotiriadis and Nelson Lang, founders of The Pita Pit, had a different idea. Why not let customers build their own sandwiches from a list of ingredients? In other words, let them have any meats, cheeses, sauces, and vegetables they wish, in any combination they prefer. The result? A new concept in dining, and one that is quickly gaining popularity. On the other hand, schemas can facilitate creativity and opportunity recognition because they help us to relate new information to what we already know—and perhaps come up with an entirely new combination.

Prototypes, too, can facilitate or hinder creativity and opportunity recognition. For instance, consider a new product I (Robert Baron) recently purchased—a rotary grater for parmesan cheese known as the Microplane. Over the years, I have purchased many cheese graters and none has worked well: All tend to jam up and to compress the cheese instead of grating it. This one, though, works like a dream (see Figure 3.4). Why? Because the cutting edges are modelled on high-quality woodworking tools. Why didn't someone think of this sooner? Perhaps because the prototype for cheese grater did not include this type of blade. In this case, an existing prototype interfered with creativity—and the development of an excellent new product. In other cases, prototypes can facilitate creativity by providing a framework for interpreting new information (e.g., by relating it to existing prototypes).

Limited Capacity to Process Information: Why Total Rationality Is Rarer Than You Think

Now that we have outlined what is, in a sense, the production facilities for creativity and opportunity recognition, we should call your attention to one other basic aspect of human cognition—the fact that it has limited capacity to process (i.e., deal with, interpret) information at any given time. So although our ability to add to the knowledge stored in memory and other mental systems seems unlimited, there appear to be fairly firm limits on how much information we can handle at once. This restriction results from the fact that *working memory*—the short-term system we described earlier—can hold only a limited amount of information at once. Because this system seems to be the contact point between what we are thinking about right now and information stored in memory, it creates a bottleneck in our efforts to make sense of our ongoing experience—and to create something new.

As a result of this limited capacity to process information, we often adopt mental shortcuts—tactics for stretching our limited capacity as far as possible. These tactics are helpful from the point of view of conserving precious mental capacity, but they can also lead us into serious errors. Further, our tendency to rely on such shortcuts is strongest at times when our cognitive systems are strained to the limit—when we are required to process large amounts of information in a short period of time (e.g., make important decisions quickly or on the basis of incomplete information). If this situation sounds like one faced by many entrepreneurs much of the time, it is! For this reason, it has been suggested that entrepreneurs may be more susceptible to these cognitive biases and errors than people in many other fields or occupations.[13] We will refer to the potential role of these errors in various aspects of entrepreneurship in later chapters, so it is useful to briefly describe some of them here.

Although many mental shortcuts exist, among the most useful are **heuristics**—simple rules for making complex decisions or drawing inferences in a rapid and seemingly effortless manner. Perhaps the most important of these is the *availability heuristic*. This mental rule suggests that the easier it is to bring information to mind, the more important or accurate we perceive it to be, and hence the greater its impact on our subsequent judgments or decisions. Further, the more information we can bring to mind, the greater the importance we assign to it.[14] Although this heuristic

LEARNING OBJECTIVE

3 Explain why we tend to use heuristics and other mental shortcuts, and how these shortcuts can influence entrepreneurs.

seems reasonable, it can lead to important errors, primarily because dramatic or unusual information is easier to recall than more mundane information. Thus, it may influence our thinking and our decisions to a greater extent than is justified. For instance, imagine an entrepreneur who is trying to choose a key employee. There are several applicants, one of whom is much more expressive and outgoing than the others. Later, when trying to remember the interviews, the entrepreneur finds it easier to recall what this person said, and that may tip the decision in this person's favour, even though other applicants are actually better qualified.

In addition to heuristics, there are many other tilts or potential errors in our thinking that result from the same general tendency to conserve our limited processing capacity. Among these, three are especially common and dangerous: the *optimistic bias*, the *confirmation bias*, and the *illusion of control*.[15] In its most basic form, the optimistic bias refers to the tendency to expect things to turn out well even when there is no rational basis for such expectations. Susceptibility to the optimistic bias may be one reason why some persons choose to become entrepreneurs: They expect to attain success even though the odds are strongly against them.[16] One common form of this bias is known as the *planning fallacy*—the tendency to believe that we can complete more in a given period of time than we actually can. Do you ever observe this tendency in your own thinking? Unless you are very unusual, you probably do. The planning fallacy, and other aspects of the tendency to be overoptimistic, has been observed among both entrepreneurs[17] and venture capitalists.[18]

The *confirmation bias* is even more insidious in its impact. This bias refers to the tendency to notice, process, and remember information that confirms our current beliefs (or, at least is consistent with them) much more readily than information that disconfirms our current beliefs. In other words, all too often, we live in a self-constructed echo chamber—the only information that gets through is information that strengthens our current views. Clearly, this bias is a very dangerous tendency for entrepreneurs who cannot afford to ignore information contrary to their current

Table 3.1 Potential Sources of Error in Human Cognition

Because we possess limited capacity to process information, we often adopt mental shortcuts to stretch this capacity and to reduce our effort. As shown here, this tendency underlies many different potential errors in our thinking.

SOURCE OF POTENTIAL ERROR	DESCRIPTION OF ERROR	EXAMPLE
Representative heuristic	A mental rule of thumb suggesting that the more closely an event or object resembles typical examples of some concept or category, the more likely it is to belong to that concept or category	An individual is assumed to belong to some occupation or group because she or he resembles the stereotype for that group or occupation.
Availability heuristic	A mental rule of thumb in which the importance or probability of various events is judged on the basis of how readily information concerning them can be brought to mind, or how much information can be readily recalled	People assume that the chances of dying in a fire or airplane crash are greater than those of dying in an automobile accident because the media report fatal fires and airplane crashes more dramatically than automobile accidents, thus making them easier to remember.
Anchoring-and-adjustment heuristic	A cognitive rule of thumb in which existing information is accepted as a reference point but then adjusted to take account of various factors	Negotiators accept their opponent's opening offer as a heuristic framework for further bargaining.
Confirmation bias	The tendency to notice and remember information that confirms our views	An entrepreneur becomes increasingly convinced that an idea for a new product is viable because he notices and remembers only information that supports this view.
Optimistic bias	The tendency to assume that things will turn out well even though there is no rational basis for this prediction	Entrepreneurs believe that the odds they will succeed are much higher than they actually are.
Planning fallacy	The tendency to assume that we can accomplish more in a given period of time than is true (or to underestimate the amount of time it will take to complete a project)	An entrepreneur assumes that each stage in starting a new venture will take less time to complete than is actually true.
Escalation of commitment (sunk costs)	The tendency to stick with decisions that yield negative results even as the negative results continue to mount	An entrepreneur continues efforts to market a product in a specific way even though these efforts produce a mounting string of failures.
Affect infusion	Emotions have powerful effects on thinking (e.g., when in a good mood, we notice and remember positive information; while when in a bad mood, we notice and remember negative information)	An entrepreneur who is in a bad mood when she interviews a job applicant recalls mainly negative information about this person; in contrast, she recalls mainly positive information about an applicant she interviews while in a good mood.

beliefs—for instance, market information or information about actual or potential competitors.

The *illusion of control* refers to the tendency to assume that our fate is under our control to a greater extent than is actually the case—to believe that we have more control over what happens to us than rational considerations suggest. Research findings indicate that this belief may be another important factor in many persons' decisions to become entrepreneurs; they believe that the fate of the new ventures they start is largely under their control and so underestimate the potential impact of economic conditions, competitors, and many other factors that are, in fact, largely outside their influence.[19]

These beliefs are only a small sample of the many potential sources of error in human cognition that have been uncovered in careful research. Others are summarized in Table 3.1. The main point of the present discussion is simply this: Because we must deal with a basic dilemma—restricted capacity to process information in the face of large amounts of information—many aspects of our cognition are far from entirely rational. On the contrary, they are subject to a wide range of tilts and biases that do indeed save effort, but also increase the odds of serious errors. Successfully navigating through these dangerous waters is crucial for entrepreneurs, so we will have reason to refer to this basic theme at many points in this book. (For discussion of one potential cognitive error that can be especially dangerous for entrepreneurs, see the **Danger! Pitfall Ahead!** section.)

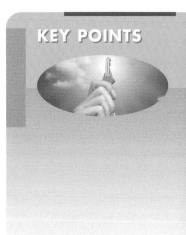

KEY POINTS

- Cognitive processes provide the foundation for creativity and opportunity recognition.
- Memory involves cognitive systems for storing information. Working memory can retain limited amounts of information for short periods of time. Active processing of information occurs in working memory, so it is the system in which consciousness exists.
- Long-term memory holds vast (perhaps unlimited) amounts of information for long periods of time. Such information can be factual or procedural in nature.
- Because our capacity to process information is limited, we often adopt shortcuts to reduce mental effort. These include heuristics and various tilts in our thinking (e.g., the confirmation bias). These shortcuts do save effort, but they can lead to serious errors.
- Among these shortcuts, one of the most dangerous for entrepreneurs is sunk costs (escalation of commitment)—a tendency to stick with decisions that yield increasingly negative results.

CREATIVITY: ESCAPING FROM MENTAL RUTS

Now that we have provided you with the necessary toolkit concerning human cognition, we can turn to one of the two central topics of this chapter: creativity (the generation of ideas that are both new and useful). A cognitive perspective offers important new insights into the nature of this crucial process and how, precisely, it occurs.

DANGER! PITFALL AHEAD!

"Too Much Invested to Quit": The Potentially Devastating Effects of Sunk Costs

Have you ever heard the phrase "Throwing good money after bad"? It refers to the fact that in many situations, people who have made a bad decision—one that is yielding negative outcomes—tend to stick to it even as the evidence for its failure mounts. They may even commit additional time, effort, and resources to a failing course of action in the hope of somehow turning it around. This tendency to become trapped in bad decisions is known as sunk costs or escalation of commitment and is very common; it happens to investors who continue to hold on to what are clearly bad stocks and to people in troubled relationships, who often remain in them when all their friends urge them to withdraw.[20] Escalation of commitment also happens in decision-making groups. They, too, find it difficult to admit that they made a mistake and so cling to bad decisions that generate increasingly negative results. Research findings indicate that such effects—sometimes described as collective entrapment (a group becomes trapped in a bad decision)—are especially likely to occur in cases where groups have exerted a lot of effort to make the initial decision and so feel strongly committed to it.

Why do such effects occur? For several reasons. First, sticking with a decision is, initially, quite rational. Giving up too quickly can be a mistake, and if the decision was made carefully to start with, it makes sense to continue with it, at least for a while. As losses mount, though, other processes that are not so rational come into play. People are unwilling to admit that they made a mistake because doing so will cause them to lose face and look foolish. Similarly, those who made the initial decision want to justify their actions, and the best way to do so is to continue on the current course and somehow make it turn out well.

Whatever the precise basis for escalation of commitment, it poses a very real danger to entrepreneurs. New ventures generally have limited resources, so there is little capacity to absorb mounting losses. Further, in any decision made by several persons, some will feel more responsible for this choice than others, with the result that dissension may occur among members of the founding team. Those who back away from the decision, claiming that they were against it all along, may come into conflict with those who feel more strongly committed to it. Overall, the results may be devastating for the new venture, so clearly, escalation of commitment is one cognitive error entrepreneurs should try to avoid.

What steps can entrepreneurs take to minimize the risk of this kind of error? Several have been found to be useful. One involves deciding, in advance, that if losses reach certain limits, or negative results continue for a specific period of time, no further resources will be invested and the decision will be changed. This decision is hard to carry out, but it is similar to stop-loss orders in the stock market: It does tend to limit the losses that will be sustained. Another strategy involves charging persons other than the ones who made the original decision with the task of deciding whether to continue. Because they did not make the original commitment, they are often less committed to it. A third approach involves creating a culture in which people do not feel that they will lose face if they reverse earlier decisions now found to be poor ones. Rationally, this approach makes a lot of sense, but as you can guess, it can be difficult to implement.

Overall, it is clear that escalation of commitment and collective entrapment in bad decisions represent serious threats to the success of new ventures. For this reason, entrepreneurs should be fully aware of these potential pitfalls and take active steps to avoid them. Doing so can be a challenging task, but one well worth the effort: The companies they save will be their own!

Creativity: Generating the Extraordinary

Suppose you were asked to name people high in creativity: Who would be on your list? When faced with this question, many persons come up with names such as Albert Einstein, Leonardo da Vinci, Thomas Edison, and Sigmund Freud. They worked in very different domains, so what do they all have in common? Essentially, this: All created something almost everyone agreed was *new*—theories, inventions, and other contributions that did not already exist. As we noted earlier, however, newness is not enough. Most researchers who have studied *creativity* define it as involving two key aspects: the items or ideas produced are both novel (original,

LEARNING OBJECTIVE

4   Define creativity and explain the role that concepts play in it.

Close to Home © 2001 John McPherson. Reprinted by permission of Universal Press Syndicate. All rights reserved.

SPLOOSH!

YOU'VE GOT MAIL!

8-17

At the National E-Mail Addiction Rehabilitation Center.

Figure 3.5 Creative Ideas Are Both Novel *and* Useful

The idea illustrated here is certainly new, but it is not useful or practical. Therefore, it does not meet the basic criteria for being described as creative.

unexpected) and appropriate or useful—they meet relevant constraints.[21] By this definition, the action shown in Figure 3.5 does not illustrate true creativity. Although the idea it involves is original, it really isn't practical. The Canadian Patent Office applies the same criteria to patent applications: Not only must an idea be new, but it must be useful, too.

Creativity is important for several reasons: It provides new knowledge, products, and other advances that can improve the quality of human life. It is somewhat surprising to learn, therefore, that until recently, it was *not* the subject of systematic research. Why not? Primarily because our understanding of human cognition was not sufficiently advanced to offer a solid framework for interpreting creativity in terms of basic cognitive processes. During the past two decades, this situation has changed greatly, and at present, there is general agreement that creativity in all domains—science, medicine, the arts, and day-to-day living—emerges from a relatively small set of basic cognitive processes. What are these processes? Most research suggests that two are central. One involves the stretching or expanding of internal mental structures we construct to organize information. The second involves the operation of various facets of human intelligence.

Concepts: Building Blocks of Creativity

The amount of information in long-term memory is vast, so in order to make it easier to retrieve and use this information, we organize it in various ways by creating internal mental structures to hold it. These structures take many different forms, but among them, **concepts**—categories for objects or events that are somehow similar to each other in certain respects—are especially important. Consider, for instance, the words "bicycle," "airplane," "automobile," and "elevator"; all are included in the concept "vehicle." Similarly, the words "shoes," "shirts," "jeans," and "jackets" are all included in the concept "clothing." As you can see, the objects within each of these concepts differ greatly, but are also similar to each other in certain underlying respects (e.g., all vehicles are used to move people from one point to another). In a sense, then, concepts act as kinds of filing systems in memory, and once established, can help us to store new information. For instance, if you observed an entirely new kind of clothing you had never seen before, you would probably have no difficulty including it in the concept "clothing."

Concepts exist in memory in hierarchical networks that reflect the relationships between them. For instance, the concept "animals" includes birds, fish, and insects. Animals, in other words, is higher in our hierarchy of concepts than birds, fish, and insects. Birds, in turn, include penguins and canaries. Similarly, fish include sharks and salmon. Insects include butterflies and mosquitoes. The same is true for many other concepts; they, too, are organized into a hierarchical structure.

The fact that we store information in memory in an organized manner has two major implications for creativity—one positive and the other negative. On the plus side of the ledger, such internal structure enhances our ability to retrieve the vast amount of knowledge included in long-term memory, which gives us better access to the raw materials from which new ideas can emerge. On the downside, however, the fact that knowledge is organized in memory often constrains our thinking, assuring that, in general, it stays pretty much within what have sometimes been described as mental ruts. In other words, the internal structures we have created for ourselves are so strong that we find it very difficult to escape from, or think outside, them. Here's a striking example. In the mid-1970s, engineers and scientists at Sony Corporation were charged with the task of developing music CDs. They made great progress but ultimately gave up for the following reason: The CDs they produced stored fully 18 hours of music, and that was viewed as being too large to be marketable. Why did the CDs hold so much? *Because the engineers made them the same size and shape as existing LP records!* Although they were brilliant scientists and engineers, they simply could not escape from the mental ruts created by their past experience to realize that the new CDs could be any size they wished!

Here's yet another and perhaps even more amazing example of how cognitive organization can interfere with creativity. The Inca of South America had a very advanced civilization—one whose achievements astounded the Spaniards who first encountered them. But one invention they did not possess was wheeled vehicles; items to be transported were loaded on animals or dragged on poles—no carts or wagons existed. Yet—and here's the really surprising fact—Inca children played with models of wheeled carts! So the Inca had the *idea* of putting wheels on vehicles, but for some reason, they viewed this design as suitable only for toys! It is hard to imagine a more dramatic illustration of the power of mental ruts to constrain human thought.

If the impact of mental ruts can be this strong, you may be wondering, how do people ever escape from them? How, in short, does creativity ever occur? The answer seems to involve the fact that concepts can sometimes be expanded, thus paving the way for creativity. In other words, creativity emerges when basic mental processes allow for the expansion or transformation of concepts so that something new appears. This transformation did not occur among the Inca, who seemed unable to expand the concept of wheeled toy into wheeled full-scale wagons, but it does occur and can be encouraged. Specifically, concepts can be stretched or expanded in several different ways.

First, they can be *combined*, with the result that something very new is generated. For instance, consider the concept of the luxury SUV. The concept of an all-wheel drive, off-road vehicle has been combined with the concept of a luxury vehicle to produce something that never existed before—and is currently very popular. When concepts that appear to be initially opposite are combined, the result can be novel indeed—at least, when they are first introduced (e.g., nonalcoholic beer).

Concepts can also be *expanded*. In fact, this is often what happens with new products—even ones that represent a major breakthrough. For instance, the first railroad cars looked very much like the horse-drawn carriages they replaced. The concept of carriages had been expanded to include a vehicle for moving people, but what resulted was very similar to the original concept in appearance, if not means of propulsion. Similarly, early television sets were often placed in beautiful wooden cabinets because they were a form of home entertainment like radios and phonographs, and that's how those items had been presented to consumers.

A third way in which concepts can be changed or expanded is through *analogy*. Analogies involve perceiving similarities between objects or events that are otherwise dissimilar. For instance, statements such as "Knowledge is like a light in the dark" or "My love is like a red, red rose" involve analogies. Knowledge is not really like a light, and lovers are not like red roses—except in special ways. By making such comparisons, however, it is sometimes possible to break out of the mental ruts described earlier. The history of science, technology, and the arts are filled with examples of creative advances based, in part, on analogy. For instance, Rutherford's view of the hydrogen atom as similar to a planetary system in some respects (a large nucleus in the centre with electrons revolving around it) and de Mestral's invention of Velcro after examining how burrs clung to his clothing with minute hooks are examples of reasoning by analogy that led to important advances. When concepts are stretched through analogy, in short, creativity is encouraged and important advances can result (see Figure 3.6).[22]

Does the creativity shown by entrepreneurs emerge from the same processes? There seems little doubt that it does; after all, why should entrepreneurs present an exception to a pattern shown over and over in science, medicine, and the arts? In short, we agree with Robert Bresson, a French film director, who once noted: "An old

Figure 3.6 Expanding Concepts Through Analogies: An Important Source of Creative Theory

When Swiss scientist Georges de Mestral looked at the burrs that stuck to his clothes after walking through fields, he noticed that the burrs had tiny hooks that became attached to the threads of the fabric. Through analogy, he reasoned that he could create a useful means of attaching things to each other with a similar system of tiny plastic hooks—and Velcro was born!

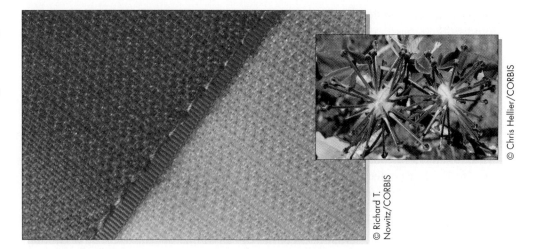

thing becomes new if you detach it from what usually surrounds it." When concepts are separated from the hierarchical mental structures of which they are a part by combining them with other concepts, by expanding them, or through analogy, they may indeed become new— or at least, point the way toward acts of creativity that, in the hands of energetic and motivated entrepreneurs, generate something truly new.

Creativity and Human Intelligence

Another important factor in creativity (and in opportunity recognition, too) is human intelligence. Here's a vivid illustration of this point:

> *Two individuals, a university professor and an entrepreneur, are walking in the woods when they spot a ferocious grizzly bear charging in their direction. The professor, whose field is physics, estimates the speed of the bear and the speed at which they can run away from it. He then states: "Stop running. There's no way we'll ever be able to escape from that bear. He will catch us in 15 seconds." The entrepreneur, however, keeps on running. When the professor asks why, the entrepreneur shouts back over his shoulder: "You're right—I can never outrun the bear. But I don't have to outrun it; all I have to do is outrun you!"*

LEARNING OBJECTIVE

5 Distinguish between analytical, creative, and practical intelligence, and explain how all three are combined in successful intelligence.

This apocryphal tale has an important moral: Intelligence is indeed an important ingredient in success, but it is not necessarily the kind of intelligence measured by standard IQ tests. Instead, it is intelligence useful in meeting the many challenges of life— challenges posed by an everchanging world. This fact is widely recognized by psychologists, who currently define **intelligence** as individuals' abilities to understand complex ideas, to adapt effectively to the world around them, to learn from experience, to engage in various forms of reasoning, and to overcome a wide range of obstacles. As you can see, this definition suggests that intelligence has several different facets: It is not a unitary phenomenon. In fact, it is now widely recognized that human intelligence can be divided into several different kinds:[23] *analytic* intelligence, which involves the abilities to think critically and analytically (this is the kind measured by traditional IQ tests); *creative* intelligence, which involves the ability to formulate new ideas and gain insights into a wide range of problems (this is the kind shown by scientific geniuses and inventors such as Einstein, Newton, and Edison); and **practical intelligence**, which involves being intelligent in a practical sense (persons high in such intelligence are adept at solving the problems of everyday life and have street smarts). Another component in this mixture may be what is sometimes described as *social intelligence*, which involves the ability to understand others and get along well with them.

A growing body of evidence suggests that in order to be creative—and successful— entrepreneurs need a balanced mixture of all three components, something one expert in human intelligence, Robert Sternberg, terms **successful intelligence**.[24] Specifically, entrepreneurs need *creative* intelligence to come up with new ideas, *practical* intelligence to identify ways to develop these ideas, and *analytic* intelligence to evaluate the ideas and determine whether they are worth pursuing (see Figure 3.7).[25]

Although Sternberg does not specifically mention social intelligence—the skills required to get along effectively with others—there is little doubt that it, too, plays a role. We will consider this topic in more detail in Chapter 4. Here, we will simply note that growing evidence suggests that social intelligence, too, is a key ingredient in entrepreneurs' success. Without it, entrepreneurs can experience major problems in obtaining the financial and human resources they need to convert their dreams into reality.[26] So this aspect of intelligence, too, is important.

In sum, human intelligence does indeed play a role in creativity and in entrepreneurship, but in a more complex way than was once assumed. The intelligence required by entrepreneurs to be creative and to found successful new ventures is much richer and more multifaceted than the kind measured by standard IQ tests. In this respect, informal observation about entrepreneurs (and other creative persons) is correct: Such individuals do not necessarily shine in settings that require mainly analytical intelligence (e.g., in school); rather, their intellectual assets are more apparent in practical settings such as the modern world of business.

Encouraging Creativity: The Confluence Approach

Now that we have considered the role of practical and successful intelligence in creativity, it seems appropriate to consider another important question: "What can be done to enhance it?" Perhaps the best way of answering this question is by considering the factors that contribute to its occurrence; to the extent these factors are maximized, then creativity, too, should be encouraged. So, what factors have been found to contribute to creativity? As we have already noted, the field of cognitive science suggests that basic cognitive processes underlie creative thought. Creativity emerges from the operation of several kinds of memory, the expansion or merging of concepts, and related processes.[27]

Although the cognitive approach to creativity provides important insights into the factors that contribute to it, a somewhat broader view that includes additional factors has gained increased acceptance in recent years. This view is known as **confluence approach**, and as its name suggests, it proposes that creativity emerges out of the confluence (i.e., convergence) of several basic resources:[28]

- *Intellectual abilities*—the ability to see problems in new ways, the ability to recognize which ideas are worth pursuing coupled with persuasive skills—being able to convince others of the value of these new ideas (a combination of successful and social intelligence)

- *A broad and rich knowledge base*—a large store of relevant information in memory; without such knowledge, the cognitive foundations for creative thought are lacking

LEARNING OBJECTIVE

6 List several factors that influence creativity, as described by the confluence approach.

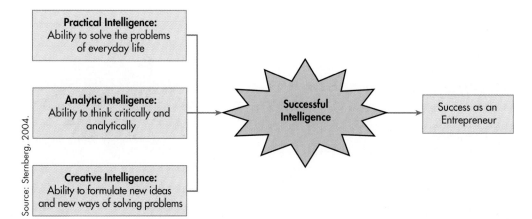

Source: Sternberg, 2004.

Figure 3.7 Successful Intelligence: A Basic Requirement for Entrepreneurs

One expert on human intelligence, Robert Sternberg, has recently suggested that in order to succeed, entrepreneurs need a high level of successful intelligence—a good blend of practical, analytic, and creative intelligence.

- *An appropriate style of thinking*—a preference for thinking in novel ways, and an ability to see the big picture—to think globally as well as locally; in essence, a propensity for escaping from mental ruts

- *Personality attributes*—such traits as willingness to take risks and to tolerate ambiguity; these traits help individuals to consider ideas and solutions others overlook

- *Intrinsic, task-focused motivation*—creative people usually love what they are doing and find intrinsic rewards in their work

- *An environment that is supportive of creative ideas*—one that does not impose uniformity of thought and one that encourages change

The confluence approach suggests that to the extent these factors are present, creative thought can emerge (see Figure 3.8). A large body of evidence offers support for this view, so it appears to be quite useful.[29] This approach, in turn, suggests several techniques you can use to increase your own creativity, and so enhance the likelihood that you will generate ideas that can be the basis for successful new ventures.

First, and most important, it is clear that new ideas do *not* emerge out of a vacuum. Rather, they derive from combining, stretching, or viewing existing information in a new way. This means that in order to be creative, it is essential to have lots of information at your disposal. There are many ways of gaining a broad and rich knowledge base, but research findings indicate that among the most useful from the point of view of becoming an entrepreneur are (1) having varied work experience (e.g., the more jobs people have held, the more likely they are to become self-employed[30]), (2) having lived in many different places,[31] and (3) having a broad social network—many friends and acquaintances who can share their knowledge with you.[32] All of these factors increase the amount of information individuals have at their disposal and make them more creative. So, if you want to enhance your own creativity, you might consider structuring your life so as to broaden your own knowledge base—the foundation from which creative ideas spring.

Second, as the confluence approach suggests, you should cultivate a style of thinking that helps you break out of mental ruts. This way of thinking is more difficult than it sounds because it is always easier to think in routine ways than to question our own beliefs. One way of doing so is to make sure that the people with whom you spend time are *not* all highly similar to yourself. To the extent they are, you will tend to agree with one another about most issues and will not challenge each others' beliefs. If, instead, you count among your friends people from different backgrounds and occupations, and who have contrasting views on a wide range of issues, this exposure can help you develop flexible, open modes of thought—which, in turn, can enhance your creativity.

Figure 3.8 Creativity: The Confluence Approach

The confluence approach suggests that creativity stems from the convergence of several factors. The most important of these include a broad and rich knowledge base, an appropriate style of thinking, certain personality attributes, and high intrinsic motivation.

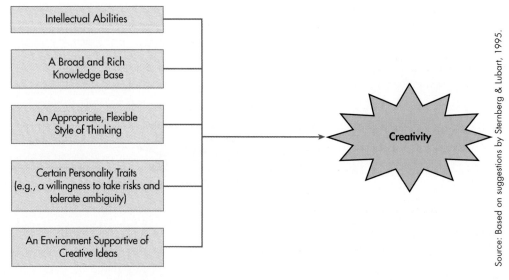

Source: Based on suggestions by Sternberg & Lubart, 1995.

Third, you should try to work in environments that encourage rather than discourage creativity. One reason many people choose to become entrepreneurs is that they feel stifled by the corporate world, which often leaves little room for imagination or originality. The very best organizations, in contrast, tolerate or even encourage innovation among their employees. They also often tend to be more open about distributing information to employees. Many studies suggest that working in such jobs can broaden your knowledge base while simultaneously encouraging you to think creatively.[33]

In sum, there are a number of steps you can take to increase your own tendency to think creatively. To the extent you make these practices part of your daily life, you will become more creative and increase your ability to come up with ideas that can lead to successful ventures. Creativity is impressive, and in the hands of the right persons, it can literally change the world. But we now know that creativity stems from factors that are far from mysterious, and that are, to an important degree, under our own control.

KEY POINTS

- Creativity involves producing ideas that are both novel and appropriate.
- Existing evidence suggests that creative thought emerges from the combination and expansion of concepts, and from reasoning by analogy.
- To be creative and succeed, entrepreneurs need successful intelligence—a good balance of analytic, practical, and creative intelligence. They also need a high degree of social intelligence—the ability to get along well with others.
- The confluence approach to creativity suggests that creativity emerges out of a convergence of several factors (intellectual abilities, a broad and rich knowledge base, appropriate style of thinking, etc.).
- This approach and others suggest concrete steps you can take to increase your own creativity and, hence, your capacity for formulating new ideas that can lead to successful business ventures.

OPPORTUNITY RECOGNITION: A KEY STEP IN THE ENTREPRENEURIAL PROCESS

As we noted in Chapter 1, identification of a potentially valuable opportunity is a key initial step in the entrepreneurial process. Entrepreneurs' decisions to found new ventures often stem from their belief that they have identified an opportunity no one else has yet recognized, and so can benefit from being first to enter the marketplace.[34] Because it is the start of the entrepreneurial process, it is not at all surprising that opportunity recognition has long been a central concept in the field of entrepreneurship. Until recently, however, little effort has been made to examine it as a *process*. Rather, opportunities have been defined largely in economic terms: Any idea for a new product, service, raw material, market, or production process that can be successfully exploited so as to generate economic benefits for stakeholders has been viewed as constituting an opportunity.[35] Although this view certainly makes sense, defining opportunities entirely from an economic perspective overlooks several key questions.

First, it largely ignores the question of *how* this process occurs; in other words, how do specific persons go about identifying opportunities that have been generated by shifting economic, technological, and social conditions (described in Chapter 2)? Clearly, this development is an active process involving human perceptions and cognition, so understanding how it occurs might well suggest ways of enhancing its occurrence—techniques for helping would-be entrepreneurs identify opportunities that will benefit not only them, but millions of persons who ultimately use the new products or services they develop.

Second, and closely related, why are some persons better at this process—at identifying opportunities—than others? The opportunities generated by economic and technological conditions are there for anyone to notice; yet, only some individuals do so. What is it about these persons that allows them, and not others, to perform this task? Third, all opportunities are certainly not equal in potential value; some are blind alleys leading to economic disaster, while others have real potential for generating personal and societal wealth. Why, then, are some individuals so much better than others at separating the wheat from the chaff—that is, at discerning which opportunities provide real potential for economic gains? In this section, we will review existing evidence concerning these issues. As we will soon see, this evidence suggests that two factors—having better access than others to certain kinds of information and being able to use this information effectively—play a crucial role.[36] For this reason, we will consider these factors first. In addition, however, cognitive processes, too, influence opportunity recognition.[37] When entrepreneurs conclude that they have noticed an opportunity, this declaration implies that they believe they have recognized something out there that exists and is worth developing, but that other persons have not yet detected. Theories and concepts in cognitive science that focus on perception and related processes offer intriguing insights into the nature of opportunity recognition, so we will consider these, too. Finally, we will comment on ways in which you, as budding entrepreneurs, can enhance your own ability to spot opportunities worth pursuing.

One more point before proceeding: Recently, there has been a debate in the field of entrepreneurship over the question of whether opportunities exist in the external world or are created by human minds.[38] We believe that there is, in fact, no basis for controversy over this issue. As we noted in Chapter 2, opportunities, as a potential (i.e., a pattern that could be observed) come into existence in the external world as a result of changes in knowledge, technology, markets, political, and social conditions. However, they remain merely a potential until they emerge within specific human minds as the result of active cognitive processes. So in a sense, opportunities both exist out there and are the creation of human thought. Choosing between these two ideas is not necessary, because both are valid. Now, back to our discussion of opportunity recognition as a process.

Access to Information and Its Effective Use: The Core of Opportunity Recognition

LEARNING OBJECTIVE

7 Explain the role of access to information and utilization of information in opportunity recognition.

The question of why some people and not others discover opportunities is both intriguing and practical: If we can understand why certain people recognize opportunities that others don't yet notice, this knowledge can provide important insights into how this process can be enhanced. In other words, it may offer valuable clues as to how individuals can increase their ability to recognize opportunities.

Research on this question offers fairly clear answers, all revolving around the central role of information. Specifically, it appears that some people are more likely than others to recognize opportunities because (1) they have better access to certain kinds of information, and (2) they are able to utilize this information once they have it.

Greater Access to Information

With respect to the first of these points (greater access to information), it appears that specific persons gain increased access to information useful for identifying opportunities in several ways. For example, they may have jobs that provide them with cutting-edge information that is not widely available to others. Jobs in research and development or marketing appear to be especially valuable in this respect.[39] Another way in which individuals gain superior access to information is through varied work and life experience—factors that, because they contribute to individuals' knowledge base, also increase their creativity.[40] For example, in a study of young Canadian software firms, Eileen Fischer of York University and I (Becky Reuber) observed that firms that had founders with more international experience established more foreign strategic partnerships and entered foreign markets more quickly after start-up.[41] Yet another way in which specific persons gain enhanced access to information is through a large social network.[42] Indeed, Per Davidsson, of the Brisbane Graduate School of Business, and Benson Honig, of Wilfrid Laurier University, found that people who are members of a business network, such as a trade association or a chamber of commerce, and those with business owners as friends or neighbours, are more apt to discover and exploit entrepreneurial opportunities.[43] As you may know from your own experience, other people are a valuable source of information, and often the information they provide cannot be acquired easily in any other way. Finally—and not surprisingly—persons who discover opportunities are often ones who actively search for them. They do not just wait for opportunities to drop into their laps; rather, they go out and look for them—often in places others overlook. In this respect, Gaglio and Katz[44] have suggested that entrepreneurs—and especially successful ones—possess a *schema* (mental framework) that assists them in being alert to, and therefore recognizing, opportunities. As we noted earlier, schemas are a kind of mental scaffold built up through experience, which help us to process information efficiently because they provide a framework into which new information can be readily placed. In other words, schemas assist us in linking new information to information already stored in memory, which, in turn, makes it easier to retain the new information and to use it in various ways.

Applying this concept to opportunity recognition, Gaglio and Katz suggest that some persons possess a schema of entrepreneurial alertness—an internal mental framework that helps them search for and notice changes that might yield valuable opportunities, changes in markets, technology, competition, and so on. The result? They are more likely to recognize opportunities than other persons. In sum, many factors give specific persons an edge where access to useful kinds of information is concerned, which, in turn, increases the likelihood that they will recognize potentially valuable opportunities.

Superior Utilization of Information

Greater access to valuable information is not the entire story, however. Entrepreneurs who recognize opportunities not only have greater access to information than other persons, they are also better at using such information. First, because of their greater access to information, they often have richer and better integrated stores of knowledge than other persons—for instance, more information (in memory) about markets and how to serve them.[45] This knowledge, in turn, enhances their ability to interpret and use new information because not only do they have more information at their disposal, but it is also better organized. As we noted earlier, large quantities of well-organized information play a key role in creativity. After all, it is hard to stretch information or combine it in new ways if it is not present or if it is not well-organized. Persons who identify opportunities have been found to possess richer and better organized stores of information, so it is not surprising that they are better able to perceive opportunities others often miss. In addition, individuals who recognize opportunities may also be better at the process of improvisation—at formulating plans and strategies on the fly, as they go along.[46] In other words, they don't necessarily engage in a systematic or detailed search for opportunities; rather, recognition of these opportunities emerges out of their continuing efforts to adapt to, and deal with, ever-changing conditions around them. A superior ability to use information in opportunity recognition can come from experience. Davidsson and Honig, for example, also found that people with previous start-up experience are more likely to discover and exploit new opportunities.[47]

Other cognitive processes, too, play a role. For instance, persons who found new ventures are more likely to be higher in intelligence than persons who do not. Moreover, entrepreneurs have been found to be higher in intelligence even when their I.Q. was measured many years in the past—when they were, on average, 12 years old![48] Additional evidence suggests that entrepreneurs are especially likely to be higher than other persons in practical intelligence—the ability to solve the

Figure 3.9 Opportunity Recognition: The Central Role of Information

Opportunity recognition stems, to an important degree, from greater access to information and greater capacity to utilize it.

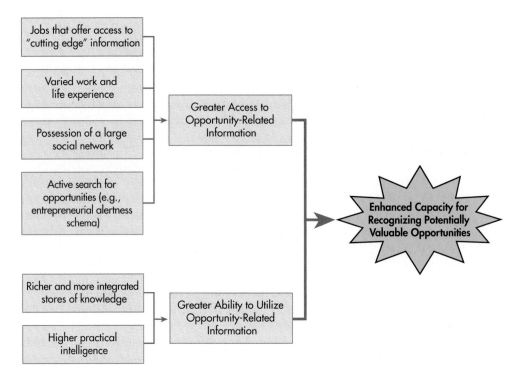

varied problems of everyday life.[49] Finally, and again, far from surprising, entrepreneurs are higher in creativity than other persons.[50] In other words, they are more adept at combining the information at their disposal into something new.

In sum, it seems clear that a key component in opportunity recognition is information—greater access to it and better cognitive tools for putting it to good use (see Figure 3.9 for a summary of these points). In this sense, the answer to the question "Why some people and not others?" with respect to opportunity recognition is far from mysterious: It stems from basic cognitive processes and well-practised skills with which we are all very familiar.

Opportunity Recognition: Additional Insights from Cognitive Science

LEARNING OBJECTIVE

8 Describe signal detection theory and distinguish between hits, false alarms, and misses.

In earlier chapters, we noted that opportunities emerge from a complex pattern of changing conditions—changes in knowledge, technology, economic, political, social, and demographic conditions. In other words, opportunities come into existence at a given point in time because of a combination of conditions that did not exist previously, but is now present. Opportunities are only a potential, however, until one or more persons connects the dots between diverse and seemingly unrelated changes or events to form the perception of a pattern that links them together—until one or more persons perceives the existence of the opportunity.[51] If this view is indeed true, then two important theories relating to human cognition can help us understand the process through which specific persons identify opportunities.

One is known as **signal detection theory**,[52] and it is concerned with a very basic question: "How do we decide whether there really *is* anything out there to notice?" This is an important question because opportunities don't always leap out at entrepreneurs—or anyone else. On the contrary, opportunities are often hard to discern against a background of noise. So a key task faced by would-be entrepreneurs is deciding whether an opportunity is or is not actually present. Signal detection theory suggests that in such situations—individuals attempting to determine whether a stimulus is present or absent—four possibilities exist: (1) The stimulus does indeed exist and the perceiver concludes (correctly) that it is present (this is known as a *hit* or *correct identification*); (2) the stimulus does exist but the perceiver fails to recognize it (this is known as a *miss*); (3) the stimulus does not exist and the perceiver concludes, erroneously, that it is present (this is a *false alarm*); (4) the stimulus does not exist and

Actual Presence of Opportunity

		Yes	No
Judgment About Presence	Yes	**Hit** Opportunity is present and is recognized.	**False Alarm** Opportunity is not present but is judged to be present.
	No	**Miss** Opportunity is present but is not judged to be present.	**Correct Rejection** Opportunity is not present and is judged to be absent.

Figure 3.10 Signal Detection Theory and Opportunity Recognition

Signal detection theory is concerned with the basic question, "How do we decide whether a stimulus is or is not present?" It suggests that there are four possibilities, which, in the context of opportunity recognition are as follows: An opportunity is present and we recognize it (a hit); an opportunity is present and we overlook it (a miss); there is no opportunity present and we realize that none exists (a correct rejection); or there is no opportunity but we conclude that one exists (a false alarm).

the perceiver correctly concludes that it is not present (a *correct rejection*—another kind of hit). (See Figure 3.10 for a summary of these possibilities.)

The theory further notes that many factors determine the rate at which individuals experience hits, misses, and false alarms in any given situation. Some of these are physical and relate to the properties of the stimuli (e.g., the brighter a light or the louder a sound, the easier it is to be certain that it is present). Other factors, however, reflect the current state of the person making this judgment (e.g., is this person fatigued? highly or weakly motivated to make correct judgments?). Still other factors involve the subjective criteria such persons apply to the task—whether they are more concerned about attaining hits or more concerned about avoiding false alarms, for instance. Perhaps at this point, a concrete example will be helpful.

Consider a security officer at a busy airport. A routine electronic scan of a busy terminal provides data suggesting that a bomb may be present, but the data are far from conclusive. What does she do next? One alternative is to keep the airport open while conducting a careful search. That will prevent delays for many travellers, but it runs the risk of tragic consequences if a bomb does in fact exist: Hundreds of people may be killed in an explosion. Another alternative is to close the airport and conduct an even more thorough search. But what if the airport is closed, and the search turns up nothing? Thousands of travellers will have been inconvenienced, and if the airport is a major one, closing it may disrupt the entire air travel system—all for nothing.

What will the security officer do? Because public annoyance is strongly preferable to being responsible for the deaths of hundreds of travellers if a bomb actually explodes, she would probably set her subjective criterion for concluding that there is a serious danger quite low. In other words, she would accept even weak data suggesting that a bomb may be present as sufficient grounds for closing the airport. The security officer, in brief, would much rather experience false alarms (closing the airport when there is no reason to do so) than misses (not closing it when there really is a bomb present).

In other situations, the opposite might be true: Misses may be preferable to false alarms. For instance, consider the case of a radiologist examining medical scans in order to determine whether a cancerous tumour is or is not present in a 90-year-old patient. The radiologist does not want to overlook tumours that exist and could, potentially, kill the patient if not removed (that would constitute a miss), but the costs of false alarms are even higher: This type of exploratory surgery is extremely dangerous for someone 90 years old and, if the cancer is a relatively slow-growing type, the patient might well die of other causes before the cancer becomes fatal. Under these circumstances, the radiologist might well set a relatively high criterion for concluding that a stimulus is present (i.e., he would require very clear evidence that a tumour is present before recommending exploratory surgery).

Now that we have described the basic concepts of signal detection theory, we can explain why it is directly relevant to opportunity recognition. Entrepreneurs are strongly motivated to obtain hits—to recognize opportunities that actually exist. But they also wish to avoid false alarms—perceiving opportunities that do not in fact exist and that, if pursued, will waste their time, effort, and resources. Further, they also desire to avoid misses—overlooking opportunities that actually exist. So in a

LEARNING OBJECTIVE

9 Explain the difference between a promotion focus and a prevention focus, and describe the effects these contrasting perspectives may have on entrepreneurs' efforts to discover valuable opportunities.

sense, signal detection theory provides a very useful framework for understanding how opportunity recognition actually occurs.

But where do entrepreneurs set their personal criteria for deciding whether opportunities are, or are not, present? In other words, what factors determine whether they are primarily motivated to attain hits, avoid false alarms, or avoid misses? Another cognitive theory, known as **regulatory focus theory**,[53] offers an answer. Briefly, this latter theory suggests that in regulating their own behaviour to achieve desired ends (something entrepreneurs do all the time!), individuals adopt one of two contrasting perspectives:[54] a *promotion focus*, in which their primary goal is attaining positive outcomes, or a *prevention focus*, in which their primary goal is avoiding negative outcomes. Many studies[55] indicate that individuals differ in their personal preferences for a promotion or prevention focus. In addition, people can be induced to adopt one or the other of these two foci by situational factors (e.g., instructions to focus either on achieving gains or avoiding losses[56]).

When regulatory focus theory is combined with signal detection theory, it generates intriguing insights into the process of opportunity recognition. Specifically, it suggests that entrepreneurs who adopt a promotion focus (an emphasis on accomplishment) will be more concerned with attaining hits (recognizing opportunities that actually exist) and with avoiding misses (failing to recognize an opportunity that exists), while entrepreneurs who adopt a prevention focus will concentrate mainly on avoiding errors—on avoiding false alarms (pursuing opportunities that don't really exist) and on correct rejections (correctly recognizing when opportunities do not exist).

Is either of these patterns better from the point of attaining success? Not really; both offer advantages and disadvantages.[57] However, it seems possible that overall, entrepreneurs who are successful at identifying valuable opportunities adopt a mixture of these two perspectives: They are eager to identify real opportunities (hits), but they are also motivated to avoid false alarms, which implies that they have better cognitive systems or structures not only for recognizing opportunities, but for evaluating them, too—for estimating their potential economic value.[58] In contrast, entrepreneurs who are less successful at identifying valuable opportunities may adopt a pure promotion focus: They focus on attaining hits (recognizing real opportunities) and are less concerned about the dangers of false alarms. These and related predictions are summarized in Table 3.2.

Together, signal detection theory and regulatory focus theory shed intriguing light on why some entrepreneurs are more adept than others at recognizing viable opportunities. In essence, those entrepreneurs who can realize an opportunity's potential have a more realistic view of the risks involved and their chances of achieving success. They are strongly motivated to maximize hits—to correctly identify real opportunities. At the same time, though, they are also strongly motivated to avoid the false alarms and the dangers of wasting their time, effort, and resources pursuing opportunities that don't really exist. That conclusion brings us back to the quote presented at the start of this chapter: "When written in Chinese the word *crisis* is composed of two characters. One represents danger and the other represents opportunity." These words, spoken by John F. Kennedy, propose that danger and opportunity are two sides of the same coin. The findings of cognitive science agree with this view, suggesting that in entrepreneurship, as in many other spheres of life,

Table 3.2 Predicted Motivation to Identify Hits, Misses, False Alarms, and Correct Rejections Among Successful and Unsuccessful Entrepreneurs

A key difference between successful and unsuccessful entrepreneurs may relate to their adoption of one of two styles of regulatory focus, and to the effects this approach has on their motivation to obtain hits, correct rejections, avoid misses, and avoid false alarms.

SUCCESSFUL ENTREPRENEURS (Mixed Promotion and Prevention Focus)		UNSUCCESSFUL ENTREPRENEURS (Pure Promotion Focus)	
High motivation to attain:	Hits Correct identification of false alarms	High motivation to attain:	Hits Avoidance of misses
Moderate motivation to attain:	Correct rejections	Low motivation to attain:	Correct identification of false alarms
Low motivation to attain:	Avoidance of misses		Correct rejections

THE VOICE OF EXPERIENCE

Some Thoughts on Avoiding False Alarms

Joanne Papari is the founder of Biochem Environmental Solutions, the largest Canadian company in the production and servicing of washroom hygiene systems, and the first Canadian firm in this field to successfully challenge the market dominance of multinationals through the launch of new and innovative products. Biochem is the only such company in the world to provide matching fragrances for all products. The company, which is based in Concord, Ontario, holds multiple patents and was the first company in the industry to become ISO 14000 certified. Born and raised in Greece, Joanne came to Canada at age 18 to study chemical engineering at the University of Windsor. After graduating in 1984, she was the first woman hired as a sales representative by a large chemical manufacturer. In just three months, Joanne became the top salesperson in Canada, and in the years that followed she became the top sales representative in North America. After 12 years of working in a corporate environment, Joanne founded Biochem Environmental Solutions in 1996. Her firm has achieved double-digit growth each year, and by 2004, it had secured approximately 30 percent of the Canadian market. Papari won the Canadian Woman Entrepreneur of the Year Award for Innovation in 2004.

If there is one thing no entrepreneur can afford, it is wasting precious time, resources, and energy pursuing false alarms—opportunities that don't really exist, or—if they do—are impossible to develop. In a recent interview, I asked Joanne Papari how she avoided such traps.

Reuber: "A potential problem for all entrepreneurs is that of wasting their time, effort, and money on a 'false alarm'—an idea for a new product or service that looks good, but is actually not feasible. How do *you*, personally, go about distinguishing between ideas that are truly good ones and ideas that are likely to be false alarms?"

Papari: "That really *is* a big issue for entrepreneurs, because no one can afford to make huge mistakes. It is essential to look at the idea from a pragmatic perspective. I focus on two key issues. First, can it be implemented? Is it feasible? Second, how much does it cost to implement? Are my customers willing to spend that much on it? There is no point in developing a state-of-the-art product if it is too expensive for your customers."

Reuber: "How do you go about deciding whether a new product idea can be implemented?"

Papari: "I have to be convinced that the product will work effectively. We build a prototype of the base technology and we test it in-house to determine the performance advantages and disadvantages. Typically, a prototype looks like a rudimentary working model—it won't look good enough to place in a customer's workplace. So, we need to test it ourselves. It can often cost over $250,000 to build a mould for a new product, and I don't want to do that until I'm sure that the product is feasible and will yield measurable performance advantages."

Reuber: "How do you address your second issue and determine whether or not a new product will be too expensive for your target market?"

Papari: "You have to know your market very well. We survey all our customers on a quarterly basis. We ask whether existing products meet their expectations, and what other products they are interested in. We ask them to identity one new thing we could do that would be useful to them. I study these survey results very carefully. Also, when I'm at customer sites, or prospective customer sites, I spend a lot of time talking to people about their company's needs and how these might change in the future. I also gain a good understanding of how much they're willing to pay for our products."

Reuber: "So your advice to budding entrepreneurs about avoiding false alarms centres mainly around collecting data about product ideas and your customer base, and taking the time to analyze the data and reflect on its implications."

Papari: "That's right. I'm an engineer and like to analyze things. I have to be convinced, through logic and data, that a new product yields tangible benefits that our customers want, at a price they are willing to pay."

Commentary: We agree with Joanne Papari's advice. An important way to avoid false alarms is to subject your ideas to systematic scrutiny. You need to know what information is most meaningful. You need to put systems in place to collect it that are both effective, yielding reliable data, and efficient in terms of time and cost. You need to understand how different pieces of information fit together to give you an overall picture of a new idea's market potential. Although you have to have confidence in your own judgment and recognize that in the final analysis, the decision is yours, moving ahead without solid information can be a mistake.

victory does not necessarily go to the strongest or the swiftest, but rather to those whose judgment is most closely aligned with reality. (How do successful entrepreneurs avoid false alarms? Some important insights are offered by Joanne Papari, founder of Biochem Environmental Solutions. See **The Voice of Experience** section.)

Practical Techniques for Increasing Opportunity Recognition

We will now conclude on a very practical note: How can you increase your own ability to recognize potentially valuable opportunities? Though we still have a lot to learn about opportunity recognition as a process, existing evidence points to several steps that should prove very helpful in this respect:

LEARNING OBJECTIVE

10 List several steps you can take as an individual to increase your skill at recognizing potentially valuable opportunities.

■ *Build a broad and rich knowledge base.* The capacity to recognize opportunities, and to be creative, depends in large measure on how much information you have at your disposal. The more you possess, the more likely you are to recognize the connections and patterns that constitute opportunities—before others do so. Learn everything you can, whenever you can; the result will be an enhanced capacity to recognize opportunities.

■ *Organize your knowledge.* Knowledge that is organized is much more useful than knowledge that is not organized. As you acquire new information, you should actively seek to relate it to what you know so that connections between existing and new information come clearly into focus. Information that is connected and organized in this manner is easier to remember—and to use—than information that it is not organized.

■ *Increase your access to information.* The more information you receive on a regular basis, which is potentially related to opportunities, the more likely you are to recognize opportunities that have just emerged. You can increase your exposure to information by holding jobs that put you on the cutting edge (e.g., jobs in research and development or marketing), by building a large social network, and by having rich and diverse work—and life— experiences.

■ *Create connections between the knowledge you have.* Research findings indicate that the more richly interconnected knowledge structures are, the more readily their inherent information can be combined into new patterns. This theory suggests that establishing such connections between information stored in memory and other cognitive systems can be a useful strategy. One way in which such connections can be formed involves what is known as deep processing—actively thinking about different information and connections between them. This way of thinking is something you can readily practise, and the result may be an increased ability to recognize emerging opportunities.

■ *Build your practical intelligence.* Entrepreneurs are sometimes accused of being dreamers—people who think so large that they lose touch with reality. In fact, this perception is far from the truth. Entrepreneurs are usually people high in practical intelligence—the ability to solve the highly varied problems of everyday life. Practical intelligence is definitely not set in stone—it can be cultivated. The best way to increase it is to avoid accepting the solutions to problems suggested by mental ruts. Try, instead, to think of new and better ways to handle various problems. The result may be an increase in your own practical intelligence—and hence your ability to recognize opportunities.

■ *Temper eagerness for hits with wariness of false alarms.* It has long been assumed that entrepreneurs are optimists—that they suffer from the optimistic bias to a greater extent than other persons (i.e., they expect positive results even when there are no rational grounds for such predictions). In fact, there is a healthy grain of truth in this idea. This view implies that it is important for entrepreneurs to focus not only on the potential gains offered by hits—by recognizing opportunities that really do exist—but also on the potentially devastating costs of pursuing false alarms (opportunities that aren't really there). In other words, if you want to be successful as an entrepreneur, and at identifying genuine opportunities, fight against your own tendencies to be optimistic, and consider the downside, too. Doing so may go against your personal inclinations, but the result may be that you avoid one of the most dangerous pitfalls lying in wait for unsuspecting entrepreneurs: the quicksand of illusory opportunities.

KEY POINTS

- In the past, opportunities have been viewed primarily in economic terms. This view is reasonable, but largely ignores such questions as how the process of opportunity recognition actually occurs, and why some persons are better at it than others.

- A cognitive perspective addresses these and other questions. It suggests, for instance, that information—access to it and the capacity to utilize it—plays a crucial role in opportunity recognition.

- Two cognitive theories—signal detection theory and regulatory focus theory—offer further insights into the cognitive foundations of opportunity recognition. Signal detection theory addresses the basic question: "Is an opportunity really present?" and suggests that entrepreneurs seek to maximize hits (recognizing opportunities that exist) while avoiding false alarms.

- Regulatory focus theory suggests that successful entrepreneurs may be more adept than unsuccessful ones at combining two contrasting perspectives (promotion and prevention focus) in their search for opportunities.

- As a nascent entrepreneur, there are several steps you can take to increase your ability to recognize valuable opportunities, including building a broad, rich, and organized knowledge base; increasing your access to information; actively searching for opportunities; increasing your practical intelligence; and tempering eagerness for hits with a healthy fear of false alarms.

Summary and Review of Key Points

- Cognitive processes provide the foundation for creativity and opportunity recognition.
- Memory involves cognitive systems for storing information. Working memory can retain limited amounts of information for short periods of time. Active processing of information occurs in working memory, so it is the system in which consciousness exists.
- Long-term memory holds vast (perhaps unlimited) amounts of information for long periods of time. Such information can be factual or procedural in nature.
- Because our capacity to process information is limited, we often adopt shortcuts to reduce mental effort. These include heuristics and various tilts in our thinking (e.g., the confirmation bias). These shortcuts *do* save effort, but they can lead to serious errors.
- Among these shortcuts, one of the most dangerous for entrepreneurs is sunk costs (escalation of commitment)—a tendency to stick with decisions that yield increasingly negative results.
- Creativity involves producing ideas that are both novel and appropriate.
- Existing evidence suggests that creative thought emerges from the combination and expansion of concepts, and from reasoning by analogy.
- To be creative and succeed, entrepreneurs need successful intelligence—a good balance of analytic, practical, and creative intelligence. They also need a high degree of social intelligence—the ability to get along well with others.
- The confluence approach to creativity suggests that creativity emerges out of a convergence of several factors (intellectual abilities, a broad and rich knowledge base, appropriate style of thinking, etc.).
- This approach and others suggest concrete steps you can take to increase your own creativity and, hence, your capacity for formulating new ideas that can lead to successful business ventures.
- In the past, opportunities have been viewed primarily in economic terms. This view is reasonable, but it largely ignores such questions as how the process of opportunity recognition actually occurs and why some persons are better at it than others.
- A cognitive perspective addresses these and other questions. It suggests, for instance, that information—access to it and the capacity to utilize it—plays a crucial role in opportunity recognition.
- Two cognitive theories—signal detection theory and regulatory focus theory—offer further insights into the cognitive foundations of opportunity recognition. Signal detection theory addresses the basic question: "Is an opportunity really present?" and suggests that entrepreneurs seek to maximize hits (recognizing opportunities that exist) while avoiding false alarms.
- Regulatory focus theory suggests that successful entrepreneurs may be more adept than unsuccessful ones at combining two contrasting perspectives (promotion and prevention focus) in their search for opportunities.
- As a nascent entrepreneur, there are several steps you can take to increase your ability to recognize valuable opportunities, including building a broad, rich, and organized knowledge base; increasing your access to information; actively searching for opportunities; increasing your practical intelligence; and tempering eagerness for hits with a healthy fear of false alarms.

Glossary

Concepts: Categories for objects or events that are similar to each other in certain respects.

Confluence Approach: A view suggesting that creativity emerges out of the confluence (i.e., convergence) of several basic resources.

Creativity: The generation of ideas that are both novel (original, unexpected) and appropriate or useful (they meet relevant constraints).

Heuristics: Simple rules for making complex decisions or drawing inferences in a rapid and seemingly effortless manner.

Human Cognition: The mental processes through which we acquire information, enter it into storage, transform it, and use it to accomplish a wide range of tasks.

Idea Generation: The production of ideas for something new; very close in meaning to creativity.

Intelligence: Individuals' abilities to understand complex ideas, to adapt effectively to the world around them, to learn from experience, to engage in various forms of reasoning, and to overcome a wide range of obstacles.

Memory: Our cognitive systems for storing and retrieving information.

Opportunity Recognition: The process through which individuals conclude that they have identified the potential to create something new that has the capacity to generate economic value (i.e., potential future profits).

Practical Intelligence: Being intelligent in a practical sense; persons high in such intelligence are adept at solving the problems of everyday life and have street smarts.

Prototypes: Mental representations of categories of events or objects.

Regulatory Focus Theory: A theory that suggests that in regulating their own behaviour to achieve desired ends, individuals adopt one of two contrasting perspectives: a promotion focus (main goal is accomplishment) or a prevention focus (main goal is prevention of losses).

Schemas: Cognitive frameworks representing our knowledge and assumptions about specific aspects of the world.

Signal Detection Theory: A theory suggesting that in situations where individuals attempt to determine whether a stimulus is present or absent, four possibilities exist: The stimulus exists and the perceiver concludes that it is present; the stimulus exists but the perceiver fails to recognize it; the stimulus does not exist and the perceiver concludes, erroneously, that it is present; or the stimulus does not exist and the perceiver correctly concludes that it is not present.

Successful Intelligence: A balanced blend of analytic, creative, and practical intelligence. Successful intelligence is the kind of intelligence needed by entrepreneurs.

Sunk Costs or Escalation of Commitment: The tendency to become trapped in bad decisions and stick to them even though they yield increasingly negative results.

Discussion Questions

1. People are not very good at describing information stored in procedural memory (the kind of memory that allows you to perform skilled tasks, such as playing a musical instrument). Why do you think this is so?

2. Many people who are afraid of flying in airplanes are not afraid to drive their own cars. When asked, they often answer: "Because there is greater danger of being killed in airplanes." This is not true—there is actually a greater chance of being killed in an automobile. Do you think the availability heuristic might play a role in this error?

3. Repeat entrepreneurs—people who start one successful venture after another—seem to have a knack for recognizing good opportunities. Do you think they may have better prototypes for opportunities than other people? If so, how did they acquire them?

4. Can you think of people you have known who were high in analytic intelligence (the kind measured by IQ tests) but low in practical intelligence? What about the opposite pattern—have you known people high in practical intelligence but low in analytic intelligence? Which would make better entrepreneurs? Why?

5. In your opinion, do opportunities exist out there in the external world? Or are they purely a construction of human thought? Why?

6. Have you ever been trapped in mental ruts—forced by your own experience and training to view a situation or problem in a way that blocked your creativity? If so, what should you have done to escape from this kind of cognitive trap?

InfoTrac Exercises

1. **Colorado Creative Music.**

   Rachel Deane Canetta; Joan Winn.

   Entrepreneurship: Theory and Practice, Spring 2002 v26 i3 p101(14)

   Full Text: COPYRIGHT 2002 Baylor University

   Article A88587641

   1. What opportunities is Darren Skanson pursuing?

   2. Does he exhibit creativity or entrepreneurial alertness?

3. When is he adopting a promotion focus and when is he adopting a prevention focus? Does he have a good balance of these two perspectives? Why or why not?

2. **Opportunity Recognition: An Exploratory Investigation of a Component of the Entrepreneurial Process in the Context of the Health Care Industry**

   Richard L. McCline; Subodh Bhat; Pam Baj

   Entrepreneurship: Theory and Practice, Winter 2000 v25 i2 p81

   Record: A74524634

Full Text: COPYRIGHT 2000 Baylor University

1. According to the text, how can you increase your ability to recognize opportunities?

2. It is suggested that there is a three-part measure of entrepreneurial-attitude orientation after the tradition established in social psychology. In this line of research, an attitude is believed to have what three components?

3. What two new exploratory scales were developed for the health care study?

GETTING DOWN
TO BUSINESS

What Is Your Prototype for an Opportunity?

In our discussion of opportunity recognition, we suggested that individuals may possess prototypes for opportunities. In other words, we have mental representations that capture the essence of what we believe opportunities to be. To the extent this is true, then one reason why some people may be better at recognizing opportunities is that they possess clearer or better developed prototypes with which to compare potential opportunities.

What is your prototype of an opportunity like? To find out, follow these steps:

1. List the features you think are required for something to qualify as an opportunity. (Hint: These might include newness, feasibility, etc.)

   a. Feature:

   b. Feature:

   c. Feature:

   d. Feature:

   e. Feature:

   (Continue with others if necessary.)

2. Now, rate how central you think each of these features is—in other words, how important is each feature you listed for recognizing an opportunity? Rate each feature by assigning each with a number from 1 to 5, where 5 = highly central and 1 = not very central.

3. Next, ask several of your friends to carry out the same steps. To what extent did you list the same or similar features? To what extent did you rate these features the same in terms of their centrality to the idea of opportunity?

4. If you can, find an entrepreneur and ask this person to also list five features of an opportunity. Then, compare this person's list to yours and to those produced by your friends.

5. Do you think the list of features you have compiled can be helpful to you in identifying opportunities for new ventures in the future?

Are You Promotion-Focused or Prevention-Focused? Testing Your Own Regulatory Focus

Research findings indicate that people have preferences for a promotion focus or a prevention focus. Those who show a preference for a promotion focus tend to concentrate on achievement—on attaining goals they find desirable. Those who show a preference for a prevention focus tend to concentrate on avoiding negative outcomes and on minimizing risks. Neither is better, but each does have important implications for becoming an entrepreneur. Early on, a promotion focus may be better because it can facilitate the search for opportunities. Later, a prevention focus may be useful because it helps entrepreneurs avoid false alarms. To find out where you stand on this dimension, follow these instructions:

Event Reaction Questionnaire

This set of questions asks you about specific events in your life. Please indicate your answer to each question by circling the appropriate number below it.

1. Compared to most people, are you typically unable to get what you want out of life?

     1   2   3   4   5
   never or seldom   sometimes   very often

2. Growing up, would you ever cross the line by doing things that your parents would not tolerate?

     1   2   3   4   5
   never or seldom   sometimes   very often

3. How often have you accomplished things that got you psyched to work even harder?

     1   2   3   4   5
   never or seldom   a few times   many times

4. Did you get on your parents' nerves often when you were growing up?

     1   2   3   4   5
   never or seldom   sometimes   very often

5. How often did you obey rules and regulations that were established by your parents?

     1   2   3   4   5
   never or seldom   sometimes   always

6. Growing up, did you ever act in ways that your parents thought were objectionable?

     1   2   3   4   5
   never or seldom   sometimes   very often

7. Do you often do well at different things that you try?

     1   2   3   4   5
   never or seldom   sometimes   very often

8. Not being careful enough has gotten me into trouble at times.

     1   2   3   4   5
   never or seldom   sometimes   very often

9. Do you often do well at different things that you try?

     1   2   3   4   5
   never or seldom   sometimes   very often

10. Not being careful enough has gotten me into trouble at times.

1	2	3	4	5
never or seldom		sometimes		very often

11. When it comes to achieving things that are important to me, I find that I don't perform as well as I ideally would like to do.

1	2	3	4	5
never true		sometimes true		very often true

12. I feel like I have made progress toward being successful in my life.

1	2	3	4	5
certainly false				certainly true

13. I have found very few hobbies or activities in my life that capture my interest or motivate me to put effort into them.

1	2	3	4	5
certainly false				certainly true

Scoring: Here's how to score your answers: Add your scores for items 1, 3, 7, 9, 10, and 11 and take an average: This is your Promotion Focus Score. Now add the scores for items 2, 4, 5, 6, and 8 and average these: This is your Prevention Focus Score. Which is higher? If the Promotion Focus Score is higher, that is your preferred regulatory focus. If the Prevention Focus Scores is higher, then that is your preferred regulatory focus. Remember: Neither is better, but both are relevant to becoming an entrepreneur—and to being successful in this role.

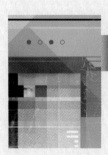

Enhanced Learning

You may select any combination of the resources below to enhance your understanding of the chapter material.

- **Appendix: Case Studies** – Twelve cases provide opportunities to apply chapter concepts to realistic entrepreneurial situations. These brief cases call for careful analysis of real business problems and ask you to think about potential solutions.

- **Video Case Library** – Nine cases are tied directly to video segments from the popular PBS television series Small Business School. These cases and video segments (available on the Entrepreneurship website at http://www.entrepreneurship.nelson.com) give you unparalleled access to today's entrepreneurs, with expert advice and insights on how to start, run, and grow a business.

- **Management Interview Series Video Database** – This video interview series contains a wealth of tips on how to manage effectively. Access to the database and practical exercises are available on the book support website at http://www.entrepreneurship.nelson.com.

Notes

1   Shane, S. 2003. *A general theory of entrepreneurship: The individual–opportunity nexus.* Aldershot, United Kingdom: Edward Elgar.

2   Rotman Canadian Woman Entrepreneur of the Year Awards, 2002 Winners. http://www.cweya.com/pastwinners2002.htm#bertrand.

3   Who we are. http://www.muttluks.com.

4   Herron, L., & Sapienza, H.J. 1992. The entrepreneur and the initiation of new venture launch activities. *Entrepreneurship Theory and Practice* 17(1): 49–55.

5   Matlin, M.W. 2002. *Cognition.* 5th ed. Fort Worth, TX: Harcourt College Publishers.

6   Haxby, J.V., Horwitz, B., Ungerleider, L.G, Maisog, J.M., Pietrini, P., & Grady, C.L. 1994. The functional organization of human extrastriate cortex: A PET-rCBF study of selective attention to faces and locations. *Journal of Neuroscience* 14(11): 6336–6353.

7   Stake Technology (to Become SunOpta Inc.) to Acquire Pro Organics Marketing, Inc. 2003. *The Soy Daily.* http://thesoydailyclub.com/Financial/stake10102003.asp

8   http://www.proorganics.com.

9   Rotman Canadian Woman Entrepreneur of the Year Awards, 2003 Winners. http://www.cweya.com/pastwinners2003.htm#boyle.

10 Shepherd, D.A., & DeTienne, D.R. 2001. Discovery of opportunities: Anomalies, accumulation and alertness. In W.D. Bygrave et al. (eds.). *Frontiers of Entrepreneurship Research* (pp.138–148). Babson Park, MA: Center for Entrepreneurial Studies.

11 Shepherd, D.A., Zacharakis, A., & Baron, R.A. 2003. VCs' decision processes: Evidence suggesting more experience may not always be better. *Journal of Business Venturing* 18(3): 381–401.

12 Zacharakis, A.L., & Shepherd, D.A. 2001. The nature of information and overconfidence on venture capitalists' decision making. *Journal of Business Venturing* 16(4): 311–332.

13 Baron, R.A. 1998. Cognitive mechanisms in entrepreneurship: Why and when entrepreneurs think differently than other people. *Journal of Business Venturing* 13(4): 275–294.

14 Rothman, A.J., & Hardin, C.D. 1997. Differential use of the availability heuristic in social judgment. *Personality and Social Psychology Bulletin* 23(2): 123–138.

15 Kunda, Z. 1999. *Social cognition: Making sense of people.* Cambridge, MA: MIT Press.

16 Busenitz, L.W., & Barney, J.B. 1997. Differences between entrepreneurs and managers in large organizations: Biases and heuristics in strategic decision-making. *Journal of Business Venturing* 12(1): 9–30.

17 Krueger, N.F., Jr. 2003. The cognitive psychology of entrepreneurship. In Z. Acs & D.B. Audretsch (eds.). *Handbook of entrepreneurial research* (pp. 105–140). London: Kluwer Law International.

18 Zacharakis, A.L., & Shepherd, D.A. 2001. The nature of information and overconfidence on venture capitalists' decision making. *Journal of Business Venturing* 16(4): 311–322.

19 Simon, M., Houghton, S.M., & Aquino, K. 2000. Cognitive biases, risk perception, and venture formation: How individuals decide to start companies. *Journal of Business Venturing* 15(2): 113–134.

20 Ross, J., & Staw, B.M. 1993. Organizational escalation and exit: Lessons from the Shoreham nuclear power plant. *Academy of Management Journal* 36(4): 701–732.

21 Lubart, T.T., & Sternberg, R.J. 1995. An investment approach to creativity: Theory and data. In S.M. Smith, T.B. Ward, & R.A. Finke (eds.). *The creative cognition approach* (pp. 269–302). Cambridge, MA: MIT Press.

22 Ward, T.B. 2004. Cognition, creativity, and entrepreneurship. *Journal of Business Venturing* 19(2): 173–188.

23 Sternberg, R.J., & Grigorenko, E.L. 2000. *Practical intelligence in everyday life.* New York: Cambridge University Press.

24 Sternberg, R.J. 1999. (ed.). *The nature of cognition.* Cambridge, MA: MIT Press.

25 Sternberg, R.J. 2004. Successful intelligence as a basis for entrepreneurship. *Journal of Business Venturing* 19(2): 189–201.

26 Baron, R.A., & Markman, G.D. 2000. Beyond social capital: How social skills can enhance entrepreneurs' success. *Academy of Management Executive* 14(1): 106–116.

27 Simon, M., Houghton, S.M., & Aquino, K. 2000. Cognitive biases, risk perception, and venture formation: How individuals decide to start companies. *Journal of Business Venturing* 15(2): 113–134.

28 Sternberg, R.J., & Lubart, T.I. 1995. *Defying the crowd: Cultivating creativity in a culture of conformity.* New York: Free Press.

29 Sternberg, R.J., & Lubart, T.I. 1995. *Defying the crowd: Cultivating creativity in a culture of conformity.* New York: Free Press.

30 Sternberg, R.J. 2004. Successful intelligence as a basis for entrepreneurship. *Journal of Business Venturing* 19(2): 189–201.

31 Lerner, M., & Hendeles, Y. 1993. New entrepreneurs and entrepreneurial aspirations among immigrants from the former USSR in Israel. In N. Churchill, S. Birley, W. Bygrave, J. Coutriaux, E. Gatewood, F. Hoy, & W. Wetzel (eds.). *Frontiers of entrepreneurship research.* Babson Park, MA: Babson College.

32 Johansson, E. 2000. Self-employment and liquidity constraints: Evidence from Finland. *Scandinavian Journal of Economics* 102(1): 123–124.

33 Klepper, S., & Sleeper, S. 2000. *Entry by spinoffs.* Working Paper, Carnegie Mellon University.

34 Durand, R., & Coeurderoy, R. 2001. Age, order of entry, strategic orientation, and organizational performance. *Journal of Business Venturing* 16(5): 471–494.

35 Dollinger, M.J. 2003. *Entrepreneurship.* 3rd ed. Upper Saddle River, NJ: Prentice-Hall.

36 Shane, S. 2000. Prior knowledge and the discovery of entrepreneurial opportunities. *Organizational Science* 11(4): 448–469.

37 Sarasvathy, D., Simon, H., & Lave, L. 1998. Perceiving and managing business risks: Differences between entrepreneurs and bankers. *Journal of Economic Behavior and Organization* 33(2): 207–225.

38 Krueger, N.F., Jr. 2003. The cognitive psychology of entrepreneurship. In Z. Acs & D.B. Audretsch (eds.). *Handbook of entrepreneurial research* (pp. 105–140). London: Kluwer Law International.

39 Sternberg, R.J. 2004. Successful intelligence as a basis for entrepreneurship. *Journal of Business Venturing* 19(2): 189–201.

[40] Blanchflower, D., & Oswald, A. 1998. What makes an entrepreneur? *Journal of Labor Economics* 16(1): 26–60.

[41] Reuber, A.R., & Fischer, E. 1997. The role of management's international experience in the internationalization of smaller firms. *Journal of International Business Studies* 28(4): 807–825.

[42] Aldrich, H. 1999. *Organizations evolving*. London: Sage.

[43] Davidsson, P., & Honig, B. 2003. The role of social and human capital among nascent entrepreneurs. *Journal of Business Venturing* 18(3): 301–331.

[44] Gaglio, C., & Katz, J. 2001. The psychological basis of opportunity identification: Entrepreneurial alertness. *Small Business Economics* 16(2): 95–111.

[45] Klepper, S., & Sleeper, S. 2000. *Entry by spinoffs*. Working Paper, Carnegie Mellon University.

[46] Hmieleski, K.M., & Corbett, A.C. 2003. *Improvisation as a framework for investigating entrepreneurial action*. Paper presented at the Meetings of the Academy of Management, August, 2003, Seattle, WA.

[47] Davidsson, P., & Honig, B. 2003. The role of social and human capital among nascent entrepreneurs. *Journal of Business Venturing* 18(3): 301–331.

[48] Van Praag, C., & Cramer, J. 2001. The roots of entrepreneurship and labour demand: Individual ability and low risk aversion. *Economica* 68(269): 45–62.

[49] Sternberg, R.J. 2004. Successful intelligence as a basis for entrepreneurship. *Journal of Business Venturing* 19(2): 189–201.

[50] Hyrsky, K., & Kangasharju, A. 1998. Adapters and innovators in non-urban environment. In P. Reynolds, W. Bygrave, N. Carter, S. Manigart, C. Mason, G. Meyer, & K. Shaver (eds.). *Frontiers of entrepreneurship research*. Babson Park, MA: Babson College.

[51] Baron, R.A. 2004. Opportunity recognition: Insights from a cognitive perspective. In J.E. Butler (ed.). *Opportunity identification and entrepreneurial behavior* (pp. 47–74). Greenwich, CT: Information Age Publications.

[52] Swets, J.A. 1992. The science of choosing the right decision threshold in high-stakes diagnostics. *American Psychologist* 47(4): 522–532.

[53] Brockner, J., Higgins, E.T., & Low, M.B. 2004. Regulatory focus theory and the entrepreneurial process. *Journal of Business Venturing* 19(2): 203–220.

[54] Higgins, E.T., 1998. Promotion and prevention: Regulatory focus as a motivational principle. In M.P. Zanna (ed.). *Advances in experimental social psychology* (Vol. 30, pp. 1–46). New York: Academic Press.

[55] Higgins, E.T., & Silberman, I. 1998. Development of regulatory focus: Promotion and prevention as ways of living. In J. Heckhausen & C.S. Dweck (eds.). *Motivation and self-regulation across the life span* (pp. 798–113). New York: Cambridge University Press.

[56] Liberman, N., Idson, L.C., Camacho, C.J., & Higgins, E.T. 1999. Promotion and prevention choices between stability and change. *Journal of Personality and Social Psychology* 77(6): 1135–1145.

[57] Brockner, J., Higgins, E.T., & Low, M.B. 2004. Regulatory focus theory and the entrepreneurial process. *Journal of Business Venturing* 19(2): 203–220.

[58] Fiet, J.O., Gupta, M., & Zurada, J. 2003. *Evaluating the wealth creating potential of venture ideas*. Paper presented at the Babson-Kaufman Entrepreneurship Research Conference, June 2003, Babson Park, MA.

ESSENTIAL SKILLS FOR ENTREPRENEURS: ENHANCING SOCIAL COMPETENCE, CREATING TRUST, MANAGING CONFLICT, EXERTING INFLUENCE, AND DEALING WITH STRESS

LEARNING OBJECTIVES

After reading this chapter, you should be able to:

1 Describe several social skills and explain how social competence (which is composed of these skills) can influence entrepreneurs' success.

2 Describe the difference between calculus-based trust and identification-based trust, and explain their roles in the development of cooperative working relationships.

3 Define conflict and describe its major causes.

4 Explain how entrepreneurs can effectively manage conflict, especially affect-based conflict.

5 Describe the techniques that individuals use most frequently to influence others in work settings.

6 Describe various techniques that people use for gaining compliance—for getting others to agree to requests they have made—and the basic principles on which these rest.

7 Define stress and describe its major causes.

8 Describe the adverse effects of stress, and explain several techniques entrepreneurs can use to reduce the level of stress they experience.

All photos this page © PhotoDisc, Inc.

"Marvelous is the power which can be exercised, almost unconsciously, over a company, or an individual, or even upon a crowd by one person gifted with good temper, good digestion, good intellects, and good looks."
(Anthony Trollope, 1863)

About ten years ago, I (Robert Baron) obtained two patents for the new product described earlier in this book (in Chapter 1)—a desktop unit that combined air filtration with additional features (e.g., noise control). Because I had only limited manufacturing experience, I decided that the best way to bring this invention to market was to license my patents to an established business. I contacted a number of companies that appeared to be appropriate as potential corporate partners, and was soon invited to visit several of them. As luck would have it, it was the third one I visited that ultimately licensed both patents. The events of that day are stamped indelibly on my memory.

When my partner Fred and I arrived, we waited for about 30 minutes, and were then brought to a room where the top people in the company were already seated: the president and CEO, the COO, the vice president for engineering, and the vice president for marketing. After brief introductions all around, the CEO turned to me and said: "OK, professor, show us what you've got." I then made a presentation during which I described the benefits of my invention and demonstrated its major features. Was I enthusiastic? Absolutely! Did I wax poetic? I don't know, but I sure gave it a try! When I was done, the president rose and announced: "OK, thanks. Now, we're going to leave the room, but we'll be back in a few minutes." At that point, he and the other executives filed out, leaving my partner and me to wonder what was happening. We didn't wait long, because less than 10 minutes later they returned. When the president held out his hand and smiled, I knew that things had gone well. "OK, professor," he said, "we definitely want your product. I'll leave you to work out the details with Neville and Stan" (the V.P. for engineering and the COO).

In the months that followed, I got to know the president of the company quite well, and on one occasion I asked him how he made his decision so quickly. His answer was revealing: "Your prototype was good, and we had agreed before you came that you had something new that fit with our other products. But it was the way you handled yourself during the meeting that mattered most to me. I could tell right away that you knew the product and technology very well. More importantly, I could see that you are a high-energy person who gets things done. And I figured, 'OK, I can work with this guy; he's a man of his word.' You can bet that I'd never make a deal with someone I didn't trust or who couldn't get me excited about his product."

I learned many things from that experience, but perhaps the most important is this: Success often involves much more than technical knowledge, business acumen, and incredibly hard work; in many cases, it also requires *personal skills* that allow individuals to get along effectively with others. In a sense, that's what the opening quote suggests: Being able to get along with others is a highly valuable skill. In our view, it is truly essential for entrepreneurs. Think, for a moment, about what the founders of new ventures actually do. First, and foremost, they must get along well with each other—they must be able to work together cooperatively without experiencing the kind of angry, emotional conflicts that can destroy even the best of working relationships. In addition, they have to interact effectively with many other people—venture capitalists, potential customers, suppliers, and prospective employees, to name just a few. They must be able to persuade or influence these people (e.g., to get them to share their views or to say "yes" to various requests), to develop trust and cooperative working relationships with them, and to manage conflicts when they occur. If entrepreneurs cannot carry out these tasks effectively, the chances that their new venture will succeed may drop precipitously.

In short, in order to run a successful new venture, entrepreneurs need a wide variety of skills that, together, contribute to what has often been termed the **social capital** of their organizations—an important resource or asset that derives from close relationships among individuals in organizations or other social structures, relationships characterized by liking, mutual trust, and close identification with each other and the organization.[1] In this chapter, we will focus on several of the most important of the skills that contribute to the development of high levels of social capital in new ventures—and, in doing so, provide new ventures with sustainable competitive advantage.[2] These skills include a general ability to get along well with others (often

86

known as *social competence*[3]), the ability to develop cooperative working relationships with others (built on mutual trust) and to manage conflict, and the capacity to influence others—to persuade them or induce them to say "yes" to various requests. In addition, because entrepreneurs are truly *the* most valuable resource in their new ventures, we will also consider an additional topic—stress management.[4] Stress is often very high in new ventures, and unless it is managed effectively, it can place the health and well-being of the founding team at risk. So learning to deal with stress and reduce its potentially harmful effects is another valuable skill, with beneficial effects not just for entrepreneurs, but for family, friends, and loved ones who care deeply about them and want them to realize their dreams.

GETTING ALONG WELL WITH OTHERS: BUILDING SOCIAL COMPETENCE

HERMAN®

"Experienced! Are you kidding? I've had 12 jobs this year alone!"

HERMAN reprinted by permission of Newspaper Enterprise Association, Inc.

Figure 4.1 Social Skills: A Key Ingredient in Personal Success

Will this person get the job? Probably not! His lack of social skills will probably count heavily against him with the interviewer. Social skills also affect the outcomes people experience in many other business contexts, and can play an important role in entrepreneurs' success.

Look at the cartoon in Figure 4.1. Do you think the applicant will get the job? Almost certainly, he will not. Why? In part because he is presenting himself in a very unfavourable light—one that may well convince the interviewer that he is not a good bet as a new employee. In essence, he is going to miss this potential opportunity because of poor social skills—an inability to get along well with others. As we will soon note, social skills have been found to influence the outcomes people experience in a wide range of business situations, so they are clearly important. Before describing these effects, let's take a closer look at what these skills involve. After that, we will examine their impact on entrepreneurs' efforts to run successful new ventures.

The Nature of Social Skills

In essence, the term **social skills** refers to a set of competencies (discrete skills) that enable individuals to interact effectively with others.[5] Previous research on such skills indicates that many different ones exist, and that all are potentially useful to individuals in interacting with others. However, it is also clear that some of these skills are more directly relevant than others to the activities performed by entrepreneurs. (Some, in contrast, are more useful in purely social rather than business contexts.) Previous research has identified five social skills that may be especially helpful to entrepreneurs:[6]

> **LEARNING OBJECTIVE**
>
> 1 Describe several social skills and explain how social competence (which is composed of these skills) can influence entrepreneurs' success.

- *Social perception.* Accuracy in perceiving others, including accurate perceptions of their motives, traits, and intentions. In other words, social perception refers to skill in reading others accurately.

- *Expressiveness.* Skill at expressing one's own reactions and emotions clearly so that they can be readily understood by others. This skill is very useful in generating enthusiasm in others.

- *Impression management.* Proficiency in the use of techniques for inducing positive reactions in others when we first meet them—for making a good first impression.

- *Persuasion and influence.* Skill at using various techniques for changing others' attitudes or behaviour in desired directions.

- *Social adaptability.* The ability to adapt to a wide range of social situations and to feel comfortable with individuals from a wide range of backgrounds.

Because these skills are often correlated (i.e., persons high in one skill are often high in other skills), they are often described by the summary term **social competence**. In other words, persons high in several social skills are described as being high in social competence, while those lower in several social skills are described as being relatively low in social competence. We will adopt that terminology in the current discussion.

The Impact of Social Competence on Entrepreneurs

Now that we have described several basic social skills, let's turn to their relevance to, and possible usefulness for, entrepreneurs.

Social Perception

Turning first to social perception, research findings suggest that this aspect of social competence is very helpful in many business contexts. For instance, interviewers high in social perception do a better job of choosing the best applicants than interviewers who are low in this skill,[7] and managers who are adept at reading their subordinates are better able than those who are low in such skill to identify the causes of substandard performance (e.g., whether it stems from lack of motivation, a lack of necessary resources, or other causes). Accurate identification of the causes of poor performance is a necessary first step in selecting effective corrective actions.[8]

Skill in social perception is also relevant to the activities entrepreneurs perform in attempting to build their new ventures. For example, consider the process of negotiation. Entrepreneurs engage in this activity frequently, especially during the early days of their new ventures' existence.[9] They must negotiate with partners, prospective employees, venture capitalists, suppliers, customers, and many others. As we will note in Chapter 5, research findings suggest that individuals who are skilled at social perception often find it easier to determine when their opponents are being honest and when, in contrast, these persons are bending the truth for their own advantage. Because knowledge of an opponent's actual break-even point plays an important role in successful negotiations,[10] it seems possible that proficiency in social perception may be an important plus for entrepreneurs, and can contribute significantly to their success.

Social perception is also relevant to another important task performed by entrepreneurs: choosing partners and key employees. As we will note in Chapter 5, individuals often attempt to conceal their true motives and intentions, and usually strive to place themselves in a favourable light. The ability to cut through such subterfuge—to perceive others accurately despite their efforts to conceal such information—can be invaluable to entrepreneurs when choosing partners and hiring key employees. In short, being adept at perceiving others accurately can be of considerable benefit to entrepreneurs in all these contexts, and provide them with an important competitive edge.

Expressiveness

Existing evidence suggests that persons high in the ability to express their emotions clearly often gain important advantages. For instance, physicians high in expressiveness are more popular with patients than those who are less expressive,[11] and salespersons who are high in expressiveness are often much more successful than those who are more deadpan. For instance, in a study conducted with Toyota salespersons, those who were high in expressiveness sold many more cars than those low in expressiveness (see Figure 4.2).[12] For entrepreneurs, being high in expressiveness may be an important means of generating enthusiasm in others—VCs, prospective customers, potential employees. In fact, venture capitalists often say that they invest in people who display passion when presenting their business plans. So again, expressiveness may be an important plus in terms of building a successful company.

Impression Management

A third social skill, impression management, has also been found to confer important advantages on those who can use it well. People employ many different techniques to create favourable impressions on others—everything from efforts to enhance one's own appearance and image through flattery to presenting gifts during an initial meeting. Skill with respect to impression management has been found to enhance the outcomes experienced by job applicants (they are more likely to get the job)[13] and to boost the ratings received by employees in annual performance reviews.[14] Skill at impression management may also be extremely helpful to entrepreneurs in their efforts to obtain needed capital. In describing how they go about making the decision whether to support a particular project, venture capitalists often report that how entrepreneurs present themselves during face-to-face meetings and presentations is one of the factors they consider—one to which they give considerable weight.[15, 16]

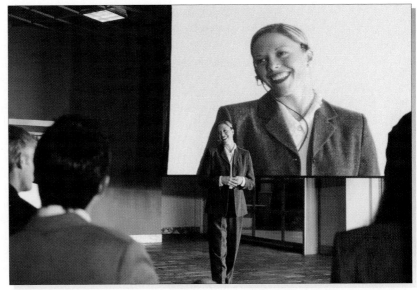

Figure 4.2 Expressiveness: A Plus in Many Business Contexts

Persons who are high in expressiveness gain an important advantage in many contexts. For instance, salespersons who are more expressive tend to be more successful, and physicians who are more expressive are more popular with patients. Entrepreneurs, too, may benefit from being expressive, especially in contexts where it is important for them to generate enthusiasm in others.

Influencing Others

Skill in terms of influencing or persuading others has been found to be highly valuable in many business contexts. Persons who are high in persuasiveness generally attain higher success in many occupations—sales, law, and medicine—than persons lower in this skill.[17] Again, this aspect of social competence may be useful to entrepreneurs in a wide range of contexts—everything from influencing their partners through convincing employees to expend even more effort on the job.

Social Adaptability

Have you ever known someone who was comfortable in almost any social situation? If so, this person was probably high in social adaptability. Persons high in this aspect of social competence are able to talk to anyone about anything, introduce themselves to strangers with minimal discomfort, and adjust to a wide range of new social situations. For them, the word "shy" is an unknown, unfamiliar concept, and they can fit comfortably into almost any social context. A large body of research findings suggests that persons high in such abilities attain greater success and more rapid promotions in many different contexts than persons low in such abilities;[18] indeed, it has even been found that professors high in social adaptability receive significantly higher ratings from their classes than professors low in social adaptability.[19]

Social adaptability can be helpful to entrepreneurs in many ways. For instance, entrepreneurs must often make many cold calls to strangers—potential customers and suppliers, to name just a few. These persons may be totally unfamiliar with the entrepreneur and his or her company, yet entrepreneurs must approach them and attempt to form business relationships. A high level of social adaptability can be very beneficial to entrepreneurs in this context.

In sum, being high in social competence can contribute to entrepreneurs' success in many different ways. The skills encompassed by social competence can help entrepreneurs to get along effectively with others and to successfully perform many activities required for building a successful company. We should note that this conclusion is far from mere speculation: Recent findings indicate that entrepreneurs who are rated by people who know them well as being high in social competence are actually more successful, in terms of the profitability of their new ventures, than entrepreneurs who are lower in such competence.[20]

Now, here's the most encouraging part: Social competence is definitely not set in stone. As is true for all the skills we will describe in this chapter, it is open to modification—and improvement. Almost anyone can enhance social skills through a little practice. Special programs for building social skills have existed for decades—in fact, the famous Dale Carnegie programs focus, to a large degree, on building the social skills described here. In addition, many psychologists and other professionals specialize in helping people improve their social skills.

Although outside assistance of this kind is very useful, you can also improve your social skills yourself with a little help from friends or family who are willing to give you their honest reactions. One useful technique is to have someone videotape you while you interact with other people in a variety of contexts. Almost everyone is surprised by what they see on such tapes. For instance, many people are shocked to find that they cannot accurately read their own facial expressions. They believe that they are showing their feelings and emotions clearly but, in fact, they are not. Similarly, on viewing tapes of their own behaviour, many persons are surprised to see how obvious their efforts at impression management or persuasion are. With a little practice, most people can substantially improve these and other aspects of their own social competence. Of course, the more help you receive, the better, but the key point is this: You *can* do better with respect to these key personal skills if you try. Given the benefits enhanced social competence can confer on entrepreneurs and their new ventures, this is effort very well spent indeed. For example, as we will explain in Chapter 6, people typically obtain capital from others with whom they have some kind of social tie, and entrepreneurs who have better social competence are better at creating such links. (How important are social skills to entrepreneurs? For the thoughts of one highly successful entrepreneur on this issue, see **The Voice of Experience** section in this chapter.)

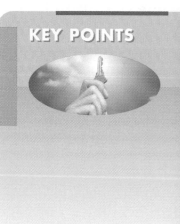

KEY POINTS

- To run a successful new venture, entrepreneurs need a variety of personal skills that are helpful in building their company (e.g., social competence, the ability to develop trust and cooperative working relationships with others, and the ability to effectively manage conflicts).
- Social competence, the ability to get along well with others, encompasses a number of discrete social skills.
- Among these, the most relevant for entrepreneurs are social perception, expressiveness, impression management, skill at influencing others, and social adaptability.
- A large body of evidence indicates that persons high in these aspects of social competence experience more favorable outcomes in a wide range of business contexts. Further, entrepreneurs high in social competence tend to be more successful than those low in such competence.
- Social competence can be readily enhanced through appropriate training, so entrepreneurs should carefully consider devoting effort to this task—doing so may yield important benefits for both entrepreneurs and their new ventures.

THE VOICE OF EXPERIENCE

In 1984, Linda Knight was a registered nurse passionate about home nursing because of its holistic approach to patient care. Realizing that the market for home nursing would grow, she founded a home-based nursing agency to service rural areas in southwestern Ontario. Throughout Knight's first decade as an entrepreneur, regulations governing home health care were changing, and her company needed to adapt to keep up. In 1996, with the Ontario government returning to a competitive model of home care service delivery, Knight's company was renamed CarePartners and aggressively entered this new competitive market. Ten years later, in 2006, CarePartners has 580 nurses working in 10 regions of Ontario and annual sales exceeding $12 million. In 2001, Knight was awarded a Rotman Canadian Woman Entrepreneur of the Year Award for Impact on the Local Economy. In a recent interview, she talked with me about the skills that have been important to the success of her business.

Reuber: "Many factors contribute to entrepreneurs' success—for example, the quality of their idea for a new venture, the entrepreneurs' experience and background, the availability of financing, and so on. How important are people skills in this mix?"

Knight: "If you want to grow your business, I would put them as number one in importance. People have to see you as a leader and want to follow you. They need to have confidence that their leader is strong."

Reuber: "How do you build a management team that can grow with the business?"

Knight: "This was a particularly salient issue for us. People are naturally drawn to people who are like them, but what you need are people who have what you don't have. Early on, I found a key person who was perfect, and very different than me. She paid close attention to detail and got things done. But, because we were so different, there was always friction between us. Then, as we added more managers, there was more friction still. The turning point came when we had a student from Queen's University come in to do a project about us. As part of the project, the student gave all managers a Myers-Briggs personality assessment and found that we spanned all personality types. His conclusion was 'You guys will be dynamic if you don't kill each other first!' That was a turning point for CarePartners because we understood our differences and had a language to work them out."

Reuber: "How important is your company culture?"

Knight: "To quote Heather Reisman, 'Culture is everything. Everything else can be copied.' We are in an oligopoly, with 14 companies like us competing for each region, and are differentiated primarily by our culture. We try to stay as 'uncorporate'

as possible. I was a nurse and understand what our nurses live every day. To keep this understanding fresh, I still do some home visits each year. We want our nurses to feel cared and valued as individuals. This is particularly important since we don't pay as well as the hospitals. People have to want to work for us. We send everyone a birthday card and even send flowers when they go the extra mile. As the company grows, it gets more difficult to maintain individualization, and so we have split into 10 smaller companies, one for each region. Each region has its own administrative staff, and does its own staffing, work scheduling and billing."

Reuber: "What are some team-building tactics you use?"

Knight: "I believe that everyone wants to have a best friend at work and so we make sure there is time to socialize. Each region has a potluck dinner during Nurses Week, and a Christmas party which the company pays for. We enter teams in charity events, such as the Relay for Life cancer run. Probably most importantly, though, we really listen to our employees. Once a year we have a comprehensive program review, and the entire management team visits each region for a day. This gives them a chance to talk about issues they are having, such as cases that are difficult to service, or staffing issues, and really be heard. We get useful information from these sessions, and leave with set of action items so we can address their concerns. We also do regular focus groups with nurses so that we understand what they want from us. We're starting to have regular quality circles in each region to make sure that feedback from the front line gets back to us."

Reuber: "Have you ever had to deal with conflict in CarePartners?"

Knight: "I've learned that conflict is very difficult for women to deal with. Remember that we're a very female company. There is one man on our management team, and we have 5 male nurses out of 580! When I first started the company, I spent many sleepless nights worrying about conflict and thinking of ways to avoid it. We're better at it now, and can terminate people when they're not delivering high-quality service. Interestingly enough, nurses on the front line want weak performers to be let go, but when you actually terminate them, it can be destabilizing, and so you need to deal with the aftermath."

Reuber: "When do you have to use your persuasion skills?"

Knight: "I like the thrill of the chase—winning a new region. Once we've won it, my management team needs to get things set up to make it work, and sometimes that is difficult. So, it's often a process of debate to decide whether or not we really want to win a contract."

continued

Reuber: "What are some lessons you'd like to pass on to aspiring entrepreneurs?"

Knight: "Recognize that where you start is not necessarily where you'll end up. I started out with a passion for home nursing, and never thought I'd be managing such a big company. There are some difficult periods along the way and you need to keep going to get through them. Perhaps the most difficult period is early on, when things are going well, but it's all on your shoulders. It gets easier when you can afford to hire more managers. Managing 50 people was more difficult for me than now, with 580, because I was doing it by myself. Second, you need to have dogged determination. The possibility that your business won't work is something that simply doesn't register on your radar. Finally, people need to be prepared for how

consuming this is. When you own your own business, you have a huge puzzle, which you're constantly turning in your mind."

Commentary: What Linda Knight is saying, in essence, is that to launch a new venture, and run it successfully, you need a great product or service *and* the ability to get along well with other people—to influence them, motivate them, earn their trust, and stimulate their commitment and enthusiasm. Making sure the product/service is excellent is the first key task for entrepreneurs—one they cannot readily delegate to others, at least in the early days of their company. But building a successful business also involves managing its internal relationships. These tasks all require excellent people skills, and entrepreneurs who possess such skills gain an important advantage over those who do not.

WORKING EFFECTIVELY WITH OTHERS: BUILDING TRUST AND MANAGING CONFLICT

Most new ventures are started not by a single entrepreneur, but by several cofounders. Indeed, often there is strength in numbers: Teams of talented, highly motivated people working closely together can accomplish much more than they could by working alone. For these benefits to be realized, however, two important conditions must be met: (1) The people involved must work together cooperatively—they must pool their efforts and direct their activities toward the same goals—and (2) The inevitable conflicts that arise when bright, energetic people work together many hours each day must be handled effectively so that they do not interfere with teamwork and cooperation. These observations suggest that among the skills essential for entrepreneurs wishing to build their new ventures into successful organizations are those relating to establishing close, cooperative working relations with others and skills relating to the effective management of conflict. Such skills help entrepreneurs build the social capital of their new ventures, and recent findings indicate that organizations high in social capital (i.e., organizations with high levels of trust, liking, and mutual identification among the persons working in them) are more effective and successful than ones low in social capital.[21] Both of these topics will be considered in this discussion.

Building Cooperation: The Key Role of Trust

If people can often accomplish more by working together than by working separately, why—you may be wondering—isn't cooperation the name of the game? Why, in other words, is cooperation less common than purely utilitarian considerations would suggest? One answer involves a simple fact: Some goals cannot be shared. Two companies seeking orders from the same potential customer both want the same result (the order!), but they cannot cooperate to attain it. On the contrary, they must compete vigorously against each other because this is clearly a winner-takes-all situation. Many other instances of this type exist and, in them, cooperation cannot occur.

In many other contexts, however, cooperation between individuals or organizations *is* possible. Whether it develops, however, depends on a number of different factors. For instance, some persons are simply more competitive than others, and will cooperate (i.e., work together as part of a team) only when there is no other choice. Similarly, within an organization, some reward structures encourage

© 2003 Tribune Media Services, Inc. All Rights Reserved. Reprinted with permission.

  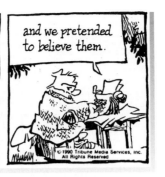

Figure 4.3 Trust: A Rare Commodity in the World of Business—and in Many Other Spheres of Life

There are many situations when trust—confidence in the words and actions of others—is low. Low levels of trust, in turn, make it difficult to develop cooperative working relationships.

cooperation between individuals (reward structures in which raises and bonuses are distributed to teams) while others discourage such coordination (systems in which rewards are distributed on the basis of individual performance). Perhaps the most important factor in the development of cooperative working relationships, however, is **trust**—one person's degree of confidence in the words and actions of another.

When we say that one person trusts another, we imply that the first person believes that the second will do what he or she says he or she will do, and will generally behave in predictable ways that are understandable in terms of the relationship between them. Moreover, the first person expects that the second will not act in ways that are harmful to her or his interests or well-being—as the characters in Figure 4.3 are doing!

Actually, there seem to be two distinct kinds of trust.[22] One—known as **calculus-based trust**—is based on deterrence. When we expect that others will act in the ways they promise because they know they will be punished for doing otherwise, we are demonstrating calculus-based trust. For instance, a customer of a new venture may believe an entrepreneur's statement about when an initial order will be shipped, because of calculus-based trust. Both the customer and the entrepreneur know what will happen if the order is late: The customer may not order from the new venture again.

A second type of trust, in contrast, is the kind that develops in relationships when people work together over long periods of time and feel that they know and understand each other's motives and needs. This type of trust is known as **identification-based trust**, and when it exists, individuals expect others to behave as they promise to behave not because they will be punished for failing to do so, but because they believe that the person they trust has their well-being at heart. Clearly, this is the kind of trust that entrepreneurs want to exist between themselves and their cofounders, and between themselves and key employees (and all employees!) of their new ventures. The advantages of identification-based trust are obvious: When such trust exists, people can be depended upon to do the right thing—which in this case means they can be depended upon to act in ways that are beneficial to the company as a whole rather than to themselves only. Figure 4.4 illustrates the difference between calculus-based and identification-based trust.

Needless to add, describing identification-based trust as a goal is one thing; attaining it is quite another. How can entrepreneurs build such trust into their working relationships? Several steps have been found to be useful. First, it is important to act as you promise. For example, if you promise to get something done by a specific time, you should try hard to do so. If you miss deadlines once in awhile, people may overlook it. But if you miss deadlines regularly, others' trust in you will be reduced. So, consistency between your words and your actions is one important trust-building step. For instance, if an entrepreneur repeatedly promises a customer that orders will be delivered at specific times but regularly fails to meet these targets, the customer's trust in the entrepreneur may be undermined.

Second, follow agreed-upon procedures. For people to trust you, it is not enough for you to do what you say you will do; in addition, you should do it in the

LEARNING OBJECTIVE

2   Describe the difference between calculus-based trust and identification-based trust, and explain their roles in the development of cooperative working relationships.

Figure 4.4 Two Kinds of Trust

Calculus-based trust rests on deterrence: One person trusts another because if that person fails to behave as promised, she or he will be punished in some way. This view implies that this person will behave as promised only when the threat of punishment is present. The other kind of trust, identification-based trust, is based on one person's belief that another has the first person's interests at heart, and will not do anything harmful to that person. When this kind of trust exists, threat of punishment and surveillance are not necessary.

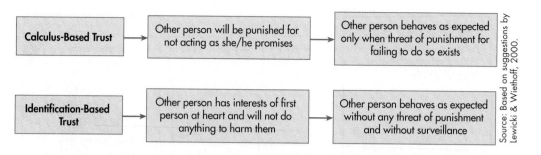

Source: Based on suggestions by Lewicki & Wiethoff, 2000.

way they expect, and the way you have outlined or suggested. For instance, suppose that an entrepreneur is trying to hire a marketing expert. She promises her cofounders that she will hire someone through a series of competitive interviews. (We will describe this process in Chapter 12.) In fact, though, she happens to meet someone at a party who is an expert in marketing and hires this person on the spot. Even if the new employee is highly competent, she may reduce her cofounders' trust in her; after all, she has *not* proceeded in the way they expected and on which they had previously agreed.

Third, trust can be built by engaging in what are known as **organizational citizenship behaviours**—employee behaviours that go beyond the role requirements of their jobs and that are not directly or explicitly recognized by formal reward systems.[23] Clearly, this is a kind of behaviour many entrepreneurs demonstrate: They frequently engage in actions that demonstrate their deep and lasting commitment to the new venture—everything from working incredibly long hours and investing their entire personal fortunes in it, to forming very close and trusting relationships with initial employees—treating them more like family members or friends than employees. In a sense, then, they are models of organizational citizenship behaviour to others in the new venture, and this attitude can contribute strongly to high levels of trust. For instance, consider Ron Schaich, founder of Panera Bread—a rapidly growing chain of bakery-cafés that sell high-quality bread and sandwiches. Schaich, who previously had founded another company with its roots firmly in bread—Au Bon Pain—is a model of commitment for his employees, many of whom are skilled bakers who share his passion for first-rate bread. As he puts it: "Nourishment for the soul ... that's what we do. I believe if you give people something special, something worth going out of the way for, they'll buy it. This belief is rooted in tradition ... in a fundamental commitment to handcrafter bread." Schaich's commitment to—and love for—high-quality bread is well-known to employees of Panera Bread, and he demonstrates it in personal visits to many of Panera's stores. His commitment and high standards help inspire employees, and have been a positive factor in Panera's success and rapid growth.

Finally, because identification-based trust requires that people understand and appreciate each others' motives and needs, it is important to discuss these with others as a basis for building trust. Where trust is concerned, in other words, ambiguity is not a good thing. To trust you, other people have to conclude that they know you, and how you are thinking. So a degree of openness is important from the point of view of establishing identification-based trust. For instance, if an entrepreneur discovers that his cofounder has entered into discussions for a cooperative arrangement with another company but hasn't discussed these tentative plans with him, his trust in this person may be weakened.

Managing Conflict: Heading off Trouble at the Pass

There is an old saying to the effect that "When emotions run high, reason flies out the window." In other words, when people experience strong emotions, they stop thinking rationally—or predictably. A corollary to this saying might be, "And when they do, they stop recognizing their own self-interest." These thoughts are certainly true where certain kinds of conflict are concerned. **Conflict** is generally defined in management science as a process in which one party perceives that another party has

LEARNING OBJECTIVE

3   Define conflict and describe its major causes.

taken or will soon take actions that are incompatible with its interests, and it takes two basic forms. In one, known as affective or emotional conflict, a strong element of anger or disliking is introduced into the situation. The two sides may or may not have opposing interests, but one thing is clear: They are upset with each other, do not trust each other, and experience strong, negative emotions (see Figure 4.5). A second kind of conflict, known as **cognitive conflict**, in contrast, is one in which individuals become aware of contrasting perspectives or interests, but focus on the issues and not on one another. For example, members of a board of advisers for a new venture may disagree about what advice to give the entrepreneurs with respect to marketing strategies without becoming upset or angry with one another: Their focus is on the

Christopher Bissell/Stone/Getty Images

Figure 4.5 Affect-Based Conflict

When conflict involves a strong emotional component, it may be especially difficult to resolve. Moreover, the persons involved may lose sight of their own self-interest as a result of the intense negative emotions they experience.

issues, not on personalities. Research findings indicate that cognitive conflict can be constructive—it can induce both sides to consider each other's positions and possible solutions very carefully. The result may be a resolution acceptable to both sides. Affective conflict, in contrast, generally produces negative results.[24] In fact, when it is intense, such conflict can badly shatter working relationships and dissipate trust that has been painstakingly built up over months or even years.

Conflict is definitely relevant to entrepreneurs and their efforts to build strong, successful businesses. Indeed, recent findings suggest that when affective conflict is high between cofounders of a new venture, the venture's performance may be significantly impaired.[25] Clearly, this is an event entrepreneurs should strongly strive to avoid. In order to prevent such conflicts from erupting, it is useful to understand why they occur, so we will first consider the potential causes of such conflicts. We will then turn to ways of preventing them and managing them effectively if they do occur. Please note that in this discussion we will focus on **affective conflicts**—conflicts that involve a large emotional component rather than conflicts that emerge from incompatible interests or goals.

Causes of Affective Conflict

Because trust has a strong upside, it is not surprising to learn that distrust has opposite effects. In fact, basic distrust between individuals or groups is a key cause of angry conflicts between them.[26] A closely related cause is preexisting grudges. Often, people import anger and resentment stemming from previous situations into a current one, with the result that what might otherwise be minor conflicts erupt into intense and angry ones.

Additional causes of conflict involve what can be viewed as largely social factors—sources having more to do with relationships between people than with opposing interests or economic concerns. One such factor that plays a role in this respect is what have been termed faulty attributions—errors concerning the causes behind others' behaviour.[27] When individuals find that their interests have been blocked (e.g., their recommendations were rejected and those of another person accepted), they generally try to determine why this occurred. Was it bad luck? A lack of planning on their part? A lack of needed resources? Or was it due to intentional interference by another person or group? If they conclude that the latter is true, then the seeds for an intense conflict may be planted—even if other persons actually had nothing to do with the negative outcomes they have experienced. In other words, erroneous attributions concerning the causes of such outcomes can, and often do, play an important role in conflicts, and sometimes cause them to occur when they could readily have been avoided.

Another social cause of conflict involves the tendency to perceive our own views as objective and resting firmly on reality, but those of others as biased or even irrational. As a result of this tendency, we tend to magnify differences

LEARNING OBJECTIVE

4 Explain how entrepreneurs can effectively manage conflict, especially affect-based conflict.

between our views and those of others, and so also exaggerate conflicts of interest between us.

Finally, we should note that personal traits or characteristics, too, play a role in conflict. For example, Type-A individuals—people who are highly competitive, always in a hurry, and quite irritable—tend to become involved in conflicts more often than calmer and less irritable Type-B persons.[28] These conflicts can be a particularly severe problem for entrepreneurs, who are more likely than others to be Type-A personalities.[29]

Overall, then, affective conflicts stem from several different sources. Fortunately, all of these can be diminished by a high degree of trust between cofounders or between entrepreneurs and their employees. When we have a high degree of identification-based trust in others, we tend to perceive their actions as stemming from positive rather than negative causes; at the least, we give them the benefit of the doubt. This approach can reduce the likelihood of emotion-laden conflict. Similarly, high levels of trust help to counter the tendency to perceive others' views as biased, self-centred, or worse. Basically, then, we are suggesting that there is a close link between trust within a new venture and the likelihood of affective conflict within it. The higher the trust, the less likely it is that such conflicts will develop. Once again, then, it seems clear that efforts to develop high levels of trust in a new venture between cofounders and between founders and employees are well worth the time and energy.

Techniques for Resolving Conflicts That Do Occur

Although trust can reduce the incidence of affective conflicts, it cannot reduce such conflicts to zero. Some conflicts, at least, will have to be resolved rather than avoided. Many techniques for resolving conflicts exist, but for entrepreneurs, the most relevant and useful resolution involves **negotiation**—a process in which the opposing sides exchange offers, counteroffers, and concessions, either directly or though representatives.[30] If the process is successful, a solution acceptable to both sides is attained and the conflict is resolved. If, instead, bargaining is unsuccessful, a costly deadlock may result and the conflict will intensify.

When the parties to a negotiation represent different companies, countries, or social groups (e.g., labour and management), the primary goal for each side may be to maximize its own outcomes, often at the cost of the opponent. Within a new venture, however, this approach makes little or no sense. Take, for example, an entrepreneur negotiating with her venture capitalist over a disagreement that they have concerning the new venture's strategy. Winning the argument with the VC might do the entrepreneur more harm than good, especially if the venture capitalist comes away from the discussions with the idea that the entrepreneur was difficult and not worthy of the same attention as other entrepreneurs in the VC's portfolio. Rather than win the debate, the two sides to any conflict should focus on obtaining what is known as a **win-win solution**—one that is acceptable to both sides and that meets the basic needs of both. Any other resolution will almost certainly be short-lived, and will, moreover, produce harmful consequences for the new venture. How can such solutions be obtained? Although there are no hard-and-fast rules, the following guidelines have been found to be useful:

■ *Avoid tactics that reflect a win-lose approach* (one in which each side attempts to maximize its own outcomes). Among the tactics to be avoided are these: (1) beginning with an extreme initial offer—one that is very favourable to the side proposing it; this strategy may put the recipient of the extreme offer at a disadvantage, but will also generate feelings of anger and resentment; (2) the big lie technique—trying to convince the other side that one's break-even point is much higher than it is so that they offer more than would otherwise be the case; and (3) convincing the other side that you have an out—if they won't make a deal with you, you can go elsewhere and get even better terms. These and related strategies tend to throw kerosene on the flames and are counterproductive in terms of reducing the intensity of affective conflict.

■ *Uncover the real issues.* As we noted earlier, many affective conflicts do not stem from opposing interests. Rather, they involve social and cognitive factors (grudges, faulty attributions concerning the cause of others' actions). A useful technique for reducing such conflicts, then, is to identify their true causes. This practice can require a lot of effort, but can ultimately save a lot of time—and frustration!

■ *Broaden the scope of the issues considered.* Often, persons negotiating with each other have several issues on the table at once. Therefore, reciprocal concessions are possible: One side gives ground on one or more issues, while the other gives ground on others. For instance, if an entrepreneur is negotiating with a prospective employee, there may be several issues on the table: salary, stock options, fringe benefits, working hours, and so on. Perhaps the entrepreneur finds it easier to make concessions with respect to stock options and working hours than salary or fringe benefits. The potential employee might be willing to trade off immediate pay for these benefits; at the very least, it is worth considering such logrolling, as it is sometimes termed.

In sum, it is best to avoid affective conflicts within a new venture: The potential costs are simply too high. When such conflicts do occur, however, savvy entrepreneurs can see them for what they are—dangerous traps for their working relationships with cofounders, employees, customers, VCs, and others—and then they can take steps such as the ones outlined here to defuse these conflicts, to resolve them, and to prevent them from doing irreparable harm to the company they are working so hard to grow. (For a disturbing example of what can happen when people who work together do not attempt to avoid or resolve affective conflicts, see the **Danger! Pitfall Ahead!** section.)

DANGER! PITFALL AHEAD!

How to Create an Affective Conflict When There Is None

Back in the mid-1990s, Delta Air Lines, like many other large carriers, was going through hard times, and for the first time in its history had to cut a number of jobs throughout the company. When asked by reporters to comment on the extent to which this had upset employees, Delta CEO Ronald W. Allen remarked, "So be it." This callous remark proved very costly. Delta's employees were furious, and let everyone—the media, passengers, and government officials—know about it. In fact, within a few days of Allen's remark, thousands of Delta employees donned "So Be It" buttons, and wore them proudly as a sign of their anger and contempt for Allen. Morale plunged, and the heat was truly on for Allen. In fact, the board of directors declined to renew his contract so that soon he, too, was out of a job.

What was going on here? A textbook illustration of affective conflict—a conflict that may have started with divergent interests, but which quickly escalated into a bitter dispute in which basic issues were quickly submerged in a tide of angry emotion. Consider the situation in the cold light of reason: Both Allen and Delta's employees wanted to save the company from a mounting sea of red ink. Yet, although some of their major interests coincided, Allen managed to drive a wedge between top management and Delta's employees—one that could only be healed by his departure.

There is an important message in these events for entrepreneurs: If affective conflict can prove so costly for a huge company like Delta Air Lines, imagine how devastating it can be when it occurs between members of the founding team or between this team and key employees. For this reason, being familiar with techniques for avoiding and defusing affective conflict is an important skill that entrepreneurs should definitely acquire—and practice!

KEY POINTS

- Trust is an essential ingredient in building cooperative working relationships. Two kinds of trust exist: calculus-based trust and identification-based trust.
- Calculus-based trust is based on the belief that if others do not act as they say they will, they will be punished. In contrast, identification-based trust is based on the belief that the person in question has our best interests at heart.
- Calculus-based trust can be increased by acting as you promise to act, following agreed-upon procedures, and being open about your own motives and needs.
- Conflict is a process in which one party perceives that another party has taken or will take actions that are incompatible with its interests. It takes two basic forms: affective or emotional conflict, which involves a strong element of anger or disliking, and cognitive conflict, which focuses on issues rather than people.
- Affective conflicts stem from many causes, including distrust; long-standing grudges; social factors, such as faulty attributions about the causes of others' behaviour; and individual difference factors (e.g., the Type-A behaviour pattern).
- The most useful means of resolving conflicts is negotiation—a process in which the opposing sides exchange offers, counteroffers, and concessions, either directly or through representatives.
- For negotiations to succeed, the participants should adopt a win-win perspective and avoid such tactics as extreme offers and the big lie technique. They should also seek to uncover the real issues and to broaden the scope of the issues discussed.

INFLUENCING OTHERS: FROM PERSUASION TO VISION

How many times each day does each of us attempt to influence others—to change their views or their behaviour? How many times each day are we, in turn, exposed to influence attempts from other persons? Whatever the number is, it is very large. Every time you hear or see a commercial, or look at an ad in a newspaper or magazine, you are being exposed to an influence attempt (see Figure 4.6). Every time you ask someone for a favour or try to change a friend's mind about some issue, you are attempting to exert some type of influence (or, because it is directed toward other persons, *social influence*).

Organizations—including new ventures—are no exception to this general rule: They, too, are the scene of countless attempts by one or more persons to influence one or more others. Clearly, being successful at this task can yield important benefits; getting others to think the way you do or to agree to your requests can be very helpful in terms of reaching your goals. This is certainly true for entrepreneurs running new ventures. Virtually every day, they come into contact with people they wish to influence—VCs, potential customers, suppliers, government officials, and many others. Further, in most cases, they have no direct power over these persons—they can't order them to do what they want. Rather, they must try to produce the results they want through their own skills with respect to influence. To the extent entrepreneurs can refine these skills, therefore, the more successful their companies are likely to be.

In this discussion, we will take a closer look at social influence and the many ways in which it is exerted. We believe that general knowledge of these techniques can prove useful in two key ways. First, this information can help you to choose among them more effectively, matching the appropriate technique to the specific situation. Second, such knowledge can help you recognize these tactics when they are used by other persons, and so can assist you in protecting yourself against them.

Figure 4.6 Influence: A Fact of Modern Life

Each day, we are exposed to countless attempts to influence us—to change our attitudes or behavior. In return, we engage in many attempts to influence others, people with whom we live or work. Many of these influence attempts take place in work settings.

© Corel

Tactics of Influence: Which Ones Are Most Common?

As you probably know from your own experience, people use many different strategies to influence others in work settings. Here is a brief description of the strategies that are used most frequently:[31]

LEARNING OBJECTIVE

5 Describe the techniques that individuals use most frequently to influence others in work settings.

- *Rational persuasion*—Using logical arguments and facts to persuade another that a view is correct or accurate.

- *Inspirational appeal*—Arousing enthusiasm by appealing to the recipient's values and ideals.

- *Consultation*—Asking for participation in decision making or in planning a change.

- *Ingratiation*—Getting someone to do what you want by putting that person in a good mood or getting that person to like you.

- *Exchange*—Promising some benefits in exchange for complying with a request.

- *Personal appeal*—Appealing to feelings of loyalty and friendship before making a request.

- *Coalition-building*—Persuading by seeking the assistance of others, or by noting the support of others.

- *Legitimating*—Pointing out one's authority to make a request, or verifying that the request is consistent with prevailing organizational policies and practices.

- *Pressure*—Seeking compliance by using demands, threats, or intimidation.

When are these various tactics used? Research findings suggest that different strategies are preferred depending on whether influence attempts are directed at targets who are higher, lower, or equivalent to oneself in terms of status or position.[32] For example, in large organizations, people generally use rational persuasion, consultation, or personal appeals when dealing with others equal to or above them in rank, but are more likely to use pressure tactics or inspirational appeals when trying to influence subordinates.

What do entrepreneurs do? Some evidence[33] suggests that they frequently use inspirational appeals. Why? Because they often face the task of convincing others to share their beliefs about what the emerging organization can, and will, become. In other words, they must convince other people (VCs, prospective employees, potential customers) to accept their vision of what might be, without much to back it up aside from their personal conviction or passion. In this context, inspirational appeals can be a very useful tactic. Indeed, recent findings indicate that the more clearly entrepreneurs can state their vision, the more successful their new ventures will be.[34]

Other Tactics of Influence: From Ingratiation to the Foot in the Door

Although the tactics described earlier are important, they are far from the entire picture where influence is concerned. Many other techniques are used for gaining compliance—for getting others to say "yes" to specific requests. Because compliance is often a goal for entrepreneurs (e.g., when they seek financial support, orders from customers, or attempt to hire new employees), it is worth taking a brief look at some of these tactics. Many tactics exist, but all of them derive from a small number of basic principles: [35]

LEARNING OBJECTIVE

6 Describe various techniques that people use for gaining compliance—for getting others to agree to requests they have made—and the basic principles on which these rest.

- *Friendship/liking.* The more other persons like us, the more willing they are to agree to our requests; several techniques for gaining compliance are based on this simple fact (e.g., flattery, ingratiation, efforts to enhance our own appearance). For example, as we will discuss in Chapter 6, people are more likely to obtain capital from someone with whom they have a direct social relationship. That is one example of how friendship makes it easier to gain compliance—in this case, compliance with the entrepreneur's request for money.

■ *Commitment/consistency.* Individuals wish to be consistent in their beliefs and actions. Thus, once they have adopted a position or committed themselves to a course of action, they experience strong pressure to comply with requests that are consistent with these initial commitments. In fact, they may find it virtually impossible to refuse such requests because doing so would force them to reject or disown actions or beliefs they previously adopted.

■ *Scarcity.* As a general rule, opportunities, objects, or outcomes that are rare or hard to obtain are more highly valued that those that are common or easy to attain. Thus, requests that emphasize scarcity or the fact that some object, opportunity, or outcome is hard to obtain or will soon no longer be available are sometimes difficult to resist.

■ *Reciprocity.* Individuals generally experience powerful pressures to reciprocate benefits they have received from others. As a result, requests that activate this principle are more likely to be accepted than requests that do not.

These basic principles appear to underlie many tactics of influence. For example, ingratiation and impression management are closely related to the principle of liking/friendship. The basic idea here is simple: First get others to like you, and once they do, ask them to do what you want.

The principle of commitment/consistency has been found to play an important role in several common, and often highly successful, tactics for gaining compliance. One of these is the *foot-in-the-door tactic*—starting with a small request, and once it is accepted, escalating to a larger request. For instance, an entrepreneur using this technique might at first ask a potential customer to accept a free sample of the new venture's product. Only later would she attempt to convert this favourable reception into a sizeable order. Another tactic based on commitment/consistency is the *lowball*—attempting to change a deal or agreement by making it less attractive to the target person after it is negotiated. This latter tactic is often used by salespersons, and it goes something like this. An attractive deal is offered to a customer. Once the customer accepts, the salesperson indicates that the sales manager or someone else in the company has rejected that arrangement, and offers a less desirable one to the customer. Rationally, people should walk away from such changes, but often, they don't: They feel committed to their initial decision, so they accept the less attractive deal.

Turning to the principle of scarcity, such tactics as *playing hard to get* and the *fast-approaching deadline technique* are widely used in the world of business. Job applicants who mention that they are under consideration for other positions or are very satisfied with their current position are using the hard-to-get tactic to manipulate important organizational outcomes in their favour. Similarly, large signs suggesting that special sale prices will only be in effect for a short period of time are often effective, and are based on the principle of scarcity (see Figure 4.7). Entrepreneurs sometimes use this tactic, too. For instance, they may tell a potential customer that they are offering a special price for a limited amount of time, thus putting pressure on this person to order now, before it is too late and the special deal has been withdrawn.

Finally, the principle of reciprocity is related to a tactic of influence known as the *door-in-the-face tactic*. In this strategy, individuals start with a request that is very large and certain to be rejected. Then they scale down their request to a more acceptable one, thus putting the target person under considerable pressure to reciprocate this concession. In fact, their concession is not a real one, but the tactic often works. Here's an example: A highly qualified prospective employee requests a 5 percent equity share in a new venture as part of his signing package. The entrepreneur refuses, offering only 1 percent. The prospective employee then backs down to 2 percent, which is the figure he wanted all along. Relieved, the entrepreneur accepts—and has, by doing so, fallen under the sway of the door-in-the-face technique.

Figure 4.7 The "Fast-Approaching Deadline" Technique

Several techniques for influencing others are based on the principle of scarcity: The suggestion that something people want is in short supply. Signs like the one shown here are using one procedure based on this principle: If people don't act quickly, they will lose out on a special price or special deal.

© Getty Images/PhotoDisc

As we noted earlier, knowing about these tactics is useful in two respects. By choosing them carefully to match specific situations, you may increase the likelihood of getting what you want—agreement to your requests by other persons. For instance, suppose that an entrepreneur is trying to persuade a customer to place an order in a market where all existing products, including the entrepreneur's, are highly similar. Here, tactics such as ingratiation (getting the customer to like the entrepreneur) might be useful. In contrast, when trying to get a repeat, and larger, order from a customer, the entrepreneur might remind this person that she placed a smaller order before, thus reminding this person of the initial commitment that was made to the new venture's products. Of course, it is possible to use more than one tactic simultaneously, but the general rule remains the same: The better the match between the tactic chosen and the particular situation, the more likely it is to succeed.

In addition, knowing about these tactics can help entrepreneurs protect themselves against their use. For instance, if a supplier has made a favourable deal with an entrepreneur, but then seeks to change it in a way that is less favourable to the entrepreneur, it could be that the low-ball tactic is being used; savvy entrepreneurs will walk away from such situations if they have any choice at all.

In sum, entrepreneurs often seek to exert influence over others—to change the way they think or act. For this reason, the more skilled entrepreneurs are with respect to persuasion and other tactics of influence, the more likely they are to attain success. And once again, we should note that almost anyone can, with a little careful practice, get better at this task. So understanding how influence works can be a valuable skill that entrepreneurs may wish to develop.

KEY POINTS

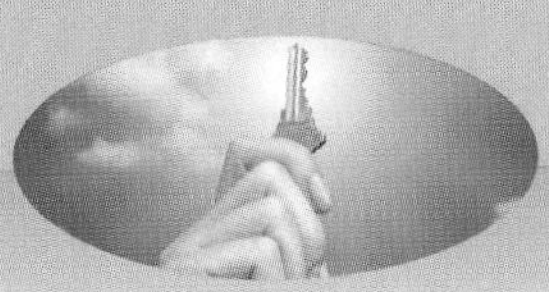

- **Each day we attempt to influence the way others think or act, and are exposed, in turn, to many efforts to influence us.**
- **Many different tactics for exerting social influence exist, but among the most frequently used are rational persuasion and consultation. Various pressure tactics are used less often.**
- **Many other tactics for exerting social influence exist; most of these are based on several basic principles: friendship/liking, consistency, scarcity, and reciprocity.**
- **Familiarity with these techniques can help entrepreneurs use them effectively themselves, and also protect themselves against these tactics when used by others.**

MANAGING STRESS: HOW ENTREPRENEURS CAN SURVIVE TO ENJOY THE FRUITS OF THEIR LABOUR

Here is an intriguing puzzle: Most entrepreneurs make strenuous efforts to protect their new venture's resources, both intellectual and physical. As we'll see in Chapter 7, they seek patents and trademarks, and they frequently purchase security systems to guard valuable equipment or raw materials. Yet, when it comes to their company's most precious resource—themselves—entrepreneurs often show a very different pattern. Rather than protecting this irreplaceable asset, they expose it to countless hazards: They work incredibly long hours, eat and sleep irregularly, and give up every enjoyable activity (from spending time with family and loved ones through hobbies) to work on their company. Certainly, we don't wish to seem critical of this steadfastness of purpose—far from it. There is a high dropout rate from start-up activities because of the time and energy required.

Indeed, Professors Monica Diochon of St. Francis Xavier University, Teresa Menzies of Brock University, and Yvon Gasse of Laval University, tracked more than 150 Canadian entrepreneurs who were in the process of starting a business in 2000.

Less than one-third of these people had an operating business after 12 months, and after 2 years, only 30 percent either had a business or were still trying to start one. People said they gave up because they were working too hard and wanted to achieve more balance in their life.[36] These results indicate that managing stress is important in getting a successful venture off the ground. By exposing themselves to incredibly high levels of stress for prolonged periods of time, entrepreneurs sometimes put their personal health at risk. It goes without saying that if their health is undermined so, too, is the future of their new venture. For this reason, we believe it is crucial for entrepreneurs to know something about stress—its causes, effects, and most importantly, how to manage it—another important skill for entrepreneurs to acquire. Those are the topics we will consider next.

Stress: Its Nature and Causes

LEARNING OBJECTIVE

7   Define stress and describe its major causes.

What precisely is **stress**? Definitions differ, but most experts agree that it refers to a pattern of emotional states and physiological reactions occurring in response to demands from many different events in our lives—our jobs, our families, our relationships, and so on. More specifically, these demands generate stress when the persons exposed to them engage in cognitive appraisal (i.e., they assess the situation) and conclude that they may soon be unable to deal with the demands upon them—when, in short, they feel in danger of being overwhelmed (see Figure 4.8). We're sure that this feeling is familiar to you, because everyone experiences it from time to time; we're also certain that you recognize it as a very unpleasant state—one you'd like to avoid or reduce as quickly as possible.

The specific conditions that generate stress are known as *stressors*, and many of these exist. One important source of stress is the demands of our jobs. Table 4.1 shows that the biggest stressor among Canadian workers is having too many demands at work and having to work too many hours as a result. The study did not specifically examine entrepreneurs, but we expect entrepreneurs to be particularly vulnerable to this stressor. Although people start their own business to be their own boss and have more control over their lives than when they are working for others, this autonomy does not usually translate into fewer working hours. Entrepreneurs are responsible for demands from all their stakeholders—for example, customers, suppliers, partners, employees, investors—and crises can arise with little warning. It is not surprising, therefore, that entrepreneurs report long working hours. A 2005 study by CIBC World Markets indicates that self-employed Canadians work an average of 56 hours per week, and 24 percent work more than 70 hours per week![37]

Other sources of stress will be all too familiar to you, such as the difficulties of juggling different roles we must play simultaneously (e.g., employee and parent; student and spouse). These roles often place incompatible demands on us—and so generate the feeling that we will soon be overwhelmed by them, which is the core of stress. This problem is especially serious for entrepreneurs, who often find that the demands of running their new ventures and the extremely long hours they work make it impossible to devote the time and attention they would prefer to their families. Sadly, these

Figure 4.8 Stress: Its Basic Nature

Stress occurs when various events in our lives (known as stressors) induce a pattern of emotional states and physiological reactions that are accompanied by the growing belief that we will not be able to cope with the demands of these events. The result can be highly unpleasant—and downright dangerous to our personal health.

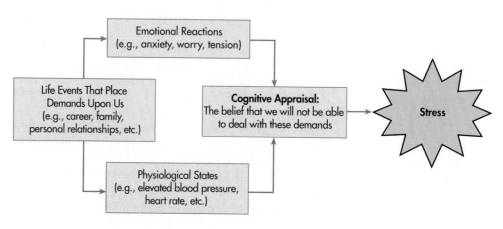

THE MAIN SOURCES OF WORKPLACE STRESS	
SOURCE	*% OF PEOPLE*
Too many demands or hours	34%
Poor interpersonal relations	15%
Lack of job security	13%
Risk of accident or injury	13%
Introduction of new technology	10%

Source: Perspectives on labour and income, Volume 4, No. 6, Statistics Canada, June 2003.

Table 4.1 Sources of Workplace Stress

A study of 25,000 Canadians, in 2000, found that working Canadians feel most stressed by having too many demands on their time and working too many hours.

demands are often a cause of great stress both for entrepreneurs and the people they love most—and can produce negative effects, such as divorce or difficulties in dealing with children.

Responsibility for others is another key source of stress. For instance, several years ago, many newspapers ran a story about one entrepreneur who continued to pay his employees after a fire that destroyed his factory. Why? Because he felt deeply responsible for their well-being and experienced a great deal of stress over the economic hardships they faced. Sadly, this generosity ultimately caused him to go bankrupt, so we're not recommending such selfless practices; rather, we report this incident because it illustrates just how stressful responsibility for others can be.

Another major cause of stress is the feeling that we do not have the social support we need—that other people are not there to help us if we need them. All these sources of stress relate to events that happen in work settings; in addition, of course, stress often comes from our personal lives, too: family obligations; romantic relationships; personal debts; even major holidays, such as Christmas, can all be sources of stress.

Although everyone is exposed to these conditions to some degree, it is clear that entrepreneurs experience exceptionally high levels of stress. The long hours that they work isolate them from their family and friends (their network of social support), and the economic worries they must confront (e.g., "Can we pay our rent this month?") are truly staggering. When the uncertainty of trying to create something new—often in the face of unrelenting competition—is added to the picture, it is clear that many entrepreneurs are exposed to very high levels of stress. Actually, we should say "expose themselves to very high levels of stress," because starting their own business is the personal choice they have made; in contrast to persons who work for existing organizations, stress is not dropped on them from the outside—entrepreneurs choose it as a way of life—or at least, as a temporary way of life.

The Adverse Effects of Stress

Common sense suggests that anything that feels as bad as stress and produces high levels of physiological arousal is probably harmful to our health. Indeed, a very large body of scientific evidence points to the conclusion that prolonged exposure to stress *is* harmful. In fact, medical authorities now believe that stress plays an important role in from 50 to 70 percent of all forms of physical illness.[38] The role of stress is particularly clear with respect to heart disease and strokes, but it is also involved in such varied illnesses as ulcers, diabetes, and even cancer. So clearly, stress is harmful to living things—including entrepreneurs!

In addition to its adverse effects on health, stress interferes with performance on many different tasks. Although low levels of stress can sometimes enhance performance, especially on purely physical tasks requiring strength or speed, moderate or high levels of stress—especially if continued for long periods of time—reduce performance on a wide range of tasks.[39] Stress has also been implicated in what is sometimes described as *desk rage*—intense and often senseless lashing out at others in response to stressful conditions on the job.[40] Such reactions can be especially harmful to a new venture, where people work in close proximity many hours each day, and temper explosions by a stressed-out entrepreneur can have devastating effects on

LEARNING OBJECTIVE

8 Describe the adverse effects of stress, and explain several techniques entrepreneurs can use to reduce the level of stress they experience.

Figure 4.9 Burnout: A Key Adverse Effect of Stress

When individuals are exposed to very high levels of stress over prolonged periods of time, they may develop burnout—a pattern that can have devastating effects on the performance of a new venture.

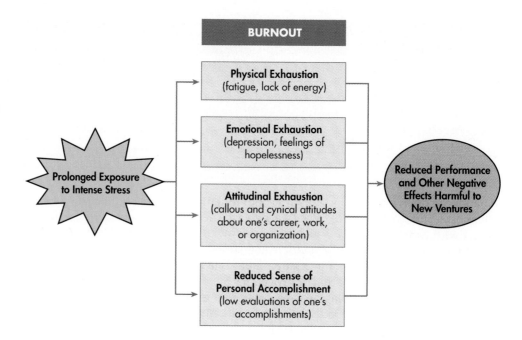

trust and morale. Finally, stress is a major cause of *burnout* (see Figure 4.9), a complex pattern of emotional, physical, and mental exhaustion that afflicts people who are exposed to stress for prolonged periods of time.[41] People suffering from burnout feel fatigued much of the time, and lose all enthusiasm for their work. In addition, they often feel hopeless and express cynical attitudes about their field and other people working in it. For instance, I once had a friend, a physician who was clearly suffering from burnout. He frequently made comments such as: "Doctors know nothing and never help anyone; they are just a money-grubbing bunch of parasites." How serious is burnout? Suffice it to say that many studies suggest that if an organization acquires a substantial number of persons suffering from burnout, its effectiveness will soon drop off the charts.[42] This threat almost certainly applies to new ventures, too. Although entrepreneurs are known for their enthusiasm, high levels of stress can ultimately undermine passion; if the founders of a new venture suffer from burnout, it seems fair to say that the heart of the new venture itself has been consumed.

All in all, it is clear that stress produces many harmful effects. Entrepreneurs, who often accept incredibly high levels of stress as a normal part of their existence, are directly in the crosshairs where these adverse effects are concerned. True, they are probably on the high end of a dimension of stress-tolerance or stress-resistance. But because they are certainly the most precious resource their new ventures possess, we think it is only prudent for them to take steps to protect themselves from the ravages of prolonged exposure to intense levels of stress. With that thought in mind, we will now describe some of the things entrepreneurs can do to protect their own health—and ensure that they will survive long enough to enjoy the fruits of their very hard labour.

Personal Techniques for Managing Stress

Stress-management techniques that you can build into your own life fall into two major categories: physical and behavioural. With respect to physical stress-management techniques, steps that strengthen personal health can be very helpful. We're sure you will find two of these steps familiar: eating a healthy diet and getting into good physical shape. The fact that they are so familiar, though, shouldn't prevent you from recognizing their value. Research findings indicate that people who exercise regularly and eat a healthy diet are far less likely to experience health problems when exposed to high levels of stress than persons who do not exercise regularly or do not eat a healthy diet. For instance, in one impressive study, a large group of college students was tested for physical fitness.[43] In addition, the same students provided information on the level of stress they were experiencing in their lives. Finally, an objective measure of their personal health was obtained from records at the university health centre. Results (see Figure 4.10) indicated that for students rated low in physical fitness, high levels of stress led to increased visits to the university health centre for physical illnesses. Among those rated high in physical fitness, however, increased stress did not produce similar harmful effects on health. This study and many others provide evidence for the following conclusion: Being in good physical condition can be an important means of warding off the adverse effects of stress. The message for entrepreneurs is clear: Taking the time to exercise regularly (as little as 20 to 30 minutes 3 to 4 times a week is often sufficient) is time well spent.

Several behavioural techniques (those relating primarily to changes in our own thinking and behaviour) have been found to be very useful for coping with stress. The first technique focuses on efforts to curtail excessive worrying. Surveys indicate that almost 90 percent of all people feel that they worry too much. The key issue, though, is not the sheer volume of worry; rather, it is *what* people tend to worry about. In many cases, they report worrying about things that are either unimportant or not directly under their control. The result is that they add unnecessarily to their own levels of stress. To the extent this tendency is reduced, stress, too, can be lowered. For example, suppose an entrepreneur worries about having enough cash flow to meet the payroll. Clearly, having enough cash flow is important and it is at least partly under the entrepreneur's control (e.g., she can avoid buying new equipment for awhile if cash is truly short.) But now suppose that the same entrepreneur worries a lot about the possibility that a large competing company will come up with a better product. Certainly, a threat from a competitor is important, but because there is not much she can do about it right now, there is little point in worrying about it. We're sure you get the main point: Worry only (or at least mainly) about important things that are at least partly under your control. Worrying about other combinations is mainly a waste of energy—and a cause of unnecessary stress. (The **Getting Down to Business** exercise (at the end of this chapter) will provide you with practice in this skill.)

Another useful behavioural technique involves what is known as the *incompatible reaction procedure*. When stress rises, so does physiological arousal, with the result that people's behaviour tends to become increasingly intense: They speak faster and in a louder voice, and tend to tense their muscles. Consciously countering these natural inclinations can be very helpful. In other words, when faced with events that are very stressful, you should consciously try to speak more slowly and quietly, and consciously try to adopt a relaxed rather than tense posture. The result? The cycle of rising stress and rising tension can be broken, at least temporarily. It turns out that this is all we need: temporary breaks from stress. Research findings indicate that these breaks are often sufficient to reduce the harmful effects that would otherwise occur.

Finally, managing stress often involves taking a step back from stressful situations and reminding oneself that even if things do not turn out as we wish—we do

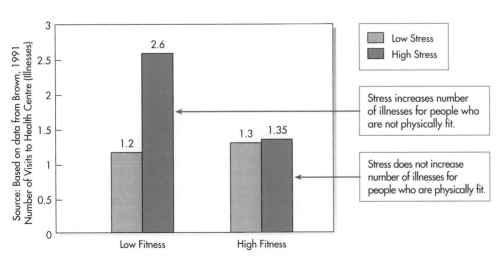

Figure 4.10 Being Physically Fit: One Useful Technique for Managing Stress

Students who were physically fit showed little increase in frequency of illness when exposed to high levels of stress. In contrast, students who were not physically fit showed a much larger increase in illness.

not get the financing we seek—it is *not* the end of the world. Human beings have a strong tendency to engage in what is sometimes termed *awfulizing*—they magnify the adverse effects of not being successful or perfect out of all proportion. The result? Even minor setbacks are interpreted as devastating calamities, and this perspective greatly magnifies the intensity—and adverse impact—of stress. Entrepreneurs are passionate about their ideas and companies, so we are certainly not suggesting that they should reduce their commitments. But seeing current situations in perspective— against a broader backdrop—can help lessen the tendency to perceive any and all setbacks as catastrophes; that approach, in turn, can help lower stress to more tolerable levels. For instance, suppose an entrepreneur fails to secure an order from a customer after weeks of effort. Is it the end of the world? Probably not. There are other customers out there and other ways to market the new venture's products that may be more successful (see Chapter 10). So an adaptive response to this situation is for the entrepreneur to think: "Bad luck! But it's not the end of the world." A much less adaptive reaction would be to think: "This is a catastrophe! How can we ever recover from this giant setback?"

In sum, although stress is an inevitable aspect of starting a new venture, there are several steps entrepreneurs can take to manage this potentially harmful process. Though these approaches differ greatly in form, they all rest, to some extent, on acceptance of the following basic principle: *No, we can't always change the world (make it the way we wish), but we can change our reactions to it.* In other words we can choose whether, and to what degree, to be upset or disturbed by various disappointments, and can choose either to manage the stress we inevitably experience or to let it dominate our thinking and our lives. The choice is always ours, and savvy entrepreneurs—those who want to remain in good health so that they can ultimately enjoy the rewards of their hard work—will definitely choose the former.

KEY POINTS

- Stress refers to a pattern of emotional states and physiological reactions occurring in response to demands from many different events in our lives.
- Stress exerts adverse effects on health, task performance, and psychological well-being. Entrepreneurs, who are exposed to high levels of stress for prolonged periods of time, are clearly at risk for such effects.
- A number of steps are helpful in managing stress, including physical techniques, such as eating a healthy diet and getting into good physical shape; and behavioural techniques, such as avoiding excessive and unnecessary worry, taking short breaks away from stressful situations, and avoiding the tendency to magnify the adverse effects of setbacks or disappointment.
- Entrepreneurs can readily use these and many other techniques to manage stress, and so assure that they will survive in good health to enjoy the fruits of their labour.

Summary and Review of Key Points

- To run a successful new venture, entrepreneurs need a variety of personal skills that are helpful in building their company (e.g., social competence, the ability to develop trust and cooperative working relationships with others, and the ability to effectively manage conflicts).

- Social competence, the ability to get along well with others, encompasses a number of discrete social skills.

- Among these, the most relevant for entrepreneurs are social perception, expressiveness, impression management, skill at influencing others, and social adaptability.

- A large body of evidence indicates that persons high in these aspects of social competence experience more favourable outcomes in a wide range of business contexts. Further, entrepreneurs high in social competence tend to be more successful than those low in such competence.

- Social competence can be readily enhanced through appropriate training, so entrepreneurs should carefully consider devoting effort to this task—doing so may yield important benefits for both entrepreneurs and their new ventures.

- Trust is an essential ingredient in building cooperative working relationships. Two kinds of trust exist: calculus-based trust and identification-based trust.

- Calculus-based trust is based on the belief that if others do not act as they say they will, they will be punished. In contrast, identification-based trust is based on the belief that the person in question has our best interests at heart.

- Calculus-based trust can be increased by acting as you promise to act, following agreed-upon procedures, and being open about your own motives and needs.

- Conflict is a process in which one party perceives that another party has taken or will take actions that are incompatible with its interests. It takes two basic forms: affective or emotional conflict, which involves a strong element of anger or disliking, and cognitive conflict, which focuses on issues rather than people.

- Affective conflicts stem from many causes, including distrust; long-standing grudges; and social factors, such as faulty attributions about the causes of others' behaviour; and individual difference factors (e.g., the Type-A behaviour pattern).

- The most useful means of resolving conflicts is negotiation—a process in which the opposing sides exchange offers, counteroffers, and concessions, either directly or through representatives.

- For negotiations to succeed, the participants should adopt a win-win perspective and avoid such tactics as extreme offers and the big lie technique. They should also seek to uncover the real issues and to broaden the scope of the issues discussed.

- Each day we attempt to influence the way others think or act, and are exposed, in turn, to many efforts to influence us.

- Many different tactics for exerting social influence exist, but among the most frequently used are rational persuasion and consultation. Various pressure tactics are used less often.

- Many other tactics for exerting social influence exist; most of these are based on several basic principles: friendship/liking, consistency, scarcity, and reciprocity.

- Familiarity with these techniques can help entrepreneurs use them effectively themselves, and also protect themselves against these tactics when used by others.

- Stress refers to a pattern of emotional states and physiological reactions occurring in response to demands from many different events in our lives.

- Stress exerts adverse effects on health, task performance, and psychological well-being. Entrepreneurs, who are exposed to high levels of stress for prolonged periods of time, are clearly at risk for such effects.

- A number of steps are helpful in managing stress, including physical techniques, such as eating a healthy diet and getting into good physical shape; and behavioural techniques, such as avoiding excessive and unnecessary worry, taking short breaks away from stressful situations, and avoiding the tendency to magnify the adverse effects of setbacks or disappointment.

- Entrepreneurs can readily use these and many other techniques to manage stress, and so assure that they will survive in good health to enjoy the fruits of their labour.

Glossary

Affective Conflicts: Conflicts that involve a large emotional component rather than conflicts that emerge from incompatible interests or goals.

Calculus-Based Trust: Trust based on deterrence. When we expect that others will act in the ways they promise because they know they will be punished in some way for doing otherwise, we are demonstrating calculus-based trust.

Cognitive Conflict: Conflicts in which individuals become aware of contrasting perspectives or interests, but focus on the issues and not on one another.

Conflict: A process in which one party perceives that another party has taken or will take actions that are incompatible with its interests.

Identification-Based Trust: Trust based on the belief that others will behave as they promise to behave, not because they will be punished for failing to do so, but because they have the trusting person's well-being at heart.

Negotiation: A process in which opposing sides exchange offers, counteroffers, and concessions, either directly or through representatives.

Organizational Citizenship Behaviours: Employee behaviours that go beyond the role requirements of their jobs and that are not directly or explicitly recognized by formal reward systems.

Social Capital: An important resource that derives from relationships among individuals in organizations or other social structures. Social capital involves close interpersonal relationships among individuals, characterized by mutual trust, liking, and identification.

Social Competence: A summary term for an individual's overall level of social skills.

Social Skills: A set of competencies (discrete skills) that enable individuals to interact effectively with others.

Stress: A pattern of emotional states and physiological reactions occurring in response to demands from many different events in our lives.

Trust: One person's degree of confidence in the words and actions of another person—confidence that this person will generally behave in predictable ways that are understandable in terms of the relationship between them.

Win-Win Solution: A solution that is acceptable to both sides and that meets the basic needs of both.

Discussion Questions

1. If you had to choose between having excellent people skills and having a truly great product or service (versus a mediocre one), which would you prefer?

2. If people can readily acquire improved social skills, why don't they make the effort to do so? How can they enhance their own social skills?

3. Trust between cofounders of a new venture is often essential to the venture's success. Suppose that for some reason, one of the cofounders loses her or his trust in another cofounder. Can such trust ever be restored? How?

4. Conflicts often start out as rational discussions over legitimate differences of opinion or perspective (cognitive conflict), but then shift quickly into angry disputes (affective conflict). How can this costly change be avoided?

5. Beginning with an extreme initial offer in negotiations can often lead to better outcomes for the person using this strategy; yet, we recommend against its use. What is the potential downside of using this tactic during negotiations?

6. After the CEO of Delta Airlines made his famous, insensitive remark about his reaction to laying off a large number of employees ("So be it."), he was faced with an immediate storm of anger from the company's employees. Was there anything he could have done to defuse this anger and save his own job?

7. What tactics of influence do you think are most useful to entrepreneurs when seeking financing for their companies? When attempting to build their customer base? Why?

8. Have you ever known any persons suffering from burnout? What were they like? Would you like to have them in your new venture?

InfoTrac Exercises

1. **Employee Conflicts Can't Be Ignored** (conflict resolution)

   HR Briefing, April 15, 2003 p7(1)

   Record: A99983489

   Full Text: COPYRIGHT 2003 Aspen Publishers, Inc.

   1. According to the text, what types of conflicts are easiest to resolve and why?
   2. According to the article, how can managers begin to hold employees accountable for their part in conflicts?
   3. What steps can managers take to begin to resolve conflicts?

2. **How to Sell an Idea**

   Ted Pollock

   Supervision, June 2003 v64 i6 p15(2)

   Record: A102677212

   Full Text: COPYRIGHT 2003

   1. Why do some people have a hard time selling their ideas?
   2. What steps can you take to show others that your idea has merits?
   3. What steps can you take to ensure you're communicating an idea most effectively?

GETTING DOWN
TO BUSINESS

Assessing Your Own Social Competence

Good social skills are a major plus for everyone, but they are especially important for entrepreneurs, who must interact with a large number of persons they did not know before starting their new venture. How do you rate with respect to social skills? To find out, ask at least five friends to rate you on each of the following dimensions. They should use the following scale for their ratings: 1 = very low, 2 = low, 3 = average, 4 = high, 5 = very high. They should place their ratings in the space before each dimension.

_____ **Social perception:** The ability to read other persons accurately.

_____ **Expressiveness:** The ability to express emotions clearly, so that other people can readily recognize them.

_____ **Skill at influencing others:** The ability to change others' views or behaviour in desired directions.

_____ **Impression management:** The ability to make a good first impression on others.

_____ **Social adaptability:** The ability to adapt to, and feel comfortable in, any social situation.

Next, average the ratings your friends have provided. Dimensions on which you scored lower than 3 are areas where you have room for improvement. How can you enhance these skills? It is best to seek the help of a professional—for instance, a psychologist who specializes in improving social skills—but you can at least get started by viewing videotapes of yourself as you interact with other people. These tapes will probably contain some major surprises, because most of us are not very good at recognizing how we come across to others. These surprises, in turn, may suggest specific things you can do to improve. For instance, if you are low in expressiveness, you can practise being more open in terms of expressing your feelings. Similarly, if you seem nervous on the tapes (e.g., if you fidget), you can work on changing these behaviours. Improving your own social skills is a challenging task, and one that takes time, but the potential benefits are so great that it is definitely worth the effort.

Don't Worry... Be Happy!

Here's a saying we like very much: "Worry is interest paid on problems in advance." Although this is not always true—there are things worth worrying about—research findings indicate that more than 80 percent of the topics or issues people worry about are ones they should probably not be worrying about. Excessive worry generates high levels of stress, which can be harmful to personal health.

To find out whether you are worrying too much, list all the things you worry about on a sheet of paper. Then, place each of these items in one of the following four quadrants.

	Things That Are Unimportant	**Things That Are Important**
Things I Can Control		
Things I Cannot Control		

What should you be worrying about? Rationally, only items that fit into the upper-right hand quadrant—ones that are both important *and* at least partly under your control. If you are worrying about items in the other three quadrants, it is time for a change; you are indeed worrying too much!

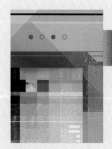

Enhanced Learning

You may select any combination of the resources below to enhance your understanding of the chapter material.

- **Appendix: Case Studies** – Twelve cases provide opportunities to apply chapter concepts to realistic entrepreneurial situations. These brief cases call for careful analysis of real business problems and ask you to think about potential solutions.
- **Video Case Library** – Nine cases are tied directly to video segments from the popular PBS television series Small Business School. These cases and video segments (available on the Entrepreneurship website at http://www.entrepreneurship.nelson.com) give you unparalleled access to today's entrepreneurs, with expert advice and insights on how to start, run, and grow a business.
- **Management Interview Series Video Database** – This video interview series contains a wealth of tips on how to manage effectively. Access to the database and practical exercises are available on the book support website at http://www.entrepreneurship.nelson.com.

Notes

1   Nahapiet, J., & Ghoshal, S. 1998. Social capital, intellectual capital, and the organizational advantage. *Academy of Management Review* 23(2): 242–266.

2   Erikson, T. 2002. Entrepreneurial capital: The emerging venture's most important asset and competitive advantage. *Journal of Business Venturing* 17(3): 275–290.

3   Baron, R.A. 2000. Psychological perspectives on entrepreneurship: Cognitive and social factors in entrepreneurs' success. *Current Directions in Psychological Science* 9(1): 15–18.

4   Frese, M. 1985. Stress at work and psychosomatic complaints: A causal interpretation. *Journal of Applied Psychology* 70(2): 314–328.

5   Weber, A.L., & Harvey, J.H. (eds.). 1994. *Perspectives on close relationships*. Boston: Allyn & Bacon.

6   Nahapiet, J., & Ghoshal, S. 1998. Social capital, intellectual capital, and the organizational advantage. *Academy of Management Review* 23(2): 242–266.

7   Eder, R.W., & Ferris, G.R. (eds). 1989. *The employment interview*. Newsbury Park, CA: Sage.

8   Heneman, R.L., Greenberger, D.B., & Anonyuo, C. 1989. Attributions and exchanges: The effects of interpersonal factors on the diagnosis of employee performance. *Academy of Management Journal* 32(2): 466–476.

9   Carter, N.M, Gartner, W.B., & Reynolds, P.D. 1996. Exploring start-up event sequences. *Journal of Business Venturing* 11(3): 151–166.

10 Thompson, L. 1998. *The mind and heart of the negotiator*. Upper Saddle River, NJ: Prentice-Hall.

11 Friedman, H.S., Riggio, R.E., & Casella, D.F. 1988. Nonverbal skills, personal charisma, and initial attraction. *Personality and Social Psychology Bulletin* 14(1): 203–211.

12 Friedman, H.S., Prince, L.M., Riggio, R.E., & DiMatteo, M.R. 1980. Understanding and assessing nonverbal expressiveness: The affective communications test. *Journal of Personality and Social Psychology* 39(2): 333–351.

13 Stevens, C.K., & Kristof, A.L. 1995. Making the right impression: A field study of applicant impression management during job interviews. *Journal of Applied Psychology* 80(5): 587–606.

14 Giacalone, R.A., & Rosenfeld, P. 1989. *Impression management in the organization*. Hillsdale, NJ: Lawrence Erlbaum Associates.

15 Hall, J., & Hofer, C.W. 1993. Venture capitalists' decision criteria in new venture evaluation. *Journal of Business Venturing* 8(1): 25–42.

16 Zacharakis, A.L., & Meyer, G.D. 1995. The venture capitalist decision: Understanding process versus outcome. In J. Hornaday, F. Tarpley, J. Timmons, & K. Vesper (eds.). *Frontiers of entrepreneurship research* (pp. 115–123). Wellesley, MA: Babson Center for Entrepreneurial Research.

17 Wayne, S.J., & Ferris, G.R. 1990. Influence tactics and exchange quality in supervisor-subordinate interactions: A laboratory experiment and field study. *Journal of Applied Psychology* 75(5): 487–499.

18 Kilduff, M., & Day, D.V. 1994. Do chameleons get ahead? The effects of self-monitoring on managerial careers. *Academy of Management Journal* 37(4): 1047–1060.

19 Baron, R.A., & Byrne, D. 2002. *Social psychology*. 10th ed. Boston: Allyn & Bacon.

20 Baron, R.A., & Markman, G.D. 2003. Beyond social capital: The role of entrepreneurs' social competence in their financial success. *Journal of Business Venturing* 18(1): 41–60.

21 Leana, C.R., & Van Buren, H.J. 1999. Organizational social capital and employment practices. *Academy of Management Review* 24(3): 538–555.

22 Lewicki, R.J., & Wiethoff, C. 2000. Trust, trust development, and trust repair. In M. Deutsch & P. T. Coleman (eds.). *The handbook of conflict resolution* (pp. 86–107). San Francisco: Jossey-Bass.

23 Podsakoff, P.M., MacKenzie, S.B., Paine, J.B., & Bachrach, D.G. 2000. Organizational citizenship behaviors: A critical review of the theoretical and empirical literature and suggestions for future research. *Journal of Management* 26(3): 513–563.

24 Amason, A.C., & Sapienza, H.J. 1997. The effects of top management team size and interaction norms on cognitive and affective conflict. *Journal of Management* 23(4): 495–516.

25 Ensley, M.D., Pearson, A.W., & Amason, A.C. 2002. Understanding the dynamics of new venture top management teams' cohesion, conflict, and new venture performance. *Journal of Business Venturing* 17(4): 365–386.

26 Thompson, L. 1998. *The mind and heart of the negotiator*. Upper Saddle River, NJ: Prentice-Hall.

27 Baron, R.A. 1988. Attributions and organizational conflict: The mediating role of apparent sincerity. *Organizational Behavior & Human Decision Processes* 41(1): 111–127.

28 Baron, R.A. 1989. Personality and organizational conflict: The Type A behavior pattern and self-monitoring. *Organizational Behavior and Human Decision Processes* 44(2): 291–208.

29 Begley, T., & Boyd, D. 1987. A comparison of entrepreneurs and managers of small business firms. *Journal of Management* 13(1): 99–108

30 Leana, C.R., & Van Buren, H.J. 1999. Organizational social capital and employment practices. *Academy of Management Review* 24(3): 538–555.

31 Yukl, G., & Tracey, J.B. 1992. Consequences of influence tactics used with subordinates, peers, and the boss. *Journal of Applied Psychology* 77(4): 525–535.

32 Yukl, G., Falbe, C.M., & Youn, J.Y. 1993. Patterns of influence behavior for managers. *Group & Organization Management* 18(1): 5–28.

33 Gartner, W.B., Bird, B.J., & Starr, J.A. 1992. Acting as if: Differentiating entrepreneurial from organizational behavior. *Entrepreneurship Theory and Practice* 16(3): 13–32.

34 Baum, J.R., Locke, E.A., & Kirkpatrick, S. 1998. A longitudinal study of the relation of vision and vision communication to venture growth in entrepreneurial firms. *Journal of Applied Psychology* 83(1): 43–54.

35 Cialdini, R.B. 1994. Interpersonal influence. In S. Shavitt & T.C. Brock (eds.). *Persuasion* (pp. 195–218). Boston: Allyn & Bacon.

36 Diochon, M., Menzies, T.V., & Gasse, Y. 2005. Canadian nascent entrepreneurs' start-up efforts: Outcomes and individual influences on sustainability. *Journal of Small Business and Entrepreneurship* 18(1): 53–74.

37 Tal, B. 2005. For love or money? A study of entrepreneurship in Canada. *CIBC World Markets*, October 11, 2005. http://research.cibcwm.com/economic_public/download/sb-flom-10112005.pdf.

38 Cohen, S., & Williamson, G.M. 1991. Stress and infectious disease in humans. *Psychological Bulletin* 109(1): 5–24.

39 Motowidlo, S.J., Packard, J.S., & Manning, M.R. 1986. Occupational stress: Its causes and consequences for job performance. *Journal of Applied Psychology* 71(4): 618–629.

40 Desk Rage. 2000. *Business Week*, November 27: 12.

41 Maslach, C. 1982. *Burnout: The cost of caring.* Englewood Cliffs, NJ: Prentice-Hall.

42 Gaines, J., & Jermier, J.M. 1983. Emotional exhaustion in high stress organizations. *Academy of Management Journal* 26(4): 567–586.

43 Brown, J.D. 1991. Staying fit and staying well: Physical fitness as a moderator of life stress. *Journal of Personality and Social Psychology* 60(4): 555–561.

PART 2

ASSEMBLING THE RESOURCES

It is one thing to have an idea for a new product or service, but quite another to turn it into an actual new venture. In this section, we describe the resources needed to actually launch a new company: managerial resources—the people whose skills, knowledge, motivation, and energy will provide the forward momentum of the new venture; financial resources—the capital needed to launch the business; intellectual property protection—the assets that help to protect your ideas against imitation; and the business plan—which helps entrepreneurs plan their venture goals and strategies and obtain support from potential stakeholders.

ALL PHOTOS THIS PAGE © PHOTODISC, INC.

CHAPTER 5

ESTABLISHING AN EFFECTIVE MANAGEMENT TEAM

LEARNING OBJECTIVES

After reading this chapter, you should be able to:

1 Explain the difference between similarity and complementarity and the relevance of these concepts to the task of choosing cofounders in a new venture.

2 Explain why entrepreneurs should conduct a careful self-assessment as part of the process of choosing potential cofounders.

3 Define "impression management" and describe various tactics used by individuals for this purpose.

4 Define "self-serving bias" and explain how it plays an important role in perceived fairness.

5 Explain the difference between constructive and destructive criticism.

6 Describe sources of error in the interpretation of information by decision-making groups. Be sure to include early favourites, group polarization, and groupthink.

7 Describe various techniques for countering the effects of these sources of error.

All photos this page © PhotoDisc, Inc.

"Union may be strength, but it is mere blind brute strength unless wisely directed." (Samuel Butler, 1882)

Although the popular view of entrepreneurs suggests that they are loners—energetic and creative people who prefer to do things in their own, unique way—most new ventures (more than two-thirds) are actually started by teams of entrepreneurs working closely together.[1] This news is not surprising: Cooperation and teamwork often allow individuals to accomplish tasks they could never accomplish alone. The fact that many entrepreneurs choose to work with cofounders, however, raises an intriguing question: Is the whole greater than the sum of its parts in this context, as it is in many others? In other words, are new ventures started by teams of entrepreneurs more successful than those started by individuals? Although no definite answer to this question currently exists, we agree with Samuel Butler, whose quotation suggests that teams are indeed a plus, but only when the persons involved work together wisely—and well. This view, in turn, implies that two tasks are crucial for entrepreneurs who decide to work with others (cofounders) to convert their ideas into reality. First, they must choose these persons carefully, selecting cofounders who will help them to reach their goals. Second, they must work effectively with these people so that the potential benefits of teamwork can actually be obtained.

Clearly, it is much easier to state these goals than to attain them. Choosing excellent cofounders and developing good working relationships with them are complex tasks requiring considerable effort. In our view, this is effort well spent because the success of any new venture depends, to an important degree, on the human resources it assembles—the knowledge, skills, talents, abilities, reputations, and social networks of its cofounders, plus those brought to it by initial, early employees. Research findings indicate that these and related factors play an important role in the launch and success of new ventures.[2] How, then, can these important tasks be performed effectively? How can entrepreneurs assemble the managerial resources needed to launch a successful new venture? These questions are the central focus of this chapter; in order to answer them in a useful way, we will consider four closely related topics.

First, we will examine the issue of complementarity versus similarity: Should entrepreneurs choose cofounders who are similar to themselves in various respects or those who are different in complementary ways, providing what the entrepreneurs themselves lack in terms of knowledge, skills, or abilities? As we will note later in this discussion, both similarity and complementarity offer advantages, but we believe that emphasizing complementarity may, in many instances, be a better strategy because it provides new ventures with a strong and diverse base of human resources. In any case, the process of choosing appropriate cofounders should certainly start with a careful self-assessment by prospective entrepreneurs. The reason for this requirement can be stated simply: In a very real sense, it is impossible for entrepreneurs to know what they should look for in cofounders unless the entrepreneurs know what they already have.

After considering why and how entrepreneurs should engage in careful self-assessment, we will turn to the task of actually choosing cofounders. This task requires skill in assessing others accurately and is far trickier than you might at first imagine. Most people are quite adept at managing their image and appearing to be what they are not, so being able to cut through such tactics is a skill worth developing. (In fact, this is a theme that we will be concerned about throughout this book. We will return to this topic in Chapter 11, where we explain why entrepreneurs often franchise their businesses to avoid dealing with employees who misrepresent their abilities.)

Third, we will turn to the issue of establishing effective working relationships with cofounders and new employees. This task requires such preliminary steps as a clear division of roles and obligations, plus careful attention to basic principles of fairness and effective communication.

Finally, we will close with a brief discussion of group decision making. We will examine how groups interpret facts and information. As you'll soon see, performing this task is neither simple nor straightforward because there are many factors that influence—and sometimes strongly distort—the accurate interpretation of information, and the decisions based on such interpretation. We will examine several of the most important of these factors and suggest ways of minimizing the dangers they pose.

If these four issues are managed effectively, a new venture can begin life with the pool of managerial resources it needs to grow and prosper; if, instead, these issues are *not* managed effectively, a new venture may begin with serious handicaps—from which it may never be able to recover.

SIMILARITY VERSUS COMPLEMENTARITY: "KNOW THYSELF" REVISITED

LEARNING OBJECTIVE

1 Explain the difference between similarity and complementarity and the relevance of these concepts to the task of choosing cofounders in a new venture.

It is a basic fact of life that people feel most comfortable with, and tend to like, others who are similar to themselves in various ways. In fact, a very large body of research evidence points to two intriguing conclusions regarding the appeal of similarity: (1) almost any kind of similarity will do—similarity with respect to attitudes and values; demographic factors, such as age, gender, occupation, or ethnic background; shared interests—almost anything; and (2) such effects are both general and strong. For instance, similarity has been found to influence the outcome of employment interviews and performance ratings: In general, the more similar job applicants are to the persons who interview them, the more likely they are to be hired. Correspondingly, the more similar employees are to their managers, the higher the ratings they receive from them.[3] You can probably guess why similarity is so appealing: When people are alike on various dimensions, they are more comfortable in each other's presence, feel that they know each other better, and are more confident that they will be able to predict each others' future reactions and behaviour. In short, everything else being equal, we tend to associate with, choose as friends or cofounders, and even marry people who are similar to ourselves in many respects.

Entrepreneurs are definitely no exception to this similarity-leads-to-liking rule. In fact, most tend to select people whose background, training, and experience is highly similar to their own. This is far from surprising: People from similar backgrounds speak the same language—they can converse more readily and smoothly than persons from very different backgrounds. Often, they already know one another because they have attended the same schools or worked for the same companies. The overall result is that many new ventures are started by teams of entrepreneurs from the same fields or occupations: Engineers tend to work with engineers; entrepreneurs with a marketing or sales background tend to work with others from these fields; scientists tend to work with other scientists, and so on (see Figure 5.1).

In one sense, similarity can be an important plus: As we will note in a later section, effective communication is a key ingredient in good working relations, so the fact that birds of a feather tend to flock together in starting new ventures offers obvious advantages. On the other hand, however, the tendency for entrepreneurs to choose cofounders whose background and training are highly similar to their own has several serious drawbacks. The most important of these disadvantages centres around redundancy: The more similar people are, the greater the degree to which their knowledge, training, skills, and aptitudes overlap. For instance, consider a group of engineers who start a company to develop a new product. All have technical expertise, which is extremely useful in terms of designing a product that actually works. But because they are all engineers, they have little knowledge about marketing, legal matters, or regulations concerning employees' health and safety. Further, they may know very little about writing an effective business

Figure 5.1 Similarity in Founding Teams of Entrepreneurs

Because people find it more pleasant and comfortable to work with others who are similar to themselves, teams of entrepreneurs often consist of persons with similar background, training, and experience. This tendency can be detrimental to the success of the new ventures they found.

Jupiter Images

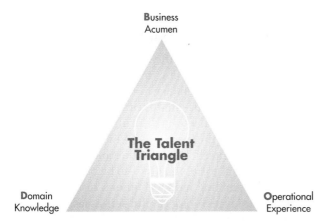

Figure 5.2 The Talent Triangle
Successful founding teams need business acumen, operational experience, and domain knowledge.

plan, which, as we will see in Chapter 8, is often crucial for obtaining required financial resources and determining how to operate a company effectively. Moreover, although all of them have excellent quantitative skills, they are not proficient at preparing written documents or in selling their ideas; as is often the case with persons from a technical or scientific background, they are better with numbers than words. Further, because all were trained in the same field (and may even have studied at the same school), they have overlapping social networks: They tend to know the same people and, hence, have a limited range of contacts from whom they can obtain needed resources—information, financial support, and so on.

By now the main point should be clear: What this particular team of entrepreneurs—or any other group—needs for success is a very wide range of information, skills, aptitudes, and abilities. This diversity is less likely to be present when all members of the founding team are highly similar to one another in important ways. Ideally, what one team member lacks one or more others can provide so that, as the quote offered at the start of this chapter suggests, the whole is indeed greater than the sum of its parts because the team can pool its knowledge and expertise. Rule number one for entrepreneurs in assembling their founding teams, then, is this: *Don't yield to the temptation to work solely with people whose background, training, and experience are highly similar to your own. Doing so will be easy and pleasant in many ways but it will* not *provide the rich foundation of human resources the new venture needs.*

According to Sean Wise, Managing Director of Ernst & Young's Entrepreneurial Business Centre in Toronto, strong founding teams exhibit business acumen, operational experience, and domain knowledge (see Figure 5.2),[4] Someone with business acumen may not have industry-specific experience, but contributes skill and experience in managing companies: making sound human resources decisions, dealing with investors, and developing growth strategies. Another person with operational experience brings skill and experience in executing plans; for example, setting up distribution channels, implementing information technology, and managing cash flow. Finally, someone with domain knowledge is needed for an in-depth knowledge of the industry and its players and an understanding of how the new firm's value proposition can meet or exceed customer expectations.

KEY POINTS

- In general, people tend to like, and feel more comfortable around, persons who are similar to themselves in various ways.
- This tendency leads entrepreneurs to select cofounders whose background, training, and experience closely match their own.
- Because a wide range of knowledge, skills, and experience among the founding team is advantageous to new ventures, selecting cofounders on the basis of complementarity rather than similarity is often a more useful strategy.
  The strongest founding teams have business acumen, operational experience, and domain knowledge.

Jupiter Images

Figure 5.3 Self-Reflection Does Not Always Equal Self-Knowledge

We cannot determine many of our most important abilities or traits directly, through self-reflection. Rather, we can only gain such information from other persons, whose reactions provide us with valuable insights into our relative standing on many important dimensions (e.g., intelligence, energy, charm, talent, etc.).

LEARNING OBJECTIVE

2 Explain why entrepreneurs should conduct a careful self-assessment as part of the process of choosing potential cofounders.

Self-Assessment: Knowing What You Have Helps Determine What You Need

Now that we have clarified the dangers associated with the potential downside of choosing to work exclusively with cofounders similar to oneself, we will take a step back and briefly examine a related issue: the importance in this process of an accurate self-assessment. As we noted earlier, it is difficult, if not impossible, to know what you need from prospective cofounders without first understanding what you, yourself, bring to the table. For this reason, a crucial initial step for all entrepreneurs—to be performed *before* beginning the task of assembling required human resources (cofounders or additional employees)—is a careful **self-assessment**, an inventory of the knowledge, experience, training, motives, and characteristics the entrepreneur possesses and can contribute to the new venture.

Self-assessment is far from a simple task: The dictum "Know thyself" sounds straightforward, but in reality, it is exceedingly difficult to put into actual practice for two major reasons. First, we are often unaware of at least some of the factors that affect our behaviour. The powerful effect of similarity is a prime example of this fact. Often, people are drawn to others, including prospective cofounders, because of subtle similarities—they are alike in various ways but are not fully aware of these similarities.

In short, they know that they like each other and find it pleasant to work together, but don't really know why. To the extent we are unaware of the factors that influence our behaviour and reactions, the task of knowing ourselves becomes complex.

Second, and perhaps even more important, we do not gain knowledge of our major traits, abilities, or even attitudes directly, through self-reflection. Rather, we gradually gain insight into these important aspects of ourselves through our relations with other persons. Only they—and their reactions to us—can tell us how intelligent, energetic, charming, or well-informed about various topics we are. There are no direct physical measures of these and many other attributes, so we have to gather them, gradually, from what other people tell us, directly or indirectly (see Figure 5.3).

Although acquiring clear self-knowledge is a complex task, we can perform it quite well—if we take the trouble to do so. There are concrete steps you, as a prospective entrepreneur, can take to develop an accurate view of your own human capital—the resources you bring to any new venture you choose to launch. You can complete several key portions of this personal inventory yourself, but for others, you will need the help of people who know you well—and hence, can provide insights you can't readily acquire alone. Remember: The reason for engaging in this activity is to understand what you already have—your own human capital—so that you can determine what you need from other persons, including potential cofounders.

- *Knowledge base.* This is a good place to begin, because it is something you can do alone. Ask yourself the following questions: "What do I know?" "What information and knowledge do I bring to the new venture?" Here, your education and experience are directly relevant and can suggest what you know and what you don't know; and therefore, what you need to acquire from others, including potential cofounders.

- *Specific skills.* Quite apart from your knowledge base are specific skills—proficiencies that enable you to perform certain tasks well. Are you very good with numbers? Adept at making oral presentations? Good with people? Everyone has a unique set of skills, and you should try to understand—and inventory—yours as a preliminary step in developing your new venture.

- *Motives.* This step is more difficult, but also quite important. Why do you want to start a new venture? Because you like a challenge? Because you fervently believe in your new product? To earn a huge fortune? To escape from corporate life and become self-employed? You can hold all of these motives at the same time, but it is useful to ponder their relative importance to you because if your personal motives do not match those of potential cofounders, you may be laying the foundation for serious future problems.

- *Commitment.* This focus is related to motivation, but not identical to it. Commitment refers to the desire to seeing things through—to continue even in the face of adversity—and to reach your personal goals relating to the new venture (e.g., the objectives listed under motives). Recent findings indicate that commitment is an important factor in new venture success.[5]

- *Personal attributes.* Here is where you will need help from other persons because only they can tell you where you stand on a number of key dimensions. Human beings differ along a tremendous number of dimensions, but in recent years, it has become increasingly clear that five personal attributes are the most central, and most relevant in business contexts. These are known as the **Big Five dimensions of personality**,[6] and growing evidence suggests two important facts about them: They are indeed central—in fact, they are so basic that where a person stands on these dimensions is usually apparent even after knowing a person for only a few minutes; and these dimensions of personality are indeed strongly related to many aspects of behaviour in business settings, including job performance.[7] What are these dimensions? Briefly, they can be described as follows:

  - *Conscientiousness.* The extent to which individuals are hardworking, organized, dependable, and persevering versus sluggish, disorganized, and unreliable.

  - *Extraversion-introversion.* The degree to which individuals are gregarious, assertive, and sociable versus being reserved, timid, and quiet.

  - *Agreeableness.* The extent to which individuals are cooperative, courteous, trusting, and agreeable versus uncooperative, disagreeable, and belligerent.

  - *Emotional stability.* The degree to which individuals are insecure, anxious, depressed, and emotional versus calm, self-confident, and secure.

  - *Openness to experience.* The extent to which individuals are creative, curious, and have wide-ranging interests versus practical and with narrow interests.

As we noted earlier, these dimensions are important. For instance, they have been found to be linked to work performance across a large number of occupations.[8] In general, conscientiousness shows the strongest association with task performance: The higher individuals are on this dimension, the higher their performance. Recent findings indicate that the higher entrepreneurs are in conscientiousness, the more likely are their new ventures to survive.[9] Emotional stability, too, is related to task performance, although not as strongly or consistently; again, the more emotionally stable individuals are, the better their performance.

Other dimensions of the big five are also linked to task performance, but in more specific ways. For instance, agreeableness and extraversion are both positively related to the interpersonal aspects of work (e.g., getting along well with others). Especially relevant to entrepreneurs is the fact that individuals' standing on several of the big five dimensions of personality is related to performance of the teams to which they belong.[10] Specifically, it has been found that the higher the average scores of team members on conscientiousness, agreeableness, extraversion, and emotional stability, the higher the teams' performances (as rated by managers). Finally, we should note that two of these dimensions—openness to experience and conscientiousness—are related to creativity and innovation.[11] Openness to experience seems to facilitate such behaviour while conscientiousness can reduce it.

How can you assess your own standing on these dimensions? Performing the Getting Down to Business exercise at the end of this chapter is a good start. By following the instructions in that exercise, you will gain helpful insights into where you stand on each of the big five dimensions. Your ratings, in turn, can help you determine what qualities you need in prospective cofounders. In general, conscientiousness and emotional stability are important pluses in almost any context. Further, people high in agreeableness are easier to get along with than people low on this dimension. Keeping these points in mind, you will probably want to choose cofounders who are high in these characteristics. But for other dimensions, complementarity may be worth considering. For instance, if you are high in extraversion and have good people skills, it is less crucial that your cofounders be high on this dimension, too; one good spokesperson may be all you need most of the time.

Similarity or Complementarity: A Final Word

So which should you seek in prospective team members, similarity or complementarity? The answer depends largely on the dimensions you are considering. Complementarity is very important with respect to knowledge, skills, and experience. In order to succeed, new ventures must acquire a rich and useful inventory of human resources. Choosing cofounders whose knowledge and experience complement your own can be very useful in attaining this important goal. On the other hand, similarity, too, offers benefits: It enhances ease of communication and facilitates good personal relationships. Similarity with respect to motives is very important: If the cofounders of a new venture have sharply contrasting motives or goals, conflict between them is almost certain to develop.

Over all then, we suggest a balanced approach: Focus primarily on complementarity with respect to knowledge, skills, and experience, but bring similarity into the picture with respect to personal characteristics and motives.[12] This strategy will provide good symmetry between acquiring the broad range of human resources new ventures require and establishing a good working environment in which all members of the founding team can work hard to convert their vision into reality.

Good luck with your personal inventory—and with the task of choosing excellent cofounders. As you proceed, keep the words of Lao-Tzu, a philosopher of ancient China, firmly in mind: "He who knows others is clever; He who knows himself has discernment."

KEY POINTS

- In order to choose cofounders who bring knowledge, skills, and attributes complementary their own, entrepreneurs must first conduct a careful self-assessment of their own human capital.
- This task is difficult because often we are unaware of the causes of our own behaviour and also because in many instances, we can acquire understanding of our own characteristics only from others' reactions to us.
- Entrepreneurs' self-assessment should carefully consider their knowledge base, specific skills, motives, and personal attributes (e.g., where they stand on each of the Big Five dimensions of personality).
- In choosing cofounders, it is often useful to focus on complementarity with respect to knowledge, skills, and experience, but on similarity with respect to personal characteristics and motives.

CHOOSING COFOUNDERS: MAXIMIZING THE NEW VENTURE'S MANAGERIAL RESOURCES

As we noted in the preceding section, it is considerably harder to "know thyself" than you might at first assume. With a little hard work, however, it is possible to formulate an accurate inventory of your own human capital—what you bring to the new venture in terms of knowledge, skills, experience, and personal characteristics.

This exercise, in turn, can help you determine what you need from other persons (e.g., cofounders, employees) in terms of these basic dimensions. Once you have drawn a bead on this issue, though, things do not necessarily get simpler, because knowing what you need is no guarantee that you will find it—or that you will recognize it when you do. Superb cofounders do not appear, conveniently, just when you need them. On the contrary, identifying such persons usually requires considerable work. Accomplishing this task is very worthwhile, because choosing badly can have disastrous consequences. (Please see the **Danger! Pitfall Ahead!** section below for further discussion of this issue.) These points raise an important, practical question: How should entrepreneurs go about selecting potential cofounders—what guidelines should they use in assembling the managerial resources required for their new ventures? Answering this question involves many activities, but perhaps most central among these is developing skill at what is known as **social perception**—the process through which we come to know and understand other persons.[13]

Social perception is a key task because unless we form accurate perceptions of others, it is impossible to determine whether, and to what extent, others offer the knowledge, skills, and characteristics we seek. For this reason, developing skill at this task is very useful for entrepreneurs. In fact, recent evidence indicates that entrepreneurs who are adept at social perception (ones who are good at perceiving others accurately) attain greater financial success than ones who are less proficient.[14]

Unfortunately, perceiving others accurately is more difficult than it sounds because other people do not always portray themselves accurately. On the contrary, they often seek to disguise their true feelings or motives and frequently seek to present themselves in a favourable light. If we accept these external masks at face value, we can be seriously misled. In order to perceive others accurately, therefore, we must learn to be adept at distinguishing reality from image where other people are concerned. In this respect, developing skill at dealing with two related issues—**impression management** and **deception**—is extremely useful.

Impression Management: The Fine Art of Looking Good—and How to Recognize It

At one time or another, virtually everyone engages in efforts to make a good first impression on others—to present themselves in a favourable light.[15] To accomplish this goal, individuals use a wide range of tactics. Most of these, however, fall into two major categories: *self-enhancement*—efforts to increase their appeal to others, and *other-enhancement*—efforts to make the target person feel good in various ways.

Specific strategies of self-enhancement include efforts to boost one's physical appearance through style of dress, personal grooming, and the use of various props (e.g., eyeglasses, which have been found to encourage impressions of intelligence; see Figure 5.4).[16] Additional tactics of self-enhancement involve efforts to appear highly skilled, or describing oneself in positive terms, for instance, explaining how daunting obstacles were overcome.

In other-enhancement, individuals use many different tactics to induce positive moods and reactions in others. A large body of research findings suggests that such reactions, in turn, play an important role in generating liking for the person responsible for them.[17] The most commonly used tactic of other-enhancement is flattery—making statements that praise the target person, his or her traits, accomplishments, or the organization with which the target person is associated.[18] Such tactics are often highly successful, provided they are not overdone. Additional tactics of other-enhancement involve expressing agreement with the target person's views, showing a high degree of interest in this person, doing small favours for them, asking for their advice and feedback in some manner, or expressing liking for them nonverbally (e.g., through high levels of eye contact, nodding in agreement, and smiling).[19]

These are not the only strategies people use; for instance, individuals sometimes employ intimidation—pretending to be dangerous or angry in order to wring concessions from others. This tactic does not generate positive reactions

LEARNING OBJECTIVE

3   Define "impression management" and describe various tactics used by individuals for this purpose.

© Getty Images/PhotoDisc

Figure 5.4 Impression Management in Action

At one time or other, almost everyone engages in impression management—efforts to present themselves in a favourable light. To accomplish this goal, people use many different tactics. Careful grooming—which is often effective—is just one of these tactics.

toward the people using it, but it does often produce the results they desire. Have you ever known anyone who relies on this approach? Such persons are far from rare, and they often enter meetings with an approach suggesting: "I'm mad as hell and am not going take anymore!" If this tactic is recognized for what it is, its impact is reduced; but it does work well in many situations, at least for some persons.[20]

Do other tactics of impression management, too, actually succeed? The answer, provided by a growing body of literature, is clear: *yes*, provided they are used with skill and care. For example, one large-scale study involving more than 1,400 employees found that social skills (including impression management) were the single best predictor of job performance ratings and assessments of potential for promotion for employees in a wide range of jobs.[21] Overall, then, it appears that impression management tactics often do enhance the appeal of persons who use them effectively. The use of these tactics, however, involves potential pitfalls: If such tactics are overused, or used ineffectively, they can backfire and produce negative rather than positive reactions from others. For instance, people often form very negative impressions of others who play up to their superiors, but treat subordinates with disdain and contempt—sometimes known as the *slime effect*.[22] The moral of these findings is clear: Although tactics of impression management often succeed, sometimes they can boomerang, adversely affecting reactions to the persons who use them.

By now, it should be obvious that being able to cut through these various tactics of impression management is very important for prospective entrepreneurs engaged in the task of choosing prospective cofounders and initial employees. Accepting others' statements about their skills, experience, and past accomplishments without *due diligence* (carefully checking on the accuracy of such information) can lead entrepreneurs to form inflated views of the persons using such tactics. Similarly, failing to recognize flattery, exaggerated agreement or similarity, and related tactics can lead entrepreneurs to go with their hearts instead of their heads when assembling the initial team for their new venture. Developing the ability to recognize such tactics when they are used requires considerable practice, but simply calling them to your attention is useful, because some research findings indicate that where impression management is concerned, "to be forewarned is to be forearmed."

Certainly, we are not suggesting that you adopt a cynical approach to other persons—that, too, can be harmful—however, accepting the information or outward façade presented by strangers without due diligence is not only naïve but it can be very costly to the fortunes of a new venture. As Peter Dunley, a humorist of the early 20th century put it, "Trust everybody, but cut the cards." (For a discussion of this important issue, see the **Danger! Pitfall Ahead!** section.)

What about the use of deception by entrepreneurs? Is this ever justified? Ethically, the answer is clear: *No!* Intentionally misleading others by withholding information or providing false information is contrary to widely accepted standards of business ethics.[23] But it is clear that some unscrupulous persons, representing themselves as entrepreneurs, do engage in deceptive practices.

Recently, business fraud has become a serious problem for e-tailers—companies that sell their products or services on the Internet. These entrepreneurs are currently being hit with a double whammy—not only is the economy weak, but there is also growing concern among consumers about deception on the Internet. Newspapers and TV news shows have recently carried many reports of cases in which online shoppers' credit card numbers have been hijacked, or in which unsuspecting shoppers have been the victims of bait and switch: They order and pay for one item, but receive another of much lower quality. Clearly, the persons who engage in such practices are not entrepreneurs: They are criminals. But there is a danger that their unscrupulous actions will reflect negatively on legitimate e-tailers. So far, there has been no large-scale defection from e-commerce sites, but since fraud is even harder to detect on computers than in person, only time will tell whether this problem will have a long-term chilling effect on new ventures that do the bulk of their business on the Web.

DANGER! PITFALL AHEAD!

The Partner Who Wasn't What He Claimed: When Social Perception Fails

In 1991, I (Robert Baron) became an entrepreneur. I had an idea for a new product (the air cleaner I described in Chapter 1) and believed that it might well have a substantial market. I realized that I did not have the knowledge and experience I needed to develop this opportunity alone, so I immediately launched efforts to identify one or more appropriate cofounders. Friends urged me to talk to the director of my university's technology park because he might be a good source of contacts. He directed me to a group of entrepreneurs running a small company that manufactured air cleaners. All of them claimed to have a lot of expertise with respect to design, manufacturing, and intellectual property rights—just what my self-assessment told me I needed most. So I entered into an agreement with one of them to start a new company and begin the process of seeking a patent for my invention. Why did I choose this particular person? Mainly because I liked his candour—he seemed very down-to-earth—and because I thought that he could provide just what I needed most. Not only did he claim to have had lots experience in product design and manufacturing, but he had also run his own marketing company. That seemed just about perfect, so we moved ahead with our plans to found a new venture.

We agreed that in this venture, I would put up the needed funds to get the patent, so he would be a junior partner, holding about 20 percent of the shares. Because he had already helped me to design the new product, we applied for the patent jointly, as co-inventors. We received the patent, and that's when my major surprises began. It soon became clear that my new partner knew much less about manufacturing than he originally claimed. In fact, he did not really have a clue as to the costs involved in manufacturing our product. When these costs turned out to be more than $2 million, we decided to license our technology to a large company rather than try to make the product ourselves. We divided our duties in the new venture very clearly: I would deal with our corporate partner and focus on building markets for our product, while my cofounder would run the day-to-day operations. But all too soon it became obvious that he either would not, or could not, handle these tasks. Our phones went unanswered (we were doing considerable business in direct sales to consumers), our financial records were a mess, and shipments of our product were painfully slow—if they happened at all. Gradually, I had to take over all these activities. The final result was that I ended up running the entire show—but sharing the profits with my partner, who often complained about the pitiful return he was getting for his valuable time!

Truly, I learned some painful lessons from these events, and when our agreement with the manufacturer expired, I told my partner that I could not continue and wanted to dissolve the company. He agreed, and that was the end of our working relationship. Looking back, I can see that although I did a fairly good self-assessment and understood what I needed from a cofounder, I then proceeded to make every mistake in the book. I did not do appropriate due diligence, did not try to separate verbal claims from reality, and did not try to determine when I was receiving the truth and when I was not. Don't misunderstand: I don't think my former partner harboured evil intentions toward me; on the contrary, I think that he was basically honest, but was lacking in self-knowledge and was seriously confused about what he could supply to our new venture. Still, I would have saved myself a lot of personal grief if I had followed the advice presented in earlier sections of this chapter. Will I do better the next time? Absolutely! After all, I don't see how I could do much worse!

Putting such instances of outright fraud aside, it is important to note that in order to assemble the resources they need (financial and otherwise), entrepreneurs—even those who are 100 percent legitimate—sometimes do stretch the truth to a degree. Often, this fabrication of the truth takes the form of expressing greater optimism about their new ventures than current facts merit. Convincing others to get on board in one way or another is a challenging task and sometimes requires emphasizing the upside while minimizing the downside. In a sense, then, entrepreneurs must often walk a fine line between enthusiasm and optimism on the one hand, and intentional misrepresentations on the other. This balancing act is a difficult task, but one the founders of new ventures should approach with care; as one venture capitalist recently told us, "I try to balance sincerity against trust. If entrepreneurs are being super-optimistic, I don't mind, as long as I think, they are also sincere. If I think they are trying to mislead me, though, trust flies out the window and the game is over as far as I'm concerned."

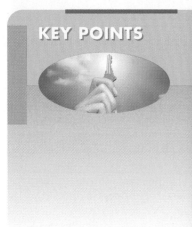

KEY POINTS

- In order to choose excellent cofounders, entrepreneurs must perform the task of social perception well—they must form accurate perceptions of other persons.
- Social perception is often a difficult task, because others do not always portray themselves accurately. They often engage in impression management—various tactics designed to place them in a favourable light. Entrepreneurs should take careful note of these tactics when choosing cofounders and should carefully check claims and information provided to them by these persons.
- Entrepreneurs often confront deception—efforts by others to actively mislead them.
- Although they are sometimes tempted to do so, entrepreneurs should avoid engaging in deception themselves. This practice is unethical and will ultimately undermine trust in the entrepreneurs and their new ventures.
- If entrepreneurs do not choose cofounders carefully, they can experience disastrous results—as one of the authors did in connection with his own start-up company.

UTILIZING THE NEW VENTURE'S MANAGERIAL RESOURCES: BUILDING STRONG WORKING RELATIONSHIPS AMONG THE FOUNDING TEAM

Assembling the resources needed to perform a task is an essential first step; indeed, there is no sense in starting unless the required resources are available or easily obtained on the fly. But it is only the beginning; the task itself must then be performed. The same principle holds true for new ventures: Assembling the necessary managerial resources—an appropriate pool of knowledge, experience, skills, and abilities—is only the beginning. The people who constitute the founding team must then work together in an effective manner if the new venture is to succeed. Unfortunately, this key point is often overlooked, or at least given very little attention, by new entrepreneurs. They are so focused on the opportunity they have identified and wish to develop that they pay scant attention to building strong working relationships with one another—working relationships that will permit the new venture to utilize its human resources to the fullest. Growing evidence suggests that such relationships are an essential ingredient in new ventures' success.[24] For instance, in one recent study of 70 new ventures, higher levels of cohesion among the founding team (positive feelings toward one another) were strongly associated with superior financial performance by these new ventures.[25] As another example, consider the case of a young Canadian firm entering foreign markets. Although internationalization can bring about exciting opportunities for growth, entering foreign markets can be difficult to manage: there are likely to be cultural and linguistic differences to become accustomed to, regulatory constraints and paperwork to deal with, and higher product-market costs to fund. Professor Eileen Fischer of York University and I (Becky Reuber) studied the internationalization of almost 200 young Canadian food-processing and software product firms and found that the integration of the top management team made a difference to the effectiveness of the firm's internationalization. When top managers interacted more frequently and made decisions jointly, foreign market sales contributed to a greater extent to overall firm growth.[26]

In view of such evidence, a key question arises: How can strong working relationships between founding team members be encouraged? Although there is no simple answer to this question, three factors appear to play a crucial role: a clear initial assignment of roles (responsibilities and authority) for all team members; careful attention to the basic issue of perceived fairness; and developing effective patterns and styles of communication (especially with respect to feedback) among team members.

Roles: The Clearer the Better

A major source of conflict in many organizations is uncertainty concerning two issues: responsibility and jurisdiction. Disagreements—often harsh and angry ones—often develop concerning who is accountable for what (responsibility) and who has the authority to make decisions and choose among alternative courses of action (jurisdiction).[27] One effective way of avoiding such problems is through the clear definition of **roles**—the set of behaviours that individuals occupying specific positions within a group are expected to perform, and the authority or jurisdiction they wield. Once established, clear roles can be very useful. For instance, consider a new biotechnology venture with two cofounders. One is a practising physician with a specialty in cardiology; the other holds an M.B.A. To maximize their effectiveness as a team, these individuals should negotiate clearly defined roles at the outset. One possibility: the M.D. runs the laboratory, because it conducts medical research and he is intimately familiar with the rules and regulations governing such activities; in addition, he is responsible for interfacing with other physicians and for choosing the drugs on which to focus—after all, he is an expert on the symptoms and causes of various medical conditions. The other founder, in contrast, handles business-related aspects of the company (e.g., purchase and maintenance of equipment, setting up the company's computer systems), and because of his business expertise, oversees hiring of new persons and financial tasks ranging from securing new capital through maintaining required records. If these roles are specified clearly in advance, the cofounders will truly work in a complementary manner—each will provide unique skills, experience, and knowledge that the other does not possess, or possesses to a lesser degree. The result? The company will operate smoothly and efficiently.

Imagine, however, that the M.D. decides that he should take an active hand with respect to the company's finances. Such interest would not be surprising because bright, talented people are often challenged to try something that they haven't done before. Because the M.D. lacks knowledge in this area, he will have to spend considerable time acquiring a working knowledge of financial statements, tax regulations, and so on. This use of time is inefficient. Moreover, his partner, who holds an M.B.A. degree, may find the physician's aspirations to be irritating at the least, and downright insulting at worst. The result? Conflict between the cofounders may occur, and the company will likely operate at lower efficiency.

The moral is clear: Once the founding team has come together to form the new venture, its members should stick to the principle of complementarity: dividing responsibilities and authority in accordance with each founder's expertise and knowledge. Anything else may well prove costly and detract from the new venture's success. The practice of complementarity sounds very simple, but the sad fact is that many entrepreneurs are highly energetic, capable people, accustomed to running the show in their own lives. Unless they can learn to coordinate with their cofounders, they may run the risk of seriously weakening their own companies.

A Note on Role Conflict

As we have just noted, it is important for entrepreneurs to establish clear-cut roles for all cofounders; this delineation facilitates coordination between the cofounders and helps to maximize the value of the new venture's human capital. But entrepreneurs, like everyone else, have roles outside their companies as well as within them. For instance, they may be spouses, significant others, or parents; they are certainly sons and daughters to their own parents. It is a classic finding in the field of human resource management that the roles that all of us hold sometimes make incompatible demands upon us; in other words, we experience *role conflict*—contrasting expectations about behaviour and responsibilities held by different groups of persons.[28] Spouses and significant others, for example, expect us to be around to fill their emotional needs at least some of the time; similarly, children have legitimate expectations for their parents.

Dealing with role conflict can be a very stressful task—and a difficult juggling act—for entrepreneurs, who must devote so much of their time to running their new ventures. Role conflict can be a very serious matter with important consequences; if the significant people in entrepreneurs' lives cannot come to terms with the heavy demands on the entrepreneurs' time and energies, serious interpersonal problems can result. These difficulties, in turn, can add to entrepreneurs' stress and reduce their overall performance. Clearly, getting one's spouse, significant others, children, and other family members on board is a task no entrepreneur can afford to overlook. The importance of this issue is emphasized by one highly successful entrepreneur in this chapter's **The Voice of Experience** section.

Perceived Fairness: An Elusive but Essential Component

Try this simple exercise: Think back over your past life and remember a specific occasion when you worked with one or more persons on some project. The context is unimportant—it can be any kind of project you wish—but try to recall an incident in which the outcome was positive: The project was a success. Now, divide 100 points between yourself and your partners according to how large a contribution each person made to the project. Next comes the key question: How did you divide the points? If you are like most people, you gave yourself more points than your partners. (For example, if you had one partner, you took more than 50 points; if you had three, you took more than 33.3 points, and so on).

LEARNING OBJECTIVE

4 Define "self-serving bias" and explain how it plays an important role in perceived fairness.

Now, by way of contrast, try to recall another incident—one in which you also worked with partners, but in which the outcome was negative: The project failed. Once again divide 100 points between yourself and your partners, according to how large a contribution each person made to the project and its outcome. In this case, you may well have given others more points than yourself. If you showed this pattern, welcome to the club: You are demonstrating a very powerful human tendency, often known as the **self-serving bias**. In this tendency, we attribute successful outcomes largely to internal causes (our own efforts, talents, or abilities) but unsuccessful ones largely to external causes (e.g., the failings or negligence of others, factors beyond our control).[29] This bias has been found to be a strong one, and it has serious implications for any situation in which people work together to achieve important goals. Specifically, it often leads all the persons involved to conclude that they have not been treated fairly. Why? Because participants in the relationship tend to accentuate their own contributions and minimize those of others, they conclude that they are receiving less of the available rewards than is justified. Further, because each person has the same perception, the result is often friction and conflict between the persons involved.

In other words, this tendency raises thorny questions relating to *perceived fairness*—a key issue for entrepreneurs. Because of the self-serving bias (plus other factors, too), we all have a tendency to assume that we are receiving less than we deserve in almost any situation. In other words, we perceive that the balance between what we contribute and what we receive is less favourable than it is for other persons. In specific terms, we perceive that the ratio between what we are receiving and what we are contributing is smaller than that for others. In general, we prefer this ratio to be the same for all, so that the larger any person's contributions, the larger their rewards—a principle known as **distributive justice**. Most people accept this principle as valid, but the self-serving bias leads us to cognitively inflate our own contributions—and hence to conclude that in fact, we are not being treated fairly (see Figure 5.6).

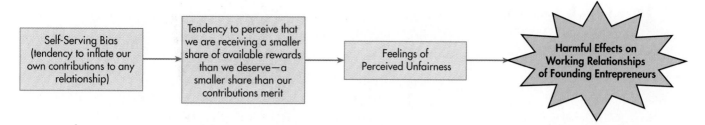

Figure 5.5 Self-Serving Bias and Perceived Unfairness

Because most of us have a strong tendency to perceive our contributions to any relationship as larger than they are, we also tend to perceive that we are receiving a smaller share of available rewards than is appropriate. In other words, we conclude that we are being treated unfairly. This perspective can be a serious problem for founding teams of entrepreneurs.

What do people do when they perceive that the distribution of rewards is unfair? Many different things, none of which is beneficial to a new venture. The most obvious tactic is to demand a larger share; because others do not view these demands as legitimate, conflict is the likely outcome. Another approach is to reduce one's contributions—to reduce effort or shirk responsibility. This response, too, can be highly detrimental to the success of a new venture. An even more damaging reaction is to withdraw, either physically or psychologically. Disaffected cofounders sometimes pull out of new ventures, taking their experience, knowledge, and skills with them. If they are essential members of the team, their departure can mark the beginning of the end for the ventures in question.

All these threats are bad enough, but even worse is the recent finding that although people tend to focus relatively little attention on the issue of fairness when things are going well (e.g., they are getting along well with their cofounders), they devote increasing attention to this issue when things begin to go badly.[30] In short, when a new venture is succeeding and reaching its goals, members of the founding team may show little concern over distributive justice. If things go badly, however, they begin to focus increasing attention on this issue, thus intensifying interpersonal friction.

Given the existence of this cycle, it is truly crucial for the founding teams of new ventures to consider the issue of perceived fairness very carefully. Cofounders should discuss this issue regularly to assure that as roles, responsibilities, and contributions change (which they will inevitably do over time), adjustments are made with respect to equity, status, and other rewards to reflect these changes. This reassessment is a difficult task because all members will tend to accentuate their own contributions (recall the powerful self-serving bias). Because the alternative is the very real risk of tension and conflict between the founding team members, and because conflict is often a major waste of time and energy,[31] it is certainly a task worth performing well—and one that will help the new venture utilize its human resources to the fullest.

Fairness can be a particularly sensitive issue when entrepreneurs hire family members, because non-family employees might feel that family employees work less and are better treated or better-compensated. Canadian researchers have provided many insights on the dynamics of family firms. With respect to the issue of fairness, Professor Lloyd Steier, of the University of Alberta, points out that altruism, as well as economic motivation, is likely to be present when family members are hired, which can stop family members from taking advantage of each other.[32] After examining a large of body of past research on family businesses, Professors Chrisman and Chua, of the University of Calgary, and Professor Sharma, of Wilfrid Laurier University, concluded that, indeed, altruism in family firms is not necessarily a bad thing.[33] Altriuism can go both ways, and family members might be the most willing employees to sacrifice in the short term to support the longer term survival of the firm. Further, Professor Reginald Litz, of the University of Manitoba, makes the point that neither businesses nor families are static, and it is frequently the case that family members enter or leave a company.[34] Therefore, it is important to establish perception of fairness among family members, and not just between family and non-family managers. This issue is discussed by John Stanton, founder of the Running Room, in the Voice of Experience section of this chapter.

THE VOICE OF EXPERIENCE

Some Thoughts on Whom You Want on Board for the Ride

In 1982, John Stanton was an out-of-shape, overweight, chain-smoking food company executive in Edmonton who decided that he had to change his lifestyle. He took up running and quickly became frustrated with buying running shoes at large sporting goods stores because of the poor customer service. Believing that there was a sizeable market of people who wanted to buy high-quality shoes from knowledgeable staff, he opened a small store in the living room of an old house in Edmonton: the first Running Room. That was in 1984, and by 2006, the Running Room had 80 locations throughout Canada and the United States, staffed by 800 employees. In 2004, Stanton was named to Maclean's magazine's Canada Day Honour Roll, as one of ten Canadians making a difference in our nation for his contribution to health through fitness; and the Running Room was recognized by the Retail Council of Canada as the 2004 Canadian Innovative Retailer. He's written four books and contributes generously to social causes. This level of activity and business growth is not possible without a solid management team in place. In a recent interview, John Stanton talked with me about team-building.

Reuber: "What skills were you first looking for when you started to build a management team?"

Stanton: "Two things: communication skills and people who care about other people. I wanted managers who were genuinely interested in helping other people. I wanted them to think of their jobs as fun rather than hard work. Otherwise, they wouldn't fit with the culture I wanted to develop, a culture that emphasizes building community."

Reuber: "When you hire managers, what qualities do you look for?"

Stanton: "Again, there are two key things. I look for people who are self-starters because they have to be able to carry their own work load. I also look for people who are team players. Lots of people say they are team players, but when it comes right down to it, they have a high need for control. Communication in our company is heavily team-based. When we're working on an initiative, such as a store opening, a marathon, or even a book, we set up a team folder on our computer system. There might be 15 to 20 people on a team folder. The folder shows task assignments and everyone's calendars and so a person's progress is visible to everyone else. Our managers have to be able to live with that level of transparency and accountability."

Reuber: "There is research indicating that cohesion among management team members is good, because it facilitates communication and the sharing of ideas, but too much cohesion can lead to groupthink, and people stop questioning a group consensus even when it's misguided. Have you ever seen this in a management team?"

Stanton: "I have seen it, especially in cases where leaders hire only people just like them. Cohesion in our management team is established and maintained because people go running or walking together on a regular basis. But it's important to select managers with different personalities and talents so you gain the advantage of different perspectives. I've said that when you hire a General Sales Manager, you should hire a cocker spaniel, but when you hire a CFO, you should hire a pit bull. The cocker spaniel and the pit bull may not see eye to eye on everything, but they play very different roles in our company and both perspectives are essential."

Reuber: "Your sons are part of your management team. What should people keep in mind when bringing family members into a business?"

Stanton: "The most important thing to watch is perceptions of fairness. Bringing in a family member has to be perceived as fair within the company if you want to retain the authority and responsibility of other key people. You need to work this. You can't just pop a family member into the business, they need to be trained and prepared for their role in the business. They have to have their own area of responsibility which leverages their strengths. Hiring a family member in the business also has to be perceived as fair within the family, especially among siblings. Families and businesses are living, breathing entities and so situations change. A son or daughter might be uninterested in the business at one point, but become interested later on, and it's important to be able to welcome them back."

Reuber: "How important is family support when someone is starting a business?"

Stanton: "Absolutely essential! When I started The Running Room, I gave up the safety net and security of a corporate job, such as a pension, bonuses, and medical insurance, and suddenly I had to mortgage my house. Five years into the business, we hit some bad times and things got tough. I came home from work one day and said to my wife that I didn't know if I was going to be able to make the payroll, and the $1.57 I had in my pocket was our total worth! She said something that has stayed with me since. She said that we started our marriage together many years ago and still had the most important things in life. That's true today: family, good health, making a difference in the community, and having fun are what are really important."

Reuber: "What are some lessons you'd like to pass on to aspiring entrepreneurs?"

Stanton: "Find the courage to do it. Don't say 'shoulda, coulda, woulda.' Don't look at starting a business as a gamble, look at it as a calculated risk. The courage to get into the water,

continued

and not being afraid to make a mistake, is what sets entrepreneurs apart. Also, make sure you have fun. I live life not knowing if I'm working or playing."

Commentary: We think that the points made by Mr. Stanton are insightful and accurate. A strong, shared culture, respect for different talents and personalities, perceptions of fairness and effective communication systems are essential for a well-functioning management team. In addition, an entrepreneur's family and close friends are part of their team. If these people aren't fully on board, entrepreneurs are likely to experience intense role conflict, which, in turn, can drain their energy, distract them from running their business, and damage those around them.

Effective Communication

Perceived unfairness is not the only cause of costly conflicts between members of a new venture's founding team. Another major factor involves faulty styles of communication. Unfortunately, individuals often communicate with others in a way that angers or annoys others, even when it is not their intention to do so. This happens in many different ways, but one of the most common—and important—occurs when delivering feedback, especially negative feedback, in an inappropriate manner. In essence, there is only one truly rational reason for delivering negative feedback to others: to help them to improve. Yet, people often deliver negative feedback for other reasons: to put others in their place, to cause others to lose face in front of others, to express anger and hostility, and so on. The result of such negative feedback is that the recipient experiences anger or humiliation, which can be the basis for smoldering resentment and long-lasting grudges.[35] When negative feedback is delivered in an informal context, rather than formally (e.g., as part of a written performance review), it is known as *criticism*, and research findings suggest that such feedback can take two distinct forms: *constructive criticism*, which is truly designed to help the recipient improve, and *destructive criticism*, which is perceived—rightly so—as a form of hostility or attack.

What makes criticism constructive or destructive in nature? Key differences are outlined in Table 5.1. As you can see from this table, constructive criticism is considerate of the recipient's feelings, does not include threats, is timely (occurs at an appropriate point in time), does not attribute blame to the recipient, is specific in content, and offers concrete suggestions for improvement. Destructive criticism, in contrast, is harsh, includes threats, is not timely, blames the recipient for negative outcomes, is not specific in content, and offers no concrete ideas for improvement. Table 5.1 also provides examples of each type of criticism.

Research findings indicate that destructive criticism is truly damaging: It generates strong negative reactions in recipients and can initiate a vicious cycle of anger, the desire for revenge, and subsequent conflict. The message for entrepreneurs is

> **LEARNING OBJECTIVE**
>
> 5   Explain the difference between constructive and destructive criticism.

Table 5.1 Constructive Versus Destructive Criticism

Constructive criticism is negative feedback that can help the recipient improve. Destructive criticism, in contrast, is far less likely to produce such beneficial effects.

CONSTRUCTIVE CRITICISM	DESTRUCTIVE CRITICISM	EXAMPLES
Considerate—protects self-esteem of recipients	Inconsiderate—harsh, sarcastic, biting	Constructive: "I was disappointed in your performance." Destructive: "What a rotten, lousy job!"
Does not include threats	Includes threats	Constructive: "I think improvement is really important." Destructive: "If you don't improve, you are history!"
Timely—occurs as soon as possible after the poor or inadequate performance	Not timely—occurs after an inappropriate delay	Constructive: "You made several errors in today's report." Destructive: "I've been meaning to tell about the errors you made last year."
Does not attribute poor performance to internal causes	Attributes poor performance to internal causes	Constructive: "I know that a lot of factors probably played a role in your performance." Destructive: "You failed because you just don't give a damn!"
Specific—focuses on aspects of performance that were inadequate	General—a sweeping condemnation of performance	Constructive: "The main problem was that the project was late." Destructive: "You did a really terrible job."
Focuses on performance, not the recipient	Focuses on the recipient	Constructive: "Your performance was not what I expected." Destructive: "You are a rotten performer!"
Offers concrete suggestions for improvement	Does not offer concrete suggestions for improvement	Constructive: "Here's how I think you can do better next time around." Destructive: "You'd better work on doing better!"

clear: Effective communication between cofounders is one essential ingredient in establishing and maintaining effective working relationships. If it is lacking, serious problems may result. For instance, consider a new venture started by partners who have followed the complementarity principle: One is an engineer and the other has a background in marketing. Although the marketing cofounder has selected his partner carefully, he harbours negative feelings about engineers ("They never think about people!"). As a result, he criticizes the engineer's designs for new products harshly. The engineer is offended by this treatment, so he begins to make changes in the company's products without informing his cofounder. Because the marketing entrepreneur doesn't know about these changes, he can't get customer input before they are made. The result? The company's products fail in the marketplace, and soon the new venture is in deep trouble. This is just one example of how faulty communication between members of the founding team can produce disastrous effects. The main point should be clear: Strong efforts to attain good, constructive communication between cofounders are very worthwhile.

One final question: Is all conflict between founding cofounders bad? Absolutely not. Conflict between team members, when focused on specific issues rather than personalities and when held within rational bounds, can be very useful. Such rational conflict can help to focus attention on important issues, motivate both sides to understand each other's view more clearly, and can, by encouraging both sides to carefully consider all assumptions, lead to better decisions.[36] In sum, conflict between founding team members is not necessarily a bad thing. Rather, it—like all other aspects of the new venture's operations—should be carefully managed so that benefits are maximized and costs held to a minimum. Overall, strong and effective working relationships between founding members are a powerful asset to any new venture, so efforts to foster them should be high on every founding team's must-do list.

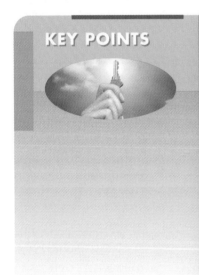

KEY POINTS

- Once an appropriate founding team is assembled, these individuals must work together effectively if their new venture is to succeed.
- One key ingredient in establishing strong working relationships is the development of clearly defined roles that specify the responsibilities and jurisdiction of each entrepreneur.
- Because of the self-serving bias and other factors, individuals often perceive that they are not being treated fairly by others—that they are not receiving a share of available rewards that is commensurate with the scope of their contributions (i.e., that distributive justice is lacking).
- Reactions to such perceived unfairness range from demanding more or doing less, to actual withdrawal from the relationship. Because all of these reactions are inimical to the success of a new venture, entrepreneurs should take active steps to assure that all members of the founding team feel that they are being treated fairly.
- Another ingredient in strong working relationships is effective communication. In particular, entrepreneurs should avoid delivering destructive criticism to one another because such negative feedback often leads to feelings of hostility and intense conflict.

INTERPRETING INFORMATION: POTENTIAL PITFALLS FOR DECISION-MAKING GROUPS

We noted in Chapter 3 that, as human beings, we are definitely *not* perfect information-processing machines. On the contrary, our thinking, reasoning, and decision making are often influenced by errors and biases that prevent these processes from being completely rational. Thus, when making decisions, entrepreneurs must work hard to hold these errors to a minimum. Otherwise, entrepreneurs stand the real risk of misinterpreting the information they have gathered, and, therefore, reaching false conclusions or decisions. In Chapter 3, we described several of these potential errors and biases that can affect our thinking. Because most new ventures are founded by teams of founders, we also need to consider the processes that can strongly affect decision making by groups. Among the factors that can badly distort the interpretation of information, four stand out as most important: the tendency to accept early favourites, group polarization, groupthink, and a tendency to ignore unshared information.

Accepting Early Favourites: Or, Why the Initial Majority Usually Wins

Most people believe—often implicitly—that decisions made by groups are safer and more accurate than decisions made by individuals. After all, group members can help keep each other from going off the deep end, and one member's misinterpretation of available information can be readily corrected by one or more other members whose interpretation is more accurate. Unfortunately, research findings concerning decisions by groups suggest that these potential benefits often fail to materialize. On the contrary, what often happens in groups is that the final decision reached is the one favoured by the initial majority—a choice sometimes known as the **implicit favourite**.[37] In other words, there is a tendency for groups (and individuals, too) to begin with a bias toward one interpretation or decision and then to move toward accepting it. In fact, as the process unfolds, other interpretations or options, known as **confirmation candidates**, are suggested and rejected. These are alternatives that are not really considered seriously; rather, they are raised mainly for the purpose of helping groups convince themselves that the initial favourite is indeed correct. The moral for entrepreneurs is clear: When trying to interpret information for use as a basis for decisions, be very wary of a drift toward the implicit favourite. Although it may ultimately prove to be the right decision, it is crucial to consider alternative interpretations or decisions carefully to avoid jumping to conclusions by prematurely closing the decision-making process.

Group Polarization: Why Groups Often Do Go off the Deep End

Earlier, we noted that many people assume that groups are less likely to make extreme decisions than individuals. In fact, precisely the opposite seems to be true. When several persons discuss information in order to reach a group decision, they show a strong tendency to shift toward views more extreme than the ones with which they began. This phenomenon, known as **group polarization**, seems to occur in many different contexts.[38] There appear to be two major reasons why group polarization occurs. First, during group discussion of information, most arguments presented are those favouring the group's initial preference or leaning. As a result of hearing such arguments, members literally persuade one another that the view favoured initially is correct, and so they shift toward this position with increasing strength. One old saying captures this effect very neatly: "We all say it's so, we all say it's so, we all say it's so, so it *must* be so!" This result is precisely what happens in many decision-making groups, as members convince each other that their interpretation of available information is correct.

A second reason why group polarization occurs involves the desire, shared by virtually everyone, to be better than average. We all want the views we hold to be better than those held by other groups' members. What does better mean in this context? It depends on the specific group, but in general, being better means holding the view favoured by the majority even more strongly than the members of other groups. Again, this tendency causes group members—and the decision-making group itself—to shift further and further toward extremity.

> **LEARNING OBJECTIVE**
>
> **6** Describe sources of error in the interpretation of information by decision-making groups. Be sure to include early favourites, group polarization, and groupthink.

Group polarization effects appear to be strong, and they are hard to resist. For this reason, entrepreneurs should be on guard against their occurrence; once these effects take hold, they can lead to truly disastrous decisions. For instance, there is some indication that group polarization played a role in Apple Computer's decision *not* to license its software to other manufacturers—a decision that ultimately cost it most of the personal computer market when Microsoft chose the opposite route, thus permitting many companies to produce computers using their operating system. We will consider ways of minimizing group polarization as part of a general discussion of techniques for improving the entire process of interpreting information and making decisions.

Groupthink: When Too Much Cohesion among Group Members Is a Dangerous Thing

In this chapter we have emphasized the importance of good relationships between members of a new venture's founding team.[39] Like anything else, a high level of cohesion among group members can cut both ways and can pose a serious threat to effective decision making. When cohesion (unity) among group members is very high, the group runs the real risk of falling prey to **groupthink**—a strong tendency for decision-making groups to close ranks, cognitively, around a decision, assuming that the group *can't* be wrong, that all members must support the decision strongly, and that any information contrary to the decision should be rejected.[40] Once this collective state of mind develops, groups become unwilling—perhaps even unable—to change their decisions, even if external events suggest that these decisions are very poor. Individuals suppress their doubts so they are not perceived as disloyal or threatening to group solidarity.

For example, the recent sponsorship scandal in Canadian politics has been called an example of groupthink.[41] After the Quebec referendum of 1995, the Sponsorship Program was set up by the federal government to increase the presence of Canada in Quebec and decrease the attractiveness of separation. A sense of urgency, strong group loyalty to an in-group aimed at reducing the power of an out-group, and perceptions of invulnerability led to a situation where little attention was paid to the responsibilities and accountabilities associated with the use of public funds. In contrast to the program's goal of boosting the fortunes of the Liberal Party, the results of groupthink did it much harm.

Ignoring Unshared Information

One major advantage of groups is that members can pool their information and experience. In other words, each has something unique to contribute, and combining members' unique knowledge increases the pool of information available. Presumably, the richer this pool, the better the decisions the group can make. This theory makes eminent good sense, but in fact, it turns out that groups do not automatically share information held by individual members. On the contrary, when groups discuss an issue and try to reach a decision, they tend to consider information shared by most if not all members and generally tend to ignore information that is known to only one or a few members. Why? Partly because information known to most members has a high probability of being reported by one or more members: Because most people know this information, it is very likely that one or more will state it. In addition, people tend to prefer information that confirms their existing knowledge, and group members encourage this process by agreeing with such statements. The result is that groups never become aware of unique information held by individual members, and so cannot use it in their decisions.[42] Ultimately, this practice can lead to misinterpretation of information and very poor decisions.

Surprisingly, this tendency for groups to ignore information held by one or a few members occurs even in contexts involving life-and-death decisions. For instance, teams of interns and medical students tend to discuss more shared than unshared information, and juries, too, discuss information known to most members while ignoring information known to one or a few members.[43] Because entrepreneurs need to employ all the information at their disposal—some of which they have gathered through great effort—this tendency, too, can be a costly one with devastating results for new ventures. For instance, if the founding team of a new venture simply discusses information already known to all members, the decisions reached about a wide range of issues, ranging from new product developments through financing, may be adversely affected, with harmful consequences for the new venture.

Improving Group Decisions: Techniques for Countering the Pitfalls

If our discussion of potential pitfalls in group decision making sounds discouraging, this is by design: It is very important for you, as nascent entrepreneurs, to be aware of these dangers; ignoring them can be costly—or even fatal—to new ventures. Being optimists by nature, though, we want to end on a positive note by reporting that there are effective techniques for countering all of these traps—techniques you can use to protect your own decisions from their impact.

One strategy that is especially useful is the **devil's advocate technique**.[44] In this procedure, one founding team member is assigned the task of disagreeing with and criticizing whatever plan or decision is the initial favourite. This tactic induces members to think carefully about the information available and the decisions toward which they are leaning; using this tactic can slow the shift toward initial favourites. It is also effective in countering groupthink, by suggesting very clearly that the group has *not* attained consensus and by focusing discussion on the fact that it is indeed possible to hold alternative views.

Another useful technique for improving the interpretation of information and group decision making involves asking group members to list all pertinent information known to them before beginning the discussion. This exercise reduces the tendency to ignore unshared information and limits the amount of time spent discussing views shared by most members, thus reducing the likelihood of reciprocal persuasion and the development of group polarization effects.

A third technique that new ventures can adopt—one that is often very helpful—is to appoint individuals with technical or business experience to a board of advisers. The advice and guidance provided by these individuals can help founding teams improve the decisions they make—provided the founders are wise enough to listen! The advice of an outside board of advisers can be extremely valuable; not only do these people have expertise that may not be present among members of the founding team, but they are also on the outside looking in. They are less subject to the effects of group polarization, groupthink, and other factors that can affect decisions by groups. For all these reasons, they can be a big plus for new ventures.

LEARNING OBJECTIVE

7 Describe various techniques for countering the effects of these sources of error.

KEY POINTS

- Once information is obtained, it must be interpreted—understood so that it can be used as a basis for making good decisions and mapping future strategy.
- Unfortunately, many sources of bias and error can affect the interpretation of information, thus leading to bad decisions. Entrepreneurs must make strenuous efforts to avoid these errors.
- One common source of error is the tendency of decision-making groups to drift toward acceptance of the group's initial preference—the implicit favourite.
- A second source of error in the interpretation of information by groups is group polarization—a strong tendency to shift toward views more extreme than the ones with which they began.
- Another potential source of error in decision-making groups is groupthink—a strong tendency for decision-making groups to close ranks, cognitively, around a decision, assuming that the group can't be wrong, that all members must support the decision strongly, and that any information contrary to the decision should be rejected.
- Although a key advantage of groups is that they can pool information held by individual members, such sharing of information does not always occur. In fact, groups often fail to share information known to only one or a few members. Instead, they tend to discuss information already known to most members, which can lead to poor decisions.
- Several procedures for reducing these potential errors exist, including the devil's advocate technique. Another involves appointing a board of advisers who, as outsiders, are less subject to forces that can distort group decisions.

Summary and Review of Key Points

- In general, people tend to like, and feel more comfortable around, persons who are similar to themselves in various ways.
- This tendency leads entrepreneurs to select cofounders whose background, training, and experience closely match their own.
- Because a wide range of knowledge, skills, and experience among the founding team is advantageous to new ventures, selecting cofounders on the basis of complementarity rather than similarity is often a more useful strategy.
- In order to choose cofounders who bring knowledge, skills, and attributes complementary to their own, entrepreneurs must first conduct a careful self-assessment of their own human capital.
- This task is difficult because often we are unaware of the causes of our own behaviour and, because in many instances, we can acquire understanding of our own characteristics only from others' reactions to us.
- Entrepreneurs' self-assessment should carefully consider their knowledge base, specific skills, motives, and personal attributes (e.g., where they stand on each of the Big Five dimensions of personality).

- In choosing cofounders, it is often useful to focus on complementarity with respect to knowledge, skills, and experience, but on similarity with respect to personal characteristics and motives.
- In order to choose excellent cofounders, entrepreneurs must perform the task of social perception well—they must form accurate perceptions of other persons.
- Social perception is often a difficult task, because others do not always portray themselves accurately. They often engage in impression management—various tactics designed to place them in a favourable light. Entrepreneurs should take careful note of these tactics when choosing cofounders and should carefully check claims and information provided to them by these persons.
- Entrepreneurs often confront deception—efforts by others to actively mislead them.
- Although they are sometimes tempted to do so, entrepreneurs should avoid engaging in deception themselves. This practice is unethical and will ultimately undermine trust in the entrepreneurs and their new ventures.

- If entrepreneurs do not choose cofounders carefully, they can experience disastrous results—as one of the authors did in connection with his own start-up company.
- Once an appropriate founding team is assembled, these individuals must work together effectively if their new venture is to succeed.
- One key ingredient in establishing strong working relationships is the development of clearly defined roles that specify the responsibilities and jurisdiction of each entrepreneur.
- Because of self-serving bias and other factors, individuals often perceive that they are not being treated fairly by others—that they are not receiving a share of available rewards that is commensurate with the scope of their contributions.
- Reactions to such perceived unfairness range from demanding more or doing less, to actual withdrawal from the relationship. Because all of these reactions are inimical to the success of a new venture, entrepreneurs should take active steps to assure that all members of the founding team feel that they are being treated fairly.
- Another ingredient in strong working relationships is effective communication. In particular, entrepreneurs should avoid delivering destructive criticism to one another because such negative feedback often leads to feelings of hostility and intense conflict.
- Once information is obtained, it must be interpreted—understood so that it can be used as a basis for making good decisions and mapping future strategy.

- Unfortunately, many sources of bias and error can affect the interpretation of information, thus leading to bad decisions. Entrepreneurs must make strenuous efforts to avoid these errors.
- One common source of error is the tendency of decision-making groups to drift toward acceptance of the group's initial preference—the implicit favourite.
- A second source of error in the interpretation of information by groups is group polarization—a strong tendency to shift toward views more extreme than the ones with which they began.
- Another potential source of error in decision-making groups is groupthink—a strong tendency for decision-making groups to close ranks, cognitively, around a decision, assuming that the group can't be wrong, that all members must support the decision strongly, and that any information contrary to the decision should be rejected.
- Although a key advantage of groups is that they can pool information held by individual members, such sharing of information does not always occur. In fact, groups often fail to share information known to only one or a few members. Instead, they tend to discuss information already known to most members, which can lead to poor decisions.
- Several procedures for reducing these potential errors exist, including the devil's advocate technique. Another involves appointing a board of advisers who, as outsiders, are less subject to forces that can distort group decisions.

Glossary

Big Five Dimensions of Personality: Basic dimensions of personality that have been found to strongly affect behaviour in a wide range of situations.

Confirmation Candidates: Alternatives that are not really considered seriously; rather, they are raised mainly for the purpose of helping groups convince themselves that initial favourite is indeed correct.

Deception: Efforts to mislead others by withholding information or presenting false information.

Devil's Advocate Technique: A procedure for improving group decision making in which one group member is assigned the task of disagreeing with and criticizing whatever plan or decision is the initial favourite.

Distributive Justice: A principle of perceived fairness suggesting that all parties to a relationship should receive a share of the available rewards commensurate with the scope of their contributions.

Group Polarization: The tendency for members of decision-making groups to shift toward views more extreme than the ones with which they began.

Groupthink: The strong tendency for decision-making groups to close ranks, cognitively, around a decision, assuming that the group can't be wrong, that all members must support the decision strongly, and that any information contrary to the decision should be rejected.

Implicit Favourite: The decision initially favoured by the majority of a decision-making group that becomes the group's final decision.

Impression Management: Tactics used by individuals to make a good first impression on others.

Roles: The set of behaviours that individuals occupying specific positions within a group are expected to perform.

Self-Assessment: An inventory of the knowledge, experience, training, motives, and characteristics the entrepreneur possesses and can contribute to the new venture.

Self-Serving Bias: The tendency to attribute successful outcomes largely to internal causes (our own efforts, talents, or abilities) but unsuccessful ones largely to external cause (e.g., the failings or negligence of others).

Social Perception: The process through which we come to know and understand other persons.

Discussion Questions

1. In general, we tend to like people who are similar to ourselves in various ways. Why can this sometimes be counterproductive for entrepreneurs when choosing partners?

2. Do you think that because of their relative standing on the Big Five dimensions of personality, some persons are more suited to become entrepreneurs than others? What characteristics would describe someone who is suited to become an entrepreneur? What characteristics might make someone unsuited to becoming an entrepreneur?

3. What tactics of impression management do you use? Which are most successful? Why?

4. How good are you at recognizing attempts at deception by other persons? What clues do you use to try to determine whether others are telling the truth or lying?

5. Everyone wants to be treated fairly. Can you think of factors other than the share of available rewards you receive that could lead you to conclude that you were being treated fairly or unfairly by others? (Hint: Do the procedures used to distribute rewards matter?)

6. Do you ever criticize others for any reason aside from a desire to help them? When? What effects does this criticism produce?

7. It is widely believed that groups are less likely to go off the deep end than individuals when making decisions. Do you think it's true? If not, what processes, working together, could push groups toward extreme (and poor) decisions?

InfoTrac Exercises

1. **Resource Complementarity in Business Combinations: Extending the Logic to Organizational Alliances** (technical) *Jeffrey S. Harrison; Michael A. Hitt; Robert E. Hoskisson; R. Duane Ireland.*

   Journal of Management, Nov–Dec 2001 v27 i6 p679(12)

   Record: A81598446

   Abstract: Organizations are combining resources through acquisitions and alliances in record numbers. Since publication of our original study in 1991, research has confirmed that resource complementarity creates the potential for greater synergy from acquisitions and alliances, leading to higher long-term firm performance as an end result. The valuable, unique, and inimitable synergy that can be realized by integrating complementary resources provides an opportunity for the firm to create competitive advantages that can be sustained for a period of time. In addition, complementary resources present opportunities for enhanced learning as well as the development of new capabilities. However, we also suggest that the existence of complementary resources is a necessary but insufficient condition to achieve synergy. The resources must be effectively integrated and managed to realize the synergy. © 2001 Elsevier Science Inc. All rights reserved.

   1. According to the text, which characteristic is more likely to lead to a successful founding team—similarity or complementarity? Why?

   2. What evidence do the authors of the article offer to support their view that complementarity leads to more successful alliances?

   3. According to the article, what benefits result from complementarity?

2. **Offer Constructive Criticism ... Without Sounding Like a Jerk**

   Info-Tech Advisor Newsletter, Sept 3, 2002 pNA

   Record: A92303209

   Full Text: COPYRIGHT 2002 InfoTech Research Group Sources: (Business Finance Magazine article, ITtoolkit.com article, Software Development Magazine article)

1. According to the text, what is the only truly rational reason for delivering negative feedback?
2. What are the effects of destructive criticism according to the text and the article?
3. List steps from the text and article that you can use to make your feedback more constructive.

GETTING DOWN
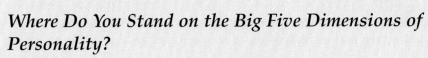
TO BUSINESS

Where Do You Stand on the Big Five Dimensions of Personality?

A large body of evidence indicates that the Big Five dimensions of personality are both basic and important. Where people stand on these factors has a strong impact on their behaviour in many situations—and the success they attain. Where do you stand on each of these dimensions? To find out, ask several people who know you well to rate you on each of the following items. Ask them to use a 7-point scale for these ratings, where 1 = lowest and 7 = highest. Their ratings are a very rough indication of where you stand on each of the Big Five dimensions of personality. (Note: Because this is an informal exercise, please interpret the findings with a healthy degree of caution.)

DIMENSION	RATING QUESTIONS (TO BE ANSWERED BY PEOPLE WHO KNOW YOU WELL)
Conscientiousness	How reliable is [your name]? How neat and orderly is _____? How carefully does _____ complete jobs?
Extraversion	How much excitement does _____ prefer? How readily does _____ make new friends? How cheerful and friendly is _____?
Agreeableness	How trusting of others is _____? How courteous is _____ toward others? How cooperative is _____?
Emotional stability	How much does _____ worry? How often does _____ become emotionally excited? How confident and secure is _____?
Openness to experience	How much does _____ like change? How much curiosity does _____ have?

Choosing the Right Partner

Many new ventures are founded by two or more persons, so it is clear that choosing a good partner (or partners) is an important task for entrepreneurs. In order to choose wisely, you need three basic pieces of information: (1) a clear self-assessment (what you bring to the table in terms of skills, abilities, knowledge, etc.), (2) a clear picture of what you need from potential partners, and (3) an ability to assess others accurately so that you can tell whether they have what you need. This exercise should help you to gather all three kinds of information.

1. **Self-assessment.** Rate yourself on each of the following dimensions. Be as honest and accurate as possible! For each dimension, enter a number from 1 to 5 (1 = very low; 2 = low; 3 = average; 4 = high; 5 = very high).

    a. Experience related to your new venture _____ (enter a number from 1 to 5)
    b. Technical knowledge related to your new venture _____
    c. People skills (skills useful in getting along with others, persuading them, etc.) _____
    d. Motivation to succeed _____
    e. Commitment to the new venture _____
    f. Personal attributes that suit you to becoming an entrepreneur _____
    g. Personal attributes that do not suit you to becoming an entrepreneur _____

2. **What you need in a partner.** Taking account of the ratings in part 1, list what you need from your partners. For instance, if you are low in technical knowledge, you would want such knowledge in your partner; if you are low in people skills, you would want a partner high on this dimension, and so on.

    a.
    b.
    c.
    d.
    e.
    f.

3. **How good are you at social perception?** Can you assess other people accurately? To find out, indicate the extent to which each of the following statements is true of you (1 = not true at all; 2 = not true; 3 = neither true nor false; 4 = true; 5 = very true).

    a. I can easily tell when other people are lying.
    b. I can guess others' true feelings, if they want to conceal these from me.
    c. I can recognize others' weak spots.
    d. I'm a good judge of other people.
    e. I can usually recognize others' traits accurately by observing their behaviour.
    f. I can tell why people have acted the way they have in most situations.

    Add your answers. If you scored 20 or higher, you see yourself as good at social perception. To find out whether this assessment is accurate, ask several people who know you well to rate you on the same items. In other words, change the items to read: "_____ can easily tell when other people are lying" (your name goes in the blank). If their ratings agree with yours, congratulations—you are good not only at assessing others, but also at assessing yourself!

Enhanced Learning

You may select any combination of the resources below to enhance your understanding of the chapter material.

■ **Appendix: Case Studies** – Twelve cases provide opportunities to apply chapter concepts to realistic entrepreneurial situations. These brief cases call for careful analysis of real business problems and ask you to think about potential solutions.

■ **Video Case Library** – Nine cases are tied directly to video segments from the popular PBS television series Small Business School. These cases and video segments (available on the Entrepreneurship website at http://www.entrepreneurship.nelson.com) give you unparalleled access to today's entrepreneurs, with expert advice and insights on how to start, run, and grow a business.

■ **Management Interview Series Video Database** – This video interview series contains a wealth of tips on how to manage effectively. Access to the database and practical exercises are available on the book support website at http://www.entrepreneurship.nelson.com.

Notes

1. Cooper, A., Woo, C., & Dunkelberg, W. 1989. Entrepreneurship and the initial size of firms. *Journal of Business Venturing* 4(5): 317–332.

2. Davidsson, P., & Honig, B. 2003. The role of social and human capital among nascent entrepreneurs. *Journal of Business Venturing* 18(3): 301–331.

3. Greenberg, J., & Baron, R.A. 2003. *Behavior in organizations.* 8th ed. Upper Saddle River, NJ: Prentice-Hall.

4. Wise, S. 2006. The talent triangle. http://www.theglobeandmail.com/servlet/story/RTGAM.20060517.wwisewords0517/BNStory/specialSmallBusiness/home?pageRequested=all&print=true.

5. Erikson, T. 2002. Entrepreneurial capital: The emerging venture's most important asset and competitive advantage. *Journal of Business Venturing* 17(3): 275–290.

6. Mount, M.K., & Barrick, M.R. 1995. The Big Five personality dimensions: Implications for research and practice in human resources management. In K.M. Rowland & G. Ferris (eds.). *Research on personnel and human resources management* (vol. 13, pp. 153–200). Greenwich, CT: JAI Press.

7. Hurtz, G.M., & Donovan, J.J. 2000. Personality and job performance: The Big Five revisited. *Journal of Applied Psychology* 85(6): 869–879.

8. Salgado, J.F. 1997. The five-factor model of personality and job performance in the European community. *Journal of Applied Psychology* 82(1): 30–43.

9. Ciavarella, M.A., Buchholtz, A.K., Riordan, C.M., Gatewood, R.D., & Stokes, G.S. 2004. The Big Five and venture survival: Is there a link? *Journal of Business Venturing* 19(4): 465–483.

10. Barrick, M.R., Stewart, G.L., Neubert, M.J., & Mount, M.K. 1998. Relating member ability and personality to work-team processes and team effectiveness. *Journal of Applied Psychology* 83(3): 377–391.

11. George, J.M., & Zhou, J. 2001. When openness to experience and conscientiousness are related to creative behavior: An interactional approach. *Journal of Applied Psychology* 86(3): 513–524.

12. Keller, R.T. 2001. Cross-functional project groups in research and new product development: Diversity, communications, job stress, and outcomes. *Academy of Management Journal* 44(3): 547–555.

13. Baron, R.A., & Byrne, D. 2002. *Social psychology.* 10th ed. Boston: Allyn & Bacon.

14. Baron, R.A., & Markman, G. 2003. Beyond social capital: The role of entrepreneurs' social competence in their financial success. *Journal of Business Venturing* 18(1): 41–60.

15. Ferris, G.R., Witt, L.A., & Hochwarter, W.Q. 2001. Interaction of social skill and general mental ability on job performance and salary. *Journal of Applied Psychology* 86(6): 1075–1082.

16. Terry, R.L., & Krantz, J.H. 1993. Dimensions of trait attributions associated with eyeglasses, men's facial hair, and women's hair length. *Journal of Applied Social Psychology* 23: 1757–1769.

17. Davidsson, P., & Honig, B. 2003. The role of social and human capital among nascent entrepreneurs. *Journal of Business Venturing* 18(3): 301–331.

18. Kilduff, M., & Day, D.V. 1994. Do chameleons get ahead? The effects of self-monitoring on managerial careers. *Academy of Management Journal* 37(4): 1047–1060.

19. Wayne, S.J., & Ferris, G.R. 1990. Influence tactics and exchange quality in supervisor-subordinate interactions: A laboratory experiment and field study. *Journal of Applied Psychology* 75(5): 487–499.

20. Olson, J.M., Hafer, C.L., & Taylor, L. 2001. I'm mad as hell and I'm not going to take it anymore: Reports of negative emotions as a self-presentation tactic. *Journal of Applied Social Psychology* 31(5): 981–999.

21. Wayne, S.J., Liden, R.C., Graf, I.K., & Ferris G.R. 1997. The role of upward influence tactics in human resource decisions. *Personnel Psychology* 50(4): 979–1006.

22. Vonk, R. 1998. The slime effect: Suspicion and dislike of likeable behavior toward superiors. *Journal of Personality and Social Psychology* 74(4): 849–864.

23. Buchholz, R.A. 1989. *Fundamental concepts and problems in business ethics.* Englewood Cliffs, NJ: Prentice-Hall.

24. Ensley, M.D., Pearson, A.W., & Amason, A.C. 2002. Understanding the dynamics of new venture top management teams: Cohesion, conflict, and new venture performance. *Journal of Business Venturing* 17(4): 365–386.

25. Cooper, A., Woo, C., & Dunkelberg, W. 1989. Entrepreneurship and the initial size of firms. *Journal of Business Venturing* 4(5): 317–332.

26. Reuber, A.R., & Fischer, E. 2002. Foreign sales and small firm growth: The moderating role of the management team. *Entrepreneurship Theory and Practice* 27(1): 29–46.

27. Cropanzano, R.D. 1993. (ed.) *Justice in the workplace.* Hillsdale, NJ: Erlbaum.

28. Greenberg, J., & Baron, R.A. 2003. *Behavior in organizations.* 8th ed. Upper Saddle River, NJ: Prentice-Hall.

29. Brown, J.D., & Rogers, R.J. 1991. Self-serving attribution: The role of physiological arousal. *Personality and Social Psychology Bulletin* 17(5): 501–506.

30 Grote, N.K., & Clark, M.S. 2001. Perceiving unfairness in the family: Cause of consequences of marital distress? *Journal of Personality and Social Psychology* 80(2): 281–289.

31 Tjosvold, D. 1993. *Learning to manage conflict: Getting people to work together productively.* New York: Lexington Books.

32 Steier, L. 2003. Variants of agency contracts in family-financed ventures as a continuum of familial altruistic and market rationalities. *Journal of Business Venturing* 18(5): 597–618.

33 Chrisman, J.J., Chua, J.H., & Sharma, P. 2005. Trends and directions in the development of a strategic management theory of the family firm. *Entrepreneurship Theory and Practice*, 29(5): 555–575.

34 Litz, R.A. 1995. The family business: Towards definitional clarity. *Family Business Review* 8(2): 71–81.

35 Baron, R.A. 1993. Criticism (informal negative feedback) as a source of perceived unfairness in organizations: Effects, mechanisms, and countermeasures. In R. Cropanzano (ed.). *Justice in the workplace: Approaching fairness in human resource management* (pp. 155–170). Hillsdale, NJ: Erlbaum.

36 Thompson, L. 1998. *The mind and heart of the negotiator.* Upper Saddle River, NJ: Prentice-Hall.

37 Nemeth, C., Connell, J.B., Rogers, J.D., & Brown, K.S. 2001. Improving decision making by means of dissent. *Journal of Applied Social Psychology* 31(1): 45–58.

38 Burnstein, E. 1983. Persuasion as argument processing. In M. Brandstatter, J.H. Davis, & G. Stocker-Kriechgauer (eds.). *Group decision processes* (pp. 103–122). London: Academic Press.

39 Ensley, M.D., Pearson, A.W., & Amason, A.C. 2002. Understanding the dynamics of new venture top management teams: Cohesion, conflict, and new venture performance. *Journal of Business Venturing* 17(4): 365–386.

40 Janis, I.L. 1982. *Victims of groupthink.* 2nd ed. Boston: Houghton Mifflin.

41 Baker, C. 2004, February, 22. Groupthink at the core of Adscam. *Winnipeg Free Press.*

42 Gigone, D., & Hastie, R. 1993. The common knowledge effect: Information sharing and group judgment. *Journal of Personality and Social Psychology* 65(5): 959–974.

43 Larson, J.R., Jr., Foster-Fishman, P.G., & Franz, T.M. 1998. Leadership style and the discussion of shared and unshared information in decision-making groups. *Personality and Social Psychology Bulletin* 24(5):482–495.

44 Hirt, E.R., & Markman, K.D. 1995. Multiple explanations: A consider-an-alternative strategy for debiasing judgments. *Journal of Personality and Social Psychology* 69(6): 1069–1086.

CHAPTER 6

FINANCING NEW VENTURES

LEARNING OBJECTIVES

After reading this chapter, you should be able to:

1 Explain why it is difficult for entrepreneurs to raise money from external investors.

2 Identify specific solutions to venture finance problems created by uncertainty and information asymmetry, and explain why these solutions work.

3 Explain why entrepreneurs typically raise very little start-up capital.

4 Create proforma financial statements and cash flow statements and conduct breakeven analysis.

5 Define debt and equity financing and explain how they differ.

6 Describe the different sources of capital for new ventures.

7 Describe the equity finance process from start to finish.

8 Explain why equity financing in new ventures is typically staged.

9 Describe how venture capitalists calculate the cost of the capital that they provide to new ventures.

10 Explain why direct and indirect social ties are important to raising money from external investors.

11 Identify the behaviours and actions that successful entrepreneurs engage in to encourage investors to back them, and explain why these behaviours and actions are effective.

All photos this page © PhotoDisc, Inc.

> "Money, it turned out, was exactly like sex; you thought of nothing else if you didn't have it and thought of other things if you did." (James Baldwin, *Nobody Knows My Name*, 1961)

In July 1996, Alex Laats, a technology licensing officer at MIT, and two undergraduate students, Pehr Andersen and Chris Gadda, founded a company named NBX Corporation to make an Internet telephone. Although none of the entrepreneurs had started a previous company, they raised $16.7 million in venture capital, and used the money to build a company that was later sold to 3Com for $80 million. How did three inexperienced entrepreneurs raise millions of dollars of venture capital and build a company?

It happened like this: While he was working at the MIT technology licensing office, Alex Laats met a venture capitalist named Charles Harris. Harris was impressed with Laats and tried to hire him for his venture capital firm, Harris and Harris. Because Laats decided he'd rather be an entrepreneur than a venture capitalist, he turned down the offer. So Harris told Laats to look him up when he had a venture he wanted to start.

In the summer of 1996, Laats called Harris to talk about financing NBX. Harris agreed to provide $500,000.

When Laats left the technology licensing office to start NBX, he agreed to license the Internet phone technology from MIT in return for 5 percent of the company. As a result, Phil Rotner, who worked in the MIT treasurer's office, became responsible for managing MIT's investment in NBX.

One of Rotner's responsibilities was to manage the investments of MIT's endowment in venture capital funds, which put him in contact with a lot of venture capitalists. This relationship proved valuable in the fall of 1996 when NBX Corporation needed to raise additional capital. Harris and Harris couldn't provide all of the additional $3.5 million that NBX Corporation needed, and Laats and Harris began to search for other venture capital firms to provide money.

Harris called Bill Laverack, a partner at J.H. Whitney, a venture capital firm that was very closely tied to Harris and Harris. Because of his relationship with Harris, Laverack supported funding NBX Corporation, figuring if Harris thought it was a good investment, it probably was. In addition, Laverack had close ties to Rotner because MIT was the largest investor in J.H. Whitney's most recent venture capital fund. Based on his relationships with Harris and Rotner, Laverack convinced his partners at J.H. Whitney to finance the second round of NBX.

By October 1997, NBX was running out of capital again. This time it was looking for $12.7 million and needed another investor. Laverack figured that they should try Morganthaler Ventures because of J.H. Whitney's relationship with that firm. Rotner also thought this was a good choice because MIT was a big investor in Morganthaler's fund, and Rotner sat on Morganthaler's advisory board.

The partners at Morganthaler Ventures thought NBX Corporation was a good investment, but there were a lot of good companies in the Internet phone business at that time. They almost didn't invest, but agreed to do so largely on the basis of Morganthaler's relationship with MIT and J.H. Whitney.

The moral of this story is that financing a new venture depends very much on social ties. NBX obtained several stages of venture capital that it otherwise wouldn't have received because of social ties between the founders and investors or between earlier investors and later investors. Given the advantages that venture capital offers new firms (see Table 6.1), one might say NBX's success depended on social relationships.

Table 6.1 Why Entrepreneurs Seek Venture Capital

Venture capital backing offers a wealth of advantages for new firms, from enhanced credibility to operating assistance.

TYPE OF ADVANTAGE	REASONING
Capital	Venture capital is a major source of high-risk capital for new ventures.
Credibility	The prestige of venture capital backing makes it easier for entrepreneurs to persuade customers, employees, and suppliers of the value of their new businesses.
Connections to investment bankers	Because of the high volume of initial public offerings that they back, venture capitalists have close ties to investment bankers, which can facilitate a company going public.
Connections to suppliers and customers	Venture capitalists often link the companies that they finance together as suppliers and customers of each other.
Assistance in recruiting the management team	Venture capitalists have strong ties to executive search firms and can help entrepreneurs attract CEOs and other senior management talent.
Operating assistance	Many venture capitalists were former entrepreneurs and have significant experience building new companies.

Social ties were very important to the founders of NBX because they helped to raise a large amount of venture capital. But why did it matter that the founders obtained this type of financing? As Table 6.1 indicates, venture capital provides entrepreneurs with a wealth of advantages, from serving as a major source of money for high-risk new businesses to demonstrating the credibility of the new business, to providing connections to important stakeholders, to giving assistance running a new business. We will talk more about venture capital later in the chapter, but for now just remember that venture capital backing provides a lot of value to new firms.

The remainder of this chapter will expand on the new venture financing process. In the first section, we will discuss why it's so difficult for entrepreneurs to raise the money they need for their new ventures. Two broad categories of problems—**information asymmetry**, or the fact that entrepreneurs know more about their opportunities than investors, and **uncertainty**—make raising money difficult, and demand specific arrangements that you will need to understand if you're going to raise external capital for your start-up.

In the second section, we will describe the amount, source, and type of capital that new ventures typically raise. We will explain why entrepreneurs usually raise a small amount of initial capital and then obtain additional financing later. We will teach you important tools for the financial analysis of your new venture, including estimating the amount and use of start-up capital, proforma financial statements, cash flow statements, and breakeven analysis. We will also discuss the difference between *debt* and *equity* financing, and explain why entrepreneurs typically obtain equity financing in the early days of their ventures. Finally, we will outline the variety of sources of financing that entrepreneurs tap.

In the third section, we will describe the structure of venture finance for the high-potential ventures that typically receive *business angel* and *venture capital* financing. In particular, we will outline the equity financing process from initial contact with investors to receiving money. We will also explain why equity investors typically stage financing, and how they establish a price for their capital.

In the fourth section, we will return to the discussion that we started in the beginning of this chapter about social capital and the behavioural side of raising money. We'll explain why having direct or indirect social ties to investors is important to raising money, and we'll outline the actions and behaviours that successful entrepreneurs use to encourage venture capitalists or others to back them.

WHY IS IT SO DIFFICULT TO RAISE MONEY? THE PROBLEMS OF UNCERTAINTY AND INFORMATION ASYMMETRY

Most entrepreneurs will tell you that the single most difficult part of starting a company is raising money. In fact, when researchers have asked entrepreneurs what their biggest concerns were in starting their new companies, the most common response is "raising money." When the researchers have asked entrepreneurs what kind of help would have been most valuable in the firm formation process, the most common answer is help with obtaining capital.[1]

But why is raising money for a new venture so difficult? The answer lies in what entrepreneurs are asking investors to do. As we indicated in Chapter 3, entrepreneurs identify uncertain new venture opportunities based on information that other people either do not have or do not recognize. As a result, investors must make decisions about funding new businesses of very uncertain value with less information than the entrepreneur has. This uncertainty and information asymmetry creates problems in financing new companies. Because entrepreneurs who want to raise money from external investors need to overcome these problems, it is important that we explain to you what they are.

Information Asymmetry Problems

The fact that entrepreneurs have or recognize information about their business opportunities that investors don't have or can't recognize creates three problems for raising money. First, entrepreneurs are reluctant to disclose information to investors,

LEARNING OBJECTIVE

1 Explain why it is difficult for entrepreneurs to raise money from external investors.

requiring investors to make decisions on limited information. Entrepreneurs need to keep secret the information about their opportunities and their approaches to exploiting them. If other people learned this information, then they could pursue the same opportunities. Moreover, investors have the money necessary to exploit the opportunities (otherwise the entrepreneurs wouldn't be talking to them about financing). So entrepreneurs don't want to tell investors too much about their opportunities or ways of exploiting them, lest the investors exploit the opportunities without them. As a result, entrepreneurs keep information about their opportunities hidden, and investors have to make decisions about financing ventures with less information than entrepreneurs have.[2]

Second, the information edge that entrepreneurs have makes it possible for them to take advantage of investors. Entrepreneurs can use their superior information to obtain capital from investors and use it for their own gain instead of for the benefit of the company.[3] For example, suppose an entrepreneur tells his investor that he needs a large expense account to entertain clients. The investor can't really know whether the entrepreneur needs the expense account because clients in that industry will not make purchases unless they are wined and dined or because the entrepreneur likes fine food and wine and will use the expense account as a way to dine out. Why? Because the entrepreneur supplies the information about the need for the expense account, and it might not be true.

Third, the investor's limited information about the entrepreneur and the opportunity creates the potential for a problem called **adverse selection**. Adverse selection occurs when a person is unable to distinguish between two options; for example, between two people, one who has a desired quality, and the other who doesn't. Because it's not possible to distinguish between the two people, the one without the desired quality has an incentive to misrepresent her attributes and say that she has the desired quality. For example, some entrepreneurs have what it takes to build a successful new company and some don't. If investors can't tell one from the other, those without the ability to build successful companies will mimic the behaviour of the others to get financing. For instance, they will pretend to possess skills, information, or experience that they really don't have. To protect themselves, investors charge a premium to pay for the losses incurred from backing the wrong people. Because talented entrepreneurs don't want to pay this premium, they withdraw from the financing market, leaving only the entrepreneurs that investors don't want to back, creating adverse selection.[4]

Uncertainty Problems

Investors also face a variety of problems because new ventures are very uncertain. First, they have to make judgments about the value of opportunities and the ability of entrepreneurs on the basis of very little actual evidence. The factors that determine which ventures will become valuable investments—such as the demand for the new product, the financial performance of the firm, the ability of the entrepreneur to manage the company, and so on—cannot be known for certain until after entrepreneurs obtain financing and start to exploit their opportunities.[5] When the entrepreneur doesn't have a patented technology or a long track record of building successful businesses (which is the case for most ventures), then the investor has to make a determination on the basis of very little hard evidence, making the financing decision very risky.[6]

Second, entrepreneurs and investors often disagree about the value of new ventures. Because new ventures are uncertain, no one really knows how profitable—if at all—a new venture will be. Therefore, investors make their financing decisions on the basis of their own perceptions about the profitability and attractiveness of ventures, which are almost always lower than those of the entrepreneur.[7] Why? Remember in Chapter 5, when we indicated that entrepreneurs are overoptimistic about their ventures? To motivate themselves to undertake the hard work of starting a company, entrepreneurs often convince themselves that their ventures' chances are better than they actually are. So when entrepreneurs negotiate with investors, who aren't overly optimistic, they often face difficult bargaining over the value of the venture.

Third, investors want to make sure that entrepreneurs will pay up if their ventures prove not to be valuable, especially if they are lending money to the venture. That way, the investor is risking less. Obviously, the entrepreneur can't tap the venture for funds to pay back the investor if the venture proves to be a failure. So investors ask entrepreneurs to provide **collateral**, or something of value that can be sold if the venture fails—such as the entrepreneur's home![8] (See Figure 6.1.) The problem with this arrangement is that many entrepreneurs need capital because they don't have anything of value; otherwise, they would finance the new firm themselves.

Why did we mention these uncertainty and information asymmetry problems, which might seem like abstract concepts? Because, by discussing these problems, we can make it easier for you to understand how investors solve them and you can learn why venture finance works the way that it does.

Figure 6.1 Investors Want Collateral When They Provide Debt Financing

Many entrepreneurs mortgage their homes to provide collateral to obtain the capital that they need to start their businesses.

Solutions to Venture Finance Problems

Don't worry. The new venture finance business is alive and well. Investors have solved the information asymmetry and uncertainty problems described above. In this section, we will outline the solutions that they've come up with, so that you can learn what you will have to do to raise money when you start your new venture.

Self-Financing

When you raise money to finance a new venture, investors will want you to invest your own money in the venture as well. The amount of capital that you contribute doesn't really matter. What's important is that you put in an amount that is a large percentage of your net worth. So if you have $10,000 to your name, investors will want it all invested in the business; but you'll have to kick in closer to $1 million if that's what you're worth.

Why do you have to put in a lot of your own capital when you are raising money from other people? After all, you probably don't want to risk losing your own money in a failed venture. Actually, that's precisely the point. You know more about the venture opportunity than any investor. So if you don't think a venture is a good enough idea to risk losing your own money, then why should investors risk theirs? Moreover, investors are worried that unscrupulous entrepreneurs will take advantage of them. Suppose that an entrepreneur put none of her own money in a new venture and then used the investor's capital to buy a fancy convertible, which she then used purely for personal pleasure or convenience. The investor really wouldn't have any way to stop this behaviour. But the investor could discourage the entrepreneur from doing it in the first place. By making the entrepreneur invest her own money along with theirs, investors give the entrepreneur an incentive to be careful with the venture's capital. If the entrepreneur invests in the venture, it wouldn't just be the investor's money that was wasted on gas for the convertible; it would also be the entrepreneur's.[9]

Although making entrepreneurs self-finance is useful for mitigating venture finance problems, it is not a complete solution, especially for very large ventures. Most people don't have enough money to self-finance large venture opportunities. For example, when Fred Smith started Federal Express, he needed tens of millions of dollars to assemble trucks, aircraft, and an information management system. He just wasn't rich enough to finance Federal Express out of his own pocket. He

Howard Sandler/Shutterstock

LEARNING OBJECTIVE

2 Identify specific solutions to venture finance problems created by uncertainty and information asymmetry, and explain why these solutions work.

needed to raise capital from others. Because entrepreneurial self-finance isn't a complete solution to the problems that investors face, investors use a variety of other mechanisms to manage information and asymmetry problems.

Contract Provisions

To protect themselves against the problems that uncertainty and information asymmetry create, investors include a variety of provisions in their contracts with entrepreneurs. First, they include covenants on entrepreneurs' behaviour. **Covenants** are restrictions on someone's actions (see Figure 6.2). Common covenants in new venture finance include precluding the entrepreneur from purchasing or selling assets or shares without investors' permission, as well as **mandatory redemption rights**, which require the entrepreneur to return the investors' capital, when requested.[10] Second, investors employ **convertible securities**, or financial instruments that allow investors to convert preferred stock, which receives preferential treatment in the event of a liquidation, into common stock, at the investor's discretion.[11] Third, investors use **forfeiture** and **antidilution provisions**. Forfeiture provisions require entrepreneurs to lose a portion of the ownership of their ventures if they fail to meet agreed-upon milestones.[12] Antidilution provisions require entrepreneurs to provide investors with additional shares in the new venture so that the investor's percentage of ownership is not reduced in later rounds of financing. Fourth, investors give themselves **control rights** to the new ventures that they finance. Control rights provide the discretion to determine how to use a venture's assets. Investors typically take a disproportionate share of control rights—for instance, they own 30 percent of the shares of the company, but take 51 percent of the seats on the board of directors. Finally, investors make it difficult for entrepreneurs to leave the company without investors' permission, or to retain much ownership of the new venture if they leave. This is accomplished by requiring long **vesting periods**, during which time entrepreneurs cannot cash out of their investments. All of these tools minimize the likelihood that entrepreneurs will act against the interest of the investors, either by restricting the entrepreneur's behaviour or by reducing the incentive to act contrary to the investors' interests. These tools also make entrepreneurs bear more of the uncertainty of the new venture, shielding investors against some of the risk of financing new companies.

Specialization

To better choose which new ventures to invest in, and to manage those investments after they're made, investors in new firms tend to specialize in two ways. First, they specialize by industry, with some focusing, for example, on the software industry and others on biotechnology. Second, many investors specialize by the stage of development of the venture, with some investors concentrating on making small investments very early in the lives of new firms, and others focusing on making larger, later-stage investments.[13] Specialization helps investors by providing them with contacts among suppliers, customers, and experts who can help evaluate the ventures that they are thinking of backing, and by ensuring that the ventures are on the right track once they have invested in them. Moreover, by specializing, investors can learn the key success factors at a particular stage of a firm's life or in a particular industry—information that makes them better able to assist and monitor new firms. Therefore, specialization helps investors overcome both information asymmetry and uncertainty problems in new venture finance.

Figure 6.2 Investors Require Entrepreneurs to Agree to Restrictive Covenants

Investors require entrepreneurs to agree to certain terms and conditions in return for financing.

DILBERT reprinted by permission of United Feature Syndicate, Inc.

Geographically Localized Investing

Unlike investors in the stock market, who often think nothing of buying shares in a foreign company traded on the stock exchange, investors in new ventures almost always make investments in companies located near them. The rule of thumb is typically not to invest in a venture more than a two-hour drive from one's office.

Why do venture investors limit their investments to local entrepreneurs? First, localized investing makes it easier to for investors to be heavily involved in new companies. Investors want entrepreneurs to give them regular updates about their ventures, and often have to step into the day-to-day operations of new firms if something starts to go wrong.[14] In fact, investors will replace the entrepreneurial team with new management if they need to, a change that requires intense involvement to accomplish.

Second, local investing makes it easier to pick the right companies to back. Investors find it easier to develop a network of sources of information about good start-ups if they focus on a constrained area. Moreover, because investors have to assess the value of information provided by entrepreneurs, they use their contacts to confirm entrepreneurs' claims about their business ideas, their talents, and so on.[15]

Syndication

Many investors in new ventures, particularly venture capitalists and business angels, choose to **syndicate**; that is, to attract other investors to join in them in making investments. Syndication allows investors to diversify their risks by putting smaller amounts of money into a variety of companies rather than putting large sums of money into one or two firms. Syndication also helps investors gather information about entrepreneurs and investors. By syndicating, investors can gather information from a greater variety of different people with different experience and knowledge,[16] as well as check their decisions against the decisions of others.[17] Both of these activities help investors to make better investment decisions.

KEY POINTS

- The problems of uncertainty and information asymmetry make it difficult for entrepreneurs to raise money from external sources.
- Information asymmetry means that investors must make decisions with less information than the entrepreneur has, that entrepreneurs can take advantage of investors, and that entrepreneurs can engage in adverse selection.
- Uncertainty means that investors have to make decisions about new ventures on very little actual evidence, that entrepreneurs and investors will disagree on the value of new ventures, and that investors will want assurance that the entrepreneur can pay up if the opportunity proves not to be valuable.
- Investors have established several solutions to the financing problems generated by information asymmetry and uncertainty, including self-financing, contract provisions, syndication, specialization, and geographically localized investing.
- Self-financing reduces entrepreneurs' incentive to act against the interests of investors, and provides collateral for new ventures.
- Covenants, mandatory redemption rights, convertible securities, control rights, and forfeiture and antidilution provisions are all contract provisions that help to protect investors against uncertainty and information asymmetry problems in venture finance.
- Investors syndicate their investments to diversify their risks and to gather information that reduces the problems generated by information asymmetry.
- Specialization and geographically localized investing provide investors with information and control that protects them against opportunistic entrepreneurs.

AMOUNTS AND SOURCES OF CAPITAL: HOW MUCH AND WHAT TYPE DO YOU NEED?

An entrepreneur will need to ask three important questions before starting a venture: How much money do I need? Where should I get that money? What type of arrangements do I need to make to obtain that capital? To answer these questions, you need to know about the amount and timing of new venture finance, the differences between debt and equity financing, and the sources of new venture finance. In this section, we provide answers to these questions, gleaned from academic research and expert entrepreneurs.

Amount of Start-Up Capital

LEARNING OBJECTIVE

3   Explain why entrepreneurs typically raise very little start-up capital.

If you read the newspaper regularly, you might be surprised to learn that most new ventures do not require much start-up capital. The financing process for the typical start-up is very different from what is described by *The Financial Post* for new ventures that make the pages of that newspaper. It has been estimated that the average Canadian business requires less than $50,000 in startup capital.[18] However, this amount varies according to the type of business. Amar Bhide, an entrepreneurship professor at Columbia University, distinguishes between asset-based start-ups and hustle-based start-ups.[19] Asset based start-ups compete on the basis of the proprietary assets they own, such as patents, locations, and brands. Most technology-based businesses and consumer goods firms fall into this category. Hustle-based start-ups compete on the basis of the entrepreneur's hustle—persuasiveness, personal selling skills, reputation, and expertise. Most service-based businesses fall into this category, at least initially. Asset-based start-ups generally require higher start-up capital, because the founding team needs to build the assets early. For example, when David Ossip founded Workbrain, a scheduling software company, in 1999, he and his family invested an initial $1 million to develop a prototype that could be installed at test customer sites. On the basis of the prototype test results, Workbrain was able to raise an additional $4 million from investors.[20]

Start-up requirements were much different for Jody Steinhauer, who founded The Bargains Group in the late 1980s. With a cash investment of only $1,000, a cellphone, and a fax machine, she built a company that procures clearance wholesale clothing for customers, such as Winners.[21] Rather than building assets such as technological prototypes, she needed to build a complex network of suppliers. Of course, entrepreneurs starting asset-based businesses need to exhibit hustle and persuasiveness, and entrepreneurs starting hustle-based businesses need to build barriers to entry, but this classification is useful for thinking about the magnitude of start-up funds necessary to get different types of ventures off the ground.

Estimating Financial Needs: Start-Up Costs, Proforma Financial Statements, Cash Flow Statements, and Breakeven Analysis

Okay, so you may not need that much capital to start a business. But how do you figure out how much money you'll need for your new business? Entrepreneurs use four important tools to figure these things out: a list of start-up costs and use of proceeds, proforma financial statements, cash flow statements, and breakeven analysis. Not only will you need to learn to use these tools to start your business, but you'll also have to put these projections into your business plan if you want to raise money. Any reputable investor will want to see this information as part of the process of evaluating your business.

List of Start-Up Costs and Use of Proceeds

One of the first things that you will need to do on the financial side of your new business is create a list of start-up costs, or costs that would need to be incurred to get the business off the ground. Examples of start-up costs are the cost of buying the equipment that you'll need to get going—ovens for a bakery, trucks for a delivery service, and so on—as well as inventory or supplies. Because you probably will have to incur costs to produce and sell your product or service, you'll need some working capital to tide you over through the period when cash is flowing out but none is flowing in. Any working capital that your business will need to get off the ground also needs to be included in your start-up costs. Furthermore, if you need to buy any long-term assets for your new business, such as a building in which to operate, that expense will need to be included as a start-up cost as well.

Once you have estimated your start-up costs, then you can figure out a couple of things that are important to raising money and getting your venture off the ground. First, you can determine the total amount of money that you are going to need to get started. This estimate is crucial to figuring out where to obtain the capital that you need. Second, you can determine how you will use the capital once you receive it. For instance, will you use the proceeds from an investment or a loan to buy equipment or a building? Or will you use the capital to obtain initial inventory and supplies? Identifying how you will use your start-up capital is important because you aren't going to be able to obtain financing until you can show investors how you are going to use their money.

Proforma Financial Statements

Now we can get down to the bottom line. After an entrepreneur estimates the start-up costs and the use of funds, the next step on the financial side of the new business is the creation of the venture's projected financial statements (including the entrepreneur's projected bottom line!). Entrepreneurs need to create proforma financial statements for their new businesses. Proforma financial statements provide projections (usually for three years) of the financial condition of the new venture based on the information that the entrepreneur has collected about the market, customers, competitors, product development, operations, and other parts of the business. Proforma income statements estimate the profit and loss for the new business. Proforma balance sheets show the financial structure of the business and allow founders and investors to conduct ratio analysis. Most experts recommend that you calculate the income statement for your business monthly or at least quarterly, and estimate the venture's balance sheet at least quarterly. Industry Canada's online tool, Performance Plus, enables entrepreneurs to compare their financial data with industry averages (http://sme.ic.gc.ca/epic/internet/inpp-pp.nsf/en/Home).

When developing their proforma financial statements, most entrepreneurs learn two lessons fairly quickly. First, the estimates of profit or loss shown in income statements depend very much on the quality of the entrepreneur's sales estimates. Therefore, accurate financial statements depend very much on accurate market analysis. In Chapter 10, we will discuss in great detail how to estimate market size and sales in a new venture. This information will be important when creating the income statement for your new venture.

Second, the estimates of profit and loss shown in income statements also depend very heavily on accurate estimates of costs. Most entrepreneurs get into trouble because of the natural tendency to underestimate costs. Remember that sales are generated through activities such as advertising and hiring people, which create costs. So any increases in sales that you project in your financial statements should be accompanied by increases in costs.

In addition, businesses in a particular industry tend to have very similar relationships between costs and sales. Therefore, when you're creating your new business's financial statements, you should carefully compare your financial statements with those of other businesses in your industry. Are your numbers realistic? For example, you project sales of $1,000,000 per year and plan to hire one saleswoman, but other firms in your industry report average sales of $300,000 per year per salesperson. Take another pass at the numbers. Odds are that your venture is not going to be more than three times as good as the average firm in your industry at generating sales. We hope

LEARNING OBJECTIVE

4 Create proforma financial statements and cash flow statements and conduct breakeven analysis.

that you will do well, but potential investors will be skeptical of any claims that you make that are much better than industry averages.

To help you to develop your proforma financial statements (and remind you of what you did in accounting class), we provide an example of a balance sheet and income statement in Table 6.2.

Cash Flow Statements

CIMITYM. Do you know what that stands for? "Cash is more important than your mother." Many venture capitalists provide this abbreviation to the entrepreneurs that they back to make sure they realize how important cash flow management and cash flow statements are to new ventures. Because most venture capitalists believe that cash flow is more important than their portfolio company founders' mothers (okay, probably not really, but it makes a point), we need to spend some time discussing cash flow management.

Cash flow statements are calculations of the amount of cash that your new venture has at a given point in time. You'll need cash flow statements to manage your new business. If a company has negative cash flow, it will be unable pay its bills and will become insolvent.

Managing cash flow is difficult because income statements do not measure the amount of cash in a business. As a result, many a business has become insolvent while remaining profitable. How is this possible? Many expenses in your income statement, such as depreciation, affect profit and loss, but do not involve real cash flows. So your business can have a profit or loss through depreciation of assets that is not reflected in actual cash flows. Moreover, cash inflows and outflows don't always occur at the same time as revenues and expenses are incurred. Sales, in particular, often occur long before customers pay for those sales, as is the case when customers buy on credit or are simply late in paying their bills.

Let's look at an example. Suppose you started a furniture business. In the first month of the life of your business, you sell a couch for $2,000 that cost you $1,000 to

Table 6.2 Proforma Financial Statements

This table shows the proforma income statement and balance sheet for Campus Pies, a new venture that sells fruit pies made according to grandma's secret recipe.

CAMPUS PIES BALANCE SHEET		
	12/31/05	12/31/06
Cash	$ 22,143	$ 26,218
Accounts receivable	$ 14,807	$ 15,801
Inventory	$ 6,284	$ 10,113
Property and equipment	$500,000	$500,000
Less: Accumulated depreciation	($ 47,901)	($ 74,112)
Total Assets	$495,333	$478,020
Accounts payable	$ 7,212	$ 8,216
Notes payable	$412,500	$412,500
Total Liabilities	$419,712	$420,716
Stockholders' equity	$ 75,621	$ 57,304
Total Liabilities and Equity	$495,333	$478,020

CAMPUS PIES INCOME STATEMENT 12/31/06	
Sales	$147,213
Less: Cost of goods sold	$119,612
Gross profit	$ 27,601
Less: Operating expenses	($103,400)
Less: Depreciation	($ 26,211)
Net Loss	($102,010)

obtain. Therefore, you book a profit of $1,000. However, your customer pays you after 30 days, following your 30-days-same-as-cash plan. As a result, your business doesn't have positive cash flow in the first month. If you had to pay $1,000 cash to obtain the couch, you'll have negative $1,000 cash flow in the first month of your business.

This example illustrates that it is important for you to estimate your new business's cash flow as well as its income. You create a cash flow statement from your income statement, so you do not need to keep two sets of books: one based on accrual accounting for the bank, investors, and tax officials, and one based on cash accounting to monitor your cash flow. To convert information from your income statement to your cash flow statement, follow these steps, as Table 6.3 illustrates:

1. Take your net profit and add back depreciation.
2. Subtract increases in accounts receivable or add decreases in accounts receivable.
3. Subtract increases in inventory or add decreases in inventory.
4. Add increases in accounts payable or subtract decreases in accounts payable.
5. Subtract decreases in notes/loans payable or add increases in notes/loans payable.
6. The resulting figure is your net cash flow.

Suppose your analysis reveals that your venture will have negative cash flow. What can you do to keep your business from becoming insolvent? The short answer is that you can improve your venture's cash flow. How? First, you can minimize your accounts receivable by offering customers discounts for paying quickly, limiting the credit that you extent to customers, and selling your receivables to companies that purchase accounts receivable at a discount in return for immediate cash. Second, you can reduce the raw material and finished products inventory that you hold to meet unanticipated customer demand. Third, you can control your spending by avoiding nonessential expenditures, such as nice furniture for your office, by leasing equipment instead of buying it, by recycling and reusing equipment and supplies, and by adding employees slowly. Fourth, you can delay your accounts payable. For instance, you can incur the extra cost of obtaining credit from your suppliers by

Table 6.3 Net Cash Flow

This table shows the conversion of information in Campus Pies' income statement to a cash flow statement.

STEP	CALCULATION FOR CAMPUS PIES	RESULT
Take net profit (net loss) from the income statement.	($102,010)	($102,010)
Add depreciation.	($102,010) + $ 26,211	($ 75,799)
Calculate the increase in accounts receivable between 12/31/05 and 12/31/06.	$ 15,801 – $ 14,807	$ 994
Subtract the increase in accounts receivable from the result in line 2.	($ 75,799) – $ 994	($ 76,793)
Calculate the increase in inventory between 12/31/05 and 12/31/06	$ 10,113 – $ 6,284	$ 3,829
Subtract the increase in inventory from the result in line 4.	($ 76,793) – $ 3,829	($ 80,622)
Calculate the increase in accounts payable between 12/31/05 and 12/31/06	$ 8,216 – $ 7,212	$ 1,004
Add the increase in accounts payable to the result in line 6.	($ 80,622) + $ 1,004	($ 79,618)
Calculate the decrease in notes payable between 12/31/05 and 12/31/06.	$412,500 – $412,500	$ 0
Subtract the decrease in notes payable from the result in line 8.	($ 79,618) – $ 0	($ 79,618)
Net cash flow for the year ended 12/31/06.		($ 79,618)

giving up on early payment discounts. Although it might cost you a little more to approach your business in this way, you might be able to keep the business solvent when cash outflows are larger than inflows.

Breakeven Analysis

Another tool that entrepreneurs need to master is **breakeven analysis**, which calculates the amount of sales that you need to achieve to cover your costs. Breakeven analysis also lets you figure out the increase in sales volume that you would need if you were to increase your business' fixed costs. To calculate your breakeven level of sales, take the following steps:

1. Determine the sales price (per unit) of your product or service.
2. Estimate the variable cost (per unit) of your product or service.
3. Subtract the variable cost per unit from the sales price to calculate your contribution margin (per unit).
4. Estimate your business's fixed costs.
5. Divide the fixed costs by the contribution margin percentage to calculate the breakeven sales volume.

Therefore, the breakeven point in terms of units sold can be calculated using the formula:

total fixed costs / (unit sales price – unit variable costs).

Table 6.4 provides an example to illustrate the calculation of the breakeven level of sales. Play around with the numbers shown in the example. You'll soon realize that the higher the proportion of your costs that are fixed, the higher your breakeven level of sales will be. So remember that buying fixed assets is going to increase your fixed costs, your breakeven level of sales, and the risk of your new venture.

To summarize: The biggest issue about raising money isn't getting enough money to *start* the business. That's relatively easy. What's more difficult is getting enough money at the right times during the early life of the venture to make sure that the venture doesn't run out of cash. Almost all new ventures experience negative cash flow from operations early in their lives. Negative cash flow means that the operation of the business uses more cash than the business generates. It will kill a new business unless the entrepreneur can obtain additional capital. The key to avoiding negative cash flow is to look for money when you don't need it. In fact, experienced entrepreneurs often say that you should look for money before you need it, and raise more money than you think you need. As the **Danger! Pitfall Ahead!** section indicates, it often takes awhile to find money, especially if your business really needs cash.

Table 6.4 Breakeven Analysis

This example shows the calculation of the breakeven level of sales for Campus Pies.

STEP	INFORMATION	CALCULATION
Determine the sales price (per unit) of your product or service.	Sales price is $10.00 per pie.	
Estimate the variable cost (per unit) of your product or service.	Variable cost is $3.00 per pie.	
Subtract the variable cost per unit from the sales price to calculate your contribution margin (per unit).	Contribution margin per unit is $7.00 per pie.	$10.00 – $3.00 = $7.00
Estimate your business's fixed costs.	Fixed costs are $500,000.	
Divide the fixed costs by the contribution margin percentage to calculate the breakeven sales volume.	Breakeven level of sales is 71,429 pies.	$500,000 / 7.00 = 71,429
Interpretation	As sales exceed 71,429 pies, Campus Pies earns a profit. Sales of fewer than 71,429 pies result in a loss.	

DANGER! PITFALL AHEAD!

The Hazards of Raising Too Little Money

When I (Scott Shane) taught at the DuPree College of Management at Georgia Tech, an M.B.A. student came to my office one day asking for advice on financing his new company, which had just developed a new inventory management software program. The student had just received a phone call from an Atlanta-area venture capital firm that wanted to finance his venture, and he wanted to talk to me about the terms he had been offered.

The venture capital firm proposed providing the new venture with $1 million in financing in return for 30 percent of the company. The plan would be to use the investors' capital to refine the prototype of the software, do a beta test, and launch the product. However, the student wasn't sure he should take the financing offer. He had only asked for $500,000 in seed capital; and he had only wanted to give up 10 percent of the company to get the money. His plan had been to use $500,000 in capital to refine the prototype and then seek more capital when the beta test began. Moreover, he had a business angel willing to take those terms.

I urged the student to take the venture capital financing, arguing that it is more important to raise enough capital than to get the best valuation of the new company. But the student was stuck on the terms. "Why," he asked, "should I give up 30 percent of the company to get $1 million when I could give up 10 percent of the company to get $500,000? If I do two financing rounds at $500,000, I'd still have 80 percent of the company left. And besides, the venture will be so much further developed by the time of the next round, that I'll get the next round of money for even less equity." I explained that the venture might run into a rough spot along the way, and that he might not be able to raise the money he needed later. "Take the money when you can get it," I said. "You never know when it will be offered to you again."

The student decided to go with the business angel's offer, and put the $500,000 he received toward developing the software. Unfortunately, it proved to be a lot harder to develop the software than the student had originally thought, and he ran through his capital very quickly. When the money started running out, the student went out looking for additional financing. However, because the beta test didn't look good, not very many investors were interested, and the student couldn't find anyone to give him the capital he needed.

The entrepreneur in this story scraped by for six more months by selling equipment and giving employees stock in place of their paycheques. But that wasn't enough. After spending $750,000, he still didn't have a working beta version of his software, and he was out of capital. Although the student probably could have solved the software problems in a few more months, no one would give him the $250,000 that he needed to keep going. So he had to close up shop.

The moral of this story: Always raise more money than your venture needs, and obtain capital when you don't need it. Moreover, make sure that your estimate the **burn rate**, the pace at which you use funds, conservatively. A good rule of thumb: It will almost always be twice as high as you originally thought! Raising enough money is essential to allowing your venture to survive and grow; to respond to unforeseen circumstances and change directions; to take the best approach to developing the business—hiring the best people, buying the best equipment and so on; and to project an image to external stakeholders of a stable, dependable and legitimate new venture.[22] If you don't raise enough money when money is easy to raise, chances are that you will run out of cash. It's almost impossible to raise money when you really need it.

Types of Capital: Debt versus Equity

When new ventures are very young, they rarely obtain **debt** financing, and tend to obtain **equity** financing instead. Debt is a financial obligation to return the capital provided plus a scheduled amount of interest; equity is a portion of ownership received in an organization in return for money provided. New ventures tend to be financed by equity for two reasons. First, until ventures have generated positive cash flow, they have no way to make scheduled interest payments. As a result, entrepreneurs need to raise money in a way that doesn't require them to make fixed payments on that capital—that is, to obtain equity investments. Second, debt financing at a fixed rate of interest encourages people to take risky actions when investors can't observe entrepreneurs' decisions. Why? If an entrepreneur fails, she can't lose any more money than she put into the venture (although the entrepreneur could lose her house if she put it into the venture by pledging it as collateral on a loan), so her downside loss is the same regardless of how much risk she takes. However, because the entrepreneur pays the same amount of

> **LEARNING OBJECTIVE**
>
> **5** Define debt and equity financing and explain how they differ.

© Getty Images/ PhotoDisc

Figure 6.3 Asset-Based Financing Is an Important Source of Capital for New Ventures

Entrepreneurs finance certain types of equipment, such as trucks, through asset-based lending in which the equipment itself provides collateral on the loan.

interest on debt regardless of how well her venture does, she keeps all of the returns from success. Thus, with debt, she has an incentive to take high risk–high return actions. In contrast, with equity investments, the entrepreneur would have to share any greater benefit that accrues from success at risky actions and so won't be as inclined to take them.

Occasionally, new ventures do obtain debt financing. When new ventures receive this type of financing early in their lives, it tends to be one of three varieties. The first is debt guaranteed by the entrepreneur's personal assets or earning power, as is the case when an entrepreneur uses credit cards or a home equity loan to finance the business. The second is **asset-based financing** (see Figure 6.3). Asset-based financing is debt that is secured by the equipment that it is used to buy. Many products, such as trucks, computers, and photocopiers, can be financed this way. (We will talk more about asset-based lenders later.) The third is supplier credit. In many industries, suppliers offer credit to entrepreneurs to obtain inventory and equipment, as is the case when a restaurant supplier finances a restaurant entrepreneur. The supplier provides the kitchen equipment, and will take it back if the entrepreneur fails to pay interest and principal on the loan to pay for it.

A recent study by Professors Stewart Thornhill, of the University of Western Ontario, and Allan Riding, of the University of Ottawa, together with Guy Gellatly, of Statistics Canada, examined the capital structure of more than 2,500 young Canadian firms. The researchers found that firms in high-knowledge industries had a significantly lower debt-to-equity ratio than firms in low-knowledge industries. The explanation for this finding is that firms operating in high-knowledge industries are operating in an environment of greater uncertainty. Their most important assets, such as R&D and human expertise, are intangible and therefore are both less liquid and more difficult to use as collateral. As a result, such firms have less access to debt financing.[23]

Sources of Capital

LEARNING OBJECTIVE

6 Describe the different sources of capital for new ventures.

Entrepreneurs have a wide variety of sources of capital for their new businesses. Because these sources are very different from one another, and all have advantages and disadvantages, it is important to be familiar with these sources, and to know when they are most useful to entrepreneurs. This section of the chapter describes the different sources of capital for new ventures.

Savings

The single most important source of capital for new ventures is the entrepreneur's own savings. Researchers have shown that approximately 70 percent of all entrepreneurs finance their new businesses with their own capital.[24] A recent Industry Canada study shows that the start-up of 66 percent of small and medium-sized enterprises in the country are financed by the savings of the owner (see Figure 6.5).

Friends and Family

Many entrepreneurs turn to their friends and family members to raise the capital that they need to finance their businesses. Although asking one's father-in-law for the money to buy equipment for a new business is a TV-sitcom standard, this scenario also appears to be true for financing real ventures. In many industries, particularly retail businesses and restaurants, entrepreneurs raise a lot of their capital from family members. Usually these financing arrangements are informal, with the entrepreneur promising to pay the money back when it's possible. However, in some cases, raising money from friends and family members can be systematic, with the entrepreneur signing promissory notes and paying interest, or selling shares of the company to obtain capital.

Business Angels

Business angels are private individuals who invest in new ventures. The typical business angel is a former entrepreneur. Business angels generally invest between $10,000 and $200,000 per venture in businesses that are geographically close to where they live and work, and in industries that they know well. They tend to demand a lower return on their investment than venture capitalists because they are less financially motivated. In addition to having the goal of making money, many business angels invest in new companies to stay involved with the entrepreneurial process. Because of their business experience, they can be valuable mentors to first-time entrepreneurs.

Venture Capitalists

Venture capitalists are people who work for organizations that raise money from large institutional investors, like university endowments and company pension funds, and invest those funds in new firms. Venture capital firms are generally structured as limited partnerships in which a fund is established for a fixed period of time, typically 10 years. The institutional investors, who provide the capital, are called limited partners because their participation is limited to providing money. The venture capitalists themselves, who make investment decisions in start-ups and manage those investments, are called general partners. At the end of the life of a venture capital fund, the venture capital firm returns the capital invested to the institutional investors plus a percentage of any profits from investing in the start-ups (usually 80 percent). The general partners keep the other 20 percent and also take a management fee (typically 2 percent of the capital in the fund annually) for managing the investments. The terms and conditions for venture capital investments should be spelled out in the company's unanimous shareholders' agreement.

In addition to providing money to new firms, venture capitalists provide assistance in operating new businesses; help to identify key employees, customers, and suppliers; and assist with operations and strategy formulation and implementation. A study of Silicon Valley start-ups by University of British Columbia professor Thomas Hellmann and Stanford University professor Manju Puri indicates that venture capitalists aid in the professionalization of new firms, in terms of human resource policies, the adoption of stock option plans, and the hiring of a VP of sales and marketing.[25] Because venture capital–backed start-ups are more likely to go public than other start-ups, venture capitalists develop strong relationships with investment bankers who underwrite initial public offerings. As a result, venture capitalists also help new firms to go public.

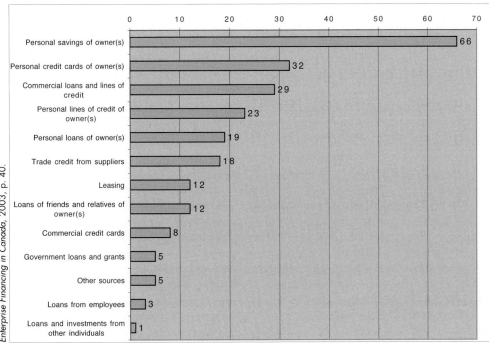

Source: Adapted from Industry Canada. *Small and Medium-Sized Enterprise Financing in Canada*, 2003, p. 40.

Figure 6.4 Where Entrepreneurs Obtain Initial Capital for Their New Businesses

This graph shows the percentage of Canadian entrepreneurs that use each of the listed sources of capital. Two-thirds of start-ups rely heavily on the entrepreneur's savings and personal credit cards as sources of initial capital.

Although venture capitalists offer a lot to new companies, they are also very demanding investors. Very few businesses meet their criteria for financing. In general, only businesses with a great deal of growth potential are interesting to this class of investors. As Table 6.5 shows, to receive venture capital backing, a new venture typically needs to operate in a high-growth industry, possess a proprietary competitive advantage, offer a product with a clear market need, and be run by an experienced management team with a plan to go public.

Moreover, venture capitalists impose a large number of restrictions on the behaviour of entrepreneurs. Venture capitalists often require entrepreneurs to issue convertible preferred stock, which allows the venture capitalist to have liquidation preference in the event that the venture does not do well, but allows common stock ownership in the event that the venture succeeds. Venture capitalists also include a large number of covenants in their agreements with entrepreneurs. For instance, they typically bar entrepreneurs from purchasing assets or issuing or selling shares without their permission, and demand mandatory redemption rights that require entrepreneurs to give them their investment back at any time. Finally, venture capitalists employ forfeiture provisions that cause entrepreneurs to lose ownership if their performance falls below target goals, and antidilution provisions that transfer shares from entrepreneurs to their investors if the venture fails to meet performance targets. Given the demands that venture capitalists place on entrepreneurs, and venture capitalists' focus on extremely high-potential companies, you will need to evaluate very carefully whether venture capital financing is appropriate for your new company.

Corporations

Many companies make strategic investments in new companies. By making these investments, they can obtain access to new companies' products or technology. In return, the established companies provide important marketing and manufacturing

Table 6.5 What Venture Capitalists Want

Venture capitalists have clear preferences in the types of businesses and entrepreneurs that they finance.

DIMENSION OF THE OPPORTUNITY	VENTURE CAPITALISTS' PREFERENCES	REASONING
Investment size	$3 million to $15 million	Transaction costs are high on small investments, but large investments are risky.
Screening	Invest in less than 1 percent of proposals	Very few ventures meet performance standards that venture capitalists demand.
Industries	High technology	Technology provides the high rate of growth that venture capitalists demand.
Control rights	More control than is proportional to the number of shares owned	Investors want to have the ability to make decisions about the direction of the company.
Ownership	Less than 50 percent	Investors do not want to undermine the incentives of the entrepreneur.
Competitive advantage	Proprietary advantage, such as a patent or exclusive contract	Investors need to be able to see the competitive advantage to know it exists.
Exit strategy	Plan for initial public offering or acquisition by established company	Venture capitalists need to cash out and return capital to the investors that provided it.
Management	Experienced entrepreneurs	Investors want to back people who understand how to build companies.
	Complementary team that balances aspects of business	Investors want a team that understands the industry and spans the functional areas of business critical to the venture.
Market	Large and growing market with no existing competitors	The venture needs a large and growing market to avoid direct competition.
Product	Product or service that meets a clear market need in a way that is demonstrably better than existing alternatives and provides high gross margins	Investors want to make sure that there is a clear need and that the new venture alternative will justify customer switching.

support for new ventures, as well as improve the latter's credibility. Another advantage of corporate investors is that they generally offer better valuation than financial investors, such as venture capitalists and business angels. However, entrepreneurs need to be careful. Corporations provide favourable financial terms, relative to other investors, because they want to obtain access to the intellectual property and products developed by new companies. Therefore, entrepreneurs have to protect their intellectual property when obtaining financing from large corporations.

Banks

University of Ottawa professors Barbara Orser and Allan Riding, together with Carleton University professor George Haines, have studied the banking environment for Canadian firms, and observed that small firms, young firms, and firms in the retail and service sectors are both less cost-efficient and more risky for banks than large, established firms and firms in other sectors. As a result, such firms have more difficulty in obtaining credit and face higher interest rates and more stringent terms.[26] In general, banks are not in the business of lending money to start-up companies. However, commercial banks do provide a variety of types of capital to new businesses under the right circumstances. First, banks occasionally provide new companies with standard **commercial loans**, particularly after those companies have begun to generate positive cash flow and when entrepreneurs can secure those loans with property, equipment, or other assets. A commercial loan is a form of financing in which the borrower pays interest on the money borrowed. Second, banks sometimes provide new companies with **lines of credit**, or agreements to allow entrepreneurs to draw up to a set amount of money at a particular interest rate, whenever they need it. Lines of credit are usually used to finance inventory or accounts receivable. Despite these examples, bank loans are relatively rare for very new businesses; positive cash flow is necessary to pay interest on a loan. As shown in Figure 6.5, many start-ups rely on individual debt financing, such as personal credit cards, personal lines of credit, and personal loans.

Asset-Based Lenders

Asset-based lenders provide financing by using the assets themselves as collateral for the loan. Take, for example, a new business that needs to purchase some computers and trucks. Both of these assets can be financed by asset-based lenders who offer loans at a certain percentage of the value of the assets (typically around 60 percent). For example, an entrepreneur could purchase ten computers and two trucks by pledging the computers and trucks as collateral against the loan, and borrow about 60 percent of the value of that equipment.

Factors

Factors are specialized organizations that purchase the accounts receivable of businesses at a discount (usually 1 or 2 percent). Because customers in many industries have between 30 and 90 days to pay their bills, new businesses often turn to factors to obtain capital immediately. With factoring, the new venture sells its accounts receivables to the factor for 98 to 99 percent of what they're worth, and receives the cash value of those receivables immediately.

Government Programs

Federal, provincial, and municipal governments offer a variety of programs to finance new businesses (see Figure 6.5). Canada Business, an information service

Figure 6.5 The Government Can Be an Important Source of Capital for Entrepreneurs

Federal, provincial, and local governments offer a wide array of programs to provide capital to entrepreneurs or to help them to obtain capital from the private sector. Hattie Dunstan, of the University of Guelph, started a jewellery business with summer funding from the Youth Entrepreneurs Program of Ontario's Ministry of Economic Development and Trade.

Courtesy of Hattie Dunstan

NEL

operated by the federal government, provides a comprehensive listing of financing sources available to Canadian entrepreneurs by public sector organizations (http://www.canadabusiness.gc.ca). Most of these programs provide loans-based assistance with lending terms tailored to the needs of small or young businesses. For example, the Business Development Bank of Canada (http://www.bdc.ca) is a financial institution owned by the federal government that will provide start-up loans to Canadian entrepreneurs who have a viable business plan and invest some money themselves. Some of the loans-based programs are oriented towards specific client bases. For example, the Aboriginal Development Fund provides loans to start, expand, and modernize aboriginal businesses in Atlantic Canada, and the Urban Entrepreneurs with Disabilities Initiative provides loans to entrepreneurs with disabilities who are living in major cities in Alberta, Saskatchewan, or Manitoba.

A second group of programs, often related to innovation or the development of technology, can provide partial funding of a project. For example, the GeoConnections/ GeoInnovations Program funds the development of geomatics applications and related technologies, while CANtex provides both repayable and non-repayable funds to help textile companies make their production processes more efficient. A third group of programs provide specialized assistance. For example, Trade Routes provides Canadian entrepreneurs in arts and culture sectors with specialized information to assist them in developing their firms' export potential and increasing their international sales. Many government programs provide a combination of loans, grants, and/or specialized services. For example, the Export Development Corporation (http://www.edc.ca) provides trade financing and risk management services (e.g., insurance) to Canadian companies doing business in foreign markets, and the Women's Enterprise Centre of B.C. provides loans, training, and counselling for women who are starting, purchasing, or growing a business in British Columbia. There are also programs oriented specifically to young entrepreneurs. For example, the Young Entrepreneurs Program of Ontario provides students 15 to 29 years of age with start-up funds, training, and mentoring to start and operate a summer business. Because there are so many government programs customized for particular client groups and industry sectors, it is important to check the programs currently available for you and your particular business concept.

KEY POINTS

- New ventures typically require very little start-up capital, but tend to demand larger amounts of capital later, as they experience negative cash flow from operations.
- To manage the financial side of new businesses, entrepreneurs estimate start-up costs and uses of funds, create proforma financial statements, generate cash flow statements, and undertake breakeven analysis.
- New ventures are generally financed by equity rather than by debt because they lack sufficient cash flow to pay interest, and because debt financing at a fixed rate of interest encourages entrepreneurs to take risky actions with investors' funds.
- Entrepreneurs have a wide variety of capital sources available to them, including their own savings, their friends and family, business angels, venture capitalists, corporations, banks, asset-based lenders, factors, and government programs.

THE STRUCTURE OF VENTURE FINANCE

Because we want you to develop a high-potential new venture—one that has the chance to make a lot of money and provide useful products or services to a large number of people—we think that it's important to describe the process by which high-potential new ventures acquire external financing. In this section, we'll describe the typical equity financing process for entrepreneurs who obtain capital from business angels and venture capitalists (because debt financing is fairly uncommon in high-potential ventures at their early stages). We focus on how the process works with venture capitalists and business angels because we can't really describe the process for raising money from your friends and family. That would depend a lot on those people, and we don't know your aunts, uncles, and roommates.

In addition to describing the financing process in general, we want to make sure that you understand a key part of the financing process—the staging of capital—so we'll talk about that in detail. We'll also discuss how much equity investors are going to take from you in return for their money, and explain how they calculate the cost of capital.

The Equity Financing Process

In general, the financing process begins with an initial introduction of the entrepreneur to the investor. Although angels and venture capitalists often receive hundreds and even thousands of business plans each year, they ignore most of them. Typically, these investors don't even consider investments unless the ventures are referred by someone the investors know and trust. Investors generally first evaluate business plans by checking to see who referred the venture. If they consider the referral to be a good one, then they will take a quick look at the business plan; typically, this quick look involves glancing at the executive summary of the business plan to see what the business is, what market it will operate in, what market need it's filling, and the product or service it's offering. Investors will weed out 95 percent of the plans they receive from this type of quick scan.

LEARNING OBJECTIVE

7 Describe the equity finance process from start to finish.

For the remaining 5 percent of plans, the investor undertakes a more formal investigation, looking for characteristics that make a venture a desirable one for external financing. So what are investors looking for? Two things: The first is an excellent venture team, the second is an excellent business opportunity.

On the venture team side of the equation, investors want to see evidence that the entrepreneur is motivated and passionate about the business, as well as honest and trustworthy. However, seeing this evidence is a relatively limited screen. Not having these characteristics might eliminate an entrepreneur from further consideration. But it doesn't weed out many people; most entrepreneurs are honest, trustworthy, motivated, and passionate about their businesses.

The real screen on the team side of the equation is experience. Investors look for entrepreneurs who they think can build companies. In general, they favour people who have started and built companies before, and who have a lot of experience in the industry they are entering.[27]

On the opportunity side of the equation, investors look for factors that demonstrate the value of the venture opportunity and the entrepreneur's ability to capture that value. We'll talk more about these factors in Chapters 7, 8, 10, and 11, but, in general, they include such things as a large market, product acceptance, an appropriate strategy, a way to protect the entrepreneur's intellectual property against imitation, a well-designed production plan, a compelling description of a product, and so on.[28] In particular, investors favour new ventures that have an externally observable competitive advantage, such as a patent, because such assets are easier to evaluate than intangible things like the entrepreneur's willingness to work hard.[29]

Once the investors are fairly sure that they would like to invest in a new venture, they conduct **due diligence**. Due diligence is a legal term that refers to the effort by investors to verify information about the new venture. It typically includes an investigation of (1) the business—the market, the business model, the intellectual property; (2) the legal entity—the organizational form, board of directors, patents, trademarks; and (3) the financial records—the company's financial statements.

If the new venture passes the due diligence hurdle, then the investor will negotiate the terms of the investment with the entrepreneur. This negotiation usually focuses on the amount of equity that the investor will receive in return for providing capital. We will explain how venture capitalists and angel investors decide on the amount of ownership that they want in return for their investment. But first, we need to explain why the initial investment the entrepreneur receives will be small relative to the total amount of investment that a successful firm will ultimately receive, and why the investors make those investments in small pieces over time.

Staging of Investment

LEARNING OBJECTIVE

8 Explain why equity financing in new ventures is typically staged.

New ventures typically raise money from investors in a series of stages, rather than all at once. That is, investors provide a small amount of money to create an **option**—a right, but not an obligation—to make additional investments later. Why? First, investing in new ventures is very risky for investors. To minimize their exposure to this risk, investors put in a small amount of money and see what happens to this initial investment. This way, the most that the investor can lose is the small amount of the initial investment.

The entrepreneur uses the initial investment to reach a **milestone**, or set target that they need to achieve for investors to consider additional financing. Examples of milestones to achieve with initial capital are the development of a prototype for the product or service, obtaining customer feedback through a survey or focus group, organizing the relevant venture team, hiring employees, and so on. If the milestone is achieved, the investor puts more money in. If the milestone isn't met, the investor discontinues investment in the venture.

Second, **staging** helps to protect investors against efforts by entrepreneurs to use their information advantage to gain at the expense of the investor. By putting money into a new venture over time, the investor has the opportunity to gather information about how the venture is doing before investing further. If the entrepreneur does anything that the investor doesn't like, such as using the money for private gain (throwing lavish parties, for example) or if the entrepreneur adopts too risky a strategy because it's not his money at risk, the investor can decide not to put more money in.[30] However, if the investor invested upfront the entire amount of money that the entrepreneur needed in the venture, then this option would lost.

Last, staging helps investors manage the uncertainty of investing in new ventures. In the very early stages of a new venture—right after the discovery of the opportunity and before a product or service has been developed—new ventures are very difficult for investors to evaluate because so little information is available. Over time, however, as a new venture develops, information about the product, the entrepreneur's management style, the firm's strategy, and so on become clearer, making it easier for investors to evaluate the venture. Because uncertainty is reduced as the venture develops, delaying most of the investment until after the venture has reached key milestones allows the investor to manage the uncertainty of investing in new ventures.[31] Table 6.6 summarizes the staging of venture finance.

The Cost of Capital

LEARNING OBJECTIVE

9 Describe how venture capitalists calculate the cost of the capital that they provide to new ventures.

How much will you pay to obtain capital for your new venture? Obviously this is an important question for entrepreneurs, and the answer is a lot! Over the past 40 years or so, equity investors in new ventures have demanded an annual rate of return of between 20 and 100 percent, depending on the venture's stage of development.

Why do investors in new ventures demand—and receive—such high rates of return? After all, even Tony Soprano, HBO's popular waste management entrepreneur, doesn't get this kind of return from his investments. There are several reasons: First, new ventures are extremely risky—and returns are inversely related to risk. Very few new ventures are ultimately successful, and investors need a high return to make up for all of the failures that they back. In fact, a rule of thumb used by investors in new ventures is that only one in ten succeeds, requiring the successful venture to pay a high rate of return to make up for the capital lost on the other nine. Second, investors in new ventures can't diversify their risks very well. Most investors in new ventures need to

STAGE	CONDITION OF THE VENTURE	SOURCES OF CAPITAL	USES OF CAPITAL	COST OF CAPITAL
Pre-seed stage	The entrepreneur has an idea, but has not yet formed a company or written a business plan.	Entrepreneur Friends and family Business angels Corporations	Write a business plan. Form a company.	70–100% rate of return
Seed stage	The entrepreneur has formed a legal entity, has a partial venture team, and has written a business plan.	Entrepreneur Friends and family Business angels Venture capitalists Corporations	Develop a prototype of the product. Fill out the venture team. Conduct market research.	60–80% rate of return
First stage	The entrepreneur has organized the company, and the product development and initial market research are complete.	Entrepreneur Friends and family Business angels Venture capitalists Corporations	Make initial sales. Establish production. Buy fixed assets.	40–60% rate of return
Second stage	The entrepreneur has produced and sold initial versions of the product, and the organization is up and running.	Business angels Venture capitalists Asset-based financiers Corporations	Scale up production. Hire additional people for sales and for production.	20–40% rate of return

Table 6.6 Stages of Financing

Investors stage financing to new ventures. Each stage has different sources of financing, different uses of capital, and different expected rates of return.

focus on a particular industry and geographic location to develop enough expertise to manage their investments. Therefore, their investments are dependent on the overall performance of a particular industry—remember the collapse of Internet ventures?— and the vagaries of the local economy. Third, investors demand an **illiquidity premium**, or extra compensation for the fact that they can't sell their investments. (As you probably know, there's no market for shares of start-ups like there is for publicly traded stocks.) Fourth, as we have said earlier, entrepreneurs have information about new ventures that they don't share with investors. Because that information advantage allows some entrepreneurs to take advantage of investors, investors demand a premium for making investments when they have an information disadvantage. Fifth, entrepreneurs are often overoptimistic when they project the future prospects of their new ventures, so investors demand a high rate of return to discount these overoptimistic projections. Sixth, unlike investors in the stock market who are largely passive, investors in new ventures provide several types of assistance to new ventures, including identifying customers, attracting suppliers, and hiring senior management, and investors want compensation for providing this assistance.[32]

The main factor that determines the rate of return that investors receive for financing new ventures is the stage of venture development. As Figure 6.6 shows, the rate of return goes down as the venture moves to later stages of development because uncertainty is reduced as ventures develop. However, the

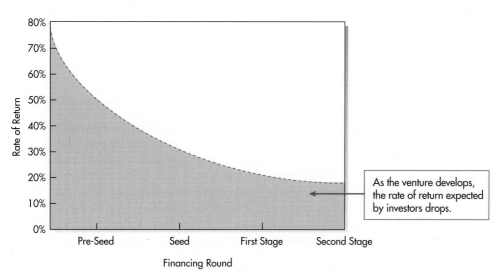

Financing Round

Figure 6.6 Rates of Return and Financing Rounds

The rate of return that investors demand decreases as the venture becomes more developed.

As the venture develops, the rate of return expected by investors drops.

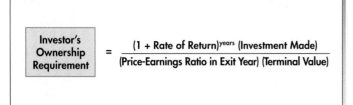

$$\text{Investor's Ownership Requirement} = \frac{(1 + \text{Rate of Return})^{\text{years}} (\text{Investment Made})}{(\text{Price-Earnings Ratio in Exit Year}) (\text{Terminal Value})}$$

Figure 6.7 The Formula for the Investor's Expected Share of a New Venture

Venture capitalists use this method to calculate how much ownership in a new venture they demand in return for their investment.

maturity of the venture isn't the only factor that influences the cost of capital. Investors also factor in their perception of the capabilities of the venture team and the quality of the business opportunity, including the size and growth rate of the market. Investors weigh the amount of capital required and the risk that is imposed on them. Founders' objectives for how the venture exit will occur and their desire for control, as well as their ability to bargain with investors, also influence the rate of return.

The cost of capital provided to new ventures can be calculated a number of different ways. However, the most common way used by professional investors is called the **venture capital method**. This method, shown in Figure 6.7, is as follows: First, the investor looks at the business plan's forecasted earnings and estimates the venture's level of income in the year that the new business is expected to be acquired or go public. Second, the investor calculates the appropriate price-earnings ratio for acquisitions and public offerings in the same industry as the new venture. Third, the investor estimates the **terminal value** of the investment by multiplying the projected income by the price-earnings ratio. Fourth, the investor uses the appropriate **discount rate**, based on the desired rate of return for the investment, and calculates the net present value of the terminal value. Fifth, the investor specifies the portion of ownership that they will take by dividing the investment amount by the net present value of the terminal value.

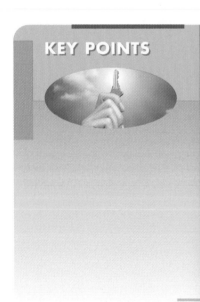

KEY POINTS

- Equity financing by business angels and venture capitalists follows a common process that typically begins with a referral, and is followed by an initial screening, a deeper investigation, due diligence, and ends with the negotiation of the terms of the investment.
- Equity investors in new ventures typically stage their investments to minimize risk, to minimize the potential for entrepreneurs to take advantage of the investors' lack of information, and to manage uncertainty.
- Investors in new ventures demand high rates of return to compensate for high risk, limited ability to diversify, illiquidity, information asymmetry, entrepreneurial overoptimism, and a need for investor involvement in the new venture's development.
- Venture capitalists and business angels typically use the venture capital method to calculate how much equity to demand in return for their investment.
- The venture capital method involves taking the business plan's forecasted earnings in the year that the entrepreneur projects the exit, calculating the appropriate price-earnings ratio, multiplying these numbers to estimate the terminal value, calculating the present value of that number on the basis of the investor's discount rate, and dividing the investment amount by the net present value figure.

SOCIAL CAPITAL AND THE BEHAVIOURAL SIDE OF VENTURE FINANCE

This chapter began with a story about how three entrepreneurs used their social relationships to obtain capital. Although we have spent most of this chapter discussing the more structural and economic factors involved in venture finance, both research and entrepreneurial experience show that raising money depends heavily on the social and behavioural factors that lie behind the story that introduced this chapter. In this section, we'll turn to a discussion of how and why social relationships, and certain behaviours and actions, help entrepreneurs to raise money from external investors.

Social Ties and the Process of Raising Money

Entrepreneurs typically raise money from people they know, tapping their social networks for contacts to sources of capital. Researchers have shown, for example, that investors are much more likely to provide capital to entrepreneurs with whom they have a direct business or social tie—that is, people with whom they have done business before, or their roommates in college—than to people to whom they have no tie.[33] Moreover, indirect social ties, or ties to people who can refer an entrepreneur to an investor (for example, a lawyer who does work for a venture capitalist) also increases the likelihood that an entrepreneur will receive financing from an investor. [34]

Why do social ties matter to raising money for new ventures? There are several reasons: First, if the investor knows the entrepreneur, then the entrepreneur will be less likely to try to take advantage of the investor. Social relationships make people act in a less self-interested way by creating a sense of obligation and generosity.[35] Most people know that a good way to kill a friendship is by taking advantage of a friend; this principle influences relationships with investors as well as relationships with roommates.

Second, social ties provide a way to invoke sanctions against people who harm others. Just like a group of friends might rally to your defence or take actions against someone who hurt you, investors use their social networks to keep entrepreneurs in line. Entrepreneurs who break the rules or take advantage of investors are quickly blackballed by the investing community.[36]

Third, social relationships provide an efficient way to gather information about people. Social networks transmit information quickly and cheaply, particularly about hard-to-observe qualities, like a person's competence or honesty.[37] So a referral from a reputable source provides an efficient way of figuring out who the good guys are.[38]

Fourth, social ties—whether direct or indirect—create positive attributions about people. When someone refers you to a third party, that referral elevates you in the eyes of the person who is going to meet you. Why? Because you have been singled out as someone important. People meeting you for the first time are predisposed to thinking that you are better than people who weren't referred to them. Similarly, if you already know someone and you are their friend, you'll tend to make positive attributions about their actions in a new setting. So if you are a good doubles partner of a venture capitalist, the positive feelings of the venture capitalist toward your net game will be carried over when you ask him for money.[39]

In short, social ties to investors really do help you to raise money (see Figure 6.8). Therefore, in practical terms, you should go first to those investors you know if you are serious about raising money. You should work your contacts. Getting referrals to investors is a central part of the process of financing a new company.

Behaviours and Actions That Encourage Investors

Entrepreneurs sometimes forget that the investors from whom they are trying to raise money are people. Just like other human beings, investors are influenced by the behaviours and actions of others. Although you probably don't need us to tell you that it would be hard to persuade investors to give you money if you met them without having washed for a month or if you cursed at them when you greeted them, you might not be aware of the more subtle behaviours and actions that entrepreneurs can engage in to positively or negatively influence investors.

In Chapter 5, we discussed the importance of impression management to entrepreneurs. Nowhere is that more important than in raising money. To obtain capital, an entrepreneur needs to generate the impression of being trustworthy and competent, and that the venture is going to be successful. Successful entrepreneurs recognize that no entrepreneur can provide irrefutable evidence that the venture will succeed and that investors, like everyone else in this world, are influenced by appearances as well as actual performance.[40] Successful entrepreneurs are careful to generate a good impression with investors.

> **LEARNING OBJECTIVE**
>
> **10** Explain why direct and indirect social ties are important to raising money from external investors.

> **LEARNING OBJECTIVE**
>
> **11** Identify the behaviours and actions that successful entrepreneurs engage in to encourage investors to back them, and explain why these behaviours and actions are effective.

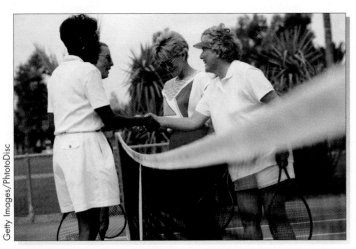

Getty Images/PhotoDisc

Figure 6.8 Social Ties Are Important to Facilitating Access to Capital

Entrepreneurs are more likely to receive venture capital or angel financing if they are referred to the investor by someone the investor knows and trusts.

They use many of the general impression management strategies that we discussed in Chapter 5. For instance, successful entrepreneurs are careful to create a good story about their ventures in their business plans so that they can persuade investors of the value of their ideas. They use effective verbal and nonverbal communication mechanisms, and avoid inadvertent negative cues, such as failing to smile or looking uncomfortable.

But successful entrepreneurs do more than just use these interpersonal techniques. They create a sense of urgency among investors so that they can generate momentum in favour of their business.[41] They also frame their business ideas in ways that make them more appealing to investors. For instance, they describe their businesses in ways that focus attention on their potential value and away from their potential risks, by making associations between their businesses and things that are familiar to investors.[42] An entrepreneur with a space tourism business, for example, might focus attention on the types of exotic vacations, such as safaris, that investors are familiar with, rather than on the dangers of space flight.

This is where a good business plan comes in, and why your professor told you that it's important to write a persuasive one if you hope to raise money. Your business plan needs to communicate the message of your business—why the need is there, how you are going to solve it, why you are going to make money, and so on—in a clear and compelling way. Remember that investors are people and that a good presentation and cogent argument will often convince people to do something that they might otherwise not do.

KEY POINTS

- Entrepreneurs typically raise money from people they know because social ties reduce the likelihood that entrepreneurs will take advantage of investors, because social networks provide an effective way for investors to sanction entrepreneurs, because social relationships provide an efficient way to transfer information, and because social ties create positive attributions about people.
- Successful entrepreneurs use impression management strategies to encourage investors to back them. They create good stories about their ventures in their business plans, and use effective verbal and nonverbal communication.
- Framing business ideas in ways that focus attention on potential and away from risks and creating urgency also encourages investors to back entrepreneurs.

Summary and Review of Key Points

- The problems of uncertainty and information asymmetry make it difficult for entrepreneurs to raise money from external sources.

- Information asymmetry means that investors must make decisions with less information than the entrepreneur has, that entrepreneurs can take advantage of investors, and that entrepreneurs can engage in adverse selection.

- Uncertainty means that investors have to make decisions about new ventures on very little actual evidence, that entrepreneurs and investors will disagree on the value of new ventures, and that investors will want assurance that the entrepreneur can pay up if the opportunity proves not to be valuable.

- Investors have established several solutions to the financing problems generated by information asymmetry and uncertainty, including self-financing, contract provisions, syndication, specialization, and geographically localized investing.

- Self-financing reduces entrepreneurs' incentive to act against the interests of investors, and provides collateral for new ventures.

- Covenants, mandatory redemption rights, convertible securities, control rights, and forfeiture and antidilution provisions are all contract provisions that help to protect investors against uncertainty and information asymmetry problems in venture finance.

- Investors syndicate their investments to diversify their risks and to gather information that reduces the problems generated by information asymmetry.

- Specialization and geographically localized investing provide investors with information and control that protects them against opportunistic entrepreneurs.

- New ventures typically require very little start-up capital, but tend to demand larger amounts of capital later, as they experience negative cash flow from operations.

- To manage the financial side of new businesses, entrepreneurs estimate start-up costs and uses of funds, create proforma financial statements, generate cash flow statements, and undertake breakeven analysis.

- New ventures are generally financed by equity rather than by debt because they lack sufficient cash flow to pay interest, and because debt financing at a fixed rate of interest encourages entrepreneurs to take risky actions with investors' funds.

- Entrepreneurs have a wide variety of capital sources available to them, including their own savings, their friends and family, business angels, venture capitalists, corporations, banks, asset-based lenders, factors, and government programs.

- Equity financing by business angels and venture capitalists follows a common process that typically begins with a referral, and is followed by an initial screening, a deeper investigation, due diligence, and ends with the negotiation of the terms of the investment.

- Equity investors in new ventures typically stage their investments to minimize risk, to minimize the potential for entrepreneurs to take advantage of the investors' lack of information, and to manage uncertainty.

- Investors in new ventures demand high rates of return to compensate for high risk, limited ability to diversify, illiquidity, information asymmetry, entrepreneurial overoptimism, and a need for investor involvement in the new venture's development.

- Venture capitalists and business angels typically use the venture capital method to calculate how much equity to demand in return for their investment.

- The venture capital method involves taking the business plan's forecasted earnings in the year that the entrepreneur projects the exit, calculating the appropriate price-earnings ratio, multiplying these numbers to estimate the terminal value, calculating the present value of that number on the basis of the investor's discount rate, and dividing the investment amount by the net present value figure.

- Entrepreneurs typically raise money from people they know because social ties reduce the likelihood that entrepreneurs will take advantage of investors, because social networks provide an effective way for investors to sanction entrepreneurs, because social relationships provide an efficient way to transfer information, and because social ties create positive attributions about people.

- Successful entrepreneurs use impression management strategies to encourage investors to back them. They create good stories about their ventures in their business plans, and use effective verbal and nonverbal communication.

- Framing business ideas in ways that focus attention on potential and away from risks, and creating urgency also encourage investors to back entrepreneurs.

Glossary

Adverse Selection: In a market where buyers cannot accurately gauge the quality of the product that they are buying, it is likely that the marketplace will contain generally poor quality products. Adverse selection was first noted by Nobel Laureate George Akerlof in 1970.

Antidilution Provisions: Contract provisions that require entrepreneurs to provide investors with additional shares in a new venture so that the investor's percentage of ownership is not reduced in later rounds of financing.

Asset-Based Financing: A type of loan in which the assets being purchased are used as collateral for the loan.

Breakeven Analysis: An analysis indicating the level of sales and production required to cover all costs.

Burn Rate: The pace at which a new venture uses capital provided by investors.

Business Angel: A person who invests in new ventures as a private individual.

Cash Flow Statements: A written statement of actual or projected cash inflows and outflows over a specific period of time, given certain levels of sales and costs.

Collateral: Something of value that an entrepreneur pledges to sell to reimburse investors in the event that there are insufficient proceeds from a venture to return the investors' principal.

Commercial Loan: A form of bank financing in which the borrower pays interest on the money borrowed.

Control Rights: The right to decide how to use a venture's assets.

Convertible Securities: Financial instruments that allow investors to convert preferred stock, which receives preferential treatment in the event of a liquidation, into common stock at the investor's discretion.

Covenants: Restrictions on the behaviour of entrepreneurs contractually agreed upon by investors and entrepreneurs.

Debt: A financial obligation to return money provided plus a scheduled amount of interest.

Discount Rate: The annual percentage rate that an investor reduces the value of an investment to calculate its present value.

Due Diligence: The review of a new venture's management, business opportunity, technology, legal status, and finances prior to investment.

Equity: The ownership of a company, which takes the form of stock. It also equals assets minus liabilities or net worth.

Factors: Specialized organizations that purchase the accounts receivable of businesses at a discount.

Forfeiture Provisions: Contract terms that require an entrepreneur to lose a portion of the ownership of the venture if agreed-upon milestones are not met.

Illiquidity Premium: Additional return demanded by investors to compensate them for the fact that an investment cannot be sold easily.

Information Asymmetry: The imbalance in knowledge about something between two parties.

Line of Credit: An agreement to allow entrepreneurs to draw up to a set amount of money at a particular interest rate whenever they need it.

Mandatory Redemption Rights: Contract terms that require an entrepreneur to return the investors their capital, when requested.

Milestone: A jointly agreed-upon goal between entrepreneurs and investors that the entrepreneur needs to meet to receive another stage of financing.

Option: A right, but not an obligation, to make a future investment.

Staging: The provision of capital in pieces conditional on the achievement of specified milestones.

Syndicate: The sharing of an investment across a group of investors.

Terminal Value: The estimated value of a new venture at the time that the investment is liquidated in an initial public offering or an acquisition.

Uncertainty: A condition in which the future is unknown.

Venture Capitalist: A person who works for an organization that raises money from institutional investors and invests those funds in new firms.

Venture Capital Method: How venture capitalists calculate the amount of equity that they will take in a new venture in return for their investment of capital.

Vesting Periods: Periods of time during which entrepreneurs cannot cash out of their investments.

Discussion Questions

1. What can entrepreneurs do to fool venture capitalists and how can venture capitalists fight back?

2. What is the hardest thing about raising money for a new business? What makes financing a new business so difficult?

3. Why should an entrepreneur agree to give up 40 percent of her company when she used her own blood, sweat, and tears to get it started?

4. How can a new company be profitable and still fail? What can you do to reduce the chances of this happening?

5. Why will you have more trouble raising debt for your new business than you'll have raising equity?

6. What can you do to make yourself and your new business more attractive to potential investors?

InfoTrac Exercises

1. **What's Wrong with Risk-Averse Venture Capitalists?** (strategy)

   John Ellis

   Fast Company, July 2003 p54(1)

   Record: A102835146

   Full Text: COPYRIGHT 2003 Gruner & Jahr USA Publishing. All rights reserved.

   1. According to the article, why is the venture capital paradigm changing?

   2. What key changes does Daniel L. Burstein predict in the venture capital paradigm?

   3. Do you agree with Burstein? Or with the author of the article? Why?

2. **Don't Count on Venture Capital, Family and Friends More Likely to Help** (The Orlando Sentinel)

   Barry Flynn

   Knight Ridder/Tribune News Service, June 24, 2003 pK1986

   Record: CJ104170537

   Full Text: COPYRIGHT 2003 Knight Ridder/Tribune News Service Byline: Barry Flynn

   1. According to the article, why do most new businesses fail?

   2. What sources of capital are most readily available to entrepreneurs?

   3. What factors do venture capitalists look for before making an investment?

GETTING DOWN
TO BUSINESS

Creating Proforma Balance Sheets, Income Statements, and Cash Flow Statements

As we explained in this chapter, you will need to develop proforma financial statements for your new business. The following steps will lead you through this exercise.

Step One: Develop 3-year proforma balance sheets for your new business, following the format shown here.

Your Company Name _____

	12/31/06	12/31/07	12/31/08
Cash			
Accounts Receivable			
Inventory			
Property and Equipment			
Less: Accumulated Depreciation			
Total Assets			
Accounts Payable			
Notes Payable			
Total Liabilities			
Stockholder Equity			
Total Liabilities and Equity			

Step Two: Develop 3-year proforma income statements for your new business, following the format shown here.

Your Company Name _____

	12/31/06	12/31/07	12/31/08
Sales			
Less: Cost of Goods Sold			
Gross Profit			
Less: Operating Expenses			
Less: Depreciation			
Net Profit (Loss)			

Step Three: Develop 3-year cash flow statements for your new business, following the format shown here.

1. Take your net profit on 12/31/06 and add back depreciation.
2. Subtract increases in accounts receivable or add decreases in accounts receivable.
3. Subtract increases in inventory or add decreases in inventory.
4. Add increases in accounts payable or subtract decreases in accounts payable.
5. Subtract decreases in notes/loans payable or add increases in notes/loans payable.
6. The resulting figure is your net cash flow for 2004.
7. Repeat for the other years.

Calculating Your Breakeven Level of Sales

In this chapter, we discussed the importance of conducting a breakeven analysis for your new venture. Breakeven analysis allows you to figure out how much sales volume you need to achieve to cover your costs. This exercise will help you to calculate the breakeven level of sales for your new venture so that you may include the information in a feasibility study. Follow these steps to do the calculation:

1. Determine the sales price (per unit) of your product or service. _____
2. Estimate the variable cost (per unit) of your product or service. _____

3. Subtract the variable cost per unit from the sales price to calculate your contribution margin (per unit). _____

4. Divide the contribution margin (per unit) by the sales price (per unit) to estimate your contribution margin percentage. _____

5. Estimate your business's fixed costs. _____

6. Divide the fixed costs by the contribution margin percentage to calculate the breakeven sales volume. _____

Evaluate your breakeven level of sales. Is it large or small? How does it compare to the average sales level of firms in your industry? How large a percentage of total sales in the market is your breakeven sales volume?

Cost of Capital

In this chapter, we discussed the venture capital method of calculating your venture's cost of capital. This exercise will help you to calculate your new venture's cost of capital so that you can include the information in a feasibility study. Follow these steps to calculate your venture's cost of capital and report the proportion of equity that the investor would take to provide you with the capital that you need. Show all steps in the process of calculating this estimate.

1. Use your proforma income statements to estimate the venture's level of income in the year that you would expect the business to be acquired or go public.

2. Calculate the appropriate price-earnings ratio for acquisitions and public offerings in the same industry as the new venture.

3. Estimate the terminal value of the investment by multiplying the projected income by the price-earnings ratio.

4. Use the appropriate discount rate, based on the desired rate of return for the investment, to calculate the net present value of the terminal value.

5. Specify the portion of ownership that investors will take by dividing the investment amount by the net present value of the terminal value.

Enhanced Learning

You may select any combination of the resources below to enhance your understanding of the chapter material.

- **Appendix: Case Studies** – Twelve cases provide opportunities to apply chapter concepts to realistic entrepreneurial situations. These brief cases call for careful analysis of real business problems and ask you to think about potential solutions.

- **Video Case Library** – Nine cases are tied directly to video segments from the popular PBS television series Small Business School. These cases and video segments (available on the Entrepreneurship website at http://www.entrepreneurship.nelson.com) give you unparalleled access to today's entrepreneurs, with expert advice and insights on how to start, run, and grow a business.

- **Management Interview Series Video Database** – This video interview series contains a wealth of tips on how to manage effectively. Access to the database and practical exercises are available on the book support website at http://www.entrepreneurship.nelson.com.

Notes

1 Blanchflower, D., & Oswald, A. 1998. What makes an entrepreneur? *Journal of Labor Economics* 16(1): 26–60.

2 Casson, M. 1995. *Entrepreneurship and business culture.* London: Edward Elgar.

3 Shane, S., & Stuart, T. 2002. Organizational endowments and the performance of university start-ups. *Management Science* 48(1): 154–170.

4 Amit, R., Glosten, L., & Muller, E. 1990. Entrepreneurial ability, venture investments, and risk sharing. *Management Science* 38(10): 1232–1245.

5 Arrow, K. 1974. Limited knowledge and economic analysis. *American Economic Review* 64(1): 1–10.

6 Bhide, A. 2000. *The origin and evolution of new businesses.* New York: Oxford University Press.

7 Wu, S. 1989. *Production, entrepreneurship and profits.* Cambridge, MA: Basil Blackwell.

8 Blanchflower, D., & Oswald, A. 1998. What makes an entrepreneur? *Journal of Labor Economics* 16(1): 26–60.

9 Barzel, Y. 1987. The entrepreneur's reward for self-policing. *Economic Inquiry* 25(1): 103–116.

10 Gompers, P. 1997. *An examination of convertible securities in venture capital investments.* Working paper. Harvard University.

11 Shane, S. 2003. *A general theory of entrepreneurship: The individual opportunity nexus.* London: Edward Elgar.

12 Hoffman, H., & Blakely, J. 1987. You can negotiate with venture capitalists. *Harvard Business Review* (March–April): 6–24.

13 Barry, C. 1994. New directions in research on venture capital finance. *Financial Management* 23(3): 3–15.

14 Sahlman, W. 1990. The structure and governance of venture capital organizations. *Journal of Financial Economics* 27(2): 473–521.

15 Sorenson, O., & Stuart, T. 2001. Syndication networks and the spatial distribution of venture capital investments. *American Journal of Sociology* 106(6): 1546–1588.

16 Ibid.

17 Lerner, J. 1994. The syndication of venture capital investments. *Financial Management* 23(3): 16–27.

18 Bygrave, W.D., & Hunt, S. A. 2005. 2004 Financing report. *Global Entrepreneurship Monitor*, Babson College and London Business School. http://www.gemconsortium.org/document.asp?id=365.

19 Bhide, A. 1994. How entrepreneurs craft strategies that work. *Harvard Business Review* (March/April): 151–161.

20 Spence, R. 2004. The perfect startup. *PROFITguide.com*, April 16. http://www.canadianbusiness.com/entrepreneur/startup_guide/article.jsp?content=20040416_134133_4956.

21 About us. http://www.bargainsgroup.com/about.aspx.

22 Baum, J. 1996. Organizational ecology. In S. Clegg, C. Hardy, & W. Nord (eds.). *Handbook of organizational studies* (pp. 77–114). London: Sage.

23 Thornhill, S., Gellatly, G., & Riding, A. 2004. Growth history, knowledge intensity and capital structure in small firms. *Venture Capital* 6(1): 73–89.

24 Aldrich, H. 1999. *Organizations evolving.* London: Sage.

25 Hellmann, T., & Puri, M. 2002. Venture capital and the professionalization of start-up firms: Empirical evidence. *Journal of Finance* 57(1): 169–197.

26 Haines, G.H., Orser, B.J., & Riding, A.L. 1999. Myths and realities: An empirical study of banks and the gender of small business clients. *Canadian Journal of Administrative Sciences* 16(4): 291–307.

27 Shane, S. 2003. *A general theory of entrepreneurship: The individual-opportunity nexus.* London: Edward Elgar.

28 Ibid.

29 Bhide, A. 2000. *The origin and evolution of new businesses.* New York: Oxford University Press.

30 Giudici, G., & Paleari, S. 2000. The optimal staging of venture capital financing when entrepreneurs extract private benefits from their firms. *Enterprise and Innovation Management Studies* 1(2): 153–174.

31 Sorenson, O., & Stuart, T. 2001. Syndication networks and the spatial distribution of venture capital investments. *American Journal of Sociology* 106(6): 1546–1588.

32 Fuerst, O., & Geiger, U. 2003. *From concept to Wall Street: A complete guide to entrepreneurship and venture capital.* Upper Saddle River, NJ: Prentice Hall.

33 Shane, S., & Cable, D. 2002. Network ties, reputation, and the financing of new ventures. *Management Science* 48(3): 364–381.

34 Shane, S., & Stuart, T. 2002. Organizational endowments and the performance of university start-ups. *Management Science* 48(1): 154–170.

35 Uzzi, B. 1996. The sources and consequences of embeddedness for the economic performance of organizations: The network effect. *American Sociological Review* 61(4): 674–698.

36 Stuart, T., & Robinson, D. 2000. *The emergence of interorganizational networks: Probation until reputation.* Working paper. University of Chicago.

37 Burt, R. 1992. *Structural holes: The social structure of competition.* Boston: Harvard University Press.

38 Fernandez, M., & Weinberg, N. 1997. Sifting and sorting: Personal contacts and hiring in a retail bank. *American Sociological Review* 62(6): 883–902.

39 Shane, S. 2003. *A general theory of entrepreneurship: The individual-opportunity nexus.* London: Edward Elgar.

40 Dees, G., & Starr, J. 1992. Entrepreneurship through an ethical lens: Dilemmas and issues for research and practice. In D. Sexton & J. Kasarda (eds.). *The state of the art of entrepreneurship* (pp. 89–116). Boston: PWS–Kent.

41 Bhide, A. 2000. *The origin and evolution of new businesses.* New York: Oxford University Press.

42 Roberts, E. 1991. *Entrepreneurs in high technology.* New York: Oxford University Press.

CHAPTER 7

INTELLECTUAL PROPERTY: PROTECTING YOUR IDEAS

LEARNING OBJECTIVES

After reading this chapter, you should be able to:

1 Explain why product development in new firms is difficult, but why new firms tend to be better than established firms at product development in most industries.

2 Explain why established firms find it easy to imitate entrepreneurs' intellectual property quickly and at a low cost.

3 Define a patent, explain what conditions are necessary for an inventor to patent an invention, and outline the pros and cons of patenting.

4 Define an industrial design and explain what conditions are necessary for an invention to be an industrial design.

5 Define a trade secret, explain what conditions are necessary for an invention to be a trade secret, and outline the pros and cons of trade secrets.

6 Define a trademark, describe why trademarks are useful to entrepreneurs, and explain how an entrepreneur can obtain a trademark.

7 Define a copyright and describe how it protects an entrepreneur's intellectual property.

8 Describe a first-mover advantage and explain the conditions under which it provides a useful form of intellectual property protection.

9 Describe complementary assets and explain when it is better for an entrepreneur to obtain control over complementary assets than to be innovative.

Capturing the Profits from New Products and Services
　The Product Development Process
　New Firm Advantages at Product Development
　Ease of Imitating Entrepreneurs' Intellectual Property

Legal Forms of Intellectual Property Protection
　Patents
　Industrial Designs
　Trade Secrets
　Trademarks
　Copyrights

Other Strategies of Intellectual Property Protection
　Learning Curves, Lead Time, and the First-Mover Advantage
　Complementary Assets

All photos this page © PhotoDisc, Inc.

"Every man with an idea has at least two or three followers." (Brooks Atkinson, *Once Around the Sun*, 1951)

In the early 1990s, Bjorn Jakobson, a Swedish entrepreneur, invented a baby-carrying device. It was a very useful product because it allowed a person to carry a baby but still have one's hands free to do other things (see Figure 7.1). As an experienced entrepreneur, Jakobson knew that other companies would soon try to imitate his product and that obtaining a patent would be a good way to protect the product against imitation. In particular, he wanted to patent it in the United States, where there was a large potential market for the device.

However, the U.S. Patent and Trademark Office had already issued eight patents for baby carriers. In 1951, Vera Maxwell received a patent on her infant carrier, followed by D.J. Hershman, who patented hers in 1966. In 1979, Sandra Hathaway patented a child carrier with an enveloping structure and suspension strap.[1] In 1983, Patricia Purtzer and William Lauer patented an infant carrier with a detachable pouch.[2] In 1990, Allison Poole and Jodi Badagliacca patented their infant carrier. In 1993, Junice Dotseth patented a baby carrier with head support,[3] and James Bicheler and Kenneth Morton patented another style of baby carrier. Finally, in 1996, Hakan Bergqvist patented still another baby carrier. Jakobson was concerned about these inventions. He knew that to obtain a patent, his baby carrier had to be something that hadn't already been invented by someone else.

At first glance, it might appear that Jakobson wouldn't be able to patent his new product because so many other people had already patented baby carriers. But, Jakobson knew that patents only protect what is stated in their claims. As we will explain in greater detail later in the chapter, a claim is the part of the patent that identifies the invention that is protected against imitation. As long as Jakobson didn't claim the same features as the other baby carriers, he could patent his baby carrier.

By carefully examining the claims of the previous baby carrier patents, Jakobson discovered that the prior inventions were different from his in several ways. As a result, he was able to claim the invention of "a baby carrier comprising two closed strap loops which are mutually connected at a point, the strap loops adapted to extend around respective shoulder regions of a user such that the point is located on a rear side of the user, a carrier piece which is connected to the strap loops both at an end part of the carrier piece and at laterally spaced sides of the carrier piece so as to form a baby supporting pouch, a pair of insert tongues secured to said strap loops, releasable fasteners providing connections between the strap loops and the laterally spaced sides of the carrier piece which, when released, enable the carrier piece to be dropped down fully around its end part, and a clasp secured to said end part of said carrier piece and including sleeves for respectively receiving said insert tongues so that said insert tongues are releasably interlocked with said clasp and a bar lock which a free length of the end part of the carrier piece is adjustable."[4]

As you probably noticed, Jakobson's patent claims are pretty narrow. This narrowness means that another person could patent another baby carrier even after Bjorn received his patent, as long as they did not violate the specific claims in his patent. In fact, just over five months after Jakobson's patent issued, Kevin Kohn of Atlanta, Georgia, filed a patent on another baby carrier.[5] The moral of this story for entrepreneurs is that a patent only protects what is stated in its claims. Even when other people have patented similar inventions previously, entrepreneurs can patent new products. But, remember that what goes around comes around. If an entrepreneur has to write narrow claims to avoid violating a previous patent, his patent will only protect the invention against a narrow range of imitators.

Figure 7.1 The Baby Bjorn: A Patented New Product

Many customers have found Bjorn Jakobson's baby carrier to be a very valuable new product, motivating the inventor to obtain a patent to protect it against imitation by others.

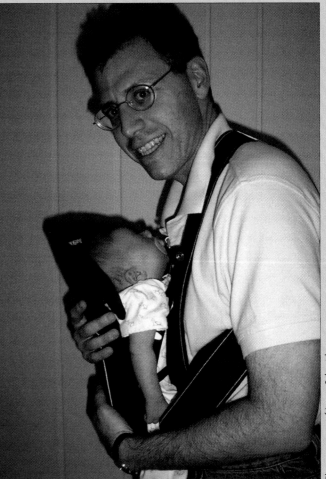

Photo courtesy of Lynne Schneider.

The remainder of this chapter will examine how entrepreneurs protect their intellectual property. In the first section, we will explain why protecting intellectual property is so important to entrepreneurs—because most of the time, entrepreneurs' only advantages over established firms lie in product development. We will also explain how the product development process works, and why new firms tend to be better at it than established firms, at least in most industries. This section will also discuss why it's very easy for people to imitate entrepreneurs' intellectual property.

In the second section, we will describe four legal forms of intellectual property protection: patents, trade secrets, trademarks, and copyrights. We'll explain how these tools work and the pros and cons of using each.

In the final section of the chapter, we will discuss forms of intellectual property protection that don't depend on legal barriers—first-mover advantages and complementary assets. We'll explain how these strategies work, and when entrepreneurs should use them to protect their intellectual property.

CAPTURING THE PROFITS FROM NEW PRODUCTS AND SERVICES

Protecting their intellectual property is very important for entrepreneurs because, most of the time (with the few exceptions we will describe in Chapter 10 about serving new markets), the only advantages entrepreneurs have over established firms lie in product development. In general, established firms are much better than new firms at marketing and manufacturing.

But just being better than established firms at product development is not enough for entrepreneurs to be successful. If entrepreneurs can't protect their **intellectual property**, which are the core ideas about their new product or service, then it doesn't matter whether they are better than established firms at product development. The established firms can wait for the entrepreneurs to complete their product development and then imitate the entrepreneurs' new products and services. In this section, we'll explain why it is very difficult for entrepreneurs to protect their intellectual property, and offer some suggestions for approaches that successful entrepreneurs have found to be effective. But first we need to explain how product development occurs and why new firms tend to be better at this activity than established firms.

The Product Development Process

Once an entrepreneur has identified an opportunity to pursue and has obtained at least the initial resources to begin pursuit of the opportunity, it is time to engage in **product development**. Product development is the process by which the entrepreneur creates the product or service that will be sold to customers.

Developing a new product or service is not easy. Even if a clear need has been recognized among potential customers, the entrepreneur still has to create a solution to that need, which can be produced and marketed for less than the customer would be willing to pay for it. That, of course, is easier said than done. For example, you probably know that cancer is a major medical problem and that people would clearly pay for a drug to treat it. Knowledge that this customer need exists doesn't mean that you can come up with a drug to treat cancer. Moreover, even if you could come up with the formula for a cancer-fighting drug, you might not be able to produce it in a cost-effective manner. For example, Taxol is a cancer drug made from the bark of the yew tree. Because yew trees are relatively rare and it takes a lot of the bark to make the drug, Taxol is very expensive. Taxol isn't a very good solution to many types of cancer, even if it were shown to be effective in treating these diseases. Medical insurers only cover the use of Taxol for very serious types of cancer that it works particularly well at treating. For other types of cancer, Taxol isn't a cost-effective solution.

LEARNING OBJECTIVE

1 Explain why product development in new firms is difficult, but why new firms tend to be better than established firms at product development in most industries.

The development of a new product or service is also difficult because it's very uncertain. Entrepreneurs don't know if the product development path will lead to a successful new product or service. In many cases, millions or even billions of dollars can be spent to develop a new product or service that doesn't work. For example, Motorola spent more than a billion dollars on a satellite-based portable phone system and then scrapped the system because it didn't work well enough to attract the necessary volume of customers.

Other times, the product development path is successful, but at developing something different from what people set out to produce. For example, when Merck was seeking to develop a drug to treat prostate problems, they found that the drug that they developed, Propecia, had the side effect of stimulating hair growth. As a result, Merck ended up developing a drug to treat baldness rather than a drug to treat prostate problems.

What does the difficulty and uncertainty of product development mean for entrepreneurs? Basically, it means that entrepreneurs are most effective at product development if they quickly screen new product opportunities to identify the most promising ones. Rather than invest heavily in the evaluation of different product opportunities, entrepreneurs do well to actually integrate their analysis with action to develop the new product.

For instance, suppose you thought of making a device to download music from the Internet and play it, like an MP3 player. Instead of conducting extensive laboratory research to decide what features to put into the prototype—testing different features and comparing them to one another on a technical basis—before making the prototype and going into production, you'd be better off building the prototype without spending a lot of time on research. By showing your best guess to some customers, you could use their feedback to figure out what you need to change before production. This approach would integrate your analysis about product features with action to get customer feedback, and avoid wasting a lot of time and money in the laboratory testing alternatives that might never matter. In addition, to avoid getting stuck in a dead end, successful entrepreneurs don't make large, sunk investments in particular product development paths, but instead maintain flexibility by limiting their investments in any one course of action.

The difficulty and uncertainty of product development also means that luck is an important part of product development. In addition to the lucky break that Merck received in the discovery of the hair growth potential of its prostate drug, successful product development also involves other types of luck, such as good timing. For example, new companies were in the process of completing the development of new computer-based voting machines just as the hanging chad controversy in the 2000 U.S. presidential election occurred. These companies had a significant advantage over companies that had completed their product development two years earlier and could not interest customers in their new products.

What is the lesson to be learned about the role of luck in product development? It isn't that we can teach you how to be lucky—if we could do that, we'd probably become professional gamblers instead of textbook authors. Rather, it is to point out that you can do everything right in product development and still fail if you are unlucky. In addition to making sure that you understand the costs and risks involved in developing a new business based on a new product or service, we want to emphasize the importance of approaching product development with a strategy of staying flexible and minimizing your investment of time and money. If there is any lesson that can be learned from the importance of luck, it's that having another chance is very valuable.

New Firm Advantages at Product Development

Product development is extremely important to entrepreneurs because it is one of the few aspects of producing and delivering a product where established firms don't have the upper hand. The advantage of new firms at product development is important because, in general, established firms are better than new firms at manufacturing products. Established firms tend to have better access to capital, which allows them to buy better equipment. They also develop tacit knowledge about production processes from years of operation that new firms cannot replicate overnight. As a result, new firms are often much less efficient and less effective at manufacturing than established firms. Moreover, established firms also have advantages of economies of scale because they have built their manufacturing operations up over time. These scale advantages allow them to manufacture products at a lower cost than new firms.

Established firms also tend to be better at marketing than new firms (except, as we will describe in Chapter 10, for products in completely new markets). In already existing markets, established firms are better than new firms at marketing because they have access to previously developed knowledge of customer needs and preferences that help them sell their products more effectively. For example, they often know how to target customers using information on the customers' previous purchasing patterns. In addition, established firms gain reputations that enhance their ability to sell new products. Established firms also have developed social ties with their customers, who are likely to be resistant to switching to new suppliers. Finally, they have marketing assets in place—such as an established sales force or retail outlets—that allow them to launch new products at a lower cost than new firms, which don't yet have these assets.

New firms make up for these marketing and manufacturing advantages of established firms with their superiority at product development. New firms tend to develop new products more easily and cheaply than more established firms because they don't have the bureaucratic structures and rules and procedures that established firms have developed over time—for example, rules about how different parts of the organization should work together and communicate. Such rules often hinder new product development. As a result, new firms can transfer information back and forth between marketing and product design people more easily, facilitating the communication and coalition building that is important to success at any creative activity.[6]

Small and start-up firms also can offer better incentives to their employees to work hard to develop new products because they can more easily provide equity as an incentive. Not only does equity motivate people to work hard to get the new product or service developed quickly, but it also allows new firms to attract talented product development people, who want the chance to make a lot of money.[7] Large, established firms can rarely match the equity incentives of new, small firms. Giving adequate amounts of equity to motivate people is difficult in large established organizations because the equity in these firms is already allocated to investors, leaving little of it to allocate to product development people. In addition, the amount that the stock price of a new firm can rise in response to the successful efforts of product development people is much larger than the amount that the stock price of a large, established firm can rise in response to the efforts of these same people because the stock price of large firms is driven by the performance of the overall business. As a result, product development people simply can't earn the kind of capital gains on stock in established firms that they can on stock in new firms.[8]

Last, new and small organizations have a great deal of flexibility, which helps them to develop new products when the unexpected occurs. Sometimes customers change their preferences in ways that people can't predict. Other times, people discover that a particular process isn't really technically feasible. These changes require product developers to change course. Just as it is easier to shift course in a small speedboat than in an ocean liner, it is easier for new and small organizations to make these changes than it is for large, established firms.

Having said all of this, we need to add a caveat. New, small firms aren't always better than large, established firms at developing new products. There are some industries in which large, established firms are better than new, small firms at product development (see Table 7.1). To be an effective entrepreneur, you need to know about these important exceptions to the product development rules that we just presented.

So what makes large, established firms better than new, small firms at product development in some industries? First, large, established firms tend to be much better at new product development in industries where production is concentrated in the hands of a few firms because these firms control access to the customer base. Second, large established firms also tend to be better at product development in industries that are capital and advertising intensive. As we explained in Chapter 6, new and

Table 7.1 When Do Small Firms Develop New Products?

Large firms are better at innovation in some industries, whereas small firms are better at innovation in others.

INDUSTRY	RATIO OF LARGE FIRM TO SMALL FIRM INNOVATIONS
Aircraft	31.000
Pharmaceutical preparations	9.231
Photographic equipment	8.778
Office machinery	6.710
Surgical appliances and supplies	4.154
Industrial inorganic chemicals	4.000
Semiconductors	3.318
Toilet preparations	2.278
Environmental controls	2.200
Special industry machinery	2.048
Radio and TV equipment	1.153
Surgical and medical instruments	0.833
Electronic components	0.740
Fabricated metal products	0.706
Electronic computing	0.696
Industrial trucks and tractors	0.650
Valves and pipefitting	0.606
Instruments to measure electricity	0.596
Optical instruments and lenses	0.571
Scientific instruments	0.518
Plastics products	0.268
Measuring and controlling devices	0.067

Source: Based on information contained in Table 1 of Acs, Z., & Audretsch, D. 1988. Innovation in large and small firms: An empirical analysis. *American Economic Review* 78(4): 680.

small firms have a much harder time raising capital than large, established firms, making them disadvantaged in industries that demand a lot of capital. Similarly, as we explained in Chapter 2, advertising depends heavily on economies of scale, making advertising-intensive industries much more favourable to large, established firms than to new, small firms. Third, new and small firms tend to be less effective at product development when industries are very research and development intensive, probably because they cannot afford to maintain large research laboratories.[9]

The lesson for entrepreneurs is quite straightforward. There isn't much of anything that entrepreneurs can do to compete with established firms in industries in which new firms are worse than established firms at product development because they are already worse than established firms at marketing and manufacturing. That's why we see so few new aircraft, pharmaceutical, and photographic equipment manufacturers, and we see even fewer successful ones. However, in industries in which entrepreneurs are better than established firms at developing new products—such as medical devices, computers, and scientific instruments—entrepreneurs have a chance to compete with established firms by taking advantage of their superior ability to develop new products. That is, they can compete if they can protect their intellectual property, a point to which we will turn in a moment.

Ease of Imitating Entrepreneurs' Intellectual Property

As we just explained, in many industries, new firms are better than established firms at developing new products and services. So why do new firms rarely reap large profits from coming up with new products or services? Why do they often lose out

LEARNING OBJECTIVE

2 Explain why established firms find it easy to imitate entrepreneurs' intellectual property quickly and at a low cost.

to established firms that were worse than they are at product development? The answer is that, with a few exceptions, most entrepreneurs' new products and services, or the intellectual property underlying them, is very easy to imitate, and can generally be copied at a fairly low cost. In fact, research by Richard Levin, now president of Yale University, and his colleagues showed that the typical unpatented process innovation could be duplicated at less than 50 percent of the cost of developing the original innovation more than 40 percent of the time. For product innovations, the numbers were even stronger, with the typical unpatented product innovation being duplicated at less than 50 percent of the original development cost more than 52 percent of the time. In addition, most of the time, a large number of firms can duplicate an entrepreneur's intellectual property. Levin and his colleagues found that almost half the time, the typical product or process innovation could be imitated by between six and ten competitors.[10]

Competitors have a wide variety of methods that they can use to imitate an entrepreneur's intellectual property at a low cost. When the entrepreneur develops a new product, the competitors' engineers can purchase that product, take it apart, figure out how it works, and produce the same thing in a process called **reverse engineering**. Competitors can also hire away the entrepreneur's employees and suppliers or just have informal conversations with them as a way to gather information about an entrepreneur's new products and services. For example, Hewlett-Packard (HP) recently had its latest printer cartridge design copied before it had even launched the new product because one of its competitors obtained a copy of the product prototype from one of HP's suppliers. (The ease of getting information from suppliers and employees is one reason why it is so important for entrepreneurs to use nondisclosure and employment agreements, which are the subject of this chapter's **Danger! Pitfall Ahead!**) Moreover, competitors often can work on their own new product development and can imitate entrepreneurs' intellectual property simply by knowing that something new has been developed and by putting their engineers and product development staff to work on copying the new product.[11]

Even patenting a technology, which we will discuss in more detail later in the chapter, does not stop imitation. In fact, because inventors are required to disclose how their inventions work in return for receiving a patent, patenting actually makes it easier for competitors to imitate the entrepreneur's intellectual property. As we will explain a little later in the chapter, the advantage of patents doesn't lie in making imitation difficult; it lies in making imitation illegal.

Our message to prospective entrepreneurs is pretty simple: You need to recognize that it takes only a short time for competitors to imitate your intellectual property. Figure 7.2 shows the number of months that competitors need to imitate a new product, at least according to one research study. So what should you do? The next two sections of the chapter discuss some ways that successful entrepreneurs

Figure 7.2 Industries Differ Significantly in the Amount of Time It Takes Rivals to Understand How to Imitate a New Product

In most industries, it takes competitors less than 12 months to figure out how to imitate a new product.

Source: Based on information contained in Table II of Mansfield, E. 1985. How rapidly does industrial technology leak out? *Journal of Industrial Economics* 34(2): 220.

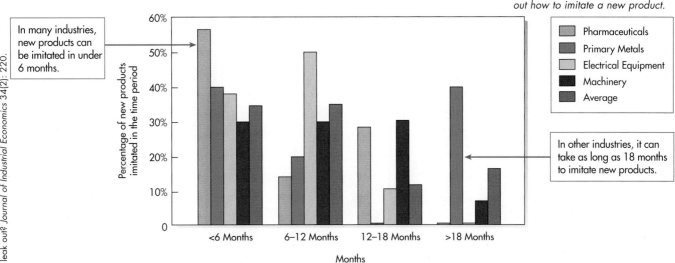

In many industries, new products can be imitated in under 6 months.

In other industries, it can take as long as 18 months to imitate new products.

DANGER! PITFALL AHEAD!

Nondisclosure and Noncompete Agreements

When I (Scott Shane) taught at the Sloan School at Massachusetts Institute of Technology (MIT), an M.B.A. student came to my office one day asking for advice on starting a new company to produce a tissue grasper, a medical device that surgeons could use to hold back tissue during an operation. The student's invention had a unique design that made it much better than alternative tissue graspers. In fact, he had already talked to several surgeons about the product, and they were all wildly enthusiastic about it.

The student's story sounded very promising; he had a very good business opportunity for starting a company. As I began to describe MIT's 50K business plan competition to the student and suggested that he enter it as a way to get his new company started, he asked a question that began to raise a red flag. "How can I be sure that I won't have any trouble from my former employer if I start the company?" he asked. "Why are you concerned?" I replied. He explained to me that before going back to school for his M.B.A., he had worked for a large, medical device company. Although he had refined the tissue grasper in a product development class at MIT, he had designed the initial version of it while he was working at this company. The student explained that his former employer wasn't interested in pursuing the development of the tissue grasper and had no intention of patenting it. But, he explained, that as an employee, he had signed **nondisclosure** and **noncompete agreements**. The first agreement precludes a person from disclosing to others any information valuable to the employer that was developed while working at the company, typically for three to five years from the termination of employment. The second agreement bars a person from working for a company that competes with the employer for a set

period of time, often one to two years. I told the student that he should have a lawyer look over his nondisclosure and noncompete agreements before he did anything else with his new venture.

The lawyer's verdict was that the student might be able to get around those agreements because noncompete agreements cannot bar employees from making a living in their profession. However, it would be something of a battle because the noncompete and nondisclosure agreements make it difficult to start a company based on knowledge developed in one's prior employment, particularly if the entrepreneur would compete against that employer. More importantly, he didn't recommend trying to start a company to make the tissue grasper. Not only would the legal fees take a lot of money the student didn't have, but also as long as the nondisclosure and noncompete agreements were unresolved issues with the former employer, it would be very difficult for the student to raise capital. Most venture capitalists and business angels simply avoid start-ups that are saddled with such legal obstacles.

The moral of this story is that you need to be careful about making agreements with your current employer if you plan to start a company later. Noncompete and nondisclosure agreements can preclude you from using ideas that you developed during that employment to start a new company (see Figure 7.3). However, there is a bright side to all this. If you start a company and you hire employees, you can get them to sign noncompete and nondisclosure agreements, which will help you to keep them from quitting and starting their own companies to make use of the ideas that they develop while working for you. You can obtain templates for such agreements on the Internet, but it is wise to check with a lawyer to make sure the agreement is enforceable in your province or territory.

Figure 7.3 Entrepreneurs Must Make Sure That They Have the Right to Use the Intellectual Property That Will Form the Basis of Their New Companies

Many would-be entrepreneurs do not realize that the employment agreements that they have signed with the companies where they work preclude them from using technology that they developed to start a new company.

DILBERT reprinted by permission of United Feature Syndicate, Inc.

keep other firms from copying their intellectual property. The following sections will help you to develop a plan for managing your new venture's intellectual property.

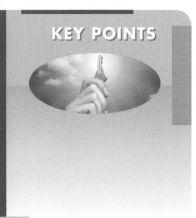

KEY POINTS

- New firms are better than established firms at product development because they do not have a bureaucratic structure, can offer better incentives to employees, and have greater flexibility.
- In industries in which established firms are better than new firms at product development, entrepreneurs have very little chance to succeed because established firms are better than new firms at marketing and manufacturing.
- New firms often fail to profit from developing new products and services because their intellectual property is easy, inexpensive, and not very time-consuming to imitate.
- Established firms can imitate entrepreneurs' intellectual property by reverse engineering entrepreneurs' products, by hiring their employees and suppliers, by having informal conversations with those people, and by conducting their own product development.

LEGAL FORMS OF INTELLECTUAL PROPERTY PROTECTION

Entrepreneurs have several legal forms of intellectual property protection available to them. Although none of these completely deters competitors from imitating their intellectual property, all of them help to protect intellectual property in some way. Successful entrepreneurs understand the advantages and disadvantages of these tools—patents, industrial designs, trade secrets, trademarks, and copyrights. In this section, we will explain what these tools can do and what they can't do so that you can choose the best way to use them to protect the intellectual property in your new venture. More information can be obtained from the Canadian Intellectual Property Office's website at http://www.cipo.gc.ca.

LEARNING OBJECTIVE

3 Define a patent, explain what conditions are necessary for an inventor to patent an invention, and outline the pros and cons of patenting.

Patents

A **patent** is a legal right granted by a national government that allows an inventor to preclude others from using the same invention for a maximum of 20 years from the date of application, in return for disclosing how the invention works. For an invention to be patented in Canada, certain conditions must be met: The invention must be novel; it must not be obvious to a person trained in the relevant field; and it must be useful. In addition, to obtain a patent, the invention must be secret at the time that the patent application has been made. If you disclosed the invention publicly, you have only a year to file the patent application.[12]

So what can you patent? You can patent a product (e.g., a snowboard); an apparatus (e.g., the binding on a snowboard); a process (e.g., a manufacturing process to make a snowboard); or a composition, such as a chemical formula (e.g., wax for a snowboard). You can't patent a business idea, such as the idea of selling fast food through a drive-through window. Also, you can't patent something that doesn't work. Recently, the courts in the United States have allowed inventors to patent business methods, such as Amazon.com's One-Click system, which permits repeat purchasers to make purchases without reentering information about themselves,[13] but business methods patents are more restricted in Canada.[14] In 2002, the Supreme Court of Canada held that higher life forms are not patentable because they are more than a composition of matter.[15] However, processes for producing a higher life form, such as plant cross-breeding, are patentable.[16]

To obtain a patent, an inventor files an application with Canada's Patent Office. Patent projection starts on this filing date. The date is important because if two inventors submit an application for the same invention, the one with the first filing date has priority.[17] Because the patent rules are complex and the whole process can take up to three years, many inventors seek assistance from a registered patent agent.[18] Approximately 30,000 patent applications are submitted each year. The initial application needs to provide little more than a description of the invention. If you have provided the required information and the required fee, then your application is pending, and the Patent Office will assign a filing number and filing date to your application. The next step is to submit a full application to be examined. Your application is made public 18 months after submission. This provides some initial protection of the invention and therefore helps the entrepreneur to obtain financing and to deter competition while the regular patent application is being processed.[19] Because the inventor needs to demonstrate that the invention is novel, the inventor or the patent lawyer searches through existing patents to determine the **prior art**. Prior art is the set of previous patented inventions that are related to the new invention. If your invention builds on prior art, you have to cite it in your patent. For example, the patent for the Baby Bjorn described at the beginning of the chapter cited the patents on previous baby carriers because Bjorn Jakobson built upon their features when he invented his baby carrier. The phrase "built upon" is important. To obtain a patent, your invention has to improve upon prior art. If your invention does exactly what the prior art does, then your device isn't an invention and you won't be able to obtain a patent.

The most important aspect of this process is determining the set of **claims**, or statements about what was invented. Inventors and their patent lawyers write these claims very carefully and try to make them as broad as possible. Why? Because, as we explained at the beginning of the chapter, a patent precludes other people from duplicating only those things stated in the claims. Therefore, a claim for a device that heats metal, for example, will protect an inventor against a much wider range of imitators than a claim for a device that heats steel. In the first case, the patent would preclude other parties from using a device to heat any type of metal; in the second case, the patent would only preclude others from using only those devices that heat steel, and others would be free to develop devices that heat iron, copper, aluminum, and so on.

Patents are very valuable tools for entrepreneurs, but they have some important disadvantages that you need to know. Table 7.2 summarizes the advantages and disadvantages of patents. Pay careful attention to the disadvantages: Many entrepreneurs get into trouble because they don't realize what they are. Among the important disadvantages of patents is the fact that they are costly to defend, are not always effective, require disclosure of the invention, and can be invented around.

The cost of patents is particularly important to entrepreneurs. The cost to obtain a patent is $15,000 or more when all legal fees are considered. Moreover, in many cases, more than one patent is required to protect a product or service, greatly increasing this cost. Furthermore, an entrepreneur is likely to want patent protection in multiple countries. To enforce a patent, an entrepreneur needs to defend it against infringement by others by going to court. This process involves hiring lawyers who develop a court case to show that another party infringed the patent or violated the monopoly right of the patent holder. Not only is the value of a patent dependent on how vigorously you defend it, but also failure to challenge people who violate your patent can undermine its effectiveness in other cases. Because defending a patent against infringement can be a very complex undertaking, especially if the case needs to go to court, obtaining and enforcing patents can become a very expensive proposition for entrepreneurs, with total costs rising easily into the hundreds of thousands and even millions of dollars.

Take, for example, Ron Chasteen's experience with his patented snowmobile fuel-injection system. Initially, he made a deal with Polaris Industries to provide the company with his fuel-injection system. One year later, Polaris cancelled the deal, saying that it was not going to use a fuel-injection system in its snowmobiles. When Polaris started selling a snowmobile with a very similar fuel-injection system to the one he had developed, Chasteen decided he had to sue. Because the litigation costs for his case were upward of $2 million, he realized that he couldn't afford to cover

ADVANTAGES OF PATENTS	DISADVANTAGES OF PATENTS
Helps to raise capital by demonstrating the existence of a competitive advantage	Requires disclosure of the invention
Raises the cost of imitation by competitors	Provides only a temporary monopoly—20 years
Provides a monopoly right by blocking other people from doing the same thing	Can be circumvented, with competitors accomplishing the same goal, but avoiding the patent protection
Prevents a second party from using the invention as a trade secret	Requires stringent legal requirements to be valid and to show infringement, making it is difficult and costly to defend a patent, especially against large companies
	Is less effective than other mechanisms at protecting intellectual property for most types of technology
	Can be irrelevant by the time the patent is granted if the technology is fast moving
	Requires patent application in all countries of the world; otherwise people can use the disclosure made in Canada to know how to exploit the invention in other countries

Table 7.2 The Advantages and Disadvantages of Patents

Although patents provide many advantages, entrepreneurs should not always patent their inventions. In many cases, the disadvantages of patents outweigh the advantages.

the costs of a lawsuit himself. After working with five law firms and spending a lot of his own money, Chasteen finally found a law firm that would take the case on contingency. Chasteen ultimately won a $70 million judgment against Polaris, but not until 11 years after he started his case.[20]

A second disadvantage of patents is that they aren't always effective. Sometimes, there is so much prior art that an inventor can only obtain a patent on a small improvement to a technology. In addition, as we mentioned earlier, patents are only as strong as their claims, and sometimes patent examiners will only allow relatively weak claims to an invention. Topping all of this off is the fact that some technologies are advancing so fast that the new product or service is obsolete by the time that the patent issues, or so many different companies have claims to different aspects of a technology that every company is forced to license their inventions to other companies or no one can produce a product or service. Because the cost of patents stays pretty much the same regardless of how effective they are, sometimes patents are simply not effective enough to make them worthwhile.

A third disadvantage of patents is that they require disclosure of the invention. The 20-year monopoly that the government provides inventors is given in return for showing others how the invention works, thereby allowing others to make use of the inventor's discovery. To obtain a patent, the inventor has to describe the invention and how it works, providing any necessary drawings that help to demonstrate its operation. This process makes it much easier for someone else to duplicate the entrepreneur's invention, possibly undermining the entrepreneur's competitive advantage if the patent cannot be enforced.

A fourth disadvantage of patents is that they can often be invented around. To understand inventing around a patent, you first need to understand that the effectiveness of patents varies greatly across industries. In pharmaceuticals and biotechnology, for example, patents are very effective at preventing imitation, but in communications equipment, they don't work very well. Why? It has to do with how technology works. When a new drug is invented, the drug's molecular structure can be patented. As those of you who have taken chemistry and biology know, the slightest change to molecular structure can dramatically change how a drug works. For example, if you take everything on the right-hand side of the molecular structure and put it on the left-hand side, you might go from an effective drug to something that kills people instantly. (Not a recommended medical treatment!) In contrast, you could easily take everything in a cellphone that was on the right-hand side of the device and put it on the left-hand side and have a perfectly effective phone. These differences in technology make it much harder for imitators to **invent around** biological and chemical patents than to invent around electrical patents. (Inventing around a patent means coming up with a solution that does not violate a patent but accomplishes the same goal.)

The savvy entrepreneur must balance the advantages and disadvantages to determine whether or not to patent. An entrepreneur should obtain a patent when a product or service meets the conditions of novelty, nonobviousness, and value, and the advantages of patenting outweigh the disadvantages. (To obtain more information about patents and to conduct a patent search worldwide, go to the Canadian Intellectual Property Office website at http://www.cipo.gc.ca.)

We need to discuss one other major issue about patents. There is no such thing as an international patent. Because patents are granted by national governments, inventors need to obtain a patent in every country where they want to protect their inventions. Patenting an invention in Canada does not protect the invention against imitation in the United States, Japan, France, or anywhere else in the world.

Why does the need to patent in multiple countries matter for entrepreneurship? First, patenting is expensive, and the need to patent in multiple countries means that entrepreneurs have to make a very sizable investment in patent costs to protect their products or services against imitation.

Second, failure to patent in a particular country means that it is legal for someone else to imitate your invention in that country. As we explained earlier, to obtain a patent in Canada, an inventor must disclose how the invention works. In other words, any time an entrepreneur patents an invention in Canada, but not everywhere else in the world, other people are being shown exactly how to develop the product or service. As a result, the entrepreneur is helping potential competitors to exploit the invention in any unprotected country!

Luckily, there is an international treaty that eases the process of applying for patents in multiple countries. You can either file for patents in each country individually, or, more easily, you can apply for protection in Canada under the Patent Cooperation Treaty. This treaty provides protection in 89 countries, including the United States, Japan, and most of the European Union, and you can apply up to 12 months after filing in Canada and yet still be assigned your Canadian filing date. Application under the Patent Cooperation Treaty does not eliminate the need to file patents in foreign countries, but it does defer the need. Reducing the time pressure means that the new firm has more time to learn which foreign markets are most promising, to acquire a preliminary international patentability opinion, and to find the resources to pay for the foreign language translation, foreign patent agents, and foreign fees.[21]

Industrial Designs

LEARNING OBJECTIVE

4 Define an industrial design and explain what conditions are necessary for an invention to be an industrial design.

An **industrial design** consists of the features of shape, configuration, pattern, or ornament of an object. While a patent application emphasizes the function of an object, an industrial design application emphasizes the design aspects of an object. The Industrial Design Office does not assess the artistic merits of the design aesthetic, but it does assess its originality.[22] For example, the shape of a snowboard is an industrial design. The registration of the industrial design lasts 10 years, and then anyone in Canada can copy it. If you mark your product to show that it is a registered design, than you may be awarded damages in an infringement suit. If you do not mark your product, the outcome of a successful lawsuit is limited to an injunction against the other party. The registration of an industrial design is marked by ⑩, followed by the name of owner of the design.[23]

As with a patent, you need to submit an application to register an industrial design. If you do not submit an application within 12 months of the design being made public (even to your neighbours), you will lose your exclusive rights to it. The application is simpler than that for a patent and includes a written description and a graphic description (drawings and/or photographs). The process usually takes between 8 and 12 months. Ownership of the design should be settled before the application is submitted. Typically, the designer is considered the owner, but if you designed an object under contract for someone else, then that person is the only person eligible to apply for an industrial design.

Trade Secrets

A **trade secret** is a piece of knowledge that confers an advantage on a firm and is protected by nondisclosure. Examples of trade secrets are production processes, for example, the way a chemical company makes fertilizer; customer lists, such as the databases at a real estate agency; and food recipes, for example, Colonel Sanders' 11 herbs and spices at KFC.

Patents and trade secrets are mutually exclusive. An entrepreneur can't obtain a patent on something and then claim it as a trade secret. Because entrepreneurs must choose between patents and trade secrets, it is important to know the advantages and disadvantages of trade secrets.

The biggest advantage of trade secrets is that they provide a way for an entrepreneur to protect a competitive advantage without disclosing to others how the technology underlying a new product or service works. Maintaining secrecy about how to exploit an opportunity is a valuable method for preventing imitation, particularly when the entrepreneur's knowledge about the exploitation process is tacit.

However, trade secrets have several disadvantages compared to patents. First, a trade secret must be kept hidden to remain valuable. In Chapter 11, we will discuss how entrepreneurs often find it difficult to keep secret their methods of exploiting opportunities, even if they have the best intentions to do so. With trade secrets, not only does the entrepreneur face the general difficulty of keeping secret their method of opportunity exploitation, but the entrepreneur must meet strict legal standards for demonstrating that they kept information secret. Ideally, their employees must sign nondisclosure forms. The entrepreneur must have procedures for keeping information secret, such as password-protecting information on computers. It must be demonstrated that certain information was kept secret by limiting access to the information and by keeping it from the view of visitors. For example, the chemical formula for Coca-Cola is a trade secret; only three executives in the company are allowed to see the actual formula, which is kept hidden in a vault in a bank in Atlanta (see Figure 7.4).

Second, unlike a patent, having a trade secret does not provide the inventor with a monopoly right. If other people independently discover the same invention (that is, they figure out the same thing without acquiring the information illegally), they are free to use it, too. On the other hand, if the trade secret were patented, then others would be barred from using it for 20 years from the date of the patent application. What does this mean in practical terms? Say you came up with the formula for Coca-Cola while experimenting in chemistry class. Because the formula isn't patented, as long as you obtained it without stealing information from Coca-Cola, you would be free to sell that beverage to anyone you wanted. Coca-Cola might sue you, claiming that you had stolen their secret, but as long as you really figured out the formula on your own, you would win the lawsuit. Canadian intellectual property laws allow independent discovery and exploitation of trade secrets by multiple parties.

Third, to enforce a trade secret and claim damages in court, you must show a loss of an economic advantage. This is a stricter standard than with a patent, which does not require you to have an economic advantage. With a patent, all you need to do to obtain damages is show that someone copied your invention.

It can be difficult to prove a trade secret infringement. Because secrecy is not a granted right, you have to prove a breach of confidentiality. Secrecy is hard to maintain over a long period of time or among large numbers of people, and so you are vulnerable when employees leave your firm.[24] For example, in a lawsuit Wal-Mart accused Amazon.com of hiring its executives in order to steal trade secrets about its information systems. In the settlement reached, the suit was dropped when Amazon.com agreed to reassign some of the employees to different work areas.[25]

The savvy entrepreneur must balance the advantages and disadvantages to determine whether to protect a new product or service through trade secrecy. An entrepreneur should use trade secrecy when a product or service confers an advantage on a firm and is protected by nondisclosure and the advantages of trade secrecy outweigh the disadvantages.

LEARNING OBJECTIVE

5 Define a trade secret, explain what conditions are necessary for an invention to be a trade secret, and outline the pros and cons of trade secrets.

Figure 7.4 Trade Secrecy Is an Important Type of Intellectual Property Protection for New Ventures

The founders of Coca-Cola chose to protect the formula for Coke by keeping it a trade secret, rather than by patenting it. This proved to be a wise decision, as the patent would have expired close to 100 years ago, but the formula for Coca-Cola still remains a secret.

© Amy Etra/Photo Edit—All Rights Reserved.

LEARNING OBJECTIVE

6 Define a trademark, describe why trademarks are useful to entrepreneurs, and explain how an entrepreneur can obtain a trademark.

LEARNING OBJECTIVE

7 Define a copyright and describe how it protects an entrepreneur's intellectual property.

Figure 7.5 Trademarks Are an Important Source of Intellectual Property Protection for Entrepreneurs

Trademarks protect a word, phrase, symbol, or design that identifies a company's products or services. Shown here are trademarks of Kaboose, a Toronto-based family focused web-based company, and Renée's Gourmet, a Toronto-based food manufacturer.

Trademarks

A **trademark** is a word, phrase, symbol, design, or combination of these that identifies and distinguishes the goods and services of one company from those of another.[26] A good example of a trademark is the logo of the Tim Hortons name. Although trademarks don't offer the kind of intellectual property protection that patents or trade secrets offer, they are still useful because they can keep your competitors from making their products look just like yours. For example, by obtaining a trademark on its swoosh symbol, Nike can better develop its brand name. No other company can put that symbol on its sneakers, hats, shirts, and so on, making it easier for customers to recognize Nike products. Indeed, many companies view their trademark as one of their key assets.

If you register your trademark, you have exclusive rights to use it in Canada for 15 years, and this right is renewable every 15 years. If you do not register your trademark, you may still have exclusive rights to use it, but you have to establish through the courts that you have used it for a considerable period of time. This process can be expensive and time-consuming and the onus is on you, the non-registered owner, to prove you have rights that take priority over the registered owner.[27] So, it makes a lot of sense to register your trademark.

You register a trademark by filing an electronic application with the Trade-marks Office. At this time, you should have already used the trademark. The process of examining your application involves searching existing trademarks to ensure that yours is not in conflict with another trademark and providing the public with the opportunity to challenge your application. Once your trademark is registered, the protection is valid only in Canada. Because trademarks need to be registered in different countries individually, it is often useful to engage a registered trademark agent who is experienced in international registrations.

A good entrepreneur should consider trademarking a word, phrase, symbol, or design that distinguishes the new venture's goods and services from those of another. An entrepreneur should use trademarks to protect these dimensions of the business, as well as to build up the new venture's brand name (see Figure 7.5).

Copyrights

A **copyright** is a form of intellectual property protection provided to the authors of original works of authorship, including literary, dramatic, musical, artistic, and certain other intellectual work.[28] For example, when we wrote the first draft of this textbook, we obtained a copyright on the material contained in it. This copyright makes it illegal for anyone else to publish the material or use it in any way. That's why we were required to sign a contract that assigned our copyright to the publisher when as part of the agreement to publish this book.

But books aren't the only things that are copyrighted. Also copyrighted are software, databases, music, study materials, plays, pantomimes, choreography, pictures, sculptures, graphics, motion pictures, recordings, and architectural designs. The main requirement for something to be copyrighted is that it is tangible. You can copyright a written speech, but not an impromptu one. You also can't copyright titles, phrases, ideas, procedures, devices, or common property, such as standard calendars.

A copyright gives the owner of the copyright, and those people the owner designates, the right to reproduce, further derive, copy, or display the protected item. In Canada, copyright protection now extends from the time the work is created until 50 years after the death of the author. If you are a citizen or resident of Canada, your copyright protection extends to those countries that are members of the Berne Convention country, the Universal Copyright Convention, the Rome Convention (for sound recordings, performer's performance and communication signals only), and members of the World

Trade Organization (WTO).[29] Perhaps more importantly, in works made for hire—that is when someone employs someone else to produce an original work of authorship—the employer receives the copyright. This information is very valuable to entrepreneurs who need others to produce things that can be protected by copyright. For example, an entrepreneur who starts a company to sell accounting software can hold the copyright on the software even someone else is hired to write the software program.

You don't have to do anything to obtain a copyright. As soon as a document (or a CD, videotape, or anything else that can be copyrighted) is produced, it has copyright protection. You can register a copyright with the Copyright Office, but it is not necessary. In essence, you have copyright protection even before you apply. Showing the copyright symbol—©—on a document isn't necessary to obtain a copyright in Canada. However, to be protected in some other countries, you do need to show the copyright symbol, the name of the copyright owner, and the year of first publication. Marking the copyrighted work in Canada is useful to prevent others from claiming that they did not know that the work was copyrighted. A good entrepreneur must often use copyrights to protect aspects of intellectual property that cannot be protected by patents or trade secrets—such as software, databases, music, study materials, plays, pantomimes, choreography, pictures, sculptures, graphics, motion pictures, recordings, and architectural designs. When patents, industrial designs, and trade secrets are not an option to protect intellectual property, copyrights become an important way that entrepreneurs can obtain legal protection for their intellectual property.

KEY POINTS

- Legal forms of intellectual property protection include patents, industrial designs, trade secrets, trademarks, and copyrights.
- A patent is a legal right granted by the government to preclude others from making use of the same invention in return for disclosing how the invention works.
- To obtain a patent, an inventor must show that the invention works, is novel, is nonobvious to a person trained in the art, and useful. A product, process, machine, chemical formula, design, plant, piece of software, composition, or business method can be patented, but a business idea can't be patented.
- Patents provide several advantages, including a monopoly on use of the invention for 20 years; however, they also have several disadvantages, including the fact that they aren't always effective; require disclosure; and can be invented around.
- An industrial design emphasizes the design aspects of an object: its shape, configuration, pattern or ornament of an object, and provides protection from imitation for 10 years.
- A trade secret is a piece of knowledge that confers an advantage and is kept hidden. Trade secrets have the advantage of providing a way to protect tacit knowledge without disclosure, but they also have the disadvantages of requiring the entrepreneur to keep the knowledge hidden, to confer no monopoly rights, and to demand evidence that the trade secrets provide a competitive advantage.
- A trademark is an original word, phrase, design, or symbol that distinguishes the goods and services of one company from another. It belongs to the first company to register or use it.
- Copyrights are a form of intellectual property protection for original works of authorship in a wide variety of forms and last from creation of the work until 50 years after the death of the author.

OTHER STRATEGIES OF INTELLECTUAL PROPERTY PROTECTION

Although legal forms of intellectual property protection are used by many entrepreneurs, and are very useful in certain settings, patents and trade secrets are not appropriate forms of protection for certain types of intellectual property. For example, suppose an entrepreneur has come up with a new piece of computer software for Internet payment. The software might not meet the conditions required for patent or trade secret protection. However, entrepreneurs can use nonlegal strategies for intellectual property protection, such as lead time, learning curves, first-mover advantages, and complementary assets to protect their new products or services against imitation. Moreover, researchers have shown that nonlegal strategies for intellectual property protection actually are more effective than legal forms in preventing duplication of the entrepreneur's products or services. Indeed, after studying more than 500 inventions reviewed by the Canadian Innovation Centre in Waterloo, Ontario, University of Toronto professors Thomas Astebro and Kristina Dahlin concluded that the factors influencing an inventor's decision to patent were different from those influencing the commercialization decision.[30] A study conducted by Wes Cohen, a professor at Duke University, and his colleagues found that lead-time/first-mover advantages, secrecy, and complementary assets were all more effective than patents in protecting both new products and new processes against imitation.[31]

Given the superiority of nonlegal strategies for intellectual property protection, successful entrepreneurs develop and use these forms of protection more often than they use legal forms of intellectual property protection. Therefore, it is useful for you to know what these protection strategies are and how to use them. When you start your business, you will be able to develop the best approach possible to protecting your intellectual property. Let's take a closer look at several kinds of nonlegal strategies of protection.

Learning Curves, Lead Time, and the First-Mover Advantage

LEARNING OBJECTIVE

8 Describe a first-mover advantage and explain the conditions under which it provides a useful form of intellectual property protection.

A firm's competitive advantage often involves speed and the timing of activities relative to those of competitors. Three different types of advantages come from speed and timing: first-mover advantages, lead-time advantages, and learning curve advantages. A **first-mover advantage** refers to any benefit that a firm receives from being the first to offer a product in a particular market. Sometimes a first-mover advantage involves **lead time** or the benefits that are generated by doing something a few months or years before someone else. Other times, a first-mover advantage involves the learning curve. We first discussed learning curve advantages in Chapter 2. Because entrepreneurs often improve their new firms' activities as a result of their efforts to learn how to do things better, early efforts to learn often put firms at a relative advantage over their competitors. By doing something more times than others, an entrepreneur can improve the venture's performance at that activity relative to the others, giving the entrepreneur an advantage. Successful entrepreneurs know that even when the intellectual property underlying their products or services can be completely imitated by other firms, being the first firm to serve a market provides an advantage that protects the products and services against competition.

Research has shown that being the first mover can protect an entrepreneur's product or service against imitation under certain conditions. First, when a business involves scarce assets, an entrepreneur can protect the intellectual property by obtaining control of the scarce assets before others can get to them.[32] For example, certain locations are better for drilling for oil than others. Early entrepreneurs in the oil industry were able to preclude complete imitation by later firms even though the later firms were able to perfectly imitate the initial entrepreneurs' oil drilling technology. How? By buying up the land where oil was close to the surface, the early movers were able to establish much lower production costs than subsequent followers.

Although buying up land where oil is close to the surface is a good way to gain a first-mover advantage in oil production, entrepreneurs don't have to obtain control over scarce physical assets, such as land, to use this type of first-mover advantage. Entrepreneurs can also gain control over intangible assets. For instance, if there are a limited number of good suppliers of a product, an entrepreneur can exploit a first-mover advantage by signing contracts with the best suppliers, leaving the inferior suppliers to imitators.[33]

Second, being a first mover provides an entrepreneur with an advantage when products become more valuable as the number of people who use the products increases (think eBay here). In Chapter 11, will we explain that people rush to be the first mover when businesses have network externalities or when the value of the product increases as more people use the product. These types of businesses have positive feedback, so any early lead in attracting customers works in favour of the entrepreneur and against any imitator further down the road.[34] People tend to use eBay as an online auction site because it is the most popular auction site. As a result, people naturally look at eBay first for online auctions, making it easier to attract attention on that site than on others. In short, when products become more valuable as more people use them, an entrepreneur receives a first-mover advantage because the entrepreneur performs better than the imitator as volume increases. Whoever is first to market tends to continue to perform better than anyone else (see Figure 7.6).

Third, any time there are high costs to customers to switch from one product to another, first movers have an advantage. A good example is the English-language typewriter keyboard. Take a look at the keyboard on your computer the next time you type a paper. The QWERTY format (named after the first six letters on the top row) is the original format and has never been replaced, even though studies have shown that other keyboard designs allow for faster and more accurate typing. Why has this product design remained dominant even though it isn't the best performer? Because the costs to people of switching to a new keyboard are very high—they would need to be trained to type on a new keyboard, make sure all the computers they use have that keyboard, make sure computer manufacturers who supply them produce the new keyboard, and so on. The costs of switching to the better keyboard just aren't worth it for any single firm, so we all still use the first—and not the best—keyboard design.[35]

Fourth, any time people tend to be content with the status quo, being a first mover offers an advantage. People are frequently satisfied with the status quo and tend to adopt new products only if the new product is *significantly* better than the old one. If an entrepreneur is the first mover, any imitators need to come up with alternative products that are *much better* than the entrepreneur's initial product on some dimension that customers care about (quality, features, durability, and so on) to compete. Otherwise customers will not change to the new product. Being first forces any imitator to offer a better product to attract customers, and coming up with a significantly better alternative is often difficult.[36]

© EBAY INC. ALL RIGHTS RESERVED

Figure 7.6 First-Mover Advantages Are Sometimes Very Helpful in Protecting an Entrepreneur's Intellectual Property

As eBay has shown, when a business demonstrates network externalities, entrepreneurs can benefit from being the first mover.
These materials have been reproduced with permission of eBay Inc.

Fifth, being a first mover is an advantage whenever reputations are important. Do you remember the name of the second person to walk on the moon? No? That's because people tend to remember the first and not the second time something happened.[37] This is just as true for new products as it is for people who walk on the moon. The first product in a market tends to make a larger and more long-lasting impression on customers, providing an advantage to the company producing it.[38] As a result, companies that are later moving have to invest more heavily in advertising than the first mover to obtain the same amount of product recognition.[39] Moreover, the first product in a market often becomes the standard against which customers compare all subsequent products, giving the first mover the advantage of being the default option.[40] For example, studies in the United States have shown that most customers treat Amazon.com as their default choice for online book purchases, only switching to other online booksellers when Amazon can't meet their needs.[41]

Sixth, entrepreneurs benefit from a first-mover advantage whenever the learning curve for producing a product or service is proprietary. Remember in Chapter 2 when we discussed the learning curve? We showed that the more times people do something, the better they become at doing it. If what they learn can be kept from spreading to competitors, first movers can gain significant cost advantages over any followers, by learning how to do things better, such as producing or marketing products more efficiently (see Figure 7.7).[42] Take Amazon.ca as an example. Every day Amazon learns more about how to gather and store information about its customers so that it can provide better customer service. This effort to learn about customers allows Amazon to provide better customer service at a lower cost than other online retailers.[43]

Please be careful here. Being the first mover isn't always the best approach for protecting your intellectual property. When the six conditions just mentioned don't hold, being first isn't an advantage. In that case, being first can be a problem. As many entrepreneurs have learned the hard way, being first sometimes shows other people what to do to imitate your ideas, rather than providing protection of your intellectual property. So take note of the conditions when being a first mover is a good idea, and you won't make the mistake of being first when it isn't a good idea.

Complementary Assets

LEARNING OBJECTIVE

9 Describe complementary assets and explain when it is better for an entrepreneur to obtain control over complementary assets than to be innovative.

As exciting as the first-mover story might sound, it isn't always beneficial for an entrepreneur to focus on introducing new products or services. New companies that introduce new products or services don't always profit from their introduction. In

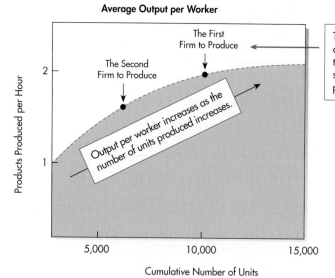

Figure 7.7 Learning Curves Provide an Important Method of Protecting an Entrepreneur's Intellectual Property

By moving ahead on the learning curve, entrepreneurs often protect their intellectual property by producing their products or services more efficiently than their competitors.

many cases, established companies imitate the new products introduced by those pioneering entrepreneurs, and they capture the profits from selling those products to customers.

Why don't new companies always profit from introducing new products or services? David Teece, a professor of business strategy at the Haas School of Business at the University of California at Berkeley, explains that the potential of new companies to profit from the introduction of new products depends on their ability to protect their intellectual property. According to Teece, three factors determine whether a new company will profit from introducing a new product: the ability to secure a strong patent; the presence or absence of a dominant design in the industry; and the presence of complementary assets in marketing and distribution.[44]

Deciding what to do about innovating is very simple if you can secure a strong patent on your intellectual property. In this situation, you will likely capture the profits from developing a new product since the strong patent precludes other companies from imitating your firm's product.[45]

But what if you cannot obtain a strong patent, either because patents tend to be weak in the industry in which you are operating or because the claims on your patent don't offer much protection? Then it is important to know whether the industry has converged on a dominant design. As we will explain in Chapter 10, a dominant design is a common approach or standard to making a product, on which all firms in an industry have agreed. In industries that have converged on a dominant design, then the firms that control the complementary assets are the ones that profit from the introduction of the new products.[46]

As we explained in Chapter 2, complementary assets are assets that must be used along with an innovation to provide a new product or service to customers, typically including manufacturing equipment, and marketing and distribution facilities. For example, in the auto industry, the internal combustion engine is a dominant design. The major automakers—Ford, General Motors, and DaimlerChrysler—control the auto manufacturing plants and the dealerships where cars are sold. As a result, entrepreneurs who develop new designs for cars don't do very well. No matter how innovative the entrepreneurs are, the fact that patents are weak in the auto industry means that the major auto companies can imitate what the entrepreneurs do. Once they successfully imitate the innovators, their manufacturing and marketing advantages can drive the entrepreneurs out of business.

Once a dominant design exists, new products have to follow a standard form that adheres to that design. If established companies can imitate the entrepreneur's new product, and they control the marketing and manufacturing facilities in the industry, it is very easy for them to exploit the same product as the entrepreneur less expensively by taking advantage of their complementary assets.

The only way that entrepreneurs can compete effectively under these circumstances is to build up their own complementary assets quickly. But in industries such as automobile manufacturing where manufacturing plants cost hundreds of millions of dollars and thousands of dealerships are spread throughout the country, it is almost impossible for entrepreneurs to successfully compete based on their complementary assets.

What's the message here? Sometimes it is better to control complementary assets than to be the innovator of new products. Entrepreneurs need to remind themselves of this message, because they tend not to do as well when controlling complementary assets is the key to success in an industry. Moreover, if they are going to try to compete in an industry in which controlling complementary assets is the key to success, then they need to know that they should focus on developing those assets. To help you figure these things out, Table 7.3 summarizes the conditions under which entrepreneurs will be more successful if they focus on gaining control over complementary assets and the conditions in which they will be more successful if they are innovative.

Table 7.3 The Choice Between Controlling Complementary Assets and Being Innovative

Under certain conditions, entrepreneurs are better off investing their resources in being more innovative than in controlling complementary assets; under other conditions, the reverse is true.

COMPLEMENTARY ASSETS ARE MORE IMPORTANT . . .	BEING INNOVATIVE IS MORE IMPORTANT . . .
When patents are not very effective	When patents are very effective
When a dominant design already exists in the industry	Before a dominant design exists in the industry
When learning curves are shallow or not proprietary	When learning curves are steep or proprietary
When knowledge is codified	When knowledge is tacit
When products are observable in use and so are easy to imitate	When products are not observable in use and so are difficult to imitate

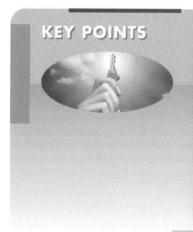

KEY POINTS

complementary assets.

- A first-mover advantage is any type of benefit that a firm receives from being the first to offer a product or service in a market. First-mover advantages are particularly useful to entrepreneurs when key assets are scarce; when products become more valuable as more people use them; when customer switching costs are high; when imitators need to offer higher quality than initiators to attract adopters; when learning curves are proprietary; and when building a reputation is important to attracting customers.
- Complementary assets, such as marketing and manufacturing facilities, are assets that are used along with an innovative new product or service. When patents are not very effective and an industry has converged on a dominant design, control of complementary assets is important to reap the rewards of innovation.

Summary and Review of Key Points

- New firms are better than established firms at product development because they do not have a bureaucratic structure, can offer better incentives to employees, and have greater flexibility.
- In industries in which established firms are better than new firms at product development, entrepreneurs have very little chance to succeed because established firms are better than new firms at marketing and manufacturing.
- New firms often fail to profit from developing new products and services because their intellectual property is easy, inexpensive, and not very time-consuming to imitate.
- Established firms can imitate entrepreneurs' intellectual property by reverse engineering entrepreneurs' products; by hiring their employees and suppliers; by having informal conversations with those people; and by conducting their own product development.
- Legal forms of intellectual property protection include patents, industrial designs, trade secrets, trademarks, and copyrights.
- A patent is a legal right granted by the government to preclude others from making use of the same invention in return for disclosing how the invention works.
- To obtain a patent, an inventor must show that the invention works, is novel, is nonobvious to a person trained in the art, and is useful. A product, process, machine, chemical formula, design, plant, piece of software, composition, or business method can be patented, but a business idea can't be patented.
- Patents provide several advantages, including a monopoly on use of the invention for 20 years; however, they also have several disadvantages, including the fact that they aren't always effective; require disclosure; and can be invented around.
- An industrial design emphasizes the design aspects of an object: its shape, configuration, pattern or ornament of an object, and provides protection from imitation for 10 years.
- A trade secret is a piece of knowledge that confers an advantage and is kept hidden. Trade secrets have the advantage of providing a way to protect tacit knowledge without disclosure, but they also have the disadvantages of requiring the entrepreneur to keep the knowledge hidden, to confer no monopoly rights, and to demand evidence that the trade secrets provide a competitive advantage.
- A trademark is an original word, phrase, design, or symbol that distinguishes the goods and services of one company from another. It belongs to the first company to register or use it.
- Copyrights are a form of intellectual property protection for original works of authorship in a wide variety of forms and last from creation of the work until 50 years after the death of the author.
- Nonlegal strategies for intellectual property protection include first-mover advantages and complementary assets.
- A first-mover advantage is any type of benefit that a firm receives from being the first to offer a product or service in a market. First-mover advantages are particularly useful to entrepreneurs when key assets are scarce; when products become more valuable as more people use them; when customer switching costs are high; when imitators need to offer higher quality than initiators to attract adopters; when learning curves are proprietary; and when building a reputation is important to attracting customers.
- Complementary assets, such as marketing and manufacturing facilities, are assets that are used along with an innovative new product or service. When patents are not very effective and an industry has converged on a dominant design, control of complementary assets is important to reap the rewards of innovation.

Glossary

Claims: The part of a patent that states what was invented and what the patent precludes others from imitating.

Copyright: A form of intellectual property protection provided to the authors of original works of authorship, including literary, dramatic, musical, artistic, and certain other intellectual works.

First-Mover Advantage: Any benefit that a firm receives from being the first to offer a product in a particular market.

Industrial Design: An object's shape, configuration, pattern, or ornament.

Intellectual Property: The core ideas about a new product or service that make the development of these products and services possible.

Invent Around: To come up with a solution that does not violate a patent but accomplishes the same goal as the patented approach.

Lead-Time Advantage: Any benefit that a firm receives by doing something before someone else.

Noncompete Agreement: A legal document in which a person agrees not to work for a competing company for a set period of time.

Nondisclosure Agreement: A legal document in which a person agrees not to divulge a company's private information for a set period of time after termination of employment.

Patent: A legal right granted by a national government to preclude others from duplicating an invention for a specified period of time in return for disclosure of the invention.

Prior Art: Prior patents that a given patent cites as the building blocks of an invention.

Product Development: The process by which the entrepreneur creates the product or service that will be sold to customers.

Reverse Engineering: The process of taking apart a product to determine how it works.

Trademark: A word, phrase, symbol, design, or combination of these that identifies and distinguishes the goods and services of one company from those of another.

Trade Secret: A piece of knowledge that confers an advantage on a firm and is protected by nondisclosure.

Discussion Questions

1. Suppose that you are founding a new company to produce a new form of surgical scalpel. Large companies, such as Johnson & Johnson, also have the same idea. Would your company or Johnson & Johnson be better at developing the new product? Explain why.

2. Assume that you have now developed your surgical scalpel. Will it be easy or difficult for Johnson & Johnson to imitate this new product? What could they do to imitate it? What can you do to stop them?

3. Think of five inventions that could be patented. Should you patent them? What are the advantages and disadvantages of patenting each of them?

4. Suppose that you are in charge of Air Canada's computer reservation system. A venture capital–backed start-up that is creating an online airline reservation system wants to hire you as chief technology officer because of your expertise with Air Canada's reservation system. Under what conditions would you be allowed take the job?

5. Suppose that you are the first entrepreneur to develop an online dating service. Would being a first mover be an advantage in this business? Why or why not?

InfoTrac Exercises

1. **Polar Bear Battle Erupts in Canada.**

   Jewelers Circular Keystone, Feb 2001 v172 i2 p68

   Record: Jewelers Circular Keystone, Feb 2001 v172 i2 p68

   Full Text: COPYRIGHT 2001 Cahners Publishing Company

   1. According to the article, why is there a lawsuit?

   2. What are the strengths and weaknesses of each side in the lawsuit?

   3. What could Ben-Oliel have done to avoid this problem?

   4. Do some research on the internet to determine how this case was resolved.

2. **World Business Briefing Americas: Canada: Lego Loses Trademark Bid.**

   Ian Austen.

   The New York Times, Nov 18, 2005 pC4(L)

   Record: A138839627

   COPYRIGHT 2005 The New York Times Company

   1. What are the key issues in this case?

   2. What other possibilities were open to Lego when its patent expired in 1978?

   3. What are the costs, for both companies, of pursuing this lawsuit for such a long time?

GETTING DOWN
TO BUSINESS

Can You Obtain a Patent?

This chapter explained that patents are an important legal form of intellectual property protection that entrepreneurs use to keep their products and services from being imitated by competitors. Although many entrepreneurs say that they'll obtain a patent, obtaining one is far more difficult. This exercise is designed to help you determine whether you can really obtain a patent to protect your new venture's product or service. Follow these steps to evaluate whether your new venture can obtain a patent.

Step One: Explain why your product or service is patentable. State explicitly why your product or service involves an invention that is novel, nonobvious, and valuable.

Step Two: Go to the Canadian Patents Database at http://patents1.ic.gc.ca/ and conduct a search of existing patents. Search by the title of your product or service, and by what you are claiming as the invention. Has your product or service already been invented? If the answer is yes, stop here, and explain why you cannot obtain a patent. If the answer is no, go on to step 3.

Step Three: Examine the claims of the existing patents. Are they broad or are they narrow? Based on the existing claims of previous patents, specify exactly what your invention will claim. Is this claim enough to protect your product or service against imitation? Why or why not?

Obtaining a Trademark

This chapter explained that entrepreneurs often obtain trademarks in their new businesses. This exercise is designed to help you to identify a trademark as a way to protect your new business's intellectual property. Follow these steps:

Step One: Identify a word, phrase, symbol, or design that you will seek to trademark.

Step Two: Go to the Canadian Trade-marks Database at http://strategis.ic.gc.ca/cipo/trademarks/search/tmSearch.do and conduct a search of existing trademarks. Is the word, phrase, symbol, or design that you selected already trademarked? If so, please select another. If your selection has not yet been trademarked, explain the steps to take to obtain a trademark.

Step Three: Explain how your new venture will benefit from the trademark. What aspects of your intellectual property will the trademark protect? How will you make the trademark valuable?

Evaluating Nonlegal Strategies for Intellectual Property Protection

This chapter pointed out that entrepreneurs can't always use legal forms of intellectual property protection to keep others from imitating their products and services. Instead, they use a variety of strategies to protect their intellectual property. In this exercise, you will be asked to develop a plan to use nonlegal mechanisms to keep firms from imitating your new product or service. Follow these steps:

Step One: Identify any nonlegal forms of intellectual property protection that your new venture will use to keep other companies from imitating its intellectual property. Will your venture obtain a first-mover advantage? Will your venture have an advantage in lead time? Will your venture have a learning curve advantage? Will your venture control complementary assets in marketing and distribution?

Step Two: Explain why the nonlegal form of intellectual property protection that you plan to use will, in fact, protect your intellectual property. For instance, if your venture will have a first-mover advantage, explain why being a first mover is an advantage in your business. Is the business one of increasing returns? Is there limited supply? Are there high switching costs? Is reputation important? Is the learning curve proprietary? Are people biased toward the status quo? Remember to provide evidence in support of your argument.

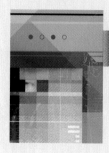

Enhanced Learning

You may select any combination of the resources below to enhance your understanding of the chapter material.

- **Appendix: Case Studies** – Twelve cases provide opportunities to apply chapter concepts to realistic entrepreneurial situations. These brief cases call for careful analysis of real business problems and ask you to think about potential solutions.

- **Video Case Library** – Nine cases are tied directly to video segments from the popular PBS television series *Small Business School*. These cases and video segments (available on the Entrepreneurship website at http://www.entrepreneurship.nelson.com) give you unparalleled access to today's entrepreneurs, with expert advice and insights on how to start, run, and grow a business.

- **Management Interview Series Video Database** – This video interview series contains a wealth of tips on how to manage effectively. Access to the database and practical exercises are available on the book support website at http://www.entrepreneurship.nelson.com.

Notes

1   U.S. Patent Number 4,139,131. http://www.uspto.gov.
2   U.S. Patent Number 4,402,440. http://www.uspto.gov.
3   U.S. Patent Number 5,246,152. http://www.uspto.gov.
4   U.S. Patent Number 5,732,861. http://www.uspto.gov.
5   U.S. Patent Number 6,009,839. http://www.uspto.gov.
6   Kanter, R, 1988. When a thousand flowers bloom: Structural, collective, and social conditions for innovations in organization. *Research in Organizational Behavior* 10: 169–211.
7   Holmstrom, B. 1989. Agency costs and innovation. *Journal of Economic Behavior and Organization* 12(3): 305–327.
8   Ibid.
9   Acs, Z., & Audretsch, D. 1988. Innovation in large and small firms: An empirical analysis. *American Economic Review* 78(4): 678–690.
10 Levin, R., Klevorick, A., Nelson, R., & Winter, S. 1987. Appropriating the returns from industrial research and development. *Brookings Papers on Economic Activity* 3(special issue): 783–832.
11 Ibid.
12 A guide to patents: Patent protection. http://strategis.gc.ca/sc_mrksv/cipo/patents/pat_gd_protect-e.html#.

13 Fuerst, O., & Geiger, U. 2003. From concept to Wall Street: A complete guide to entrepreneurship and venture capital. New York: Prentice Hall.
14 DuPlessis, D., Enman, S., O'Byrne, S., & Gunz, S. 2005. *Canadian business and the law.* Toronto: Thomson Nelson, p. 399.
15 DuPlessis, D., Enman, S., O'Byrne, S., & Gunz, S. 2005. *Canadian business and the law.* Toronto: Thomson Nelson, p. 398.
16 Manual of Patent Office Practice, Chapter 12, Canadian Intellectual Property Office. http://strategis.ic.gc.ca/sc_mrksv/cipo/patents/mopop/chap12-e.html#12.04.01.
17 DuPlessis, D., Enman, S., O'Byrne, S., & Gunz, S. 2005. *Canadian business and the law.* Toronto: Thomson Nelson, p. 401.
18 Writing a patent application. http://strategis.gc.ca/sc_mrksv/cipo/patents/e-filing/write6.htm.
19 Fuerst, O., & Geiger, U. 2003. *From concept to Wall Street: A complete guide to entrepreneurship and venture capital.* New York: Prentice Hall.
20 Paris, E. 1999. David v. Goliath. *Entrepreneur* 27(11): 20.

21 Applying in another country. http://strategis.gc.ca/sc_mrksv/cipo/patents/e-filing/appl7.htm.

22 A guide to industrial designs. http://strategis.ic.gc.ca/sc_mrksv/cipo/id/id_gd_basic-e.html#section01.

23 DuPlessis, D., Enman, S., O'Byrne, S., & Gunz, S. 2005. *Canadian business and the law*. Toronto: Thomson Nelson, p. 403.

24 Stand out from your competitors: Explore trade secrets and confidentiality agreements. http://strategis.ic.gc.ca/sc_mrksv/cipo/corp/genpub_bus-e.html#3.

25 Wolverton, T. 2005. Amazon.com, Wal-Mart settle lawsuit. *News.com*, April 5.

26 A guide to trade-marks: The basics, Registered trade-mark vs. unregistered trade-mark. http://strategis.gc.ca/sc_mrksv/cipo/tm/tm_gd_basic-e.html#section04.

27 A guide to trade-marks: The basics, Registered trade-mark vs. unregistered trade-mark. http://strategis.gc.ca/sc_mrksv/cipo/tm/tm_gd_basic-e.html#section04.

28 A guide to copyrights: Copyright protection, Automatic protection for Canadian and foreign works. http://strategis.gc.ca/sc_mrksv/cipo/cp/copy_gd_protect-e.html#8.

29 A guide to copyrights: Copyright protection. http://strategis.gc.ca/sc_mrksv/cipo/cp/copy_gd_protect-e.html#8.

30 Astebro, T & Dahlin, K. 2005. Opportunity knocks. *Research Policy* 34(9): 1404–1418.

31 Cohen, W., Nelson, R., & Walsh, J. 2000. *Protecting their intellectual assets: Appropriability conditions and why U.S. manufacturing firms patent (or not)*. NBER Working Paper No. 7552.

32 Lieberman, M., & Montgomery, C. 1988. First-mover advantages. *Strategic Management Journal* 9(special issue): 41–58.

33 Sandberg, K. 2001. Rethinking the first mover advantage. *Harvard Management Update* 6(5): 1–4.

34 Shapiro, C., & Varian, H. 1999. The art of standard wars. *California Management Review* (Winter): 8–32.

35 David, P. 1985. Clio and the economics of QWERTY. *American Economic Review* 75(2): 332–337.

36 Shankar, V., Carpenter, G., & Krishnamurthi, L. 1998. Late mover advantage: How innovative late entrants outsell pioneers. *Journal of Marketing Research* 35(1): 54–70.

37 Sandberg, K. 2001. Rethinking the first-mover advantage. *Harvard Management Update* 6(5): 1–4.

38 Boulding, W., & Christen, M. 2001. First-mover disadvantage. *Harvard Business Review* 79(9): 20–21.

39 Kerin, R., Varadarajan, P., & Peterson, R. 1992. First-mover advantage: A synthesis, conceptual framework, and research propositions. *Journal of Marketing* 56(4): 33–52.

40 Mellahi, M., & Johnson, M. 2000. Does it pay to be a first mover in e.commerce? *Management Decision* 38(7): 445–452.

41 Ibid.

42 Lieberman, M., & Montgomery, C. 1988. First-mover advantages. *Strategic Management Journal* 9(special issue): 41–58.

43 Mellahi, M., & Johnson, M. 2000. Does it pay to be a first mover in e.commerce? *Management Decision* 38(7): 445–452.

44 Teece, D. 1987. Profiting from technological innovation: Implications for integration, collaboration, licensing and public policy. In D. Teece (ed.). *The competitive challenge* (pp. 185–220). Cambridge, MA: Ballinger Publishing.

45 Ibid.

46 Ibid.

CHAPTER 8

WRITING AN EFFECTIVE BUSINESS PLAN: CRAFTING A ROAD MAP TO SUCCESS

LEARNING OBJECTIVES

After reading this chapter, you should be able to:

1 Define a business plan and explain why entrepreneurs should write one.

2 Explain how the process of persuasion plays a key role in business plans and in the success of new ventures.

3 Explain why the executive summary is a very important part of any business plan.

4 Describe the major sections of a business plan and the types of information they should include.

5 Describe the seven deadly sins of business plans—errors all entrepreneurs should avoid.

6 Explain why potential investors usually ask entrepreneurs to give verbal presentations describing their idea for new products or services and their company.

7 Describe the steps entrepreneurs can take to make their verbal presentations to potential investors truly excellent.

All photos this page © PhotoDisc, Inc.

> "There is a real magic in enthusiasm. It spells the difference between mediocrity and accomplishment." (Norman Vincent Peale, 1961)

Whether they realize it or not, most entrepreneurs accept these words as true. They are convinced that because *they* believe passionately in their ideas and their new ventures, others will, too, if given half a chance to do so. As a result, they are often dismayed when their initial efforts to obtain financial backing meet with lukewarm receptions (or worse!) from venture capitalists, business angels, and others who might readily provide the resources they need. "What's wrong with these people?" they wonder. "Can't they recognize a great thing when they see it?" The problem, of course, may not be a lack of discernment on the part of these persons. Rather, it may have much more to do with the kind of job the entrepreneur is doing in presenting her or his idea to others. Yes, the entrepreneur is enthusiastic and enthusiasm sells. But in order to induce other people—especially ones who have been taught by years of experience to view new ventures with a jaundiced eye—enthusiasm alone is rarely sufficient. In addition, entrepreneurs who want to succeed must realize that they face a very serious and very tough task, one centred around the process of persuasion—the task of inducing others to share our views and to see the world much as we do. After all, why should total strangers entrust their hard-earned money to something as risky in nature as a new venture, especially if it is going to be run by someone who has had little if any experience in starting or running a business? Would you? Unless you are like the characters shown in Figure 8.1, and have fallen in love with an idea or industry, the answer is clear: No!

If enthusiasm alone is not enough, then what can entrepreneurs do to gain the resources they need? For many entrepreneurs, a large part of the answer involves preparing a truly first-rate business plan. This document is a formal, written expression of the entrepreneur's vision for converting ideas into a profitable, going business, and in most cases, it is the entry card for serious consideration by venture capitalists, banks, and other sources of funding: Most won't even think about supporting a new venture until they have seen and carefully evaluated this document. This basic fact poses something of a dilemma for many entrepreneurs: They firmly believe in their ideas and their own ability to carry them through to success, but at the same time, they have had little practice in writing formal documents, such as business plans. In fact, unless they have a background in business (which only some entrepreneurs possess), they may not even have a clear idea about what a business plan is or what it should contain. The result? Many do not prepare such plans; in fact, statistics show that more than 60 percent of small, new companies have no business plan—or no written plans of any kind, for that matter.[1]

Figure 8.1 Overeager Investors: A Very Rare Occurrence!

Sometimes, investors rush to offer funding to start-up companies in a hot industry, as happened during the late 1990s with respect to Internet companies. In most cases, however, they are much more careful about where they put their hard-earned money!

That brings us to the main purpose of this chapter: helping you understand what a business plan is and how to write one that will assist you in attaining the support you need, financial and otherwise. In order to reach this goal, we will proceed as follows. First, we will examine the question of why you should write a business plan, even if you are in the rare and truly glorious situation of not needing financial support to get started. As we will soon note, preparing this document can be helpful in several important ways. In fact, research findings indicate that entrepreneurs who prepare excellent business plans are more likely to attain success than those who do not—for reasons that will soon become clear. For instance, one recent and very carefully conducted study found that writing business plans significantly reduced the chances of venture failure and increased the rate of new business and new product development among a random sample of Swedish entrepreneurs.[2]

After explaining why it is usually helpful to write a thorough business plan, we will turn to the task of describing this document in detail—the key sections it should contain, how these sections should be put together, and so on. Throughout this discussion, we will do more than just describe the basic requirements: We will also provide you with tips and suggestions for making your plan excellent—an instrument for transmitting your own enthusiasm and vision to others. We think this is crucial information that will serve you well as you move toward starting your own venture.

After we have described the major sections of a formal business plan, we will return to a key theme we wish to emphasize throughout this chapter: Persuasion is, indeed, the name of the game where starting a new venture is concerned. For that reason, writing an excellent business plan, though certainly a crucial activity, is only the first step in a larger process. Persuading other people to support your new venture involves several other steps as well. For instance, a plan that generates initial positive reactions on the part of venture capitalists and other investors to whom you send it (an outcome achieved by only a few percentage of all plans) will often lead to the next step: an invitation for you to make a formal presentation. This presentation often plays an important role in decisions about whether and to what extent to support your venture, so it is a task you should definitely take very seriously. How can you shine in this context? Although we agree with John Ruskin (1749) who once wrote: "He who has truth at his heart need never fear the want of persuasion on his tongue," we also know that being persuasive involves much more than personal conviction. In this section, therefore, we will provide suggestions for reaching these goals, based on both careful research and our personal experiences as entrepreneurs.

Finally, in the Appendix, we provide the example of a real, recent business plan developed by two entrepreneurs to obtain bank financing. In the Voice of Experience section, we talk with these entrepreneurs about the process of developing the business plan and the role it has played in the growth of their business.

WHY WRITE A BUSINESS PLAN? THE BENEFITS OF CLEAR-CUT GOALS

LEARNING OBJECTIVE

1 Define a business plan and explain why entrepreneurs should write one.

Make no mistake: Preparing a business plan requires a lot of hard work. In fact, it usually requires many hours of careful thought, followed by an equal or larger number of hours spent converting these thoughts into a written document. Although university professors may enjoy such activities (!), entrepreneurs often do not. Often, they are eager to get started—to launch their business and make their vision happen. Many realize that once their business has been launched, it will rarely follow the steps and time line outlined in the business plan. So why should they stop and devote so much hard work to the task of preparing a first-rate business plan, even if, as we noted earlier, they are in the rare and enviable position of *not* needing outside resources to get started? Perhaps the simplest yet most important answer we can give is this: *It is truly difficult to arrive somewhere unless you know where you want to go.* In other words, a business plan is much more than a document designed to persuade skeptical people to invest in your new venture: *It is also a detailed road map for converting your ideas and vision into a real, functioning business.* Writing a business plan requires you, as an entrepreneur, to carefully and fully address a number of complex issues relating to the process of converting your idea and its accompanying vision into reality: how your product will be produced, the price at which it will sell, how and to whom it will be marketed, how it will compare with existing or potential competitors, what financial resources are needed and how these will be used, and so on.

In other words, the term "plan" in "business plan" is really appropriate: A carefully prepared and well-reasoned business plan will indeed help you with the process of planning; it really *will* provide the road map mentioned in the title of this chapter. More specifically, a well-prepared business plan will explain what the new venture is trying to accomplish and how it will go about attaining these goals. This is the kind of information venture capitalists and others who might support a new venture often seek, and in fact, the clearer the links between the goals sought and the means for accomplishing them, the more impressive (and persuasive) the business plan will be. But remember: Entrepreneurs do not write business plans solely to persuade others to invest in their new ventures. They also write them to provide themselves with a clearer understanding of the best ways of proceeding. That, we hope you'll agree, is invaluable information that should be sought by all entrepreneurs early in the process.

Having made these points, we should now balance the scales, so to speak, by noting that a business plan is a *living document*—one that often changes—and changes often—as a new business develops. Because you can never know in advance just how your new business will develop, there is a limit to how much planning you can do. For this reason, successful entrepreneurs often avoid analysis paralysis, in which they spend countless hours in the library developing long, formal business plans with lots of data and assumptions, fancy spreadsheets, and beautiful bindings. Instead, they do just enough planning to get their new companies started, and then use the information that they gather from actually running their new ventures to refine their plans in the light of reality. In essence, the successful entrepreneur's business planning model often looks like this: (1) Develop a simple, basic business plan, (2) start the business, (3) take the information that is gained from starting and running the new business and use it to refine the plan and obtain funding as this becomes necessary.

For example, consider Alex D'Arbeloff, founder of Teradyne, a large, public, scientific instruments company. When D'Arbeloff founded his company, he wrote a short business plan only a few pages in length. He assumed that there was little benefit in developing a long, detailed business plan made up mostly of assumptions and analysis of data resting on largely unsupported assumptions. Rather, it was better to focus on the key pieces of information that he knew to be true, and get the business started. Then, once the business was up and running, he revised his business plan many times, adding new information as it was acquired. D'Arbeloff's success as an entrepreneur made him quite wealthy, and he now works as a business angel who has backed such notable companies as Lotus. As a business angel, he maintains the same philosophy that he used when he started his own company: Look for entrepreneurs who have written simple, straightforward business plans that focus on key dimensions of business opportunities that are well understood, and then treat their business plans as living documents that change and develop with the new ventures.

The advantages of this approach are obvious: Entrepreneurs can spend their time getting their business started rather than on writing a formal business plan, and thus have something tangible to sell when they finally do seek large amounts of outside funding to expand their growing businesses. (See Figure 8.2 for a summary of the model of business planning we have just described.)

So overall, is it better to start with a long, detailed business plan or a shorter and simpler one? As you can guess, the answer is "It depends." In some situations, a long and detailed plan is necessary—for instance, when large amounts of funding are required to launch the new venture. In others, a shorter and less detailed plan will suffice—as long as it provides sufficient guidance to get the business started, and it is changed on the fly to reflect new information as it becomes available. The key rule, then, is to *always* engage in careful preparation and planning, but to be flexible and to match the form of the business plan you develop to the specific needs of your new venture.

Figure 8.2 A Model of Business Planning Used by Many Successful Entrepreneurs

Many successful entrepreneurs write relatively simple business plans that are based on information they actually know rather than on lots of untested assumptions. Then they start their businesses and use the information they gain from running them to both refine their business plans and to secure additional funding as needed. The cycle continues, thus making business plans true living documents that are open to change in response to new information.

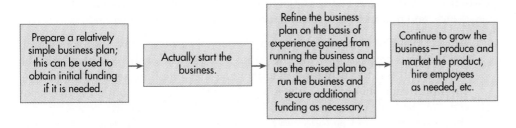

Prepare a relatively simple business plan; this can be used to obtain initial funding if it is needed. → Actually start the business. → Refine the business plan on the basis of experience gained from running the business and use the revised plan to run the business and secure additional funding as necessary. → Continue to grow the business—produce and market the product, hire employees as needed, etc.

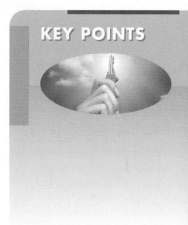

KEY POINTS

- A business plan is a formal written document that explains the entrepreneur's vision and how it will be converted into a profitable, viable business.
- Venture capitalists and other potential sources of funding generally require a formal business plan as a first step for considering investments in new ventures.
- An additional step, and one that is often very important, involves a face-to-face presentation of the plan by the entrepreneur to venture capitalists or other interested parties.
- Preparing a formal business plan is useful for most entrepreneurs because doing so encourages them to formulate specific goals and concrete plans for reaching them, and these are invaluable both for converting ideas into viable companies and for raising needed capital.
- However, many successful entrepreneurs develop a fairly simple business plan, and then refine it in the light of information they gain from actually running the new venture.

COMPONENTS OF A BUSINESS PLAN: BASIC REQUIREMENTS

Business plans are as different in their specific contents as the persons who prepare them. You will find many different business plan templates on the Internet. Overall, though, there is general agreement that they must contain a number of basic sections that, together, address key questions anyone should ask before investing in a new venture:

- *What* is the basic idea for the new product of service?

- *Why* is this new product useful or appealing—and to whom?

- *How* will the idea for the new venture be realized—what is the overall plan for producing the product, for marketing it, and for dealing with existing and future competition?

- *Who* are the entrepreneurs—do they have the required knowledge, experience, and skills to develop this idea and to run a new company?

- If the plan is designed to raise money, *how much* funding is needed, *what type of financing* is needed, *how* will it be used, and how will both the entrepreneurs and other persons realize a return on their investment?

As you can see, these are truly basic and important questions—the kind *you* would ask *yourself* before making an investment in a start-up company. A well-prepared business plan addresses all these questions and many others, too. Moreover, it does so in an *orderly*, *succinct*, and *persuasive* fashion. Pay careful attention to these terms, because they are truly crucial. As we noted earlier, the great majority of all business plans are rejected within a few minutes by experienced venture capitalists who see hundreds or even thousands of such documents each year. As a result of this experience, they employ a set of filters to determine which business plans are worthy of their time and which they can quickly discard. As an entrepreneur, you want to do everything in your power to assure that your business plan is one of the few that receive more than a cursory glance, and that requires careful attention to several basic principles:

- *The plan should be arranged and prepared in proper business form.* The plan should start with a *cover page* showing the name and address of the company and the names and contact information (telephone, e-mail, etc.) for key contact people. This information should be followed by a clear *table of contents* outlining the major sections. The table of contents should then be followed by an *executive summary*; which, in turn, should be followed by the major sections of the plan, each clearly headed and identified. Various appendices (e.g., detailed financial projections, complete résumés for the company's founders and key persons) follow, often bound separately. Overall, the entire plan should adhere to the same basic rule: It should have the appearance of a serious business document, but should *not* seek to wow readers with showy illustrations or super-creative use of type fonts and styles. Remember: The first impression you make on venture capitalists, bankers, and other people important to your company's future will be made by your business plan, so make sure that it looks like what it is: A serious document prepared by serious people!

- *The plan should be succinct.* This principle is absolutely crucial; no one—not even your own family members—will plow through hundreds of pages of dense, convoluted prose (or complex financial figures). An effective business plan, therefore, should be as short and succinct as possible. Anything more than 40 to 50 pages is almost certainly overkill, and up to a point, the shorter the better. For instance, the business plan submitted by Teradyne was six pages in length, and that for Lotus Development was ten pages. The key goal is to address the major questions listed earlier (what, why, how, who, and how much?) in a clear and intelligent manner, without needless detail or redundancy. Always keep in mind that the people you want to read your plan are busy and highly experienced: They know how to cut rapidly to the heart of what your business is all about and to tell whether you are smart enough to present it clearly.

- *The plan should be persuasive.* As we have tried to emphasize, you are facing a highly competitive situation in which you will have a small window of opportunity: Either you seize the attention of the people who read your plan early on and have additional chances to persuade them, or they conclude, within minutes, that reading further would be a waste of time. It is simply a fact of life: Experienced decision makers operate this way in many business contexts, not just with respect to evaluating business plans. For instance, research on job interviews indicates that many interviewers make their judgment about the suitability of each applicant within a minute or two.[3] Why? They simply don't have time to waste on applicants who are clearly not suitable, so they reach a decision about whether to continue the discussion very early in the process. If their decision is "this is not a suitable person," they conclude the interview very quickly. If, instead, they decide "this could be a good candidate," they keep the interview going in order to acquire more information. The same principle is at work with respect to business plans: Decisions are made very quickly by venture capitalists and other potential sources of funding and are rarely, if ever, reversed.[4] Therefore, you must begin strong, and continue strong, if you want to succeed. And the place where a business plan begins is the executive summary—the first major component of the business plan and, in some ways, the most important.

One more point: We want to emphasize that, ultimately, it is the quality of the idea behind the new venture, and the quality of the person or persons who have put it together that are crucial. If the idea is not sound and has little economic potential, experienced investors will recognize this weakness immediately, no matter how well-written or persuasive the plan appears to be. So before you decide to invest large amounts of time and effort into preparing a super-impressive business plan, you absolutely *must* get feedback on the idea behind your new venture. If the response is not encouraging, stop right there, because proceeding is almost certain to be a waste of time.

LEARNING OBJECTIVE

2 Explain how the process of persuasion plays a key role in business plans and in the success of new ventures.

The Executive Summary

LEARNING OBJECTIVE

3 Explain why the executive summary is a very important part of any business plan.

Have you ever heard the phrase "elevator pitch"? I (Robert Baron) first became familiar with it while working at a government agency (I was a program director at the National Science Foundation). I observed that many of my more experienced colleagues went to lunch at a specific time each day and that they jockeyed for position in front of the elevator. Why? Because they wanted to stand next to the division director—the person who made key decisions about how funds available to our part of the agency would be distributed—and they knew that she would be standing on the elevator when the door opened (because her office was on a higher floor). On the way down to the street, they made their elevator pitches—brief but impassioned statements about the wonderful things going on in their particular areas of science, and why funding of such work would be a great investment. The director usually made no concrete response, but in a few cases, I heard her remark, "That sounds interesting ... make an appointment so we can discuss it." That response signified great success because it meant that the one- or two-minute pitch delivered in the elevator had at least opened the door to further discussions—and the real possibility of additional funding.

The moral of such situations is clear: Often, we have just a brief opportunity to stimulate another person's interest—to get them interested enough to want to learn more. That, in essence, is the purpose of the executive summary. This part of the business plan—which should be brief and to the point (many experienced investors suggest two to three pages at most)—should provide a short, clear, and persuasive overview of what the new venture is all about. In essence, it should provide brief answers to all the questions listed earlier: What is the idea for the new product or service? Why will it be appealing—and to whom? Who are the entrepreneurs? How much funding (and in what form) are they seeking?

Can all this be accomplished within a brief format? Absolutely. But being succinct requires very careful and thoughtful writing—writing that delivers a lot of information per sentence (or even word), yet also conveys the entrepreneurs' excitement and enthusiasm. We wish we could provide you with a few simple rules for writing such a document, but in fact, we cannot: The precise contents will depend on the specific ideas you are presenting. But whatever your ideas are, the executive summary should answer key questions briefly, but in enough detail that a reader can form a clear picture of what your new venture is all about. Remember: This is an important part of the business plan, so it is worthy of special effort. It is your first and best chance (and often your only chance!) to generate interest in others, so by all means, make it your very best shot in all respects.

After the executive summary, major sections follow in an orderly arrangement. Many arrangements of these key sections are possible, but here is one that is used in many business plans and that seems quite logical. The specific order of the sections—as well as their content, however—should be dictated by the nature of your idea and what you are trying to communicate in the plan, not by any hard-and-fast preset rules.

LEARNING OBJECTIVE

4 Describe the major sections of a business plan and the types of information they should include.

■ *Background and purpose.* A section describing your idea and the current state of your business.

■ *Marketing.* A section describing the market for your product or service—who will want to use or buy it, and—most importantly—*why* they would want to do so. In other words, describe your target market and your value proposition. Business plans often have separate sections detailing the firm's communication strategy, pricing strategy, distribution strategy, and sales strategy.

■ *Competition.* Information on the existing competition and how it will be overcome, pricing, and related issues. (Sometimes the discussion on the competition is a separate section, and sometimes it is included in the marketing section.) Readers of your plan want to know what the market gap is, how you will enter the market to fill the gap, and how you will build and sustain competitive advantage against current firms and future entrants.

■ *Development, production, and location.* Where your product or service is right now in terms of development, how you will move toward actually producing or providing the product or service, and (if it is relevant to your company) where the new venture will be located. Information on operations, too, can be included in this section if it is an important factor in understanding what the business will do and why it has significant economic potential.

■ *Management.* A section describing the experience, skills, and knowledge of the new venture's management team—what you have and what additional skills may be required in the months ahead. Information on current ownership should be included here.

■ *Financial section.* This section provides information on the company's current financial state and offers projections for future needs, revenues, and other financial measures. It should also include information on the amount of funding being sought, when such funds are required, how they will be used, cash flow, and a breakeven analysis.

■ *Risk factors.* This section discusses various risks the new venture will face and the steps the management team is taking to protect against them.

■ *Harvest or exit.* Investors are interested in understanding precisely how they will gain if the company is successful, so information on this important issue (e.g., when and how the company might go public) can often be very useful.

■ *Scheduling and milestones.* Information on when each phase of the new venture will be completed should be included, so that potential investors will know just when key tasks (e.g., start of production, time to first sales, projected breakeven point) will be completed. The scheduling and milestones can be a separate section, or it can be included in other sections, as appropriate.

■ *Appendices.* Here is where detailed financial information and detailed résumés of the top management team should be presented.

To be complete, all business plans must cover these and closely related topics. However, depending on the specific nature of the new venture, the order can be altered, and the relative length adjusted. In other words, there are no hard-and-fast rules about how long or detailed each section should be; rather, the length and scope are matters of good business judgment.

Now that we've provided an overview of the key sections included in a sound business plan, we'll describe each of these sections in more detail.

Background, Product, and Purpose

Among the first pieces of information potential investors want to know are facts relating to the background of your product and your company and what, specifically, you hope to accomplish. As we noted in Chapters 2 and 3, ideas for new products or services do not arise in a vacuum; rather, such opportunities emerge out of changing economic, technological, and social conditions and are then recognized by specific persons who take action to develop them. A key question from potential investors, then, is "What is the nature of the idea driving your company and how did it arise?" The answer will often require discussing conditions in the industry in which your company is located, because these conditions, in part, have likely suggested the idea you are now seeking to develop.

For instance, suppose that an entrepreneur has developed a new material that gives the soles of shoes much better traction than any material now on the market. Potential investors will want to know why this feature is useful and who will want to use the new material (e.g., manufacturers of athletic shoes? manufacturers of medical devices for people who have been hurt in accidents or who have brittle bones?). In other words, this section of the business plan should explain what the product has to offer—why it is unique and valuable, and therefore has potential for generating future profits. Unless these issues can be addressed clearly and successfully, investors are likely to conclude that the risks far outweigh any potential benefits.

Investors also usually want basic information about the existing company—its legal form, its current ownership, and its current financial condition. After all, no one wants to invest in a new venture in which thorny issues of ownership exist, or where there is an excessively high overhead.

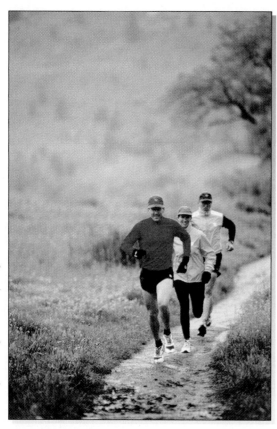

John Kelly/The Image Bank/Getty Images

Figure 8.3 Describing the New Venture's Goals or Mission

The first major section of a business plan should provide background information on the nature of the product and the start-up venture. It should also include information on the new venture's goals—a brief mission statement. For instance, a company that wants to develop a new material that gives shoes better traction might present data indicating how many athletes are injured each year in falls, and show how the company's product would help reduce the frequency of such accidents.

This section of the business plan should also address the company's goals: What does it hope to accomplish? Returning to the venture with a new material for shoes, described earlier, this section of the business plan should clarify whether the new material will be generally useful for all kinds of shoes or only for some (e.g., running shoes) and the benefits its use will confer. For instance, perhaps many thousands of persons are injured in falls each year, and perhaps many of these injuries could be prevented through use of the new material (see Figure 8.3). In that case, these potential benefits should be mentioned along with the financial benefits that will stem from the company's success. But again, the usefulness of such information depends very much on the idea behind the new venture, and it is more appropriate for some than others. Like everything else in the plan, the potential benefits should only be included if they are relevant and will contribute to both planning by the entrepreneurs and their ability to communicate the nature of the company to others.

In sum, after reading this initial section, potential investors will understand where and how the product was developed, the basic nature of the entrepreneur's company (its legal form, ownership, history), what it is that makes this product or service valuable or unique, and what the new venture will seek to accomplish—a brief statement of its mission. Together, this information provides a useful framework for understanding later sections of the business plan, so it is important that it be presented first.

Market Analysis

One reason why products fail is that no one conducted careful market analysis before they were produced; in other words, no one bothered to find out if there was a market for them—whether anyone would really want to buy or use them. The result? Disaster for the entrepreneurs who invented them and for anyone who invested in the companies that were launched to produce and sell these items.

It is not surprising, then, that sophisticated investors want to see specific and detailed information concerning marketing as part of any strong business plan. Specifically, they want information on what entrepreneurs have done to identify the market for their product (e.g., have they conducted marketing surveys? detailed market analyses?). Moreover, investors want to know how large these markets are, whether they are growing or shrinking, and how the new products or services will be promoted in these markets. This analysis often requires detailed information about *competing products*—whether they exist and, if so, how the new product will be demonstrably superior; *competing companies*—who are they, and how they are likely to respond to the entrepreneurs' new product; and *pricing*—how the new product or service will be priced relative to competing products or services, and why this pricing strategy makes sense.

For instance, consider Photowow.com, a company started by Robert Schiff in Los Angeles. Schiff's company makes large pieces of art for use in homes and businesses. This art is produced by large-format inkjet printers and can show almost anything—for instance, the buyer's children in pop montages resembling the style of a famous artist, such as Andy Warhol. This is an entirely new product, so pricing it was a challenging task and required careful consideration of existing products (e.g., art posters). Marketing, too, raised complex questions: What would be the potential market for such art? Many possibilities existed: franchises, which would want to show a picture of their founders in every outlet; corporations, which might want to have a picture of the home office in every branch. Schiff explored all these, plus others, with the help of consultants and was then able to include this information in his business plan.

In essence, this section of a new venture's business plan should be designed to convince skeptical investors that the entrepreneurs have done their homework: They have examined potential markets for their product or service carefully and have evidence indicating that consumers or other businesses (depending on the product or service) will want to buy it when it becomes available. Further, investors want to know the specifics of how the new product or service will be promoted, and at what cost. Market projections are, of course, always uncertain; no one ever knows for certain how consumers will react to new products (see Figure 8.4). But at the very least, entrepreneurs should have engaged in state-of-the-art efforts to learn why people will want to buy or use their products, and to pinpoint an effective marketing strategy. If, instead, it is simply assumed that the product or service is so wonderful that people will line up to buy it, a loud alarm will sound for sophisticated investors, and they will quickly lose interest.

Development, Production, and Location

It is not possible to market a new product or service unless it is available, so another issue that must be carefully addressed in any effective business plan is product development and production. Potential investors want information about where the new venture's products and services are in this process: Are they still under development? Are they fully developed and ready to be manufactured? If so, what are the projected costs and timetable for making the product or for delivering the service? Related issues include steps to assure quality and safety for consumers or other users (e.g., has the company applied for Underwriters Laboratory approval, or similar certification?). As I learned while running my own company, such processes can require months—and considerable fees—so investors want to know that entrepreneurs are aware of these issues and have them well in hand.

The further along a start-up company is with respect to these issues, the more attractive it will be to potential investors—not simply because the company has developed beyond the initial launch phase, but also because this progress demonstrates that the company is operating in a productive and rational manner. I (Robert Baron) recently invested in a new biotechnology company, mainly because I liked the basic idea (developing drugs for orphan diseases—ailments that afflict too few people for major drug companies to bother with) and also because I know and respect the founders. Another important consideration for me, however, was where the company stood with respect to development of effective new drugs. My conclusion was that everything was in place to allow the new venture to move ahead quickly, but only time will tell whether I was correct in this judgment. In any case, I—like other potential investors—searched for information on this issue in the company's business plan and would certainly have been less enthusiastic about investing in it if such information were not included or was too general in scope to be informative.

The Management Team

Many venture capitalists note that they would rather invest in a first-rate team with a second-rate idea than a second-rate team with a first-rate idea. Although this saying is something of an exaggeration— venture capitalists and other investors actually focus on many different issues— there is actually a substantial grain of truth in such statements. What venture capitalists are saying, in essence, is that talented, experienced, and motivated people at the top of a new venture are very important for its success. For this

Figure 8.4 Market Analysis: Sometimes Uncertain, But Always Essential

Entrepreneurs should always devote careful attention to the following question: "What is the need for our product or service? Why, in other words, would anyone want to buy or use it?" Market research can often help to answer this question. The product on the left was introduced after market research indicated that consumers would want to buy it—which is exactly what happened: It was a huge success. In contrast, the product on the right was introduced mainly because the company that produced it simply assumed that a market for it existed; in fact, consumers did not want it and the product largely failed.

© Roger Ressmeyer/CORBIS

AP/ Wide World Photos/Carlos Osorio

reason, a key section of any business plan describes the people who will run the new venture.

What, specifically, do potential investors want to know? Primarily that, taken together, these people have the experience, expertise, skills, and personal characteristics needed to run the new venture successfully. We say "taken together," because as we pointed out in Chapter 5, investors want to know that the management team has complementary skills, abilities, and experience: What one person is lacking, others provide, and vice versa. Further, investors want to be reasonably certain that the members of the team have developed good working relationships: Each has clearly assigned roles and duties, and communication between them is good. Although investors may be willing to bend these requirements to a degree—for instance, they can't really require decades of experience from a very young group of entrepreneurs—they do demand at least some of them. If the management team of a new venture is lacking in experience, for instance, they may require that the entrepreneurs hire seasoned executives to assist in running the business—in other words, that they acquire needed experience from outside the new venture team itself. Similarly, if entrepreneurs are lacking in experience, investors may place greater weight on their training, their intelligence, and their interpersonal skills. Seasoned investors know from past experience that entrepreneurs who are good at getting along with others are more likely to succeed than those who are rough around the edges and annoy or irritate the people with whom they deal. After all, why should anyone give their business to a stranger who rubs them the wrong way? Surely, it would take a vastly superior product or service to tip the balance this way. In fact, research findings indicate that entrepreneurs who are high in social skills are indeed more successful in running new ventures than ones who are not.[5]

In short, potential investors place a great deal of emphasis on the qualifications of entrepreneurs, and do everything they can to assure that the companies they fund are headed by people in whom they can have confidence. The source of such confidence is, ideally, past business experience, but if this background is lacking, potential investors will seek to assure that this potential weakness is offset by other strengths brought to the table by the founding entrepreneurs: high intelligence (social and cognitive), a high level of technical skill, and yes—energy and enthusiasm!

Financial Plans and Projections

Every section of a business plan is important—of that there can be no doubt. But one section that is absolutely certain to receive close and especially careful examination is the section dealing with financial matters. This section should include several major components, each of which must be carefully prepared. As we explained in Chapter 6, these elements provide a picture of the company's current financial state, how it will use the funds it receives from investors, and how it will manage its financial resources to reach its major objectives.

The financial section should provide an assessment of what assets the venture will own, what debt it will have, and so on. As Chapter 6 explained, such information is summarized in a **proforma balance sheet**, showing projections of the company's financial condition at various times in the future; such information should be projected semiannually for the first three years. These projected balance sheets allow investors to determine whether debt-to-equity ratios, working capital, inventory turnover, and other financial indices are within acceptable limits and justify initial and future funding of the company. In addition, as Chapter 6 explained, a **proforma income statement** should be prepared to illustrate projected operating results based on profit and loss. This statement records sales, costs of goods sold, expenses, and profit or loss, and should take careful account of sales forecasts, production costs, costs of advertising, distribution, storage, and administrative expenses. In short, it should provide a reasonable projection of operating results. Finally a **cash flow statement** showing the amount and timing of expected cash inflows and outflows should be prepared, again for a period of several years. By highlighting expected sales and capital expenditures over a specific period of time, this forecast will underscore the need for and timing of further financing and needs for working capital. These forms are summarized in Table 8.1.

Another key part of the financial section—one also discussed in Chapter 6—should be a **breakeven analysis**, a table showing the level of sales (and production) needed to cover all costs. This analysis should include costs that vary with the level of production (manufacturing, labour, materials, sales) and costs that do not vary with production (interest charges, salaries, rent, and so on). The breakeven analysis is a very important reality check for entrepreneurs who often have an overly optimistic view of how quickly their new venture can become profitable, and it is often examined with considerable care by potential investors.

Overall, the financial section of the business plan should provide potential investors with a clear picture of how the new venture will use the resources it already has, resources generated by continuing operations, and resources provided by investors to move toward its financial objectives. If there is any section in which entrepreneurs should strive to hold their enthusiasm and optimism in check, it is the financial plans and projections: Many investors have learned to view entrepreneurs' financial projections with a healthy dose of skepticism. Investors have seen too many overly optimistic predictions to view the situation otherwise; in fact, many begin by discounting entrepreneurs' projections by a minimum of 50 percent!

Critical Risks: Describing What Might Go Wrong

You probably know this saying, known as Murphy's Law: "If anything can go wrong, it will." Perhaps you have also heard the corollary: "Murphy was an optimist." Entrepreneurs, filled with enthusiasm for their new ventures, are not the most likely candidates on earth to think hard and long about what can go wrong with respect to their new ventures. On the contrary, they prefer to dwell on the upside and are often genuinely dismayed when things do *not* go according to plan, which is one reason why effective business plans should contain a section specifically focused on what might potentially go wrong—critical risks that can prevent the new venture from reaching its key objectives. Thinking about these risks is good medicine for entrepreneurs, and formulating ways of responding to these potential calamities before they occur can be constructive indeed!

What are the potential risks new ventures face? Here is a partial list:

- Price cutting by competitors, who refuse to roll over and play dead for the new venture

- Unforeseen industry trends that make the new venture's product or service less desirable—or less marketable

- Sales projections that are not achieved for a variety of reasons, thus reducing cash flow

- Design, manufacturing, or shipping costs that exceed estimates. Product development or production schedules that are not met (people problems, such as low employee motivation, can play a role in each of the last three points)

INCOME STATEMENT	CASH FLOW STATEMENT
Includes sales as they are generated.	Shows sales as "cash in" only when payment is received.
Includes depreciation.	Depreciations are added back in because it is not a cash expense.
Interest on loans is included.	Both interest and principle are included.
Beginning inventory and ending inventory are included in the calculation of cost of goods sold.	Inventory purchases are recorded as bills actually paid

Table 8.1 Income Statements and Cash Flow Statements: Some Key Differences

Income statements and cash flow statements differ in several important respects.

Figure 8.5 New Ventures Face Retaliation from Existing Firms

New ventures confront many risks. One risk is litigation from existing competitors. Even if the new venture is successful in a lawsuit, legal matters can divert the firm's management from developing the market for its products. Such lawsuits can take a long time. The lawsuit by Danish company LEGO, against Montreal-based Mega Bloks, was launched in 1996 and was not completed until 2005.

- Problems stemming from top management's lack of experience (e.g., an inability to negotiate contracts with suppliers or customers on favourable terms)

- Longer than expected lead times with respect to obtaining parts or raw materials

- Difficulties in raising additional, needed financing

- Unforeseen political, economic, social, or technological trends or developments (e.g., new government legislation or the sudden start of a major recession)

These are just a few of the many potential risks that can put new ventures badly off the track. The difficulty in identifying risks is that many are truly unexpected. In particular, entrepreneurs need to think about how rivals might react to the start of their firm (see Figure 8.5). For instance, Montreal-based Mega Bloks sells interlocking plastic blocks that can be used interchangeably with LEGO blocks. Although patent protection for LEGO blocks expired in 1988, LEGO claimed that Mega Bloks infringed on its trademark because the raised studs on the toy bricks were part of its distinctive brand.[6] LEGO launched a lawsuit in 1996 that continued until 2005, when the Supreme Court of Canada ruled in Mega Blok's favour. Mega Bloks is also undefeated in the highest courts of Greece and France, and has cases pending in Spain and Italy.[7] Lawsuits such as these are time-consuming and expensive for new firms to deal with. Although Mega Bloks' management was successful in growing the firm while managing this legal issue in jurisdictions around the world, lawsuits launched by rivals can distract a new firm's management from other market priorities.

Many of the potential risks are frightening to contemplate, so why should entrepreneurs describe them in detail in their business plans? Mainly because recognizing these dangers is the first step toward coming up with strategies to deal with them if they do in fact occur. Writing an appropriate risk-related section for their business plan obliges entrepreneurs to perform this task and take these potential risks into account.

Reaping the Rewards: Harvest and Exit

All good things must come to an end, and even the most enthusiastic of entrepreneurs realizes that at some point, they may want to leave the companies they started. This decision may come about because they have reached a stage in life where they want to sit back a bit and enjoy the fruits of their labours or, alternatively, because it is they crave the excitement of starting something new, so they may choose to launch yet another new venture. Whatever the reason, every business plan should include a section that describes both *management succession*—how the founding entrepreneurs can, ultimately, be replaced—and *exit strategies for investors*—how they can ultimately reap the benefits of having funded the new venture. Initially, ownership of a new venture is not a liquid asset: Shares cannot readily be sold to other persons. Later, however, this status can change radically if the company has an initial public offering (IPO) and its shares are subsequently traded on a national exchange. The business plan should address this and other potential exit strategies for investors, and for founders, too. In fact, this section is often very important to investors who fully understand the Arab proverb: "Think of the going out before you enter."

Scheduling and Milestones

A final section in the body of the business plan should address when major activities will be performed and key milestones reached. Again, giving careful thought to the timing of when various tasks will be performed or specific goals achieved is useful

© Peter Jones/Reuters/Corbis

both for entrepreneurs and potential investors. Identifying target dates may help entrepreneurs overcome a powerful cognitive bias known as the *planning fallacy,* which we described in Chapter 3—the tendency to assume that we can accomplish more in a given period of time than is really possible.[8] In this way, it can serve as another important reality check. From the point of view of investors, it indicates that entrepreneurs are indeed paying careful attention to the operations of their company and have developed clear plans for its future progress. What are these milestones? Included among the most important are these:

- Formal incorporation of the new venture (if this has not already occurred)
- Completion of product or service design
- Completion of prototypes
- Hiring of initial persons (sales or otherwise)
- Product display at trade shows
- Reaching agreements with distributors and suppliers
- Launch of initial production
- Receipt of initial orders
- First sales and deliveries
- Profitability

This list is just a small sample of the many milestones new ventures can include in their business plans; many others exist as well. The important point is to select milestones that make sense both from the point of view of the company's resources and the industry in which it is located.

Appendices

Because the main body of the plan should be relatively brief—as short as is adequate for presenting all essential information—several items are best included in separate appendices. Items typically included are detailed financial projections and full résumés of the founders and other members of the top management team. By including such items in appendices, entrepreneurs ensure that this important information is present for persons who wish to examine it, but at the same time keep the length of the business plan within desirable limits.

A Note on the Intangibles

In the preceding section, we described an outline of the essentials—the sections that are generally viewed as necessary for any thorough business plan. What we haven't addressed, of course, is what might be termed the *intangibles*—the extra something that leads readers of a plan to drop their slightly jaded attitude and to conclude, perhaps with some excitement, that there is indeed something here worth a closer look. We have all done a large amount of writing, so we believe that such factors as organization, clarity, choice of words, and style do indeed matter. Unfortunately, no one has yet been able to draw a bead on how these factors operate or how you can turn them to your own advantage. Given the importance of the business plan in the future of your new venture, however, we do have a concrete suggestion: Before distributing it to potential investors, have a number of people who are known to be good writers read it. If they will do it as a favour, that's great; if not, pay them for their time. Then *listen carefully to their suggestions* and revise the plan accordingly. Honestly, we can't think of anything else you can do that is likely to yield as much benefit for you and for your new venture. (What about the downside—are there specific errors you

LEARNING OBJECTIVE

5 Describe the seven deadly sins of business plans— errors all entrepreneurs should avoid.

should be careful to avoid because they can be the kiss of death to any business plan? Our answer is "Yes." And we have attempted to summarize the most important of these in the **Danger! Pitfall Ahead!** section.)

KEY POINTS

- All business plans should begin with an executive summary—a brief (two to three pages) section that provides a brief, clear, and persuasive overview of what the new venture is all about.
- Subsequent sections should include:

  Background and purpose. A section describing your idea and the current state of the business.

  Marketing. A section describing the market for the new venture's product or service, why there is a need for the product (or service) and why anyone would want to buy it, plus information on the existing competition and how it will be overcome, and pricing.

  Development, production, and location. Where the product or service is, in terms of development, how it will be produced, and (if appropriate) information on where the business will be located.

  Management. A section describing the experience, skills, and knowledge of the new venture's management team.

  Financial section. A section that provides information on the company's current financial state, and offers projections for future needs, revenues, and other financial measures, as well as a breakeven analysis.

  Risk factors. A section that discusses various risks the new venture will face, and the steps the management team is taking to protect against these threats.

  Harvest or exit. A section focused on how investors will gain if the company is successful.

  Scheduling and milestones. An overview of when each phase of the new venture will be completed, so that potential investors will know just when key tasks (e.g., start of production, time to first sales, projected breakeven point) will be completed.

  Appendices. Detailed financial information and detailed résumés of the top management team.

DANGER! PITFALL AHEAD!

The Seven Deadly Sins for New Venture Business Plans

Let us say it again: less than five minutes. That's the amount of time your plan has in the hands of many potential investors before they decide to turn thumbs up or thumbs down on it. In other words, in just a few moments, they evaluate a document that may have taken you weeks or even months to prepare. For this reason, it is absolutely imperative that you avoid errors that will doom your plan to the rejection pile no matter how good other sections of it may be. We term these the "Seven Deadly Sins of New Venture Business Plans." Here they are for you to recognize—and avoid:

Sin #1: The plan is poorly prepared and has an unprofessional look (e.g., no cover page, a cover page without contact information, glaring typos). This kind of carelessness triggers the following investor reaction: "I'm dealing with a group of amateurs."

Sin #2: The plan is far too slick (e.g., it is bound like a book, is printed on shiny paper, uses flashy graphics). This kind of glossy presentation leads investors to think: "What are they trying to hide behind all those fireworks?"

Sin #3: The executive summary is too long and rambling—it doesn't get right to the point. This excessiveness leads investors to think: "If they can't describe their own idea and company succinctly, I don't want to waste my time with them."

Sin #4: It's not clear where the product is in terms of development—does it exist or not? Can it be readily manufactured? Investors conclude: "I can't tell whether this is real or just another pipe dream; I'll pass on this one."

Sin #5: No clear answer is provided to the question: "Why would anyone ever want to buy one?" Many entrepreneurs seem to assume that their new product or service is so great that it will virtually sell itself. This type of self-assurance leads investors to think: "How naïve can you get? Even a machine that grew hair on the heads of bald men would need a marketing plan. These are truly amateurs."

Sin #6: There is no clear statement of the qualifications of the management team. This lack of information leads investors to conclude: "They probably have no relevant experience—and may not even know what relevant experience would be!"

Sin #7: Financial projections are largely an exercise in wishful thinking. This kind of optimism leads potential investors to conclude: "They have no idea about what it is like to run a company, or (even worse) they think I am incredibly naïve or stupid. Pass!" (These Seven Deadly Sins are summarized in Figure 8.6.)

The moral is clear: Keep a sharp lookout for these seven deadly errors because if you commit even one, your chance of obtaining help from sophisticated investors will drop off the bottom of the scale.

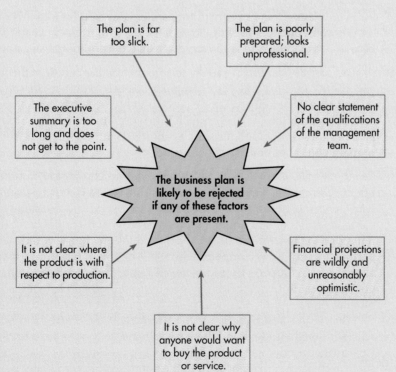

Figure 8.6 The Seven Deadly Sins for New Venture Business Plans

If one or more of these errors or problems are present in a business plan, it is likely to be rejected by potential investors, no matter how good other aspects of the plan may be.

MAKING AN EFFECTIVE BUSINESS PLAN PRESENTATION: THE BALL IS DEFINITELY IN YOUR COURT

LEARNING OBJECTIVE

6 Explain why potential investors usually ask entrepreneurs to give verbal presentations describing their idea for new products or services and their company.

LEARNING OBJECTIVE

7 Describe the steps entrepreneurs can take to make their verbal presentations to potential investors truly excellent.

Researchers who study stress agree that the way in which people think about stressful situations is a powerful determinant of how they react to them. One possible reaction is to emphasize the downside—to imagine what will happen if you simply can't cope with the stressful situation. Many people feel this way about making formal presentations: They imagine forgetting what they planned to say or harsh rejection from the audience, which causes them to experience high levels of anxiety that can, in turn, interfere with their actual performance. In contrast, another way to think about high-stress situations is to view them as a *challenge*—an opportunity to rise to the occasion and show the world what you've got. When people think about stressful situations in this way, they experience lower levels of anxiety, and their performance often matches their expectations: It *does* rise to new heights.[9]

Likewise, you should consider yourself fortunate to have the opportunity to verbally present your idea and your company to venture capitalists or other potential investors or sources of funding. The fact that you have been invited to make the presentation indicates that you have successfully passed the first major hurdle: More than 90 percent of plans do not generate an invitation to make a presentation, so you are already in a select group. Because you have done such a good job in preparing your plan, why should you doubt your ability to make a dynamite presentation? Basically, you should not; on the contrary, confidence, not doubt, should be your guiding principle. But confidence does not automatically translate into a first-rate presentation. Confidence, like writing an excellent business plan, requires a lot of preparation. Yes, some of us are better at making presentations—and at persuasion—than others, but almost all of us can improve our presentation skills if we try. Here are some concrete steps you can take (we really mean *should* take) to assure that your verbal presentation will match the high quality of your business plan—or even exceed it.

- *Remember: This really is important.* Your carefully prepared business plan has opened the door, but venture capitalists, bankers, and business angels do not give funds to business plans—they give them to people. How you handle this presentation has serious consequences for your company. It's important to keep this fact in mind because it will motivate you strongly to take the additional steps described below.

- *Prepare, prepare, and then ... prepare some more.* You are certainly the world's greatest expert on your idea and your company, but this expertise doesn't mean that you will be able to describe your ideas accurately, succinctly, and eloquently without careful preparation. Ask how much time you will have for your remarks (often it is 20 minutes or less, and it can be as short as 5 minutes in some settings) and then prepare your comments to fit this time.

- *Choose the content carefully.* What, exactly, should you try to accomplish during this brief presentation? Several areas need to be covered, but first and foremost you want to demonstrate that your product and service are unique and potentially valuable, and that you understand precisely what this value is. In this context, I'm reminded of the time I made the presentation that secured a manufacturing partner for my own company. The CEO of this large (more than $1 billion in annual sales) company turned to me and said, "OK, professor, tell us what you've got." His team of engineers had already tested our prototypes exhaustively, and his staff had read our business plan in detail, but he wanted to hear *me* summarize the nature and benefits of the product. Why? Partly, I'm sure, to find out whether I really understood them myself and also, as he later told me, to see how I performed under pressure. I had done my homework and was ready with a short presentation that got right to the point, so although many pointed questions followed later, I felt from the start that I was on the right track.

▧ *Remember that you are trying to persuade, not overwhelm.* One potential trap for many entrepreneurs—especially ones from a technical background—is to lapse quickly into technical language that only others in that technical field would understand. This approach can be a serious tactical error, because although the people you are addressing are highly intelligent and have a wide range of business experience, they may not have the specific training needed to understand highly technical descriptions. In general, it is far better to focus on the big picture—what the product does and why it is superior to other, competing products, rather than to slip into technical language that is easy and comfortable for the entrepreneur, but which may be largely unfamiliar to at least some potential investors.

▧ *Show enthusiasm—but temper it with reality checks.* Yes, you should definitely be enthusiastic; after all, this is *your* baby and *your* chance to shine, but temper your enthusiasm with hard facts and data. If you have completed marketing research, mention it briefly as you discuss marketing strategy. In any financial projections you mention, ensure that you keep at least one foot in contact with the ground; anyone can use a spreadsheet program to demonstrate sales that soon exceed the entire gross national product of the country. Your audience will certainly *not* be dazzled—or influenced—by numbers that make little or no business sense.

▧ *Rehearse!* There is no substitute for rehearsal where oral presentations are concerned. Some of these practice runs should be performed in front of friends and cofounders of your company so that you can get their feedback on how to improve. Others should be in front of people totally unfamiliar with your idea or company; that will help you find out whether your presentation makes sense to people learning about it for the first time. (When you give your formal presentation, some of the people in the audience will probably be in this situation, or—at most—they will have read your two-page executive summary.) Some rehearsals don't even require an audience. It is often helpful to deliver portions of your presentations to the four walls of your own room or office, just to make sure that you have committed major points to memory.

▧ *Don't overlook the basics.* It's amazing, but we have both personally attended many presentations that fell flat on their face because the people giving them had focused on the content, delivery, and level of their talks, but had forgotten about the basics. For instance, we have seen many talks in which the presenters spent precious time trying to figure out how to get their slides to appear on the screen, or in trying to explain charts or tables that were extremely complex or unreadable by the audience. In other cases, presenters failed to keep track of time and ran out of this precious commodity before they could make key points. *Don't overlook these basic issues.* If you do, all your hard work and careful presentation may go directly down the drain, and for very little reason.

▧ *Adopt a cooperative, helpful approach to questions.* One thing that is sure to happen during and after your presentation is that members of the audience will ask you pointed, searching questions. These questions should come as no surprise. First, you are asking them to give you money—perhaps large amounts of money. Second, they are an experienced group, who have seen lots of things go wrong with what seemed, at first, to be excellent start-up ventures. They are cautious and will have no qualms about asking you to hold forth on virtually any point made in your business plan—and also on issues not considered in the plan. Your answers to these questions are important and must make good sense, but so, too, is your attitude. If you bristle with obvious annoyance when asked a pointed question, or when the person who asks a question objects to your answer, this clash is a sign to potential investors that you may be lacking in the kind of emotional maturity they want to see in entrepreneurs, and you may *not* be a good bet. Your reaction to questions should be to take all questions seriously, answer them as best as possible, and maintain a helpful, cooperative attitude, no matter how intense the session becomes.

If you keep these points firmly in mind, we believe that you will have a good chance of making an excellent presentation—a much better chance than would be true if you ignore these points or minimize their importance. But suppose that despite your best efforts, and despite the fact that you did an excellent job, you still receive a "no" from a group on which you pinned high hopes. Should you be discouraged? Not at all. Very few entrepreneurs obtain support from the first potential investors they approach. In fact, highly successful entrepreneurs often note that their companies were rejected by many investors initially. In view of this fact, you should view rejections as an opportunity to learn, and you should try to obtain as much information as possible from them. Try to find out *why* your proposal was rejected, and whether there were aspects of the plan and your presentation that the potential investors found especially weak—or strong. Then, go back to the drawing boards and rework both your plan and your presentation. Along these lines, there are two key points you should keep firmly in mind: (1) There is almost always room for improvement, in virtually everything; and (2) success does *not* have to be immediate to be sweet. Good luck!

KEY POINTS

- Entrepreneurs should view invitations to give verbal presentations about their idea and their company as a challenge—a chance to shine—rather than as a high-stress situation in which they may be overwhelmed.
- Because such presentations are very important to the future of new ventures, entrepreneurs should take them very seriously and try to do an outstanding job.
- Steps that can help entrepreneurs accomplish this goal include selecting content carefully, avoiding technical jargon, showing enthusiasm tempered by reality, rehearsing carefully, paying careful attention to basic aspects of presentations (e.g., arriving early to set up audiovisual systems), and adopting a helpful cooperative attitude toward questions.
- Entrepreneurs should view rejections by potential investors as an opportunity to learn—to improve both their business plan and their verbal presentations.

THE VOICE OF EXPERIENCE

Business Planning Is More Important Than the Business Plan

Since writing their first business plan in 2002, Amy Ballon and Danielle Botterell have been growing Admiral Road. Recently, they talked with me about the process of writing that first business plan and the role that business planning plays in their company. Their first business plan is shown in the Appendix to this chapter.

Reuber: "How did you come to found a blanket manufacturing business?"

Admiral Road: "We had a burning desire not to continue working on Bay Street and gave ourselves three months to find an alternative. We started with a list of criteria for a start-up: it

had to have low capital-intensity, it had to be low-tech and we had to be able to balance the business with children." (In the four years after starting Admiral Road, Ballon and Botterell have each had two children, as you can see from the photo.) "We spent days and days making lists of possible businesses, and matching them against our skill sets, our interests, and what we thought market demands were. We have a regular Sunday night dinner group, and each week we would throw out ideas and find out what people thought of them. This feedback was valuable—for example, no one could see us being calm enough to run a spa! Within a month, we'd narrowed it down to a couple of choices. Amy had been a customer of the blanket business

continued

Courtesy of Admiral Road

we ended up buying and knew people who were trying to order blankets but couldn't. So, we knew that there was demand but not supply. We met with the owner to find out what happened to the business and found out that it was a side business for her that had become increasingly difficult to run because she was located in a rural area and there was a shortage of people who could sew for the company. She agreed to sell us the assets at a very reasonable price and we had a lawyer draw up a sales agreement to transfer the rights to us. The legal agreement bought peace of mind, especially with respect to the intellectual property rights of her designs, even though the lawyer probably cost half as much as all the assets cost!

Reuber: "Can you describe the process of developing the initial business plan?"

Admiral Road: "We actually did it over a weekend. On Friday, we sat down with the Ernst & Young template for a business plan and assigned sections to each of us. We worked all weekend and met with a banker on Monday. Beforehand, though, we had collected some valuable information. We talked to loans officers at five major Canadian banks to find out what was available to us as new business owners. So, we had a good idea of what they were looking for and what bank we wanted to target. (Yes, there were differences among them.) As with any business plan, the hardest element is the demand forecasts. We were lucky because we had the sales figures from the previous owner and knew how much she'd made at different shows and through different channels. Her track record also gave us a good basis to estimate costs. We'd heard through the business community that the bank, as a matter of course, would halve our sales forecasts so we doubled what we thought were the most realistic figures."

Reuber: "How did the bank react to it?"

Admiral Road: "Our banker loved it. At one point he said to the loans officer 'give them whatever they want!' We think this reflects three things. First, we weren't asking for all that much, and it was guaranteed by our personal savings, so there was little risk for him. However, he did slash some fees and do some deals for us. Second, we got the impression that 95 percent of what he sees is 'back of the napkin.' When you have a thorough, comprehensive plan, it stands out. Third, he liked our business school credentials and work experience. It's really true that bankers pay attention to the people at least as much as the plan. We still have the same banker today. It's really important to get to know your banker and nurture the relationship. We send him media articles about Admiral Road and keep him up-to-date on our plans and progress. So, if we need additional credit at any point in time, he very much understands why and is supportive."

Reuber: "Was the plan useful for anything other than getting the line of credit from the bank?"

Admiral Road: "Yes, developing the plan forced us to think in a constructive way about what we could do when. This was especially true for the marketing plan. In setting down activities against the calendar, we were forced to answer questions about what we could afford to do at different times and what would yield the biggest payoffs."

Reuber: "What is the role of a business plan now that Admiral Road is operating successfully?"

Admiral Road: "We have switched focus from the business plan to business planning. After starting the business, we spent much of 2002 and 2003 learning about the industry—how to make blankets, how to ship, how to find and retain sewers, what our most promising customer base was, a whole host of things. We were mired in the details and too busy to step back. Then, at the start of 2004, we had what we called the G2 Summit. We sat down and talked about our priorities for the business and realized that it was important to rebrand and develop a more professional image and website. A year later, at the start of 2005, we had another summit and developed a comprehensive financial model of the business and conducted sensitivity analyses to explore various growth options. This marked a transition point for Admiral Road. Up until then, business planning meant looking at most three months ahead. For the past year, though, we have held monthly planning meetings, setting goals and projections and looking ahead five years. Business planning has become increasing and critically important to the business."

Commentary: What Amy Ballon and Danielle Botterell are saying, in essence, is that business planning matters more than the business plan itself. Through the process of planning you learn more about your business, how the various parts fit together, and how it might best evolve. When entrepreneurs approach other people, such as investors or bankers, with their business plan, it becomes obvious very quickly whether they have been deeply engaged in the planning process and, as a result, truly understand their business.

Summary and Review of Key Points

- A business plan is a formal written document that explains the entrepreneur's vision and how it will be converted into a profitable, viable business.
- Venture capitalists and other potential sources of funding generally require a formal business plan as a first step for considering investments in new ventures.
- An additional step, and one that is often very important, involves a face-to-face presentation of the plan by the entrepreneur to venture capitalists or other interested parties.
- Preparing a formal business plan is useful for most entrepreneurs because doing so encourages them to formulate specific goals and concrete plans for reaching them, and these are invaluable both for converting ideas into viable companies and for raising needed capital.
- However, many successful entrepreneurs develop a fairly simple business plan, and then refine it in the light of information they gain from actually running the new venture.
- All business plans should begin with an executive summary—a brief (two to three pages) section that provides a brief, clear, and persuasive overview of what the new venture is all about.
- Subsequent sections should include:
  Background and purpose. A section describing your idea and the current state of the business.
  Marketing. A section describing the market for the new venture's product or service, why there is a need for the product (or service) and why anyone would want to buy it, plus information on the existing competition and how it will be overcome, and pricing.
  Development, production, and location. Where the product or service is, in terms of development, how it will be produced, and (if appropriate) information on where the business will be located.

  Management. A section describing the experience, skills, and knowledge of the new venture's management team.
  Financial section. A section that provides information on the company's current financial state, and offers projections for future needs, revenues, and other financial measures, as well as a breakeven analysis.
  Risk factors. A section that discusses various risks the new venture will face, and the steps the management team is taking to protect against these threats.
  Harvest or exit. A section focused on how investors will gain if the company is successful.
  Scheduling and milestones. An overview of when each phase of the new venture will be completed, so that potential investors will know just when key tasks (e.g., start of production, time to first sales, projected breakeven point) will be completed.
  Appendices. Detailed financial information and detailed résumés of the top management team.
- Entrepreneurs should view invitations to give verbal presentations about their idea and their company as a challenge—a chance to shine—rather than as a high-stress situation in which they may be overwhelmed.
- Because such presentations are very important to the future of new ventures, entrepreneurs should take them very seriously and try to do an outstanding job.
- Steps that can help entrepreneurs accomplish this goal include selecting content carefully, avoiding technical jargon, showing enthusiasm tempered by reality, rehearsing carefully, paying careful attention to basic aspects of presentations (e.g., arriving early to set up audiovisual systems), and adopting a helpful cooperative attitude toward questions.
- Entrepreneurs should view rejections by potential investors as an opportunity to learn—to improve both their business plan and their verbal presentations.

Glossary

Breakeven Analysis: An analysis indicating the level of sales and production required to cover all costs.

Business Plan: A written expression of the entrepreneur's vision for converting ideas into a profitable, going business.

Cash Flow Statement: A written statement of actual or projected cash inflows and outflows over a specific period of time, given certain levels of sales and costs.

Persuasion: The task of inducing others to share our views and to see the world much as we do.

Proforma Balance Sheet: A form showing projections of the company's financial condition at various times in the future.

Proforma Income Statement: A form illustrating projected operating results based on profit and loss.

Discussion Questions

1. Since writing a business plan requires a lot of work, why should entrepreneurs do it? Why not just get the company started? Which approach would you prefer, and why?

2. Why is the executive summary at the start of a business plan so important? What should be its primary goal or goals?

3. Why it is important to explain where the new product or service is with respect to the production process (e.g., is an idea? a prototype? in production?)?

4. Why it is so important for a business plan to fully describe the experience and expertise of the new venture's management?

5. How much optimism should be built into financial projections? What is the potential downside of including too much optimism?

6. Why should business plans include a full disclosure and discussion of potential risk factors? Isn't this just calling attention to negatives that might prevent investors from providing financial support?

7. Some people are better than others at giving verbal presentations. Should entrepreneurs consider this factor when choosing potential cofounders?

InfoTrac Exercises

1. **The Ins and Outs of Turnons and Turnoffs.** (The Company Doctor) (developing sound business plans that will attract potential investors) (column)

   Scott Clark

   Long Island Business News, May 7, 1999 v46 i19 p35A(1)

   Record: A54896541

   Abstract: Many entrepreneurs develop, assemble, or present business plans that represent their life's dream so poorly that they fail to attract the interest of potential investors. All business plans ever written feature elements that will engage readers' interest, that may turn them on, or turn them off. Suggestions pertaining to business plan writing may help entrepreneurs to engage the immediate attention and, perhaps, the support of potential financiers.

   1. According to the article, what two purposes should a business plan achieve?

   2. What aspects of the Admiral Road business plan, presented in the appendix to this chapter, might be turnoffs to potential stakeholders?

   3. What aspects are likely to be turnons to potential stakeholders?

2. The dos and don'ts of fund raising. Barbara Jorgensen.

   Electronic Business, May 2001 v27 i5 p29

   Record: A74361522

   Abstract: More and more companies need to seek funds from venture capital companies but most don't have a clue as to the best way of going about doing so. Companies must take care to do an accurate presentation to venture capital companies, paying particular attention to important details such as their niche and importance in the market. This article also give as ten reasons why companies fail to get funding.

1. According to the text, what should you emphasize when presenting your business plan to potential stakeholders?

2. What are the most frequent problems with business plans?

3. Where should a business plan be optimistic and where should it be pessimistic?

GETTING DOWN
TO BUSINESS

Writing a Great Executive Summary

A first-rate executive summary is an important ingredient in any good business plan. Excellent summaries catch the attention and interest of potential investors who generally decide, on the basis of the executive summary, whether to continue reading— or to move on to the next business plan in the pile. For this reason, learning how to write an excellent executive summary is a very useful skill for entrepreneurs. Follow these steps to improve your skill with respect to this important task.

1. **Write an executive summary for your new venture.** Be sure that it is no more than two to three pages long.

2. **Now, ask several people you know to read it and comment on it.** In particular, ask them to rate the summary on the following dimensions. (Ratings should use a 5-point scale: 1 = very poor; 2 = poor; 3 = neutral; 4 = good; 5 = excellent.)

   a. It provides a clear description of the new product or service.

   b. It explains why the new product or service will be appealing in specific markets.

   c. It identifies these markets and explains how the product will be promoted in them.

   d. It explains where the product is with respect to production.

   e. It explains who the entrepreneurs are and describes their background and experience.

   f. It explains how much funding the entrepreneurs are seeking and the purposes for which it will be used.

3. **Obtain the average score on each dimension.** The features on which you scored low (3 or below) are the areas that you should work on. Prepare an improved executive summary and have a different group of people rate it.

4. **Continue the process until the ratings on all dimensions are 4 or 5.**

Describing the New Venture's Management Team—And Putting It in a Favourable Light

Potential investors consider the quality of a new venture's management team to be a crucial factor—perhaps the most crucial—in their decision about whether to provide funding for it. Therefore, not only is it important to assemble an excellent team but it is essential to describe it fully and in terms that are as positive as possible. Unfortunately, some entrepreneurs don't seem to recognize the importance of this task. They fail to list past accomplishments or experience, and are just too modest overall. Carrying out the following steps can help you avoid these errors—and increase your chances of obtaining the funding you seek.

1. **List each member of the top management team of your new venture.**

2. **Describe their role in the new venture—what, specifically, will they do?**

3. **Next, ask each to provide information on the following items:**

    a. Where and when did they received their degrees, and in what fields.

    b. A description of all relevant experience—experience that is in any way relates to the tasks they will perform. This experience can include work experience, offices held in social and professional organizations, experience in running previous businesses (even small, informal ones), writing experience—almost anything that is relevant to their role in the new venture.

    c. Honours, awards, and prizes they have received (academic, business, athletics, etc.).

    d. Personal references—the more experienced, well-known, and prestigious, the better.

    e. Anything else in their background or experience that is relevant to their role in the new venture and places them in a favourable light (e.g., famous relatives? famous friends or associates?).

4. **Match the information that you have about the members of the top management team to the roles that you defined.** Make sure to include all the information that supports their ability to fulfill these roles, but don't include information that isn't relevant to the role. (For example, don't say that your head of marketing was the president of her high school chess club.)

5. Finally, show the finished product to other members of the top management team and brainstorm with them about whether it presents your strengths in a way that will be obvious to potential investors. If it does not, go back to the drawing board and start again!

Enhanced Learning

You may select any combination of the resources below to enhance your understanding of the chapter material.

- **Appendix 1: Case Studies** – Twelve cases provide opportunities to apply chapter concepts to realistic entrepreneurial situations. These brief cases call for careful analysis of real business problems and ask you to think about potential solutions.
- **Video Case Library** – Nine cases are tied directly to video segments from the popular PBS television series Small Business School. These cases and video segments (available on the Entrepreneurship website at http://www.entrepreneurship.nelson.com) give you unparalleled access to today's entrepreneurs, with expert advice and insights on how to start, run, and grow a business.
- **Management Interview Series Video Database** – This video interview series contains a wealth of tips on how to manage effectively. Access to the database and practical exercises are available on the book support website at http://www.entrepreneurship.nelson.com.

Notes

1   Mancuso, J.R. 1975. *How to write a winning business plan.* Englewood Cliffs, NJ: Prentice-Hall.

2   Delmar, F., & Shane, S. (2003). Does business planning facilitate the development of new ventures? *Strategic Management Journal* 24(12): 1165–1185.

3   Fletcher, C. 1979. Impression management in the selection interview. In R.A. Giacalone & P. Rosenfeld, P. (eds.). *Impression management in the selection interview* (pp. 269–272). Hillsdale, NJ: Erlbaum.

4   Zacharakis, A.L, & Shepherd, D.A. 2001. The nature of information and overconfidence on venture capialists' decision making. *Journal of Business Venturing* 16(4): 311–332.

5   Baron, R.A., & Markman, G.D. 2003. Beyond social capital: The role of entrepreneurs' social competence in their financial success. *Journal of Business Venturing* 18(1): 41–60.

6   McNish, J. 2005. Mega Bloks v. LEGO. *globeandmail.com*, November 23.

7   Marotte, B. 2005. Top court quashes LEGO big against toy rival. *Globe and Mail*, November 18: B5.

8   Buehler, R., Griffin, D., & MacDonald, H. 1997. The role of motivated reasoning in optimistic time predictions. *Personality and Social Psychology Bulletin* 23(3): 237–247.

9   Greenberg, J., & Baron, R.A. 2003. *Behavior in organizations.* 7th ed. Upper Saddle River, NJ: Prentice-Hall.

In this section, we present a real business plan written by Amy Ballon and Danielle Botterell, two Toronto-based entrepreneurs who decided to leave Bay Street to open their own business in 2002 (see the Voice of Experience in Chapter 8 for their insights on business planning). Ballon and Botterell purchased the assets of an existing blanket manufacturer and used these assets to found Admiral Road. They used their own funds to purchase the business, and wrote the business plan to think through their development plan and to obtain a line of credit from a bank (see Figure A8.1). You can find out more about Admiral Road from the company's website at http://www.admiralroad.com.

ADMIRAL ROAD BUSINESS PLAN

1. Executive Summary

Admiral Road is a mail-order company that produces a high quality and attractive product that serves as a personalized alternative to mass-produced products for the gift or home accessory buyer.

Purchased as an established business, Admiral Road offers tested products to a receptive customer base via mail order or at craft shows. The Company has plans to sell its products via the Internet and to target corporate accounts and suitable retailers.

Admiral Road's margins are attractive and the Company expects to be net income positive in its first year of operation. The principals of the Company have solid business backgrounds and extensive personal networks through which to market the products.

2. Background

Admiral Road began when the principals, Amy Ballon and Danielle Botterell, purchased a fleece blanket and accessory business from Mazooma Inc. of Huntsville,

Courtesy of Admiral Road

Courtesy of Admiral Road

Figure A8.1 Venture Business Plans Need to Convey Clear Business Objectives

The founders of Admiral Road used their business plan to obtain funds to develop a logo and image for their business and to invest in professional photographs of their products, such as their moose blanket.

Ontario. The owner of Mazooma designed the product line and first marketed it at the Toronto One of A Kind Craft Show in December 1998, during which she generated approximately $20,000 of revenue. She continued to operate the fleece business by mail order in conjunction with her Huntsville retail store until she experienced a labour shortage, which caused her to stop producing the blankets in late 2000.

Both of the principals of Admiral Road were customers of Mazooma's blanket business. When Mazooma stopped providing the blankets, Admiral Road perceived a market niche and approached Mazooma about a purchase. The purchase was completed on March 13th, 2002 and all rights of ownership were legally transferred. During the negotiations to purchase Mazooma, the principals spent considerable time with the owner of Mazooma. During these sessions, the success and viability of each product was discussed, as was pricing, marketing and other key elements to running the business. The owner of Mazooma was extremely forthcoming and the sessions were very valuable.

As part of the purchase of Mazooma's blanket business, Admiral Road bought a mailing list with approximately 1700 customer names on it, as well as supplier lists, the exclusive rights to all of the designs, catalogue and web site artwork and the hard assets of the business (sewing machines, design table, etc.). By purchasing the Mazooma blanket business—a known and proven entity—rather than starting a business from scratch, the principals of Admiral Road believe that considerable time and funds were spared in the learning process.

3. Product

Admiral Road produces a Canadian handmade fleece product. The product line includes blankets, pillows and accessories for babies, children, adults and pets. The emphasis is on quality, bright and beautiful colours, and designs that are comforting and fun. The products are reasonably priced and yet upscale. Items in the catalogue range in price from $24 to $105 (see Exhibit 1).

Exhibit 1 Admiral Road Catalogue

4. Market Analysis

4.1 Customer Analysis

Admiral Road's products will appeal to a number of different customer groups.

4.1.1 BUYER OF BABY GIFTS

With the current product line, the best selling item is the Baby Name Blanket—a fleece blanket featuring brightly coloured appliquéd animals and the child's name. At $39, it makes an excellent gift from a grandparent, friend, or someone attending a baby shower. Our research shows that the price point on this product reflects the amount most people want to spend on a gift for a newborn.

While there are many options for gifts for babies, very few offer a personalized touch, which is a huge contributing factor to the popularity of the blankets.

4.1.2 HOME OR COTTAGE OWNER

Admiral Road's fleece product designs are unique as well as beautiful, comfortable and durable. With motifs such as oak leaves and cottages, the big blankets and quilts are perfect accessories for casual rooms in homes or cottages. Buyers will also appreciate the ease of caring for Admiral Road products.

4.1.3 TOURISTS

Admiral Road's products are designed with a distinctly Canadian flair. Purchasing a throw or a pillow adorned with a moose or a polar bear will serve to remind tourists of Canada while enjoying a comfortable and well-made product. Tourists will be able to access Admiral Road's products through craft shows initially and later through retailers to whom the Company is wholesaling.

4.1.4 RETAILERS

Admiral Road will seek out retailers across Canada with whom the products would fit well. Participating in craft shows is an excellent way to make contacts with appropriate retailers.

4.1.5 CORPORATE CLIENTS

As did its predecessor, Mazooma, Admiral Road will serve companies who wish to send unique and personal gifts to their client. The Company has already made contact with several potential corporate clients and has secured a relationship with one.

Regardless of the specific customer's attributes, Admiral Road's products will appeal to those wishing to pay a slight premium for original home accessories, each of which is handmade in Canada. Admiral Road customers will be looking for a one-of-a-kind product, rather than something mass-produced. Customers will appreciate the personalized nature of the children's and pet products, as well as the ability to have any product personalized.

4.2 Market

Admiral Road views the market potential as very broad. The Company will focus its marketing efforts on craft shows, personal contacts, and corporate clients in Southern Ontario for the remainder of 2002. Additionally, the Company will market and sell its products via the Internet. Beginning in 2003, Admiral Road will participate in craft shows outside of Ontario and will focus on wholesaling, while continuing to solicit corporate clients.

4.3 Competitors

While there are a limited number of providers of fleece blankets for infants in the local market, the Company's research shows that there are no comparable personalized products on the market. Additionally, while there is a company offering fleece blankets in Canada, its customer, marketing and design focus are very different than that of Admiral Road.

5. Marketing and Sales Channels

5.1 Marketing:

In developing the marketing plan, Admiral Road has defined its mission statement as follows: To design and produce Canadian-made textile products for babies, kids, adults and pets in a manner that emphasizes quality, fashion and fun and serves as an alternative to mass-produced products.

The marketing objectives of Admiral Road are three-fold. The first objective is to make customers in the Ontario market aware of the Admiral Road brand and product through participation in various craft shows and a launch event. Admiral Road has had replies from nine major craft shows and gained acceptance into each one. The first three craft shows were extremely successful. The second objective is to capitalize on the 1,700-person mailing list that was purchased as an asset of the former business. These existing customers will be contacted with a mailing and a follow-up telephone call. Finally, Admiral Road will promote the company name and product in the broader market using a company web site. The Company has registered the domain name "admiralroad.com."

5.2 Marketing Strategy

The marketing strategy is to create a fleece product line centred around the concepts of quality and fun. Various promotional activities will be used to support the mail order business and managed by the full-time efforts of the two principals. Marketing concepts include participation in Ontario craft shows, a launch event, a catalogue, a mailing to existing mailing list customers, promotional fliers, an email campaign, local television appearances and print media write-ups.

5.3 Sales channels:

In Year 1, distribution channels include a launch event and eight major craft shows in Ontario. Product will also be available by contacting Admiral Road directly by telephone and through the web site. The Company will also target corporate sales through the extensive personal networks of the principals. Additionally, wholesaling to retailers will be pursued via participation in craft shows and targeting selected appropriate partners. The marketing schedule has been planned for the remainder of 2002 (see Exhibit 2).

6. Management Team

Admiral Road's management team combines business expertise with creative talent. Formerly employed as management consultants, Amy Ballon and Danielle Botterell are both graduates of the MBA program at the University of Toronto. Before returning to business school Amy and Danielle held responsible positions at TSE 100 firms (see Exhibit 3).

There are many craftspeople in Ontario, many of whom make beautiful products. There are however, very few craftspeople with solid business experience and know-how. Admiral Road believes that it is uniquely positioned and qualified to grow its business exponentially.

The principals have known each other for more than 12 years and are aware of the challenges of partnership. A partnership agreement as well as a commitment to the business and a friendly relationship is in place to mitigate this challenge.

7. Funding Requirements

The Principals have each contributed $12,500 to the business for a total of $25,000 in start-up capital. To date, the Company has incurred approximately $25,000 in expenses, which includes the purchase of the Mazooma business and its assets, hard

Exhibit 2 Admiral Road Marketing and Media Calendar

		May				Jun				Jul					Aug				Sep					Oct				Nov				Dec			
		6	13	20	27	3	10	17	24	1	8	15	22	29	5	12	19	26	2	9	16	23	30	7	14	21	28	4	11	18	25	2	9	16	23
1	Catalogue prod'ctn	■																																	
2	Send Launch Invites		■																																
3	Toronto Show																																		
4	Burlington Show				▢																														
5	Web site launch						■																												
6	Launch Party						■																												
7	Hamilton Show																																		
8	Goderich Show																																		
10	Barrie Show															▢																			
9	Shaw Show																																		
11	Mailing to existing list																		■																
12	Ottawa Show																																		
13	One of a Kind Show																														▢				
14	TV appearance																														■				

■ Internal event

▢ Craft Show

AMY S. BALLON

Employment

Admira Road Designs
Owner, March 2002 - Present
- Negotiated the purchase of an existing mail-order fleece blanket and pillow business
- Prepared marketing materials including packaging and a catalogue
- Developed new designs and product ideas
- Accepted to all craft shows to which the Company has applied

Mercer Management Consulting, Toronto, Ontario
Associate, 2000 – 2002
- Led a module to redesign marketing processes at a major U.S. regional bank that identified opportunities for increased efficiency
- Identified revenue growth opportunities for a major Canadian cultural institution that resulted in organizational change and an improved ability to target clients
- Prepared numerous presentations for business development purposes
- Managed and oversaw the work of analysts

TD Bank, Corporate and Investment Banking Group, Toronto, Ontario
Summer Associate, International Trade Finance, Latin America, Summer 1999
- Closed $45 million in trade finance transactions generating over $1 million in revenue
- Prepared financial and business analyses to assess the Bank's relationships in Latin America
- Developed a business case to judge the viability of opening a Representative Office in Latin America

Nesbitt Burns, Investment Banking Department, Toronto, Ontario
Coordinator, Financial Services Group, 1997 - 1998
- Advised Great-West Life in its $3.1 billion acquisition of London Life as a member of the project team
- Assisted in the research and preparation of presentations for clients in the financial services sector

Diefenbach Elkins Vandenberg (Corporate Design Consultancy), Toronto, Ontario
Account Executive, 1995 - 1996
- Compiled research data for *Bell Canada* on the strategic positioning of its retail stores
- Developed a positioning paper for *Saudi Aramco* on the branding of its retail gas stations
- Oversaw the production of promotional materials for various clients

Moment Magazine, Washington, D.C.
Marketing Assistant, 1994 - 1995
- Coordinated advertising for a national magazine with a circulation of 40,000

- Implemented a distribution program that provided communities with low-cost subscriptions and increased monthly circulation by 25%

EDUCATION

University of Toronto, MBA, 2000
- President of the Graduate Business Council – the elected students' representative to the faculty, administration and business community
- Winner of the Concordia International Case Competition

McGill University, BA, Political Science, 1994
- *Graduated with Distinction*

The Hebrew University, Jerusalem, Israel, 1992-1993

ACHIEVEMENTS

- Trained for and successfully completed dozens of road races including six full marathons:
- Boston 2001 (Time: 3:31), Boston 2000 (3:39), Toronto 1998 (3:38), Chicago 1997 (3:42), Washington, D.C. 1996, (3:55), Toronto 1995 (4:33)

Volunteer Activities
Proofreader, Ontario Roadrunner Magazine, 1997 - 2000
Department Coordinator, Nesbitt Burns' United Way Campaign, 1997-1998; raised over $175,000
Chairperson, Chevrolet Mother-Daughter Walk for the Heart and Stroke Foundation, 1996 - 1997

Special Skills and Interests
- Language study; French, Spanish, German, Hebrew, Arabic and Latin
- Traveled throughout the former Soviet Union, Europe, Southeast Asia and the Middle East

---

DANIELLE S. BOTTERELL

PROFESSIONAL EXPERIENCE

Owner
Admiral Road Designs, Toronto, Ontario   Present
- Negotiated the purchase of an existing mail-order fleece blanket and pillow business
- Prepared marketing materials including packaging and a catalogue
- Developed new designs and product ideas
- Accepted to all craft shows to which the Company has applied

Associate
Mercer Management Consulting Toronto, Ontario   Fall 2001-March 2002

Associate, Investment Banking
RBC Dominion Securities, Toronto, Ontario   Summer 2000

- Key team member for a $350 million public-private infrastructure project
- Created complex financial models and presentations for senior client management in healthcare, retail, and auto sectors
- Designed, researched and completed a bank-wide product profile used for marketing purposes

Director, Investor Relations and Corporate Communications
TrizecHahn Corporation, Toronto, Ontario

- Managed relationships with key investors and media contacts
- Led a cross-divisional team in the implementation of an integrated company-wide web site
- Crafted speeches, news releases and other key corporate documents
- Created monthly IR/market activity report for Peter Munk and senior management
- Drafted and coordinated entire production of annual and quarterly reports
- Created and maintained IR content for corporate web site
- Negotiated key contracts and managed all supplier relationships for IR department
- Prepared department budget

Director of Investor Relations
Minorca Resources Inc., Toronto, Ontario

- Initial development of corporate communications program
- Assumed role of key contact for portfolio managers, analysts, and retail investors
- Handled all investor relations activities for two equity issues totaling $90 million
- Worked with management team and investors in restructuring of equity deal
- Handled crisis communications for shareholders and media following post-Bre-X collapse
- Developed corporate image through drafting and production of annual and quarterly reports
- Drafted, disseminated and filed press releases
- Scripted and arranged all investor meetings and presentations
- Prepared regulatory filings and contact with stock exchange market surveillance teams

---

EDUCATION

Masters of Business Administration
Joseph L. Rotman School of Management, Toronto, Ontario
Elected Class President   2000-2001

Canadian Securities Course

Bachelor of Arts, Honours, Political Science
McGill University, Montreal, Quebec

Diplome, Niveau II
Université d'Aix-Marseille III, Aix en Provence, France

LANGUAGE STUDY

French (fluent), Mandarin, German

PROFESSIONAL DEVELOPMENT

Canadian Investor Relations Institute (CIRI): Board of Directors   1998-1999
                        Chair,   Membership   1998-1999
                        Committee   Member   1997
- Attended three annual CIRI conferences
- Attended seminars on Corporate Disclosure, Stock Exchange workings, Media Interaction
- Planned and attended seminars on IR web sites, effective investor kits, media relations and IR fundamentals
- Attended Northern Miner mining seminars, guest speaker at Northern Miner Investor Relations Conference

COMMUNITY INVOVLEMENT

Campaign Chair: TrizecHahn United Way Campaign 1998 – raised $50,000
Corporate Committee member: Kids' Help Phone - 1998-1999
Organizing Committee member: Fundraising Gala for the Toronto International Film Festival –1997

INTERESTS

Golf
Running – trained for and completed New York City marathon – November 2000
Reading – about 50 books a year

---

assets such as a computer, telephones and fleece inventory, as well as administrative expenses. The capital also covers all initial marketing expenses including the fees to participate in craft shows as well as a budget for a launch event.

Exhibit 3 Résumés of Principals of Admiral Road

The Company has generated approximately $8,000 of revenue to date. At this time, the Company is seeking a line of credit to finance the following:

▦ The placement of an advertisement in a North American publication;

▦ The building of an e-commerce web site;

▦ A logo/identity for the business;

■ Professional photography of our product line for use in print and web advertising; and

■ Booth space at the prestigious One of a Kind Craft Show.

8. Financial Projections

Exhibit 4 shows that Admiral Road expects to have Pro Forma 2002 revenues of nearly $100,000, with a net income of more than $43,000.

The Company currently has no debt.

9. Risks

Risks are associated with all new business ventures. In the case of Admiral Road two risks have been identified. First, the barriers to entry are quite low. Craftspeople would find it relatively easily to imitate the product by purchasing fleece and reproducing the Company's designs. However, this risk is somewhat mitigated by operational and financial expertise of the principals that is required for the successful widespread distribution of the product. The other risk is the dissolution of the partnership. To mitigate this risk the principals have drawn up a Partnership Agreement that outlines the terms of business should the partnership dissolve.

Exhibit 4 Admiral Road Projected Financials

Assumptions

1 **Depreciation:**

Computer	$ 1,200
Telephones	$ 200
Sewing Machines	$ 900
Other Equipment	$ 300
Total	$ 2,600
Industrial Machine	$ 1,400 over 20 years

All equipment is straight-line depreciated over 3 years

2 **Sales, General & Administrative Expenses/Month**

Telephone/Internet	$ 210
Car Insurance, Gas	$ 300
Craft Shows	$ 350
Mailing/Promotion	$ 200
Total	$ 1,060

3 **Tax Rate**   35%

4 **Custom Orders**

10% of orders are custom at approximately $10 revenue, $1 cost per order

5 **Growth Rate**

2003	50%
2004	25%
2005	15%

6 **Projected % of Revenue**

Cost of Goods Sold	17%
SG&A	13%

	May	June	July	August	September	October	November	December	Total	Pro Forma 2002
2002										
Revenue	$ 1,962.00	$ 6,640.00	$ 6,640.00	$ 6,640.00	$ 3,964.00	$ 3,964.00	$ 18,718.00	$ 18,718.00	$ 67,246.00	$ 97,506.70
COGS	$ 329.99	$ 1,251.37	$ 1,251.37	$ 1,251.37	$ 547.61	$ 547.61	$ 3,241.18	$ 3,241.18	$ 11,661.69	$ 16,909.45
Gross Profit	$ 1,632.01	$ 5,388.63	$ 5,388.63	$ 5,388.63	$ 3,416.39	$ 3,416.39	$ 15,476.82	$ 15,476.82	$ 55,584.31	$ 80,597.25
SG&A	$ 1,060.00	$ 1,060.00	$ 1,060.00	$ 1,060.00	$ 1,060.00	$ 1,060.00	$ 1,060.00	$ 1,060.00	$ 8,480.00	$ 12,720.00
EBITDA	$ 1,553.95	$ 4,328.63	$ 4,328.63	$ 4,328.63	$ 2,356.39	$ 2,356.39	$ 14,416.82	$ 14,416.82	$ 48,086.25	$ 67,877.25
Depreciation	$ 78.06	$ 78.06	$ 78.06	$ 78.06	$ 78.06	$ 78.06	$ 78.06	$ 78.06	$ 624.44	$ 866.67
EBIT	$ 1,475.89	$ 4,250.58	$ 4,250.58	$ 4,250.58	$ 2,278.33	$ 2,278.33	$ 14,338.76	$ 14,338.76	$ 47,461.81	$ 67,010.58
Interest	$ -	$ -	$ -	$ -	$ -	$ -	$ -	$ -	$ -	$ -
Taxes	$ 516.56	$ 1,487.70	$ 1,487.70	$ 1,487.70	$ 797.42	$ 797.42	$ 5,018.57	$ 5,018.57	$ 16,611.63	$ 23,453.70
Net Income	$ 959.33	$ 2,762.87	$ 2,762.87	$ 2,762.87	$ 1,480.91	$ 1,480.91	$ 9,320.20	$ 9,320.20	$ 30,850.17	$ 43,556.88

	2003	2004	2005
Revenue	$ 146,260.05	$ 182,825.06	$ 210,248.82
COGS	$ 24,864.21	$ 31,080.26	$ 35,742.30
Gross Profit	$ 121,395.84	$ 151,744.80	$ 174,506.52
SG&A	$ 19,013.81	$ 23,767.26	$ 27,332.35
EBITDA	$ 102,382.04	$ 127,977.54	$ 147,174.18
Depreciation	$ 866.67	$ 866.67	$ 866.67
EBIT	$ 101,515.37	$ 127,110.88	$ 146,307.51
Interest	$ -	$ -	$ -
Taxes	$ 35,530.38	$ 44,488.81	$ 51,207.63
Net Income	$ 65,984.99	$ 82,622.07	$ 95,099.88

		Baby Blankets	Kid Blankets	Big Blankets	Cozy	Pillows	Mini	Custom	Total
May	Units	30	4	2	0	5	20	6.1	
	Revenue	$ 1,170.00	$ 196.00	$ 150.00	$ -	145	$ 240.00	$ 61.00	$ 1,962.00
	COGS	$ 138.91	$ 32.54	$ 28.45	$ -	$ 32.80	$ 91.20	$ 6.10	$ 329.99
June	Units	75	15	10	5	10	100	21.5	
	Revenue	$ 2,925.00	$ 735.00	$ 750.00	$ 525.00	290	$ 1,200.00	$ 215.00	$ 6,640.00
	COGS	$ 347.28	$ 122.03	$ 142.23	$ 96.74	$ 65.59	$ 456.00	$ 21.50	$ 1,251.37
July	Units	75	15	10	5	10	100	21.5	
	Revenue	$ 2,925.00	$ 735.00	$ 750.00	$ 525.00	290	$ 1,200.00	$ 215.00	$ 6,640.00
	COGS	$ 347.28	$ 122.03	$ 142.23	$ 96.74	$ 65.59	$ 456.00	$ 21.50	$ 1,251.37
August	Units	75	15	10	5	10	100	21.5	
	Revenue	$ 2,925.00	$ 735.00	$ 750.00	$ 525.00	290	$ 1,200.00	$ 215.00	$ 6,640.00
	COGS	$ 347.28	$ 122.03	$ 142.23	$ 96.74	$ 65.59	$ 456.00	$ 21.50	$ 1,251.37
September	Units	70	10	2	2	10	0	9.4	
	Revenue	$ 2,730.00	$ 490.00	$ 150.00	$ 210.00	290	$ -	$ 94.00	$ 3,964.00
	COGS	$ 324.13	$ 81.36	$ 28.45	$ 38.70	$ 65.59	$ -	$ 9.40	$ 547.61
October	Units	70	10	2	2	10	0	9.4	
	Revenue	$ 2,730.00	$ 490.00	$ 150.00	$ 210.00	290	$ -	$ 94.00	$ 3,964.00
	COGS	$ 324.13	$ 81.36	$ 28.45	$ 38.70	$ 65.59	$ -	$ 9.40	$ 547.61
November	Units	300	18	8	10	30	250	61.6	
	Revenue	$ 11,700.00	$ 882.00	$ 600.00	$ 1,050.00	870	$ 3,000.00	$ 616.00	$ 18,718.00
	COGS	$ 1,389.11	$ 146.44	$ 113.78	$ 193.48	$ 196.78	$ 1,140.00	$ 61.60	$ 3,241.18
December	Units	300	18	8	10	30	250	61.6	
	Revenue	$ 11,700.00	$ 882.00	$ 600.00	$ 1,050.00	870	$ 3,000.00	$ 616.00	$ 18,718.00
	COGS	$ 1,389.11	$ 146.44	$ 113.78	$ 193.48	$ 196.78	$ 1,140.00	$ 61.60	$ 3,241.18

PART 3

LAUNCHING THE NEW VENTURE

All new ventures must adopt a specific legal form, so choosing among these forms is a key step in actually launching a new venture. Once launched, new ventures need three key ingredients to succeed. They need specific marketing plans that help them to actively sell their products or services. They need an overall strategy for gaining and holding competitive advantage, and for overcoming the disadvantages faced by new companies that must compete with larger, well-established firms. Finally, because growing ventures require an ever-expanding labour force, entrepreneurs must be able to successfully recruit, motivate, and retain high-quality employees.

ALL PHOTOS THIS PAGE ©
PHOTODISC, INC.

CHAPTER 9

THE LEGAL FORMS AND LEGAL ENVIRONMENTS OF NEW VENTURES

LEARNING OBJECTIVES

After reading this chapter, you should be able to:

1 Describe the major forms of business ownership—sole proprietorship, partnerships, corporations—and explain the advantages and disadvantages of each.

2 Define franchising and describe the advantages and disadvantages of becoming a franchisee.

3 Describe the legal principles governing franchise agreements and the information disclosure that potential franchisees should insist upon.

4 Describe current trends in franchising, such as smaller outlets in nontraditional locations, co-branding franchising, and international franchising.

5 Describe the basic components of business contracts, and explain what happens if these obligations are not met.

6 Describe the basic components of a risk management strategy and how you might go about selecting a lawyer.

The Legal Forms New Ventures Can Take
   Sole Proprietorship: One Company, One Owner
   Partnerships: Different Forms, Different Benefits
   Corporations: Limited Liability, But at a Cost

Franchising
   The Benefits of Becoming a Franchisee
   Drawbacks of Becoming a Franchisee
   Legal Aspects of Franchising
   The Future Shape of Franchising

The Legal Environment of New Ventures:
Some Basics
   Business Contracts: Their Essential Components
   Basic Elements of a Contract
   Obligations under Contracts
   Risk Management

All photos this page © PhotoDisc, Inc.

> "The business of the law is to make sense of the confusion of what we call human life—to reduce it to order but at the same time to give it possibility, scope, even dignity." (Archibald MacLeish, 1978)

When I started my first company in 1992, I (Robert Baron) didn't give much thought to the legal form it should take. I was certain from the word "Go!" that it should be a corporation. Why? Mainly for two reasons. First, I had been working for more than 25 years, so I had built up a reasonable amount of personal property (my house, stocks, real estate holdings). I realized that a corporation would protect these assets if, for some reason, the company did not succeed and ended up in debt. Second, I had experience with several other forms of ownership—joint ventures, various kinds of partnerships—and had found that they all suffered from serious drawbacks. For instance, I had been a limited partner in past investments where the controlling general partners had done pretty much as they pleased—including diverting the partnership's funds to their personal use. I wanted to avoid these problems, so I decided to make my new business a corporation. As I quickly discovered, though, incorporation was more complicated—and expensive—than I had guessed. Many decisions had to be made: How would stocks be distributed? Would there be one kind of stock or several? No, forming a corporation was not easy; yet, it still seemed the right way to go. Ultimately, I discovered still additional problems; for instance, dissolving the corporation nine years later turned out to be a nightmare of endless paperwork. Along the way, I found filing the required financial statements to be a difficult chore—especially in the early, hectic days when we were first getting started.

Looking back, and knowing what I know now, I realize that I actually had several choices aside from forming a corporation. In other words, my new venture could have taken one of several different legal forms. In fact, there are many legal issues that entrepreneurs need to consider. We agree with the quote and share MacLeish's conviction that laws do often bring order to the turmoil of daily life, and also realize that many entrepreneurs know very little about legal matters. Our goal for this textbook is not to turn you into legal experts, but to familiarize you with some of these legal issues. In Chapter 7, we examined legal issues concerning intellectual property protection. In this chapter, we look at the legal forms a venture can take, including the option of becoming a franchisee, as well as the basic elements of contract law and risk management. New ventures are as subject to these laws as large, mature companies. So please *do* look before you leap: The business you save may be your own.

THE LEGAL FORMS NEW VENTURES CAN TAKE

The next time you pick up your dry cleaning, look at the moving belt that brings your clothing to the front counter. If it says "Railex," you are face-to-face with a product manufactured by a company started by my (Robert Barron's) Uncle Sid (see Figure 9.1). In fact, several members of my family, including my grandfather and at least three uncles, started businesses and were—or are—entrepreneurs. Most of them chose to make their new ventures corporations, but my grandfather's business took a different form: It was a straightforward partnership, which he started with one other person. As I'll note later, this decision got him into serious difficulties and ultimately led to the demise of a profitable company. But that's getting ahead of the story. Let's turn now to an overview of the major legal forms new ventures can take, and the advantages and disadvantages offered by each.

Sole Proprietorship: One Company, One Owner

By far the simplest form of business ownership is the **sole proprietorship**— a situation in which a business is owned and managed by one individual. Almost all sole proprietorships are small companies. The appeal is obvious. Such businesses are simple to create—you just open for business. If you want to operate a business under a name different from your name, you

Figure 9.1 Entrepreneurship in Robert Baron's Family

One of my uncles is a founder of the Railex Corporation. He and his brothers chose to make their company a corporation.

© Getty Images/ PhotoDisc

Source: © The New Yorker Collection 1984 Dean Vietor from cartoonbank.com. All Rights Reserved.

"Now that you've demonstrated your clout, let's get on with the negotiations."

LEARNING OBJECTIVE

1 Describe the major forms of business ownership—sole proprietorship, partnerships, corporations—and explain the advantages and disadvantages of each.

Figure 9.2 Conflict between Partners: A Major Source of Problems for Partnerships

When partners disagree over important issues and experience conflict, the effects can be devastating for their company.

---

need to register the business name with the provincial government (unless you are operating a business in Newfoundland and Labrador). The Canada Business Service Centre website, http://www.cbsc.org, lists the registration and licensing requirements for each province and territory. The costs involved in setting up a sole proprietorship are very low—you just open for business—and this simplicity, too, is a decided advantage: There is little paperwork. In fact, owners do not have to file a separate tax return because revenues and expenses are reported on the owner's personal tax return. Business losses are deductible against other income. A third benefit of being the sole owner of a business is total control over its operations: As an owner, you make all the decisions and, of course, you get to keep all the profits. If, one day, you decide to the close the business, you just stop operating the business. Clearly, then, there are important pluses to being a sole proprietor: Entrepreneurs who choose this route are truly their own bosses, and as we noted in Chapter 1, that is one reason why many people choose to become entrepreneurs in the first place.

These benefits come at a considerable cost, however. The most important of these is that owners of sole proprietorships are subject to **unlimited personal liability**: They are personally liable for all debts incurred by the business. Not only can you lose your entire investment if the business fails, but you can also lose most of your personal assets, too, if the business is deeply in debt. Although most provinces permit owners to retain some equity in their homes or car, everything else is fair game for debtors, and the owner can be forced to sell them to pay off the debts the business has incurred.

A second disadvantage involves the fact that when individuals run a business by themselves, they represent the sum total of its management resources: If they lack the knowledge or skill needed to run the business successfully, they must either hire someone who has the skill they lack, or the business may fail. Similarly, if the owner becomes ill or incapacitated, or if she or he chooses to retire, the business terminates unless there is a family member, close friend, or employee willing and able to operate it. Finally, sole proprietorships face a big disadvantage in obtaining capital: The business has no stocks that can be sold to investors, and banks and other financial institutions may be reluctant to issue loans because of the risks involved (e.g., the business will halt or terminate if something happens to the owner). The assets of the business (e.g., a piece of equipment) can be sold when the owner wishes to dissolve the firm, but the business itself cannot be sold because it is not a legal entity. In sum, although nearly all of us daydream about owning our own business and being our own boss, sole proprietorship is generally not a suitable legal form for a new venture that we hope to nurture into a large financial success.

Partnerships: Different Forms, Different Benefits

As noted earlier, the business started by Robert Baron's grandfather was a **partnership**, which, in the legal sense of this term, is an association of two or more people who do business together for the purpose of making a profit. It is assumed that the co-owners (partners) will share the profits, assets, and liabilities of the business in accordance with agreed-upon terms. What are these terms? They can be anything the partners choose. For instance, partners could decide to divide the profits 50-50, 90-10, or according to any other formula they prefer. Whatever the terms, however, these should be stated as clearly as possible in a written **partnership agreement**, a document written with the assistance of a lawyer and that states all of the terms under which the partnership will operate. The partnership agreement should spell out all the details—especially the areas about which bitter disagreements can emerge, such as how profits will be divided, what each partner will contribute, how decisions will be made, how disputes will be resolved, and how the partnership can be dissolved. Specifically, a standard partnership agreement will generally include the following kinds of information:

1. Name of the partnership
2. Purpose of the business
3. Location of the business
4. Names of the partners and their legal addresses
5. Duration of the partnership
6. Contributions of each partner to the business at the creation of the partnership and later
7. An agreement on how profits and losses will be distributed
8. An agreement on salaries or drawing rights against profits for each partner
9. Procedures for expanding or dissolving the business
10. Information on how the assets will be distributed if the partners choose to dissolve the partnership
11. How each partner can sell her or his interest in the business
12. What happens if one of the partners is disabled or absent
13. How alterations or modifications to the partnership agreement can be made

In other words, the partnership agreement covers all the major issues that are likely to arise as the partners seek to run their new venture; therefore, entrepreneurs are advised to seek legal counsel when drafting such an agreement. If partners do not prepare a written partnership agreement, regulations specified under the provincial Partnership Act will apply.[1] This law specifies the rights and general obligations of partners and focuses on three key elements: ownership interest in the business, sharing of the business's profits and losses, and the right to participate in managing the operation of the partnership. Under the Partnership Act, each partner has a right to:

1. Share in management and operations of the business
2. Share in any profits the business earns
3. Receive interest on additional advances made to the business
4. Receive compensation for expenses incurred on behalf of the partnership
5. Have access to the books and records of the partnership
6. Receive a formal accounting of the partnership's business affairs

In addition, the Partnership Act specifies that each partner is obligated to:

1. Share in any losses
2. Work for the partnership without salary
3. Submit differences concerning the conduct of the business to a majority vote or arbitration
4. Give the other partner complete information about all activities of the business
5. Provide a formal accounting of the partnership's business activities

What are the advantages and disadvantages of a partnership? On the plus side of the ledger, partnerships are easy and inexpensive to establish: Owners must simply obtain required business licences and complete a few forms. Similarly, partnerships provide a high level of flexibility: Partners can choose to divide profits and responsibilities in any way they choose. If the partners have complementary skills and knowledge, these can contribute to the successful operation of the business. Moreover, because each partner can contribute equity, the pool of financial resources available is expanded. Finally, partnerships are not subject to federal taxation; rather, net income or losses are *passed through* to the partners as individuals. This arrangement avoids the double taxation to which many corporations are exposed (taxation at the corporate level *and* at the individual level; we will return to this topic later in our discussion of corporations).

On the minus side, partners generally have unlimited liability, just as if each were a sole proprietor. (The exception is *limited partners* in a *limited partnership*.) Second, it is often difficult to continue a partnership if one of the partners becomes ill, becomes disabled, or dies. This situation is especially difficult when the partnership agreement restricts how each partner can dispose of his or her share of the business. Often, it is required that the partner wishing to sell must first offer it to the remaining partner or partners. If these remaining partners do not have the necessary funds, they may be forced to seek a new partner or to dissolve the partnership, which is what happened to my grandfather. During the Depression of the 1930s, his company (which manufactured clothing) remained profitable. When his partner became seriously ill, and my grandfather could not purchase his share, it became necessary to terminate the business. The same situation might have developed if my grandfather and his partner had experienced personal conflicts—a situation that often arises in partnerships when the partners disagree over important issues (see Figure 9.2). In short, partnerships definitely involve major risks, and any entrepreneur contemplating this form of ownership should consider these risks with care and seek legal advice in drafting a partnership agreement.

Limited Partnerships

Because partnerships cannot sell stocks (as can corporations), they often experience difficulty in raising needed capital. One solution to this problem is to form a **limited partnership**, in which one or more partners are *general partners* who manage the business and others are *limited partners* who invest in the business but forego any right to manage the company. Such persons share in the profits in accordance with terms stated in the *limited partnership agreement* (which they sign when they become partners and register with the provincial government), but they have limited liability: They can only lose what they have invested. In contrast, the general partners have unlimited liability. In a sense, then, limited partnerships offer a combination of the benefits of partnerships and the benefits provided by corporations. One potential problem, however, is the danger that the general partners will run the business in a way that benefits them personally, while harming the interests of limited partners.

Limited Liability Partnerships

A *limited liability partnership* (L.L.P.) is used by professionals, such as accountants and lawyers, who are not permitted to incorporate but want to enjoy the advantages of limited liability for legal actions brought against other partners. For example, an accountant in a limited liability partnership is liable for her own negligence, but not personally liable for the negligence of her partners. In this kind of partnership, all partners are limited partners. As with all partnerships, the partnership itself pays no tax; rather, all profits and losses are passed through to the limited partners, who pay any taxes due as individuals. Limited liability partnerships are permitted in Alberta, Saskatchewan, Manitoba, Ontario, Quebec, and Nova Scotia.

Figure 9.3 Most Canadian Firms Are Incorporated

Most Canadian firms are incorporated: 68% of small businesses (firms with fewer than 100 employees) are incorporated, while 32% are unincorporated joint ventures, partnerships, or sole proprietorships. For medium-sized enterprises (firms with 100 to 500 employees), the percentage of incorporated businesses is even higher, at 84%.

Source: Industry Canada (Industry Canada's Small Business Policy Branch Strategic Plan 2003–04 to 2005–06).

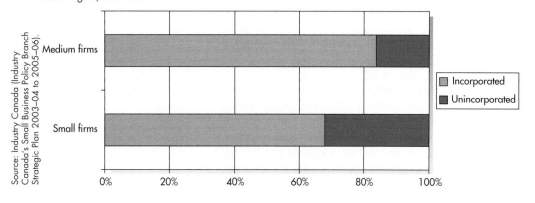

KEY POINTS

- Sole proprietorships are the simplest form of business ownership: ownership by one person.
- Sole proprietorships are easy and inexpensive to establish, but the persons who own them are subject to unlimited liability for the business's debts, and in many cases, the business cannot continue if the owner becomes ill or incapacitated.
- Partnerships are an association of two or more persons who co-own a business. All partnerships should have a partnership agreement outlining the rights and obligations of all partners.
- In a partnership, at least one person must be designed as a general partner; this person has unlimited liability. In a limited partnership, one person is the general partner and all the others are limited partners.
- In a limited liability partnership, all persons are limited partners. Such partnerships are restricted to professionals practising together (e.g., lawyers, accountants).

Corporations: Limited Liability, But at a Cost

Most Canadian companies are incorporated (see Figure 9.3). A key advantage of corporations is that they are a form of business ownership that allows owners (persons holding stocks in them) to receive profit while at the same time providing the significant advantage of limited liability: No matter how great the debts of the corporation, shareholders' liability is limited to the amount of their investment. In legal terms, **corporations** are separate legal entities apart from their owners, entities that may engage in business, make contracts, own property, pay taxes, and sue and be sued by others. Canadian entrepreneurs have the choice of incorporating provincially or federally. Provincially incorporated businesses have the right to carry out business in only one province, but fairly simple licensing procedures will extend its ability to conduct business in other provinces. Federally incorporated businesses can operate anywhere in Canada; consequently, businesses that operate nationally and internationally may have lower administrative costs with federal incorporation.[2]

Entrepreneurs can form a corporation without the assistance of a lawyer. In fact, Corporations Canada has a system that enables people to incorporate online, at http://strategis.ic.gc.ca/epic/internet/incd-dgc.nsf/en/Home. A corporation is a complex legal entity, however, and the services of a good lawyer are usually essential. Registration of a corporation generally requires that the persons creating it provide the following information:

- The corporation's name

- Names and addresses of the persons incorporating

- Official address of the corporation

- Capital stock authorization—the number of stocks to be issued and the types (if more than one) of stock available

- Restrictions (if any) on transferring stocks

- Names and addresses of the officers and directors of the corporation

- Restrictions (if any) on the corporation's activities

- Provisions that the entrepreneur wants to add to the articles of incorporation. For example, if the entrepreneur wants the corporation to remain private, provisions should be added to restrict the number of shareholders to 50 or fewer and to disallow the selling of stocks to the public.

Once this information has been submitted and the required fees paid, the corporation receives a certificate of incorporation. The shareholders then must hold a meeting to formally elect directors. The directors, in turn, appoint the corporate officers.

Advantages of Corporations

We have already described a key advantage offered by corporations: limited liability for stockholders. In the past, shareholders had no personal liability for debts or actions of the corporation. However, recent court decisions have interpreted statutory provisions in such a way that entrepreneurs—owners of small corporations—are increasingly liable for legal claims against the corporation, such as with respect to environmental offences. In other words, forming a corporation no longer offers shareholders total immunity to claims relating to these issues. For instance, if an incorporated start-up venture is creating an environmental hazard through its operations, the owners of the company as well as the corporation itself may be subject to prosecution for these violations. This kind of liability is a sobering fact, and one that entrepreneurs should consider carefully.

Another key advantage of corporations is the ability to attract capital. Because they can sell stocks, corporations can raise additional funds by doing so, as necessary. Similarly, corporations can continue indefinitely, long beyond the presence—or even lives—of their founders. Finally, stocks are transferable; they can be sold to someone else. If the stocks are traded publicly on a stock exchange, such liquidity can be very high. We will return to the issue of creating a public corporation in Chapter 13, in our discussion of exit strategies for entrepreneurs.

Disadvantages of Corporations

Like all forms of ownership, however, corporations also have a downside. First, it can be complex and expensive to start a corporation; lawyer's fees and government fees can exceed $2,500 in many cases. Even more important, because corporations are separate legal entities, any profits they earn can be subject to *double taxation*: The corporation itself must pay taxes on these profits, and then, if the profits are distributed to individual shareholders, these persons must pay tax on them again, as individuals.

Corporations, unlike partnerships or sole proprietorships, are subject to many legal and financial requirements. Corporate officers must record and report certain types of management decisions and actions, and must report financial data to both the federal and provincial governments. Corporations must hold annual meetings, and managers are required to consult with the board of directors about major decisions. If the stocks of the company are traded publicly, the corporation must file quarterly and annual reports with the relevant provincial or territorial security commission. Although corporations are a very useful form of business ownership, they have important drawbacks, too.

Table 9.1 Major Forms of Business Ownership

The three major forms of business ownership and their key features are summarized here.

	SOLE PROPRIETORSHIP	PARTNERSHIP	CORPORATION
Owner's liability	Unlimited	Unlimited for general partners, limited for limited partners	Limited
Number of owners	1	2 or more	Any number, but fewer than 50 if a private corporation
Tax liability	Proprietor pays at individual rate	Partners pay at individual rate	Double tax: corporation pays tax and shareholders pay tax on dividends
Transferability of ownership	Assets, but not ownership, are transferable	Needs to be specified in partnership agreement. May require consent of partners	Fully transferable
Continuity of business	Ends on death of proprietor or upon termination by proprietor	Dissolves upon death or retirement of general partner	Perpetual
Cost and ease of formation	Low; easy	Moderate and complex because of the need for a partnership agreement	Moderate and complex
Ability to raise capital	Limited	Moderate	Very high

In sum, several forms of business ownership are open to entrepreneurs. All offer a mixed pattern of advantages and disadvantages, so the task of choosing between them should be approached carefully—and with considerable caution. Also, it is important for entrepreneurs to note that they are not locked in forever to the form they select initially: Some changes are easier to make than others (e.g., from sole proprietorship to partnership, from one form of partnership to another), but there is no reason to stick with an initial choice if conditions change and it becomes clear that a change would be advantageous. We have covered a lot of ground in this section, so before proceeding, please examine Table 9.1 carefully; it provides an overview of the types of business ownership we have discussed, and of the advantages and disadvantages they offer.

KEY POINTS

- Corporations are legal entities apart from their owners, entities that may engage in business, make contracts, own property, pay taxes, and sue and be sued by others.
- One key advantage of corporations is that they provide limited liability to their owners. Another key advantage of corporations is the ability to attract capital. However, corporations, unlike partnerships or sole proprietorships, are subject to many legal and financial requirements.

FRANCHISING

If you walk down any commercial street in virtually any town or city in Canada, you will probably see signs like the ones in Figure 9.4. If you recorded the names of all the businesses jostling each other for space—and your attention!—you would almost certainly find that a large percentage of them are ones you already know: Canadian Tire, Second Cup, Color Your World, Giant Tiger, First Choice Haircutters, Shoppers Drug Mart, Tim Hortons, M&M Meat Shops, Fionn MacCool's Irish Pub, and East Side Mario's, to mention just a few. Moreover, you would see the same names, and the same businesses, no matter where you happened to be. The reason for this is obvious: **Franchising** is a tremendously popular form of business ownership today, and all these companies are franchises born in Canada. What is franchising? In essence, it is a system of distribution in which legally independent business owners (*franchisees*) pay fees and royalties to a parent company (the *franchisor*) in return for the right to use its trademark, sell its products or services, and, in many cases, to use the business model and system it has developed. How popular is franchising? In Canada, there are more than 950 franchisors, which, together, operate more than 85,000 separate outlets (stores, restaurants, hotels, etc.). Roughly 85 percent of these outlets are located in Ontario, Quebec, and British Columbia. Together, franchises account for more than $70 billion in annual sales.[3] Indeed, Canada constitutes the world's second most developed franchise market, after the United States. Franchising is indeed very big business.

LEARNING OBJECTIVE

2 Define franchising and describe the advantages and disadvantages of becoming a franchisee.

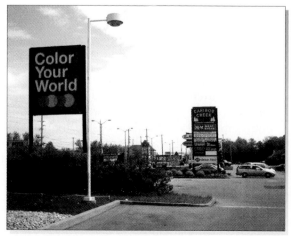

Photo: Indu Ghuman

Figure 9.4 Franchising: Definitely Big Business in Canada

As a walk or a drive down any commercial street or road suggests, franchising is very popular in Canada. In fact, there are more than 85,000 separate franchise outlets at the current time, and the number is growing rapidly.

Photo: Indu Ghuman

Photo: Indu Ghuman

Figure 9.5 Franchising Is a Popular Growth Strategy in the Food Industry

Franchisors provide franchisees with business advantages, such as a brand name, standardized operations, and buying power, which are particularly important in the restaurant industry.

The franchisee is provided with a complete business system: a trademarked name, the products or services to be sold, the buildings in which the business will be operated, a marketing strategy, methods of actually operating the business, quality control, and assistance in actually running the business. Franchising is found in many different industries: business service firms, hotels, car rental agencies, and beauty aid retailers, but is probably best known for its role in the restaurant industry (see Figure 9.5). Franchisees who enter into an agreement with a franchisor virtually receive a turnkey operation: The franchisor sets up the business, trains the franchisee on how to run it, and then often helps the franchisee to operate it. In a sense, this type of business is the farthest away from our definition of entrepreneurship, but as you can readily see, it offers important benefits for the franchisees—especially if they have little or no prior experience in running a business.

The Benefits of Becoming a Franchisee

We have already mentioned some of the benefits of franchising for franchisees—they become associated with a well-known brand name or product and receive, to varying degrees, help in setting up and running a business. In essence, they benefit from the past experience of the franchisor, who, if successful, has identified an effective and profitable business model and put it into operation hundreds or even thousands of times. But this is only part of the total picture; franchisees also gain additional benefits from their association with the franchisor. These benefits are summarized in the following sections.

Training and Support

Have you ever heard of Hamburger University? It is the facility run by McDonald's corporation to train new franchisees. During a 14-day period, new franchisees receive instruction in everything from how to clean grills correctly to how to manage their businesses. Other major franchisors run similar operations —for instance, Color Your World runs a six-week training program to build expertise on products; retail marketing and promotion; and business operations, such as inventory management and financial management.[4] Clearly, such training can be invaluable to new franchisees, and for many, the fees they pay for such training is money well spent. (As we will see, however, this benefit is not always the case and can be a source of serious conflict between franchisees and franchisors.)

Standardized Products and Services

If you buy a doughnut in a Tim Hortons outlet in Cochrane, Alberta, it will be virtually identical to one you purchase at a Tim Hortons outlet in Cochrane, Ontario. Why? Because major franchisors insist that products sold under their name meet strict standards (see Figure 9.6). This standardization is a big plus for franchisees, because it means that they do not have to work hard to convince potential customers that they are selling good products or services: The name on the door does this job for them. In contrast, it may take years for independent business owners to build a solid reputation in their local communities— and then, of course, these reputations are only good within a limited geographic area.

Reprinted with the kind permission of the Pita Pit Limited. Source: www.pitapit.com.

Figure 9.6 Product Standardization Is an Advantage But Can Also Be a Disadvantage for Franchisees Who Want to Develop Their Own Products

The Pita Pit, started in Kingston, Ontario, has a standardized menu focused on pita sandwiches.

National Advertising

Major franchisors launch equally major advertising campaigns—promotions that consumers recognize and, on occasion, like. For instance, Tim Hortons had a very well-known Rrroll Up The Rim To Win marketing campaign, and from time-to-time airs the True Stories series of television commercials nationally. Such campaigns are not free to franchisees: Usually, they pay a fee or a percentage of their sales to support them. But given the fact that these campaigns appear on national television and are developed by top-notch advertising companies, this expense can be a bargain, and an important plus contributing to franchisees' success (see Figure 9.7).

Buying Power

Can you imagine how many pounds of potatoes are purchased by McDonald's Corporation each year? How about the number of napkins and pieces of cutlery purchased by major food chains? The point of these statistics is simple: Major franchisors have huge buying power. They can negotiate very favourable prices for the items they need, which they then supply to their franchisees. Most pass along at least a portion of these savings to their franchisees—after all, they want these individuals to succeed. Although franchisees must purchase their supplies and equipment from the franchisors, this arrangement is often a very good deal, which helps hold costs below those paid by independent businesses that do not benefit from this centralized buying power.

Financial Assistance

Although major franchisors do not generally loan money to potential franchisees, they do often help them in less direct ways. For instance, they assist them in establishing relationships with banks, investors, and other sources of funds. Moreover, they do sometimes offer highly qualified franchisees such benefits as in-house construction loans (e.g., in the hotel industry) and even short-term loans to cover franchising fees, which in some cases can be very large.

Site Selection and Territorial Protection

The location of any business can be crucial, and is especially true for retail operations, which is what most new franchises are. Major franchisors often conduct careful site analyses to help pinpoint good locations for new outlets, and franchisees benefit from this expertise: Their businesses open in locations that draw on a large potential market.

Figure 9.7 National Advertising: An Important Benefit for Franchisees

Major franchisors often launch national advertising campaigns, which include television commercials, magazine ads, fliers, and billboards. These campaigns help increase business for their franchisees.

Image courtesy of Indu Ghuman

One problem for any new business is nearby competition. Major franchisors help to reduce this risk for franchisees by offering franchisees *territorial protection*—an assurance that no additional, competing outlets will be opened within a specified distance. This condition helps avoid dilution of sales and contributes to the success of new franchise outlets. Recent findings suggest, however, that many new franchisors won't offer this type of protection to franchisees because it hinders the franchisor's flexibility.[5]

A Business Model That Works

Perhaps most important of all, successful franchisors provide new franchisees with a proven business model. In other words, franchisees do not have to learn by trial and error—the usual way in which new businesses grope their way to success. On the contrary, the business models of major franchisors have been honed and perfected through experiences gained in thousands of previously opened outlets. The result is that the methods and systems supplied to new franchisees really do *work*. As long as the franchisees follow these methods and supply the required level of hard work and commitment, their chances of success are increased; at least, their chances are often higher than what is likely for the owners of independent small businesses who must learn on the fly and often only manage to get it right after spending considerable time on the brink of failure.

Drawbacks of Becoming a Franchisee

Given the immense popularity of franchising, it is clear that growing numbers of people recognize the advantages. But becoming a franchisee is certainly not an unmixed blessing; there are also serious drawbacks to entering into this kind of business relationship. Here are some of the key disadvantages.

Franchise Fees and Royalties

Franchisees need considerable capital to purchase a franchise operation. For example, an M&M Meat Shop operation requires an investment of approximately $300,000, to cover the franchise fee, store start-up costs and initial inventory and working capital. Even that investment pales by comparison with the amount required to open a new hotel in one of the leading franchise chains: more than $10 million! So start-up costs for franchisees are often quite high. On top of this initial investment, franchisees must pay royalties to the franchisor, usually based on a percentage of gross sales; for example, royalties for M&M Meat Shop franchisees are 3 percent of gross sales, and they pay an additional 2 percent of gross sales monthly into a marketing fund.[6] In general, these fees must be paid even if the outlet is not profitable, so some franchisees find themselves facing a situation where the franchisors make money while they barely make ends meet—or worse. In such cases, it is as if they are simply an employee of the franchisor, working hard to make profits for this company rather than themselves. This arrangement is certainly not why franchisees chose to open a business in the first place, so those who face this situation can tell you—with lots of pain—about the potential downside of franchising.

Enforced Standardization

Many franchisees suffer from a basic misunderstanding: They believe that at first they will follow the strict guidelines established by the franchisor, but later, after they get the hang of running the business, they will be able to branch out and do things their way. In fact, this kind of independence is not an option. Many franchise agreements require franchisees to run their businesses in a specific way, and violations of the rules can lead to serious consequences, including revocation of the franchise. I once knew of a McDonald's outlet that was frequently dirty—the floors, the tables, even the bathrooms. I was not surprised when one day, signs proclaiming "Under

New Management" appeared. The previous owner's inability or unwillingness to adhere to the company's strict guidelines concerning cleanliness had ultimately cost him his franchise—and the large fees he had paid to open this outlet (more than $500,000).

Restricted Freedom over Purchasing and Product Lines

Franchisees also have little or no choice with respect to where they purchase their supplies: These must be obtained from the franchisor or sources specified by the franchisor, and franchisees have little or no choice over the products they sell. If the franchisor decides to introduce a new product and it is one the franchisee thinks will not be popular locally, she or he can seek approval to refrain from offering it, but the final decision rests with the franchisor. So, for instance, if a large pizza franchisor decided to introduce kiwi fruit pizza, its franchisees would be required to add it to the menu and to stock the ingredients—even if they never sold a single kiwi pizza.

On the other side of the ledger, some highly successful franchisors invite input from franchisees—and really listen to it. In fact, at Subway—named the number one franchise by *Entrepreneur* magazine in 2006, for the fourteenth time—franchisees serve on the advertising board and in the purchasing coop. They meet about every four months to discuss the direction of the company and have had a major hand in shaping its strategic plan. So, franchisees are not necessarily left out in the cold in terms of having input into how the parent company—and their own franchises—are run. Indeed, it was a Chicago franchisee who suggested and pilot tested the advertising campaign starring Jared, the young man who lost weight by eating Subway products, which emphasized Subway's image as the choice of health-conscious consumers.[7]

Poor Training Programs

Many major franchisors run excellent training programs for new franchisees. The quality of such programs varies greatly across the industry, however, and many franchisees complain that they have paid large fees for training and then received very little in return. Clearly, this situation can be discouraging for franchisees, so the general rule of "check before you invest" clearly applies here.

Market Saturation

Some experts feel that the golden age of franchising, at least in some industries, has already passed. Prime locations for fast-food restaurants, motels, auto service facilities, and many other kinds of franchises are already occupied, and new outlets are being placed in less desirable locations. Is that true? No one knows for sure. Again, it is important for potential franchisees to check carefully the analysis of a location they are thinking of acquiring.

Lower Ability to Coordinate across Individual Units

We should briefly mention one further disadvantage faced by franchisees—especially those who own units in large franchise chains. Research findings indicate that such chains are less effective at coordinating their price and advertising as compared to corporations that own a large number of outlets (e.g., a restaurant chain that does not franchise its units).[8] Why? Because each individual owner receives spillover effects from efforts to improve sales through pricing or advertising, which reduces the incentive to coordinate with others and, overall, reduces effectiveness relative to corporate chains.

In sum, franchising, as a route to business ownership, offers a mixed assortment of potential benefits and potential drawbacks. Franchisees benefit from the brand name, quality control, and national advertising provided by the franchisor, but must pay large fees, continuing royalties, and give up any dreams about operating a business the way they prefer. Moreover, one study indicates that franchisees actually make less money than independent entrepreneurs in the same industry.[9] Finally, we should note that despite all the advantages a franchise can offer, rates of failure are quite high among franchisees; indeed, one recent study that obtained data from 800 franchise systems and 250,000 individual outlets over a 4-year period found turnover rates in excess of 10 percent per year.[10] (Turnover refers to a transfer from an existing owner to a new franchisee, a cancellation of the franchise agreement, a failure to renew a franchise agreement by the franchisor, or a reacquisition—the franchisor purchases the unit from the franchisee.) These failures stem from many factors, but central among them seems to be a basic misfit between the skills, abilities, and motives of the franchisee and the requirements of running a successful franchise unit.[11]

So, is becoming a franchisee for you? Or would you prefer to run your own business, make your own mistakes, and take the risks of learning as you go? Only you as an individual can answer this question, and to a large extent, it depends on the relative, subjective weights you place on receiving expert help, becoming part of a going concern, and personal freedom to run your business as you choose. Some people, like one couple described in a recent magazine article,[12] move back and forth between the two roles. This couple—call them Jack and Diane (not their real names)—tried running their own business (a golf apparel website) first. It failed because they were unwilling to quit their current jobs to become full-time entrepreneurs. They still wanted to run their own business, so they compromised this dream and purchased a franchise—an automobile quick-oil-change operation. They viewed this option as a way to leverage their plan to run their own business by acquiring necessary capital from the franchise.

In short, the decision to become a franchisee is complex and should reflect not only economic realities, but personal dispositions and preferences as well. Remember: this choice, once made, is *not* set in stone; people can—and often do—switch from one role (franchisee) to the other (independent business owner) at different points in their lives.

Legal Aspects of Franchising

LEARNING OBJECTIVE

3 Describe the legal principles governing franchise agreements and the information disclosure that potential franchisees should insist upon.

Whenever an industry booms, government regulations cannot be far behind, and franchising is no exception to this general rule. In Canada, the relationship between a franchisor and a franchisee is a contractual relationship, which is governed by contract law. In Ontario and Alberta, there is specific franchise legislation, designed primarily to protect franchisees.[13] The legislation emphasizes the need for good faith and fair dealing in franchise relationships. In particular, the Ontario legislation spells out the information that must be provided to potential franchisees 14 days before the franchisee enters into a binding agreement or pays any money. Important items that must be disclosed are summarized in Table 9.2. As you can see, this information is important to potential franchisees in making their decision about whether to proceed. Among the information that must be included is full disclosure of information about the franchisor and its officers, the financial history of the franchisor, franchise fees and continuing payments (e.g., royalties, service fees, training fees, etc.), information on restrictions concerning the goods or services franchisees are permitted to sell, territorial protection, obligations of the franchisor, and a description of the conditions under which the franchisor can repurchase the franchise or refuse to renew it. If you are considering the possibility of purchasing a franchise, you should examine such information carefully, and then ask additional questions of the franchisor. It is also very useful, if possible, to talk with current franchisees, who can give you important insights into how the franchisor treats franchisees, and to what extent it helps them achieve success. In any case, entering into an agreement with a franchisor is a very serious decision, and should only be made after careful consideration and only after doing your homework (e.g., checking into the current financial state of the franchisor, its competition, and so on).

1	Information about the franchisor's previous business experience, and the previous experience of its offices, directors, and partners
2	Information on previous convictions or pending charges against the franchisor, its officers, directors, and partners
3	Information on any bankruptcies or insolvency proceedings involving the franchisor, its officers, directors, and partners
4	Information about the initial franchise fee and other start-up costs
5	Information on continuing payments franchisees must make
6	Information about quality restrictions on goods, services, equipment, supplies, inventory, and other items used in the franchise and where franchisees may purchase them
7	Description of any financial assistance available from the franchisor
8	Description of any territorial protection for the franchisee
9	Information about the franchisor's intellectual property rights
10	Contact information for current Ontario franchisees as well as for anyone who has ceased to be a franchisee in the past year
11	Description of conditions related to the renewal and termination of the franchise agreement and transfer of the franchise
12	Franchisor's audited financial statements for the most recent year

Table 9.2 Information Franchisors Must Disclose to Potential Franchisees

In Ontario, provincial law requires franchisors to disclose all of the information described here to potential franchisors. This information must be supplied at least fourteen days before they sign a contract.

The Future Shape of Franchising

Any economic activity that is growing as rapidly as franchising is also very likely to be experiencing rapid change—which is definitely true with respect to franchising. Here, briefly, are some of the trends that are currently emerging.

Smaller Outlets in Nontraditional Locations

Smart businesses go where the customers are, and major franchisors have begun to put this principle into operation. As a result, they are opening scaled-down outlets in places where a full-scale operation would not be appropriate. Franchise outlets are appearing in grocery stores, on university and college campuses, in high school cafeterias, in hospitals, in zoos, and in theatres (see Figure 9.8). These outlets put the products or services they sell directly in the path of potential customers, and so encourage them to buy. This trend is a new one, so it seems likely to continue for some time.

Co-Branding Franchising

Because many businesses have heavy volume at certain times of day or at certain times of the year but lower volume at other times, franchisors are *co-branding* many products to make more efficient use of costly retail space. For instance, rest areas along Highway 401 generally contain multiple franchises, all selling different but compatible products. One combination I have seen in the rest areas is Wendy's and Tim Hortons. The basic idea is that people eat more of each product at different times of the day and less at other times. For instance, they tend to eat doughnuts and drink coffee in the morning, but consume hamburgers at lunch or dinner. By taking advantage of these different patterns of consumption, the cost of renting expensive real estate can be spread across a greater volume of total sales.

International Franchising

In recent years, franchisors have moved into international markets. For instance, if you travel through Europe, you will see the familiar Golden Arches of the McDonald's Corporation not only in large cities, but increasingly in smaller towns, too. Indeed, Meng Sun, an M.B.A. graduate from the University of Calgary was the first McDonald's franchisee in China.[14] But, as many franchisors have discovered, exporting their products or services is not always simple. In fact, products or services that sell very well in North America sometimes seem strange or unpleasant to customers in other countries. Even brand names can be

LEARNING OBJECTIVE

4 Describe current trends in franchising, such as smaller outlets in nontraditional locations, co-branding franchising, and international franchising.

Figure 9.8 Franchise Outlets in Nontraditional Locations: A New Trend in Franchising

A recent trend in franchising is to place small outlets in places where they are convenient for potential customers, such as this Williams Coffee Pub outlet on the campus of McMaster University.

Photo: Indu Ghuman

a source of difficulty. For example, some years ago, Chevrolet was puzzled by the cool reception its Nova automobile received in Latin America—until someone pointed out that "No va" means "Doesn't go" in Spanish! So, franchisors who do not carefully investigate local tastes and customs can run into serious problems. The huge success of franchise outlets in Russia, China, and other international markets, however, suggests that international franchising is a trend that will continue in the years ahead.

A Huge Expansion in the Kinds of Business Being Franchised

At one time, most franchises were located in the food and retail trade industries—McDonalds, Pizza Hut, Tim Hortons, and Canadian Tire spread from coast to coast and became household words. Recently, however, franchising has expanded into virtually every corner of the economy. For instance, there are now franchises providing business services (e.g., Shred-It and Print Three), franchises providing home services (e.g., Nutri-Lawn) and franchises providing educational services (e.g., Kumon Math & Reading Centers). Other areas in which the number of franchises is growing rapidly include health services (e.g., Take Thirty), home improvements (e.g., 1-800-Got Junk?), real estate (e.g., Royal Lepage), and shipping (e.g., Pak Mail). Overall, franchisors now offer potential franchisees a truly staggering array of businesses to operate, and there is no sign that this expansion will end soon.

In sum, franchising is an immensely popular way for ambitious persons to own his or her own business without coming up with an idea for a new product or service and without developing his or her own, unique business model. It is also a potentially high-growth strategy for an entrepreneur who wants to expand the scope of his or her business venture, as we shall discuss in Chapter 11. For these reasons, it seems likely to remain a large and growing activity for many years to come.

KEY POINTS

- Franchising is a system of distribution in which semi-independent business owners (franchisees) pay fees and royalties to a parent company (the franchisor) in return for the right to use its trademark, sell its products or services, and, in many cases, use the business model and system it has developed.
- Franchising offers important benefits to franchisees including training and support, standardized products, national advertising, site selection, and a business model that works.
- However, franchising also has a downside: Franchisees must pay substantial fees and royalties, they must deal with enforced standardization, and they have restricted freedom over purchasing and product lines.
- Franchising is regulated by contract law and by specific franchising legislation in Ontario and Alberta.
- All prospective franchisees should obtain extensive information about the franchisor and franchise agreement before signing the franchise agreement.
- Current trends in franchising include smaller outlets in nontraditional locations, co-branding franchising, international franchising, and a large expansion in the kinds of businesses being franchised.

THE LEGAL ENVIRONMENT OF NEW VENTURES: SOME BASICS

LEARNING OBJECTIVE

5 Describe the basic components of business contracts, and explain what happens if these obligations are not met.

Business Contracts: Their Essential Components

Another aspect of the law with which entrepreneurs should be familiar is governing **contracts**—promises that are enforceable by law. *Contract law* is a body of laws designed to assure that parties entering into contracts comply with the provisions in them; it also provides remedies to those parties harmed if a contract is broken.

A contract does not have to be written to be legal and enforceable. Indeed, many contracts are oral. In Canada, only contracts dealing with the following issues must be in writing: (1) the leasing or sale of land, (2) paying someone else's debt, (3) contracts with a fixed term greater than one year, or (4) contracts that involve the sale of goods greater than a certain value (which varies provincially and is generally between $30 and $50). If a contract is not written, it is only enforceable if there is some way to prove its existence, such as the testimony of witnesses.

Basic Elements of a Contract

A contract must meet four basic requirements in order to be binding on the parties involved:

- *Legality.* The contract must be intended to accomplish a legal purpose. For instance, you cannot write a contract to sell illegal drugs because doing so itself is not legal.

- *Agreement.* A legal contract must include a legitimate offer and a legitimate acceptance, which is known as a *meeting of the minds* in legal terminology. If, for instance, an entrepreneur offers to sell some product to a customer for a specific price and the customer accepts, this agreement is a contract. If there is no acceptance by the customer, then there is no contract.

- *Consideration.* Something of value must be exchanged between the parties involved to constitute a contract. If nothing of value is exchanged, then the agreement is about a gift and does not constitute a contract. For instance, suppose that a customer is so pleased with the product or service provided by an entrepreneur that she says, "I like your product so much that I'm going to give it free advertising." If she does not deliver on this promise, the entrepreneur cannot legally demand that she do so, because her offer did not involve the exchange of anything of value—it was a gift.

- *Capacity.* Not all persons have the capacity to legally enter into a contract. Minors or persons who are intoxicated or who have diminished mental ability cannot be bound by contracts. So if an entrepreneur makes a deal with a customer who is clearly intoxicated (and several witnesses can testify to this fact), the entrepreneur cannot insist that the customer honour the agreement: The fact that the customer was intoxicated at the time means that the contract was not valid.

Obligations under Contracts

If you have a contract with someone and that person fails to comply with the terms of the agreement, what can you do? Legally, this is known as a **breach of contract**, and several options are available. In most cases, the damaged party can sue for, and obtain, money or some specific action by the other party as compensation for the damages sustained. The goal is to restore the damaged party to the condition that would have existed if the contract had been fulfilled. In most cases, the amount of money awarded to the damaged party (the *plaintiff*), is an amount that reflects the monetary extent of the damage.

If money alone is not enough to restore a person to the desired state, a judge may order *specific performance* by the person who violated the contract. This type of remedy is only available when money will not compensate for the damages incurred. It requires the person who violated the contract to do exactly what that person originally agreed to do. For instance, suppose that an entrepreneur sells a business to another person and signs a noncompete agreement indicating that that there will be no intention to start or own a similar business in a specific geographic area for a certain period of time. Later, though, this person starts such a business. This action is a violation of the noncompete agreement (which is a contract), and under these circumstances, a judge may rule that money is not enough to compensate the purchaser for the harm done and may issue an injunction—a court order that prohibits the entrepreneur from operating the new business for the duration of the original agreement.

Risk Management

LEARNING OBJECTIVE

6 Describe the basic components of a risk management strategy and how you might go about selecting a lawyer.

Entrepreneurs should understand how they are going to manage the legal risks of business ownership. To do this, they need to identify the legal risks, assess the probability and severity of a loss associated with each risk, and implement measures to minimize their exposure to a risk.[15] When the expected loss is large, entrepreneurs may choose to avoid the risk altogether. For example, a business owner might choose to avoid setting up a production facilities in countries with an unpredictable political or legal environment. Second, entrepreneurs can reduce risks by using tactics to reduce the probability or severity of a loss. For example, an entrepreneur might implement strict training and quality control measures for a production facility in order to reduce the exposure to product failures. Finally, entrepreneurs can manage risk by transferring risk to another party. Purchasing insurance is one example of risk transference, but many risks are difficult to insure against. Entrepreneurs can also transfer some risk to their customers by contractually limiting the damages the firm is responsible for under different circumstances. For example, software producers can require online customers to agree to licensing terms by clicking on an "I Accept" button before they are permitted to download software.[16]

Contract law is very complex and so the most basic risk management strategy is to have a trained lawyer draw up a contract that is certain to meet the requirements of a particular situation. This advice, in turn, raises an intriguing question: How can entrepreneurs choose a good lawyer? There is no simple answer, but there are some definite do's and don'ts well worth considering:

- Do *not* choose a lawyer for your company simply because he or she is someone you know; this person, despite being a friend, may lack the skills and experience you need in many business contexts.

- Do *not* choose, as a lawyer for your company, the lawyer who has handled other, unrelated matters for you (real estate transactions, estate planning, divorce); this lawyer may be skilled in these areas, but may not necessarily be skilled with respect to business law.

- Do seek a lawyer by asking other people in business for referrals; they are likely to steer you to a lawyer or law firm that has the skills you need.

- Provincial law societies offer lawyer referral services.

- Do ask potential lawyers to describe their experience; if they are reluctant to do so, look elsewhere!

These are just general guidelines; choosing a lawyer is a personal decision and should reflect your own preferences. But do be certain to obtain the services of a lawyer who has worked with entrepreneurs and small businesses before; such a person will understand the many legal pitfalls that can threaten new ventures, and help you steer clear of them.

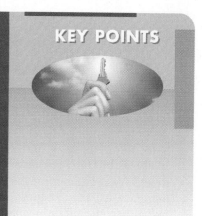

- Entrepreneurs should be familiar with the laws governing contracts—promises that are enforceable by law.
- Key elements of contracts are legality (the contract must be designed to accomplish a legal purpose), agreement (a legitimate offer and legitimate acceptance), consideration (something of value must be exchanged), and capacity (the persons involved must be capable of entering into a contract).
- If contracts are violated, the damaged party usually seeks redress in the form of monetary damages, but in some circumstances, can be awarded damages in the form of a specific performance by the party that violated the contract.
- Entrepreneurs can manage the legal risks associated with their business, by avoiding risk, reducing risk, and transferring risk.
- In choosing a lawyer for a new venture, it is usually best to select one who has experience with new ventures.

Summary and Review of Key Points

- Sole proprietorships are the simplest form of business ownership: ownership by one person.
- Sole proprietorships are easy and inexpensive to establish, but the persons who own them are subject to unlimited liability for the business's debts, and in many cases, the business cannot continue if the owner becomes ill or incapacitated.
- Partnerships are an association of two or more persons who co-own a business. All partnerships should have a partnership agreement outlining the rights and obligations of all partners.
- In a partnership, at least one person must be designated as a general partner; this person has unlimited liability. In a limited partnership, one person is the general partner and all the others are limited partners.
- In a limited liability partnership, all persons are limited partners. Such partnerships are restricted to professionals practising together (e.g., lawyers, accountants).
- Corporations are legal entities apart from their owners, entities that may engage in business, make contracts, own property, pay taxes, and sue and be sued by others.
- One key advantage of corporations is that they provide limited liability to their owners. Another key advantage of corporations is the ability to attract capital. However, corporations, unlike partnerships or sole proprietorships, are subject to many legal and financial requirements.
- Franchising is a system of distribution in which semi-independent business owners (franchisees) pay fees and royalties to a parent company (the franchisor) in return for the right to use its trademark, sell its products or services, and, in many cases, use the business model and system it has developed.
- Franchising offers important benefits to franchisees including training and support, standardized products, national advertising, site selection, and a business model that works.
- However, franchising also has a downside: Franchisees must pay substantial fees and royalties, they must deal with enforced standardization, and they have restricted freedom over purchasing and product lines.
- Franchising is regulated by contract law and by specific franchising legislation in Ontario and Alberta.
- All prospective franchisees should obtain extensive information about the franchisor and franchise agreement before signing the franchise agreement.
- Current trends in franchising include smaller outlets in nontraditional locations, co-branding franchising, international franchising, and a large expansion in the kinds of businesses being franchised.
- Entrepreneurs should be familiar with the principles governing contracts—promises that are enforceable by law.
- Key elements of contracts are legality (the contract must be designed to accomplish a legal purpose), agreement (a legitimate offer and legitimate acceptance), consideration (something of value must be exchanged), and capacity (the persons involved must be capable of entering into a contract).
- If contracts are violated, the damaged party can usually seek redress in the form of monetary damages, but in some circumstances, can be awarded damages in the form of a specific performance by the party that violated the contract.
- Entrepreneurs can manage the legal risks associated with their business, by avoiding risk, reducing risk, and transferring risk.
- In choosing a lawyer for a new venture, it is usually best to select one who has experience with new ventures.

Glossary

Breach of Contract: A legal term referring to situations in which two parties have a legal contract and one fails to comply with the terms of the agreement.

Contracts: Promises that are enforceable by law.

Corporations: Legal entities separate from their owners that may engage in business, make contracts, own property, pay taxes, and sue and be sued by others.

Franchising: A system of distribution in which legally independent business owners (franchisees) pay fees and royalties to a parent company (the franchisor) in return for the right to use its trademark, sell its products or services, and use the business model and system it has developed.

Limited Partnership: A partnership in which one or more partners are general partners who manage the business and others are limited partners who invest in the business but forego any right to manage the company.

Partnership: Two or more people who do business together for the purpose of making a profit.

Partnership Agreement: A document written with the assistance of a lawyer, and that states all of the terms under which the partnership will operate.

Sole Proprietorship: A type of business ownership in which a business is owned and managed by one individual.

Unlimited Personal Liability: Occurs when business owners are personally liable for all debts incurred by the business.

Discussion Questions

1. Recent court decisions have challenged the view that persons who own stocks in corporations have limited liability for debts or actions of the corporation. What are the consequences of these court rulings for entrepreneurs?

2. Would you ever become a limited partner in a limited partnership? Why? Why not?

3. Suppose that one of your customers promises you an order but then does not place it. Can you sue this customer under contract law?

4. How can a franchisor considering the possibility of entering a foreign market find out, in advance, whether its products or services will be well-received in this new market?

InfoTrac Exercises

1. **Canada's franchise ombudsman initiative: the Canadian franchise community is embarking upon a new approach to dispute resolution with a pilot franchise ombudsman project.**

   Edward N. Levitt.

   Franchising World, April 2002 v34 i3 p26(2)

   Record: A85031981

   Full Text: COPYRIGHT 2002 International Franchise Association

   If you go to the website of the CFA, you can find out more information about this program: http://www.cfa.ca/page.aspx?url=OmbudmansProgram.html

   1. What is the purpose of the Franchise Ombudsman Program?

   2. Why is the program needed?

   3. Does the existence of this program make you more wary of becoming a franchisor or a franchisee? Why or why not?

   4. Explain the funding model for the program and its rationale. Does this funding model make sense to you?

2. **Damages in contract and tort would-have-beens and would-have-dones.**

   Joost Blom.

   The Advocate, May 2005 v63 i3 p391(12)

   Record: A133369486

   Full Text: COPYRIGHT 2005 Vancouver Bar Association (Canada)

   1. What is the basic rule of compensation for a breach of contract?

   2. What are some difficulties in determining what might have happened, hypothetically, if a breach of contract had not occurred?

   3. What is the difference between the assessment of damages under a contract and the assessment of damages under a tort?

   4. Explain why a knowledge of how damages are assessed is relevant to people starting new firms.

GETTING DOWN
TO BUSINESS

Choosing the Best Form for Your New Venture

Many entrepreneurs assume that the best form for their new venture is a corporation. In fact, though, this assumption may not be true. Other options exist and choosing among them depends on the goals the entrepreneur wants to reach and which features of these many business forms are more important to the entrepreneur. Which of these business forms is best for your new venture? To gain practice in deciding, answer each of the following questions:

1. How many owners will there be?

2. Is it important for you to have limited liability? (For instance, this may be relatively important to you if you have lots of personal wealth; if you do not, it may be less important.)

3. Is transferability of ownership important or unimportant?

4. Do you anticipate that your new venture will pay any dividends? If so, how important is it to you that such dividends will be subject to double taxation?

5. If you decide to leave the business, do you care whether it can continue to operate without you?

6. How important is keeping the costs of forming the business low?

7. How important is the ability to raise additional capital in the future as needed?

Consider your answers in terms of the features of various business forms summarized in Table 9.1. On the basis of this information, rule out business forms that would definitely *not* meet your goals or requirements, and then choose among the remaining ones on the basis of how close a match they provide to these goals.

Is Franchising for You?

Franchising is a rapidly expanding activity. In fact, new franchises are being started every day, and the number is now in the thousands. Just because franchising is popular, though, doesn't necessarily mean that it is for you. To decide whether you should consider this option for owning your own business, answer the following questions:

1. How important is it to you to get help in starting your business—such things as training and support, standardized products, national advertising, site selection, and a proven business model that works? (These are the kinds of help often offered by successful franchisors.)

2. How important is it to you to really be your own boss—to be able to make decisions about running your business, the nature of your products or services, suppliers, advertising, and so on? (The freedom to make these decisions will usually not be possible if you are a franchisee.)

3. How important is it to you to receive ongoing help in running your business— such things as assistance in hiring and training employees, continuous feedback on what you are doing right and what you are doing wrong, etc.?

4. What are your ultimate goals with respect to running your own business—to make money and have a secure life? Create something really new that changes people's lives? Obtain the personal freedom that can only come from being your own boss?

5. How important is it to you that the products or services you offer are well-known to potential customers—that they recognize the name over the door even if they have never visited your business before?

Consider your answers carefully in the light of the discussion in this chapter of the benefits and drawbacks to becoming a franchisee. Only you can decide whether franchises offer what you want out of running a business—and out of life. But answering these questions carefully and fully will at least help you make this decision in a rational manner. Whatever your choice—independent business or franchise—good luck!

Enhanced Learning

You may select any combination of the resources below to enhance your understanding of the chapter material.

- **Appendix: Case Studies** – Twelve cases provide opportunities to apply chapter concepts to realistic entrepreneurial situations. These brief cases call for careful analysis of real business problems and ask you to think about potential solutions.
- **Video Case Library** – Nine cases are tied directly to video segments from the popular PBS television series Small Business School. These cases and video segments (available on the Entrepreneurship website at http://www.entrepreneurship.nelson.com) give you unparalleled access to today's entrepreneurs, with expert advice and insights on how to start, run, and grow a business.
- **Management Interview Series Video Database** – This video interview series contains a wealth of tips on how to manage effectively. Access to the database and practical exercises are available on the book support website at http://www.entrepreneurship.nelson.com.

Notes

1 DuPlessis, D., Enman, S., O'Byrne, S., & Gunz, S. 2005. *Canadian business and the law*. 2nd ed. Toronto: Thomson Nelson.

2 DuPlessis, D., Enman, S., O'Byrne, S., & Gunz, S. 2005. *Canadian business and the law*. 2nd ed. Toronto: Thomson Nelson.

3 These figures are taken from Industry Canada's Strategis website: http://strategis.ic.gc.ca/epic/internet/inimr-ri.nsf/en/gr127348e.html.

4 Franchise profile: Color Your World. http://www.franchisedirectory.ca/onefranchiseProfile.asp?FranchiseID=NAT1DPIM.

5 Azoulay, P., & Shane, S. 2001. Entrepreneurs, contracts and the failure of young firms. *Management Science* 47(3): 337–358.

6 Franchise information. http://www.mmmeatshops.com/en/franchiseinfo/index.asp.

7 Torres, N.L. 2006. Staying Power: Why is Subway still on top? *Entreprenuer* (January) and entrepreneur.com. http://www.entrepreneur.com/article/0,4621,325101,00.html.

8 Michael, S.C. 2002. Can a franchise chain coordinate? *Journal of Business Venturing* 17(4): 325–341.

9 Bates, T. 1995. A comparison of franchise and independent small business survival rates. *Small Business Economics* 7(5): 377–388.

10 Holmberg, S.R., & Morgan, K.B. 2003. Franchise turnover and failure: New research and perspectives. *Journal of Business Venturing* 18(3): 403–418.

11 Stanworth, J., & Curran, J. 1999. Colas, burgers, shakes, and shirkers: Towards a sociological model of franchising in the market economy. *Journal of Business Venturing* 14(4): 323–344.

12 Maddocks, T.D. 2003. Driving forward. Jack and Diane look for new ways to get their small-business dreams moving. Will franchising be the right direction? *Entrepreneur* (March): 86, 88.

13 DuPlessis, D., Enman, S., O'Byrne, S., & Gunz, S. 2005. *Canadian business and the law*. 2nd ed. Toronto: Thomson Nelson.

14 Gray, S., & Fowler, G.A. 2005, July. Chinese entrepreneurs eye fast-food franchises. *StartupJournal.com*.

15 DuPlessis, D., Enman, S., O'Byrne, S., & Gunz, S. 2005. *Canadian business and the law*. 2nd ed. Toronto: Thomson Nelson.

16 DuPlessis, D., Enman, S., O'Byrne, S., & Gunz, S. 2005. *Canadian business and the law*. 2nd ed. Toronto: Thomson Nelson.

CHAPTER 10

MARKETING IN A NEW FIRM

LEARNING OBJECTIVES

After reading this chapter, you should be able to:

1 Identify a real customer need and explain why an entrepreneur should seek to develop a product or service that meets a real need.

2 Explain why entrepreneurs need marketing information before beginning their ventures, and describe ways they can gather this information.

3 Define perceptual mapping and explain how its results can assist entrepreneurs in designing their products.

4 Explain conjoint analysis and indicate what information it provides for entrepreneurs.

5 Explain why entrepreneurs use different techniques to assess customer preferences in new and established markets, and identify those different techniques.

6 Explain how large and growing markets help entrepreneurs.

7 Define the new product S-curve, and explain why it is important for entrepreneurs to understand the relationship between effort and product performance.

8 Describe the typical new product adoption pattern and explain how it influences entrepreneurial action.

9 Define "crossing the chasm" and explain why and how entrepreneurs "cross the chasm."

10 Explain how entrepreneurs should choose the customers on whom to focus their initial efforts.

11 Define a "dominant design" and a "technical standard" and explain how they influence the performance of new ventures.

12 Explain why personal selling is a very important part of entrepreneurs' marketing strategies.

13 Describe how entrepreneurs price new products.

All photos this page © PhotoDisc, Inc.

"Try novelties for salesman's bait, for novelty wins everyone." (Goethe, Faust: Part I, 1808, Tr. Philip Wayne)

Recently, many publishers have been telling authors that electronic books will soon replace real books. This happened to me (Scott Shane) last year, when one large publisher suggested that I write an electronic textbook. The basic idea was simple: Students would purchase an access code that would allow them to view and download their textbook from a special Internet site. Students could then, at their discretion, highlight various sections, enter notes to help their studying, print individual chapters, or do anything else they wished to their electronic textbooks. I was a little skeptical; books are, after all, very convenient products. They can be carried through airport security without setting off alarms, can be read almost anywhere, even in places where no source of power is available, and they have additional uses, too—for instance, they can be used to prop open doors and can even serve as makeshift fly-swatters!! All these features led me to wonder: Would students really give up regular books for e-books in the next few years? The answer was quick in coming: No! Sales of the e-book versions of most texts are miniscule. Given a choice, students overwhelmingly choose books in their traditional form.

This outcome raises an intriguing question: Why did people invest millions of dollars in these ill-fated e-book projects? Didn't they do their homework first, to find out if anyone would want to buy this kind of product? The answer is complex and contains important lessons for entrepreneurs. In essence, here is what happened: The companies involved did try to find out, in advance, whether students would buy these books—they conducted marketing research. But, as is frequently the case when entrepreneurs pursue new technology, it is very difficult to gauge the market for something that hasn't yet been introduced. Moreover, as the S-shaped curve in Figure 10.1 shows, when new products based on new technologies are introduced, they are often inferior in performance to existing alternatives and therefore are not adopted by mainstream customers. Only after further development has been undertaken to improve the new product's performance does it begin to perform better than the existing alternatives, and mainstream customers begin to adopt it in large numbers. The moral of this story is that talking to customers is only one part of the process of developing and marketing a new product. Gathering information in a way that generates useful answers, and understanding how new product performance develops, are also very important.

Figure 10.1 The Transition from Traditional Books to E-Books

When a new product based on a new technology is introduced, it often has inferior performance to the product it replaces. However, the new product makes up for this initial disadvantage as effort is put into improving it.

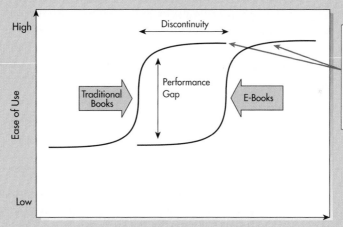

Up to this point, traditional books are easier to use, but as e-books are further developed, they may pass traditional books in terms of ease of use

The remainder of this chapter will expand on marketing in a new firm. Marketing is an extremely important activity for entrepreneurs. Indeed, Laurentian University professors Rolland LeBrasseur and Terry Zinger recently tracked start-ups in Northern Ontario and found that greater marketing capabilities were associated with a higher likelihood of survival over the first three years.[1] In the first section of the chapter, we will discuss how entrepreneurs assess markets and customer needs. We will explain why it is important for entrepreneurs to develop new products or services to meet *real* customer needs—truly solving unsolved customer problems or offering products or services that are significantly better than existing alternatives. We will outline techniques that entrepreneurs use to assess markets and customer needs—focus groups, surveys, perceptual mapping, focus groups, conjoint analysis, observation, discussions with users and experts, extrapolation of trends, and so on—and explain why the choice of one technique or another depends on whether your product or service will open up a new market or will be used in an existing market.

In the second section, we will discuss market dynamics and explain what entrepreneurs need to know about them. We will explain why it is so important for entrepreneurs to estimate the size and growth rate of the market that they are entering when they begin their new ventures. We will outline the advantages that new firms have over established firms in entering new markets. We will also discuss how new products develop in the S-shaped pattern first described at the beginning of the chapter, and explain what this pattern of product development means for entrepreneurs, particularly for their timing of market entry.

In the third section, we will discuss how entrepreneurs achieve mainstream market acceptance for their new products and services. We will describe the typical adoption pattern for new products and services and explain why it is normally distributed, with few adoptions occurring early, many more later on, and then fewer later still. We will discuss how entrepreneurs transition from the early adopters of new products and services to the early majority of adopters, explain why it is important for entrepreneurs to focus on a single product or service when their ventures begin, and describe how they should choose which customers to target first. The third section will also discuss dominant designs for new products and how the tendency of products to converge on a single design over time influences the performance of new ventures. Finally, in this section we will explain how technical standards influence new product adoption and how entrepreneurs can get customers to adopt their products as the technical standard in the market that they are targeting.

In the final section of the chapter, we will focus on the marketing process in new companies. We will discuss why entrepreneurs focus on personal selling as their main marketing tool, as opposed to relying heavily on advertising or brand name reputation to sell their products the way that many established companies do. This section will also discuss how entrepreneurs price their new products, focusing on the influence of the new venture's cost structure and supply and demand for products in the market.

ASSESSING THE MARKET

Successful entrepreneurs do not launch companies and begin to offer new products and services without first gathering information about the market and customer preferences. In particular, successful entrepreneurs ensure that there is a real need for their new product or service, assess customer preferences for the attributes of the new product or service that they are considering offering, and identify the key dimensions of customer needs that their product or service is meeting.

Starting with a Real Need

LEARNING OBJECTIVE

1   Identify a real customer need and explain why an entrepreneur should seek to develop a product or service that meets a real need.

Successful entrepreneurs develop new products and services that are based on real customer needs. This sounds pretty obvious, right? Maybe, but surprisingly few entrepreneurs develop products that meet a real need; most end up failing to generate any sales. Why? Most entrepreneurs become enamoured of the idea of starting a company and do not pay enough attention to whether they can provide a product or service that is better than existing alternatives.

For example, when I (Scott Shane) was teaching at the Sloan School at MIT, one student proposed a business to provide Internet delivery of soap and shampoo. This being MIT, the other students in the class immediately assumed that he was going to come up with a complex electronic system for this product, and asked how he intended to put electronic sensors in the soap and shampoo dispensers so that the toiletries would automatically be ordered when they ran low. The student responded that he wasn't going to use electronic sensors; his business idea was just that people would go onto the Internet and order shampoo and soap when they ran low. When I asked why there was a need to order shampoo and soap over the Internet, as opposed to just going to the grocery store to get these items, the student answered that he could never remember to buy toiletries when he went to the grocery store, and figured that this problem would be solved by Internet toiletry delivery.

In reality, however, there is no need for this service. Unlike this student, most people *can* remember to stop at the drugstore or supermarket to buy toiletries. Even the most absent-minded people can run out to a 24-hour supermarket or drugstore to get these items at the last minute—especially when the alternative is to wait three days for UPS to deliver the online order of soap! So, although this entrepreneur thought he was serving customers, his business idea did not meet a *real* customer need.

What does it mean for a *real* customer need to exist? It's a real need when customers have a problem that they want solved, but no existing products or services can resolve it. For example, a drug that cures lung cancer would meet a real need. Nothing today treats this disease very well, and people who have the disease would like a cure. A product or service also meets a real need when it is so much better at solving a problem that customers are motivated to switch to the new product or service from an existing alternative. Notice that we said "so much better at solving." Because people tend to prefer the status quo, a new product or service has to be much better than an old one to get people to switch to it. Just slightly better is rarely enough to motivate customers to change. For example, a microchip that triples computer-processing speed would meet a real need, but one that improved processing speed by 2 percent probably would not.

How do successful entrepreneurs determine whether there is a real customer need for a new product or service? In general, they follow a four-step process. First, they look for customer problems. We will talk more about this a little later in the chapter, but basically, successful entrepreneurs search out problems that customers have that aren't being solved adequately. What gets customers frustrated? What makes them complain? Those things are usually the sign of a problem that represents a real customer need. For example, are people in the accounting departments of several companies complaining that the software they use is inadequate to manage both their payroll and inventory? If customers complain that they need to integrate records from different aspects of their business and existing accounting software can't do this, then customers might really need better, more integrated software.

Once the entrepreneur has figured out that customers have a real problem that is not being solved, the second step is to come up with a true solution to that problem. Otherwise, from an entrepreneur's perspective, it doesn't really matter that customers have an unsolved problem. In our accounting software example, it wouldn't matter that customers want software to integrate inventory and payroll records if the entrepreneur can't write software that would integrate the two any better than existing accounting software. If the entrepreneur's software were no better than existing alternatives, there would be no reason to start a new business to produce software.

But suppose that the customers have a real problem, and the entrepreneur has a true solution to that problem; the third step in the process is to figure out the economics of satisfying the customer's need. For example, it would only make sense to start a new business to offer a solution to the customer need for integrated accounting software if the entrepreneur could offer a product at a price that customers would pay, and could still make a profit. If the entrepreneur could develop the solution, but it would cost more than customers would be willing to pay for it, then starting a company to offer the new software wouldn't be worthwhile.

The final step in the process is to identify any alternatives to the entrepreneur's solution that exist or will emerge in the very near future. This step is often the hardest for entrepreneurs to manage because people tend to convince themselves

Jupiter Images

Figure 10.2 To Succeed, a New Business Must Satisfy a Real Customer Need

Because people believe that they should take all possible steps to improve their pets' health and extend their pets' lives, there is a need to manage the high cost of complex veterinary procedures with pet insurance.

LEARNING OBJECTIVE

2 Explain why entrepreneurs need marketing information before beginning their ventures, and describe ways they can gather this information.

that the solutions that they come up with are better than those offered by anyone else. However, successful entrepreneurs know that they need to critically compare their solutions to those offered by others, keeping their egos from getting involved. To do this well, entrepreneurs often need to talk directly to potential customers or third parties to receive a realistic opinion on the value of their solutions in comparison to other alternatives. For example, our accounting software entrepreneur might show both her software and alternative software to accounting software experts and ask for their opinions. Only if the entrepreneur's new product or service were actually better than the alternatives would there be a reason to start a new business.

Pethealth, a pet insurance company founded by Mark Warren in 1999, in Oakville, Ontario, is a good example of a company established to exploit a real customer need (see Figure 10.2). Mark had been living in Great Britain where pet insurance was popular. When he returned to Canada with four dogs, he found that pet insurance products, largely available through veterinarians, were not well developed. Pet owners increasingly want to extend their pets' lives with costly medical procedures and would rather pay a known, fixed premium than be faced with an unexpected expensive bill. Warren's focus on continuous innovation to meet customer needs has paid off. Pethealth now has 25 percent of the North American market in pet insurance, with 2004 sales of $11.3 million (80 percent from the United States). In 2005, it was second on *Profit Magazine*'s list of Canada's 100 Fastest-Growing Companies.[2]

MARKET INFORMATION: DETERMINING WHAT YOUR CUSTOMERS REALLY WANT

Daniel J. Borstein, a well-known historian, once remarked (1961): "We read advertisements ... to discover and enlarge our desires. We are always ready ... to discover, from the announcement of a new product, what we have all along wanted without really knowing it." Borstein was a historian but, in a sense, he was a good psychologist, too, because the findings of modern cognitive science confirm his words: Often, we are not very good at describing our needs or, to put it slightly differently, at identifying the factors that affect our behaviour. For instance, we know that we like (or dislike) something—a new product, a prospective employee, a new idea—but we aren't clear as to why we have these reactions.

This peculiarity raises a perplexing question for entrepreneurs. On the one hand, they need marketing information before launching their companies—information on how potential customers will react to and evaluate the products or services they provide, and who these potential customers really are. (As we will note later, there can be some interesting surprises in this respect, because new products or services are often adopted by customers different from those the entrepreneurs initially anticipate.) Marketing information and a detailed marketing plan explaining how the new product or service will be promoted are usually included in business plans, and venture capitalists and other potential investors often read this information carefully. Further, existing evidence suggests that new ventures that draw a careful bead on specific markets or specific geographic areas are more successful than those that do not focus their efforts and products in this way.[3] Even before the company reaches the stage of marketing a new product, it needs to gather information from potential customers. This step raises an important question that entrepreneurs should begin considering before they launch a new venture: How can such information be gathered? The overall answer is: Through several different techniques. None is perfect, but together, they can give entrepreneurs a useful handle on how potential customers will react to their product, and why they will—or will not—be willing to buy it.

Direct Techniques for Gathering Market Information: Surveys, Perceptual Mapping, and Focus Groups

The most obvious approach to finding out how people will react to a new product or service is simply to ask them. This technique is true for most products except those that are really novel and create new markets. Marketing such products requires different techniques, which we will discuss later in this section. However, just asking customers how they feel about a new product also creates some problems even when the product isn't totally new, because it can yield jumbled information that is difficult to interpret. Even worse, it is a basic principle in the field of marketing, and in the study of human behaviour generally, that the answers you get from people depend strongly on the questions you ask.

For instance, consider the Stapleless Stapler, which was patent-protected and produced by a company that no longer exists. Perhaps the entrepreneur who invented it tried to gather marketing information before launching the new venture. But consider what the entrepreneur would have learned if questions such as these had been posed to prospective customers: "Isn't it a nuisance when a stapler runs out of staples?" "Do you ever cut yourself or break a nail trying to pull staples out of documents?" The answers might well suggest that people are greatly dissatisfied with existing staplers; in fact, though, these are petty annoyances that are more than offset by the convenience of this product. Yet, the entrepreneur might not realize this because she or he has asked loaded questions almost certain to put the new product in a favourable light. Although this observation may sound absurd—who would fall prey to such obvious traps?—it isn't really that far-fetched: Cognitive science indicates that we are all subject to a strong confirmation bias—a powerful tendency to notice and collect information that confirms our beliefs and preferences. So, never underestimate the power of commitment to an idea (or product): The dangers of falling in love with one's own invention are all too real to overlook.

In order to obtain useful marketing information about their new products or services, therefore, entrepreneurs need to approach this task in a more systematic manner and assure that they do indeed ask appropriate questions that do not load the dice in favour of the conclusions they want to reach (e.g., that their new product is one consumers badly want and will rush out to buy). There are several techniques for obtaining such information, as described below.

Customer Surveys

One useful way to obtain marketing information is to have persons in the target group (the people you expect to be future customers) compare your product with existing ones. This comparison can be done by showing them each product and asking them to rate each one on a number of different dimensions (e.g., low to high in terms of quality, usefulness, value, etc.). In such surveys, it is often common practice to use five-point scales: Each product is rated as Very Low, Low, Moderate, High, or Very High on each dimension being considered. If the questions on such surveys are chosen carefully and the people who evaluate the products and respond to the questions are truly representative of potential customers, valuable information can be obtained.

Please note, though, that such surveys rest on an assumption that is sometimes very shaky: that we already know the dimensions along which potential customers perceive and evaluate products. Sometimes the result is obvious. For instance, a travel alarm that fails to keep accurate time or fails to go off at the time set is useless, so accuracy and reliability are almost certainly key dimensions for such a product. Size, too, probably matters—although it is difficult to tell in advance whether customers weight this as heavily as accuracy and reliability. Perhaps they are willing to trade off size for a loud alarm, for instance. With respect to other products—especially very new ones, however—it is often difficult to tell, in advance, what features will be most important to customers. To get at this very basic question, another technique is often useful—one known as perceptual mapping.

LEARNING OBJECTIVE

3 Define perceptual mapping and explain how its results can assist entrepreneurs in designing their products.

Perceptual Mapping: Identifying Key Product Dimensions

Have you ever left your keys, eyeglasses, or chequebook somewhere in your home or apartment and then not been able to find them? If so, welcome to the club. Almost everyone has experiences like this, and some of us have them every day! The commonness of this experience suggests an interesting possibility for a new product: a small device that can be attached to items such as keys or eyeglasses, and can then be triggered to emit an audible (or visible) signal by a handheld control device. Sound interesting? In fact, the idea is not new: Several products that accomplish this feat already exist, but none has been very successful to date, which raises an intriguing question: Why not? What is it about these existing products that fails to satisfy the needs of potential customers, so that they are not rushing out to buy these products? More importantly, how would an entrepreneur who wants to fill this need find out just what's lacking in existing products so that she or he can design a better one?

This is where **perceptual mapping** enters the picture.[4] Perceptual mapping refers to a kind of diagram of potential customers' perceptions—a map that reveals the key dimensions along which they perceive products and evaluate them. The central idea is this: When people choose among existing, competing products, they are obviously comparing them on various dimensions and then selecting the product that they perceive most favourably on some, or all, of these dimensions. But what, exactly, are these dimensions? Some are obvious, such as price, perceived quality, and various aspects of a product's appearance. But others are not so easy to discern. For instance, consider the devices for locating lost objects, mentioned earlier. On what dimensions are potential customers evaluating them? Several possibilities come to mind: size, loudness (or brightness) of the signal they emit, ease with which they can be attached to various objects, and so on. But these are just guesses: Until we conduct careful market research, we really don't know whether potential customers are actually comparing and evaluating the products on these dimensions or on others we haven't been able to guess. To find, out we use perceptual mapping.

Focus Groups: Understanding How Consumers Perceive and Evaluate Products

Although it can be a complex process and can be carried out in several ways, one popular means of conducting consumer surveys involves **focus groups**—groups of about 8 to 12 people who are similar to potential customers and who meet for one to two hours to describe their perceptions of and reactions to relevant products. Focus groups are conducted by a moderator, whose task is to elicit a broad range of opinions from participants. The moderator accomplishes this task by creating a relaxed, friendly atmosphere for the discussion, and by assuring that all participants get a chance to express their views. The moderator also probes for the meaning of statements people make—the thoughts, ideas, and reactions behind the words. The basic goal is to identify the key dimensions along which focus group members perceive and evaluate various products. In order to reach this objective, a procedure known as the repertory grid is often used. Each product being considered is listed on a separate index card. The deck is then shuffled and three cards are chosen, often by a participant in the focus group. The moderator then asks members of the focus group to describe ways in which any two of the products are similar and the third is different. This discussion leads to initial identification of a dimension that people use to perceive the product. For instance, for item-locator devices, size might emerge as one dimension and weight as another. The process is repeated with new sets of three cards until no new dimensions appear. Then, after the key dimensions have been identified, participants rate the products along each of these dimensions and discuss these ratings until consensus is reached.

The overall result is identification of the dimensions with which products of the type being considered are actually perceived and evaluated by potential customers, plus relative rankings of the products in question along these dimensions. Results are then often presented in the form of a chart, such as the one in Figure 10.3. Each item is rated on each dimension, and comparisons between them can then be made.

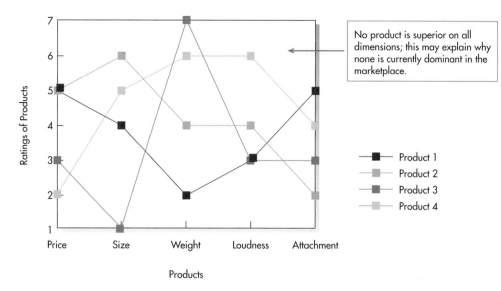

Figure 10.3 Perceptual Maps for Object Locators: No Clear Winner

Products for locating lost objects vary along several key dimensions (price, size, weight, loudness of signal), but no single product is high on all these dimensions. The fact that there is no clear winner may explain why none of these products has yet generated large sales. (Please note: Such charts should be interpreted with a healthy degree of caution; they provide rough estimates of customers' preferences—not precise measurements of them.)

As you can see, none of the products is an obvious winner—products that score high on one dimension often score low on others, and vice versa. This result suggests why none of the products considered in this focus group has reaped large sales: None does a good overall job of meeting customer needs. A product that scored high on several of the key dimensions, in contrast, might well be more successful—which, in turn, can constitute a major opportunity for astute entrepreneurs. Please note: Such charts are definitely not a magic formula for understanding customer preferences—far from it. Interpreting human judgments is always a complex matter, and market research is often more art than science; at best, it provides a general guide to consumers' views and reactions—not precise measurements of these in the sense that physical measurements can be precise. So please interpret charts such as the one shown in Figure 10.3 with a healthy degree of caution. Still, the entrepreneur who launches a new venture without attempting to determine, in advance, how potential customers will react to a new product or service is on very shaky ground indeed. For this reason, market information is an essential, not a luxury, and should definitely be part of entrepreneurs' pre-launch agendas.

Conjoint Analysis: Determining Which Dimensions Are Most Important

Why do customers choose one product over another? Presumably, because the product they select offers an optimal combination of features—high rankings along the dimensions customers view as most important. But which of these dimensions weigh most heavily on customers' preferences and decisions? Price? Size? Weight? What about various combinations of these features? For instance, will customers accept larger size in return for a lower price?

Simply asking consumers "Which dimensions are most important to you?" will not solve this puzzle. Although people *believe* that they can explain why they behave as they do, a large body of evidence indicates that, in fact, they are not very good at this task: They don't really know the reasons they make various decisions.[5] For instance, recently, I (Scott Shane) visited a relative who had just purchased a huge SUV—one of the largest on the market. As he manoeuvred this gigantic vehicle through dense city traffic, I asked him why he had decided to buy it. His answer? "I don't know … it just makes me feel good to drive it." I'm sure he had reasons for choosing this SUV, but he could certainly not describe them to me clearly.

A solution to this mystery is provided by **conjoint analysis**.[6] Conjoint analysis asks individuals to express their preferences for various products that are specially chosen to offer a *systematic array* of features. In the previous section, we

LEARNING OBJECTIVE

4   Explain conjoint analysis and indicate what information it provides for entrepreneurs.

presented the example of a lost-object locator. Perceptual mapping showed that people had different preferences about price, size, loudness of the locator signal, weight, and battery life. To determine the relative importance of each of these dimensions for consumers, entrepreneurs could present examples of locator devices (real, or perhaps just in photos or other images) to potential customers and ask them to indicate the likelihood that they would purchase each one. The products are specifically designed so that they are low or high on each of the key dimensions.

For instance, one product would be high on the first dimension (price), but would be low on the others: size, loudness, weight, and battery life. A second would be low on price, as well as low on all the others, and so on. Because there are five different dimensions, this would generate a large number of products: 2 (low, high) × 2 (low, high) × 2 (low, high) × 2 (low, high) × 2 (low, high) = 32. Consumers might be shown pairs of items and asked to choose between them. Alternatively, they could be shown one at a time and asked to indicate the likelihood that they would purchase it (e.g., on a seven-point scale where 1 = very unlikely to buy it and 7 = very likely to buy it). As you can see, if the number of dimensions is large (e.g., 7 instead of 5) and if the products can be high, moderate, or low on each, the number of combinations would quickly get out of hand (e.g., 3 × 3 × 3 × 3 × 3 × 3 × 3 = 2,187).

To reduce this problem, conjoint analysis often uses a *fractional factorial design*—only a fraction of all the combinations are presented to consumers. How is this fraction chosen? Largely on the basis of preliminary evidence from perceptual mapping. For instance, if perceptual mapping suggested that price, size, and loudness of signal are the most important dimensions, these would be fully represented in the array of products, while other dimensions might be represented only in combination with others. The data gathered by conjoint analysis (participants' ratings of each product or choices between them) are then analyzed statistically (e.g., by regression analysis). The results of such analyses indicate the relative importance of each variable (i.e., size, weight, loudness, etc.) in participants' decisions.

Although the statistical details of conjoint analysis are beyond the scope of this discussion, the overall strategy is straightforward: Instead of asking potential customers to tell us which dimensions are most important to them in choosing between various products, they actually make these choices, and their selections or stated preferences provide the information we seek.

Conjoint analysis can provide extremely valuable marketing information to entrepreneurs. Once they know what features are most important to consumers, entrepreneurs can build these features into their new products, and therefore maximize their chances of success. In contrast, just going to market without gathering this information often leads to problematic results.

Observation as a Technique for Gathering Market Information: The Entrepreneur as Sherlock Holmes

In one famous story involving Sherlock Holmes, Sir Arthur Conan Doyle's famous detective, Holmes amazes Dr. Watson by stating—correctly, it turns out—that one physician's practice is in decline while that of another physician, whose office is next door, is on the rise. When Watson asks Holmes how he knew this, Holmes points to the steps leading into the two offices: One shows much more recent wear than the other. "Elementary, my dear Watson," Holmes remarks (see Figure 10.4).

In this case, Holmes has used direct observation for learning about the preferences of patients—who can be viewed as the physician's customers. Similarly, if they are perceptive, entrepreneurs, too, can profit from direct observation for gathering such information. For example, before expanding his Israeli cracker business into North American markets, Peter Shamir spent six months in different types of stores watching how North Americans bought crackers. He

Figure 10.4 Direct Observation: Often Useful

Sherlock Holmes often used observation to solve mysteries. In one of his many adventures, he correctly determined that one physician was much more popular than another, whose office was next door. How did he do it? By noticing that the steps leading to the popular doctor's office showed greater recent wear than those leading to his neighbour's office. In a similar manner, entrepreneurs can use direct observation to gather information about potential markets for their new products or services.

Index Stock Imagery, Inc.

learned that customers in the cracker aisle of big supermarkets decided which cracker to buy in about 10 seconds, but people lingered over products longer in the deli aisle and in smaller stores, such as health food stores and gourmet shops. The insights from this observation led him to launch his product successfully in smaller stores.[7]

This type of data—and data collected through the other techniques described here—is called primary data when it is collected specifically for the entrepreneur's purpose. Entrepreneurs often augment primary data with secondary data—data they do not collect themselves, and which has not been collected specifically for their purposes, but can still be very useful. For instance, entrepreneurs can examine the sales of competing products to see whether any trends emerge—some rising in popularity, others declining. Such trends may suggest that certain features or combinations of features are gaining or losing appeal to potential customers. Similarly, entrepreneurs can examine data (e.g., from the Statistics Canada website or Industry Canada's Strategis website) to see how demographic populations or industrial sectors are changing. In some cases, these changes can even suggest the basis for a successful company.

For instance, consider Brian Scudamore, CEO of 1-800-Got Junk. This Canadian company, which is now located in more than four Canadian provinces and 38 American states, helps people get rid of ... their junk! Because most of us are incredibly weak when it comes to deciding to get rid of things we have had for years but no longer use, you might wonder how Scudamore came up with this idea. Mainly on the basis of indirect marketing information. He noticed, for instance, that storage facilities were experiencing a sharp drop in business. This trend suggested to him that more people were getting rid of their unneeded possessions at a higher rate than in the past. Why? Perhaps tough economic conditions play a key role: An increasing number of persons were concluding that they could no longer afford to pay to store items they did not use or want. By carefully observing these trends (forms of indirect market information), Scudamore was able to come up with the idea for his new company, and to cash in handsomely on the new "Get rid of it!" ethic that seemed to be emerging.

Which Technique Should You Choose?

So how do entrepreneurs know what techniques to use to gather information from customers? The first step is to determine the kind of market that they're targeting. Is the target market already well established, for example, the market for automobiles? Or is the target market new, such as the market for Internet-based auction houses in the early 1990s? When the target market is already established, the process of assessing the market and customer preferences is much easier, and generally involves using focus groups and surveys. When the target market is established, customer preferences are not very uncertain because the basic characteristics of those preferences are known. For instance, anyone who wants to sell automobiles today pretty much knows what the market wants in a car. In addition, when the target market is established, customers find it much easier to communicate their preferences to entrepreneurs. This exchange of information makes it much easier to establish good survey and focus group questions. The second step is to figure out what kind of new product or service you are developing. Is your solution to customer needs already known and understood or is it a novel solution? For example, a faster processing computer chip made of silicon would be a well-known and understood solution because existing computer chips are made of silicon. In this example, the entrepreneur is producing a faster chip that works more or less the same way as previous chips. But there have been times when computer manufacturers offered novel solutions to the problem of making computers process information faster, as occurred when computer manufacturers shifted from using vacuum tubes to transistors and again from transistors to

LEARNING OBJECTIVE

5 Explain why entrepreneurs use different techniques to assess customer preferences in new and established markets, and identify those different techniques.

microchips. In the case of both of these transitions, the solution to the customer problem was based on new science and engineering and so was not well known or well understood by customers.

Similar to the case with a known target market, when knowledge of the solution is well known, the process of assessing the market and customer preferences is much easier. Entrepreneurs can again rely on focus groups and survey techniques. Table 10.1 summarizes when different approaches to gathering information about customer preferences work the best. As the table shows, when the target market and solutions are well known, traditional market research techniques are quite effective. In contrast, when the target market and solutions are not well known, traditional market research techniques tend to do very poorly. Under these conditions, the people in the focus groups and surveys don't know enough to provide useful answers. For instance, when the laser and the photocopier first appeared, potential customers surveyed about these products said that there would be no use for them. In large part, they responded this way because they could not envision the ways in which these products would ultimately be used.

So what should you do when the market or the solution you are offering is really novel? Under these circumstances, successful entrepreneurs have discussions with industry experts and extrapolate trends to determine which features to include in new products and services. But be careful. These techniques appear to work best when the market or the solution is really new. When the market or the solution is well known, traditional market research techniques work better. You really have to know your target market and your product before deciding which techniques to use or you will get yourself into some serious trouble.

What about situations in which either the target market or the solution is known, but the other is not? The entrepreneur needs to use a blend of traditional market research techniques and futurist approaches. In these cases, anthropological expeditions, in which entrepreneurs put themselves in the shoes of the customer, or in-depth conversations with early adopters and lead users of new products, or partnering with customers to develop the products often prove to be very effective strategies for learning about customer preferences.[8]

Before concluding our discussion of market research techniques, we would like to make two points. The first is that marketing information—even if excellent in every respect—is no guarantee of success. To the extent a product or service is truly new, it may be difficult for consumers to compare it with existing products. History is filled with products that were designed for one use and one market but, in fact, found success with a different use or in a different market. For instance, consider personal computers. When IBM launched this new product in 1981, the company was absolutely convinced that it would be used only in business contexts: After all, who would want this business tool for home use? Within a few short years, however, it became clear that consumers were much more inventive at developing uses for a personal computer than IBM's engineers—or their marketing division!—ever dreamed.

Table 10.1 Market Research Techniques Depend on the Type of Market

Entrepreneurs use different techniques to learn about customer needs in new and existing markets.

	EXISTING MARKET	NEW MARKET
Philosophy of market research	Deductive data analysis	Intuition
Techniques for gathering customer information	Focus groups, surveys, mall studies	Industry experts, trend extrapolation, future scenarios
Examples	New types of toothpaste, new car models	Internet auction houses, telephone

Source: Based on information contained in Barton, D. *Commercializing Technology: Imaginative*

Here's another one: Silly Putty was developed, quite by accident during World War II, when chemists were searching for a silicone-based rubber substitute. It was unsuitable for that use, but soon—and unexpectedly—became a popular children's toy. Recently, however, it has found another market: as an aid to stress-reduction among harried adults.[9]

Busy executives seem to find bouncing and stretching the elastic substance quite relaxing. But small amounts (the package for children contains 14 grams) are not enough to satisfy these adult appetites, so they buy it in bulk. In fact, groups of Silly Putty fans join together to order the manufacturer's minimum bulk amount, which gives each person 4.5 kilograms or more of the bouncing wonder. Certainly, Silly Putty is a dramatic example of a product that has found a new market niche—one its makers probably never dreamed would emerge. So yes, market information is often very helpful to entrepreneurs, but it is just one of several kinds of information they need in order to achieve the success they dream of.

The second point is that there are costs as well as benefits in collecting market information. Given the importance to entrepreneurs of gathering and analyzing information from customers, most entrepreneurs try to gather customer information before they launch their new products. But some entrepreneurs do not gather adequate information before moving forward. Certainly, some of these entrepreneurs don't gather adequate information from customers before they start because they haven't taken entrepreneurship courses and read books like this one that explain why doing so is important. However, entrepreneurs often know that gathering information from customers is important, but fail to gather this information because of the time and money pressures that they face. Sometimes, entrepreneurs don't gather information from customers because they don't have enough money to pay for focus groups, interviews, surveys, or other efforts to obtain customer information and still pay for the costs of developing the product itself. Other times, entrepreneurs don't gather information because they are worried that another entrepreneur will get to the market before them or because they are concerned that the opportunity will disappear before they can get their product out. For example, an entrepreneur in the fashion industry might want to survey customers about her new fall line of clothing, but realizes that if she spends the time gathering information, she will be unable to get her clothing into retail stores until after Halloween, clearly too late to launch a fall line. The moral of this story is that gathering information from customers is important, but entrepreneurs often need to make difficult choices between spending their limited capital on assessing customer needs or spending it on other things, and between gathering information or meeting windows of opportunity in the market before they close (see Figure 10.5).

Figure 10.5 Entrepreneurs Need to Analyze Market Needs

Entrepreneurs often face a tension between meeting a market window and conducting the market research necessary to learn about the market.

DILBERT reprinted by permission of United Feature Syndicate, Inc.

KEY POINTS

- Entrepreneurs are most successful when they start a company that meets a real need: either solving a customer problem that no product or service has yet solved, or being so much better at solving the problem than an existing product or service that customers are motivated to switch.
- Before launching a new venture, entrepreneurs need reliable marketing information—information on how potential customers will react to and evaluate the products or services they provide.
- Because people are not very successful at identifying the factors that influence their behaviour, simply asking them why they like or dislike various products is not an effective approach.
- Perceptual mapping, one technique for identifying the dimensions along which customers evaluate various products, is often a useful initial step.
- One useful procedure for gathering such information is focus groups—groups of about 8 to 12 people who are similar to potential customers and who meet for one to two hours to describe their perceptions of and reactions to relevant products.
- Conjoint analysis is a useful technique for determining the relative importance, in the customer's preferences and decisions, of the dimensions that they consider important.
- Through the effective use of conjoint analysis, entrepreneurs can design products that will have high appeal to potential customers, and so maximize the chances of success of their new ventures.
- In addition to gathering their own marketing information, entrepreneurs can also use indirect or secondary data, information gathered by others.
- When markets are new, entrepreneurs assess customer preferences differently from when markets are already established; entrepreneurs need to adopt the right assessment techniques for the type of market they are targeting.
- Although marketing data are often useful to entrepreneurs, gathering it is no guarantee of success, especially with respect to new products or services, because consumers may find comparing new products to existing products a difficult task, and unexpected uses for such products may quickly emerge.

MARKET DYNAMICS

Successful entrepreneurs realize that all markets are not equal. They understand that some markets, such as the market for golf clubs, are larger than other markets, such as the market for ping pong paddles. Successful entrepreneurs also realize that markets grow at different rates; for instance, the market for SUVs is currently growing much faster than the market for muscle cars. Last, they recognize that markets evolve as new products are born, mature, and grow old. Therefore, successful entrepreneurs understand the dynamics of the markets that they are thinking of entering before they begin their companies and launch their new products or services; this preparation ensures that they adopt the right marketing strategy for that market. In this section, we introduce you to some of the key market dynamics that successful entrepreneurs exploit to their advantage.

Knowing Your Market: The Importance of Market Size and Market Growth

LEARNING OBJECTIVE

6 Explain how large and growing markets help entrepreneurs.

One basic question that entrepreneurs need to ask when developing a marketing plan for their new venture is "How large is the market?" A large market is important because new businesses have a fixed cost to get started. The smaller the market, the lower will be the potential sales for the new venture and the higher share of the market the entrepreneur will need to obtain just to cover the cost of getting started. Moreover, a new venture can enter a large market without drawing a lot of attention from competitors, who notice what's going on in the market much more easily in small markets. Because the new venture often is not yet ready to compete—its products haven't been developed, its employees haven't been hired, and so on—going in under the radar, as venture capitalists call it, is very important.

Entrepreneurs also need to determine how quickly the market is growing. A rapidly growing market is advantageous to entrepreneurs because it affects the sales process. In a stagnant market, the only way for a company to make sales is to take customers away from other companies. However, in a rapidly growing market, a company can grow quickly by serving customers who had not previously been customers in the market. It is much easier to capture new customers than customers served by other firms because in the latter case, the other firms will compete with you to keep their customers. In addition, a rapidly growing market is beneficial to entrepreneurs because rapid growth means a larger volume of customers, providing the benefits of volume purchasing and scale economies that lower the entrepreneur's costs.

Existing versus New Markets

Although entrepreneurs can develop new products and services for existing markets using known solutions, they are far better off focusing on creating new products and services for new markets using new solutions. Why? The answer is that entrepreneurs are not the only people who develop new products and services. The managers of established companies do the same thing, often with more people and money behind the projects. To introduce a new product or service successfully, entrepreneurs not only need to satisfy a market need but they need to do so better than competitors. It also really helps if the entrepreneur can introduce a new product or service that established companies aren't trying to develop.

When markets already exist, or new products are based on known solutions to customer problems, new firms are at a real disadvantage relative to established companies. Because established companies have already sold their products to customers, they have already gathered a large amount of information about customer preferences. Have you ever used a store card at a retailer like Staples? That credit card allows the retailer to know exactly what you purchased, when you purchased it, how much you spent, whether it was on sale, whether you used a coupon, and so on. This information makes it pretty easy for Staples to figure out what your preferences are when they launch a new product, especially in comparison to an entrepreneur who is competing with Staples and is launching a new product for the first time.

When the market is new or the solution to customer needs is novel, however, entrepreneurs can offset the advantages that existing companies have in understanding customer preferences. Dorothy Leonard Barton, a professor at the Harvard Business School, has explained that existing companies have three major disadvantages when serving new markets with novel solutions to customer needs.[10] The first, which she calls **core rigidities**, means that companies do well at things that they are accustomed to doing, not at doing things that are new. Existing companies aren't very good at coming up with new products to serve new markets or that are based on new solutions to customer needs, because they have a hard time breaking away from old ways of doing things.

The second disadvantage of established firms, which Professor Barton calls **tyranny of the current market**, means that established companies have a hard time coming up with new products for new markets because they listen to their customers. This might sound strange—after all, your marketing textbook probably told you how important it is to listen to your customers, and it is if you want to continue to serve your *existing* customers. However, listening to *existing* customers will make it difficult for a company to come up with new products for *new* markets. The reason? A firm's existing customers will always ask for improvements to current products, not for products for new markets. As a result, existing customers will keep established companies focused on making improvements to current products rather than on looking for ways to target new customers.

The third disadvantage of established firms is something Professor Barton calls **user myopia**. This term refers to customers of existing firms seeing only very narrow needs or solutions. Typically, they might see their own needs, but not the needs of other potential customers. This focus creates big problems when a new product is very useful for a different market. For example, when Halloid Corporation, the precursor to Xerox, introduced the first photocopy machine, its representatives went to the only people who reproduced documents at the time—offset printers—and asked them what they thought of the machines. The printers responded that they had no use for them; offset printing worked just fine. Fortunately, Halloid Corporation didn't listen to the printers because this was a classic case of user myopia. Sure, offset printing worked just fine for printers, who didn't need photocopiers. But, as you know, there was a huge need for photocopiers—in schools, offices, libraries, and so on. The printers didn't see this use because they couldn't see the needs and preferences of other segments of the market.[11]

The lesson here is counterintuitive. Although entrepreneurs often want to pursue established markets with well-known solutions to customer needs because it is easier, that isn't necessarily the best approach. Entrepreneurs are likely to have an advantage over established companies when they launch products based on novel solutions to customer needs in new markets. When established companies have sold products based on an older solution for a long time or when the market is so new and demand so unknown that it is very difficult to do much market research, entrepreneurs who launch businesses with novel products tend to do very well.

Timing the Market: The S-Curve Story

LEARNING OBJECTIVE

7 Define the new product S-curve, and explain why it is important for entrepreneurs to understand the relationship between effort and product performance.

As we explained in the beginning of the chapter, products have life cycles that influence the ability of entrepreneurs to enter markets with new products. Researchers have shown that when products are first introduced, they are often inferior to alternative products on many of the dimensions that are important to customers, like quality, reliability, and performance.[12] For example, the first automobiles could not travel as far or go as fast as the typical horse and buggy that people used for transportation at the time. However, firms work their way up the learning curve as they figure out how to improve their products. They add new features, improve speed, enhance reliability, or otherwise make the new products better along the dimensions that customers care about.

Initially, this improvement is slow because learning new things is difficult. Many ideas about how to improve the product turn out to be dead ends. Moreover, as soon as people solve one problem, they often face another, precluding them from gaining rapid performance improvement. For example, when people built the first airplanes, each initial effort to improve the wings and the engines yielded only a few feet of additional flight. But after working through a variety of design problems, the early airplane entrepreneurs figured out the key solutions to wing and engine problems, and flight performance improved dramatically. This rapid improvement in performance continues for a while, until it reaches a level of diminishing returns, where each amount of effort to improve yields very little benefit in terms of performance. For example, making an airplane capable of flying one additional mile takes much more of an investment than it took to get earlier airplanes to increase their range from one to two miles. As you probably figured out, this pattern of new product performance is shaped like an "S." Researchers call it the **S-curve**.[13] In Figure 10.6, we show the S-curve for computer memory.

We have just described the S-curve for a successful new product. If things always worked the way we just described, then companies would produce new products all of the time, knowing that they would eventually perform better than the older products they already have. However, new products don't always end up performing better than old ones—or they do, but it takes so long that it isn't worthwhile developing the new

Source: Based on information in Foster, R. 1986. *Innovation: The Attacker's Advantage.* New York: Summit

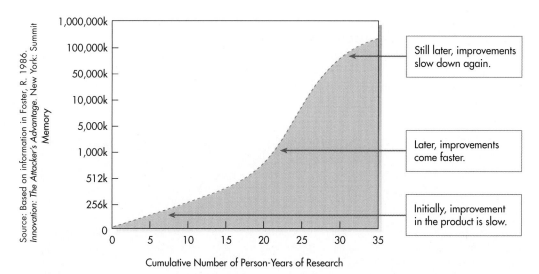

Figure 10.6 The S-Curve for Computer Memory

Entrepreneurs need to be aware that their new product introductions are often inferior to existing alternatives when they are first introduced; new products improve as people put more effort into their development.

product. For instance, in the 1970s, many people thought that nuclear power would replace fossil fuels, such as oil and coal, in making electricity. Unfortunately for them, the entrepreneurs developing nuclear power plants ran into large obstacles in improving the safety of the plants. As a result, nuclear power has never achieved superior performance to oil and coal in producing electricity on all the dimensions that customers care about. Although it might succeed in attaining these goals some day in the future, the fact that it hasn't for 30 years has meant that entrepreneurs who tried to launch companies to make electricity using nuclear power in the 1970s were unable to replace alternative products, like coal and oil, in a short enough time frame to survive.

The product development S-curve has important implications for entrepreneurs. First, introducing novel products is very difficult for entrepreneurs because new products start out with a performance inferior on the dimensions that customers care about compared with the existing product alternatives. To survive this early period, entrepreneurs need to find a source of capital that can sustain them until they can develop their new product's performance, or find a market segment that doesn't care that much about the performance of the new product and is willing to adopt it.

Second, entrepreneurs need to recognize that new product improvement is a function of effort, not time. Unless someone invests in the development of the new product, it will never become as good as the existing product alternatives. Often, the entrepreneur can't simply wait until the product is good enough to compete with existing products. If the entrepreneur doesn't produce the new product, it will never be as good as existing alternatives.

Third, identifying the point of acceleration in the S-curve is an important entrepreneurial skill. By knowing when a new product's performance is about to take off, the entrepreneur can better time hiring employees, expanding manufacturing, and raising capital. More importantly, entrepreneurs need to predict whether the S-curve will accelerate. If the new product's performance does not improve rapidly, it will never overtake existing products in terms of the performance that customers prefer. Similar to the example with nuclear power, new products that do not improve rapidly will not replace existing products, such as coal and oil, and so it is not a very good product for entrepreneurs to develop.

Successful entrepreneurs also know that established firms will not compete with them to develop new products that lie at the early part of the S-curve. Because the new product begins with inferior performance to the products that established firms already have, the established firms have little incentive to change their products. In fact, the inferiority of the new product often leads managers of established firms to believe that the new product will always have very limited appeal to customers and is something that they do not need to worry about. Worse come to worst, the managers of established firms figure that they can always improve their own products to compete with the new product. Established firms will almost always opt for improving their own product rather than adopting the new product because they have investments in the technology and human resources used to produce the older product. As a result, they will be unwilling to shift to the new product until after it has proved its superiority over the old one, at which point the entrepreneur has a big head start.[14]

KEY POINTS

- Entrepreneurs are more successful in large and growing markets because large markets amortize the fixed cost of getting started over a larger number of units, and because it is easier to sell in more rapidly growing markets.
- Entrepreneurs are better off targeting new markets than established markets because established firms face three obstacles in assessing new markets: core rigidities, the tyranny of the current market, and user myopia.
- The performance of new products follows an S-shape. Initially, a large amount of effort is required to achieve small improvements in product performance. Then performance improvements accelerate, with a small amount of effort leading to large improvements in performance. Ultimately, a large amount of effort is again required to achieve small improvements in performance as the product confronts the law of diminishing returns.
- The product S-curve is important to entrepreneurs because new products begin with inferior performance to existing products, requiring entrepreneurs to obtain a source of capital to keep their ventures alive as they improve new product performance. The S-curve also shows that the improvement in new products is a function of effort, not time. Finally, it demonstrates the importance of timing organizing activities to the acceleration of the S-curve.
- Established companies rarely compete with entrepreneurs to develop new products on the early part of the S-curve because the new product generally begins with inferior performance to the established company's existing products, and because the managers of established firms often believe that they could always improve the performance of their existing products to compete with new products.

ACHIEVING MARKET ACCEPTANCE

LEARNING OBJECTIVE

8 Describe the typical new product adoption pattern and explain how it influences entrepreneurial action.

To be successful, entrepreneurs must have large numbers of customers accept and adopt their products and services. Acquiring this customer base requires that entrepreneurs know which customers will adopt products when, and which characteristics the product must attract to gain acceptance from a particular segment of the market. Given their limited resources, entrepreneurs often need to focus on a single set of customers and need to know how to pick the right set of customers. Finally, entrepreneurs must be aware of any dominant design or technical standard that is in place or likely to come into place in their market before they get started.

Adoption Patterns: Understanding Which Customers Adopt When

Entrepreneurs are understandably thrilled when they are able to sell their first product or service. A first sale is quite an achievement—one that many entrepreneurs never accomplish. However, for entrepreneurs to really succeed with their new businesses, they need to do more than achieve a first sale. They need to achieve broad adoption of their new products or services.

How do entrepreneurs achieve broad acceptance of their products? The first step lies in understanding how customers adopt new products. In general, the adoption of new products and services follows a normal distribution, like the one shown in

Figure 10.7. A small group of customers are innovators, who are the earliest customers of new products and services. Early adopters follow the innovators. The majority of customers adopt after that, followed by a smaller group that are laggards, who adopt new products pretty late in the process.[15] Although the adoption of products doesn't always work as precisely as is shown in our figure, largely because of differences in individual tastes and preferences, this pattern is a good starting point for entrepreneurs. On average, across the vast majority of products, adoption patterns follow the normal distribution shown in the figure.

In fact, you have probably seen this adoption pattern at work. Think about the adoption of iPods. You probably know someone who was an innovator—someone who bought one of the very first iPods to come out. You also probably have some friends who were early adopters. They bought their iPods before most of the people you know bought them. Most of your friends probably bought their iPods around the same time, because most people are in the early or late majority of adopters. Last, we suspect that you know some people (your parents, perhaps?) who are laggards who still have not purchased an iPod.

Why does this adoption pattern matter to entrepreneurs? Understanding adoption patterns helps to understand how to introduce new products and services. One thing that entrepreneurs need to know about Figure 10.7 is that different groups adopt products for different reasons.[16] Innovators often feel that they need every new device and piece of technology on the market. They tend to be intrigued by new products and adopt them so that they can explore what is new. In many cases, they purchase new products before they are formally marketed, even offering to purchase prototypes and beta tests. These customers are very insensitive to price. They want to try what is new, and often there are no alternatives yet available at any price. Early adopters tend to appreciate the value of new products and adopt them without much marketing effort by sellers. Although these people do not need new products as quickly as the innovators, they do claim to have greater needs for new product features than the majority of ultimate adopters. They base their buying decisions on their intuition about the value of new products and do not require much information to make their purchasing decisions. The early majority appreciates the value of new products, but also is influenced by practicality. They often want to see references from satisfied customers or endorsement by celebrities and other famous people before purchasing. The late majority tends not to be comfortable with new products and is driven to purchase by other considerations. They will wait for a product to become well established before purchasing it. Only when they are shown that the value of having the product clearly outweighs the cost do they adopt the product. The laggards avoid new products. In fact, they will do everything that they can to avoid adopting them. In many cases, laggards only adopt new products because the old products that they have been using are no longer available, as is the case with

Figure 10.7 The Typical Pattern of Adoption of New Products

Most new products face a normal distribution of adopters. Few customers adopt early or late in the adoption cycle; most customers adopt in the middle of the cycle.

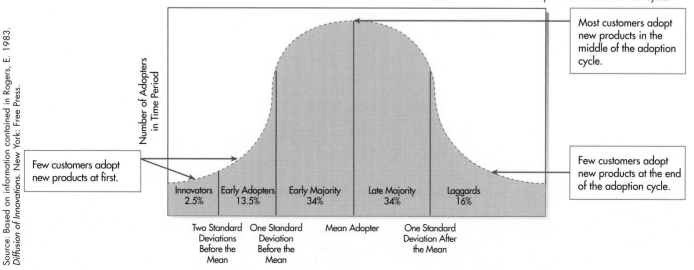

Source: Based on information contained in Rogers, E. 1983. *Diffusion of Innovations.* New York: Free Press.

many very late adopters of computers who only adopted when typewriters became difficult to buy.[17]

Because different groups of customers adopt new products for different reasons, entrepreneurs need to know where the market is on the adoption curve when they start their new businesses and introduce their new products. If the early majority is not yet adopting the product, it might be too early for the entrepreneur to try large-scale promotion based on references from satisfied users or celebrity endorsements. In contrast, if the late majority is already adopting the product, the entrepreneur better have well-established support for the product if she hopes to get customer acceptance.[18]

In addition, entrepreneurs need to adjust their marketing message to fit the needs of the segment of customers who are adopting at the time. In general, this means offering more information and more support as part of marketing new products as the customer base shifts more toward late adopters who need this information and support to make their buying decisions.

Moving from Early Adopters to the Early Majority

LEARNING OBJECTIVE

9 Define "crossing the chasm" and explain why and how entrepreneurs "cross the chasm."

Transitioning from early adopters to the early majority is very important for entrepreneurs. In most markets, the innovators and the early adopters are too small a group to sustain new firms. Firms that sell only to them tend to die. But, because adopters of new products tend to follow a normal distribution, there is a very big increase in the number of customers when the entrepreneur moves from early adopters to early majority. Transitioning to the early majority allows new firms to get the volume of sales that they need to survive. Moreover, innovators and early adopters often demand customization of products. As a result, serving only these groups often becomes cost-ineffective for entrepreneurs who really need to develop products for larger volume markets to make a profit on them. Furthermore, profit margins are the highest at the middle of the adoption bell curve for many markets because the increase in volume of sales that occurs when firms transition to the early majority allows them to dramatically lower costs through higher volume of purchases and economies of scale. Last, the high cost of equity capital that many entrepreneurs incur to finance their business requires the transition to the early majority, or the level of sales revenue of the new firm is insufficient to pay back investors.[19]

Despite its importance, making the transition from early adopters to early majority is difficult for entrepreneurs, which led Geoffrey Moore, a well-known marketing consultant, to call it "crossing the chasm." Entrepreneurs find crossing the chasm difficult because the needs and demands of innovators and the early adopters are very different from the needs and demands of the early majority. The early majority often wants to purchase solutions to their problems, not just novel products and services. For instance, in computer software, the innovators and early majority might purchase novel software alone, but the early majority will often want training and support, manuals, a customer service hotline, and so on.[20]

So how do successful entrepreneurs cross the chasm? First, they build the complete solution to customer needs described earlier, rather than offering just the product itself. Second, they focus on a single niche because they will not be able to offer the complete system that customers want if they try to serve too many niches at once. Third, entrepreneurs communicate the information about their solution to customers in a clear and effective way so that customers understand that the new company intends to be the market leader in solutions to this particular customer need (see Figure 10.8).[21]

LEARNING OBJECTIVE

10 Explain how entrepreneurs should choose the customers to focus their initial efforts on.

Focus: Choosing the Right Customers to Target First

To be successful, entrepreneurs need to focus. As we explained in the previous section, entrepreneurs need to focus to cross the chasm. Focusing is also essential in new businesses because entrepreneurs have limited resources. Because raising capital is difficult and costly, entrepreneurs rarely have enough capital for pursuing multiple

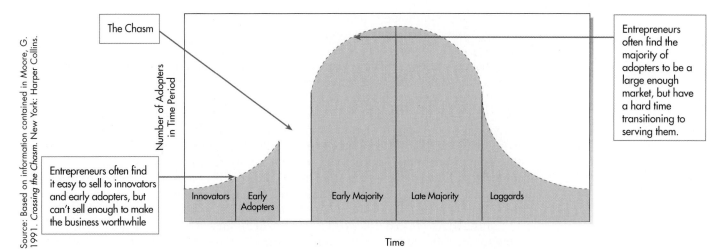

Source: Based on information contained in Moore, G. 1991. *Crossing the Chasm.* New York: Harper Collins.

The Chasm

Entrepreneurs often find it easy to sell to innovators and early adopters, but can't sell enough to make the business worthwhile

Entrepreneurs often find the majority of adopters to be a large enough market, but have a hard time transitioning to serving them.

Number of Adopters in Time Period

Innovators | Early Adopters | Early Majority | Late Majority | Laggards

Time

Figure 10.8 Crossing the Chasm

Entrepreneurs often find it easy to sell their new products to innovators and early adopters, but find it difficult to transition to the early majority.

market segments at the same time. Moreover, as entrepreneurs have to gather a lot of information about markets and customers to develop new products and services and pursue their opportunities, they rarely have enough time to gather information about a number of market segments at the same time. Even the most determined entrepreneurs just can't work much more than 100 hours per week!

But focusing is only beneficial if you focus on the right customers. How should an entrepreneur choose where to focus? By considering the customer. This approach involves figuring out which customers need to buy the product or service. Customers need to buy if the product or service gives them something that improves their productivity, reduces their costs, or gives them something that they could not have before.[22] For example, a courier service has a need to buy a global positioning system because it allows drivers to develop more precise routes and make their deliveries more efficiently. Similarly, a cookie business has a need to buy new product packaging that allows them to improve the storage life of their cookies, because the company makes more money if its products can be kept longer on store shelves.

CV Technologies of Edmonton is one company that found the right customers to target after a false start with the wrong customers. Founded in 1993, CV Technologies is a research-oriented company that produces COLD-fX, a ginseng-based cold and flu remedy. The company initially wanted to sell or license the rights to COLD-fX to pharmaceutical companies, but the pharmaceutical companies were uninterested. In 1996, however, the general manager of the Edmonton Oilers found the product in a natural food store. Because professional athletes often have stressed immune systems, his players were eager to try it. Dr. Shan, the company's co-founder, agreed to supply the Oilers with COLD-fX if they agreed to provide research data on its effectiveness. The combination of scientific data and celebrity athlete endorsements allowed CV Technologies to cross the chasm from the early adopters (the athletes) to reach the early majority among the 55 percent of Canadians that regularly buy natural over-the-counter treatments.[23]

Dominant Design: Product Convergence and Its Effect on New Ventures

Many markets have **dominant designs**. A dominant design is an arrangement that all companies producing a product will choose as the way of bringing together the different parts of a product or service.[24] A good example of a dominant design is the internal combustion engine. Once this design was introduced, all automobile makers adopted this design, and it hasn't changed since then.

Why should entrepreneurs care about dominant designs? Because they influence an entrepreneur's likelihood of success. William Abernathy, a former professor at Harvard Business School, and Jim Utterback, a professor at the Sloan School at MIT, explain that products evolve through periods of incremental change, punctuated by radical breakthroughs. Radical breakthroughs are a new way of making something

LEARNING OBJECTIVE

11 Define a "dominant design" and a "technical standard" and explain how they influence the performance of new ventures.

or a fundamentally new product design or architecture. Take computers as an example. Initially, computers used vacuum tubes. For many years, computer manufacturers made incremental improvements to vacuum tubes so that they would perform better and better. The computer manufacturers initially had different designs for vacuum tubes, but then converged on a single common design. Then the computer industry experienced a radical shift—to transistors. After that radical shift, computer manufacturers had different designs for their products. Then they converged on a dominant design for transistors, and again made incremental improvements, making the transistors better and better. Then there was another radical shift, this time to integrated circuits. For a while, computer manufacturers had different integrated circuit designs, but ultimately converged on a dominant design. Again, after the dominant design, the computer makers made incremental improvements to the integrated circuit, reducing their size and increasing their processing speed.[25]

This pattern we just described is important because it very much affects the right time for an entrepreneur to start a new company. Every time there is a radical technological shift in an industry, new firms rush in and begin to compete because this is the point in the evolutionary cycle that is most favourable to new firms. Because there is no dominant design, new firms aren't handicapped by having to adopt a design that existing firms, who have more experience than they do, already use. Moreover, once firms converge on a dominant design, they shift their basis of competition to efficiency and scale economies because the product design has become standardized. This shift favours established firms over new firms, which are not as efficient and often can't operate on the same scale as established firms.[26] How powerful are the effects of a dominant design? For a dramatic illustration of the far-reaching impact they command, please see the **Danger! Pitfall Ahead!** section.

Technical Standards: Getting Customers to Adopt Your Design as the Market Standard

In many industries, entrepreneurs must produce products or services that meet a **technical standard**. A technical standard is an agreed-upon basis on which a product or service operates. For example, the gauge of a railroad track is standard to make sure that all producers of railroad cars can operate on the same track.

The most important thing for entrepreneurs to know about technical standards is that getting the market to adopt your product design as the technical standard will make you super rich. One of the most famous technical standards is the Windows computer operating system. Bill Gates became one of the richest men in the world largely because almost 80 percent of computers in the world operate the Windows operating system.

Those of you who are interested in becoming rich will be reassured to know that there are things that you can do to increase the likelihood that your market will adopt your product design as the technical standard. First, entrepreneurs can discount their prices when the new product is initially introduced, attracting more customers than if they charged a high price. Having this high volume is useful for attracting suppliers because many suppliers would prefer to work with the largest producers who have the largest volume (for example, many software producers preferred Windows to the Macintosh operating system and would only write their software for Windows). Therefore, firms that generate the most customers quickly often stay ahead of competitors because suppliers prefer them to other alternatives. By being ahead of alternatives, the product becomes the technical standard in the industry.[27]

A second action that entrepreneurs can take to make their products the technical standard is to build relationships with producers of **complementary products**. Complementary products are products that work together, such as recorded movies and videotape recorders, or computer hardware and computer software. When VCRs first came out, Sony was locked in a major battle with Matsushita over whose VCR format would become the technical standard. Sony had the Betamax, and

Matsushita had VHS. VHS became the technical standard, and Betamax disappeared, largely because of a very wise decision by Matsushita. The executives at Matsushita pushed hard to get their standard adopted by the new video rental shops that were springing up around the country. In contrast, Sony didn't seem to care. Because recorded movies were an important complementary product to the VCR, once people started to rent movies and rental shops began to offer VHS tapes, most customers adopted the VHS standard and the Sony Betamax failed.[28]

A third action entrepreneurs can take to get their products adopted as the technical standard is to get to the market quickly rather than get to the market with the best version. Often this early introduction means starting with a simplified product that doesn't have all the best technology or features. It also means signing contracts with already existing manufacturers to produce the product for you rather than building new manufacturing plants from scratch. Finally, it involves simplifying the product so that mass production can occur.[30]

Getting to market quickly with less than perfect products is difficult for many entrepreneurs, who make the mistake of waiting to enter the market until they can make sure that their products are as close to perfect as they can get them. Sometimes this waiting period makes sense, but getting to market fast is a better approach when technical standards are up for grabs. As long as customers are more likely to switch

DANGER! PITFALL AHEAD!

Stymied by the Dominant Design: The Story of Electric Vehicles

Did you know that there were once more electric-powered vehicles in North America than gasoline-powered ones? According to David Kirsch, a business historian and entrepreneurship professor at the University of Maryland, in 1900, vehicles using gasoline-powered internal combustion engines were actually the least common type. Steam-powered vehicles were the most common (have you ever seen a Stanley Steamer at an automobile museum?) and electric-powered vehicles were the second most common.[29] In 1900, very few people thought that the internal combustion engine would become the dominant design in automobiles. Electric- and steam-powered vehicles performed much better than gasoline-powered ones: They had greater range and could pull heavier loads. In fact, newspapers and magazines from that time period extolled the virtues of the electric vehicle and were often quite critical of the internal combustion engine. Many people predicted that the entrepreneurs who had founded electric- and steam-powered vehicle companies would become very wealthy, and those who formed gasoline-powered vehicle companies were destined to bankruptcy. But, as you probably know, the reverse occurred. The founders of the companies that made gasoline-powered vehicles went on to great wealth, and the entrepreneurs who lead the steam- and electric-powered vehicle companies ended up on the dustbin of history.

So what happened? Convergence on the dominant design that we have been talking about. Although electric and steam vehicles had better technical performance than gasoline-powered vehicles, they weren't as good as gasoline-powered vehicles for touring. In the early 20th century, many North Americans discovered the joy of driving for the fun of it. Electric vehicles weren't great for touring because they had batteries that had to be recharged. If a person went touring in the wrong direction, there was no place to recharge the car battery. Steam-powered vehicles tended to break down a lot on the terrible roads of the day. When people went touring, they preferred gasoline-powered cars, as long as they remembered to bring extra gasoline. As more people began to tour in gasoline-powered cars, other entrepreneurs began to serve them by building gasoline stations so that they could refuel their cars. Over time, as more and more people began to use gasoline-powered cars, the alternative product designs became less and less popular. The makers of those types of cars ran into financial trouble and went out of business, until ultimately the only design of car that anyone drove was a gasoline-powered car. The moral of this story for entrepreneurs is that industries often converge on a dominant design; those firms that produce the dominant design tend to survive and grow while other firms tend to fail, even if all the experts thought that the other product designs were better than the dominant design.

to the new version of a company's products than to those produced by a competitor, the entrepreneur is better off entering the market quickly with an incomplete product than waiting until a completed product is available. Waiting too long lets customers adopt another product design as the technical standard and makes it very hard for the entrepreneur to break into the market later.

KEY POINTS

- Customers tend to follow a normal distribution in the adoption of new products and services, and can be divided into five groups, which adopt new products for different reasons: innovators, early adopters, early majority, late majority, and laggards.
- Entrepreneurs often find it difficult to transition from selling to the early adopters to selling to the early majority, a concept called "crossing the chasm," because the early majority have different needs and demands from innovators, most notably the desire for a whole solution to their problems.
- Successful entrepreneurs cross the chasm by building a complete solution to customer needs, by reducing the scope of their product offerings to focus on a single niche, and by communicating information about their solution to customers in a clear and effective way.
- Entrepreneurs consider the customer to choose the right segment to focus on initially, selecting those with the greatest need to buy as their initial target market.
- Many new products converge on a dominant design, or arrangement that all companies producing a product will choose, as the way of bringing together the different parts of the product. New companies are most successful if they are founded before an industry converges on a dominant design, which leads to competition on the basis of efficiency and scale economies.
- In many industries, products must conform to a technical standard, or an agreed-upon basis on which a product operates. Because having your product design adopted as the technical standard is beneficial, entrepreneurs often try to get their design adopted as the standard through price discounting, building relationships with the producers of complementary products, and by getting to market quickly.

THE MARKETING PROCESS IN A NEW COMPANY

Perhaps the two most important aspects of the marketing process in a new company are selling and pricing. Much as people like to say, "a product sells itself," most new products don't. Entrepreneurs have to know how to sell to others. Entrepreneurs also have to figure out how to price their new products or services if they want to introduce them successfully. Although there are certainly other aspects of the marketing process in a new company, these two dimensions are central to that activity, and probably account for most of the entrepreneur's marketing activity in the early days of the venture.

Personal Selling: The Central Component of Entrepreneurial Marketing

Personal selling is an effort by the entrepreneur to sell a product or service through direct interaction with customers. Although people often think of advertising, creating brand names, and building sales forces when they think of marketing, those aspects of marketing often occur relatively late in the life of a new venture. In the very beginning, most of the marketing effort by a new business consists of efforts by the entrepreneur to persuade customers to buy the new company's products or services (see Figure 10.9). For this reason, it is important for you to know what activities make people effective at selling.

LEARNING OBJECTIVE

12 Explain why personal selling is a very important part of entrepreneurs' marketing strategies.

Successful entrepreneurs understand that effective selling proceeds in the following way: First, the entrepreneur generates customer interest in the product or service. This interest is usually sparked by letting customers know that the entrepreneur has a product or service that will meet a need that they have. For example, suppose target customers are architects who want a better way to see what a building design will look like than constructing models out of mylar and foam. The entrepreneur can generate interest among target customers by letting them know that she has developed computer software that generates three-dimensional images of buildings. By explaining that she has a solution to the customer's need, the entrepreneur can generate customer interest.[31]

Second, the entrepreneur identifies the customer's requirements for purchasing a new product. In the architectural example we just discussed, is the customer computer savvy or does she also want manuals and a customer support hotline along with the architectural design software? By determining customer requirements, the entrepreneur can figure out what aspects of the new product or service offering will sell the customer. Knowing what the customer needs is a very important step in the sales process, and one that many people overlook. In their rush to persuade customers, entrepreneurs often forget to ask customers their requirements. As a result, they often tell customers about the wrong features of their products or services and hinder their ability to make sales.

The third step in the process is to overcome customer objections. Customers rarely purchase new products without challenging something that entrepreneurs tell them. To make the sale, entrepreneurs need to provide good answers to the objections and hesitations that customers have.[32] For example, architects might question whether the entrepreneur provides adequate customer support, whether the software can be linked to existing CAD/CAM software, or whether the product is easy to use. By providing explanations to these questions that customers feel are adequate and persuasive, the entrepreneur can make the customer feel comfortable enough to buy the new product or service.

The final step in the process is to close the sale. Many entrepreneurs often forget to close their sales, continuing to discuss the product until after the customer has expressed a conditional commitment to purchase.[33] As a result, they talk themselves out of a sale by making the customer feel that they are wasting their time. So how does the entrepreneur close a sale? When the customer has shown a conditional commitment to purchase, by indicating that they like the product or would like to have it, the entrepreneur should move to close the sale. Typically closing a sale involves asking closing questions, such as "Would you like to pay for that with a credit card or cash? Would you like to pick up the product or have us deliver it? Would you like one or two units?" These types of questions lead the discussion to its natural completion.

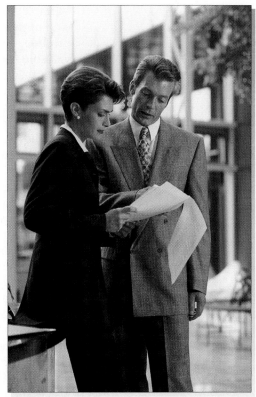

Digital Vision/Getty Images

Figure 10.9 Personal Selling Is Central to Successful Marketing by Entrepreneurs

Direct personal selling is the entrepreneur's most important marketing tool—more important than advertising, building a brand name, or other marketing devices used by larger and more established companies.

Pricing New Products: The Role of Cost Structure and Supply and Demand

Entrepreneurs must set a price for their new products. Setting a price involves several important steps. First, the entrepreneur must determine the costs of the product and set a price that is greater than cost. Otherwise, the entrepreneur will not make a profit. Many an entrepreneur has failed to set prices relative to costs and has gone out of business while selling up a storm.

To understand the costs, the entrepreneur must make sure to calculate both **fixed costs** and **variable costs**. Fixed costs are costs for items such as facilities and equipment that do not change with the number of units that they produce.

Variable costs are costs that are incurred on each unit that is produced, like a commission given to a salesperson or the cost of packaging for each shipped product. Although entrepreneurs are generally pretty good at estimating their variable costs, they often have trouble calculating the portion of their per unit costs that represent a share of the fixed cost. This difficulty occurs because the entrepreneur does not know how much volume will be produced. The more volume that the new venture produces, the lower the per unit portion of fixed costs. In fact, one of the reasons that many entrepreneurs fail is that they believe that they will produce a much larger volume than they actually do. As a result, the per unit portion of their fixed costs becomes very high, leading costs to exceed revenue.

Second, the entrepreneur needs to pay attention to the market conditions. Most products sell within a limited range that creates a floor and ceiling on prices. The entrepreneur must make sure that the products can be sold within that range. If the entrepreneur's costs are too high to price within the existing range for products, the business probably shouldn't be launched because it will have a hard time attracting customers.

But what about the totally new products we talked about earlier in the chapter? Even for these products, the entrepreneur probably doesn't want to price the product above the range of existing products or services on the market. Why? One reason is that there is really no such thing as a product without alternatives, and a reasonable price is necessary to encourage customers to switch from those alternatives to the new product. For example, when the telephone was first developed, people still had the alternative of using the telegraph or mail to communicate. Similarly, when e-mail was first introduced, people could still use fax machines and telephones to communicate. If the entrepreneurs who first launched these products had priced them much higher than the alternative products on the market, then customers would not have been willing switch to the new product. A second reason is the same one we offered earlier in the chapter when we were talking about technical standards. Whenever entrepreneurs would benefit from widespread adoption of their products—such as the case when the most popular product becomes the technical standard—it is a good idea to price the product at a reasonable level to encourage customers to buy it. By encouraging customer adoption, the low price generates the advantages that come from large sales volume. A third reason is, as we said earlier, that most truly new products perform much worse than existing alternatives when they are first introduced. If a new product performs worse than existing alternatives and is priced higher than those alternatives, then customers have no reason to try the new product.

Third, the entrepreneur must understand how customers trade off product attributes and price. Because no two products are exactly the same, customers are often willing to pay more for one product than for another. The price difference between the two products can be attributed to the different attributes of the two products. This comparison is relatively easy to do if two products are the same on all dimensions except one. But what if they have three different features—range, size, and brand name? Then assessing the price that each of these attributes represents is much more difficult. Entrepreneurs have a particularly difficult time accurately assessing the value of intangible attributes of competing products. For example, historically, business customers might be willing to pay more for an IBM computer because it is backed by the IBM brand name. Intangibles, such as customer service or brand name reputation, often account for differences in the price of otherwise similar products (see Figure 10.10).

Last, the entrepreneur must factor in hidden costs or discounts in pricing. For example, if a competitor offers a 2 percent discount to customers paying immediately, rather than in 90 days, this discount affects the net price. Similarly, if competitors generally offer credit to customers, then the cost of raising the capital to provide this credit needs to be factored into the price. In short, setting a price for a new product involves figuring out one's costs and not pricing below them, knowing what

© Reuters/CORBIS

© Reuters/CORBIS

alternative products sell for and not pricing above them, figuring out the value to customers of different product attributes and using that information to accurately price the components that your product has, and factoring in any hidden costs or discounts that come from credit terms.

Figure 10.10 Pricing Is an Important Part of Entrepreneurial Marketing

Entrepreneurs need to set an appropriate price for their new product or service; only the most foolish would try to sell a Kia sports car for the price of a Ferrari.

KEY POINTS

- Personal selling, or efforts to market a product or service to customers through direct interaction, is perhaps the most important marketing method available to entrepreneurs.
- Effective personal selling involves a process that begins with generating customer interest in the product or service, followed by identifying customer requirements, overcoming objections, and closing the sale.
- Entrepreneurs set the prices of their new products by considering several factors: their cost structure, the supply and demand conditions in the market in which they operate, customer trade-offs between product attributes and price, and hidden costs and discounts.

Summary and Review of Key Points

- Entrepreneurs are most successful when they start a company that meets a real need: either solving a customer problem that no product or service has yet solved, or being so much better at solving the problem than an existing product or service that customers are motivated to switch.

- Before launching a new venture, entrepreneurs need reliable marketing information—information on how potential customers will react to and evaluate the products or services they provide.

- Because people are not very successful at identifying the factors that influence their behaviour, simply asking them why they like or dislike various products is not an effective approach.

- Perceptual mapping, one technique for identifying the dimensions along which customers evaluate various products, is often a useful initial step.

- One useful procedure for gathering such information is focus groups—groups of about 8 to 12 people who are similar to potential customers and who meet for one to two hours to describe their perceptions of and reactions to relevant products.

- Conjoint analysis is a useful technique for determining the relative importance, in the customer's preferences and decisions, of the dimensions that they consider important.

- Through the effective use of conjoint analysis, entrepreneurs can design products that will have high appeal to potential customers, and so maximize the chances of success of their new ventures.

- In addition to gathering their own marketing information, entrepreneurs can also use indirect or secondary data, information gathered by others.

- When markets are new, entrepreneurs assess customer preferences differently from when markets are already established; entrepreneurs need to adopt the right assessment techniques for the type of market they are targeting.

- Although marketing data is often useful to entrepreneurs, gathering it is no guarantee of success, especially with respect to new products or services, because consumers may find comparing new products to existing products a difficult task, and unexpected uses for such products may quickly emerge.

- Entrepreneurs are more successful in large and growing markets because large markets amortize the fixed cost of getting started over a larger number of units, and because it is easier to sell in more rapidly growing markets.

- Entrepreneurs are better off targeting new markets than established markets because established firms face three obstacles in assessing new markets: core rigidities, the tyranny of the current market, and user myopia.

- The performance of new products follows an S-shape. Initially, a large amount of effort is required to achieve small improvements in performance. Then performance improvements accelerate with a small amount of effort, leading to large improvements in performance. Ultimately, a large amount of effort is again required to achieve small improvements in performance as the product confronts the law of diminishing returns.

- The product S-curve is important to entrepreneurs because new products begin with inferior performance to existing products, requiring entrepreneurs to obtain a source of capital to keep their ventures alive as they improve new product performance. The S-curve also shows that the improvement in new products is a function of effort, not time. Finally, it demonstrates the importance of timing organizing activities to the acceleration of the S-curve.

- Established companies rarely compete with entrepreneurs to develop new products on the early part of the S-curve because the new product generally begins with inferior performance to the established company's existing products, and because the managers of established firms often believe that they could always improve the performance of their existing products to compete with new products.

- Customers tend to follow a normal distribution in the adoption of new products and services, and can be divided into five groups, which adopt new products for different reasons: innovators, early adopters, early majority, late majority, and laggards.

- Entrepreneurs often find it difficult to transition from selling to the early adopters to selling to the early majority, a concept called "crossing the chasm," because the early majority have different needs and demands from innovators, most notably the desire for a whole solution to their problems.

- Successful entrepreneurs cross the chasm by building a complete solution to customer needs, by reducing the scope of their product offerings to focus on a single niche, and by communicating information about their solution to customers in a clear and effective way.

- Entrepreneurs consider the customer to choose the right segment to focus on initially, selecting those with the greatest need to buy as their initial target market.

- Many new products converge on a dominant design or arrangement that all companies producing a product will choose as the way of bringing together the different parts of the product. New companies are most successful if they are founded before an industry converges on a dominant design, which leads to competition on the basis of efficiency and scale economies.
- In many industries, products must conform to a technical standard, or an agreed-upon basis on which a product operates. Because having your product design adopted as the technical standard is beneficial, entrepreneurs often try to get their design adopted as the standard through price discounting, building relationships with the producers of complementary products, and by getting to market quickly.
- Personal selling, or efforts to market a product or service to customers through direct interaction, is perhaps the most important marketing method available to entrepreneurs.
- Effective personal selling involves a process that begins with generating customer interest in the product or service, followed by identifying customer requirements, overcoming objections, and closing the sale.
- Entrepreneurs set the prices of their new products by considering several factors: their cost structure, the supply and demand conditions in the market in which they operate, customer trade-offs between product attributes and price, and hidden costs and discounts.

Glossary

Complementary Products: Complementary products are products that work together, such as DVDs and DVD players, or computer hardware and computer software.

Conjoint Analysis: A technique for determining the relative importance of various dimensions in customers' evaluations of specific products.

Core Rigidities: The fact that companies tend to do well at things that they are accustomed to doing, not things that are new.

Dominant Design: A common approach or standard to making a product on which firms in an industry have converged; for example, many software companies design their products to operate with Microsoft Windows.

Fixed Costs: Costs of items such as facilities and equipment that do not change with the number of units sold.

Focus Groups: Groups of 8 to 12 people who are similar to potential customers and who meet for one to two hours to describe their perceptions of and reactions to relevant products.

Perceptual Mapping: A technique for identifying the key dimensions along which potential customers evaluate products.

Personal Selling: An effort by an entrepreneur to sell a product or service through direct interaction with customers.

S-Curve: A graphical depiction of the typical pattern of performance improvement of new products or services as a function of the amount of effort put into them.

Technical Standard: An agreed-upon basis on which a product or service operates.

Tyranny of the Current Market: The fact that listening to customers will make it difficult for companies to come up with new products for new markets because a firm's current customers will always ask for improvements to current products, not new products for new markets.

User Myopia: The fact that customers can only see very narrow needs or solutions, typically only their own needs, not those of other market segments.

Variable Costs: Costs incurred for each unit that is sold.

Discussion Questions

1. The most straightforward way to obtain information on how potential customers will react to a new product is simply to ask them. Why is this method sometimes misleading?

2. In this chapter, we noted that marketing information, even if it is excellent in every respect, is no guarantee of success. Why is this so? Is there any kind of information that could guarantee success for new ventures?

3. Think of some new products or services. Is there a real need for them? Why or why not? Try to rank order the new products or services that you came up with. For which ones is the need greater than the others? Why?

4. Suppose that you have an idea for a new service—one that will help couples plan their wedding. How could you use perceptual mapping to decide which kind of information and help would be most attractive to potential customers?

5. Assume that you have an idea for developing a business to create a new communication device to replace e-mail. How should you assess customer needs for the product? How would your assessment process differ from the one that you'd use if you were developing a business to create a new breakfast cereal?

6. Suppose you've developed a new product or service and the market size today is only $100,000.

Should you pursue the new product or service? Why or why not?

7. Assume that you've just started a new company to sell Reading Week trips to Fort Lauderdale. What should you to do to market your product and make your first sales?

8. Suppose you've developed a new computer software package for inventory management. You've made some initial sales to innovators and early adopters. How are you going to make sales to the early majority of customers?

InfoTrac Exercises

1. **Early Adopters: Geeks or Pioneers?** (full disclosure) (how to buy cutting-edge technology products) (Column)

   Stephen Manes

   PC World, May 2003 v21 i5 p170(1)

   Record: A99910443

   Full Text: COPYRIGHT 2003 PC World Communications, Inc.

   1. According to the text, why do early adopters tend to adopt new products?

   2. According to the article, what distinguishes smart early adopters from "hapless geeks who overpay for new but inadequate products"?

   3. What price do early adopters sometimes have to pay for their product choices?

2. **The Internet and Personal Selling**

   Paul N. Romani

   American Salesman, March 2003 v48 i3 p3(8)

   Record: A98265212

Full Text: COPYRIGHT 2003 National Research Bureau

   1. According to the text, what role does personal selling play in entrepreneurial marketing?

   2. Based on your reading of the article, do you think that the Internet can take the place of personal selling for an entrepreneur? Why or why not?

   3. Why did eToys fail as a new online venture?

3. **Forget Focus Groups: Just Watch Users, Innovator Says** (news)

   Tom Kelley, product innovator, IDEO Product Development Inc.)

   Machine Design, March 20, 2003 v75 i6 p28(1)

   Record: A99378451

   Full Text: COPYRIGHT 2003 Penton Media, Inc.

   1. According to the text, what role do focus groups play in innovation?

   2. According to Tom Kelly, what is the value of focus groups in product innovation?

   3. What approach does Kelly take to innovation?

GETTING DOWN
TO BUSINESS

Identifying a Real Need for a New Product or Service

In this chapter, we discussed the importance of identifying a product or service that meets a real customer need. This exercise will help you to develop a product or service that meets a customer need. Please follow these steps to complete the exercise.

Step One: In one paragraph, describe the new product or service that your business will create.

Step Two: List the features that your product or service will have (consider things like price, size, weight, and so on).

1.

2.

3.

4.

5.

Step Three: Specify how you will collect information from customers about their needs. Will you observe customers? Will you conduct focus groups? Will you conduct interviews? Will you distribute surveys?

Step Four: Collect information from customers about their needs, following the methodology you said that you would follow in step 2.

Step Five: Match customer needs to the features of your product or service. Does your product or service have attributes that meet the needs of the customer? If yes, explain why. If not, consider how you will modify the product or service to meet the needs of customers.

Step Six: Describe the optimal combination of features that customers want in your product or service. Use conjoint analysis, if you want. Otherwise, simply consider which features are particularly important to customers and make sure that those features are included in your product or service.

Developing a Marketing Plan

As this chapter explained, entrepreneurs need to develop plans to estimate market size and to convince potential customers to adopt their new products or services. To help you create a marketing plan for your new venture, we have designed this exercise. Please follow these steps:

Step One: Gather data on sales of similar products or services in your market over the past five years. Plot these data over time. Describe the shape of demand growth in your market over time. Use this information to project demand over the next five years. Estimate the size of your market over the next five years.

Step Two: Identify the market niche you will focus on. Explain how you will choose your customers. Make sure to explain why customers have a compelling reason to buy.

Step Three: Identify the early adopters of your product or service. Explain why this segment of the market will adopt. Make sure to match the needs of early adopters to the characteristics of your product in explaining why the initial segment of the market will adopt your product or service. Also be sure to include any evidence from your customer feedback that explains why the features of your product or service will lead initial customers to adopt.

Step Four: Explain how your new venture will transition to mainstream customers. Explain what your venture will do to attract mainstream customers. How will you advertise and promote your product or service? What support will you provide along with your product or service? How will you achieve market leadership?

Step Five: Estimate the number of customers that your venture will attract over the next five years, and project your new venture's sales growth. Remember to consider the typical S-shaped curve of customer adoption. In addition, estimate the amount of resources that you will need to invest to attract customers over the next five years.

Step Six: Gather information on the share of the market held by the top three competitors, and use this information to calculate your projected market share over the next five years.

Learning to Sell

As we explained in this chapter, much of successful marketing in a new business involves personal selling. If you want to be a successful entrepreneur, you'll need to learn how to sell. This exercise will help you practise learning how to sell.

Step One: Find a partner in the class. The two of you will alternate being the customer and the salesperson.

Step Two: Identify a list of 10 things that you will try to sell (for example, a baseball cap, a car, tickets to Reading Week in Fort Lauderdale, and so on). Each of you will take five of these and try to sell them to the other.

Step Three: Try to sell your partner on the first object. Start by generating customer interest in the product or service. As we indicated earlier in the chapter, interest is usually created by letting customers know that you have a product or service that will meet a need that they have.

Next, identify the customer's requirements for purchasing a new product. By determining customer requirements, you can determine which aspects of the new product or service offering will sell your partner. Remember to ask your customers about their requirements.

The third step in the process is to overcome your customer's objections. Customers rarely purchase new products without challenging something that entrepreneurs tell them. To make the sale, you'll need to provide good answers to your partner's objections and hesitations.

The final step in the process is to close the sale. When your customer has shown a conditional commitment to purchase by indicating an affinity for the product or a desire to own it, move to close the sale. Typically, concluding a sale involves asking closing questions, such as "Would you like to pay for that with a credit card or cash? Would you like to pick up the product or have us deliver it? Would you like one or two units?"

Enhanced Learning

You may select any combination of the resources below to enhance your understanding of the chapter material.

- **Appendix: Case Studies** – Twelve cases provide opportunities to apply chapter concepts to realistic entrepreneurial situations. These brief cases call for careful analysis of real business problems and ask you to think about potential solutions.
- **Video Case Library** – Nine cases are tied directly to video segments from the popular PBS television series Small Business School. These cases and video segments (available on the Entrepreneurship website at http://www.entrepreneurship.nelson.com) give you unparalleled access to today's entrepreneurs, with expert advice and insights on how to start, run, and grow a business.
- **Management Interview Series Video Database** – This video interview series contains a wealth of tips on how to manage effectively. Access to the database and practical exercises are available on the book support website at http://www.entrepreneurship.nelson.com.

Notes

1. LeBrasseur, R., & Zinger, T. 2005. Start-up survival and management capability: A longitudinal analysis of micro-enterprises. *Journal of Small Business & Entrepreneurship* 18(4): 409–422.

2. Spence, R. 2005. Profit 100 profiles: The fastest five. *Profit Magazine* 24(3): 49–59.

3. Wesson, T., & DeFigueiredo, J.N. 2001. The importance of focus to market entrants: A study of microbrewery performance. *Journal of Business Venturing* 16(4): 377–403.

4. Knott, A.M. 2002. *Venture design*. Philadelphia: Entity Press.

5. Baumeister, R.F. (1998). The self. In D.T. Gilbert, S.T., Fiske, & G. Lindzey (eds.). *Handbook of social psychology* 4th ed., vol. 1 (pp. 680–740). New York: McGraw-Hill.

6. Green, P., & Rao, V. 1971. Conjoint measurement for quantifying judgmental data. *Journal of Marketing Research* 8(3): 355–363.

7. Macht, J. D. 1998. The new market research. Inc. 20(10): 86–93.

8. Barton, D. 1994. *Commercializing technology: Imaginative understanding of user needs*. Harvard Business School Note 9-694-102.

9. Warren, S. 2002. When grown-ups go for Silly Putty they do it in a big way. *The Wall Street Journal*, September 11: A1, 9

10. Barton, D. 1994. *Commercializing technology: Imaginative understanding of user needs*. Harvard Business School Note 9-694-102.

11. Ibid.

12. Foster, R. 1986. *Innovation: The attacker's advantage*. New York: Summit Books.

13. Ibid.

14. Ibid.

15. Rogers, E. 1983. *Diffusion of innovations*. New York: Free Press.

16. Ibid.

17. Moore, G. 1991. *Crossing the chasm*. New York: Harper Collins.

18. Rogers, E. 1983. *Diffusion of innovations*. New York: Free Press.

19. Moore, G. 1991. *Crossing the chasm*. New York: Harper Collins.

20. Ibid.

21. Ibid.

22. Ibid.

23. Pearson, K. 2005. How COLD-fX got so hot. *Profit Magazine* 24(5): 46–48.

24. Utterback, J. 1994. *Mastering the dynamics of innovation*. Cambridge: Harvard Business School Press.

25. Tushman, M., & Anderson, P. 1986. Technological disconti-nuities and organizational environments. *Administrative Science Quarterly* 31(3): 439–465.

26. Utterback, J. 1994. *Mastering the dynamics of innovation*. Cambridge: Harvard Business School Press.

27. Arthur, B. 1996. Increasing returns and the new world of business. *Harvard Business Review* 74(4): 100–109.

28. Cusumano, M., Mylonadis, Y., & Rosenbloom, R, 1992. Strategic maneuvering and mass market dynamics: The triumph of VHS over beta. *Business History Review* 66(1): 51–94.

29. Kirsch, D. 2000. *Electric vehicles and the burden of history*. New Brunswick, NJ: Rutgers University Press.

30. Arthur, B. 1996. Increasing returns and the new world of business. *Harvard Business Review* 74(4): 100–109.

31. Bhide, A. *Selling as a systematic process*. Harvard Business School Note 9-935-091.

32. Ibid.

33. Ibid.

CHAPTER 11

STRATEGY: PLANNING FOR COMPETITIVE ADVANTAGE

LEARNING OBJECTIVES

After reading this chapter, you should be able to:

1 Define a competitive advantage and explain why an entrepreneur needs to have one to be successful.

2 Describe a new firm strategy and explain why entrepreneurs need one to protect their profits from opportunity exploitation.

3 Distinguish between efforts to keep others from learning about or understanding the business idea and barriers to imitation, and explain why both are important to entrepreneurs.

4 Define Arrow's paradox and explain the problem of disclosure.

5 List several barriers to imitation that entrepreneurs use.

6 Identify the conditions that favour franchising from the point of view of both the entrepreneur with an opportunity to exploit and potential franchisees.

7 Describe the strategic actions that entrepreneurs take to manage information asymmetry and uncertainty in the entrepreneurial process.

8 Explain why entrepreneurs often start their businesses on a small scale and expand if they are successful.

9 Explain how alliances and partnerships with established firms help entrepreneurs to exploit their opportunities.

10 List actions that entrepreneurs undertake to make their new ventures appear more legitimate, and explain why they take these actions.

All photos this page © PhotoDisc, Inc.

> "What sets us against one another is not our aims—they all come to the same thing—but our methods, which are the fruit of our varied reasoning." (Saint-Exupery, *Wind, Sand and Stars*, 1939)

Entrepreneurs develop business ideas to sell something that meets a market need and to introduce that product or service successfully into the mainstream market. However, just satisfying a market need does not mean that an entrepreneur will earn a profit. To make money, the entrepreneur also needs to develop a strategy that protects the business idea against competition. This chapter focuses on the entrepreneur's strategy.

What makes a strategy effective in protecting a business idea against competition? Existing evidence suggests that the answer involves two key types of action: (1) precluding others from gaining access to or understanding information about how to exploit the opportunity; and (2) creating barriers to the exploitation of the opportunity by others, even if they have access to information about the opportunity and understand how to exploit it.[1]

Robert Baron certainly used both of these types of strategic action when he developed the air filtration product that we discussed in Chapter 1. How did he preclude others from gaining access to or understanding information about the opportunity? He kept that information secret (see Figure 11.1). By not describing to other people where the information that triggered his recognition of the opportunity came from—the problem in his daughter's dorm room, details of his research about how the physical environment affects human behaviour, and his conversations with companies where he had worked— Baron minimized the chance that others would gain access to the information that led him to learn of the opportunity. Furthermore, he kept others from understanding how to exploit the opportunity by

making sure that he did not show other entrepreneurs or established companies, such as the manufacturers of existing air filters, how to design and manufacture a product that simultaneously filtered the air, reduced noise, and released fragrance.

How did Baron create barriers that would keep others from exploiting the opportunity in the same way that he did? By obtaining a patent on the Personal Privacy System (PPS) technology, Baron created a legal barrier that stopped others from imitating his approach to exploiting the opportunity. Even if air filter manufacturers had access to the same information that led Baron to recognize the opportunity, and even if they understood exactly how to design and manufacture the PPS product, the patent provided a legal barrier that kept the air filter manufacturers from acting. By adopting this two-part strategy, Baron protected the profits that his business idea generated against competition by others.

Figure 11.1 Entrepreneurs Should Keep Their Approaches to Exploiting Opportunities Secret

Entrepreneurs will run into problems if they talk too much about their opportunity and their plan to exploit it.

"These dreams of yours wherein you find great tubs of money, Mr. Croy—can you describe the spot a little more exactly?"

© The New Yorker Collection 1939 Garrett Price from cartoonbank.com. All Rights Reserved.

The remainder of this chapter expands on the basic ideas behind entrepreneurial strategy. The first section discusses why new firms need a **competitive advantage** to exploit an entrepreneurial opportunity successfully. A competitive advantage is an attribute that allows a firm, and not its competitors, to capture the profits from exploiting an opportunity. Even though the typical new business has no competitive advantage, you want your new venture to have one. Why? The typical entrepreneurial effort lasts less than three years, never generates a profit, and is abandoned, or ends in bankruptcy.[2] So if you want to have a successful new business rather than a typical new business, you will need a competitive advantage.

The second section will return to the theme that we started to discuss at the beginning of the chapter. We will describe how the entrepreneur precludes others from gaining access to information about the opportunity and understanding how to exploit it, as well as how the entrepreneur creates barriers to the exploitation of the opportunity by others, even if they know about the opportunity and how to develop it.

LEARNING OBJECTIVE

1 Define a competitive advantage and explain why an entrepreneur needs to have one to be successful.

The third section will discuss the organizational form that new ventures take. Although people usually think that entrepreneurs exploit opportunities by founding firms that own and operate all parts of the value chain, entrepreneurs often exploit opportunities by licensing their business ideas to others. Even when they found firms, entrepreneurs frequently rely on market-oriented modes of exploitation, such as franchising, or develop only part of the value chain, contracting with other firms to provide the rest. We will explain when entrepreneurs should choose market-oriented modes of exploitation, such as franchising and licensing, and when they are better off owning all parts of the value chain.

The last section of the chapter will discuss the strategies that entrepreneurs use to overcome the information asymmetry and uncertainty that are fundamental to the entrepreneurial process. People can never know for sure that their business idea will be successful until after they have exploited an opportunity, making the entrepreneur's pursuit of opportunity uncertain. To overcome the difficulties that uncertainty and information asymmetry generate in the pursuit of opportunity, entrepreneurs undertake several strategies that we discuss in the last section of the chapter.

COMPETITIVE ADVANTAGE: AN ESSENTIAL INGREDIENT

In Chapter 1, we explained that the entrepreneurial process begins when the entrepreneur comes up with a business idea or way to exploit an opportunity. In Chapter 2, we pointed out that entrepreneurs typically devise these business ideas because they have access to better information about the opportunity or are better able to recognize the opportunity from the information that they have. As a way to exploit their business ideas, entrepreneurs develop new products and services that customers value. This chapter focuses on ways to protect the value that the company derives from providing customers with valuable products and services.

At the very beginning of the process, no one else will have exactly the same business idea as the entrepreneur; the entrepreneur has a **monopoly** on it. A monopoly is a situation in which a firm is the only supplier of a product or service. For example, suppose that you have identified an opportunity to put a club on the edge of campus because there is no place to listen to music or dance near school. At the beginning, your club will be the only business satisfying the demand for a place in which to listen to music and dance.

What happens after you open your club? Nothing—if you are wrong about the opportunity. If there is no demand to listen to music and dance, or if you can't make a profit because you can't get a liquor licence or because the bands cost too much to book, then your club will go under, and that will be the end of the story. But what if your club is successful and you start making money? People will imitate your business idea. Your roommates, your classmates, and the owner of the local pizzeria will learn that the idea for a club is profitable. Because they, too, would like to earn profits, they might enter the market and set up clubs with the same design and the same music as your club, and close by, too.

Left unchecked, these imitators will erode your profit from exploiting the opportunity. The imitators will try to acquire the resources needed to exploit the club business idea, driving up the costs of those resources, and undermining profits. Now instead of booking a band cheaply because yours was the only gig in town, you have to outbid the other three club owners for music talent. The imitators will also target your customers by cutting the cover, offering free drinks or free food, driving down your revenues and, consequently, your profits. This process of competition will continue until there are no profits left from the exploitation of the club opportunity.

Not only can't you stop people from trying to imitate good business ideas, but also by starting a successful business you actually help them. The very act of pursuing a business idea provides other people—both individual entrepreneurs and existing companies—with the information that they need to develop a business idea that successfully exploits the same one that you have identified. In our club example, for instance, you showed the others where to put their clubs and which bands to book by operating your club.

To keep imitators from taking away the profits that you earned from coming up with a business idea that satisfies the needs of customers, you must develop a competitive advantage that deters imitation. If you can keep the information about the opportunity and how to exploit it from leaking out completely, then others will be unable to imitate your business idea completely. Similarly, if you can create some barrier that precludes others from taking action to exploit the opportunity in the same way that you did, you can also deter imitation.

In the club example, suppose that you signed an exclusive contract with all of the really good local bands. Because those bands would only play in your club, and not in the three other clubs on the edge of campus, you would have a competitive advantage. As long as people want to hear specific bands, you would have a barrier to imitation of your business idea. If the imitators can't copy your business idea completely, and that idea generates a profit, then the profits from exploiting the opportunity will remain with you.

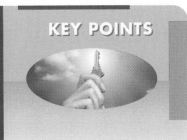

KEY POINTS

- The identification of a business opportunity that satisfies the needs of customers is not enough for an entrepreneur to earn profits; the entrepreneur also needs a competitive advantage.
- The exploitation of an opportunity will provide information to others about how to imitate the entrepreneur's business idea; imitation by others will erode the entrepreneur's profit from exploiting the opportunity.
- By developing a competitive advantage, the entrepreneur precludes others from imitating the business idea perfectly, and allows the entrepreneur to capture the profits from exploiting the opportunity.

STRATEGY: PROTECTING PROFITS FROM THE EXPLOITATION OF OPPORTUNITY

In general, entrepreneurs retain the profits from their exploitation of opportunities in two ways. First, they keep others from learning about their opportunities or understanding their business ideas for exploiting those opportunities. Entrepreneurs do this by keeping secret the information that allowed them to discover the opportunity, and by making it difficult for others to understand their methods of exploitation. Second, entrepreneurs use three types of barriers to block others from exploiting the opportunity in the same way that they do, even if the others have learned about the opportunity and understand how to exploit it: controlling resources, building a reputation for satisfying customers, and by innovating to stay ahead of competitors.[3] This section will discuss these methods for protecting a business idea against competition.

Secrecy: Keeping Others from Learning about or Understanding How to Exploit the Opportunity

Stopping others from acquiring the information that allows an entrepreneur to identify an opportunity sometimes involves keeping that information secret. For example, suppose you learned that most university students wanted to go to Cancun

LEARNING OBJECTIVE

2 Describe a new firm strategy and explain why entrepreneurs need one to protect their profits from opportunity exploitation.

LEARNING OBJECTIVE

3 Distinguish between efforts to keep others from learning about or understanding the business idea and barriers to imitation, and explain why both are important to entrepreneurs.

instead of Fort Lauderdale during Reading Week. If you were planning to start a charter travel business that sold Reading Week package tours, you might not want to share this information about the preferences of your market with others. If other people didn't know that the hot destination for Reading Week was Cancun, and not Fort Lauderdale, then they wouldn't recognize that the key to the opportunity would lie in booking hotel rooms in Cancun, and wouldn't compete with you to gain access to the necessary resources (the beachfront rooms) to exploit the opportunity.

Because the goal of keeping information about the opportunity secret is to keep others from learning that the opportunity exists, this strategy works best when there are few ways of getting the information about the opportunity other than from talking to the entrepreneur. As you probably suspected, the Reading Week example is a tough one to protect just by keeping the information about the discovery of the opportunity secret. Too many people could obtain access to information about this opportunity from sources other than you. So even if you keep the information a secret, potential competitors could still get access to this information independently and exploit the opportunity in the same way that you do.

When are there few ways to get information about the opportunity other than from the first person to identify it? In general, when identification of the opportunity requires knowledge of a new and complex process that the entrepreneur retains as a **trade secret** (see Chapter 7), other people find it difficult to gain access to the information necessary to identify the opportunity on their own. Sometimes people discover a new process for making something that other people haven't yet figured out. For example, suppose that you were working in the chemistry lab on campus and you figured out how to combine several chemicals into a formula that tripled the speed at which grass grew. You might want to start a fertilizer company to exploit your discovery. If you did, you would probably want to avoid telling other people that you had discovered this new formula for fertilizer. If other people didn't know that the new formula existed, then they wouldn't go looking for it. As a result, they wouldn't know that there was an opportunity to use the formula to produce fertilizer, and they wouldn't compete with your new fertilizer company.

The entrepreneur can also keep others from imitating the business idea if they can keep others from understanding how to exploit the opportunity, even if they have learned that the opportunity exists. Strategic management researchers call this concept **causal ambiguity** because other people do not understand the causal process that allows the entrepreneur to exploit the opportunity.[4] For example, suppose that you and everyone else in your dorm know that the people in the town where your university is located really like fruit pie. The townies' preference for fruit pie creates demand conditions that make it possible for you to start a company to sell fruit pies (remember that in Chapter 2 we explained that demand conditions influence opportunities for new businesses). If the whole dorm knows that people in the town like pie, then the information about the opportunity is not a secret. You can't stop other people from imitating your business idea simply by keeping the information about the opportunity secret.

However, what if your grandmother gave you really great recipes for making pie—recipes so great that no other pie ever tastes as good as hers? Then you could exploit causal ambiguity to keep other people from learning how to exploit this business opportunity in the same way that you do. You could start a business making pie for the people in town, using your grandma's recipes. Even though the other people in your dorm know about the opportunity—the demand for pie in the town—they would not know how to exploit that opportunity—your grandmother's recipes. As a result, you could exploit the opportunity without losing out to competition from them.

An entrepreneur's ability to keep others from understanding an opportunity usually involves some type of **tacit knowledge**. Tacit knowledge is knowledge about how to do something that is not written down, or codified. People know what they do, but not why or how they do it. That's related to tacit knowledge. For instance, you probably know how to swim. If you do, we suspect that your knowledge is tacit. Unless you are really strange, you probably don't refer to written instructions on how to do the crawl each time you go swimming. In fact, if someone asked you to explain how to swim, you probably wouldn't even be able to explain the exact steps that you follow. Why? As we explained in Chapter 3, your knowledge about how to swim is tacit and is held in procedural memory (see Figure 11.2).

Many aspects of business are tacit. A good engineer might know how to operate a manufacturing plant, but not be able to give you step-by-step instructions on how to do it. A successful salesperson might know how to make a sale, but not be able to write a sales guide. Even the pie recipe example points out the value of tacit knowledge. Grandma's recipes are codified knowledge, or knowledge that is written down in documentary form. But when your grandmother makes pie, she might also exploit tacit knowledge, knowledge of things that she does that aren't actually written in the recipe. These things make her version of the pie taste better than when you follow the same recipe that she follows.

Tacit knowledge is better than codified knowledge for creating causal ambiguity about how to exploit an opportunity. When knowledge is codified in, say, a recipe for pie, anyone who wants to imitate the entrepreneur can do so by getting hold of the recipe. Although it may be more difficult to get hold of the recipe than to figure out that the opportunity exists, it is still not as easy as figuring out how your grandmother makes such great pie when the secret isn't written in the recipe.

When an entrepreneur has tacit knowledge about how to exploit an opportunity, other people have difficulty figuring out the causal relationships that drive the processes that the entrepreneur uses to produce, distribute, and organize.[5] Unless others can get inside the entrepreneur's head, they just can't figure out what those key production, distribution, and organizational processes are. If other people can't figure out the entrepreneur's processes, they can't imitate them, which protects the entrepreneur's profits against imitation. For example, suppose that key to the successful exploitation of an opportunity to market a line of upscale yoga clothing lies in an entrepreneur's tacit knowledge about what image will sell. Even if other people started companies to sell yoga clothes, the entrepreneur would still be able to retain the profits from the opportunity if other people are not able to imitate the entrepreneur's tacit knowledge about establishing an image.

The use of causal ambiguity to keep other people from imitating a business idea is particularly effective when the tacit knowledge that the new venture is exploiting is based on rare skills or experience.[6] If large numbers of people have the skills or experience to exploit the opportunity, then some of them will probably figure out how to exploit it, even if the entrepreneur keeps the tacit knowledge secret. However, if only a small number of people have the skills or experience to exploit a particular opportunity, an entrepreneur will be able to keep others from imitating just by keeping the tacit knowledge secret.

For a discussion of another potential problem that comes from not keeping knowledge of a business idea secret that can be especially dangerous for entrepreneurs, please see the **Danger! Pitfall Ahead!** section.

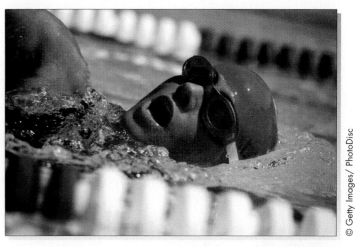

Figure 11.2 Tacit Knowledge Helps Entrepreneurs to Deter Imitation Even When Others Are Aware of the Opportunity

Much like swimming, exploiting opportunities involves tacit knowledge. Many entrepreneurs successfully keep others from imitating their business ideas by making use of tacit knowledge.

© Getty Images/ PhotoDisc

LEARNING OBJECTIVE

4 Define Arrow's paradox and explain the problem of disclosure.

Establishing Barriers to Imitation

Often, other people can imitate an entrepreneur's business idea once the entrepreneur has begun to exploit it because the entrepreneur either cannot keep the information about the opportunity secret or cannot create causal ambiguity about the way the idea is exploited. If secrecy is not a viable strategy to prevent imitation, the entrepreneur can keep others from profiting from the opportunity by creating barriers to imitation of the method of exploiting it.[8] Creating barriers to imitation is also useful,

LEARNING OBJECTIVE

5 List several barriers to imitation that entrepreneurs use.

even if the entrepreneur is trying to keep secret knowledge of the opportunity or how to exploit it. Even when people try to maintain secrecy, that secrecy is often breached; others can learn even tacit knowledge. Therefore, entrepreneurs establish three types of barriers to competition: obtaining control of the resources needed to exploit the opportunity, developing a reputation and brand name, and innovating to stay ahead of the competition (see Table 11.1).[9]

DANGER! PITFALL AHEAD!

Arrow's Paradox: The Problem of Disclosure

We just stressed the importance of keeping secret your opportunity and knowledge about how to exploit it. Although that may seem easy to do, it really isn't.

Suppose that you have come up with a great new design for a new windshield wiper, and have tested it out with several different people. They all love your new wipers, which work much better than other windshield wipers and only cost half as much to produce.

You know that you need to talk to potential customers about the wipers, so you send a letter to the major automakers telling them that you have developed a great new set of windshield wipers. One day you get a call back from the folks at one of the companies, who tell you that they'd like you to come in and talk to them. On the phone, the manager is really positive, telling you that your wiper design sounds like just the thing they have been looking for, and that they would like to buy it from you. They just need to learn a little more about the wipers. So you set up a meeting.

When you get to the meeting, a junior staffer ushers you into a huge oak-panelled conference room where seven or eight people are around the table waiting for you. Everyone is very excited to hear about your new windshield wipers.

The people at the company ask to see the prototype of your windshield wipers because they want to get a sense of what they look like. They ask you how you designed the windshield wipers because they want to make sure that the design is compatible with their vehicles. They ask you what materials you used, and how much time it took to produce the wipers because they want to make sure that the process is as good as they imagine. All the while, they keep telling you that they love your windshield wipers, and that there is going to be a big cheque in the works for you. Because you want the sale, you answer all of their questions.

At the end of the meeting, they thank you and tell you that they will be in touch soon. But a few weeks pass and you hear nothing. You call to follow up, leaving voice mails, which elicit no response. You try to reach the people in the meeting, but you get shunted off to a secretary. Finally, you realize that they are never going to buy your windshield wiper design.

What happened? You have fallen victim to Arrow's paradox.[7] Kenneth Arrow, a Nobel prize–winning economist at Stanford University, explained that disclosing knowledge is a paradox. A buyer will never buy a piece of knowledge, such as a design for a new windshield wiper, if its value is unknown. So to sell a piece of knowledge, its value has to be demonstrated. However, demonstration transfers the knowledge to someone else, and undermines the buyer's incentive to pay for it. So once demonstration has occurred, the buyer won't pay for the knowledge. Although there are a few solutions to this problem, such as patenting the technology that your business idea is based on, or getting people to sign a nondisclosure agreement— an agreement that those people you describe your idea to won't disclose it to anyone else—the problem cannot be eliminated. So we want you to pay attention to it. Many people will try to get you to disclose your business idea to them so that they can use it to exploit the opportunity that you have discovered. So please be careful. Keeping information about your opportunity and how to exploit it secret is harder than it looks.

Obtaining Control of Resources

An entrepreneur can build a barrier to competition by gaining control over the key resources that are required to exploit the opportunity.[10] For example, suppose that you came up with a business idea to sell food at sporting events on your campus. Every university has a limited number of arenas and stadiums in which the sporting events take place. If you signed a contract to lease all of the food service space—the

TYPE OF BARRIER	EXAMPLE	REASONING BEHIND WHY THE BARRIER WORKS
Control of resources	A biotech company obtaining a patent on a formula for a cold remedy	The patent legally precludes others from selling a cold remedy with the same formula
Reputation and Brand	An Internet grocer developing a reputation for delivering outstanding fresh fruit and vegetables	The reputation keeps customers from defecting to your competition
Innovation	A graphics chip manufacturer achieving two product cycles per year	To keep up with you, competitors need ongoing access to customer needs, and state-of-the-art personnel and R&D facilities to meet those needs.

Table 11.1 Entrepreneurs Deter Imitation by Building Barriers to Competition

Entrepreneurs establish several different types of barriers to competition.

key resource for exploiting this opportunity—in all of the arenas and stadiums on campus, you would be able to stop other people from exploiting the same opportunity as you.

In addition to contracting with resource providers to obtain control over key resources, you could just purchase the source of supply of that resource. This strategy would make the most sense if your opportunity depended on a key resource with a limited source of supply. Suppose, for example, that you were going to build a business selling diamond rings, like the South African company, De Beers. High-quality diamond gems can be found in only a few diamond mines in the world. By purchasing these mines, you would effectively preclude everyone else from gaining access to the gem-quality diamonds used in jewellery, just as DeBeers has done.

Sometimes entrepreneurs gain control over a resource by obtaining a legal monopoly on the process used to exploit the opportunity. For example, as discussed previously, a **patent** is an exclusive right given by the government to preclude others from duplicating an invention for a specified period of time. A permit, such as a taxi licence, gives you rights to carry out an activity in a particular geographic area and blocks others from carrying out that same activity. Some shopping centres give their tenants exusive rights to sell a particular category of goods.[11]

Establishing a Reputation and Brand Name

Entrepreneurs also create a second barrier to competition, the establishment of a favourable reputation and brand. By creating goodwill among customers, an entrepreneur can keep customers from shifting their allegiance to other firms, and thus keep the profit gained from exploiting the opportunity to themselves. For example, suppose that you developed a new type of mountain bike, and everyone agreed that your mountain bike was really excellent and wanted to buy it. The big problem for you would be that other people could imitate your mountain bike design and compete for a share of the mountain biking market and your profits. You might be able to keep customers from going to any of your competitors who imitated the design of your bike if you developed a reputation for excellent customer service and a strong brand name. These can provide a competitive advantage for your mountain bike company and allow you to preserve profits against the efforts of competitors to take them away.

One tactic is particularly useful in developing a reputation as a barrier to competition. The entrepreneur can advertise heavily to promote the attributes of a new product or service to customers. This advertising creates customer expectations about the attributes of a product or service. If imitators can't or don't copy all of these attributes, the advertising makes customers reluctant to switch to the competitors' product or service, reducing competition from other firms.

Innovation

A third barrier to competition used by entrepreneurs is innovation. Innovation involves any effort to keep the entrepreneur's product or service ahead of the alternatives offered by competitors on any dimension desired by customers, including quality, features, speed, cost, and so on. For example, an entrepreneur who has developed a piece of financial planning software could add additional features to the base model, such as tax paying, bill paying, or estate planning capability. By innovating, the entrepreneur can take advantage of the learning curve that we discussed in Chapter 2. As long as the entrepreneur can make improvements to the initial product or service sooner than competitors, the entrepreneur can retain customers by always offering attributes of the product or service that the competitors' products and services don't have.

Using Multiple Barriers Simultaneously

These methods of establishing and maintaining a competitive advantage are not mutually exclusive. Successful entrepreneurial ventures often use multiple methods simultaneously. Take, for example, Toronto-based Spin Master.[12] Spin Master was founded in 1994, by three University of Western Ontario graduates with $10,000. They've grown Spin Master into Canada's largest toy company, winning many toy and entrepreneur awards along the way. How does Spin Master maintain its advantage and guard against imitation? Perhaps most importantly, its founders have deep tacit knowledge in picking winning toys. Since this process is causally ambiguous and involves insight and intuition, it is extremely difficult for others to imitate. Second, Spin Master obtains control over critical resources by licensing toy designs from inventors. Once Spin Master obtained the merchandise rights to Teenage Mutant Ninja Turtles, for example, its competitors were blocked from them. Third, Spin Master pays attention to its brand and the reputation it has developed with different stakeholder groups. Early in the company's life, its Air Hogs toy became the third best-selling toy in North American and was praised by *Popular Science* as a technological innovation. This acclaim led Spin Master to gain a reputation as a risk-taker and an innovator among customers, retailers, and inventors. With 85 percent of Spin Master's new products coming from outside inventors, Spin Master pays particular attention to its reputation among inventors and treats them very well, both individually and during the inventor retreats it hosts. And finally, Spin Master innovates continuously. The life of a typical toy is 18 months and so every year Spin Master needs to change 70 percent of its product line. The company has recently diversified, by selling children's furniture, which has a longer shelf life than toys. Spin Master also innovates in the back office, recently implementing a $6 million enterprise resource planning (ERP) system to track products from production to store sales. In the brutally competitive toy industry, Spin Master needs to establish barriers to imitation in all of these ways in order to maintain its advantage.

KEY POINTS

- Entrepreneurs protect their business ideas against competition in two ways: by keeping others from learning about the opportunity and understanding how they exploit it, and by blocking others from exploiting the opportunity in the same way that they do.
- Efforts to stop others from learning about an opportunity involve keeping secret the information that led to the discovery of the opportunity, which works best when the information about the opportunity requires knowledge of a new process.
- The entrepreneur can keep others from imitating the opportunity by taking advantage of causal ambiguity about how to exploit the opportunity, which works best when the understanding about how to exploit the opportunity involves tacit knowledge that is held by only a few people.
- Entrepreneurs deter competition by creating three barriers to imitation of their business ideas: obtaining control of the resources needed to exploit the opportunity; developing a reputation for satisfying the needs of customers; and innovating to keep their products or services ahead of those offered by the competition.

MARKET MODES OF EXPLOITATION

One popular misconception about entrepreneurship is that people always exploit opportunities with a **hierarchical mode**: by establishing a new organization that produces and distributes new products or services. Although it is true that entrepreneurs often found **vertically integrated** companies—that is, firms that own successive stages of the value chain, including the purchase of inputs, manufacturing and production, and marketing and distribution outlets—entrepreneurs don't have to own all parts of the value chain. Instead, they can use what economists call **market-based modes** of opportunity exploitation: exploiting the opportunity via a contractual relationship between different parties.

Palm Computing provides a good example of a start-up that used a market-based mode of opportunity exploitation. Rather than build their computer organizer alone, the founders of Palm Computing sought partnerships with other companies who produced the parts for the PalmPilot according to Palm's specifications. For instance, The Windward Group, a California-based software developer, created the desktop computer applications for the PalmPilot. By partnering with other companies that created the various parts of the PalmPilot, the company's founders were able to increase their speed to market and reduce their costs—two important competitive advantages in the handheld computer market.[13]

The two most common market-based modes of opportunity exploitation are **licensing** and **franchising**. Each of these modes is appropriate in different circumstances.

LEARNING OBJECTIVE

6 Identify the conditions that favour licensing from the point of view of both the entrepreneur with an opportunity to exploit and potential franchisees.

Licensing

Licensing is a mode of business in which one business contracts with another to use the latter's business idea to make products and services for sale to end customers in return for a fee. Many entrepreneurs use licensing to exploit their business ideas. As we've seen, toy inventors license their toy designs to companies such as Hasbro and Spin Master. Process ideas as well as product ideas can be licensed. For example, Edmonton-based video game developer Bioware licenses its game engine technology to other developers. Western Economic Diversification Canada provides an online Inventors Guide that examines issues associated with inventions, including the question of whether to license or sell an invention if you do not wish to commercialize it yourself.[14] When you sell an idea, you receive a fixed payment. When you license an idea, you receive a royalty for each use of the idea. Royalties are typically 2 to 8 percent of the retail price, and the total amount you receive will depend on how many units of your product are sold.

Entrepreneurs use licensing to exploit their opportunity for three main reasons. The first reason is that they are unable to obtain sufficient resources to bring their idea to market. For example, many biotechnology entrepreneurs are unable to obtain the hundreds of millions of dollars that it takes to get a drug through all phases of regulatory approval. To finance drug development, they license their drugs to large pharmaceutical firms, such as Merck and Pfizer, who use the entrepreneur's technology to produce the actual drugs. The Spin Master example shows that this practice is not limited to high-tech sectors. Most toy inventors cannot obtain the half a million dollars it can take to commercialize a toy design, not to mention setting up production facilities and spending millions of dollars on TV ads. Instead, they focus on toy design as their part of the opportunity and license their designs to established companies that have the resources to bring the toy to market successfully.

Second, in addition to lacking sufficient funds, entrepreneurs often lack critical capabilities to bring their ideas to market. Other people or firms might have deeper knowledge of the relevant market, efficient manufacturing and distribution facilities, and/or more expertise in selling new products or services to customers. For example, a software engineer who developed a 3-D design system that would be ideal for architects might know little about bringing such a software product to market successfully. The engineer might choose to license the system to an established firm that knows how to sell software to professional service firms. This approach allows the software engineer to focus on technology development without worrying about starting a business. It is likely to be faster, easier, and cheaper for the established firm to exploit the opportunity than for the software engineer to start his own company. Indeed, researchers have found that both the entrepreneur and the licenser gain from this mode of exploitation because performance rises dramatically when people who have strong capabilities for exploiting opportunities do so in place of those who have weaker capabilities.[15]

Third, entrepreneurs also use licensing to exploit their opportunity when they need to get it to market fast. Sometimes the window of opportunity is not long enough for an entrepreneur to assemble the entire value chain in time to be able to exploit it. For instance, suppose that you designed a tread that could be put on boots and shoes to stop people from slipping in the winter. By the time you set up an entire company to manufacture and sell the treads, the winter might be over. With the market window gone, the opportunity would be lost. So, you could license your invention to an established firm with a compatible product line, such as a boot manufacturer, who can get it made and on the shelves of Canadian Tire in time for winter customers.

Licensing, however, is only feasible if you are able to disclose information about your product or technology to a potential licensee in sufficient detail for them to be able to assess it. Two aspects of your ability to disclose are critical to think about. The first is secrecy, the disclosure itself. As we mentioned in the **Danger! Pitfall Ahead!** section on Arrow's paradox, entrepreneurs often find it difficult to use market mechanisms to exploit opportunities because disclosure of their business ideas to other parties undermines the willingness the those parties to pay for the ideas. Having a patent mitigates this problem because other parties are blocked from using your product or service without your agreement. The second aspect is your ability to provide a detailed description of your product or technology. Market-based mechanisms are also more common when a business idea can be codified, or written down, in a contract. When a business idea can be described in a contract, both sides can have confidence that the legal system will enforce the agreement that they have made. However, if the business idea is too uncertain or too vague to write down, contracts are difficult to use. Not only are negotiations likely to break down as the two parties have trouble agreeing on what they buying and selling[16] but also the uncertainty of the idea makes any contract that they manage to write very difficult to enforce.

For example, suppose that you wanted to sell your business idea for a PDA-based nutrition analysis system. Users would input what they eat, and the system would provide an ongoing analysis of their nutritional intake. The idea would have value to lots of people who want to keep track of what they eat. But, if you do not yet know exactly what the system will look like and how the calculations will be made, you will have a hard time contracting with someone else to buy or license the business idea. If it turns out that your algorithms do not work properly and you cannot get endorsements from important health groups, people are unlikely to be interested in the idea. To get a licensee to sign the contract in the first place, you'd have to be willing to allow an exit clause in the contract if the licensee decides the solution you came up with is not feasible. But once you do that, then the licensee will have a way out of any contract that is signed, by saying that the idea is not feasible, and then the contract is no longer enforceable.

This possibility raises the issue that entrepreneurs need to take care in choosing a licensee. To make money, you need to find partners with the resources or capabilities that you lack, but you also need to find partners who treat you fairly and that you trust. You are in a better position to select a licensee if there are alternatives—if a number of established firms are interested in licensing your product or technology. If you and your product are more attractive to potential licensees, then you will have more bargaining power in negotiating contract terms. It is therefore important for you look at licensing from a potential licensee's viewpoint and to assess honestly what you bring to the table. In general, your product or technology will be more attractive to potential licensees to the extent that it has three key characteristics.[17] First, potential licensees prefer situations where there is intellectual property protection, such as a patent. Not only does a patent protect you from exploitation by a licensee, it protects the licensee from competition in the market. Second, potential licensees prefer to see compelling evidence that your product or technology will sell. This evidence does not need to be a large amount of market research; it could be a compelling demonstration of the product's strengths. Although potential licensees will do their own analyses, you need to be able to convince them at the outset that it is worth their time and money to look at your invention more closely. In doing so, remember that they are likely to know more about the target market than you do, because that is likely to one reason you are turning to a licensee in the first place. Third, potential licensees are attracted to products with a long life expectancy and technologies with the potential to serve as the basis for multiple products. These characteristics allow licensees to spread the costs of understanding your ideas and bringing them to market across several revenue streams.

Franchising

Franchising is a second market-based mode of exploiting a business opportunity. The franchisor develops a plan for the provision of a product or service to end customers, and another party, the franchisee, obtains the right to use the franchisor's plan in return for a fee and agreeing to oversight by the franchisor.[18] As a franchisor, you provide a variety of assets that improve sales: a brand name that helps to attract customers; scale economies in purchasing and advertising; and assistance in areas such as location selection, outlet setup and leasing, employee training, and financing.

We have discussed franchising from the franchisee's point of view in detail in Chapter 9. Here we briefly outline two reasons why an entrepreneur might choose to use franchising to exploit an opportunity. First, franchising allows you to expand the scope of your business geographically without financing the expansion yourself. Suppose, for example, that you would like to establish a chain of auto repair shops, each of which will require $500,000 in equipment. You might go to an angel investor to try to get the capital that you need to set up the repair shops. But you have an alternative. You could offer franchises to people who would open repair shops based on your specifications.

The franchising option allows you to overcome the high cost of capital by tapping franchisees as a source of capital. Franchisees pay franchisors upfront fees—in the tens, and sometimes hundreds, of thousands of dollars—to obtain the rights to use the franchisor's brand name and business format in an outlet that they, the franchisees, own.[19] Moreover, by franchising an outlet instead of owning it outright, the entrepreneur can transfer the cost of setting up the outlet to the franchisee. Indeed, Second Cup franchise agreements are limited to 10 years, and a franchisee who wishes to renew the agreement is required to spend $150,000 to $275,000 to redevelop and modernize the café (see Figure 11.3)[20] This policy transfers the initial set-up costs *and* the costs of maintaining a modern look-and-feel to the franchisees. A second reason to franchise is to ensure that the people operating your outlets are as motivated as you are to make the outlets succeed. Franchisees are themselves entrepreneurs who have put their own money in their franchise and so they are likely to be more motivated than a typical store manager to work hard, enhance customer satisfaction, and improve sales.

Figure 11.3 To Minimize the Cost of Exploiting Opportunities, Entrepreneurs Often Franchise

The Second Cup uses franchising to grow its businesses and to fund the modernization of its cafés.

Photo: Indu Ghuman

As with licensing, franchising is only possible in situation where the entrepreneur is able to specify the operations of an outlet in sufficient detail for a franchisee to copy it exactly. Further, although franchising permits the geographic expansion of cloned units, it is less suitable for other types of expansion. If you expect your growth strategy to be based on a wider or more diversified product line, then franchising is unlikely to be a suitable method to exploit your opportunity. Franchises do expand their product line—consider the new beverages offered at Second Cup outlets during the past five years—but new products need to be standardized and fit seamlessly with existing operations and outlet layouts. The primary growth mechanism for franchises stems from having more outlets.

KEY POINTS

- Entrepreneurs can, and do, exploit opportunities through market-based modes of exploitation, such as franchising and licensing.
- Entrepreneurs often use licensing when they lack the resources or capabilities to exploit the opportunity themselves, or when the window of opportunity is too short for them to exploit on their own.
- An entrepreneur who wishes to exploit an opportunity through licensing will be more attractive to potential licensees to the extent that the idea is protected by a patent, there is compelling evidence of a market for the idea, and the idea is likely to have longevity in the market.
- Both licensing and franchising require entrepreneurs to disclose information about their products and technologies to other parties. They must be able to do so in sufficient detail that a contract can be written and upheld.

MANAGING INFORMATION ASYMMETRY AND UNCERTAINTY IN THE PURSUIT OF OPPORTUNITY

LEARNING OBJECTIVE

7 Describe the strategic actions that entrepreneurs take to manage information asymmetry and uncertainty in the entrepreneurial process.

The entrepreneurial process involves a great deal of uncertainty. When entrepreneurs found their firms, they face technical uncertainty because they do not know for sure that the product or service that they are developing is going to work, or if it works, that they will be able to produce it. Entrepreneurs also face market uncertainty because they never really know for sure that customers will want their new product until after introducing it; and, even if the customers like it, it is uncertain whether they will demand a large enough volume, fast enough, and at a price at which the entrepreneur can make a profit. Last, entrepreneurs face competitive uncertainty because they do not know whether they will be able to create a competitive advantage and capture the profits from their exploitation of an opportunity, or whether other companies will take that profit away from them.[21]

The entrepreneurial process also involves significant information asymmetry between the entrepreneur and employees, investors, customers, and suppliers. Entrepreneurs identify and exploit opportunities because they have access to better information or have greater ability to recognize opportunities from that information. Moreover, entrepreneurs often keep secret their methods of exploiting opportunities to limit imitation. These two forces mean that entrepreneurs almost always have more information about their opportunities and their methods of exploiting them than their employees, investors, customers, and suppliers.[22]

Because uncertainty and information asymmetry are an important part of the entrepreneurial process, successful entrepreneurs must develop strategies for managing these dimensions of the entrepreneurial process. In this section, we discuss three important strategies that entrepreneurs use to manage this asymmetry: growth from small scale, forming alliances and partnerships with established firms, and creating legitimacy for the opportunity and the new venture.

Growth from Small Scale

There are economies of scale in advertising and production, which lower the cost structure of a new firm. Although there are benefits to operating on a large scale, most entrepreneurs do not start their businesses on a large scale (see Figure 11.4). The answer lies in the uncertainty and information asymmetry that new ventures face.

The uncertainty and information asymmetry that pervade the entrepreneurial process make it virtually impossible for entrepreneurs to establish their ventures on a large scale, and even if they could, uncertainty and information asymmetry make it very foolish to do so.[23] First, most entrepreneurs have to self-finance the development of their new ventures. Except for a few very wealthy individuals, most people do not have a large amount of savings. So even if they max out all of their credit cards (as many entrepreneurs do!), very few people could come up with all of the money that it would take to start a business on the same scale as their existing competitors (given the hundreds of millions of dollars that it would take to start a biotechnology company, the billions of dollars it would take to start a semiconductor company, or the tens of billions of dollars it would take to start an auto company).

So what do typical entrepreneurs do? Instead of starting their companies by matching the broad product lines, large manufacturing facilities, or extensive advertising of established companies in their industries, entrepreneurs generally start with small companies focused on a single product line. Then, if they do a decent job with their initial efforts, the entrepreneurs attract external investors, who give them the money to grow their ventures to the size of the other firms in the industry.

Second, investors do not like to give entrepreneurs large sums of money all at once: they tend to make relatively small investments in new ventures over time. As a result, most entrepreneurs simply cannot raise the capital that it would take to start a company that is large from day one. There is just too much information asymmetry and uncertainty, not to mention too few investors with enough capital to finance a new rail equipment company that is the size of Bombardier, or a new graphics company that is the size of ATI Technologies.

Third, starting a company is risky. Most people, entrepreneurs included, want to minimize risk. Risk in new ventures comes from making large, irreversible investments. The most that you can lose if your business fails is the amount that you put into assets that have no liquidation value. The smaller that investment is, the less that you will have at risk if the venture fails.[24] A good example of a large, irreversible investment is a steel plant. Once you take cash and use it to build a steel plant, that is what you have. You aren't going to be able to change that steel plant into a biotechnology laboratory, no matter how hard you try, even if you find that your opportunity was really in biotechnology and not in steel.

So entrepreneurs keep their risks low by making investments in things that are not irreversible, such as using generic trucks instead of specialized, custom-made

LEARNING OBJECTIVE

8 Explain why entrepreneurs often start their businesses on a small scale and expand if they are successful.

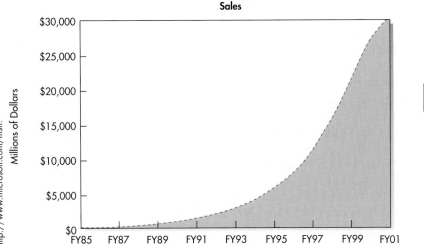

Source: Based on data available at http://www.microsoft.com/msft.

Figure 11.4 Most Entrepreneurs Start Their New Businesses on a Small Scale and Then Expand If the Initial Effort Proves Favourable

Even Microsoft, one of the world's largest companies, began as a tiny company and expanded from there.

vehicles. That way, if their businesses fail, the entrepreneurs can always sell the trucks, making the investment reversible. This strategy also explains why entrepreneurs don't purchase most of the assets that they need, and tend to lease or borrow instead.[25] A borrowed asset can be returned, and a lease cancelled, much more easily than an asset can be sold.

Unfortunately for the entrepreneur, some asset commitments are irreversible. There is just no way to get around it. For example, if you are going to make and sell a new electronic device, you don't really have much choice, but you have to take some of your money and use it to build a prototype of the device. Here, small-scale production comes into play in reducing your risk. You can minimize risk by building one prototype and, if it works, expanding to small-scale production, and, then, if that works, expanding to greater production.

Moreover, uncertainty means that entrepreneurs need to be flexible and adaptive in their strategies. Remember that, at the very beginning, entrepreneurs do not know whether they can produce a product, find a market for the product, or compete with other firms to earn profits from that product. If it turns out that they can't do these things, entrepreneurs have to change their plans. Moreover, events occur that require entrepreneurs to change their plans. For instance, you might have planned to launch a really high-end boutique hotel, but if the economy tanks, you may need to make the hotel appeal to families to get enough customers to survive. By starting small and not investing too much in any one direction until the technical, market, and competitive uncertainties are reduced, the new venture remains more flexible and adaptive, and the entrepreneur can change direction more easily.

This strategy of remaining flexible is the reason that many businesses begin as consulting or contract organizations and go into making products only if customers turn out to be interested.[26] For example, many software product firms start off as software consulting firms. By developing software for a fee, entrepreneurs are paid to learn about market requirements. It is less risky to refine the software for a wider market than to start developing software with little evidence that customers are actually interested in it.

Forming Alliances and Partnerships with Established Firms

LEARNING OBJECTIVE

9 Explain how alliances and partnerships with established firms help entrepreneurs to exploit their opportunities.

Many new firms form alliances with established firms as part of their strategy to exploit their opportunities. For instance, many new biotechnology companies engage in research and development alliances with established pharmaceutical companies.

Researchers have explained that the formation of alliances and partnerships with established firms overcomes several major problems in the exploitation of entrepreneurial opportunities.[27] First, as we mentioned earlier, in our discussion of the use of market-based modes of opportunity exploitation, opportunities are often short-lived and entrepreneurs do not have enough time to obtain external financing to build needed assets, such as manufacturing plants or retail outlets. By forming alliances with established companies, the entrepreneur can gain access to already developed assets. For example, when new biotechnology companies are in a race to be the first to develop a new drug, they often form alliances with pharmaceutical firms to gain access to research facilities and expertise because venture capitalists cannot provide them with the resources quickly enough to build these assets from scratch. In studying the alliances of young Canadian biotechnology firms, University of Toronto researchers Joel Baum, Tony Calabrese, and Brian Silverman found that business success was related to the configurations providing the best information and opportunities for learning.[28] Another situation in which young Canadian firms often form alliances is when they are internationalizing. When there is a high degree of uncertainty about foreign markets, alliance partners, with knowledge of local tastes, customs, and distribution channels, can help a young firm learn about the new market.[29]

Second, entrepreneurs simply lack the capital that they need to purchase the resources that they need, both because they must self-finance and because investors ration the capital that they provide to entrepreneurs. Alliances and partnerships with established firms provide a way to gain access to resources that they need—such as plant and equipment, sales forces, and product development expertise—but don't have the money to purchase. For example, the expertise of Vancouver-based New Line Skateparks lies in designing and constructing skate parks. However, to build a skate park you need to convince a municipality to give you the contract. New Line Skateparks teamed up with van der Zalm + Associates, a Vancouver-based landscape design firm to take advantage of this firm's track record and expertise in overall park design and pitching to city officials. Together they've completed more than 50 projects, including a $1 million park in Winnipeg.[30] Moreover, as we explained earlier in our discussion of starting on a small scale, allying with an established company that already has the equipment and facilities that the entrepreneur needs minimizes the potential downside loss that the entrepreneur would experience if the business idea turned out to be a failure.[31]

Third, an alliance or partnership with an established company helps the entrepreneur persuade others that the business idea is valuable. People tend to be skeptical of new businesses and assume that established firms are able to assess them. An entrepreneur can mitigate this problem by selling a new product or service under an established firm's brand name through an alliance or partnership (see Figure 11.5).[32] Because the established firm has a reputation to lose if the entrepreneur's product or service turns out not to be any good, potential customers see the established firm's support as evidence of the value of the new product or service, making them more willing to buy it. For example, iPod users are likely to evaluate iPod accessories introduced by new firms more favourably if it is featured on the Apple website. Using a similar logic—that high-quality people and organizations will want to form alliances only with other high quality people and organizations—York University professor Yuval Deutsch and University of British Columbia professor Thomas Ross show that having reputable directors is a signal of high quality for new firms.[33]

Establishing alliances as part of an entrepreneur's strategy involves certain hazards. In particular, alliance partners may take advantage of the entrepreneur, exploiting their size and power in the relationship. Numerous examples have been found of entrepreneurs forming partnerships with large, established companies and then finding that the alliance partners had misrepresented the assets and capabilities that they would or could bring to the relationship. A larger alliance partner can wait for the new firm to make investments in the relationship and then, exploiting the fact that those investments are sunk, extract a better deal from the entrepreneur. Alliance partners have also been known to withhold promised resources and capabilities. Entrepreneurs need to factor in these hazards when evaluating the benefits of alliances and partnerships with other firms.

Figure 11.5 Entrepreneurs Often Form Alliances and Partnerships with Established Firms

Partnering with Sears and other prominent retailers, George Foreman was able to achieve faster customer acceptance of his lean, mean, fat-grilling machine.

Legitimating the Opportunity and the New Venture

The uncertainty and information asymmetry inherent in the entrepreneurial process also means that entrepreneurs often have to generate legitimacy for their business ideas, particularly if those business ideas are novel. Legitimacy is a quality based on the belief that an idea is correct and appropriate. For example, a new company called LifeGem has just introduced a new product that allows you to take the remains of your dead relatives, cremate them, and turn them into industrial diamonds that are then placed into jewellery. (We are not kidding. We saw a segment

LEARNING OBJECTIVE

10 List actions that entrepreneurs undertake to make their new ventures appear more legitimate, and explain why they take these actions.

about this company on the Today Show). To succeed, this company will first have to convince people that taking human remains and turning them into jewellery is a correct and appropriate action before it can worry about how to manufacture the jewellery or how to price it. Although you might think that convincing people that it's okay to use human remains in this way is impossible, it probably isn't. When life insurance was first introduced, people didn't think that it was appropriate or correct for the same reasons that people think that making jewellery from the cremated remains of relatives is incorrect and inappropriate.[34] Yet life insurance became an accepted product that many people buy.

The tendency of people to resist viewing new business ideas as legitimate requires entrepreneurs to take action that demonstrates the legitimacy of their business ideas and opportunities to make them acceptable to customers, suppliers, investors, and employees. Entrepreneurs can demonstrate legitimacy in several ways. First, entrepreneurs show that their business ideas conform to existing norms. For instance, the entrepreneur who came up with the first ethanol-powered car designed it to look like other cars, changing only the engine. Why? By keeping everything else in the car the same, potential customers would view the ethanol-powered vehicle as more legitimate and acceptable than if it didn't look like a standard car.

Another way that entrepreneurs demonstrate legitimacy is to imitate the routines and procedures of existing firms so that their ventures don't look like new companies. For example, many entrepreneurs borrow the offices of existing firms when trying to meet customers, instead of meeting their clients where they do business—in their homes or their garages. They do this because people tend not to trust or believe in businesses that don't look real. By borrowing real offices, entrepreneurs show customers what looks like a regular business, not like some start-up in a garage.[35]

A third way that entrepreneurs demonstrate legitimacy for their new businesses is by engaging in collective action. Entrepreneurs often work together, through trade or industry associations, to lobby for regulatory change or to set standards. For example, the founders of Manitoba Harvest Hemp Foods participated in lobbying the Canadian government to legalize hemp seed production.[36] Entrepreneurs have an incentive to work towards common standards and designs because they make products and services less confusing to customers and reduce the level of effort to persuade customers that the opportunity is reliable and valid.[37] For example, entrepreneurs in the wireless telecommunications industry joined together to establish a trade association and standard-setting body, in part to make sure that the government and general population understood the general value of wireless devices.

A fourth way that entrepreneurs demonstrate legitimacy for their business ideas is by obtaining certification by reputable authorities. People tend to believe in the reliability and validity of statements made by people in authority, in part because those people have greater expertise than the general population, and in part because people in authority have a lot to lose if they certify the value of something that turns out to have no value. For example, rather than stating that a food product is kosher or organic, it is more effective for a food producer to have the product certified as kosher or organic, because consumers believe that certifications are credible and reliable. Sometimes certifications are exclusive and more like awards. For example, a product that is designated as an Editor's Pick from *PC Magazine* stands out from the many products that do not receive such a designation. Huggy Rao, a professor of organizational behavior at the Kellogg School at Northwestern University, showed the value of certification to new ventures in a study of automobile companies in the early 20th century. Rao showed that new automobile companies that won contests sponsored by automotive magazines were more likely to survive than their competitors.[38] Similarly, in a study of young Canadian software firms, York University's Eileen Fischer and I (Becky Reuber) observed that receiving product awards made a difference to the fortunes of young computer graphics chip companies, relative to their rivals.[39] In short, to be successful, entrepreneurs need to establish legitimacy for their new businesses just as people need to establish legitimacy for anything new that they pursue (see Figure 11.6).

Figure 11.6 Entrepreneurs Often Have to Take Actions That Legitimate Their Business Ideas

The Canada Revenue Agency certifies commercial tax preparation software packages and Internet applications each year. Since customers are likely to buy only certified products that are guaranteed to file correct tax returns, entrepreneurs should have their products certified before entering this market.

Getty Images

KEY POINTS

- Entrepreneurs engage in three strategies to manage the technical, market, and competitive uncertainty and information asymmetry that new ventures face: growth from a small scale, forming alliances and partnerships with established firms, and creating legitimacy for the opportunity and the new venture.
- Uncertainty and information asymmetry lead entrepreneurs to self-finance; lead investors to limit the size of their investments in new ventures; and require entrepreneurs to bear risk, all of which lead entrepreneurs to start on a small scale and expand if they are successful.
- Entrepreneurs form alliances and partnerships with established firms to establish the value chain quickly; to overcome capital constraints to the assembly of necessary assets; and to use established brand names to demonstrate the value of their new products and services.
- Uncertainty and information asymmetry also make it difficult for people to believe that new business ideas are appropriate and correct, leading entrepreneurs to take actions to demonstrate the legitimacy of their opportunities and business ideas. Among the different ways that entrepreneurs demonstrate legitimacy are adhering to existing rules and norms; imitating the routines and procedures of existing firms; engaging in collective actions; and obtaining certification from reputable authorities.

Summary and Review of Key Points

- The identification of a business opportunity that satisfies the needs of customers is not enough for an entrepreneur to earn profits; the entrepreneur also needs a competitive advantage.

- The exploitation of an opportunity will provide information to others about how to imitate the entrepreneur's business idea; imitation by others will erode the entrepreneur's profit from exploiting the opportunity.

- By developing a competitive advantage, the entrepreneur precludes others from imitating the business idea perfectly, and allows the entrepreneur to capture the profits from exploiting the opportunity.

- Entrepreneurs protect their business ideas against competition in two ways: by keeping others from learning about the opportunity and understanding how they exploit it, and by blocking others from exploiting the opportunity in the same way that they do.

- Efforts to stop others from learning about an opportunity involve keeping secret the information that led to the discovery of the opportunity, which works best when the information about the opportunity requires knowledge of a new process.

- The entrepreneur can keep others from imitating the opportunity by taking advantage of causal ambiguity about how to exploit the opportunity, which works best when the understanding about how to exploit the opportunity involves tacit knowledge that is held by only a few people.

- Entrepreneurs deter competition by creating three barriers to imitation of their business ideas: obtaining control of the resources needed to exploit the opportunity; developing a reputation for satisfying the needs of customers; and innovating to keep their products or services ahead of those offered by the competition.

- Entrepreneurs can, and do, exploit opportunities through market-based modes of exploitation, such as franchising and licensing.

- Entrepreneurs often use licensing when they lack the resources or capabilities to exploit the opportunity themselves, or when the window of opportunity is too short for them to exploit on their own.

- An entrepreneur who wishes to exploit an opportunity through licensing will be more attractive to potential licensees to the extent that the idea is protected by a patent, there is compelling evidence of a market for the idea, and the idea is likely to have longevity in the market.

- Both licensing and franchising require entrepreneurs to disclose information about their products and technologies to other parties. They must be able to do so in sufficient detail that a contract can be written and upheld.

- Entrepreneurs engage in three strategies to manage the technical, market, and competitive uncertainty and information asymmetry that new ventures face: growth from a small scale, forming alliances and partnerships with established firms, and creating legitimacy for the opportunity and the new venture.

- Uncertainty and information asymmetry lead entrepreneurs to self-finance; lead investors to limit the size of their investments in new ventures; and require entrepreneurs to bear risk, all of which lead entrepreneurs to start on a small scale and expand if they are successful.

- Entrepreneurs form alliances and partnerships with established firms to establish the value chain quickly; to overcome capital constraints to the assembly of necessary assets; and to use established brand names to demonstrate the value of their new products and services.

- Uncertainty and information asymmetry also make it difficult for people to believe that new business ideas are appropriate and correct, leading entrepreneurs to take actions to demonstrate the legitimacy of their opportunities and business ideas. Among the different ways that entrepreneurs demonstrate legitimacy are adhering to existing rules and norms; imitating the routines and procedures of existing firms; engaging in collective actions; and obtaining certification from reputable authorities.

Glossary

Causal Ambiguity: A lack of understanding about the underlying process through which entrepreneurs exploit opportunities.

Competitive Advantage: A business attribute that allows a firm, and not its competitors, to capture the profits from exploiting an opportunity.

Franchising: A system of distribution in which legally independent business owners (franchisees) pay fees and royalties to a parent company (the franchisor) in return for the right to use its trademark, sell its products or services, and use the business model and system it has developed.

Hierarchical Mode: A form of exploiting opportunities, in which one party owns all parts of the operation that produces and sells a product or service to end customers.

Legitimacy: A quality based on the belief that something is correct and appropriate.

Licensing: A mode of business in which one party contracts with another to use the first party's ideas to make products and services for sale to end customers in return for a fee.

Market-Based Mode: A form of exploiting opportunities in which different parts of a business, such as manufacturing and marketing, are owned by different entities and are connected by a contractual relationship.

Monopoly: A situation in which a firm is the only supplier of a product or service.

Patent: A legal right granted by a national government to preclude others from duplicating an invention for a specified period of time in return for disclosure of the invention.

Tacit Knowledge: A type of understanding that cannot be documented or even articulated. It is frequently contrasted with codified knowledge, which is a type of understanding that can be expressed in documentary form.

Trade Secret: A piece of knowledge that confers an advantage on firms and is protected by nondisclosure.

Vertically Integrated: A situation in which a firm owns successive stages of the value chain.

Discussion Questions

1. Suppose you started a company without a competitive advantage. What do you think would happen to your company? Why?

2. Think of five different new businesses. For each of these businesses, explain what you would do to increase your chances of keeping the profits received as a result of exploiting these business opportunities. Why would you choose this approach?

3. Assume that you've come up with an idea for a new restaurant specializing in chicken fingers. Should you pursue the opportunity through franchising or by establishing a chain of company-owned stores? Explain your choice.

4. When you start a new company, should you form a partnership or alliance with a large, established firm? Why or why not?

5. You've just started a new telecommunication company, and other entrepreneurs in the industry invite you to join the telecom trade association. Should you join? Why or why not?

InfoTrac Exercises

1. **Competitive Advantage Through Specialty Franchising**

   John F. Preble; Richard C. Hoffman

   Journal of Consumer Marketing, Winter 1998 v15 n1 p64(14)

   Record: A20514522

   Abstract: A competitive advantage in terms of strategy and customer responsiveness can be developed through mobile franchising. Mobile franchises tend to be more focused in their strategies in terms of geography, product, and market. They can establish their business where their clients are located or where the customer's "need" can be found. Semicustom work, fast cycle times, professional service, proximity to customer, and customer responsiveness are some of the significant elements of mobile franchises.

   1. According to the text and the article, what are the benefits of franchising for entrepreneurs?

   2. According to the article, how is competitive advantage developed through mobile franchising?

   3. What market trends are fueling entrepreneurial opportunities in mobile franchising?

2. **BlackBerry still bears fruit**

Karen Brown.

Wireless Week, Sept 15, 2004 v10 i19 p30(2)

Full Text: COPYRIGHT 2004 Reed Business Information

Record: A122460076

1. According to the article, how is Research In Motion maintaining a competitive advantage?

2. What are the advantages of its licensing deals for Research In Motion, its licensees, and BlackBerry users?

GETTING DOWN

TO BUSINESS

Developing a Strategy

This chapter discussed the importance of developing a strategy for your new venture. Without a strategy, you can still start a firm, but you're unlikely to be successful. For this reason, it's important to carefully think about your new venture strategy. Moreover, when you write a feasibility study on your venture opportunity or develop a business plan to exploit it, you'll need to specify your new venture's strategy. This exercise will help you to develop a strategy for your new venture. If you follow these steps, you will be well on your way to defining a strategy for your new venture.

Step One: In one paragraph, identify the opportunity that your new venture will exploit.

Step Two: Using the material you developed when you completed the exercises in Chapter 10, explain the customer need that your new venture's product or service will fill, and how your product or service will fill that need.

Step Three: Explain how your new venture will deter actions by other firms to meet this customer need with their products or services. Remember to consider the mechanisms discussed in this chapter: Will you develop a trade secret? Will you exploit causal ambiguity? Will you obtain control over resources through exclusive contracts, patents, government permits, or the purchase of the key source of supply? Will you build a reputation through advertising and the development of a brand name? Will you innovate and move ahead of competitors by providing superior product or service features?

Step Four: Choose your organizational form. Will you establish a vertically integrated operation or will you franchise or license? Explain your choice. How do the factors that we discussed in the chapter—cost, speed, capabilities, and information—influence your decision?

Step Five: Explain how your new venture will overcome information asymmetry and uncertainty. How will your new venture grow? Will you create alliances and partnerships with established firms? If so, why and how? How will you create legitimacy for your new venture? Will you imitate the actions of large firms? Conform to norms? Engage in collective action? Seek certification from reputable authorities?

Write down your strategy for building your business. Explain how your business will grow from its initial size at the time it is formed to the size that it will be at the time of your exit strategy. In addition, explain how you will establish legitimacy for your new venture and explain how you will overcome problems of information asymmetry and uncertainty in developing the venture.

Identifying Your Competitors

This chapter has focused on the importance of establishing a competitive advantage in your new business. To establish a competitive advantage, entrepreneurs need to identify their competitors and specify how their new venture will provide better products or services than those offered by competitors. Unfortunately, most entrepreneurs have trouble identifying their competitors and evaluating their strengths and weaknesses. This exercise is designed to help you identify your competitors, evaluate their strengths and weaknesses, and pinpoint a strategy for offering better products and services than your competitors.

Step One: List all of the competitors that your new venture will face. Be careful to approach this question from the point of view of your customer. For example, if your new venture is a bakery, list all competing bakeries in your area. Also include all other companies that offer products that your customers might choose over your own, for example, doughnut shops and ice cream parlours. Remember to consider all firms (like your own) that might enter the market in the near future.

Step Two: Summarize the products and services that each of your competitors offers. Include information about the product features, price, quality, advertising and promotion strategy, distribution methods, after-sales service, and so on.

Step Three: For each of your competitors, list their strengths and weaknesses. Make sure to approach this analysis from your customers' perspective, and be fair to your competitors. If they have real strengths, acknowledge them. For each of your competitors' strengths, explain how you will overcome it. For each of their weaknesses, explain how you will exploit it.

Step Four: Identify the current strategies of each of your competitors. Are they adding new strengths? Do they have plans to overcome current weaknesses? Be prepared to explain how you will respond to the current strategies of each of your competitors.

Gathering Information on Competitors

Most entrepreneurs find it very difficult to gather information about their competitors. As a result, they write business plans based on inaccurate or outdated information about their competitors' strategies and strengths and weaknesses. To overcome this problem, you'll need to practise gathering information about your competition. For this reason, we've developed this exercise in gathering information on competitors. Follow these steps to create a file on each of your new business's competitors.

1. **Conduct an Internet search on each of your competitors.** Take the information that you gather and divide it into categories such as strategy, products and services, problems, successes, and so on.

2. **Talk to your competitors and their customers.** Ask customers what they like and dislike about your competitors. Ask your competitors about their companies. You'll be surprised how much information people will give you. Add that information to the records that you created from your Internet search.

3. **Examine documentary sources.** Go to the library and conduct a database search on your competitors. What do articles in newspapers, magazines, and trade publications say about them? Have your competitors issued press releases that provide useful information? Have their executives made presentations or speeches that provide information about their companies? Include the information from documentary sources in your records about competitors.

4. **Examine your competitors' advertising.** What do print, radio, television, Internet, billboard, and other advertising for your competitors show about them? What about displays at trade shows or other events? Do they provide useful information about your competition? The answer is probably yes. Again, add this information to your records.

Enhanced Learning

You may select any combination of the resources below to enhance your understanding of the chapter material.

- **Appendix: Case Studies** — Twelve cases provide opportunities to apply chapter concepts to realistic entrepreneurial situations. These brief cases call for careful analysis of real business problems and ask you to think about potential solutions.

- **Video Case Library** — Nine cases are tied directly to video segments from the popular PBS television series Small Business School. These cases and video segments (available on the Entrepreneurship website at http://www.entrepreneurship.nelson.com) give you unparalleled access to today's entrepreneurs, with expert advice and insights on how to start, run, and grow a business.

- **Management Interview Series Video Database** — This video interview series contains a wealth of tips on how to manage effectively. Access to the database and practical exercises are available on the book support website at http://www.entrepreneurship.nelson.com.

Notes

1. Shane, S. 2003. *A general theory of entrepreneurship: The individual–opportunity nexus.* London: Edward Elgar.
2. Schiller, B., & Crewson, P. 1997. Entrepreneurial origins: A longitudinal inquiry. *Economic Inquiry* 35(3): 523–531.
3. Shane, S. 2003. *A general theory of entrepreneurship: The individual–opportunity nexus.* London: Edward Elgar.
4. Barney, J. 1991. Firm resources and sustained competitive advantage. *Journal of Management* 17(1): 99–120.
5. Nelson, R., & Winter, S. 1982. *An evolutionary theory of economic change.* Cambridge, MA: Belknap Press.
6. Amit, R., Glosten, L., & Muller, E. 1993. Challenges to theory development in entrepreneurship research. *Journal of Management Studies* 30(5): 815–834.
7. Arrow, K. 1962. Economic welfare and the allocation of resources for inventions. In R. Nelson (ed.). *The rate and direction of inventive activity* (pp. 609–626). Princeton, NJ: Princeton University Press.
8. Rumelt, R. 1987. Theory, strategy and entrepreneurship. In D. Teece (ed.). *The competitive challenge: Strategies for industrial innovation and renewal* (pp. 137–158). Cambridge, MA: Ballinger.
9. Casson, M. 1982. *The entrepreneur.* Totowa, NJ: Barnes & Noble Books.
10. Shane, S. 2003. *A general theory of entrepreneurship: The individual–opportunity nexus.* London: Edward Elgar.
11. Casson, M. 1982. *The entrepreneur.* Totowa, NJ: Barnes & Noble Books.
12. The material on Spin Master has been taken from the company's website (www.spinmaster.com) and Spence, R. 2005. Inside the tornado. *Profit* 24(6): 40–47.
13. Henricks, M. 1998. The modular squad. *Entrepreneur* 26(3): 74–75.
14. The Inventors Guide, Western Economic Diversification Canada. http://www.wd.gc.ca/tools/inventors/default_e.asp.
15. Teece, D. 1986. Profiting from technological innovation: Implications for integration, collaboration, licensing, and public policy. *Research Policy* 15(6): 286–305.
16. Audretsch, D. 1997. Technological regimes, industrial demography and the evolution of industrial structures. *Industrial and Corporate Change* 6(1): 49–82.
17. The Inventors Guide, Western Economic Diversification Canada. http://www.wd.gc.ca/tools/inventors/default_e.asp.
18. Shane, S., & Foo, M. 1999. New firm survival: Institutional explanations for new franchisor mortality. *Management Science* 45(2): 142–159.
19. Shane, S. 1998. Making new franchise systems work. *Strategic Management Journal* 19(7): 697–707.
20. Second Cup Royalty Income Fund Prospectus, November 23, 2004. http://www.secondcupincomefund.com/prospectus.pdf.
21. Amit, R., Glosten, L., & Muller, E. 1990. Does venture capital foster the most promising entrepreneurial firms? *California Management Review* 32(3): 102–111.
22. Shane, S. 2003. *A general theory of entrepreneurship: The individual–opportunity nexus.* London: Edward Elgar.
23. Bhide, A. 2000. *The origin and evolution of new businesses.* New York: Oxford University Press.
24. Caves, R. 1998. Industrial organization and new findings on the turnover and mobility of firms. *Journal of Economic Literature* 36(4): 1947–1982.
25. Starr, J., & MacMillan, I. 1990. Resource cooptation via social contracting: Resource acquisition strategies for new ventures. *Strategic Management Journal* 11(summer): 79–92.
26. Roberts, E. 1991. *Entrepreneurs in high technology.* New York: Oxford University Press.
27. Stuart, T., Hoang, H., & Hybels, R. 1999. Interorganizational endorsements and the performance of entrepreneurial ventures. *Administrative Science Quarterly* 44(2): 315–349.

28 Baum, J., Calabrese, T., & Silverman, B. 2000. Don't go it alone: Alliance network composition and startups' performance in Canadian biotechnology. *Strategic Management Journal* 21(3): 267–294.

29 Reuber, A.R., & Fischer, E. 1997. The influence of the management team's international experience on the internationalization behaviours of SMEs. *Journal of International Business Studies* 28(4): 807–825.

30 Giroday, G. 2005. Dude, how do we handle all these orders? *Globe and Mail Report on Small Business Magazine*, Fall: 22–25.

31 Venkataraman, S. 1997. The distinctive domain of entrepreneurship research: An editor's perspective. In J. Katz & R. Brockhaus (eds.). *Advances in Entrepreneurship, Firm Emergence, and Growth* Vol. 3 (pp. 119–138). Greenwich, CT: JAI Press.

32 Eisenhardt, K., & Schoonhoven, K. 1990. Organizational growth: Linking founding team, strategy, environment, and growth among U.S. semiconductor ventures, 1978–1988. *Administrative Science Quarterly* 35(3): 504–529.

33 Deutsch, Y., & Ross, T. 2003. You are known by the directors you keep: Reputable directors as a signaling mechanism for young firms. *Management Science* 49(8): 1003–1017.

34 Aldrich, H. 1999. *Organizations evolving*. London: Sage.

35 Starr, J., & MacMillan, I. 1990. Resource cooptation via social contracting: Resource acquisition strategies for new ventures. *Strategic Management Journal* 11 (summer): 79–92.

36 Co-founder of Manitoba Harvest Earns Prestigious "Young Entrepreneur" Award, NewsTarget.com, September 8, 2005. www.newstarget.com/z008131.html.

37 Aldrich, H. 1999. *Organizations evolving*. London: Sage.

38 Rao, H. 1994. The social construction of reputation: Certification contests, legitimation and the survival of organizations in the American automobile industry: 1895–1912. *Strategic Management Journal* 13(winter): 29–44.

39 Reuber, A.R., & Fischer, E. 2006. Don't rest on your laurels: Reputational change and young technology-based ventures. *Journal of Business Venturing*, forthcoming.

CHAPTER 12

BUILDING THE NEW VENTURE'S HUMAN RESOURCES: RECRUITING, MOTIVATING, AND RETAINING HIGH-PERFORMING EMPLOYEES

LEARNING OBJECTIVES

After reading this chapter, you should be able to:

1 Explain why information about recruiting, motivating, and retaining high-quality employees is useful to entrepreneurs.

2 Describe the relationship of number of employees to new venture success.

3 Describe the role of social networks in new ventures' efforts to hire additional employees.

4 Define "job analysis" and "job description" and explain why they are important initial steps in the search for new employees.

5 Define "reliability" and "validity" and explain why all techniques used for selection must be high on both. Describe structured interviews and explain why they are higher in validity than traditional employment interviews.

6 Describe the requirements for setting effective goals, and why it is so important to tie rewards to performance.

7 Describe the role of fairness in motivating employees.

8 Define "job enlargement" and "job enrichment" and explain why they are important in motivating employees.

9 List the relative advantages and disadvantages of temporary and permanent employees.

10 Describe various means for relating pay and other rewards to performance.

11 Define "continuance commitment," "affective commitment," and "normative commitment" and explain their role in the retention of high-quality employees.

12 Define the "control barrier" and explain why it is so important for entrepreneurs to learn how to delegate authority to others.

All photos this page © PhotoDisc, Inc.

> *"Genius begins great works; labour alone finishes them."* (Joseph Joubert, 1974–1824)

It's a sad fact of life that, often, our actions produce exactly the opposite of what we want. This fact is certainly true for entrepreneurs—especially successful ones. If you ask them why they started their own ventures in the first place, many will make statements such as these: "I hated being a small cog in a big machine" or "I really wanted more personal freedom—to be able to do things the way *I* want to do them, not the way I'm told to do them." In new ventures, at least for awhile, this is precisely what entrepreneurs' hard work and dedication yield: They *do* get to make all the decisions and run the show. But then, if the new venture is successful, a strange paradox begins to develop: As the company grows in size, entrepreneurs find their freedom and sense of control increasingly restricted. They must spend more and more of their time overseeing a business that becomes—much to their dismay—increasingly like the large, complex organizations from which they fled! Talk about getting precisely what you *don't* want in life!

One way to deal with this situation is to limit further growth—to seek a safe market niche and continue to fill it—and some entrepreneurs do indeed choose this option. For those who want to see their new ventures become as large and successful as possible, however, there is another option. Entrepreneurs can shift from being a team leader—the person who inspires members of a small group of cofounders and initial employees—to becoming a leader of many teams, a very central person in the company, but one who, of necessity, delegates key tasks to other persons.[1] This reality is often a difficult transition for entrepreneurs, delegating the implementation of their dream to other people. As we will note repeatedly, relying on others is an essential change if the new venture is to continue to grow. Ultimate and substantial success for new ventures derives not from a situation in which entrepreneurs are capable of doing everything, but rather from a smooth and orderly shift away from this early state to one in which the entrepreneur has assembled a first-rate team of employees to whom are delegated many of the growing venture's key processes.

The founding team of any new venture is a key component of its human resources. A first-rate group of founders brings a wealth of knowledge, experience, skills, and commitment to their company.[2] Further, as common sense would suggest, the larger the founding team and the more varied the experience of its members (the principle of complementarity), the greater the likelihood that the new venture will succeed. Specifically, the greater are the new venture's chances of survival[3] and the faster its rate of growth.[4] But no matter how excellent a new venture's founding team is, it cannot possibly supply all required resources or all forms of information. At the very least, new ventures often require the services of experts from outside the company—for instance, lawyers, accountants, or engineers. If the new venture is successful in obtaining financing and in building a customer base, the need for additional human resources in the form of employees beyond the founding team may soon become apparent.

LEARNING OBJECTIVE

1 Explain why information about recruiting, motivating, and retaining high-quality employees is useful to entrepreneurs.

One of the most perplexing concerns for an entrepreneur is the number of employees that should be hired. Adding employees—expanding the new venture's human resources—offers obvious advantages. New employees are a source of information, skills, and energy; further, the more employees a new venture has, the greater the number and larger the size of the projects it can undertake. There is little doubt that in many contexts, people working together in a coordinated manner can accomplish far more than individuals working alone. But adding employees to a new venture has an obvious downside, too. Employees add to the new venture's fixed expenses and raise many complex issues relating to the health and safety of such persons that must be carefully considered. In a sense, therefore, expanding the company's workforce is a double-edged sword, and the results of expanding the number of employees can truly be mixed in nature.

However, existing evidence suggests that on balance, the benefits of increasing the number of employees outweigh the costs. New ventures that start with more employees have a greater chance of surviving than those that begin with a smaller number.[5] Similarly, companies with more employees have higher rates of growth than those with fewer employees.[6] Profitability, too, is positively related to the size of new ventures. For example, the greater the number of employees, the larger the earnings of new ventures, and the greater the income generated by them for their founders.[7]

LEARNING OBJECTIVE

2 Describe the relationship of number of employees to new venture success.

We should hasten to note that these findings are all correlational in nature: They indicate that number of employees is related, in a positive manner, to several measures of new ventures' success. They do not, however, indicate that hiring new employees causes such success. In fact, both number of employees and various measures of financial success may stem from other, underlying factors, such as the quality of the opportunity being developed, commitment and talent of the founding team, and even general economic conditions (it is often easier to hire good employees at reasonable cost when the economy is weak than when it is strong). So the relationship between new venture size (number of employees) and new venture success should be approached with a degree of caution. Still, having said this, it is clear that human resources are a key ingredient in the success of start-up companies.

In other words, the entrepreneur needs to pay attention to attracting, motivating, and retaining high-quality employees. Initially, the founders perform the entire human resources function themselves—they want to choose everyone who joins their team and to play a central role in motivating and retaining these people. But at some point, they must entrust these tasks to others. If that's the case, then why should you, as current or future entrepreneurs, be interested in these tasks? After all, you will ultimately turn these tasks over to others. We think the answer involves three major points. First, the process through which entrepreneurs delegate these tasks to others is gradual rather than sudden. Thus, information on how to accomplish human resources tasks skillfully is useful to entrepreneurs during the early phases of their new venture's growth, when they *will* be performing them. Second, most entrepreneurs want to place their personal stamp on their companies, and one important way of doing this is to play an active role in establishing the systems through which first-rate employees are recruited, motivated, and retained. Third, when they delegate these tasks to others, entrepreneurs need to choose these persons well—to choose the best people. One way of assuring that the best people possible are recruited is to understand just what these individuals will do. In sum, we think there are several reasons why it's important for you to understand the nature of these tasks (recruiting, motivating, and retaining excellent employees). In the remaining sections of this chapter, therefore, we will provide you with an overview of key factors relating to these tasks. Our goal is certainly *not* to turn you into an expert on key aspects of human resource management; reaching that goal requires several years of specialized training. But we do want to arm you with basic information we believe you will find valuable as you seek to enhance the growth of your new venture and move toward achieving your personal dreams and goals.

RECRUITING AND SELECTING HIGH-PERFORMING EMPLOYEES

New ventures face serious obstacles with respect to attracting outstanding employees: As new companies, they are relatively unknown to potential employees and cannot offer the legitimacy or security of established firms. Thus, they enter the market for human resources with important disadvantages. How do start-up companies overcome these difficulties? Largely through the use of social networks. In other words, they tend to hire people they know either directly, from personal contact, or indirectly, through recommendations from people they do know and trust[8] (see Figure 12.1). This approach is helpful to new ventures in several ways.

By hiring people they know (often family members, friends, or persons with whom they have worked in the past), entrepreneurs are able to acquire human resources quickly, without the necessity for long and costly searches. Second, because they know the people they hire either directly or indirectly, it is easier for entrepreneurs to convince these individuals of the value of the opportunity they are pursuing. Third, new ventures often lack clearly established rules or a well-defined culture; having direct or indirect ties with new employees makes it easier to integrate them into this loose and changing structure.

In sum, new ventures generally hire people known to the founding entrepreneurs, either directly or indirectly, and in this way are able to expand their base of human resources in a relatively rapid and cost-effective manner.

Figure 12.1 Social Networks: A Major Source of New Employees for New Ventures

Entrepreneurs often rely on social networks as a source of new employees. The persons they hire are people they know or people who have been recommended to them by people they trust.

However, to some point, to fuel growth, entrepreneurs need to hire from outside their social networks, and new ventures are at a serious disadvantage when they enter the labour market. Because they are new, they are relatively unknown to potential employees and cannot offer the security or brand familiarity of established firms. Although there is currently little direct evidence on this issue, it seems reasonable to suggest that unless new ventures succeed in overcoming these obstacles, they may be doomed to failure—after all, they cannot grow if they fail to attract and retain essential and dedicated employees. How, then, should entrepreneurs approach this important task? To provide you with some useful guidelines, we will consider two basic questions: (1) Where should entrepreneurs search for high-quality employees? and (2) What specific techniques should they use to identify the best among them?

LEARNING OBJECTIVE

3 Describe the role of social networks in new ventures' efforts to hire additional employees.

The Search for High-Performing Employees: Knowing What You Need and Where to Look

There is an old saying suggesting, "It's hard to get somewhere unless you know where you want to go." In other words, it's hard to reach a goal unless you have defined it clearly. That's certainly true with respect to hiring high-quality employees. Before beginning a search for such persons, it is crucial to first determine just what it is that your new venture is seeking. In the field of human resource management, this recommendation implies two preliminary tasks: a **job analysis**—determining just what the job involves and what it requires in terms of specific knowledge, skills, and abilities[9]—and formulation of a clear **job description**—an overview of what the job involves in terms of its duties, responsibilities, and working conditions. In large companies, job analyses can be very detailed and lead to highly specific job descriptions, but for entrepreneurs, especially in the very hectic early days of a new venture, when founders have to do virtually everything, it is usually sufficient for them to simply have a clear idea of what the person or persons they are seeking will actually do and a brief written description of the major duties and tasks they will perform.

Why are these initial steps so important? Because they provide a basis for choosing among potential employees—for selecting those most likely to succeed in a specific job. The best choice, all other factors being equal, is the person whose knowledge, skills, and abilities provide the closest match to the requirements of the job. If they have not conducted a job analysis and formulated a clear job description for a particular position, entrepreneurs (or the persons to whom they delegate this task) will still proceed to choose among potential employees—this is a task that *must* be accomplished. However, it will be more difficult to make these choices on the basis of job requirements. Instead, for instance, they may choose the persons they find most congenial or attractive, or applicants who stand out from the crowd rather than the person best qualified for the job. For this reason, it is best to formulate a clear idea of the specific requirements of any job before beginning the search-and-selection process.

LEARNING OBJECTIVE

4 Define "job analysis" and "job description" and explain why they are important initial steps in the search for new employees.

Having said that, we should add that in some industries—those that are on the cutting edge of technological advancement, such as biotechnology, for instance—it may be very difficult to specify the requirements of various positions very precisely because conditions are changing so rapidly that the tasks people perform, too, will certainly change. But insofar as conditions will permit, it is a good idea to first determine, as precisely as possible, what is needed before beginning the search for new employees.

Once the task of specifying precisely what is needed—the skills and abilities new employees will provide to the growing venture—has been completed, the search for these persons can begin. As we noted, new ventures often fill their initial needs for additional human resources largely through their founders' social networks. In other words, they tend to hire people they know either directly, from personal contact, or indirectly, through recommendations from people they do know and trust. Referrals from current or former employees are often especially helpful in this regard. If new ventures continue to grow, however, these sources may soon prove to be inadequate: They simply do not produce a sufficient number of potential employees or those with the full array of knowledge and skills that the new venture needs.

At that point, entrepreneurs must expand their search. One method is to use advertisements in carefully selected publications. For instance, ads may be placed in trade journals that reach specific, targeted audiences. Because new ventures usually lack the resources to screen large numbers of applicants, it is generally less useful for them to advertise in mass-circulation outlets, such as large local newspapers (although, of course, there may be exceptions to this general rule). Other useful sources include visits to college and university employment centres; here, once again, it is possible to specify job requirements quite precisely and to be reasonably certain of interviewing only persons whose qualifications match these closely. In recent years, Internet sites (e.g., Jobshark.ca and Monster.ca) have been developed to assist companies in finding employees, and to assist potential employees in finding jobs. Entrepreneurs should not overlook current customers as a potential source of new employees. Customers know the new venture's products and are familiar with its operations, so they can often be a very helpful source of referrals. Finally, professional headhunters are often helpful. Venture capitalists often have working relationships with such firms to help the start-ups they fund obtain management and technical talent, so these recruitment firms can be a very useful source for entrepreneurs who have obtained financial support from VCs. Together, the sources outlined here are often sufficient to provide growing new ventures with a pool of applicants from which they can choose. And that brings us to the next important step in the process: techniques for selecting the best people in this pool.

Selection: Techniques for Choosing the Cream of the Crop

Our experience tells us that, in many cases, new ventures do a reasonably good job of assembling a pool of potential employees: Their social networks, current customers, and other sources yield a number of persons who could, at first glance, be hired. Choosing among them, however, is another story. This is a difficult task under the best of conditions, even in large organizations that have human resource departments with experts specifically trained to perform this task. Entrepreneurs, in contrast, often lack such specialized experience and, moreover, must try to fit the task of making these decisions into their extremely busy days. Further, serious mistakes—hiring an incompetent or unethical person—are even more costly for new ventures, with their limited resources, than for large, existing companies. So how can entrepreneurs accomplish this task effectively? The answer, basically, is through a combination of several techniques.

First, it is essential for us to insert a few words on the topics of reliability and validity, because these concepts are closely related to the question of selecting the best employees. **Reliability** refers to the extent to which measurements are consistent across time or between judges. For instance, if you step on your bathroom scale this morning and it reads "70 kilograms" but then you get back on it 10 minutes

LEARNING OBJECTIVE

5 Define "reliability" and "validity" and explain why all techniques used for selection must be high on both. Describe structured interviews and explain why they are higher in validity than traditional employment interviews.

later and it reads "60 kilograms," you might question its reliability; your weight hasn't changed in 10 minutes, so the scale does not seem to be providing consistent measurements. (Perhaps it needs a new battery.) A good illustration of reliability across judges is the ratings given to champion figure skaters by a panel of judges. The more the judges agree, the more we consider their ratings to be reliable (consistent).

In contrast, **validity** refers to the extent to which measurements actually reflect the underlying dimension to which they refer. For instance, consider the device shown in Figure 12.2. It purports to measure the sexiness of the person holding the bulb on the bottom. Does it really measure this dimension? Of course not; it responds to the temperature of people's hands, which is likely more a reflection of what they have been holding recently (e.g., a cup of hot coffee) than their sex appeal. Such a device is low in validity: It does not measure what it purports to measure. (In fact, it is fair to say that it has no validity.)

Reliability and validity are closely related to the task of selecting the best persons for specific jobs: Only selection tools or techniques that both reliable and valid are useful for this purpose—and legal under existing laws. In fact, if the validity of any technique used for selection is doubtful, using that technique can result in costly lawsuits; keep this fact in mind if this type of trouble is one you would rather avoid!

So where do various selection tools stand with respect to reliability and validity? Many, it turns out, are quite low on both of these dimensions. Letters of recommendation, for instance, have been found to be almost totally unrelated to actual on-the-job performance, which means that they are very low in validity. Surprisingly, the same is true for standard employment interviews—the selection technique that is by far the most widely used. Traditional interviews, which are largely unstructured in nature and proceed in any way that the interviewer wishes, suffer from several major problems that tend to reduce their validity. For instance, interviewers often make their decisions very early, after only a few minutes—well before they have had a chance to gather pertinent information about an applicant.[10] Second, if interviewers ask different questions of each applicant, and allow the length of the interview to vary greatly, how can they later compare the various applicants in a systematic manner?[11] The answer is that they can't, so validity suffers.

Additional problems involve the fact that interviewers, like everyone else, are subject to subtle forms of bias in the way they perceive applicants. A large body of evidence indicates that applicants who are attractive, applicants who are similar to the interviewer in various respects (age, background, ethnic identity), and applicants who are good at impression management tend to have a major edge over applicants who are less attractive, less similar to the interviewer, and less skilled at impression management.[12] Such factors are largely unrelated to the ability of various persons to perform the jobs for which they are being interviewed, so the validity of such interviews is questionable, at best. Despite these drawbacks, and despite the bizarre results they often yield (see Table 12.1), most companies—including new ventures—continue to employ brief job interviews as the primary means through which they choose their employees. Why is this so? Probably because most persons, including entrepreneurs, suffer from the illusion that they are highly skilled at social perception. In other words, they believe that they can form an accurate impression of others' major traits, motives, and talents on the basis of a brief conversation with them.[13] In fact, systematic research suggests that we are unduly optimistic in this regard: The task of assessing others is far more difficult and subject to many more sources of error than most people realize. We are generally less successful at this task than we believe, which calls the validity of traditional job interviews into serious question.

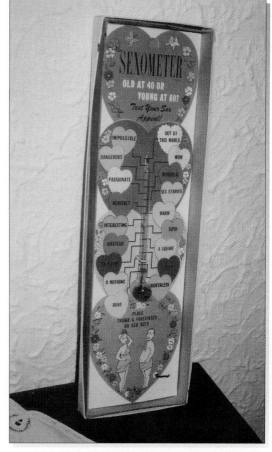

Photo courtesy of R.A. Baron.

Figure 12.2 Low Validity: An Example

Validity refers to the extent to which any measuring device or instrument actually measures what it claims to measure. The device shown here is, of course, very low in validity: It really cannot measure what it claims to measure.

Table 12.1 Interviews: Sometimes They Yield Bizarre Results!

Traditional job interviews sometimes yield unexpected—and bizarre—results. The information shown here is based on actual interviews.

• Applicant entered and asked: "Why am I here?"
• When asked about his loyalty, one applicant showed a tattoo of his girlfriend's name on his arm.
• Applicant said that if I hired him, "You will soon regret it!"
• The applicant arrived with a large snake around her neck and stated: "I take him everywhere."
• Applicant remarked: "If I am hired, I will teach you ballroom dancing for free." She then started demonstrating this skill.
• The applicant left a dry-cleaning tag on his jacket and remarked: "I wanted to show you how clean I am."
• The applicant took three calls on a cellphone during the interview and said: "I have another business on the side."
• After a difficult question, the applicant said: "I need to leave the room to meditate before answering."

Source: Adapted from information presented by Gomez-Mejia, Balkin, & Cardy, 2001.

Fortunately, the validity of interviews can be greatly improved by switching to what are known as **structured interviews**, in which all applicants are asked the same questions—ones chosen carefully to be truly job-related. Some of the questions (situational questions) ask the applicants how they would respond to particular work situations (e.g., "What would you do if you ran out of supplies?"). Others focus on job knowledge—do applicants have the necessary information. Additional questions focus on applicants' willingness to perform the job under current conditions (e.g., "What are your feelings about working overtime during very busy periods?"). Empirical evidence suggests that structured interviews are, perhaps, the most valid technique for selecting employees: Different interviewers come up with similar ratings for the same applicants, and these ratings do predict on-the-job performance. So although they are not perfect, structured interviews offer a useful technique—one that can help entrepreneurs make the correct decisions when choosing among several applicants.

Another technique for selecting employees and one that is reasonably high in validity involves **biodata**—information about employees' background, experiences, and preferences provided by employees on application forms. This information has been found to have moderate validity for predicting job performance—provided the questions asked are indeed relevant to the job in question. For instance, suppose that a job requires a lot of travel; a question on the application form might ask: "How willing are you to travel on the job?" or "How frequently did you travel in your previous job?" Clearly, applicants who are willing to travel are a better choice than those who express reluctance to travel. But remember: Information collected in this manner is useful only to the extent that it is relevant to the job in question. In addition, certain kinds of questions cannot be asked, either in person or on application forms. Questions that inquire about an applicant's family, physical characteristics, personal health, and religion can violate human rights legislation and can land an entrepreneur in hot water. As long as questions are focused directly on knowledge, skills, preferences, and experience related to the job, these problems can be avoided, and structured interviews can be a valuable tool for choosing the best persons for specific jobs.

Although we have been emphasizing the use of interviews as a tool for selecting employees, it is important to note that many companies—new ventures included—often use such meetings with job applicants for another purpose: to build the image of the company. Up to a point, this can be a good strategy. But research findings indicate that it is often a big mistake to oversell a company, whether it is a new start-up or an established corporation. Painting too positive or rosy a picture of working conditions can set employees up for major disappointments once they are on the job, which can undermine both their motivation and commitment. In general, it is much better to make sure that interviews reflect what are known as **realistic job previews**—efforts to present a balanced and accurate picture of the company to potential employees. In that way, unpleasant surprises are minimized, and new employees are more likely to remain on the job after they are hired.[14]

Why should you, as a current or future entrepreneur, want to know about these techniques and procedures? For two reasons we have already noted: (1) You will probably carry out the tasks of recruiting and selecting employees yourself, at least initially, and (2) later on, if you decide to delegate these tasks to others, you should still want to retain oversight, to ensure that these tasks are being handled correctly. Remember: Not only is recruitment of excellent employees crucial to the future of a new venture, but carrying out this task in an inappropriate manner can also put the company at risk for lawsuits stemming from violations of the laws. Clearly, then, this is one more instance where the adage "Better safe than sorry" applies—and with a vengeance.

One final point: It is absolutely crucial to carefully check all references provided by job applicants and all claims they make concerning past experience and training. All people, unfortunately, are not completely honest, and applicants for jobs at new ventures are no exception to this general rule. To be on the safe side, therefore, entrepreneurs should check at least major aspects of an applicant's resume before hiring the best candidate. In all likelihood, the information is accurate, but in a few cases, there may be some big surprises lurking around the edges!

KEY POINTS

- As new ventures grow, their requirements for additional human resources, too, increase. Often, these new employees are hired through the founding teams' social network.
- Existing evidence suggests that the greater the number of employees in new ventures, the greater their financial success. However, this relationship does not necessarily imply that increasing the number of employees causes success; rather, both success and number of employees may stem from the same underlying factors (e.g., the quality of the opportunity being exploited).
- Before beginning a search for new employees, it is very useful to carry out a job analysis and prepare a job description for each position to be filled. Only after these preliminary tasks have been completed can clarity be obtained about what needs are to be met by new employees as well as steps formulated to choose the best persons for these positions.
- In their search for new employees, entrepreneurs focus primarily on their own social networks. However, as the new venture grows, it may be necessary to turn to other sources, such as advertisements in trade publications, the Internet, and referrals from customers.
- Reliability—the consistency of measurements over time or between judges—and validity—the extent to which measurements reflect the dimension to which they refer—are important considerations in selecting employees. Only techniques high in both reliability and validity are useful for this purpose and are legal under existing laws.
- Two employee selection techniques that are high in reliability and validity are structured interviews and biodata—information about applicants' background, experiences, and preferences—gathered by means of detailed application forms.
- It is best to provide potential employees with accurate information about working conditions in a company during an interview; such realistic job previews protect new hires from unpleasant surprises when they assume their jobs. This practice also can improve employee motivation and retention.

MOTIVATING EMPLOYEES: MAXIMIZING THE VALUE OF THE NEW VENTURE'S HUMAN RESOURCES

Entrepreneurs are, by definition, highly motivated persons, and so it sometimes comes as a shock to them that everyone hired by their new ventures is not equally motivated to make the venture succeed. Early hires may well have high levels of motivation because they are acquaintances, former co-workers, or people referred to the entrepreneurs by close friends. But once a new venture begins to grow and to hire additional employees, the issue of motivation—of how to motivate these persons so that they will do their best work—arises, just as it does in every other organization. In fact, because every person on the payroll matters to a new venture, and it cannot afford to support free riders who coast along on the efforts of others, maximizing employee motivation is a key concern for entrepreneurs. In this section, we will offer some concrete suggestions for reaching this goal. Initially, most entrepreneurs use an inspiring vision of what their company can become to motivate new employees, and they are often highly skilled in this regard.[15] But this is just one technique that may be effective for building motivation, and we believe that it is very useful for entrepreneurs to at least be familiar with several others.

Before turning to these motivation boosters, however, we should say a few words about just what we mean by the term **motivation**. In the fields of human resource management and organizational behaviour, the two branches of management that have focused most attention on this topic, motivation is usually defined as the processes that arouse, direct, and maintain human behaviour toward attaining some goal. In other words, motivation refers to behaviour that is energized by, and directed toward, reaching some desired target or objective. To fully understand motivation, all four components are necessary: Nothing happens without arousal (energy), and nothing is accomplished by random flailing around; to attain specific goals, behaviour must be directed and generally continued over some period of time. Here's a simple example: Suppose that an entrepreneur wants to obtain financing for her new venture. She doesn't sit around daydreaming about this objective; rather, she takes active, energetic steps to reach it. And these steps are directed—they are not sheer random activity. For instance, she may use her network to identify possible business angels or to put her in contact with venture capitalists and other potential sources of funding. She doesn't, in contrast, go to a nearby intersection with a sign reading "Need money for a new venture" and try to solicit it from passing motorists. Further, her behaviour persists over time: She doesn't quit after one or two setbacks. On the contrary, her desire to obtain financing is strong, so she continues to try over and over again. And her efforts are directed toward a specific goal—obtaining financing. Because all four components are present—energy, direction, persistence, and a clear objective or goal—her actions illustrate the basic nature of motivation. (See Figure 12.3 for a summary of these components.) Note, by the way, that this is an example of self-motivation: The entrepreneur is motivated to obtain financing by internal factors—her own goals and desires. Because a key task for entrepreneurs is that of motivating others, we will focus primarily on this issue in the current discussion.

Reaching for the Moon—or at Least, the Next Level Up: The Key Role of Goals—and Vision

When you work on a task, do you set goals for yourself? For instance, when you began reading this chapter, did you set the goal of finishing all of it? Half? If you are like most ambitious, hard-working people the answer is probably *yes*. You probably already know that setting goals in this way can be highly motivating: They can help us maintain behaviour for long periods of time. Why? Partly because knowing where we want to get (our goal) helps us measure our progress: We can tell whether, and how quickly, we are getting where we want to be. That, it appears, helps us continue;

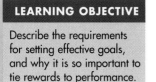

LEARNING OBJECTIVE

6 Describe the requirements for setting effective goals, and why it is so important to tie rewards to performance.

Figure 12.3 Motivation: Its Basic Components

Motivation involves four major components: arousal (activation), direction (toward some goal), maintenance of the behaviour over time (persistence), and the goal toward which energy is directed.

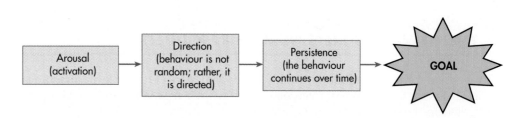

in fact, research findings indicate that the closer we get to a specific goal, the stronger our motivation to reach it may become, and the greater the effort we expend trying to finally get there.[16]

So far, we have been talking about self-set goals—the goals people set for themselves. Clearly, entrepreneurs are masters at this task: In fact, the desire to set their own goals—to have personal control over their life and their own activities—is one reason why many people become entrepreneurs in the first place.[17] In contrast to entrepreneurs, many persons are not so self-directed: They do not seek total independence and do not always set goals for themselves. Or, if they do, they set goals that are so easy to reach that they are not very motivating. Echoing this basic fact, a vast number of research studies indicate that in many business contexts, setting goals for employees is an extremely useful way to increase their motivation—and their performance. In order to be maximally helpful, though, such goals must meet certain criteria:

- They must be *challenging*—the goals must be a stretch for the people involved, so that they have to work hard to expend effort to reach them. In contrast, goals that are not challenging do not increase motivation and performance.

- They must be *attainable*—setting impossible goals that people cannot reach does not increase their motivation or performance; on the contrary, such goals often encourage people to give up because they conclude that they cannot possibly reach the stated objective.

- They must be *specific*—just telling people to do their best or increase their output is practically useless. To motivate increased effort and performance, goals must be specific (e.g., "Increase your output by 15 percent within a month," "Reduce your error rate by 20 percent within two weeks").

- They must be *accepted* by the persons involved—if people reject a goal because it is not consistent with their own wishes or objectives, it will have little if any impact on them; after all, it's not *their* goal so why should they try to attain it?

- *Feedback* concerning progress must be provided—the people involved must be kept informed about how they are doing. Are they moving toward the goal? At an acceptable pace? In the absence of such feedback, people have no idea about whether their efforts are paying off, and may soon become discouraged.

As we noted earlier, a large body of evidence suggests that setting goals that meet these criteria is a powerful technique for increasing motivation and performance.[18] Indeed, the results it produces are often nothing short of dramatic. For instance, in one recent study, operators of a pizza chain found that drivers who delivered its pizzas were not stopping fully at stop signs, thus putting themselves and the company at risk for accidents—and lawsuits. Goal setting coupled with concrete feedback was used to change this behaviour: Drivers were given the specific goal of coming to a complete stop at least 75 percent of the time (versus the 45 percent rate they showed at the beginning of the study). Further, their driving was observed, and they were given feedback about the extent to which they met this goal every week. As you can see from Figure 12.4, results were dramatic: Shortly after goal setting and feedback were instituted, the drivers' performance rose to very close to the target level. However, when feedback was discontinued, their rate dropped back down to what it had been earlier. (A control group received no goal and no feedback; as expected, their behaviour did not change during the course of the study.)

Because goal setting is relatively easy to use, it can be a powerful technique for entrepreneurs. To be effective, though, it must be applied in accordance with the guidelines described here. If these guidelines are ignored, results will probably be disappointing.

At this point, we wish to emphasize again a point we made earlier: Many entrepreneurs go beyond focusing on objectives relating to task performance. They focus instead on *vision*—on what they want to achieve, and what their company can

Figure 12.4 Goal Setting: A Highly Effective Technique for Motivating Employees

When a clear goal was established for the drivers of pizza delivery trucks and they were given feedback, their performance increased sharply. When feedback was removed, however, performance decreased to the level shown initially, before the goal was established.

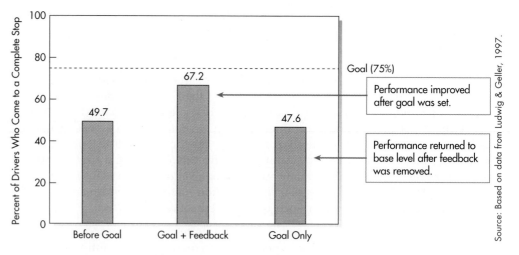

Source: Based on data from Ludwig & Geller, 1997.

become. Communicating this vision clearly to employees and others, research findings suggest, can greatly enhance the growth of new ventures.[19]

One final comment: Throughout this discussion, we have mentioned motivation and performance together. It is important to note that they are definitely *not* the same thing. Motivation is a key ingredient in the performance of many tasks, but by itself, it is not a guarantee of improved performance. For instance, if employees lack required skills or knowledge to perform a job well, they will probably be unable to do so even if their motivation is very high—that's one reason why careful selection of job applicants is so important. Similarly, even highly motivated people may not be able to do a good job with poor or faulty equipment. So keep in mind that motivation is only one of the ingredients in good performance; it is often a crucial one, but it is by no means the entire story.

Tying Rewards to Performance: The Role of Expectancies

Do you recall our discussion of the optimistic bias in Chapter 3? We noted then that, in general, people are optimistic; they believe, more than is justified by the cold light of reason, that things will turn out well and that they will experience positive outcomes in many different situations.[20] This tendency is closely related to motivation: Because people are optimistic, they generally believe that the greater the effort they expend on a given task, the better they will perform it, and that good performance will generally yield larger rewards than poor performance. In many cases, these assumptions are reasonable; in other cases, though, such assumptions can be misleading. For instance, have you ever tried to perform a task with faulty tools or when you were lacking some necessary information? In such cases, working hard does not necessarily improve performance. I recall the first time I ever tried to build a bookcase; because I didn't know enough about how pieces of wood could be joined, it didn't matter how hard I worked: What I produced was still pretty shaky.

Similarly, you have probably experienced situations in your life where good performance was not recognized or rewarded; perhaps the situation was unfair, or your good work was just overlooked.

An important theory of motivation known as **expectancy theory**[21] suggests that both of these factors, plus one additional one, play a key role in motivation. Specifically, this theory—which has been verified by many different studies—suggests that people will be motivated to work diligently on a task only when three conditions prevail: (1) they believe that expending effort will improve their performance (a condition known as *expectancy*), (2) they believe that good performance will be rewarded (a condition known as *instrumentality*), and (3) the rewards offered are ones they really want or value (*valence*). When any one of these factors is missing, motivation tends to drop to very low levels, which is eminently reasonable: Why, after all, should anyone exert effort on tasks when doing so won't improve performance, or when there is no link between the quality of one's performance and the payoffs one receives? The answer is clear: Under these conditions, they will *not* expend the effort—they will not be motivated to work hard on this particular task.

Now here is where things get interesting: Because entrepreneurs are even more optimistic than other persons[22] and also higher in the belief that they can accomplish whatever they set out to accomplish (i.e., higher in self-efficacy), they tend to assume—implicitly, but strongly—that effort and performance are closely linked and that performance and rewards are also closely related to each other. So if working hard on a task doesn't succeed at first, they tend to redouble their efforts rather than give up. If at first the value of their hard work is not recognized, they tend to strive even harder to assure that, ultimately, it is. Other persons, however, may be more inclined to experience declines in motivation when confronted with these conditions. Thus, in running their new ventures, entrepreneurs should take careful note of this factor. It suggests several practical steps that they can implement to maintain the motivation of their employees at high levels:

- Make sure that effort does indeed lead to good performance—ensure that people have the training, equipment, and knowledge they need to perform their jobs well. If these are lacking, and effort does not produce improvements in performance, employees may get discouraged, with costly results for the new venture.

- Make sure that good performance is recognized and rewarded—that there is a close link between performance and rewards. Common examples are reward systems for pay, bonuses, and other positive outcomes established for the new venture. We will return to reward systens in more detail in our discussion of steps useful in retaining first-rate employees. Here, we will merely note that when excellent performance is *not* recognized and rewarded, there is more at work than motivation—there is also a very real possibility that these people will decide to leave, which can be devastating for a new venture.

- Make sure that the rewards provided for good performance are rewards that employees really want. It may sound obvious, but remember: *Money is not the only thing people want from their jobs.* True, it is certainly important, but sometimes, people value other outcomes, such as specific kinds of fringe benefits, flexible working hours or vacation schedules, praise, and recognition. For instance, biotech start-ups often permit their scientists to publish research findings because it increases the motivation of these highly trained professionals. For this reason, many organizations are currently offering employees a broad range of benefits, including all those shown in Table 12.2. If you want to retain the best people in your company, ensuring that rewards for good performance are rewards that employees truly want is a valuable principle to remember.

In sum, to the extent that the links between effort and performance or between performance and reward are strong and clear for employees, their motivation will be high. Break or weaken these links, however, and the results may be a demoralized

BENEFITS (DESCRIPTION)	
Counselling (financial, legal, psychiatric/psychological)	Parking
Discounts on merchandise	Transportation to and from work
Tax preparation	Child adoption
Education subsidies	Clothing allowance
Child care	Subsidized food service
Housing allowance	Tool allowance
Elder care	Social and recreational opportunities
Emergency loans	Relocation expenses
Physical fitness programs	Credit union

Table 12.2 Employee Benefits: Some New Forms

In order to keep employee motivation high, it is important to offer benefits that they find desirable. Here is a sample of the vast range of benefits offered to employees by actual companies. We're sure you will find some of these surprising.

Source: Based on information presented by Henderson, 1989, Compensation management, Prentice-Hall.

and de-motivated workforce. Savvy entrepreneurs, therefore, will take careful note of these basic facts and do everything in their power to assure that conditions favouring high levels of motivation are the standard in their new ventures. Again, if they don't focus on this task themselves, they should be certain that the people to whom they delegate this task are using the techniques described here; if they are not, there may be reason for concern—and added oversight.

Fairness: An Essential Ingredient in Motivation

The summer between my freshman and sophomore years at college, I (Robert Baron) worked in the finance office of a large labour union. I was a summer fill-in, so the work was totally boring: I mainly filed forms and prepared new file folders by placing labels on them. My hours were long, and I had to punch a time clock when I arrived and when I left. I had only 45 minutes for lunch and one 15-minute break in the morning. I needed the money for college, so I would have gladly put up with all of this except for one thing: Another student also working there was treated much better. Tom, who was a year older than I was, arrived late every morning and often left early. He disappeared for long periods of time during the day, and often took two-hour lunches. Worst of all, he was given the most interesting jobs to do. The final blow came when, by mistake, I received his paycheque. When I opened the envelope and discovered that it was 50 percent higher than mine, my head nearly exploded over the unfairness of it all. "Who the heck is this guy to get such special treatment?" I wondered. I soon found out: He was the nephew of the president of the union. End of mystery—but not of my feelings of being treated unfairly.

What do you think these feelings of unfairness did to my motivation? As you can readily guess, they caused it to drop to zero. "Why should I put out effort for an organization that treats me like this?" I remember thinking. In fact, this is one of the key effects of unfairness in business contexts: The people exposed to it experience a strong drop in motivation. Even worse, they often engage in instances of theft and sabotage, partly because of their anger toward the business that has treated them unfairly and partly because this is one way to even the score, so to speak—to get what they feel they deserve, even if they have to take it themselves.[23]

This situation provides a clear illustration of one set of conditions that leads individuals to conclude that they are being treated unfairly—an imbalance between the contributions they make to the outcomes (rewards) they receive, relative to those of other persons. In general, we expect this ratio of contributions and rewards to be about the same for everyone in the group: The more each person contributes, the larger the rewards he or she receives. In other words, we seek **distributive justice** (or **equity**)— conditions under which available rewards are divided fairly among group members, according to what each has contributed to the group.[24] It was the absence of this kind of fairness that upset me in my summer job: My contributions were actually larger than those of Tom, yet his rewards were greater the mine (see Figure 12.5).

An imbalance between what they receive and what they contribute is not the only reason people feel unfairly treated, however. In addition, such feelings can arise when people feel that the procedures in dividing available rewards are not fair

Figure 12.5 Distributive Justice: A Specific Example

In deciding whether we have been treated fairly, we often focus on distributive justice—the degree to which available rewards are divided in accordance with each person's contributions (the more each contributes, the larger the rewards received). In a summer job I once held, my contributions were larger but my outcomes were smaller than those of another student. The result: I experienced strong feelings of unfairness (inequity).

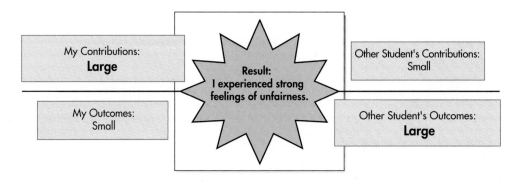

(*procedural justice*) or when they feel that the people who distribute these rewards have not explained their decisions adequately or shown enough courtesy in their behaviour (*interactional justice*).[25] Reactions to these kinds of injustice, too, are much the same: People become angry, feel resentment, and experience a drop in the desire to work hard. They may also demand larger rewards or more courteous treatment or—ultimately—take a walk and leave this exploitative workplace behind. (See the **Danger! Pitfall Ahead!** section for discussion of another, especially disturbing, kind of reaction to unfairness on the part of employees.)

LEARNING OBJECTIVE

7 Describe the role of fairness in motivating employees.

DANGER! PITFALL AHEAD!

Employee Theft: Evening the Score with an Unfair Employer

- In the restaurant business—one in which many entrepreneurs operate—theft by employees is estimated to be between 5 and 8 percent of gross sales
- A 2002 study by Ernst & Young found that 20 percent of Canadians are personally aware of people stealing from their employers.[26]
- In 2004, a study by the Retail Council of Canada found that internal theft accounted for 48 percent of retail losses and was the leading cause of retail losses.[27]
- In retail businesses around the world, more than 3 percent of employees admit that they steal every day, and 8 percent admit that they steal at least once a week.
- Fraud costs businesses in the United States more than $400 million each year.

These numbers suggest that employee theft is a major problem for many companies and that—more to the point—small businesses (including new ventures) are far from immune to this predicament. Why do employees steal? For many reasons, but research findings indicate that one of the most important reasons is that they believe they are being treated unfairly.[28] In other words, they steal because they feel that they are entitled to do so—they are merely evening the score, so to speak. Here's one disturbing example, from a small law office.

This office specialized in personal injury claims and employed a number of paralegals—people who do not hold a law degree but are trained in basic legal procedures. One of them, we'll call him Joe, was paid $7 per hour. Working conditions were terrible—to earn more money, the lawyers in the firm continually increased the number of cases they were handling, and although they earned huge fees, they did not share these with their hard-working employees. Most paralegals left after a few months, but Joe stuck it out. Why? Because he figured out a way to steal large amounts of money (more than $2,500 per month) from the company. Here's how: Because legal claims often drag on for years, clients would move away, give up, or simply forget about their cases after some period of time. So when cheques arrived to settle these cases, there was often no client to receive her or his share. Joe simply forged the names of the people and cashed their cheques. Rightfully, these leftover cheques should have gone to the company, but as Joe put it, "They were underpaying me, so I figured they owed me." In this instance, it was a small law firm that suffered financial losses, but the same pattern can certainly develop in new ventures if employees feel that they are not being treated fairly. Because struggling start-up companies need all the revenue they can generate and can ill-afford losses stemming from employee theft, it is clear that building fairness into their culture is not only the ethical thing to do—it is the most practical, too! And, of course, it is also important to have systems that monitor inventory and money.

What does this mean for entrepreneurs? Several things. First, they should be very careful to be fair to people in their new ventures. Strong efforts must be made to link rewards to performance as closely as possible, so that the greater the employees' contributions, the greater their rewards. Second, it is important to establish fair procedures for evaluating performance and distributing available rewards—procedures that are understood by all employees. We will have more to say about this issue later, but it is definitely an important where motivation is concerned. Third, there is a strong reason for treating employees with courtesy and respect. Not only is this behaviour ethically correct, but it is also an essential condition for maintaining a high level of motivation.

Designing Jobs to Make Them Motivating

Before concluding, we should briefly mention one additional technique for maintaining or increasing motivation among the employees of a new venture: designing the jobs they perform so that they are intrinsically motivating. Almost no one likes jobs that are totally routine, completely repetitious, and which they have little or no control over. People who find themselves in such jobs become clock-watchers, impatiently waiting for the day to end so that they can get back to their real lives—the things they enjoy and that matter to them (see Figure 12.6). Certainly, their jobs are low on the list.

LEARNING OBJECTIVE

8   Define "job enlargement" and "job enrichment" and explain why they are important in motivating employees.

It is all too easy for entrepreneurs, who are excited about creating something new and are typically overstimulated every day, to overlook this fact. They forget that employees may not share in their feelings and may, in fact, be bored by the tasks they perform, which suggests that some attention to **job design**—structuring jobs so that they increase people's interest in doing them (and hence their motivation)—is important. Fortunately, reaching this goal is not very difficult. Two basic steps can be very helpful in assuring that employees' jobs are not totally routine. One approach is known as *job enlargement*, and involves expanding jobs so that they include a wider variety of tasks and activities. For example, instead of having an employee pack products for shipment all day, this person can also be asked to help keep track of returns and perhaps play a role in ordering supplies needed in shipping.

The second basic technique of job design is *job enrichment*, which involves giving employees not simply more tasks, but tasks requiring a higher level of skill and responsibility. For example, the boring summer job I described earlier could have been enriched by allowing me to answer requests from members for various forms or information booklets. Those tasks would have involved a little more thought than filing endless forms, and would also have been tasks I could have done at my own pace.

We have covered a lot of ground in this discussion, but in essence, the principles we have described are very straightforward and eminently reasonable. They can be summarized as follows:

- People will work harder when they are striving to reach challenging goals they accept than when they have no clear goals to attain.

- People will work harder when they perceive clear links between their effort, their performance, and the rewards they receive, than if these links are weak or absent.

- People will work harder when they feel that they are being treated fairly (in terms of rewards, procedures, and courtesy) than when they feel they are being treated unfairly.

- People will work harder when their jobs are designed to be interesting to them.

All of these principles can be built into a new venture; indeed, new ventures have an advantage in this respect over large, existing companies in which complex and unreliable reward systems and organizational politics often get in the way. But these key ingredients in employee motivation will *not* take care of themselves. They will exist only to the extent that entrepreneurs or others to whom this task has been delegated take the time to assure their presence. Given the crucial role of employee motivation in the success of a new venture, this is a task entrepreneurs should definitely *not* neglect.

LEARNING OBJECTIVE

9   List the relative advantages and disadvantages of temporary and permanent employees.

SHOULD NEW VENTURES HIRE TEMPORARY OR PERMANENT EMPLOYEES? COMMITMENT VERSUS COST

In growing their human resources, entrepreneurs must determine whether new employees should be hired on a temporary or permanent basis. Again, there are advantages and disadvantages to both strategies. Temporary employees reduce fixed costs and provide for a great deal of flexibility: They can be hired and released as the fortunes of the venture dictate. Further, hiring temporary employees permits the new venture to secure specialized knowledge or skills that may be required for a specific project; when the project is completed, the temporary employees depart, thus reducing costs.

On the other side of the coin, there are several disadvantages associated with temporary employees. First, they may lack the commitment and motivation of permanent employees. After all, they know that they have been hired on a contract basis for a specified period of time (although the length of the contract can often be extended), so they have little feeling of commitment to the new venture: In a sense, they are visitors, not permanent residents. In addition, there is the real risk that temporary employees will acquire valuable information about the company or its opportunity and then carry this knowledge to potential competitors. Certainly, that is a serious danger for any new venture. Permanent employees, in contrast, tend to be more strongly committed and motivated with respect to the new venture and are less likely to leave.

Overall, then, the choice between temporary and permanent employees is a difficult one. Which is preferable seems to depend, to a large extent, on specific conditions faced by a new venture, such as the industry in which it operates or the opportunity it is attempting to exploit. In situations where flexibility and speed of acquiring new sets of knowledge and expertise are crucial (e.g., among software start-up companies), temporary employees may be very beneficial.[29] In situations where employee commitment and retention are more important (e.g., employees rapidly acquire skills and knowledge that increase their value to the new venture), then focusing on a permanent workforce may be preferable.[30]

Paul Venning/Iconica/Getty Images

Figure 12.6 Low Motivation: One Result of Failing to Design Jobs so That They Are Interesting to Employees

When their jobs are dull and tedious, employees generally have low motivation to perform them. This situation can be rectified through careful job design.

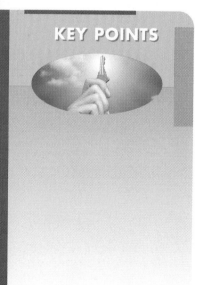

KEY POINTS

- Motivation is defined as the processes that arouse, direct, and maintain human behaviour toward attaining some goal.
- Setting goals that are specific in nature, challenging but attainable, and accepted by the persons for whom they are established is a very effective technique for increasing motivation, provided that the persons in questions also receive feedback concerning progress toward these goals.
- Expectancy theory suggests that motivation will be high when there are clear links between effort and performance and between performance and rewards, and the rewards provided are ones people actually value.
- When employees feel that they are being treated unfairly in terms of outcomes, procedures, or courtesy they receive, motivation is sharply reduced. Thus, entrepreneurs should be careful to establish these kinds of fairness in their new ventures.
- Through job enlargement and job enrichment, jobs can be designed to be interesting and motivating for the persons who perform them.
- The choice between hiring temporary and permanent employees is a complex one; both offer advantages and disadvantages. Ultimately, this decision must depend on the specific situation in which a new venture operates.

RETAINING HIGH-PERFORMING EMPLOYEES

Good people are always in demand, so new ventures face the same problems that all companies do: how to retain high-performing employees. Doing so is especially crucial for new ventures for two key reasons: Replacing good people requires time and other precious resources the new venture can ill afford, and if they leave, they may take important information with them—perhaps to competitors. For these reasons, it is truly important for new ventures to retain their key employees. Many strategies can be useful in this regard, but two are most important: (1) developing excellent reward systems, and (2) building a high level of commitment and loyalty among employees. These two strategies are related, but because they involve different actions, we will discuss them separately, taking care to note links between them.

Reward Systems: Linking Pay and Performance

When bright, talented people come to work for a new venture, they are, in essence, taking a risk: Such persons can always find good jobs in large organizations—workplaces that offer higher levels of job security. So why do they choose to join relatively risky new ventures? Several factors probably play a role: the commitment and enthusiasm of the founders, who tell a good story about their company and its potential future; and dissatisfaction with conditions in the large companies where they have previously worked. Another factor that is crucial, and the one on which we will focus here, involves potential rewards: Good people come to work for new ventures because they perceive greater potential for rewards in this setting. If this is so, then it is also true that ensuring that these beliefs are realized—or at least remain viable— is a crucial task for entrepreneurs. How can this goal be attained? Largely through the development of effective **reward systems**—systems in the new venture for recognizing and rewarding good performance.

In general terms, the kinds of systems most suitable for new ventures are described in the field of human resource management as **pay-for-performance systems** (or *incentive systems*). Such systems assume that employees differ in how much they contribute to the company's success, and that they should be rewarded in accordance with the scope of their contributions. In other words, such systems strive for the kind of distributive justice described earlier in this chapter. Several varieties of such plans exist. The most common type, *merit pay plans*, offers employees an increase in base pay, with the size of the increase being determined by their performance. The higher the performance is rated, the larger the raise. (Space limitations preclude our discussing the complexities involved in measuring and rating employees' performance, but it is crucial that these tasks be carried out in a systematic and accurate manner—far from an easy task. In fact, this matter is so complex that we recommend that entrepreneurs hire appropriate consultants to help them establish such systems of performance appraisal.)

Another type of individual pay-for-performance plan involves bonuses. In such plans, employees receive a bonus based, again, on their performance. A variant of these plans involves *awards*—tangible prizes, such as paid vacations, electronic equipment, or other desirable items. In new ventures, entrepreneurs may also provide either actual stock in the company or stock options to employees. The latter give the employees the right to purchase shares of the company at a given price. Research findings indicate that new ventures that provide equity to employees grow faster and attain greater success than those that do not, so this incentive system appears to be a technique well worth considering.[31]

All these pay-for-performance plans can be highly effective if designed and administered carefully. The advantages lie primarily in the fact that such plans translate the principles we described in our discussion of motivation into tangible actions important to employees. The link between performance and reward is strengthened, commitment to the company's goals is increased, and fairness (in terms of a balance between contributions and outcomes) is obtained. No wonder these plans often work!

Like every management procedure, however, pay-for-performance plans have a downside. Most important among these is the possibility that a "Do only what you get paid for" mentality may develop. In other words, employees may focus on whatever indicators of performance are part of the system, while neglecting everything else. For instance, in some school systems, teachers' pay has been linked to the scores their students attain on standardized tests. The result? The teachers focus on helping their students do well on these tests (e.g., by learning various test-taking tactics) rather than helping them understand the subject matter they are studying. Similarly, the number of no-shows (passengers who book tickets but don't show up) rose when airlines began compensating reservations agents on the number of reservations they booked.

Another problem with pay for performance plans is that they are hard to follow during tough economic times. When funds for raises and bonuses are severely limited—or even nonexistent—it may not be feasible to offer meaningful rewards to employees even for truly outstanding performance. Under these conditions, entrepreneurs need to be creative to hold onto their first-rate employees. People won't work hard forever without tangible rewards, so this is when effective communication with employees becomes essential. They should be fully informed about the current situation and about the entrepreneurs' plans to help things improve. In the meantime, entrepreneurs should do everything they can to demonstrate that they really do value excellent performance. For instance, they can offer nonmonetary support to hard-pressed employees, such as adopting flexible hours and creating a pool of child-care resources. The main point is that ambitious, hardworking persons can put up with difficult situations—including a gap between their performance and their rewards—on a temporary basis. But to maintain their motivation, it is important to assure employees that this state of affairs will not persist. If they conclude that it will not change, their motivation will drop, and they will head for the exit as soon as this is feasible.

In contrast to individual pay-for-performance plans, other reward systems offer incentives to teams of employees rather than to individuals. In such plans, all team members receive rewards based on the team's overall performance. This arrangement can lead to increased performance and a high level of cohesiveness among group members, but is unsatisfying to many people who prefer to float or sink on their own merits. It also encourages *free-riding* effects in which some team members do most of the work while others ride on their coattails.

Perhaps more useful to new ventures are *company-wide pay-for-performance plans*, in which all employees share in the company's profits. *Profit-sharing* plans distribute a portion of the company's earnings to employees; *employee share ownership plans* (ESOP) reward employees with stock or options to purchase the company's stock at a specific (favourable) price. These plans make employees partners in the new venture, which can work wonders for their motivation—and their desire to remain with the company. Indeed, a 1988 study by the Toronto Stock Exchange compared public companies with and without an employee share ownership plan and found that the firms with an ESOP had a higher growth rate, profit margin, return on equity, return on capital and productivity (revenue per employee).[32]

In sum, instituting an effective and fair reward system is one major technique new ventures can use to retain their best employees. Thus, this is an issue entrepreneurs should consider with care as their new ventures grow and they hire increasing numbers of employees.

Building Employee Commitment

Why do people decide to leave one job for another? The answer is definitely not as simple as "Because they can earn more money." On the contrary, the decision to leave appears to be a complex one, involving lots of thought and many factors.[33] How, then, can entrepreneurs tip this decision-making process in their favour, so that high-performing employees remain on board? A key factor involves **organizational commitment**—the extent to which individuals identify with and are involved with their organizations and are, therefore, unwilling to leave it.[34] High levels of organizational commitment are often present in new ventures, where, at least initially, employees are recruited and hired by the founders. As new ventures grow and this task is delegated to others, there is the real risk that such commitment will decrease, so nurturing organizational commitment is an important consideration entrepreneurs should not overlook.

LEARNING OBJECTIVE

10 Describe various means for relating pay and other rewards to performance.

LEARNING OBJECTIVE

11 Define "continuance commitment," "affective commitment," and "normative commitment" and explain their role in the retention of high-quality employees.

Actually, three distinct kinds of organizational commitment exist. One, known as *continuance commitment*, refers mainly to the costs of leaving. If an individual would lose a lot by leaving (e.g., some portion of a pension plan, the opportunity to see close friends), these negatives can weigh heavily in the balance and cause the employee to remain. For instance, stock contributions made by companies to retirement funds are nontaxable until employees redeem the stock. This stipulation can increase continuance commitment because employees want to remain with the company until the stock rises to high levels. Similarly, stock distributed as part of employee share ownership plans may not become fully vested for employees until some period of time has elapsed. Again, this arrangement can increase continuance commitment. A second kind of commitment is known as *affective commitment*—it refers mainly to positive feelings toward the organization. If an individual shares the values of the company and holds it in high regard, this employee is less likely to leave than someone with the opposite feelings. Finally, individuals may remain with a company as a result of *normative commitment*—they stay because of a feeling of obligation to others who would be adversely affected by their departure. All three of these forms of commitment are important to new ventures, because each tends to help in the retention of employees. Employees of new ventures often identify with their employers because they believe in what the company is doing—that's why they came there in the first place! So to the extent such feelings can be strengthened, new ventures can retain their best employees. How can this be accomplished? Research findings offer several suggestions.

First, as job design suggests, making jobs interesting and giving employees some autonomy over how they carry out their work is useful. Why would anyone become committed to an organization that assigns them to dull, routine tasks and gives them no say over their work? Second, affective commitment can be increased by aligning employees' interests with those of the company. Employee share ownership plans are highly effective in this way because, as we noted earlier, they make employees partners in the new venture. To the extent they feel that they have a stake in the new venture, employees may be very reluctant to leave. Finally, actively *listening* to employees—taking their input and suggestions seriously—can increase affective commitment. When entrepreneurs listen carefully to their employees, they send the message that the employees matter—that the company is committed to *them*. This message, in turn, encourages feelings of commitment on the part of employees.

Is building a high level of organizational commitment worth the bother? Research findings indicate that it is. The higher employees' commitment, the less likely they are to leave for another job.[35] That, after all, is what entrepreneurs want—retention of persons they have worked hard to hire and who are essential to their company's continued growth. (For the thoughts of a highly successful entrepreneur on this and other issues relating to strengthening a new venture's human resources, see **The Voice of Experience** section.)

Overcoming the Control Barrier: A Note on the Necessity of Letting Go

The need to delegate is sometimes hard for entrepreneurs to accept. Although they do want to surround themselves with the best people—to hire excellent employees—they often have a very hard time letting go—delegating authority to other people.[36] The reasons are understandable: Entrepreneurs have a passion for their companies and view them almost through the eyes of a doting parent. Just like loving parents, they find it difficult to surrender their authority and let other people control their new venture's fate by making important decisions or setting strategy. Yet—and here's the paradox—unless they can accomplish this task, they may put the future of their growing companies in jeopardy. To understand why, we need to take a brief look at how new ventures grow and move through successive stages of development.

Figure 12.7 Committed People Are Less Likely to Leave

Owning or leasing a NerdMobile emphasizes the shared goals and shared stakes among the nerds of Nerds On Site.

Photo courtesy of Nerds On Site

THE VOICE OF EXPERIENCE

Attracting, Motivating, and Retaining Nerds

In 1995, while working at Future Shop in London, Ontario, David Redekop and John Harbarenko (pictured above) saw a growing need for an on-site, friendly, non-intimidating, affordable information technology service. To meet this need, they started Nerds On Site. Ten years later, in 2005, Nerds On Site is located coast-to-coast across Canada, from St. John's to Victoria, and internationally, in 45 U.S. cities, South Africa, Australia, the United Kingdom, Germany, Bolivia, and Mexico. The company operates in four markets: residential, SOHO (small office/home office), SME (small and medium-sized enterprises), and corporate, and is affiliated with 700 nerds (independent IT consultants) worldwide. With approximately 1,000 new customers every 10 to 12 business days, increasing numbers of home businesses, and growing IT use at home and work, the secret to the growth of Nerds On Site has been the way it recruits, motivates, trains, and retains its nerds. In a recent interview, Redekop, Harbarenko, and CEO Charlie Regan talked with me about their innovative human resource management strategies.

Reuber: "How do you decide who works for Nerds On Site?"

NOS: "It's a multi-stage process. We get thousands of applications each year from around the world. All the applications go through an online assessment process where we look at their background and have simple psychometric tools that assess attitudes regarding customer service and work ethic. Once they get through this assessment process, they arrive at what we call First Step. We meet with people in a group setting and explain our business model, in 60 to 90 minutes. After breaking for coffee, the people who are still interested stay and participate in Second Step: a question-answer session with current nerds, designed to provide a detailed understanding of what it means to be a nerd. The people still with us after Second Step take an online personality test. After getting through the test, people are invited to participate in Third Step. In Third Step, an applicant shadows a current nerd at several client engagements. The nerd assesses their skills and competencies and recommends either hiring or not hiring. In this way, our current nerds decide who should become a nerd and be trusted with our brand. We need to emphasize that our nerds are *not* employees, they are independent IT consultants. We call them EntrepreNerds. We don't require that they work exclusively for us, but after a year or so, they're usually too busy to be working for anyone else."

Reuber: "What qualities do you look for?"

NOS: "We call it our CHARGE statement, and it reflects the qualities we test for and look for in applicants. C stands for CEO, confidence and competence. Our clients want decisions to be made on the spot and to be left with a secure feeling that the nerd is accountable. H stands for human engineering, the ability to build

bridges between human beings. A stands for an attitude of humility—no matter how good we are, we can learn from other people. R stands for resourceful and responsive. Our nerds need to be able to find answers on their own in order to be responsive to our clients. G stands for goal- and destination-focused, knowing where you're headed. Finally, E stands for engaging and enthusiastic all the time. The client experience is always better when carried out with engaging enthusiasm. In short, though, we're looking for creativity and passion. We want people who are up at 3 a.m. checking for a best-in-class solution to an issue they were dealing with the previous afternoon."

Reuber: "What kind of contractual arrangements do the nerds have with the company?"

NOS: "We call them the Rules of Engagement. There are four sets of rules. One set are rules about our culture; for example, how we expect clients to be treated. A second set outlines how business operations are carried out. The third set specifies how nerds should deal with each other, and the fourth set specifies the relationship between the nerds and the corporation. All nerds sign on to these rules. The rules are written by the nerds themselves and are revised quarterly. We collect everyone's suggestions for change and have a Council of Engagement, which considers the suggestions and makes recommendations for change, which are then passed around for people to comment on. The process allows the rules to be sensitive to culture; for example, some rules in South Africa differ from rules in North America."

Reuber: "Beyond the rules, how can you motivate certain behaviours?"

NOS: "We do have financially based incentives. For example, we buy all nerds a cellphone and pay for their calls, because we don't want them to hesitate in calling for help. We really want nerds to drive a NerdMobile (see Figure 12.7). Not only do 44 percent of new customers call us because they've seen one of our cars, but they help to build our brand. So, when the nerds submit their weekly billing, we pay a substantial premium to nerds who have bought or leased a NerdMobile."

Reuber: "Once a nerd is on board, what's important in keeping them?"

NOS: "Training and support are key. Our University of NERDology has over 60 professors and covers over 250 competencies. Our nerds really want to take our online courses and get certified in new competencies. We operate in four markets, so there is lots of room for personal growth within Nerds On Site. We also provide a high level of support. It is not unusual for a nerd to put out a call for help and get responses from all over the world within 20 minutes. Finally, we run a lot of pilot

continued

Photo courtesy of Nerds On Site.

projects to find better ways of doing things. Because we have a sophisticated communications infrastructure, people can find out pilot project results as soon as they become available, so they are always able to find better ways of solving problems."

Reuber: "What are some lessons you'd like to pass on to aspiring entrepreneurs?"

NOS: "You need to deliver measurable results! Until you deliver something valuable to the market, you're just talking. So, from the very beginning, think about your success metrics and how you're going to deliver them. You also need passion, or it won't be fun."

Commentary: We agree with John Harbarenko, David Redekop, and Charlie Regan. They have sophisticated systems in place to pick people who will be happy at Nerds On Site, and with whom they will be happy. First-rate people always have choices, and so it is very important to create a corporate culture that values people highly and enables them to develop and prosper. From the interview, it was obvious that these three guys on the executive team follow their own advice. They're having lots of fun with the business, learning from each other and finding new ways to grow.

Six Phases of Company Growth

Company growth is a continuous process, so dividing it into discrete phases is somewhat artificial. Still, many experts find it convenient to talk about six different phases through which many companies move:

- *Conception/existence.* This phase is the classic start-up period, during which companies emerge and move toward the point at which they can deliver a product or service. During this phase, founders do essentially everything, so the issue of delegating does not arise.

- *Survival.* At this stage of development, the new venture has become a real company; it has customers and is earning revenues. During this phase, too, the issue of delegation is relatively unimportant; although there may be a small number of employees, the founders remain central in every aspect of its operation.

- *Profitability and stabilization.* During this phase, the company attains economic health: It is earning a profit and has a growing number of employees. Functional managers are hired, but because the company is still small, the founders continue to play a key role, and delegation is just beginning to become an important issue.

- *Profitability and growth.* At this stage, the company moves toward real growth, and to reach this goal, its growing cash reserves are placed at risk (i.e., they are used to finance further growth). The founders are still central to all aspects of the company's business, but high-quality managers are needed to oversee its increasingly complex operations.

- *Take-off.* This stage is the pivotal phase of company growth from the point of view of delegation: The company is growing rapidly and becoming far too large for one founder or even a team of founders to oversee effectively. This growth necessitates the hiring of first-rate, professional managers—and these people will not come on board, or remain, if they are not given sufficient authority and autonomy to do their jobs. This phase encompasses what some authors term the **control barrier**—the founders *must* surrender at least a significant amount of control over the company to others—people they have hired, bankers, or new shareholders who have provided needed capital. If they successfully pass through this barrier, the company can continue to grow; if they do not, its fortunes may begin to decline—a pattern that is far from rare.[37]

■ *Maturity.* If founders successfully navigate their way through the control barrier, the company becomes truly mature: The new venture has, in a sense, arrived and is a significant player in its industry or market.

Here's a key point about these phases: In the early days of a new venture (the first and second phases), entrepreneurs' skills, abilities, and knowledge—their capacity to accomplish various tasks—are crucial to the success of the company. From the third phase on, however, their importance in determining the success of the company begins to decline. At the same time, though, the importance of another factor—the founders' ability to delegate—increases until, as shown in Figure 12.8, the two curves cross; at this point, the control barrier occurs. Beyond that point, success at delegating is crucial and, in fact, is closely tied with the company's ability to recruit, motivate, and retain high-quality employees and staff.

In essence, the illustration of the control barrier suggests that entrepreneurs must change their style of leadership as their companies' grow. At first, as we suggested at the start of this chapter, they act as team leaders, persons who lead a small group of highly motivated people toward shared goals—primarily through the vision they describe and endorse. Later on, they must become leaders of teams—key decision makers who, nevertheless, delegate a large degree of authority and autonomy to other persons who lead various teams within the company—separate departments or, perhaps, integrated cross-functional teams. Whatever form the growing organization takes, at some point, founders *must* truly let go. In other words, they must come to understand that control does not necessarily imply ownership of their company; on the contrary, it involves use of and access to assets.

To put it as clearly as we can, a 10 percent equity stake in a company worth $1 billion is clearly a lot more valuable to an entrepreneur than a 90 percent equity stake in a company worth $1 million! So letting go—delegating authority and trading equity for use of a much larger pool of assets—must, at some point, go hand in hand with the processes we have considered in this chapter: recruiting, motivating, and retaining first-rate people. Once the right people are on board, it is only reasonable for entrepreneurs to entrust them with key tasks; if this transfer of tasks does not occur, why should these talented, energetic people stay around? The answer is simple: They won't. Letting go in an orderly manner and at the appropriate point in time is one of the best things founding entrepreneurs can do for their companies. And this is another reason why paying careful attention to recruiting, motivating, and retaining first-rate employees is crucial to the success of new ventures: When entrepreneurs do a good job at these tasks and are surrounded by truly excellent people, the pain of letting go may be significantly reduced: After all, they realize that they are placing the fortunes of their company in very good hands!

LEARNING OBJECTIVE

12 Define the "control barrier" and explain why it is so important for entrepreneurs to learn how to delegate authority to others.

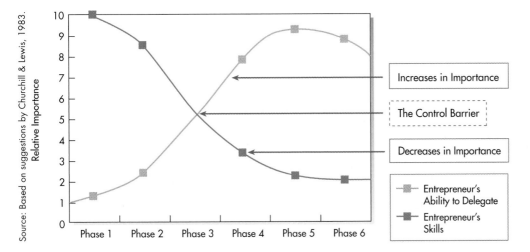

Figure 12.8 Changing Roles for Entrepreneurs as Their Companies Grow

During early phases of growth, entrepreneurs' skills, abilities, and knowledge are crucial to the success of their new ventures. During later phases, however, the importance of these factors drops, while the importance of another factor— entrepreneurs' ability to delegate— grows in importance. The two curves cross at what is sometimes described as the control barrier.

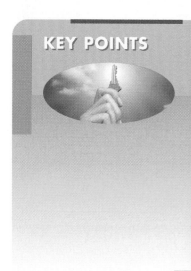

KEY POINTS

- In order to retain excellent employees, new ventures need reward systems that closely link incentives to performance.
- Pay-for-performance systems accomplish this goal by linking either individual or team performance to rewards such as pay, benefits, or equity in the company.
- Another important means for retaining excellent employees is strengthening their organizational commitment—their loyalty to the new venture—which can be accomplished in several ways.
- New ventures move through six relatively distinct phases of growth. During early phases, the entrepreneurs' skills, abilities, and knowledge play a key role in the new venture's success. In later phases, such success is closely linked to the entrepreneur's ability to cross the control barrier and delegate authority to others—the excellent employees the new ventures seeks to attract.
- Entrepreneurs who have done an excellent job with respect to recruiting, motivating, and retaining first-rate employees will often find this task easier to accomplish than entrepreneurs who have not.

Summary and Review of Key Points

- As new ventures grow, their requirements for additional human resources, too, increase. Often, these new employees are hired through the founding teams' social network.
- Existing evidence suggests that the greater the number of employees in new ventures, the greater their financial success. However, this relationship does not necessarily imply that increasing the number of employees causes success; rather, both success and number of employees may stem from the same underlying factors (e.g., the quality of the opportunity being exploited).
- Before beginning a search for new employees, it is very useful to carry out a job analysis and prepare a job description for each position to be filled. Only after these preliminary tasks have been completed can clarity be obtained about what needs are to be met by new employees, and steps formulated to choose the best persons for these positions.
- In their search for new employees, entrepreneurs focus primarily on their own social networks. However, as the new venture grows, it may be necessary to turn to other sources, such as advertisements in trade publications, the Internet, and referrals from customers.
- Reliability—the consistency of measurements over time or between judges—and validity—the extent to which measurements reflect the dimension to which they refer—are important considerations in selecting employees. Only techniques high in both reliability and validity are useful for this purpose and are legal under existing laws.
- Two techniques for selecting employees that are high in reliability and validity are structured interviews and biodata—information about applicants' background, experiences, and preferences—gathered by means of detailed application forms.
- It is best to provide potential employees with accurate information about working conditions in a company during an interview; such realistic job previews protect new hires from unpleasant surprises when they assume their jobs. This practice can also improve employee motivation and retention.
- Motivation is defined as the processes that arouse, direct, and maintain human behaviour toward attaining some goal.

- Setting goals that are specific in nature, challenging but attainable, and accepted by the persons for whom they are established is a very effective technique for increasing motivation, provided that the persons in question also receive feedback concerning progress toward these goals.
- Expectancy theory suggests that motivation will be high when there are clear links between effort and performance and between performance and rewards, and the rewards provided are ones people actually value.
- When employees feel that they are being treated unfairly in terms of outcomes, procedures, or courtesy they receive, motivation is sharply reduced. Thus, entrepreneurs should be careful to establish these kinds of fairness in their new ventures.
- Through job enlargement and job enrichment, jobs can be designed to be interesting and motivating for the persons who perform them.
- The choice between hiring temporary and permanent employees is a complex one; both offer advantages and disadvantages. Ultimately, this decision must depend on the specific situation in which a new venture operates.
- In order to retain excellent employees, new ventures need reward systems that closely link incentives to performance.
- Pay-for-performance systems accomplish this goal by linking either individual or team performance to rewards such as pay, benefits, or equity in the company.
- Another important means for retaining excellent employees is strengthening their organizational commitment—their loyalty to the new venture—which can be accomplished in several ways.
- New ventures move through six relatively distinct phases of growth. During early phases, the entrepreneurs' skills, abilities, and knowledge play a key role in the new venture's success. In later phases, such success is closely linked to the entrepreneur's ability to cross the control barrier and delegate authority to others—the excellent employees the new ventures seeks to attract.
- Entrepreneurs who have done an excellent job with respect to recruiting, motivating, and retaining first-rate employees will often find this task easier to accomplish than entrepreneurs who have not.

Glossary

Biodata: Information about potential employees' background, experiences, and preferences provided by them on application forms.

Control Barrier: Refers to the unwillingness of founders of new ventures to surrender control over the company to others.

Distributive Justice: A principle of perceived fairness suggesting that all parties to a relationship should receive a share of the available rewards commensurate with the scope of their contributions.

Expectancy Theory: A theory of motivation suggesting that in order for motivation to be high, individuals must perceive clear links between their effort and their performance and between their performance and their rewards, and the rewards offered are actually desirable.

Job Analysis: A careful analysis of a specific job to determine what it involves and what it requires in terms of specific knowledge, skills, and abilities.

Job Description: An overview of what the job involves in terms of its duties, responsibilities, and working conditions.

Job Design: The structuring of jobs so that they increase people's interest in doing them (and hence their motivation).

Motivation: The processes that arouse, direct, and maintain human behaviour toward attaining some goal. In other words, motivation refers to behaviour that is energized by, and directed toward, reaching some desired target or objective.

Organizational Commitment: The extent to which individuals identify with and are involved with their organizations and are, therefore, unwilling to leave it.

Pay-for-Performance Systems: Reward systems that assume that employees differ in how much they contribute to the company's success, and that they should be rewarded in accordance with the scope of their contributions.

Realistic Job Previews: Efforts to present a balanced and accurate picture of the company to potential employees, with the goal of improving future retention of these persons.

Reliability: The extent to which measurements are consistent across time or between judges.

Reward Systems: Systems for recognizing and rewarding good performance.

Structured Interviews: Interviews in which all applicants are asked the same questions—ones chosen carefully to be truly job-related.

Validity: The extent to which measurements actually reflect the underlying dimension to which they refer.

Discussion Questions

1. In general, when entrepreneurs are first increasing the size of their new ventures, they tend to hire people they know. Can you think of any potential problems that could result from such a strategy?

2. Why is it crucial that all techniques used to select employees be both reliable and valid?

3. When choosing excellent employees, why are structured interviews superior to regular job interviews?

4. From the point of view of goal setting, why is the strategy of telling employees "Do your best!" generally ineffective?

5. Suppose that you want to give a bonus to high-performing employees for their excellent work. How should you go about doing this?

6. Why is it important to develop high levels of organizational commitment among employees in a new venture?

7. What is the control barrier and why is it crucial that entrepreneurs cross it successfully?

8. How can success in recruiting, motivating, and retaining first-rate employees make it easier for entrepreneurs to cross the control barrier?

InfoTrac Exercises

1. **What's My Hiring Line? Here Are Some Valuable Pointers for How to Conduct a Successful Interview** (hiring line)

   Richard Ream

   Information Today, May 2002 v19 i5 p18(2)

   Record: A85410699

   Full Text: COPYRIGHT 2002 Information Today, Inc.

   1. How, as an interviewer, can you avoid a mismatch of culture?

   2. How can you assess a job's context to value the traits and skills that will increase your opportunity to make a successful hire?

   3. What steps can you take to ensure a successful interview?

2. **Light Their Fires** (motivating employees)

   William Cottringer

   Supervision, June 2003 v64 i6 p12(3)

   Record: A102677211

   Full Text: COPYRIGHT 2003 National Research Bureau

   1. According to expectancy theory, what factors play a key role in motivation?

   2. Do you agree with the following statement: "All employees have a drive to perform well"? Why or why not?

   3. What tools can a supervisor use to motivate employees?

GETTING DOWN
TO BUSINESS

Setting Motivating Goals

Setting appropriate goals for ourselves is a very important task, not just because it strengthens and maintains motivation, but also because once goals are set, the strategies for reaching them are often clarified. You are already setting goals for yourself in many areas of life, but practice in this skill—choosing effective self-set goals—can be highly beneficial to entrepreneurs, and to anyone else. Follow these instructions to gain such practice.

1. **Consider goals you have set for yourself within the past few weeks.** For each, list the goal, and then describe it. (Some examples: "I set the goal of completing a term paper by a specific date." "I set the goal of writing a draft of my business plan by a specific date.")

   Goal 1:

   Goal 2:

   Goal 3:

   Goal 4:

   Goal 5:

2. **Now, for each goal you identified, rate the extent to which it met each of these criteria.** For each goal, place a number next to each criterion using the following scale: 1 = very low in meeting this criterion; 2 = low in meeting this criterion; 3 = neither high nor low; 4 = high in meeting this criterion; 5 = very high in meeting this criterion.

   ▪ Specific: Was the goal specific? _____ (Place your rating here.)

   ▪ Challenging: Was the goal challenging? _____

   ▪ Attainable: Was the goal attainable? _____

   ▪ Feedback: Could you readily assess your progress toward reaching this goal? _____

How high are your ratings? If they are not 4 or 5 on each goal, think carefully about how you could have redefined the goal so that it met these criteria. Remember: The more closely goals meet these criteria, the better they are for enhancing motivation and performance.

Planning a Hiring Strategy: A Potential Plus for Your Business Plan

When you start your new venture—and especially if it grows as rapidly as you hope!—the chances are good that you will soon need to hire employees. Clearly, you want to do this well and attract the best people you can find. Although many entrepreneurs give little thought to this task, it is an important one; moreover, to the extent you can explain clearly in your business plan how you will accomplish it, this can be another plus in your column for venture capitalists and other investors. To start planning for your hiring strategy, complete the following steps.

1. **Job Descriptions and Analyses:** You can't hire the best people for a job until you know just what it is you want them to do. So begin by describing each position you think you will have to fill and by listing the skills, experience, and abilities required by each position.

   a. Position one:

   b. Position two:

   c. Position three:

   d. Position four:

   e. Position five:

   Continue as necessary.

2. **Attracting an Excellent Pool of Applicants:** For each position, you will want to attract a number of excellent candidates. How will you go about finding these people? In other words, what strategies will you follow to attract an excellent pool of applicants? Describe these here.

   a. Specific strategy:

   b. Specific strategy:

   c. Specific strategy:

3. **Selecting the Best Applicants:** Once you attract these candidates, how will you choose among them? In other words, what selection techniques and tools will you use (interviews, structured interviews, biodata)? Describe these and be sure to give careful consideration to whether these techniques are reliable and valid—and whether they are consistent with federal and provincial laws and regulations.

   a. Selection technique #1:

   b. Selection technique #2:

   c. Selection technique #3:

Enhanced Learning

You may select any combination of the resources below to enhance your understanding of the chapter material.

- **Appendix: Case Studies** – Twelve cases provide opportunities to apply chapter concepts to realistic entrepreneurial situations. These brief cases call for careful analysis of real business problems and ask you to think about potential solutions.

■ **Video Case Library –** Nine cases are tied directly to video segments from the popular PBS television series *Small Business School*. These cases and video segments (available on the Entrepreneurship website at http://www.entrepreneurship.nelson.com) give you unparalleled access to today's entrepreneurs, with expert advice and insights on how to start, run, and grow a business.

■ **Management Interview Series Video Database –** This video interview series contains a wealth of tips on how to manage effectively. Access to the database and practical exercises are available on the book support website at http://www.entrepreneurship.nelson.com.

Notes

1. Levie, J., & Hay, M. 2000. Life beyond the "kitchen" culture. In S. Birley & D.F. Muzyka (eds.). *Mastering entrepreneurship* (pp. 257–261). Upper Saddle River, NJ: Prentice-Hall.
2. Schefcyzk, M., & Gerpott, T.J. 2001. Qualifications and turnover of managers and venture capital-financed firm performance: An empirical study of German venture capital-investments. *Journal of Business Venturing* 16(2): 145–165.
3. Eisenhardt, K., & Schoonhoven, K. 1995. *Failure of entrepreneurial firms: Ecological, upper echelons and strategic explanations in the U.S. semiconductor industry.* Working Paper. Stanford University.
4. Reynolds, P., & White, S. 1997. *The entrepreneurial process: economic growth, men, women and minorities.* Westport, CT: Quorum Books.
5. Baum, J. 1996. Organizational ecology. In S. Clegg, C. Hardy, & W. Nord (eds.). *Handbook of organization studies.* (pp. 77–114). London: Sage.
6. Shutjens, V., & Wever, E. 2000. Determinants of new firm success. *Papers in Regional Science* 79(2): 135–159.
7. Gimeno, J., Folta, T., Cooper, A., & Woo, C. 1997. Survival of the fittest? Entrepreneurial human capital and the persistence of underperforming firms. *Administrative Science Quarterly* 42(4): 750–783.
8. Aldrich, H. 1999. *Organizations evolving.* London: Sage.
9. Buckley, M.R., & Eder, R.W. 1988. B.M. Springbett and the notion of the "snap decision" in the interview. *Journal of Management* 14(1): 59–67.
10. Judge, T.A., Higgins, C.A., & Cable, D.M. 2000. The employment interview: A review of recent research and recommendations for future research. *Human Resource Management Review* 10(4): 383–405.
11. Gomez-Mejia, L., Balkin, D.B., & Cardy, R.L. 2001. *Managing human resources.* 3rd ed. Upper Saddle River, NJ: Prentice-Hall.
12. Kacmar, K.M., Ratcliff, S.L., & Ferris, G.R. 1989. Employment interview research: Internal and external validity. In R.W. Eder & G.R. Ferris (eds.). *The employment interview: Theory, research, and practice* (pp. 32–41). Newbury Park, CA: Sage.
13. Baron, R.A., & Byrne, D. 2002. *Social psychology.* 10th ed. Boston: Allyn & Bacon.
14. Wanous, H.P., & Coella, A. 1989. Organizational entry research: Current status and future directions. In G. Ferris & K. Rowlands (eds.). *Research in person and human resources management* Vol. 7 (pp. 59–120). Greenwich, CT: JAI Press.
15. Baum, J.R., Locke, E.A., & Smith, K.G. 2001. A multidimensional model of venture growth. *Academy of Management Journal* 44(2): 292–303.
16. Locke, E.A., & Latham, G.P. 1990. *Goal setting.* Englewood Cliffs, NJ: Prentice-Hall.
17. Baron, R.A. 2004. The cognitive perspective: A valuable tool for answering entrepreneurship's basic "why?" questions. *Journal of Business Venturing* 19(2): 221–239.
18. Ludwig, T.D., & Geller, E.S. 1997. Assigned versus participative goal setting and response generalization: Managing injury control among professional pizza deliverers. *Journal of Applied Psychology* 82(2): 253–261.
19. Baum, J.R., & Locke, E.A. 2004. The relationship of entrepreneurial traits, skill, and motivation to subsequent venture growth. *Journal of Applied Psychology* 89(4): 587–598.
20. Shepperd, J.A., Ouellette, J.A., & Fernandez, J.K. 1996. Abandoning unrealistic optimistic performance estimates and the temporal proximity of self-relevant feedback. *Journal of Personality and Social Psychology* 70(4): 844–855.
21. Mitchell, T.R. 1983. Expectancy-value models in organizational psychology. In N. Feather (ed.). *Expectancy, incentive, and action* (pp. 293–314). Hillsdale, NJ: Lawrence Erlbaum Associates.
22. Simon, M., Houghton, S.M., & Aquino, K. 2000. Cognitive biases, risk perception, and venture formation: How individuals decide to start companies. *Journal of Business Venturing* 15(2): 113–134.
23. Greenberg, J. 1998. The cognitive geometry of employee theft: Negotiating "the line" between taking and stealing. In R.W. Griffin, A. O'Leary-Kelly, & J.M. Collins (eds.). *Dysfunctional behavior in organizations: Non-violent dysfunctional behavior* (pp. 147–194). Stamford, CT: JAI Press.
24. Brockner, J., & Wiesenfeld, B.M. 1996. An integrative framework for explaining reactions to decisions: The interactive effects of outcomes and procedures. *Psychological Bulletin* 120(2): 189–208.
25. Greenberg, J. 1997. *The quest for justice on the job.* Thousand Oaks, CA: Sage.
26. One in five Canadians say fraud occurs in their workplace. http://www.ey.com/global/Content.nsf/Canada/Media_-_2002_-_Fraud2002.
27. Jamieson, J. 2005. Employee theft plagues small business. CanWest News Service, October 8.
28. Greenberg, J. 1998. The cognitive geometry of employee theft: Negotiating "the line" between taking and stealing. In R.W. Griffin, A. O'Leary-Kelly, & J.M. Collins (eds.). *Dysfunctional behavior in organizations: Non-violent dysfunctional behavior* (pp. 147–194). Stamford, CT: JAI Press.

29 Matusik, S. 1997. Motives, use patterns and effects of contingent resource use in entrepreneurial firms. In P. Reynolds, W. Bygrave, N. Carter, P. Davidsson, W. Gartner, C. Mason, & P. McDougall. *Frontiers of entrepreneurship research* (pp. 359–372). Babson Park: Babson College.

30 Aldrich, H., & Langdon, N. 1997. Human resource management and organizational life cycles. In P. Reynolds et al. (eds.). *Frontiers of entrepreneurship research* (pp. 349–357). Babson Park: Babson College.

31 Levie, J., & Hay, M. 2000. Life beyond the "kitchen" culture. In S. Birley & D.F. Muzyka (eds.). *Mastering entrepreneurship* (pp. 257–261). Upper Saddle River, NJ: Prentice-Hall.

32 What is an ESOP? http://www.esop-canada.com/esop.html.

33 Mitchell, T.R., & Lee. T.W. 2001. The unfolding model of voluntary turnover and job embeddedness: Foundations for a comprehensive theory of attachment. In B.M. Staw & R.I. Sutton (eds.). *Research in organizational behavior* Vol. 23 (pp. 189–246). Oxford, UK: Elsevier.

34 Meyer, J.P., & Allen, N.J. 1997. *Commitment in the workplace: Theory, research, and application.* Thousand Oaks, CA: Sage.

35 Lee, T.W., Ashford, S.J., Walsh, J.P., & Mowday, R.T. 1992. Commitment propensity, organizational commitment, and voluntary turnover: A longitudinal study of organizational entry processes. *Journal of Management* 18(1): 15–32.

36 Churchill, N.C., & Lewis, V.L. 1983. The five stages of small business growth. *Harvard Business Review* 61(3): 30–50.

37 Levie, J., & Hay, M. 2000. Life beyond the "kitchen" culture. In S. Birley & D.F. Muzyka (eds.). *Mastering entrepreneurship* (pp. 257–261). Upper Saddle River, NJ: Prentice-Hall.

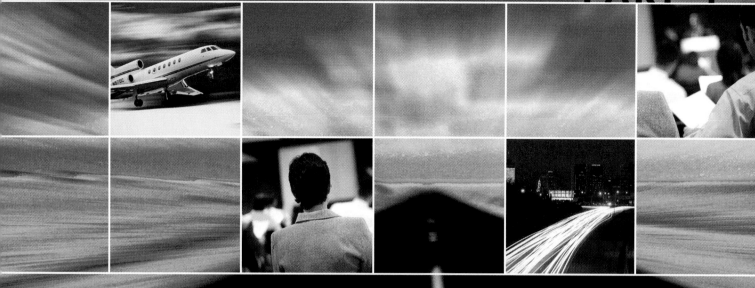

HARVESTING THE REWARDS

CHAPTER 13

When—and How—to Harvest the Rewards from Your Business

At some point in time, entrepreneurs usually begin to consider strategies to harvest the rewards of all the time, money, and energy they have invested in their venture. They may consider exiting the business altogether, by selling it to a family member, a rival, or an organization that wants to get into the market. Alternatively, they may consider going public—selling stock to the public in hopes of fuelling growth and increasing the value of their shares. Both actions require valuing the company so that negotiations with potential purchasers can proceed. Before initiating this final phase of the process, entrepreneurs should carefully consider what they want to do next, which, in turn, can be closely linked to the phase of life they have reached. Harvest strategies appropriate for young entrepreneurs in their 20s, 30s, or 40s may not be ideal for entrepreneurs who have reached a later phase of life. Although harvest strategies are primarily economic strategies, they must also take into account the preferences and current and future life styles of each individual entrepreneur.

ALL PHOTOS THIS PAGE ©
PHOTODISC, INC.

WHEN—AND HOW—TO HARVEST
THE REWARDS FROM YOUR BUSINESS

LEARNING OBJECTIVES

After reading this chapter, you should be able to:

1 Describe basic methods of valuing a business, including balance sheet methods, earnings-based methods, and the market method.

2 Describe issues entrepreneurs should consider when transferring ownership of their companies to family members or employees.

3 List the advantages and costs of an initial public offering.

4 Describe the basic nature of negotiation and explain the nature of several key bargaining tactics.

5 Explain why integrative agreements between negotiators are generally best, and explain the relationship of such agreements to the overall approach to negotiation (a win-lose approach versus a win-win approach).

6 Define "life transitions" and explain why entrepreneurs should consider their own age and phase of life before choosing an exit strategy.

All photos this page © PhotoDisc, Inc.

"All things change ... There is nothing in the whole world which is permanent. Everything flows onward ... the ages themselves glide by in constant movement." (Ovid, 10 B.C.)

In the spring of 1987, I (Robert Baron) accepted a new position at Rensselaer Polytechnic Institute in New York. I was on the faculty of Purdue University at the time, and was living happily in a house I liked very much. It sat on a small hill surrounded by hundred-year-old oak trees, and I had redone it from top to bottom after buying it five years earlier—the kitchen, bathrooms, the works. But now, it was time to leave, so I put it up for sale. At first, I saw the sale purely as an economic transaction: I knew how much money I had invested in the house and wanted that plus a reasonable profit. As potential buyers appeared, though, I began to realize that more was going on than simple economics. One possible buyer told me: "I love the house, but the first thing I'm going to do if I buy it is cut down all those little trees over there." I shuddered because I had planted those trees myself—oaks, maples, and ashes—and I saw them as my gift to future generations. "Cut them down?" I mused. "What kind of person is he *anyway*?" When he made an offer, I rejected it, even though it was close to the price I was seeking.

Another potential buyer told me: "I like your house, but I don't know about that porch. It's too narrow. I'll probably have it torn down so I can build another." Again I found myself thinking, "Do I want this person to have my house?" I had built that porch myself, and was very proud of it. When this buyer made an offer, I found myself unwilling to agree to some of the terms she suggested. The real estate market was good at the time, so ultimately, I did get a buyer who seemed to appreciate the house just the way it was; he got it, and for a very attractive price.

By now you may be wondering, "What does all this have to do with entrepreneurship?" The answer is simple: It offers important insights into the final phase of the entrepreneurial process—the time when entrepreneurs reap their well-deserved rewards through harvest strategies. Consider this: If sweat equity and other noneconomic factors sometimes play an important role with respect to the sale of houses (see Figure 13.1), imagine how powerful these factors can be when entrepreneurs consider selling the companies they have built from the ground up, out of their own vision, energy, and spirit. Because entrepreneurs often feel a deep commitment to their companies (their babies, as some describe them), they cannot readily view leaving them behind solely in economic terms.

We will take full account of this fact in the current chapter, which focuses on the various ways in which entrepreneurs can harvest their rewards from the companies they have founded. Although these strategies are basically economic arrangements, it is important to note that entrepreneurs' attitudes, values, and goals often play a crucial role in determining which of these harvest strategies they choose and the specific terms they accept. For instance, all harvest strategies involve the task of valuing a company—determining its economic worth. Is this based entirely on economic factors? Sometimes, but in many cases, additional factors enter into the equation, just as they do with respect to real estate transactions. As we have already noted, persons who put their houses up for sale often exaggerate the value of their property because of sweat equity or other psychological factors, and the same forces are at work for entrepreneurs. Often, they overestimate the value of their companies because of the time and effort they have invested in building them. Indeed, given the magnitude of this investment, the impact of these forces is far stronger than in the case of merely selling a house. Even at this very basic level, then, factors other than economics play a role.

After considering various valuation and harvest strategies, we will turn to an aspect of the process that is crucial, but often receives very little attention from entrepreneurs: negotiation. Through a process of negotiation, an entrepreneur and the potential purchasers of the company attempt

Figure 13.1 The Noneconomic Side of Economic Transactions

Many persons attach inflated values to their homes because of the effort they have invested in improving them (sweat equity) and other psychological factors. For similar reasons, entrepreneurs sometimes find it difficult to view the sale of their businesses purely in economic terms.

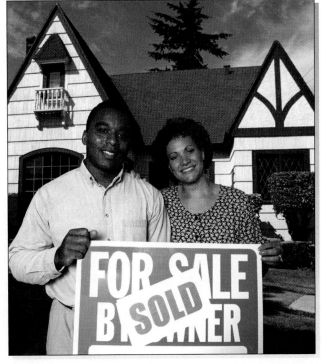

© PhotoDisc, Inc.

to arrive at an agreement acceptable to both sides. Negotiation is complex, and it is important for entrepreneurs to understand the process and the key factors affecting it. We will conclude with a discussion of the interplay between some basic facts of human life (e.g., entrepreneurs' stage of life) and the harvest strategies they choose. As human beings, we experience many changes as we move through the lifespan. Physical changes are the most obvious, but they are only a part of the total picture; as we age, we change cognitively and socially, too. The result is that our capabilities, goals, and social relationships change in subtle but important ways. For this reason, it is important for entrepreneurs to consider just where they are in this continuous process of development so that they can choose a harvest strategy that makes sense personally as well as economically.

DETERMINING THE VALUE OF A BUSINESS: A LITTLE ART, A LITTLE SCIENCE

How much is a business worth? As we noted earlier, entrepreneurs and potential buyers may have sharply different perspectives on this issue. Entrepreneurs know the business intimately and are fully aware of the effort, stress, and sacrifice that were required to build it to its present level. They also fully appreciate its **intangibles**— assets that are difficult, if not impossible, to list on the balance sheet: the goodwill the company has acquired with customers and suppliers, its reputation in the industry, its success in attracting and motivating first-rate employees. As a result, entrepreneurs often have difficulty viewing the business in purely economic terms; it looms so large in their consciousness that it is hard for them to be totally objective. The result: They tend to perceive their business as having higher value, and greater future potential, than is actually the case, and this perception can impede its sale.

How can this important obstacle be overcome? In part, by careful valuation of the company. As the heading of this section suggests, valuation is not a calculation that can be performed by a simple economic formula; in fact, experts in valuation can sometimes disagree considerably with respect to the numbers they generate. So, it is often best to value the company by using several different methods and then to negotiate a specific price on the basis of all this information. Putting such negotiations aside for the moment, let's look at three important ways of valuing a business—three ways of generating figures that can then serve as the starting point for discussions concerning a final selling price.

Balance Sheet Methods

LEARNING OBJECTIVE

1 Describe basic methods of valuing a business, including balance sheet methods, earnings-based methods, and the market method.

One basis for valuing a company is in terms of its balance sheet. In the simplest approach, net worth is calculated according to this simple formula:

Net Worth = Assets – Liabilities

The problem with this approach is that it fails to take account of the fact that the true market value of some assets may not be reflected in the balance sheet. For instance, many companies carry land and buildings on their books at prices considerably lower than their actual market value. Similarly, equipment, and fixtures may be carried at higher or lower figures than their fair market value—the cost to replace them. For this reason, valuation is usually computed by the *adjusted balance sheet technique*, in which the actual market value of assets is taken into account. This method estimates the value of such assets as inventories, supplies, and fixtures in terms of cost of last purchase and replacement value. Thus, it yields a more realistic valuation than a simple balance sheet approach.

Earnings Methods

When purchasers buy a business, they are buying not just current assets and liabilities. They are also buying future earnings—thus, another way of valuing a business is in terms of its future earnings. Three different methods of calculating the value of a business in terms of its future earnings are widely used.

Excess Earnings Method

Some businesses are more successful than others in their industry. To the extent this is the case, they have a higher value because they will generate greater future earnings. One method for calculating the value of a company, the **excess earnings method**, takes account of this fact. It estimates the extent to which a company will generate earnings in excess of the average for its industry and attributes these excess earnings to *goodwill*—an intangible asset of which entrepreneurs are highly aware, but which, as we noted earlier, is difficult to include in financial statements. The excess earnings method assumes that the extent a company is outperforming its competitors is attributable to what is termed "goodwill." It makes no effort to determine how this factor arises or what it involves; to the extent a company is generating greater-than-average profits, it is assumed to possess this intangible asset.

Here are the basic steps in calculating the value of a business through this method:

1. *Adjusted tangible net worth* is calculated (for argument's sake, let's assume it is $500,000).

2. *Opportunity cost of investing in the business is calculated.* This figure represents the costs investors will incur by investing in this business rather than others, and it consists of (1) the rate or risk-free return (usually calculated in terms of treasury bills or other similar financial instruments), (2) an adjustment for inflation, and (3) the risk allowance for investing in this particular business. The greater the risk, the higher the rate of return required by investors. A typical figure is 25 percent: Investors require a 25 percent return on their investment to justify the risks involved in purchasing an existing business. This rate of return can be higher or lower and, in fact, is open to negotiation between the entrepreneur and potential buyers.

   Finally, because by purchasing the company the buyer will forego a salary that could be earned elsewhere, this figure is added to calculate total opportunity cost.

   The opportunity cost, then, would be calculated as follows:

   $500,000 (tangible net worth) × 25% = $125,000; adding the purchaser's lost salary (which we will assume is $50,000) to this = $125,000 + $50,000 = $175,000. This figure is the total opportunity cost.

3. *Net earnings are projected.* Here, again, is where art enters the picture: The buyer must estimate the company's net earnings on the basis of past earnings, current trends, and any other factors she or he wishes to include. Let's assume that this figure is $200,000 for the upcoming year.

4. *Compute extra earning power.* Earnings over and above industry average are included here. This figure is the difference between net projected earnings ($200,000) and total opportunity costs ($175,000). As a result, extra earning power = $25,000.

5. *Estimate value of intangibles.* The extra earning power is then multiplied by a years-of-profit figure (usually three to four years) to compute the estimated value of goodwill over a period of several years. Let's assume that the buyer chooses a three-year period: 3 × $25,000 = $75,000. This figure is the extra earning power projected ahead—a measure of goodwill.

6. *Determine the value of the business.* The value of the business is then based on a simple calculation in which the adjusted tangible net worth and the value of the intangibles are summed. This calculation would yield the following: $500,000 (total tangible net worth) + $75,000 (estimated value of intangibles) = $575,000. This figure is the value of the business as computed by this method.

Capitalized Earnings Method

In this approach, expected net earnings are capitalized to determine value. This method is simpler and uses the following formula:

> Capitalized net earnings = Net earnings (after deducting owner's salary)/Rate of return. In our example, this would be $200,000 − $50,000/0.25 = $600,000. Notice that this figure is not very different from the $575,000 calculated using the excess earnings method.

Discounted Future Earnings Method

It is a basic fact of life that money received today is worth more than money that will be received in the future; after all, a bird in the hand is worth two (or at least 1.10!) in the bush. This principle is known as the *time value* of money. A third earnings-based method for valuing businesses takes account of this principle and is known as the **discounted future earnings method**. It calculates a company's value by discounting future earnings, which, after all, are far from certain. The basic steps are as follows:

1. *Future earnings are projected for five years.* Usually, in fact, three projections are made: pessimistic, most likely, and optimistic. Let's say that for our hypothetical company the most likely scenario is a total of $500,000 in earnings.

2. *These future earnings are discounted.* By how much? Again, this amount is open to negotiation, but often a figure approaching 25 percent is used. Again, this figure reflects the risk that projections will not be achieved. Discounting future earnings by 25 percent for each future year (for five years) yields a projected discounted figure of $279,000.

3. *Income beyond the fifth year is calculated.* Often, this calculation involves multiplying projected fifth-year income by 1/Rate of return. Here, the figure is $120,000 (Projected earnings)/25% = $480,000.

4. *Income beyond the fifth year is discounted by the present value factor.* This figure, and other figures for present value for years 1, 2, 3, 4, and 5, can be found in published tables that provide appropriate numbers for various discount rates (e.g., 20 percent, 25 percent, 30 percent, etc.). For our example, the figure is $480,000 × 0.26 = $124,800.

5. *Total value of the business is computed.* This calculation involves adding the present value of the company's estimated earnings and the present values of its earnings from the sixth year. This figure is $500,000 + $124,800 = $624,800.

All three methods offer advantages and all involve disadvantages. But note that given the assumptions made here, the methods do not yield wildly different values (the range is $575,000 to $624,800). This narrow range is generally true: Regardless of which method is used, if reasonable assumptions about future earnings and opportunity costs are made, similar figures will be obtained through each method. The fact that differences remain, however, suggests that entrepreneurs and potential buyers must resolve which method will be used to value the company. If agreement can't be reached on the method to be used, negotiations may well fail.

Market Method

A third major way of determining the value of a business involves comparing the price/earnings ratio of the business to that of other publicly traded companies in the same industry. This method is known as the **market value approach** or the *price-earnings approach*. Several companies comparable to the privately held company now up for sale are identified, and price/earnings ratios for those publicly traded companies obtained. This average figure is then multiplied by the estimated net earnings of the privately held company. For instance, in our example, let's assume that the average price-earnings ratio for companies similar to the business we are valuing is 3.10. Projected net earnings for the coming year are $200,000. Multiplying the two figures, we obtain 3.10 × $200,000 = $630,000. This figure is the value of the company.

One problem with this approach is the difficulty involved in identifying several publicly traded companies that are similar enough to the business up for sale to allow for meaningful comparisons. Similarly, this method compares publicly and privately held companies, and because privately held companies are basically illiquid (there is no market for their stock), assuming that the same price-earnings ratio applies is questionable; perhaps a much lower one would be appropriate. In fact, this point is precisely what buyers will argue if this is the method of valuation preferred by the entrepreneur.

SELLING OR TRANSFERRING OWNERSHIP

Recently, I (Robert Baron) invested in a start-up biotechnology company. Why did I choose to risk my hard-earned capital on this new venture? Partly because I strongly liked the business model on which the company was based. The founders have chosen to focus their efforts on developing new drugs that will be helpful in treating what are known as orphan diseases—illnesses that afflict fewer than 200,000 people in the United States. Because the number of persons suffering from such illnesses is relatively small, large pharmaceutical companies have little interest in developing drugs to treat them. If the new company in which I invested is successful in identifying such drugs, however, it will become very attractive to these giant corporations, which may then seek to acquire it. If this happens, both the founders and early investors, such as myself, will reap very large rewards. In fact, this is precisely the scenario sought by the founding entrepreneurs: They realize that they cannot possibly hope to compete head-on with huge companies in the pharmaceutical industry. For instance, they certainly cannot match the size or experience of the sales staff or marketing departments of these companies. So instead of planning to compete with them, they hope to make enough progress to become an attractive candidate for a buyout— one that will be prove highly advantageous to the founders and early investors.

Acquisition by a larger company is just one of several strategies open to entrepreneurs to transfer ownership of their businesses to other people.

One very common way for entrepreneurs to exit from the companies they have founded is to turn over the reigns to a member of their own family. This strategy makes very good sense for several reasons. First, these persons (spouses, children, brothers and sisters, parents, etc.) have often helped to build the company either through financial support or by assuming actual roles in the venture. Second, they often own large blocks of shares. Third, they have the trust and confidence of the entrepreneur and also know the company very well. Finally, one key goal for many entrepreneurs is that of building something of value for their children and other family members; given that goal, what better way to exit than by turning the company over to the people for whom it was built in the first place?

In transferring ownership of the business to a family member, entrepreneurs need to complete the transaction in a way that will minimize taxes, and so need to seek expert advice before proceeding. However, intergenerational succession is more challenging than simply minimizing taxes. Indeed, in a survey of the top executives of more than 200 family firms in Canada, Professors Jess Chua and James Chrisman of the University of Calgary, and Pramodita Sharma of Wilfrid Laurier University found that succession was their number one concern, and managing their relationship with non-family members was second.[1] It is crucial that a clear *succession plan* be adopted— a plan that spells out in detail how and when the entrepreneur will transfer ownership in the company, and control of it, to designated successors. Further, it is important that these persons be chosen carefully, and with the consent of all interested parties. Successors must be individuals who want to play an active role in the business, and must be suited for this challenging task. In particular, they must have a coherent and realistic post-succession vision for the business. After studying succession failures, Professor Danny Miller of École des Hautes Commerciales in Montreal,

LEARNING OBJECTIVE

2 Describe issues entrepreneurs should consider when transferring ownership of their companies to family members or employees.

Professor Lloyd Steier of the University of Alberta, and Isabelle Le Breton-Miller of Organizational Effectiveness Research in Montreal concluded that many successions fare badly for one of three reasons. Successors are either too attached to the way things were done in the past, too quick to reject what worked in the past, or follow indecisive and inconsistent strategies.[2] Without a well thought out succession plan, serious difficulties can arise—including costly power struggles between family members who are unhappy with the entrepreneurs' choice of successor, their role in the company, or their share of the company's stock. As a general rule, the larger and more successful the company, the more bitter and costly these disputes, so entrepreneurs should do everything in their power to avoid them.

Entrepreneurs can also choose to transfer ownership to people who are currently working in the company. Who knows and understands a company best? Presumably, its top management team—the people who run it on a day-to-day basis. They understand its products, its finances, its structure, and its prospects for the future. It's far from surprising, therefore, that when entrepreneurs decide to depart, people in the top management often see an opportunity to purchase the company. The purchase can be handled in several ways. If they have enough cash, they can purchase it outright, or negotiate an agreement in which they pay a portion initially and the balance over a period of time (a cash plus note arrangement). Alternatively, they can arrange for a **leveraged buyout**. In this arrangement, the managers interested in purchasing the company borrow from a financial organization in order to pay the owner an agreed-upon price. The new owners pledge their stock as collateral for the loan or, depending on many factors, the lenders can accept an equity position in the company to cover part or all of the funds. Because the purchasers in leveraged buyouts are already running the company, disruption is minimized. As a result, leveraged buyouts are often a popular strategy for transfer of ownership of successful companies from their founders to the top management team these founders have assembled.

Leveraged buyouts are most useful for companies that have sufficient assets to serve as collateral for the loan required to purchase them. Companies purchased through leveraged buyouts generally have dependable cash flow from operations, a high ratio of fully depreciated fixed assets (equipment, plant, etc.), an established and successful product line, and low debt—both current and long-term. If, in contrast, a company lacks these characteristics, its stock may not provide sufficient collateral for the required loan, and a leveraged buyout may not be either feasible or desirable.

Employee share ownership plans (ESOPs) also provide a useful vehicle for transferring ownership of a company to its employees over a period of years. Some governments facilitate such plans. For example, residents of British Columbia can receive a 20 percent tax credit for investing in their employer's business, up to a maximum of a $2,000 tax credit ($10,000 investment) per year.[3]

ESOPs are a useful harvest strategy when entrepreneurs wish to exit from the companies they have founded in a gradual manner rather than all at once, as often occurs in a sale to outsiders. In addition, ESOPs are useful when many employees in a company are highly committed to it and have been employed by it for long periods of time. In contrast, ESOPs are not as useful when turnover among employees is high and these employees have little or no interest in obtaining an equity position in the company that employs them.

When entrepreneurs want to sell to outsiders, they can sell to competitors or non-competitors. *Competitors* are often interested in acquisitions to expand their market share or acquire an important resource. For example, Markham-based ATI Technologies sought to acquire the technological capabilities it needed for product development through its acquisitions of graphic chipmakers Chromatic Research in 1998 and ArtX in 2000. *Non-competitors are often interested in acquisitions as opportunities* to invest their surplus cash and their management skills. For example, in 2004, Bain Capital Partners, a U.S. private equity firm, purchased 70 to 80 percent of the Montreal-based Dollarama chain from the founder, Larry Rossy, for an amount in the $1 billion range. Rossy had founded the company 12 years previously, and had built it to a chain of 350 stores in six provinces.[4]

Selling to outsiders is often a very good strategy. As we noted in Chapter 11, it is often very costly for a company to maintain its own manufacturing and distribution systems—especially when these already exist and are highly developed and efficient in other businesses. If a new venture becomes part of a larger company that already has such systems in place, these costs can be greatly reduced or even eliminated. Similarly, being part of a larger firm may offer economies of scale and scope that can be highly beneficial.

Although many potential buyers may exist for a sound business, finding them is not always a straightforward task. Sometimes, this search involves hiring a *business broker*, a company that specializes in arranging for sales of existing businesses. Alternatively, if the business is already quite large, selling it may require the services of an investment banker who can arrange the large amount of financing needed for such a sale. Whichever route is taken, sale of an existing business often involves preparation of a *selling memorandum*, a marketing document designed to attract interest in the business. Like all marketing documents, the selling memorandum should place the company in a favourable light, but it should also be accurate and refrain from claims that will, on close examination by buyers, be found to be exaggerations. It is also often useful to seek the help of professional advisers who may be aware of potential buyers not known to the entrepreneurs. For the thoughts of one entrepreneur who sold his business to a larger firm in the industry, see the **Voice of Experience** section later in this chapter.

Just as people attempting to sell a house often make repairs and improvements before putting it on the market, entrepreneurs wishing to sell their business should be sure that their company's house is in good order before putting it on the market. Among the steps entrepreneurs can take to make their company attractive to potential buyers are the following:

- Sell at the right stage of development: In general, the timing is more attractive when the company is on the way up and is growing rapidly, not when it has already reached its peak.

- Sell when the business cycle is strong.

- If the entrepreneur will be leaving after the sale and this person's talent is part of what makes the business valuable, suggest ways of compensating for this loss.

- Identify and protect all intellectual property (patents, trademarks, etc.).

- Adopt transparent and conservative accounting policies appropriate to the business sector and ensure that your accounting records are in order, so that potential buyers feel they can make a proper valuation assessment.

- Resolve any open questions that might make it difficult to estimate the value of the business—tax or other compliance issues, and legal issues.

Once potential buyers appear, the valuation of the business and the negotiation process play key roles in shaping the specific terms of the sale agreement.

KEY POINTS

- Ownership transfer or sales involve valuation of the business. Several methods for accomplishing this task exist: balance sheet methods, earnings methods, and the market method.
- The transfer of the company to family members needs to be based on a sound succession plan and tax advice.
- The transfer of the company to employees can involve a leveraged buyout or an employee share ownership plan, and can take place gradually.
- Sales to outsiders offer important advantages over continuing to run an independent company and, in fact, a venture may have greater value as part of a larger organization than it does as an independent company.

THE VOICE OF EXPERIENCE

Successful Sales Take Time

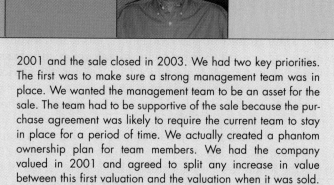

In 2003, Paul Riedlinger and his brother Bob sold a company that had been in their family for three generations. Initially known as Canadian Amplifier, the company was founded in Waterloo, Ontario, in 1926, by Paul's grandfather, William Riedlinger. It made gramophone horns, like the one pictured with the RCA dog, for Grimes Radio, a division of Electrohome. When gramophone horns were replaced by the new technology of amplifiers, the company shifted gears and started making components for wooden furniture. This move was successful until the bottom dropped out of the furniture market during the 1982 recession. At this time, Paul was completing his H.B.A. degree at the University of Western Ontario. He came into the company and started looking for a new market in which they could leverage the company's capabilities. They settled on high-end decorative ornamental mouldings and millwork. By 2001, the company, now known as The Ornamental Group (http://www.ornamental.com), was the largest supplier of decorative mouldings and millwork to The Home Depot and Lowe's Home Improvement. It supplied all the mouldings for the penthouse suites of the MGM Grand in Las Vegas. Eighty percent of the company's revenue came from the United States. In 2003, Paul and his brother sold the company to American Wood Moulding of Baltimore, Maryland. In a recent interview, Paul talked with me about the sale.

Reuber: "Why did you decide to sell the company?"

Riedlinger: "The company was so big that it wasn't fun anymore. We had 275 employees, four factories in North Carolina, a factory in Waterloo, and contract plants in China. We loved doing the custom work, but when we became so tied to Home Depot and Lowe's, there wasn't time for it. The big retailers are more focused on process than on innovation. They are concerned about vendor management and, although we provided the most profitable products in the millwork aisle, they were a small percent of the overall sales of that aisle, and so we felt vulnerable. It felt like a good time to try something else."

Reuber: "What were you looking for in a buyer?"

Riedlinger: "We were proactive in seeking out buyers. It's a small world and so we knew the other players and wanted to find a buyer that was a good match for our product. It was actually quite complicated because Home Depot and Lowe's prefer exclusive vendor relationships. We were in the strange position of supplying to both of them because no other supplier was large enough to satisfy their demand nationally in the U.S. And so we had to find a buyer who could also supply to both."

Reuber: "What did the sales process look like?"

Riedlinger: "My brother and I gave ourselves two years, and it really does take that long for a sale of any size. We started in 2001 and the sale closed in 2003. We had two key priorities. The first was to make sure a strong management team was in place. We wanted the management team to be an asset for the sale. The team had to be supportive of the sale because the purchase agreement was likely to require the current team to stay in place for a period of time. We actually created a phantom ownership plan for team members. We had the company valued in 2001 and agreed to split any increase in value between this first valuation and the valuation when it was sold. This plan worked very well. The top managers stayed committed to quality and growth and the four of them gained roughly $1 million each from the sale.

Our second priority was to develop a shortlist of suitable purchasers, and in the end we focused on two companies. One of these was Masco Corporation, based in Michigan. Masco has a history of acquisitions and, in fact, has its criteria for acquisitions posted on its website. Masco was a good fit and was interested, but they were busy with other initiatives at the time and so we started with America Wood Moulding (AWM). AWM is based in Baltimore, and is partly owned by Tenon, a New Zealand company. They were a good fit because AWM was the largest supplier of moulding to Home Depot and another Tenon company sold to Lowe's, so Tenon companies could cover our two major customers. We had a six-month lockup, when we weren't allowed to shop around while our negotiations with AWM were ongoing."

Reuber: "Did you do anything else to prepare the company for sale?"

Riedlinger: "The company was in good shape. It was debt-free and there was an excellent management team in place. We did want it to look its best, and that affected spending priorities. For example, we pushed back some acquisitions we might have done."

Reuber: "And what are you doing now?"

Riedlinger: "Since the sale was structured in two stages, it took two to three years to disengage from the company. We got part of the purchase price right away, and the rest of it two years later. In the interim, my brother and I retained shares and a seat on the Board. I went back to school and completed my M.B.A. at the University of Toronto's Rotman School of Management, in 2006. I'm looking at various opportunities. I'll keep you posted."

Commentary: Paul Riedlinger's description of the process of selling a business is insightful. There are many similarities to starting a company. You need to have a keen understanding of your target market and why other companies might buy your product (your firm). You need to be sensitive to the motivations of

continued

Photo courtesy of Paul Riedlinger

your employees during a period that might seem very unsettled to them. You need to understand the economics and how another company's business model matches the requirements of your business model. Finally, you need to understand your own motivation.

Just as motivations are critical to understanding why people start businesses, and why they start particular businesses, motivations are critical to understanding why people leave businesses and why they select particular harvest strategies.

TAKING A COMPANY PUBLIC: THE LURE OF IPOS

Entrepreneurs have a multitude of goals and an abundance of visions of the future, but many do share one major dream: reaching the point at which they can take their company public through an **initial public offering (IPO)**. In 2004, there were 87 IPOs completed in Canada, for a total value of $6.2 billion, which was the greatest IPO activity in the country since the bursting of the dot-com bubble in 2000.[5] Why is this particular harvest strategy so appealing to many entrepreneurs? Perhaps the simplest answer is that going public often generates huge amounts of cash—sometimes, more than entrepreneurs ever thought possible. The entrepreneurs can use this infusion of capital (or at least, the portion they actually receive!) for major expansion of their companies. Further, publicly traded companies quickly acquire an aura of respectability in the eyes of various stakeholders, from investors to customers, and this enhanced image can be a big plus from the point of view of gaining competitive advantage.[6] Once a company has gone public, the market in which it is traded provides continuous, updated valuation of its worth, which can both facilitate later rounds of financing and generally enhance liquidity. In addition, public companies can use stock options for their employees more easily than privately held companies, and they can also more readily use their stock to acquire other companies.

There are important advantages to IPOs, but they come at a considerable cost— one that entrepreneurs need to consider carefully. First, going public is a tremendously expensive process; indeed, it can consume as much as 25 percent of the entire value of the offering! Not only are there direct costs of underwriting the issue and meeting strict legal and accounting standards of due diligence, but there are also the costs of having top management of the company literally tied up for months, as they participate in the road show that proceeds most initial public offerings and is required by underwriters to assure that the new issue sells (see Figure 13.2).

Another potential cost is that most IPOs involve *lock-up agreements* to prevent insiders—including entrepreneurs—from cashing in on the public offering. These agreements require that entrepreneurs retain their stock for months or even years after the initial public offering. Further, shares may be underpriced initially because underwriters want initial purchasers to experience an immediate rise in stock prices. These purchasers are often preferred customers of the underwriter and, in fact, they are often the group that benefits most initially. Finally, entrepreneurs need to consider the ongoing costs of being a public company, such as meeting continuous disclosure and audit requirements.

Finally, entrepreneurs should recognize the fact that publicly traded companies are

LEARNING OBJECTIVE

3 List the advantages and costs of an initial public offering.

Figure 13.2 Participating in Roadshows: One Cost of IPOs

Prior to an initial public offering (IPO), the top management of the company must engage in extensive promotion of the company and its future prospects, in cooperation with underwriters of the IPO. This promotional activity takes them away from their regular jobs, and their absence often creates serious difficulties for the company. Shown here is LeapFrog's president and CEO Mike Wood (centre) at the New York Stock Exchange the day after its IPO.

AP Photo/Richard Drew

subject to very careful scrutiny—scrutiny that may limit the founding team's freedom to run the company as they prefer. For instance, markets tend to frown on risky business strategies so such strategies will probably have to be avoided. Further, investors expect returns in the form of dividends or capital gains, so management's attention may be diverted to focusing on these issues and on short-term strategies designed to raise earnings this year—or even this quarter—to make investors happy, rather than on longer term goals. Before going public, entrepreneurs don't have to consider such matters, but after the IPO, they absolutely must consider them with care.

A study of Canadian IPOs indicates that many companies go public too early, and so success rates and survival rates are low.[7] Canadian IPOs have tended to be smaller than IPOs in other industrial companies. In the second half of the 1990s, for example, the average value of Canadian IPO transactions was $2.5 million, compared with $74 million in France, $131 million in Germany, $93 million in the United Kingdom, and $84 million in the United States. Fewer than 35 percent of the companies that launched an IPO in Canada between 1991 and 1995 survived five years and had nets assets greater than the proceeds from the IPO. For companies with less than $1 million in net assets, the IPO was unsuccessful in 53 percent of cases, and only 6 percent of firms still existed and had net assets of at least $10 million after five years. Therefore, the timing of an IPO is absolutely critical.

In general, an IPO involves four phases of activity. During Phase 1, efforts are made to prepare the company for L-Day (listing day). This activity has been compared to preparations for prom night in high schools—a process of getting the company to look its best so that it will shine on L-Day.[8] Phase 2 involves working closely with the IPO work group (underwriters, accountants, investment bankers, lawyers) to prepare all IPO documentation (registration statement, prospectus, road show material). Phase 3 is the actual distribution exercise, which involves a two- or three-week road show by top management. Phase 4 should, ideally, continue the process by providing a constant flow of information to stock analysts and investors; this activity is needed to maintain public interest in the company and its shares. However, after the first three phases are complete, many companies are totally exhausted and find it extremely difficult to maintain this high level of activity. In addition, the need for the top management team to return to running the company may be acute, because they have been directing virtually all of their time and energies to the IPO process.

So, should entrepreneurs consider going public as a viable exit strategy? Many experts agree that the answer can be "yes" if the company truly needs large amounts of capital to grow and develop, and it is fortunate enough to possess an experienced management team that can handle the stress of the process and at the same time tell a great story to the public markets. Under these conditions, an IPO can provide entrepreneurs with the capital they need to fully realize their vision and, ultimately, with a very profitable exit route. On the other hand, many companies show excellent records of growth without an IPO (e.g., the Dollarama chain, which was subsequently purchased for more than $1 billion), so an IPO is not a necessary ingredient in long-term success.

KEY POINTS

- Entrepreneurs can harvest financial rewards from their companies through initial public offerings.
- IPOs offer important advantages (e.g., large infusions of cash) but come at a substantial cost (fees from underwriters are high, and the top management team must devote most of its energies to the IPO for several months).
- There is a low success rate among IPOs in Canada, as in most industrialized countries. It is important that entrepreneurs do not attempt to launch an IPO too early, when their venture is too small to attract investors and to bear the costs of the process.

NEGOTIATION: THE UNIVERSAL PROCESS

All harvest strategies involve **negotiation**—a process in which opposing sides exchange offers, counteroffers, and concessions either directly or through representatives. If the process is successful, an agreement acceptable to both sides is attained. If, instead, negotiations fail, the process ends, and each side seeks other parties with whom to make a deal.

Entrepreneurs engage in negotiations with others for many reasons; for example, to obtain initial funding, to write a partnership agreement, or to finalize contracts with customers and suppliers. When they decide to exit a business or to launch an IPO, they negotiate with potential purchasers of their company, or with underwriters, in order to implement the strategy they have chosen. For these reasons, it is important that entrepreneurs understand some of the basics with respect to negotiation. Specifically, they need to understand the nature of this process and how to carry it out effectively. Fortunately, the importance of negotiation as a process has been widely recognized in several different fields (management, psychology, political science), so there is a wealth of knowledge on which to draw.[9] Here, we will summarize some of the key points that, we believe, will prove especially useful to entrepreneurs.

Negotiation Tactics

We have already defined negotiation as a process in which opposing sides exchange offers, counteroffers, and concessions in an effort to obtain an agreement acceptable to both sides. Each side, of course, wishes to obtain an agreement favourable to its own interests, but each recognizes that the opponent is probably *not* going to lie down and surrender; rather, this person (or group of persons), too, will seek to maximize her or his outcomes. As a result, a key question becomes: "How can I persuade the other side to make concessions favorable to my interests?" Research findings indicate that the most basic answer involves the use of tactics that reduce the opposing side's aspirations—tactics that encourage opponents to conclude that they cannot get what they want and must, instead, settle for something much less favourable to them, but more favourable to their opponent.[10] Let's take a look at some of these tactics and also at the question of whether it is ethical to use them.

The course and outcome of negotiations are influenced by many different factors. Among the most important of these, however, are specific *bargaining tactics* that are used to reduce an opponent's goals. These include (1) beginning with an extreme initial offer—one that is very favourable to the side proposing it and is, in fact, much more favourable than this side can realistically expect to receive (e.g., an entrepreneur places a much higher value on her company than even she believes it merits); (2) the big lie technique—convincing the other side that one's breakeven point is much higher than it is so that the other side will offer more than would otherwise be the case (e.g., an entrepreneur seeks to convince a potential purchaser that he would rather continue to own the company than to sell for the price suggested by the would-be buyer); (3) convincing the other side that you have an out—another party with whom you can make a deal (e.g., an entrepreneur convinces a potential purchaser that there is another purchaser waiting in the wings—even if this is not true). Are these and related tactics ethical? Opinions differ, but research findings indicate that certain tactics are widely recognized as being unethical.[11] Here are the tactics generally considered to be most objectionable: (1) false promises—making false promises or commitments one has no intention of keeping; (2) misrepresentation—providing misleading or false information to an opponent; and (3) inappropriate information gathering—collecting information through theft, spying, etc. To the extent

> **LEARNING OBJECTIVE**
>
> 4 Describe the basic nature of negotiation and explain the nature of several key bargaining tactics.

a negotiator engages in such actions, her or his behaviour is generally viewed as unethical. According to these principles, then, an extreme initial offer is generally ethically acceptable (although risky, because if it is too extreme, it can anger or annoy an opponent), but both the big lie and fictitious claims about having an out are not ethically acceptable—they involve false statements and misrepresentation. Please note: We're not saying that negotiators do not engage in such tactics; we are merely pointing out that most people consider doing so to be a violation of ethical standards. Thus, entrepreneurs who want to protect their reputation for making future deals or running additional companies should approach these tactics with caution: Using them can work in the short run, but it may prove very costly over longer periods of time.

Although the tactics we have considered so far are among the most important, many others procedures for inducing one's opponent to make concessions during negotiations also exist. These do not focus on reducing opponent's aspirations; rather, they concentrate on inducing specific feelings and reactions in opponents—feelings or reactions that make it hard for them not to offer favourable terms to the person using such tactics. For instance, skilled negotiators often try to arrange their own concessions so that these produce pressures to reciprocate among opponents. More specifically, they make a series of small concessions on issues that they view as relatively unimportant. This approach puts subtle pressure on opponents to reciprocate—to make concessions of their own. If negotiators are truly skilled, they manoeuvre their opponents into the position where the concessions they make are precisely the ones the negotiators desire.[12]

A related tactic involves inducing *positive affect* (i.e., positive feelings or moods) among opponents. A large body of research findings indicates that when people experience positive affect, they are much more likely to agree to a request and to behave in cooperative ways.[13] How can positive affect be induced among opponents? By holding discussions in very comfortable and pleasant settings, by providing lavish refreshments, and by treating the opponents with respect and courtesy (see Figure 13.3). Again, research findings indicate that such procedures often work: They make it easier, psychologically, for opponents to move toward the positions desired by the negotiators who use them.

We could continue, but by now the main point should be clear: Many techniques for influencing the course of negotiations, and for obtaining positive outcomes from negotiations, exist. For entrepreneurs, negotiation is almost a way of life—they engage in it throughout the entrepreneurial process, from discussions with potential investors through deliberations with potential purchasers when arranging exit strategies. For this reason, understanding the nature of negotiations, and being able both to recognize various tactics and to use them effectively, is definitely well worth the effort. Please take note: Becoming a skilled negotiator requires years of practice, so our goal here is mainly that of acquainting you with the complexities of this process, not trying to turn you into experts. But being aware of the tactics we have discussed is a very good start, and will at least put you on the road toward improving what is certainly one of the most valuable skills you can develop.

Figure 13.3 Positive Affect and the Course of Negotiations

Research findings indicate that putting one's opponent in a good mood is often a useful negotiating strategy.

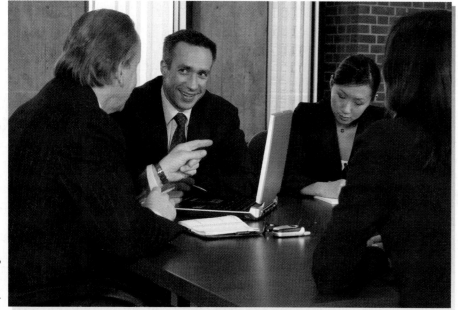

Jupiter Images

Overall Orientation towards Negotiation

Another aspect of negotiation has been found to be very important in determining the outcomes it produces. This aspect is what is generally referred to as the **overall approach to negotiation** adopted by the persons participating in it. Research findings indicate that two basic approaches exist. One approach views negotiation as a win-lose situation in which gains by one side are necessarily linked with losses for the other. The other approach, in contrast, assumes that the interests of the two sides are not incompatible and that an agreement that maximizes the outcomes of both sides can be obtained; this view is known as a win-win approach.

Not all situations offer the potential for win-win agreements, but many do provide such possibilities. If the parties to a negotiation are willing to explore all options carefully, they can sometimes attain what are known as **integrative agreements**— arrangements that maximize joint benefits—the gains experienced by both sides. Here's one well-known example: Two cooks are making different recipes, and both call for an orange; yet, the cooks have only one orange in their kitchen. What do they do? One possibility is to cut the orange in half; this works, but it leaves both chefs short of what they need. Another, and more creative (integrative) solution, is to notice that one cook needs all the juice while the other needs only the peel. So, one cook can take the peel and leave the juice for the other. This option is a much better solution, because both get what they need; in other words, the joint outcomes are considerably better. Other strategies for reaching integrative solutions are summarized in Table 13.1.

One strategy that is especially useful to entrepreneurs is *logrolling*, a technique in which each party makes concessions on issues that are relatively unimportant to it in exchange for concessions on other issues that it values more highly. Here's a concrete example: An entrepreneur wants a specific price for his company because he feels that he needs this amount in order to maintain his lifestyle in the years ahead. The potential purchaser is concerned with price, but an even more important issue for her is having the entrepreneur stay on with the company for a specified period of time, to smooth the transition. The entrepreneur would prefer to leave at once, but can handle staying on for a year—if that will help him get the price he wants. If the two sides are sharp enough to recognize this difference in the relative importance of these two issues, they can logroll: The purchaser raises her price and the entrepreneur agrees to stay on. Each side gets what is most important to it by making concessions on issues it views as less important. Again, logrolling is not always possible, but when it is—or when other integrative strategies are feasible—the outcome can be an agreement that meets the primary needs

LEARNING OBJECTIVE

5 Explain why integrative agreements between negotiators are generally best, and explain the relationship of such agreements to the overall approach to negotiation (a win-lose approach versus a win-win approach).

Table 13.1 Techniques for Reaching Integrative Agreements

Several techniques for reaching agreements that maximize joint outcomes (integrative agreements) exist, but they are not always easy to recognize. Negotiators who succeed in identifying such opportunities can often attain highly satisfactory agreements.

TECHNIQUE FOR REACHING INTEGRATIVE AGREEMENTS	DESCRIPTION AND EXAMPLES
Broadening the pie	Available resources are increased so that both sides can obtain their major goals (e.g., additional sources of funding for a purchase are obtained).
Nonspecific compensation	One side gets what it wants, and the other is compensated on an unrelated issue (e.g., entrepreneur gets the price she wants for her business, and the purchaser gets rights to patents held by the entrepreneur).
Logrolling	Each party makes concessions on low-priority issues in exchange for concessions on issues it values more highly (see text).
Cost-cutting	One party gets what it wants and the costs to the other party are reduced or eliminated (e.g., the entrepreneur gets the price he wants for the business, but the purchaser will pay this over a large number of years and in a way that makes the payments tax deductible).
Bridging	Neither party gets its initial demands, but a new option that satisfies the major interests of both sides is developed (e.g., the purchaser wants the entrepreneur to remain while the entrepreneur wants a straight sale; a new option in which the entrepreneur will train a replacement is worked out).

of both sides. That's an important point because research findings indicate that winning in a negotiation can prove costly: If one side manages to get most of what it wants (perhaps because it is bargaining from a position of real strength), the opponent may be forced to accept, but the seeds of future problems may be sown.[14] The losing side feels that it has not been treated fairly and may find various ways to even the score, either overtly or covertly. This reaction is a common occurrence in the realm of labour-management relations, where the ultimate outcome can be negative for both sides. For instance, during the 1950s and 1960s, unions representing employees in the newspaper industry staged repeated strikes, thus forcing costly concessions from the owners of many famous newspapers (e.g., the *Herald Tribune* in New York). Faced with this confrontational approach, many newspaper owners began to view the unions as totally unreasonable, and gradually concluded that it was impossible for them to earn reasonable rates of return in this industry. The result? They closed down many famous newspapers, thus costing well-paid union members their jobs and depriving the public of newspapers they had read for decades. Here's how this scenario might operate with respect to entrepreneurs. Suppose that an entrepreneur is a skilled negotiator and manages to extract exceptionally favourable terms from a purchaser. When the purchaser reconsiders this deal at a later time, he concludes that he paid far too much. As a result, he feels justified in delaying payments to the entrepreneur or in saying negative things about this person, thus harming the entrepreneur's chances of obtaining funding to start another company. For this reason alone, integrative agreement and a win-win approach are strongly preferable to agreements in which one side sets out to defeat its opponent—and does so. (For an example of what can happen when negotiators focus on winning at all costs, please see the **Danger! Pitfall Ahead!** section).

What we have been saying throughout this section, in essence, is this: Negotiation is a complex process that is affected by more than purely economic factors. As we noted in Chapter 3, human beings are not entirely rational. On the contrary, we are subject to many cognitive errors, and our thinking is often strongly influenced by our emotions.[15] For this reason, we sometimes lose sight of our basic self-interests during negotiations. These interests can be summarized in two major points: (1) obtain a favourable agreement with your opponent, and (2) avoid (insofar as possible) inducing feelings of anger, resentment, or outrage on the part of your opponent. In other words, as negotiators, we should seek fair and equitable agreements—not one-sided ones. The temptation to try to win by defeating your opponent is often great but the likelihood that negotiations will succeed is much lower when this kind of win-lose strategy is adopted by one or both sides. Moreover, any agreement that is produced from a win-lose strategy will tend to be unstable: The losing side will feel that it has been unfairly treated (perhaps tricked or exploited) and that, in turn, sets the stage for later, serious problems. Entrepreneurs who keep these basic points clearly in mind as they negotiate with potential purchasers over the sale of their company (or with anyone else over any other issue, for that matter), will ultimately obtain better and more lasting agreements than ones who revert to the standard approach of viewing their opponents as enemies against whom any and all tactics are acceptable. Obtaining integrative agreements requires more effort, thought, and greater creativity than the more obvious win-lose approach, but often, the outcome is well worth the additional cost.

DANGER! PITFALL AHEAD!

The Costs of Negotiating to Win: Watch Out for the Ankle-Biters!

Do you ever store food in plastic containers? If so, the chances are good that some of them, at least, say Rubbermaid on the lids. Until the mid-1990s, Rubbermaid had a virtual monopoly on small food-storage containers. But then something strange happened: Rubbermaid products began to disappear from the shelves of supermarkets and large discount stores, where they had previously been prominently featured. I remember when this happened, and at the time, I wondered why. Now, I know. During the mid-1990s, the price of resin, the raw material for many of Rubbermaid's products, soared, virtually doubling in only 18 months. Rubbermaid's reaction was to pass these price increases directly on to its customers, and when they protested, the company adopted a very tough negotiating stance. This position was true even with respect to giant Wal-Mart, its largest single account. In other words, Rubbermaid hung tough and viewed negotiations with its customers as confrontations in which it set out to defeat these companies.

What happened next was classic. Stung by Rubbermaid's harsh treatment, and tempted by smaller companies who passed less of the price increase for resin on to customers, Wal-Mart and other large customers reduced the amount of shelf space they devoted to Rubbermaid's products. Consumers, in turn, were not as loyal to the Rubbermaid brand as the company expected and deserted its products for lower priced containers that were now featured in the space previously occupied by Rubbermaid. Finally, Rubbermaid got the message and realized that the small companies they viewed as ankle-biters had used Rubbermaid's intransigence in negotiation with its customers to gain competitive advantage—and a larger share of this lucrative market.

Rubbermaid, of course, is a giant corporation. But the message for entrepreneurs—or anyone else entering into negotiations—is clear: If you choose to view your opponent as an enemy and seek to win the negotiation by defeating this person, get ready for some nasty surprises. It is rare in life that one side has all the power, and although you may triumph in the short run, the long-term costs may be more than you bargained for. This basic principle is as true for giant corporations as it is for individual entrepreneurs negotiating with potential purchasers of their business. So, although integrative solutions that maximize joint outcomes are often hard to obtain, they are, often by far the best, and well worth the effort.

KEY POINTS

- Negotiation is a process in which participants exchange offers and counteroffers until either an agreement is reached or negotiations deadlock. Skill in negotiating with others is very useful to entrepreneurs throughout the entrepreneurial process—from negotiating with potential investors to negotiating with potential buyers of the business.
- A key goal of negotiators is to reduce the aspiration (goals) of their opponent.
- Other tactics involve efforts to generate pressures to reciprocate concessions on the part of opponents, and inducing them to experience positive affect.
- A key factor that affects the course and outcomes of negotiations is the negotiators' overall approach to this context: win-lose or win-win. A win-win approach offers much greater opportunity for reaching integrative agreements—arrangements that maximize joint outcomes.

HARVEST STRATEGIES AND THE LIFE SPAN: DIFFERENT NEEDS—AND GOALS—AT DIFFERENT TIMES OF LIFE

Samuel Butler once wrote: "Life is like playing a violin solo in public and learning the instrument as one goes on." (1895). We agree; life does involve of a lot of ad-libbing, and we do indeed make it up as we go along. That's as true for entrepreneurs as anyone else; in fact, one could argue that they are the improvisers *par excellence.* After all, they are people who create something—viable new ventures—out of what, at first glance, appears to be nothing. Moreover, their energy, optimism, and belief in their own abilities equip them for long, productive working lives. Even entrepreneurs, however, must ultimately come face to face with the realities of the human life span. We do indeed change with the passing decades, and these changes take many different forms. Change is slow at first, but speeds up for most people after they pass the age of 50. Energy, the acuteness of our senses, and stamina all decrease—although there are huge individual differences in this respect. For instance, research findings indicate that these processes are much slower for people who stay in good physical shape than for those who do not.[16] Thus, it is possible for a physically fit person aged 60 to have more energy and stamina than a less fit person 20 or even 30 years younger. So the rate at which we decline physically, if not the decline itself, is, to some degree, under our control.

Physical changes, however, are only part of the total picture. As we move through the life span, we also change cognitively and socially, too. With respect to cognitive changes, it was once believed that memory, intelligence, and many other aspects of cognition decline with increasing age. Recent findings, however, suggest that such changes—if they occur—are much slower and smaller in magnitude than was previously assumed.[17] For instance, some aspects of memory do seem to decline with increasing age (e.g., our ability to transfer information from short-term storage into long-term memory), but others remain largely unchanged. For instance, semantic memory (general knowledge) does not decline with age and may, in fact, increase.[18] Similarly, procedural memory—the kind of memory involved in skilled motor activities—remains largely unimpaired as we age. Intelligence, too, changes only slowly, if at all, with increasing age. In fact, recent studies suggest that the only components of intelligence that decline with age are those directly related to speed—for instance, how quickly people can retrieve information from memory or perform tasks that require quick responses. In contrast, practical intelligence, a kind that is especially important to entrepreneurs, may actually increase with age rather than decline.[19]

Additional research focused on creativity, too, points to encouraging conclusions. Although most persons seem to make their major contributions during their 30s and 40s, the optimal age depends on the field in question. In highly quantitative fields such as mathematics and theoretical physics, creativity peaks occur relatively early—when people are in their 20s and 30s. In other fields of science, however, the peak is much later, occurring when scientists are in their 40s and 50s. Research findings indicate that many persons show a second peak, late in life—in the 60s, 70s, or even 80s. For instance, Picasso produced many of his famous paintings in his 60s, 70s, and even in his 80s (see Figure 13.4), and Michelangelo was painting until his death

Figure 13.4 Creativity: Does It Decline with Age?

Many famous persons—artists, scientists, composers, writers—make important contributions late in life. For instance, Pablo Picasso (shown here) produced many paintings when he was in his 70s and 80s, which suggests that creativity does not necessarily decrease with age.

© Hulton-Deutsch Collection/CORBIS

at 84. Composers, too, often show a second peak of productivity late in life. For instance, Rachmaninoff's "Symphonic Dances" was written just one year before his death, decades after he composed his most famous works.

What these examples suggest for entrepreneurs, of course, is that they can continue working productively for many decades—if they so choose—and if their families agree. That is an important point, worth emphasizing: The demanding life of an entrepreneur can take a heavy toll on family and personal relationships, and these people certainly should have a voice in this decision. In other words, entrepreneurs have more to consider than simply their own preferences. Just as the support of spouses, significant others, friends, and family members is essential at the start, so, too, is it important in deciding when and how to exit. As countless entrepreneurs recognize, you really *can't* do it alone, and it is only fair that the people who helped you along the way should have a voice in deciding when it is time to say "enough."

In any case, it is clear that at some point, all entrepreneurs face the following key question: Do I want to keep working and leading the same kind of hectic life, devoting 100 hours or more per week to my business? This is a question each person must answer for himself or herself, but research on human development across the life span suggests that most of us do reach a time when we want a simpler, less hectic life.

To summarize the main findings of this research,[20] it appears that we all pass through a series of distinct phases or eras in our lives, with each phase separated from the one before it by a turbulent transition period. One of these is the *age 30 transition*. At this time, individuals realize that they are nearing the point of no return: If they remain in their current job and life, they will have too much invested to change. Faced with this fact, people often re-examine their initial choice and either make major changes or decide that they indeed chose the best course. This response to the age 30 transition explains one reason why many entrepreneurs decide to leave their jobs with large corporations soon after turning 30.[21]

The next life transition, which occurs when people are between ages 40 and 45, is known as the *midlife transition*. It is a time when many individuals first begin to think about their own mortality. Up until this period, most view themselves as young, and life as a very long-term proposition, stretching off into a dimly visible future. After age 40, though, many persons come to see themselves as the older generation. This perspective leads them to take stock of the success of their past choices and the likelihood of reaching their youthful dreams. The result can be a major change in a person's life—divorce, remarriage, a new career. Many individuals experience yet another period of transition between the ages of 50 and 55. This *late-adult transition* marks the close of the middle years of life and the start of late adulthood. During this transition, individuals must come to terms with their impending retirement and the major changes this transition will bring. How long do they want to work? What do they want to do if they stop? These are questions most people never considered before, but begin to ponder with increasing frequency after age 50.

What does all this mean for entrepreneurs? Basically, entrepreneurs should take such factors into account in deciding how and when to exit from their companies. As human beings, we definitely have different goals and needs at different stages of our lives, and these should be carefully considered by entrepreneurs when they think about leaving the companies they have created. Young entrepreneurs—those under 40—may well want to start another company, so they are likely to choose a harvest strategy that yields significant cash on closing. Older entrepreneurs (e.g., those 50 or older) may be uncertain as to whether they want to start the whole process over again. Instead, they may consciously want to slow down and smell the roses. For such persons, a gradual exit and payments over a period of time may make more sense. And still older entrepreneurs, who are already very secure financially, may want to focus on transferring ownership in their businesses to children or other family members.

The key point is this: No single harvest strategy is best for all entrepreneurs. Rather, the choice among them, and the specific terms negotiated, should reflect not only economic realities (what is best for the company and its future), but personal

LEARNING OBJECTIVE

6 Define "life transitions" and explain why entrepreneurs should consider their own age and phase of life before choosing an exit strategy.

realities, too. These considerations should include what one researcher, Veronika Kisfalvi, has recently described as central life issues—concerns that derive from the entrepreneurs' unique life experiences and are basic themes in everything they do, including the strategies they choose for running their new ventures (e.g., desire for autonomy, success, recognition, taking action, etc.).[22] These life issues will vary from person to person, but we all have them in one form or another. Similarly, the choice among exit strategies should reflect where the entrepreneur is in life's journey, and what he or she wants to do in the years ahead. The more entrepreneurs take these factors into account, the more likely they are to be able to echo the words of Javier Perez de Cuellar (1991), former Secretary-General of the United Nations, who, in speaking of his own retirement, remarked, "I am a free man. I feel as light as a feather." That is a fitting conclusion to a life of active achievement, and one to which, we believe, all entrepreneurs are entitled. Good luck! We wish you a smooth, interesting, and fulfilling journey through the decades that define our adult lives.

KEY POINTS

- As we age, we move through distinct phases or eras of life. These phases are separated by somewhat turbulent transition periods, during which many people examine their lives in the light of changing goals.
- The harvest strategy selected by entrepreneurs should reflect their objectives and preferences in the same way that their start-ups reflected their objectives and preferences at an earlier point in time.
- To the extent that entrepreneurs take careful account of these personal factors as well as economic ones, the exit strategies they choose and then negotiate will be ones that help them achieve the major goals they seek.

Summary and Review of Key Points

- Ownership transfer or sales involve valuation of the business. Several methods for accomplishing this task exist: balance sheet methods, earnings methods, and the market method.

- The transfer of the company to family members needs to be based on a sound succession plan and tax advice.

- The transfer of the company to employees can involve a leveraged buyout or an employee share ownership plan, and can take place gradually.

- Sales to outsiders offer important advantages over continuing to run an independent company and, in fact, a venture may have greater value as part of a larger organization than it does as an independent company.

- Entrepreneurs can harvest financial rewards from their companies through initial public offerings.

- IPOs offer important advantages (e.g., large infusions of cash) but come at a substantial cost (fees from underwriters are high, and the top management team

must devote most of its energies to the IPO for several months).

- There is a low success rate among IPOs in Canada, as in most industrialized countries. It is important that entrepreneurs do not attempt to launch an IPO too early, when their venture is too small to attract investors and to bear the costs of the process.

- Negotiation is a process in which participants exchange offers and counteroffers until either an agreement is reached or negotiations deadlock. Skill in negotiating with others is very useful to entrepreneurs throughout the entrepreneurial process—from negotiating with potential investors to negotiating with potential buyers of the business.

- A key goal of negotiators is to reduce the aspiration (goals) of their opponent.

- Other tactics involve efforts to generate pressures to reciprocate concessions on the part of opponents, and inducing them to experience positive affect.

- A key factor that affects the course and outcomes of negotiations is the negotiator's overall approach to this context: win-lose or win-win. A win-win approach offers much greater opportunity for reaching integrative agreements—arrangements that maximize joint outcomes.

■ As we age, we move through distinct phases or eras of life. These phases are separated by somewhat turbulent transition periods, during which many people examine their lives in the light of changing goals.

■ The harvest strategy selected by entrepreneurs should reflect their objectives and preferences in the same way that their start-ups reflected their objectives and preferences at an earlier point in time.

■ To the extent that entrepreneurs take careful account of these personal factors as well as economic ones, the exit strategies they choose and then negotiate will be ones that help them achieve the major goals they seek.

Glossary

Balance Sheet Methods (of valuation): Methods for valuing businesses based on their balance sheets.

Capitalized Earnings Method: A method for valuing businesses based on capitalized net earnings.

Discounted Future Earnings Method: A method of valuing businesses based on discounted future earnings.

Earnings Methods: Methods of valuing businesses based on their future earnings.

Employee Stock Ownership Plans (ESOPs): Methods of transferring ownership of a company to its employees; the current owners contribute to an employee stock ownership trust. Contributions are often based on the profitability of the company.

Excess Earnings Method: A method of valuing businesses based on the extent to which a company will generate earnings in excess of the average for its industry.

Initial Public Offering (IPO): Initial sale of stock in a company to the public.

Intangibles: Assets that are hard, if not impossible, to list on the balance sheet: the goodwill the company has acquired with customers and suppliers, its reputation in the industry, its success in attracting and motivating first-rate employees.

Integrative Agreements: Arrangements that maximize joint benefits—the gains experienced by both sides.

Leveraged Buyout: Procedures for transferring ownership of a company to its current managers. The managers borrow from a financial organization in order to pay the owner an agreed-upon price.

Market Value (price-earnings) Approach: Procedures for valuing businesses based on the price-earnings ratios for comparable publicly owned companies.

Negotiation: A process in which opposing sides exchange offers, counteroffers, and concessions either directly or through representatives.

Overall Approach to Negotiation: The general attitude to negotiation adopted by the persons participating in it. Two basic patterns are a win-lose approach and a win-win approach.

Discussion Questions

1. How important do you think emotional and other nonrational factors are in shaping entrepreneurs' exit strategies? Can you think of ways in which the impact of these factors can be reduced?

2. How can entrepreneurs decide which of several family members is the best person to be their successor in running the company? Should they seek outside help in making this choice?

3. What are the advantages of selling a company to insiders (e.g., its current executives)? What are the advantages of selling a company to outsiders? On balance, do you think one of these strategies is superior to the other?

4. Sometimes, all methods for valuing a company—balance sheet, earnings, and market approaches—yield similar results. On other occasions, however, they do not. Why?

5. Many entrepreneurs work toward the goal of an initial public offering (IPO). Although an IPO can yield large amounts of cash, such offerings have a downside, too. What is the downside, and why should entrepreneurs consider it carefully before seeking an IPO?

6. Why does holding negotiations in a very pleasant environment sometimes help participants to reach an agreement?

7. What do the effects of aging have to do with entrepreneurs' choice of an exit strategy?

InfoTrac Exercises

1. **Identify All Possible Exits; Too Many Businesses Are Launched Without a Thought for the Day When the Founder Will Move On. Big Mistake, Says This Veteran Entrepreneur** (entrepreneur's byline)(advice for entrepreneurs on exit strategies)

   William J. Link.

   Business Week Online, December 6, 2002 pNA

   Record: A94978856

   Full Text: COPYRIGHT 2002 The McGraw-Hill Companies, Inc. Byline: William J. Link

   1. According to the article, what types of entrepreneurs should consider an exit strategy at start-up?

   2. What four steps are necessary to build a business for a smooth exit?

   3. Why is developing an exit strategy first important in the success of a new business?

2. **Ethnic Entrepreneurship, Transmigration, and Social Integration: An Ethnographic Study of Chinese Restaurant Owners in Rural Western Canada**

   Josephine Smart

   Urban Anthropology and Studies of Cultural Systems and World Economic Development Fall-Winter 2003 v.32 i3-4 p. 311(32).

   Record: A114856846

   Full Text: COPYRIGHT 2003 Plenum Publishiing Corporation

   1. What are some patterns in how people have come to own and operate Chinese restaurants?

   2. What are the most important factors contributing to the success and failure of the Chinese restaurants examined in this study?

   3. How and why have the harvest strategies of Chinese restaurant owners changed over time?

GETTING DOWN
TO BUSINESS

Valuing Your Company

As we saw in an earlier section, there are many ways of valuing your company. Because every entrepreneur who runs a successful business will, ultimately, exit from it, we think it is important for you to gain practice in the basics of this process—although, almost certainly, you will have the help and guidance of a financial expert when the time comes to prepare an actual valuation. Follow these steps to gain familiarity with the major valuation methods.

1. **Balance sheet method.** Using the adjusted balance sheet method, compute the net worth of your company. (Net worth = Assets – Liabilities)

2. **Earnings methods.** Choose one of the three basic earnings methods of valuation (excess earnings method, capitalized earnings, discounted future earnings method) and, following steps outlined in the text, use it to value your company.

3. **Market method.** Use the market method to value your company.

Now, compare the three figures you obtained. Do they differ? If so, why? What assumptions did you make as a basis for these calculations? Would you feel comfortable explaining these assumptions to potential purchasers of your company? Remember, valuation is just a starting point for complex negotiations with potential purchasers of your company, so our comments about negotiation certainly apply: Excessive valuations that are based on unconvincing assumptions will usually *not* help you to obtain a higher price; they may, instead, get negotiations off to a bad start. So think carefully about the assumptions you make in any method of valuation; if they are unrealistically inflated, the probably won't contribute in a positive way to reaching a satisfactory agreement.

Improving Your Negotiating Skills

Negotiation truly is the universal process; whether we realize it or not, we engage in it several times each day. For instance, do you ever divide chores between yourself and roommates or significant others? If so, you almost certainly negotiated with them about this issue. Have you ever arranged the division of tasks between yourself and co-workers, or arranged for a co-worker to cover for you while you took needed time off? Again, negotiation was almost certainly involved.

To gain insights into how often you are negotiating, and how well you are handling this process, follow these steps.

1. For one week, keep a record of all the occasions on which you engage in negotiation with others. Write down:
   a. The issue over which you negotiated
   b. The person with whom you negotiated
   c. The tactics you used during the negotiations
   d. The outcome
   e. The satisfaction of both you and the other person with the arrangement you made
2. Next, consider negotiations carefully in terms of the following questions:
   a. Are you satisfied with the tactics you used, or do you think you could have chosen better ones?
   b. What about the stability of the arrangements you negotiated—are they ones that are fully acceptable to both you and the other person? (If not, these arrangements probably won't last.)
   c. Did you use different tactics depending on your relationship with the other person? (e.g., one set of tactics with people you must deal with regularly, but another set with people you may never see again?)
3. Finally, ask yourself this question—and answer honestly: When you approached each of these situations, did you adopt a win-win approach in which you genuinely sought an agreement that would be fully satisfactory to both you and the other person? Or did you adopt a win-lose approach, in which you concentrated mainly on getting what you wanted? Remember: Agreements obtained through a confrontational, win-lose approach may be attractive in the short run, but they can come back to haunt you—with interest—later on.

Enhanced Learning

You may select any combination of the resources below to enhance your understanding of the chapter material.

- **Appendix: Case Studies** – Twelve cases provide opportunities to apply chapter concepts to realistic entrepreneurial situations. These brief cases call for careful analysis of real business problems and ask you to think about potential solutions.
- **Video Case Library** – Nine cases are tied directly to video segments from the popular PBS television series Small Business School. These cases and video segments (available on the Entrepreneurship website at http://www.entrepreneurship.nelson.com) give you unparalleled access to today's entrepreneurs, with expert advice and insights on how to start, run, and grow a business.
- **Management Interview Series Video Database** – This video interview series contains a wealth of tips on how to manage effectively. Access to the database and practical exercises are available on the book support website at http://www.entrepreneurship.nelson.com.

Notes

1. Chua, J., Chrisman, J.J., & Sharma, P. 2003. Succession and nonsuccession concerns of family firms and agency relationship with nonfamily managers. *Family Business Review* 16(2): 89–107.

2. Miller, D., Steier, L., & Le Breton-Miller, I. 2003. Lost in time: Intergenerational succession, change and failure in family business. *Journal of Business Venturing* 18(4): 513–531.

3. Programs and Services, British Columbia Ministry of Economic Development. http://www.ecdev.gov.bc.ca/ProgramsAndServices/BusinessServices/Investment_Capital/Employee_Share_Ownership/old/faq.htm.

4. Marotte, B. 2004. Bain snaps up discount chain Dollarama. *Globe and Mail*, November 26: B5.

5. PricewaterhouseCoopers Canada, Survey of Initial Public Offerings in Canada January 2004–December 2004. http://www.pwc.com/extweb/ncpressrelease.nsf/DocID/F974FA96415A736C85256F7F0054DF33.

6. Leleux, B. 2000. Riding on the wave of IPOs. In S. Birley & D.F. Muzyka (eds.). *Mastering entrepreneurship* (pp. 394–398). London: Prentice-Hall.

7. The figures on Canadian IPOs are taken from *Small and medium-sized enterprise financing in Canada*, a 2003 report by the Small Business Research & Policy Branch of Industry Canada. http://www.strategis.gc.ca.

8. Leleux, B. 2000. Riding on the wave of IPOs. In S. Birley & D.F. Muzyka (eds.). *Mastering entrepreneurship* (pp. 394–398). London: Prentice-Hall.

9. Thompson, L. 1998. *The mind and heart of the negotiator.* Upper Saddle River, NJ: Prentice-Hall.

10. Pruitt, D.G., & Carnevale, P.J. 1993. *Negotiation in social conflict.* Pacific Grove, CA: Brooks/Cole.

11. Thompson, L. 1998. *The mind and heart of the negotiator.* Upper Saddle River, NJ: Prentice-Hall.

12. Baron, R.A., & Byrne, D. 2002. *Social psychology.* 10th ed. Boston: Allyn & Bacon.

13. Isen, A.M. 1984. Toward understanding the role of affect in cognition. In R.S. Wyer & T.K. Srull (eds.), *Handbook of social cognition* vol. 3 (pp. 179–236). Hillsdale, NJ: Erlbaum.

14. Pruitt, D.G., & Carnevale, P.J. 1993. *Negotiation in social conflict.* Pacific Grove, CA: Brooks/Cole.

15. Forgas, J.P. 1995. Mood and judgment: The affect infusion model (AIM). *Psychological Bulletin* 117(1): 39–66.

16. Arking, R. 1991. *Biology of aging: Observations and principles.* Englewood Cliffs, NJ: Prentice-Hall.

17. Park, D.C., Smith, A.D., Lautenschlager, G., Earles, J.L., Frieseke, D., Zwahr, M., & Gaines, C.L. 1996. Mediators of long-term memory performance across the lifespan. *Psychology and Aging* 11(4): 621–637.

18. Shimamura, A.P., & Jurica, P.J. 1994. Memory interference effects and aging: Findings from a test of frontal lobe function. *Neuropsychology* 8(3): 408–412.

19. Sternberg, R.J., Wagner, R.K., Williams, W.M., & Horvath, J.A. 1995. Testing common sense. *American Psychologist* 50(11): 912–927.

20. Levinson, D.J. 1986. A conception of adult development. *American Psychologist* 41(1): 3–13.

21. Zimmerer, T.W., & Scarborough, N.M. 1996. *Entrepreneurship and new venture formation.* Upper Saddle River, NJ: Prentice-Hall.

22. Kisfalvi, V. 2002. The entrepreneurs' character, life issues, and strategy making: A field study. *Journal of Business Venturing* 17(5): 489–518.

Appendix: Case Studies

CHAPTER ONE

SASKCAN PULSE TRADING

For Murad Al-Katib, 2004 was a very good year. At just over 30 years old, he received an Ernst & Young Entrepreneur of the Year Award for Emerging Entrepreneur in the Prairie Region of Canada, and his business, Saskcan Pulse Trading, was awarded the Saskatchewan Business of the Year by the Saskatchewan Chamber of Commerce. In May 2005, he was named one of Canada's Top 40 Under 40.

Al-Katib's family emigrated from Turkey to Canada in 1965. He was raised in Davidson, Saskatchewan (population 1,117), where his father practised medicine. Since his family arrived in Canada before he was born, he learned to speak Turkish only because his mother insisted upon it. He received a bachelor of commerce degree with distinction, from the University of Saskatchewan (1994) and a master's degree in international management with distinction, from the American Graduate School of International Management in Phoenix, Arizona (1995). After a stint at the World Bank in Washington, D.C., he returned to Saskatchewan. As a trade development officer for Saskatchewan Trade and Export Partnership (STEP) for 5½ years, he travelled extensively to promote Saskatchewan exports.

Saskcan Pulse Trading was formed in 2001, by a company called Arbel, the largest importer and exporter of lentils in Turkey. Arbel had been buying Saskatchewan lentils to process in Turkish plants, but wanted to start processing them in Saskatchewan to reduce costs. At start-up, Al-Katib became president, CEO, and a director of the Regina-based company. He raised more than $11 million in capital to build and operate two processing facilities with five production lines for cleaning, sizing, splitting, colour-sorting, and packaging a full line of lentil, chickpea, pea, mustard, and canary seed products. The Arslan family, who own Arbel, contributed $1.15 million, and Al-Katib raised the remainder from Crown Ventures Fund, the Saskatchewan Government Growth Fund, Farm Credit Canada, and the Business Development Bank of Canada (BDC), with operating financing from the CIBC. Ownership was divided between the Arslan family (60%), the investors Crown Capital (34%), and Al-Katib (6%).

The company sells red split lentils, football red lentils, whole lentils, chickpeas, and peas. It buys products directly from producers and also buys cleaned product from other local processors. These products are an inexpensive, high-fibre source of protein and a staple of the diets of people in many parts of the world. Within a year of start-up, Saskcan Pulse Trading was selling to 21 countries.

Why "Pulse"? The Saskatchewan Pulse Growers website states that "pulse" is derived from a Latin word meaning a thick soup, and the word refers to seeds of legumes that are used as food, such as fababeans, chickpeas, lentils, peas, and beans.

Questions

1. What individual-level, group-level, and societal-level factors do you think influenced Murad Al-Katib's decision to start Saskcan Pulse Trading?

2. What individual-level, group-level, and societal-level factors do you think will influence the future success of Saskcan Pulse Trading?

Sources

http://www.saskcan.com/

http://www.saskpulse.com/

Johnstone, B. 2001. Pulse processing plant to set up here. *Leader-Post*, November 29: B9.

Johnstone, B. 2004. Regina's Al-Katib steers Saskcan Pulse to victory. Leader-Post, October 25: B4.

Martin, P. 2003. Global leader hits home run with Saskatchewan plant. *Saskatchewan Business Magazine*, September/October: 7–8.

McMurdy, D. 2005. Entrepreneur puts Sask. lentils on world map. *The StarPhoenix*, February 17: C10.

Pratt, S. 2001. Turkish proposal takes lentil splitting to new level. *The Western Producer*, November 29.

CHAPTER TWO

ANALYZING THE FOOD INDUSTRY

Chris and Robin love to cook and to eat well, and have developed several delicious relishes and chutneys that they produce in Robin's kitchen. Initially they produced just enough to give away to family and friends, but during the past year they have been selling 50 to 150 jars each weekend at a popular farmer's market. Sales have grown steadily, and they have loyal customers who make frequent purchases. Selling in the market has been invaluable in providing data on which types of relishes and chutneys are popular at different times of the year. It has also allowed them to test ideas, such as different packaging styles and different unit sizes and prices, while chatting with repeat customers.

Chris and Robin are about to graduate from university and neither has lined up full-time work. Enthusiastic friends and customers are encouraging them to launch a new business to produce and market the relishes and chutneys. An acquaintance, who owns an industrial kitchen that is not currently utilized at capacity, has offered to rent them production facilities, at a low price, until they are ready to acquire their own space.

Robin's uncle is quite pessimistic about their prospects, and has told them that the food industry is a particularly difficult segment to enter. Chris's sister is more optimistic, and has pointed out successful and entrepreneurial Canadian food manufacturers, such as Spitz in Medicine Hat, Alberta; Renée's Gourmet Foods in Toronto; and PEI Preserve Company in New Glasgow, Prince Edward Island. Their parents recommend they construct a comprehensive business plan that includes a clear and thorough assessment of the food industry. This exercise should help them understand their challenges and help position their new product line. Chris and Robin have spent two months of their spare time (while juggling schoolwork) trying to gather research to validate their idea, and are struggling to find sources of information. They realize that before any type of viable business plan can be developed, their segment of the food industry needs to be assessed. The specific elements of this type of assessment are unclear to both of them, however.

In doing their research, the partners have found the following North American Industry Classification System (NAICS) codes:

NAICS 311	Food Manufacturing
NAICS 31142	Fruit & Vegetable Canning, Pickling & Drying (includes jams and ketchup)
NAICS 31191	Snack Food Manufacturing
NAICS 31194	Seasoning and Dressing Manufacturing

Questions

1. What are useful information sources for Chris and Robin? Why are they useful? What are their limitations?

2. What elements of the industry should Robin and Chris examine?

3. What guidance is provided by successful industry examples, such as Spitz, Renée's, and PEI Preserve Company?

4. Is the food industry a good industry for launching a start-up? Why or why not?

5. Is there a source of opportunity for a new business here? If so, what is it? If not, why not?

6. Is this an opportunity that favours new firms? Why or why not?

Sources

http://www.strategis.gc.ca
http://www.spitzsales.com
http://www.renees.com
http://www.preservecompany.com
Note: This case is based on the Brand-S Business Development Plan, by Shimmy Brandes and Arjun Kumar, 2002.

CHAPTER THREE

CANJAM AND QUAKE

CanJam Trading Ltd.

CanJam Trading Ltd., headquartered in Dartmouth, Nova Scotia, was founded by Grace White in 1989. CanJam is a salt-fish and fresh-fish producer and sells to foreign markets around the world.

White was raised in Kingston, Jamaica, where both of her parents had home-based businesses. They sent her to university in Canada, where she received a bachelor of commerce degree from St. Mary's University in 1978. After graduation, she worked in the insurance industry and as a financial planner. On vacation in Jamaica, White met a processor who was having trouble sourcing Atlantic mackerel. When she returned to Halifax, she did an in-depth study of the mackerel industry. She found a year-round source of supply that could meet this processor's needs, and CanJam was born. Initially the company's main market was Jamaica, and it primarily sold underutilized products, such as tripe, pork feet and pickled pork tails, turkey necks, pickled and frozen mackerel, frozen herring, frozen and dried squid, and salt pollock. As sales increased, CanJam acquired two fish-processing plants in Nova Scotia. The company has its own branded products and will brand private-label products for customers.

By 2000, CanJam was a $50-million international trading business, exporting products from fish to corn meal to the United States, Japan, and China. White received a Women Entrepreneur of the Year award in 1993, and in 1999, CanJam was named one of Canada's top 100 women-owned businesses by *Chatelaine* magazine.

Quake Technologies

Quake Technologies, headquartered in Ottawa, Ontario, was founded in 2000, by a team led by Daniel Trépanier. Quake is a private fabless semiconductor company. It designs and sells high-speed, high-performance, mixed-signal integrated circuits that strengthen the foundations of optical networking. "Fabless" means it relies on third parties to fabricate or manufacture its products, rather than having its own manufacturing facilities.

Originally from Montreal, Trépanier received a bachelor of science degree in electrical engineering from Queen's University in Kingston, Ontario, and an M.B.A. from New York University. Prior to founding Quake, he worked at Milliren Technologies, Inc., a crystal oscillator start-up in Massachusetts, and at ANADIGICS Inc., a semiconductor company in New Jersey. His co-founders had previous work experience at Nortel Networks and Agilent Technologies.

In 2000, telecommunications analysts were forecasting that worldwide sales of optical networking systems would exceed US $23 billion by 2004. At start-up, Quake had $3 million in seed financing from an Ottawa-based entrepreneur and offices in both Ottawa and San Jose, California. Within six months of start-up, Quake had received US $12 million in financing from Mohr, Davidow Ventures, an early-stage Californian venture capital firm. In May 2001, the company raised US $30 million in a second round of financing.

In 2001, Quake was named by the Fabless Semiconductor Association (FSA) as a Fabless Start-Up of the Year, and in 2004 Quake received the FSA Outstanding Financial Performance by a Private Company award. By August 2006 Quake had 50 employees, mostly in Ottawa, and was acquired by Applied Micro Circuits Corporation in a U.S. $69 million deal. Trépanier was expected to stay on as President.

Questions

1. What conditions or factors generated these opportunities?
2. What factors do you think led Grace White and Daniel Trépanier to recognize these opportunities?
3. How is their involvement in CanJam and Quake likely to influence how Grace White and Daniel Trépanier recognize subsequent opportunities?
4. In what ways is opportunity recognition the same or different in these two industries?

Sources

Davidson, H. 2000. Where are they now?: All stars. *Profit Magazine* 19(2): 27.
www.rotman.utoronto.ca/cweya/pastwinners1993.htm#white
www.canjam.ca
www.quaketech.com
www.canadait.com

CHAPTER FOUR

TRAINING, WORK BOOTS, AND AQUACULTURE

Trevor's Training Venture

After receiving his bachelor's degree in computer science, Trevor worked for six years as an information technology (IT) professional. He worked for a government agency and then for a large national insurance company, receiving steady, regular promotions. After six years, though, Trevor was ready for a change and went back to school for his M.B.A. With his M.B.A. in hand, Trevor got a job with a prestigious consulting firm. As a consultant, he worked for five years helping companies reorganize their information technology function. Now he is thinking of starting his own business.

Trevor wants to start a company that helps clients with their information technology training requirements. He sees his target market as large organizations in the private and public sectors. From his consulting experience, he knows that IT training is difficult for such organizations, even those with high-performing IT departments, and they're very interested in outsourcing it. Initially, he would focus on project management training. For a relatively small licensing fee, a certification body in the

United States will give him access to their excellent training material, organized into three levels of knowledge. The people he trained would be able to write certification exams at all of the three levels.

Warren's Work Boot Venture

Warren is a mechanical engineer who has worked with companies in Alberta's oil sands for the past eight years. He is now a manager in charge of specialized equipment acquisition. This job involves designing required equipment, monitoring and evaluating the work of contractors who complete the design specifications, and supervising the installation of the equipment in the field. He has a reputation for being a smart and organized leader, well-liked, and well-respected by co-workers and contractors. Now he is thinking of starting his own business.

Warren wants to start a company that manufactures work boots. During his many years in the oil sands, he has owned and seen many types of work boots. In his spare time, he has played around with new designs and has come up with one that is drier and lighter than other boots on the market and, perhaps most importantly, has greater traction so that people are less likely to slip when wearing them. His cost estimates indicate that he can make a 50 percent profit on each pair of boots if he sells them for the current price of an average pair of work boots.

Adam's Aquaculture Venture

Adam has a Ph.D. in biology and has spent the past 10 years teaching and doing research in the area of genetics and molecular biology. He and his research team have come up with a technique to reduce the incidence of viruses in aquaculture businesses, such as shrimp and salmon farms. Now he is thinking of starting his own business.

Adam wants to start a business to exploit his technology by licensing it to organizations (governments, nurseries, and research institutes) worldwide. He knows that the aquaculture industry is enormously important to the economy of Canada and many other countries, and that viruses present huge and increasing costs and problems. He has seen other scientists start biotech companies while keeping their university position, and he wants to do the same. With the support of his university commercialization office, he has applied for two patents to protect the technology.

Questions

1. In order to get their businesses off the ground, Trevor, Warren, and Adam will need to persuade potential stakeholders that their business concept is a viable opportunity. What are the major stakeholder groups with which each of them needs to be most concerned?

2. What will potential stakeholders be most skeptical about? In other words, what do these entrepreneurs have to be most convincing about in order to be persuasive?

3. For each item you identify in question 2, suggest the most effective means of being persuasive to potential stakeholders.

CHAPTER FIVE

Playtime

Jennifer Li and Ann Bhusari are in their final year of graduate school. They are both completing master's degrees: Jennifer in film studies and Ann in computer engineering. Both are talented in their respective fields: Jennifer has won creative writing awards, and Ann has won prizes in programming competitions. They met several years ago and became good friends because they share a love of computer gaming.

They spend much of their leisure time playing computer games, much of their entertainment budget on computer games, and keep up with the latest developments through online publications and discussion forums. They've spent many hours discussing the computer games they'd like to see on the market, and have developed bits and pieces as hobbyists.

Now that the end of their graduate studies is in sight, Jennifer and Ann are talking about the possibility of starting Playtime, a company to develop their own computer games. They know that the market is huge. In 2002, global sales were US $30 billion, which exceeded movie box office receipts, and sales worldwide are predicted to reach US $85 billion by 2010. Although the market is perceived as being heavily dominated by male game players, a recent study of American gamers indicates that 43 percent are female, and that women over 18 years of age represent a larger portion of the game-playing population (28%) than boys ages 6 to 17 (21%).

Jennifer and Ann want to specialize in developing games for women. They suspect that their game ideas will be particularly appealing to women players and believe that there is going to be a gap in the market because games that are violent or sports-oriented (and less likely to appeal to women) are increasingly prominent on store shelves. Women represent only 10 to 15 percent of workers in the Canadian computer games industry, and critics believe that their weak presence is reflected in the way women are often portrayed in games.

More specifically, Jennifer and Ann want to specialize in *mobile* games for women to play, for example, while they commute to work on buses and subways. They believe that as women game players marry and have children, stay-at-home moms around the world will be increasingly interested in mobile games to occupy their time while they wait for their children at various activities and outings, such as piano lessons and play dates. At US $2.6 billion in 2005, global revenues from mobile games are only a fraction of global revenues from all computer games, but they are also expected to increase even more rapidly, to US $11.2 billion by 2010.

Jennifer and Ann know that it is too early for them to get financing from investors or bank loans, but their families have agreed to lend them some start-up funds. Before doing so, though, their families would like to see a business plan. As part of the business plan, Jennifer and Ann need to specify their roles, and how they expect a management team to develop as the company becomes successful.

Questions

1. What should Playtime's management team look like at start-up?

2. How do you see the management team growing over time, as the company becomes successful?

3. Should Jennifer and Ann establish an advisory board? When? Whom should they invite to be members?

4. Through your own research on the Internet, identify two Canadian companies that are similar in some important way to the company that Jennifer and Ann want to start. Compare your answers to questions 1 to 3 to the way that these companies have organized their managerial talent.

Sources

Chen, J., Patel, R., & Schaefer, R. 2002. *Information technology sector report*. Houston: Rice University.

Dyer-Witherford, N. 2004. *Mapping the Canadian video and computer game industry*. Working paper. London, Ontario: Faculty of Information & Media Studies, University of Western Ontario.

Entertainment Software Association. 2005. Essential facts about the computer and video game industry. May 18, 2005. http://www.theesa.com/archives/2006/05/2006_essential.php.

Informa Telecoms and Media, 2005. Mobile games industry worth USD 11.2 billion by 2010. Press Release, May 19, 2005. http://www.3g.co.uk/PR/May2005/1459.htm.

CHAPTER SIX

MEDNOTES

You have agreed to assist a four-person team of entrepreneurs in examining the financial requirements for their new venture. Before meeting with you, they sent you a summary of their business concept and some rough financial assumptions and projections (below).

Business Concept Summary

MedNotes will provide medical transcription services for Canadian doctors. MedNotes will provide a low-cost, high-quality alternative to current on-site (or local) medical notes transcription services, by outsourcing production to off-shore locations in Pakistan. Individuals performing this service in Pakistan, compared with those in Canada, have a stronger medical background and work at much lower wages. In addition, the time difference allows for a standard 24-hour turnaround.

The market is huge on the buyer side. Outsourcing medical transcription is an emerging industry, currently estimated at $3 billion and expected to grow to $12 billion in the next five years. Doctors are facing increased time constraints, and health care costs are rapidly escalating. Transcription costs are currently 1.5 percent of billings, and a turnaround time of two to four weeks is common. In addition, the transcriptions themselves are of low quality. Low-quality records compromise patient care and confidentiality regulations. They also limit the feasibility of future automated productivity solutions in health care.

There are currently two types of service providers in Canada: salaried on-site transcribers (or administrative assistants) and traditional Canadian transcription services. Salaried personnel are in close proximity, but they are in short supply, have a large backlog, and represent a fixed cost for hospitals. Traditional transcription services provide faster turnaround, but are more expensive than salaried personnel. There are medical transcriptions services in the United States that outsource the work to Pakistan, but they have shown little interest in the Canadian market given its smaller size, regulations, and the need to develop connections with Canadian medical networks.

Although we will provide a low-cost service, we will differentiate ourselves primarily on the basis of service quality, involving rigorous training, triple-checked proofreading, and a reward system linked both to speed and quality. Doctors will have an account manager familiar with their needs, who will be able to deal with requests for document changes and for quick turnaround time. This personalization will ensure a seamless and stress-free transcription service. We expect to gain a first-mover advantage because of the comfort issues associated with the confidentiality of medical information.

Doctors will dictate patient histories into a digital recorder. At the end of each day, the WAVE or MP3 file will be uploaded onto the company website under the doctors' accounts. A transcriber in Pakistan will download the file, listen to it, and type out the notes in a Word document. The typed notes will be uploaded back under the doctors' account where they can pick them up at their convenience. Our marketing and IT operations will be based in Toronto. We will monitor emerging technologies, such as voice recognition technology, so that we can take advantage of the most reliable and effective technologies available.

We will outsource the actual transcription services to existing companies in Pakistan. High-quality companies already exist, and there is a vast pool of English-speaking qualified medical graduates in Pakistan who want to do this type of work. We will initially have one relationship manager located in Pakistan to select and monitor our suppliers, and will add more as demand increases.

Financial Assumptions

Revenue

▪ In each of the first five years, MedNotes will sign up four average-sized Ontario hospitals. Each hospital has an average of 48 specialists, and so each year, we will provide service to roughly an additional 192 specialists, providing MedNotes with a 12.5 percent market share by the end of year 5.

▪ The average number of lines per year per doctor is 165,000 (330 days × average of 500 lines per day).

▪ We will charge our customers 14 cents per line, and we will pay a third-party supplier in Pakistan 8 cents a line to do the transcription. Both rates are fixed, with no volume discounts.

Costs

▪ Start-up costs of $137,330 include computer hardware, computer software, office equipment, office furniture, medical books, and incorporation and legal fees.

▪ Annual ongoing costs of $612,440 include:

▪ Office costs of $25,300 (leasing space, utilities, supplies)

▪ Personnel costs of $515,640 (1 administrative assistant, 2 technicians, 1 quality control supervisor, 5 account managers, and 1 offshore manager)

▪ Executive team salaries of $320,000 ($80,000 × 4)

▪ Other costs of $71,600 (insurance, market research outsourced to a third party, a T1 leased line, two toll-free lines, accounting services outsourced to a third party, legal fees, medical journal subscriptions, janitorial services)

▪ Sales commissions are 5 percent of revenues, general sales and marketing costs are 6 percent of revenues, general R&D costs are 3 percent of revenues, and "other" general costs are 2 percent of revenues.

▪ There will be 10 percent annual increases in each of the following: cost of the direct mail campaign, R&D salaries and benefits, R&D testing, and administrative salaries and benefits.

▪ There will be a 20 percent annual increase in rent and utilities.

▪ We will use straight time depreciation: 3 years for computer hardware and software and 10 years for property, plant, and equipment.

Initial Capital

The initial capital of $230,000 will be provided from the following sources:

▪ $100,000 from the founders ($50,000 each)

▪ $30,000 from a relative of one of the founders

▪ $100,000 from a bank loan, secured by the personal assets of the founders.

Questions

1. Approximately when will MedNotes become cash flow positive?
2. Calculate a rough breakeven point for MedNotes.
3. What types of financing should the founders of MedNotes anticipate?
4. What are the most important variables to examine in a sensitivity analysis? What values of these variables should the founders consider?

Exhibit 1 Income Statement By Quarter

Adapted from Shamsi, S., Norli, H., Hong, K., & Bhatia, U. 2002. MedNotes Business Plan.

	Year 1 Q1	Q2	Q3	Q4	Year 2 Q1	Q2	Q3	Q4
NET REVENUES	0	0	0	1,781,287	1,514,094	1,781,287	2,493,802	3,117,253
COST OF REVENUE	0	0	0	903,083	962,218	1,132,021	1,584,830	1,981,037
GROSS PROFIT	0	0	0	878,204	551,876	649,266	908,972	1,136,216
OPERATING EXPENSES								
Sales & Marketing	0	0	0	664,192	259,489	305,282	427,394	534,243
Research & Development	0	0	0	78,439	50,098	58,939	82,514	103,143
General & Administration	0	0	0	256,493	78,349	92,176	129,046	161,308
Total Operating Expenses	0	0	0	999,124	387,936	456,397	638,954	798,694
EARNINGS FROM OPERATIONS	0	0	0	-120,920	163,940	192,869	270,018	337,522
EXTRAORDINARY EXPENSE								
Legal fees	-25,000	0	0	0	-6,875	-6,875	-6,875	-6,875
Relocation costs	-20,000	0	0	0				
Total Extraordinary Expenses	-45,000	0	0	0	-6,875	-6,875	-6,875	-6,875
EARNINGS BEFORE INCOME AND TAXES	-45,000	0	0	-120,920	157,065	185,994	263,143	330,647

MedNotes - Capital Expenditures by Quarter

	Year 1 Q1	Q2	Q3	Q4	Year 2 Q1	Q2	Q3	Q4
Capital expenditures	200,000	40,000	40,000	0	200,000	100,000	100,000	100,000
Annual depreciation	25,524				32,857			

	Year 3 Q1	Q2	Q3	Q4	Year 4 Q1	Q2	Q3	Q4
NET REVENUES	2,271,141	2,671,931	3,740,703	4,675,879	3,028,188	3,562,574	4,987,604	6,234,505
COST OF REVENUE	1,430,035	1,682,394	2,355,352	2,944,190	$1,897,101	2,231,884	3,124,638	3,905,797
GROSS PROFIT	841,106	989,537	1,385,351	1,731,689	1,131,087	1,330,690	1,862,966	2,328,708
OPERATING EXPENSES								
Sales & Marketing	357,998	421,174	589,643	737,054	458,159	539,010	754,615	943,268
Research & Development	73,359	86,305	120,827	151,033	96,729	113,798	159,318	199,147
General & Administration	100,621	118,377	165,728	207,160	123,073	144,792	202,709	253,386
Total Operating Expenses	531,978	625,856	876,198	1,095,247	677,961	797,600	1,116,642	1,395,801
EARNINGS FROM OPERATIONS	309,128	363,681	509,153	636,442	453,126	533,090	746,324	932,907
EXTRAORDINARY EXPENSE								
Legal fees	-7,563	-7,563	-7,563	-7,563	-8,319	-8,319	-8,319	-8,319
Relocation costs								
Total Extraordinary Expenses	-7,563	-7,563	-7,563	-7,563	-8,319	-8,319	-8,319	-8,319
EARNINGS BEFORE INCOME AND TAXES	301,565	356,118	501,590	628,879	444,807	524,771	738,005	924,588

MedNotes - Capital Expenditures by Quarter

	Year 3 Q1	Q2	Q3	Q4	Year 4 Q1	Q2	Q3	Q4
Capital expenditures	100,000	200,000	100,000	150,000	200,000	200,000	100,000	150,000
Annual depreciation	42,076				45,435			

	Year 5			
	Q1	**Q2**	**Q3**	**Q4**
NET REVENUES	3,785,235	4,453,218	6,234,505	7,793,132
COST OF REVENUE	2,366,304	2,783,887	3,897,442	4,871,803
GROSS PROFIT	1,418,931	1,669,331	2,337,063	2,921,329
OPERATING EXPENSES				
Sales & Marketing	556,184	654,334	916,067	1,145,084
Research & Development	120,028	141,210	197,694	247,117
General & Administration	145,104	170,710	238,994	298,743
Total Operating Expenses	821,316	966,254	1,352,755	1,690,944
EARNINGS FROM OPERATIONS	597,615	703,077	984,308	1,230,385
EXTRAORDINARY EXPENSE				
Legal fees	-9,151	-9,151	-9,151	-9,151
Relocation costs				
Total Extraordinary Expenses	-9,151	-9,151	-9,151	-9,151
EARNINGS BEFORE INCOME AND TAXES	588,464	693,926	975,157	1,221,234

MedNotes - Capital Expenditures by Quarter

	Year 5			
	Q1	**Q2**	**Q3**	**Q4**
Capital expenditures	200,000	200,000	200,000	150,000
Annual depreciation	49,015			

MedNotes - Selected Balance Sheet Items

	Year 0	Year 1	Year 2	Year 3	Year 4	Year 5
Cash balance at start	230,000					
Accounts Receivable		957,442	1,603,158	2,337,939	3,117,253	3,896,566
Inventories		783,766	1,068,772	1,246,901	1,662,535	2,078,168
Accounts Payable		693,455	1,115,798	1,627,206	2,169,608	2,712,010

MedNotes - Variable and Fixed Costs

	Year 1	Year 2	Year 3	Year 4	Year 5
Cost of Revenue					
Variable	707,425	5,445,649	8,168,474	10,891,299	13,614,124
Fixed	195,657	214,457	243,497	268,121	305,312
Total	903,082	5,660,106	8,411,971	11,159,420	13,919,436
Operating Expenses					
Variable	285,006	1,425,030	2,137,545	2,850,060	3,562,574
Fixed	714,117	856,950	991,733	1,137,946	1,268,695
Total	999,123	2,281,980	3,129,278	3,988,006	4,831,269
Total Costss & Expenses					
Variable	992,431	6,870,679	10,306,019	13,741,358	17,176,698
Fixed	909,774	1,071,407	1,235,231	1,406,067	1,574,007
Total	1,902,205	7,942,086	11,541,250	15,147,425	18,750,705

CHAPTER SEVEN

A PATENT MATTER

Technological breakthroughs in the machine industry are commonplace. Thus, whenever one company announces a new development, some of the first customers are that company's competitors. The latter will purchase the machine, strip it down, examine the new technology, and then look for ways to improve it. The original breakthroughs always are patented by the firm that discovers them, even though the technology is soon surpassed.

A few weeks ago, Tom Farrington completed the development of a specialized lathe machine that is 25 percent faster and 9 percent more efficient than anything currently on the market. This technological breakthrough was a result of careful analysis of competitive products. "Until I saw some of the latest developments in the field," Tom told his wife, "I didn't realize how easy it would be to increase the speed and efficiency of the machine. But once I saw the competition's products, I knew immediately how to proceed."

Tom has shown his machine to five major firms in the industry, and all have placed orders with him. Tom has little doubt he will make a great deal of money from his invention. Before beginning production, however, Tom intends to get a patent on his invention. He believes his machine is so much more sophisticated and complex than any other machine on the market that it will take his competitors at least four years to develop a better product. "By that time I hope to have improved on my invention and continue to remain ahead of them," he noted.

Tom has talked to an attorney about filing for a patent. The attorney believes Tom should answer two questions before proceeding: (1) How long will it take the competition to improve on your patent? and (2) How far are you willing to go in defending your patent right? Part of the attorney's comments were as follows: "It will take us about three years to get a patent. If, during this time, the competition is able to come out with something that is better than what you have, we will have wasted a lot of time and effort. The patent will have little value since no one will be interested in using it. Since some of your first sales will be to the competition, this is something to which you have to give serious thought. Second, even if it takes four years for the competition to catch up, would you be interested in fighting those who copy your invention after, say, two years? Simply put, we can get you a patent, but I'm not sure it will provide you as much protection as you think."

Questions

1. Given the nature of the industry, how valuable will a patent be to Tom? Explain.

2. If Tom does get a patent, can he bring action against infringers? Will it be worth the time and expense? Why or why not?

3. What do you think Tom should do? Why?

Source

From Entrepreneurship: Theory, Process, Practice with InfoTrac College Edition 6th Edition by Kuratko/Hodgetts. Copyright 2004. Reprinted with permission of South-Western, a division of Thomson Learning: http://www.thomsonrights.com. Fax 800-730-2215.

CHAPTER NINE

THE PITA PIT

The Pita Pit was founded in Kingston, Ontario, in 1995 by John Sotiriadis and Nelson Lang. In 1997, they began to expand, and by the beginning of 2005, they had almost 200 locations in Canada and the United States. In the spring of 2005, the partners sold the U.S. operation (73 stores) to a group of entrepreneurs—and Pita Pit franchisees—in Idaho.

Pita Pits sell only pitas, and not other fast food, such as hamburgers. Customers can choose their own fillings and watch the pita be made on the spot to their specifications. Customers can get a pita sandwich full of low-fat protein and lots of vegetables. The menu emphasizes healthy food choices and the ingredients are fresh and natural; for example, rather than using slices of processed chicken, chicken is grilled just before the sandwich is made. On the Pita Pit website is a nutrition calculator. You can choose the ingredients for your sandwich, and then calculate the calories, carbohydrates, fat, sodium, protein, cholesterol, and fibre your sandwich contains.

Like most franchises, the location of a Pita Pit store is important to its success. However, unlike McDonald's and Tim Hortons, Pita Pits are not located on busy corners with commuter drive-throughs and lots of parking. Pita Pit customers typically walk to the store, and the Pita Pit stores located close to university and college campuses are the most successful. In both Canada and the United States, some Pita Pits are located right on campus: at the University of Western Ontario, there is a Pita Pit in both the Medical Sciences Building and the University Community. In cities where there is scarce affordable retail space around a university, it can be difficult to find a suitable location for a Pita Pit. For example, it was a difficult to find a location for a

Pita Pit in Manhattan, although eventually a spot was found in the West Village, two blocks from New York University, and the first Pita Pit in New York City opened in May 2005.

Questions

The Pita Pit has stores across Canada, and the Canadian locations are listed at http://www.pitapit.com. If possible, visit one of the stores and talk with the franchisee before addressing these questions.

1. Why are college and university students the important target market for Pita Pit?

2. As a college or university student, you are a target customer, and therefore a target franchisee. Examine the information for potential franchisees on the company's website. What do you see as the benefits and constraints of becoming a Pita Pit franchisee?

3. What additional information (not posted on the website) would you want to know before deciding to become a franchisee? How might you find this information?

4. The website lists the expected costs of opening a Pita Pit store in Canada. How do these costs compare with your estimates of the costs of setting up a similar store on your own?

Sources

Butler, J. 2005. Riggs buys restaurant chain. *Coeur d'Alene Press*, June 10, 2005. http://www.CDApress.com.

Pita Pit makes fast move. 2005. *Real Estate Weekly*, May 18. http://www.pitapit.com

CHAPTER TEN

MAKING CHOICES IN MARKET RESEARCH AND TARGETING CUSTOMERS

Manitoba Harvest Hemp Foods and Oils

Manitoba Harvest Hemp Foods and Oil is a Winnipeg-based company co-founded in 1998 by Mike Fata, Alex Chwaiewsky, and Martin Moravcik. Manitoba Harvest grows, processes, and packages hemp-based products. The company is a certified kosher and USDA-certified organic processor. You can buy its products in natural food stores, health food stores, and supermarkets across Canada and the United States, and through the company's toll-free telephone number.

Fata became interested in hemp for its health benefits (e.g., Omega-3 and Omega-6 fats) in the 1990s. However, at that time there was no market for hemp food products, and it was unclear whether they were even legal. Fata met co-founders Moravcik and Chwaiewsky when they were lobbying the federal government to legalize hemp seed production. The legal issues associated with selling hemp food products in the United States were not resolved until February 2004, when the U.S. Drug Enforcement Agency lost its case against the Hemp Industries Association. The outcome of this case had a huge impact on the industry, which grew 66 percent throughout 2004 and another 47 percent in 2005.

Despite these challenges, the company has grown more than 50 percent annually since start-up, with 2004 revenue of more than $1 million (mostly from the United States) and 2005 revenue more than $2.5 million. Manitoba Harvest is the largest integrated manufacturer of hemp food in North America, and is privately owned. Fata was awarded the 2004 Business Development Bank of Canada's Young Entrepreneur Award for Manitoba.

Source

http://www.manitobaharvest.com.

Remsoft

Remsoft is a Fredericton-based company co-founded in 1992 by Andrea and Ugo Feunekes. Remsoft develops forest management software. The Remsoft Spatial Planning System allows Remsoft's customers on five continents to set strategic and tactical forest planning objectives and to make decisions based on these objectives. Customers include major forestry companies, such as Abitibi and Weyerhaeuser; public agencies, such as Parks Canada and the Minnesota Department of Natural Resources; and First Nations groups, such as Wolf Lake First Nation and the Lake Taupo Forest Trust.

Technology is essential for effective forestry management because there are millions of variables that can affect forestry activities. Remsoft's technology allows customers to take all variables into consideration while simulating different scenarios. Through its Educational Partners Program, Remsoft makes its software available to colleges and universities through discounted educational licences.

The company now has an 80 percent market share in North America, Australia, and New Zealand. Although small in terms of number of employees (there are eight), annual sales in the privately owned company fluctuate between seven and eight digits. In November 2005, Andrea Feunekes received the Royal Bank of Canada Canadian Woman Entrepreneur of the Year Award, for innovation.

Source

www.remsoft.com

Questions

1. What type of market research would you expect to see in the initial business plan for both companies?

2. What types of customers would you expect each company to target first? How might each company target these customer groups? How might the companies plan to expand their customer base?

3. How would you expect the sales function in each company to operate?

CHAPTER ELEVEN

ABEBOOKS

When people think of used book sellers, they usually think of small, often dusty, retail stores. What is less likely to come to mind is a company that has won a Canadian Information Productivity Award; e-commerce awards from *Forbes* magazine, *Internet Retailer* magazine, and the United Nations World Summit; entrepreneurship awards from Fast Company and Ernst & Young; and was named one of Canada's top employers by *Maclean's* magazine in 2003, 2004, and 2005. Such a company is Abebooks.

Abebooks was founded in Victoria, B.C., in 1995. Ten years later, it is the world's largest marketplace for new, used, rare, and out-of-print books. The size of its operation is staggering. Abebooks has a virtual inventory of 80 million books, comprising listings from 13,500 booksellers across the world. Each day, its websites supports 3 million searches, 25,000 sales, and 200,000 new book listings. In 2005, the value of books sold by Abebooks was US $150 million. It has been profitable since start-up, without any venture capital, and it remains a private company.

Questions

To answer the following questions, you need to find out more about the history and activities of Abebooks. There are two readily available sources of information. First, look at the press releases listed on the Abebooks website (go to Company Information, then click on Press Room). Second, search the InfoTrac database of articles with "abebooks" as the search term.

1. What would you say were key advantages and disadvantages of competing as a used book seller in Victoria, B.C., in 1995?

2. How was Abebooks able to gain an initial competitive advantage in the mid-1990s?

3. How has Abebooks been able to sustain this advantage until today?

4. Why did Abebooks survive, and even thrive, after the dot-com bust in March 2000, when many e-retailers went out of business?

Source

http://www.abebooks.com

CHAPTER TWELVE

NIMA SYSTEMS

After graduating with a degree in computer science, Nick Baker and Marcia Johnson formed a consulting firm (NIMA Systems) to write software for clients. Since most of their initial clients were in the health care sector, Nick and Marcia became very experienced in the needs of this sector. After completing a large application for a stand-alone medical clinic, Nick and Marcia realized that it would not be difficult to modify the system so it could be sold to other clinics. The client supported this move and, in fact, offered to provide endorsements for prospective customers.

When they were ready to go to market, the high-quality user interface, much-needed functionality, and endorsement from a respected industry player proved to be a winning combination. In the first year, Nick and Marcia licensed the application to 10 clinics. Each licence comes with four hours of installation and training, but customers often contract to receive an additional day to make sure their clinical records are secure.

As happy as Nick and Marcia are with sales to date, they realize that they have only taken advantage of low-hanging fruit. Subsequent sales are going to be more difficult. In addition, now that they have 11 clinics using the system, customers are starting to request modifications and extensions. Rather than responding to each request individually, Nick and Marcia want to roll them into generic updates that everyone will receive. The licensing agreement states that licensees will receive any updates to the system free of charge, but does not specify how often these updates will be available. This wording gives Nick and Marcia some breathing room, but they realize that they need to specify the requirements for an update soon and release it in a couple of months.

As their business grows, Nick and Marcia are having an increasingly difficult time juggling all the demands on their time. They've started to divide responsibilities functionally, with Nick focused more on system development and Marcia focused more on sales, but even so, they are stretched. In addition, customers are not hesitant to call when they have questions about the system, and dealing with these questions eats up a frustratingly large amount of time.

Nick and Marcia are realizing that they cannot do it all themselves and need to bring other people on board. Marcia wants to continue to do sales, but she wants to hire a half-time employee to help her plan and roll out a sales strategy. Nick wants to hire a full-time programmer who can also field some of the customer calls. He also wants to acquire some networking expertise, so he can investigate some ideas he has for mobile add-on products. Rather than hiring an expert in the field as a full-time employee, he'd prefer to hire the expert on a three-month contract position. This arrangement will give him time to explore how promising his ideas are.

Questions

Federal and provincial governments enact employment legislation in Canada. In answering these questions, assume that Nick and Marcia are operating their business in your province or territory. Each province and territory has its own Business Service Centre, and you can find out about relevant legislation by going to its website. If you go to the website of the Canada Business Service Centres (http://www.cbsc.org), you can select your language of choice (English or French) and then click on the flag of a province or territory, and you will be directed to its website.

1. In hiring these three people, what rules and regulations should Nick and Marcia be aware of when:

   - Hiring someone as an employee vs. an independent contractor;

   - Carrying out the hiring process;

   - Writing employment contracts;

   - Paying employees;

   - Dismissing an employee.

2. Are there any government-sponsored employment or training assistance programs that Nick and Marcia should take advantage of?

3. What tactics should Nick and Marcia use to motivate people working for them?

CHAPTER THIRTEEN

SERIALLY HARVESTING

Lorne Abony, named one of Canada's Top 40 Under 40 for 2005, is a serial entrepreneur. By the time Toronto-born Abony had obtained a B.A. from McGill University, a law degree from the University of Windsor, and an M.B.A. from New York City's Columbia Business School, he had started and harvested several businesses. After finishing school, life as a securities lawyer seemed dull compared to starting entrepreneurial ventures, so in 1998, he started Paw.net, an early Internet-based retailer of pet supplies, which ultimately became known as Petopia.com.

Born in San Francisco during the dot-com boom, Petopia.com raised more than $100 million from venture capitalists and corporate investors. In March 2000, the firm's management filed, with the U.S. Securities and Exchange Commission, a preliminary prospectus to raise up to $100 million in an IPO. At that time, the company had 200 employees and marketing alliances with America Online, Yahoo!, and Excite@Home. Petopia was a partner of Petco, one of the largest retailers of pet supplies in the United States, with more than 500 stores. As of March 2000, Petco owned 26 percent of Petopia. Petopia was the online channel for Petco products, and Petopia shared Petco's warehouses, thereby avoiding the high costs of setting of its own facilities. Petopia was ranked top in customer relations among online pet stores. However, by October 2000, 60 percent of Petopia's employees had been laid off, and the IPO plans had been called off. In November 2000, the leading pet e-tailer, Pets.com closed. Pets.com had raised $83.5 million in an IPO earlier that year and was backed by online giant Amazon.com, which owned 30 percent of the firm. In December 2000, Petco acquired the assets of Petopia for an undisclosed price.

After Petopia closed, Abony worked for 18 months at a New York private equity firm until the right opportunity came along—which it did—in the form of a betting exchange technology. In 2002, Abony co-founded Columbia Exchange Systems (CES) with Andrew Rivkin, the founder of Toronto-based CryptoLogic, a leader in the global gaming software industry. Together they raised $1.8 million in start-up financing. Software development was based in Toronto, to take advantage of synergies with the former Cryptologic development team, but CES was headquartered in London, England, where sports betting is much more developed, accepted, and widespread than it is in North America. The company's first product was a legal sports betting exchange technology that was licensed to gaming operators in Europe and Asia so they could offer worldwide person-to-person wagering. Licensees include U.K.-based Matchedbets and Austria-based BETandWIN.com. In December 2003, CES went public on the Alternative Investment Market of the London Stock Exchange and was capitalized at approximately £13.3 million (AIM:CES). The IPO raised $11 million and the founders raised an additional $12 million in June 2004.

In July 2004, CES bought Los Angeles-based SkillJam Technologies for $8 million. SkillJam produced pay-per-play and subscription-based Internet games. Its games are based on skill (as opposed to chance) and it produces private-label gaming solutions companies, such as AOL, MSN, and Disney's Go.com. In October 2004, CES went public on the Toronto Stock Exchange under the company name of FUN Technologies (TSX:FUN). (In January 2005, the company's name was legally changed to FUN Technologies plc and it started to operate on the London Stock Exchange under that name.) The 2004 audited financial statements indicate that the company had a £750,000 loss in 2003 and a £1,126,000 loss in 2004. Before listing on the TSX, Abony raised $56 million among interested and savvy institutional investors, including the Ontario Teachers' Pension Plan. At the age of 35, he was the youngest CEO of TSX-listed companies.

In 2005, FUN Technologies continued acquiring companies (Las Vegas-based Don Best Sports, Minneapolis-based Fanball Interactive), developing partnerships (Verizon, Virgin Games, Game Show Network), and raising funds. The company published preliminary year-end results for 2005 showing revenues of £13.7 million, of which £9.4 million was from acquisitions. EBITDA (earnings before interest, taxes, depreciation, and amortization) was a positive £1.8 million, although the company expected a GAAP (generally accepted accounting principles) loss of £7 million.

In November 2005, Liberty Media purchased 51 percent of FUN Technologies for US $196 million. It's been estimated that this acquisition values Abony's share of FUN at roughly US $70 million. Liberty Media is owned by media mogul John Malone, who built the biggest cable company in the United States from his ranch near Denver, Colorado. He sold the cable company to AT&T for $60 billion, and uses Liberty Media as a vehicle for investing in content. Through Liberty Media, Malone controls 18 percent of Rupert Murdoch's company, News Corporation.

Questions

In answering these questions, you are encouraged to find out more about the current state of FUN Technologies at the company's website (http://www.funtechnologies.com) and through documents filed with Canadian securities regulatory authorities at http://www.sedar.com.

Petopia

1. When Petopia filed the preliminary prospectus in March 2000, how would the firm's management have expected the company to be valued?
2. What factors led to the cancellation of Petopia's IPO plans?
3. What assets would Petco have purchased from Petopia in December 2000?

Columbia Exchange Systems

4. Why were Rivkin and Abony able to complete such a successful IPO in England so quickly after start-up, in the era following the dot-com bubble?
5. Why do you think the founders decided to issue an IPO in Toronto in 2004?
6. Why did they change the company's name?

7. Why were Rivkin and Abony able to raise funds during 2003 and 2004 for a company that was not profitable?

8. Why do you think CES was able to buy SkillJam for $8 million?

FUN Technologies

9. By September 2005, FUN Technologies operated in London, England (6 employees), Toronto (10 employees), Las Vegas and Minneapolis (70 employees between them), and Los Angeles (55 employees). What are the advantages and disadvantages of this geographic dispersion?

10. Why would Liberty Media pay $194 million for FUN Technologies? How do you expect FUN Technologies to change after the acquisition?

11. Why did FUN Technologies agree to the acquisition? How do you expect the roles of Abony and Rivkin to change after 2005?

Sources

http://www.columbiaexchange.com

http://www.funtechnologies.com

Baker, M. 2005. Business profile: Party animal. *The (London) Telegraph*, September 18. http://www.telegraph.co.uk/money/main.jhtml?xml=/money/2005/09/18/ccprof18.x ml. Brown, J. 2000. Service, Please. *Business Week*, October 23: 48.

Bucholtz, C. 2000. Reality bites for web pet stores. *VAR Business*, October 2: 13.

Enos, L. 2000. Petco gobbles up Petopia's assets. *E-commerce Times*, December 6. http://www.ecommercetimes.com/story/5880.html.

Longley, S. 2005. Securing a second success. *eGaming Review*, December: 50-51.

Parkinson, G. 2005. Malone buys 51% of AIM-listed Fun. *The Independent*, November 23. http://news.independent.co.uk/business/news/article328750.ece.

Schwartz, J. 2000. Petopia fetches IPO. *Forbes.com*, March 14. http://www.forbes.com/2000/03/14/mu5.html

Watson, T. 2005. Fun and games. *Canadian Business* 78(6): 23–25.

Wolverton, T. 2000. Petco laps up the assets of Petopia.com. *CNET News.com*, December 5. http://news.com.com/Petco+laps+up+the+assets+of+Petopia.com/2100-1017_3-249456.html.

Wolverton, T. 2000. Pets.com latest high-profile dot-com disaster. *CNET News.com*, November 7. http://news.com.com/2100-1017-248230.html.

GLOSSARY

A

Adverse Selection: In a market where buyers cannot accurately gauge the quality of the product that they are buying, it is likely that the marketplace will contain generally poor-quality products. Adverse selection was first noted by Nobel Laureate George Akerlof in 1970.

Affective Conflicts: Conflicts that involve a large emotional component rather than conflicts that emerge from incompatible interests or goals.

Amortized: A method of distributing the cost of an investment over the number of units produced or sold.

Antidilution Provisions: Contract provisions that require entrepreneurs to provide investors with additional shares in a new venture so that the investor's percentage of ownership is not reduced in later rounds of financing.

Asset-Based Financing: A type of loan in which the assets being purchased are used as collateral for the loan.

B

Balance Sheet Methods (of valuation): Methods for valuing businesses based on their balance sheets.

Big Five Dimensions of Personality: Basic dimensions of personality that have been found to strongly affect behaviour in a wide range of situations.

Biodata: Information about potential employees' background, experiences, and preferences provided by them on application forms.

Breach of Contract: A legal term referring to situations in which two parties have a legal contract and one fails to comply with the terms of the agreement.

Breakeven Analysis: An analysis indicating the level of sales and production required to cover all costs.

Burn Rate: The pace at which a new venture uses capital provided by investors.

Business Angel: A person who invests in new ventures as a private individual.

Business Plan: A written expression of the entrepreneur's vision for converting ideas into a profitable, going business.

C

Calculus-Based Trust: Trust based on deterrence. When we expect that others will act in the ways they promise because they know they will be punished in some way for doing otherwise, we are demonstrating calculus-based trust.

Cannibalize: An effort to produce and sell a product or service that replaces a product or service that one already produces and sells.

Capital Intensive: The degree to which the production process in a firm or industry relies on capital rather than on labour.

Capitalized Earnings Method: A method for valuing businesses based on capitalized net earnings.

Case Method: A research method in which large amounts of data about one organization or specific persons are gathered and then used to reach conclusions about which factors have influenced important outcomes, such as economic success.

Cash Flow: The internally generated funds available to a firm after costs and depreciation are subtracted from revenues.

Cash Flow Statements: A written statement of actual or projected cash inflows and outflows over a specific period of time, given certain levels of sales and costs.

Causal Ambiguity: A lack of understanding about the underlying process through which entrepreneurs exploit opportunities.

Claims: The part of a patent that states what was invented and what the patent precludes others from imitating.

Cognitive Conflict: Conflicts in which individuals become aware of contrasting perspectives or interests, but focus on the issues and not on one another.

Collateral: Something of value that an entrepreneur pledges to sell to reimburse investors in the event that there are insufficient proceeds from a venture to return the investors' principal.

Commercial Loan: A form of bank financing in which the borrower pays interest on the money borrowed.

Competence-Destroying: A form of change that undermines the skills and capabilities of people who are already doing something. It is contrasted with competence-enhancing change, which enhances the skills and capabilities of people who are already doing something.

Competitive Advantage: A business attribute that allows a firm, and not its competitors, to capture the profits from exploiting an opportunity.

Complementary Assets: Assets that must be used along with an innovation to provide a new product or service to customers, typically including manufacturing equipment and marketing and distribution facilities.

Complementary Products: Complementary products are products that work together, like DVDs and DVD players, or computer hardware and computer software.

Concentration: The proportion of market share that lies in the hands of the largest firms in an industry. This concept is commonly measured by the four-firm concentration ratio, a government measure of the market share that lies in the hands of the four largest firms in an industry.

Concepts: Categories for objects or events that are similar to each other in certain respects.

Confirmation Candidates: Alternatives that are not really considered seriously; rather, they are raised mainly for the purpose of helping groups convince themselves that the initial favourite is indeed correct.

Conflict: A process in which one party perceives that another party has taken or will take actions that are incompatible with its interests.

Confluence Approach: A view suggesting that creativity emerges out of the confluence (i.e., convergence) of several basic resources.

Conjoint Analysis: A technique for determining the relative importance of various dimensions in customers' evaluations of specific products.

Contracts: Promises that are enforceable by law.

Control Barrier: Refers to the unwillingness of founders of new ventures to surrender control over the company to others.

Control Rights: The right to decide what to do with a venture's assets.

Convertible Securities: Financial instruments that allow investors to convert preferred stock, which receives preferential treatment in the event of a liquidation, into common stock at the investor's option.

Copyright: A form of intellectual property protection provided to the authors of original works of authorship, including literary, dramatic, musical, artistic, and certain other intellectual work.

Core Rigidities: The fact that companies tend to do well at things that they are accustomed to doing, not things that are new.

Corporations: Legal entities separate from their owners that may engage in business, make contracts, own property, pay taxes, and sue and be sued by others.

Covenants: Restrictions on the behaviour of entrepreneurs contractually agreed upon by investors and entrepreneurs.

Creativity: The generation of ideas that are both novel (original, unexpected) and appropriate or useful; they meet relevant constraints.

D

Debt: A financial obligation to return money provided plus a scheduled amount of interest.

Deception: Efforts to mislead others by withholding information or presenting false information.

Devil's Advocate Technique: A procedure for improving group decision making in which one group member is assigned the task of disagreeing with and criticizing whatever plan or decision is the initial favourite.

Discounted Future Earnings Method: A method of valuing businesses based on discounted future earnings.

Discount Rate: The annual percentage rate that an investor reduces the value of an investment to calculate its present value.

Discrete: A characteristic of a new product or service that makes it independent of a system of other assets necessary to use the product or service.

Distributive Justice: A principle of perceived fairness suggesting that all parties to a relationship should receive a share of the available rewards commensurate with the scope of their contributions.

Dominant Design: A common approach or standard to making a product on which firms in an industry have converged; for example, many software companies design their products to operate with Microsoft Windows.

Due Diligence: The review of a new venture's management, business opportunity, technology, legal status, and finances prior to investment.

E

Earnings Methods: Methods of valuing businesses based on their future earnings.

Economies of Scale: A reduction in the cost of each unit produced as the volume of production increases.

Employee Stock Ownership Plans (ESOPs): Methods of transferring ownership of a company to its employees; the current owners contribute to an employee stock ownership trust. Contributions are often based on the profitability of the company.

Equity: The ownership of a company, which takes the form of stock. It also equals assets minus liabilities or net worth.

Excess Earnings Method: A method of valuing businesses based on the extent to which a company will generate earnings in excess of the average for its industry.

Expectancy Theory: A theory of motivation suggesting that in order for motivation to be high, individuals must perceive clear links between their effort and their performance and their performance and their rewards, and that the rewards offered to them are actually desirable.

Experimentation: A research method in which one variable is systematically changed in order to determine whether such changes affect one or more other variables.

Export Intensity: The percentage of a firm's revenue that comes from foreign markets, or, foreign revenue divided by total revenue.

F

Factors: Specialized organizations that purchase the accounts receivable of businesses at a discount.

First-Mover Advantage: Any benefit that a firm gets from being the first to offer a product in a particular market.

Fixed Costs: Costs of items such as facilities and equipment that do not change with the number of units sold.

Focus Groups: Groups of 8 to 12 people who are similar to potential customers and who meet for one to two hours to describe their perceptions of and reactions to relevant products.

Forfeiture Provisions: Contract terms that require an entrepreneur to lose a portion of the ownership of the venture if agreed-upon milestones are not met.

Franchising: A system of distribution in which legally independent business owners (franchisees) pay fees and royalties to a parent company (the franchisor) in return for the right to use its trademark, sell its products or services, and use the business model and system it has developed.

G

Group Polarization: The tendency for members of decision-making groups to shift toward views more extreme than the ones with which they began.

Groupthink: A strong tendency for decision-making groups to close ranks, cognitively, around a decision, assuming that the group can't be wrong, that all members must support the decision strongly, and that any information contrary to the decision should be rejected.

H

Heuristics: Simple rules for making complex decisions or drawing inferences in a rapid and seemingly effortless manner.

Hierarchical Mode: A form of exploiting opportunities in which one party owns all parts of the operation that produces and sells a product or service to end customers.

Human Capital: Investment or value in human resources rather than physical assets.

Human Cognition: The mental processes through which we acquire information, enter it into storage, transform it, and use it to accomplish a wide range of tasks.

Hypothesis: An as yet untested prediction or explanation for a set of facts.

I

Idea Generation: The production of ideas for something new; very close in meaning to creativity.

Identification-Based Trust: Trust based on the belief that others will behave as they promise to behave not because they will be punished for failing to do so, but because they have the trusting person's well-being at heart.

Illiquidity Premium: Additional return demanded by investors to compensate them for the fact that an investment cannot be sold easily.

Implicit Favourite: The decisions initially favoured by a majority of a decision-making group that becomes the group's final decision.

Impression Management: Tactics used by individuals to make a good first impression on others.

Industrial Design: An object's shape, configuration, pattern, or ornament.

Information Asymmetry: The imbalance in knowledge about something between two parties.

Initial Public Offering (IPO): Initial sale of stock in a company to the public.

Intangibles: Assets that are hard, if not impossible, to list on the balance sheet: the goodwill the company has acquired with customers and suppliers, its reputation in the industry, its success in attracting and motivating first-rate employees.

Integrative Agreements: Arrangements that maximize joint benefits—the gains experienced by both sides.

Intellectual Property: The core ideas about a new product or service that make the development of these products and services possible.

Intelligence: Individuals' abilities to understand complex ideas, to adapt effectively to the world around them, to learn from experience, to engage in various forms of reasoning, and to overcome a wide range of obstacles.

Intrapreneurs: Persons who create something new, but inside an existing company rather than through founding a new venture.

Invent Around: To come up with a solution that does not violate a patent but accomplishes the same goal as the patented approach.

J

Job Analysis: A careful analysis of a specific job to determine what it involves and what it requires in terms of specific knowledge, skills, and abilities.

Job Description: An overview of what the job involves in terms of its duties, responsibilities, and working conditions.

Job Design: The structuring of jobs so that they increase people's interest in doing them (and hence their motivation).

K

Knowledge Spillovers: The accidental transfer of information about how to create new products, production processes, ways of marketing, or ways of organizing, from one firm to another.

L

Lead-Time Advantage: Any benefit that a firm receives by doing something before someone else.

Learning Curve: A relationship that measures the per-unit performance at production as a function of the cumulative number of units produced.

Legitimacy: A quality based on the belief that something is correct and appropriate.

Leveraged Buyout: Procedures for transferring ownership of a company to its current managers. These persons borrow from a financial organization in order to pay the owner an agreed-upon price.

Licensing: A mode of business in which one party contracts with another to use the first party's ideas to make products and services for sale to end customers in return for a fee.

Limited Partnership: A partnership in which one or more partners are general partners who manage the business and others are limited partners who invest in the business but forego any right to manage the company.

Line of Credit: An agreement to allow entrepreneurs to draw up to a set amount of money at a particular interest rate whenever they need it.

Locus of Innovation: The location, both within the value chain and between the public and private sector, in which efforts to apply new knowledge to the creation of new products, production processes, and ways of organizing occur.

M

Macro (Perspective): A top-down perspective that seeks to understand the entrepreneurial process by focusing largely on environmental factors (i.e., economic, financial, political factors) that are largely beyond the direct control of an individual.

Mandatory Redemption Rights: Contract terms that require an entrepreneur to return to the investors their capital, when requested.

Market-Based Modes: A form of exploiting opportunities in which different parts of a business, such as manufacturing and marketing, are owned by different entities and are connected by a contractual relationship.

Market Value (price-earnings) Approach: Procedures for valuing businesses based on the price-earnings ratios for comparable publicly owned companies.

Memory: Our cognitive systems for storing and retrieving information.

Micro (Perspective): A bottom-up perspective that seeks to understand the entrepreneurial process by focusing on the behaviour and thought of individuals or groups of individuals (e.g., founding partners).

Milestone: A jointly agreed-upon goal between entrepreneurs and investors that the entrepreneur needs to meet to receive another stage of financing.

Monopoly: A situation in which a firm is the only supplier of a product or service.

Motivation: The processes that arouse, direct, and maintain human behaviour toward attaining some goal. In other words, motivation refers to behaviour that is energized by, and directed toward, reaching some desired target or objective.

N

Negotiation: A process in which opposing sides exchange offers, counteroffers, and concessions, either directly or through representatives.

Noncompete Agreement: A legal document in which a person agrees not to work for a competing company for a set period of time.

Nondisclosure Agreement: A legal document in which a person agrees not to divulge a company's private information for a set period of time after termination of employment.

O

Opportunity: The potential to create something new (new products or services, new markets, new production processes, new raw materials, new ways of organizing existing technologies, etc.) that has emerged from a complex pattern of changing conditions—shifts in knowledge, technology, or in the economic, political, social, and demographic climates.

Opportunity Recognition: The process through which individuals conclude that they have identified the potential to create something new that has the capacity to generate economic value (i.e., potential future profits).

Option: A right, but not an obligation, to make a future investment.

Organizational Citizenship Behaviours: Employee behaviours that go beyond the role requirements of their jobs and that are not directly or explicitly recognized by formal reward systems.

Organizational Commitment: The extent to which individuals identify with and are involved with their organizations and are, therefore, unwilling to leave it.

Overall Approach to Negotiation: The general attitude to negotiation adopted by the persons participating in it. Two basic patterns are a win-lose approach and a win-win approach.

P

Partnership: Two or more people who do business together for the purpose of making a profit.

Partnership Agreement: A document written with the assistance of a lawyer, and that states all of the terms under which the partnership will operate.

Patent: A legal right granted by a national government to preclude others from duplicating an invention for a specified period of time in return for disclosure of the invention.

Pay-for-Performance Systems: Reward systems that assume that employees differ in how much they contribute to the company's success, and that they should be rewarded in accordance with the scope of their contributions.

Perceptual Mapping: A technique for identifying the key dimensions along which potential customers evaluate products.

Personal Selling: An effort by an entrepreneur to sell a product or service through direct interaction with customers.

Persuasion: The task of inducing others to share our views and to see the world much as we do.

Practical Intelligence: Being intelligent in a practical sense; persons high in such intelligence are adept at solving the problems of everyday life and have street smarts.

Prior Art: Prior patents that a given patent cites as the building blocks of an invention.

Product Development: The process by which the entrepreneur creates the product or service that will be sold to customers.

Proforma Balance Sheet: A form showing projections of the company's financial condition at various times in the future.

Proforma Income Statement: A form illustrating projected operating results based on profit and loss.

Prototypes: Mental representations of categories of events or objects.

R

R&D Intensity: The proportion of a firm's sales that are devoted to creating new scientific knowledge and applying that knowledge to the creation of new products and production processes.

Realistic Job Previews: Efforts to present a balanced and accurate picture of the company to potential employees, with the goal of improving future retention of these persons.

Regulatory Focus Theory: A theory that suggests that in regulating their own behaviour to achieve desired ends, individuals adopt one of two contrasting perspectives: a promotion focus (main goal is accomplishment) or a prevention focus (main goal is prevention of losses).

Reliability: The extent to which measurements are consistent across time or between judges.

Reverse Engineering: The process of taking apart a product to determine how it works.

Reward Systems: Systems for recognizing and rewarding good performance.

Roles: The set of behaviours that individuals occupying specific positions within a group are expected to perform.

S

Schemas: Cognitive frameworks representing our knowledge and assumptions about specific aspects of the world.

S-Curve: A graphical depiction of the typical pattern of performance improvement of new products or services as a function of the amount of effort put into them.

Self-Assessment: An inventory of the knowledge, experience, training, motives, and characteristics the entrepreneur possesses and can contribute to the new venture.

Self-Serving Bias: The tendency to attribute successful outcomes largely to internal causes (our own efforts, talents, or abilities) but unsuccessful ones largely to external cause (e.g., the failings or negligence of others).

Signal Detection Theory: A theory suggesting that in situations where individuals attempt to determine whether a stimulus is present or absent, four possibilities exist: The stimulus exists and the perceiver concludes that it is present; the stimulus exists but the perceiver fails to recognize it; the stimulus does not exist and the perceiver concludes, erroneously, that it is present; the stimulus does not exist and the perceiver correctly concludes that it is not present.

Social Capital: An important resource that derives from relationships among individuals in organizations or other social structures. Social capital involves close interpersonal relationships among individuals, characterized by mutual trust, liking, and identification.

Social Competence: A summary term for an individual's overall level of social skills.

Social Perception: The process through which we come to know and understand other persons.

Social Skills: A set of competencies (discrete skills) that enable individuals to interact effectively with others.

Sole Proprietorship: A type of business ownership in which a business is owned and managed by one individual.

Staging: The provision of capital in pieces conditional on the achievement of specified milestones.

Stress: A pattern of emotional states and physiological reactions occurring in response to demands from many different events in our lives.

Structured Interviews: Interviews in which all applicants are asked the same questions—ones chosen carefully to be truly job-related.

Successful Intelligence: A balanced blend of analytic, creative, and practical intelligence. Successful intelligence is the kind of intelligence needed by entrepreneurs.

Sunk Costs or Escalation of Commitment: The tendency to become trapped in bad decisions and stick to them even though they yield increasingly negative results.

Syndicate: The sharing of an investment across a group of investors.

Systematic Observation: A research method in which certain aspects of the world are observed systematically, keeping careful records of what is detected. This information is then used as a basis for reaching conclusions about the topics under investigation.

T

Tacit Knowledge: A type of understanding that cannot be documented or even articulated. It is frequently contrasted with codified knowledge, which is a type of understanding that can be expressed in documentary form.

Technical Standard: An agreed-upon basis on which a product or service operates.

Terminal Value: The estimated value of a new venture at the time that the investment is liquidated in an initial public offering or an acquisition.

Theory: Refers to efforts to go beyond merely describing various phenomena and, instead, to explain them.

Trademark: A word, phrase, symbol, design, or combination of these that identifies and distinguishes the goods and services of one company from those of another.

Trade Secret: A piece of knowledge that confers an advantage on firms and is protected by nondisclosure.

Trust: One person's degree of confidence in the words and actions of another person—confidence that this person will generally behave in predictable ways that are understandable in terms of the relationship between them.

Tyranny of the Current Market: The fact that listening to customers will make it difficult for companies to come up with new products for new markets because a firm's current customers will always ask for improvements to current products, not new products for new markets.

U

Uncertainty: A condition in which the future is unknown.

Unlimited Personal Liability: Occurs when business owners are personally liable for all of debts incurred by the business.

User Myopia: The fact that customers can only see very narrow needs or solutions, typically only their own needs, not those of other market segments.

V

Validity: The extent to which measurements actually reflect the underlying dimension to which they refer.

Variable Costs: Costs incurred for each unit that is sold.

Variables: Aspects of the world that can take different values.

Venture Capitalist: A person who works for an organization that raises money from institutional investors and invests those funds in new firms.

Venture Capital Method: How venture capitalists calculate the amount of equity that they will take in a new venture in return for their investment of capital.

Vertically Integrated: A situation in which a firm owns successive stages of the value chain.

Vesting Periods: Periods of time during which entrepreneurs cannot cash out of their investments.

W

Win-Win Solution: A solution that is acceptable to both sides and that meets the basic needs of both.

NAME INDEX

A

Abernathy, W., 271–72
Abetti, P.A., 18, 27
Abony, L., 375–77
Acs, Z., 53, 194
Al-Katib, M., 361–62
Alba-Ramirez, A., 27
Aldrich, H., 54, 84, 170, 307, 335, 336
Allen, N.J., 336
Allen, R.W., 97
Amason, A.C., 111, 139, 140
Amit, R., 170, 306
Andersen, P., 142
Anderson, P., 54, 283
Anderson, R.B., 6, 27
Anonyuo, C., 111
Aquino, K., 83, 335
Ardichvili, A., 27, 53
Arking, R., 360
Arrow, K., 54, 170, 290, 306
Arthur, B., 283
Ashford, S.J., 336
Astebro, T., 6, 27, 186, 195
Audretsch, D., 53, 54, 194, 306
Azoulay, P., 251

B

Bachrach, D.G., 111
Badagliacca, J., 172
Baker, C., 140
Baker, M., 377
Baker, N., 374–75
Balkin, D.B., 27, 335
Ballon, A., 214–15, 221
Balsillie, J., 7
Bamford, C., 53
Barnett, W., 54
Barney, J., 306
Barney, J.B., 83
Baron, R.A., 3, 7, 14, 27, 60, 83, 84, 86,
    111, 123, 139, 140, 201–2, 205, 220,
    231, 285, 320, 335, 339, 343, 360
Barrick, M.R., 139
Barry, C., 170
Barton, D., 265–66, 283
Barzel, Y., 170
Bates, T., 251
Baum, J., 53, 170, 298, 307, 335
Baum, J.R., 111, 335
Baumeister, R.F., 283
Bedeian, A.G., 27
Begley, T., 111

Bell, A.G., 11
Bergqvist, H., 172
Bertrand, M., 56
Bezos, J., 34
Bhide, A., 31, 53, 148, 170, 283, 306
Bicheler, J., 172
Bird, B.J., 111
Birley, S., 27
Blakely, J., 170
Blanchflower, D., 84, 170
Bollinger, M., 27
Boorstin, D.J., 256
Botterell, D., 214–15, 221
Boulding, W., 195
Bower, J., 54
Boyd, D., 111
Boyle, D., 58
Branzei, O., 27
Bresson, R., 65–66
Brockner, J., 84, 335
Brown, J.D., 112, 139
Brown, K.S., 140
Brown, R., 53
Buchholtz, A.K., 139
Buchholz, R.A., 139
Bucholtz, C., 377
Buckley, M.R., 335
Buehler, R., 220
Burnstein, E., 140
Burt, R., 170
Busenitz, L.W., 83
Butler, J., 372
Butler, S., 115, 354
Bygrave, W.D., 170
Byrne, D., 111, 139, 335, 360

C

Cable, D., 170
Cable, D.M., 335
Calabrese, T., 298, 307
Camacho, C.J., 84
Cardozo, R., 27, 53
Cardy, R.L., 335
Carland, J.C., 27
Carland, J.W., 27
Carnevale, P.J., 360
Carpenter, G., 195
Carter, N.M., 111
Casella, D.F., 111
Casson, M., 170, 306
Caves, R., 306
Chasteen, R., 180–81
Chatter, M., 14

Chen, C.C., 27
Chen, J., 366
Chrisman, J.J., 27, 127, 140, 343, 360
Christen, M., 195
Christensen, C., 54
Chua, J.H., 27, 127, 140, 343, 360
Churchill, N.C., 336
Chwaiewsky, A., 372
Cialdini, R.B., 111
Ciavarella, M.A., 139
Clark, M.S., 140
Coella, A., 335
Coeurderoy, R., 83
Cohen, S., 112
Cohen, W., 186, 195
Collins, C.J., 12, 27
Comeau, J., 27
Connell, J.B., 140
Cooper, A., 139, 335
Corbett, A.C., 84
Cramer, J., 84
Crewson, P., 306
Crick, A., 27
Cropanzano, R.D., 139
Curran, J., 251
Cusumano, M., 283

D

D'Arbeloff, A., 199
Dahlin, K., 186, 195
David, P., 195
Davidson, H., 364
Davidsson, P., 71, 84, 139
Day, D.V., 111, 139
de Mestral, G., 65, 66
De Tienne, D.R., 83
Dean, T., 53
Dees, G., 170
DeFigueiredo, J.N., 283
Delmar, F., 220
Deutsch, Y., 299, 307
Diderot, D., 15
DiMatteo, M.R., 111
Diochon, M., 101–2, 111
Dollinger, M.J., 83
Donovan, J.J., 139
Dorland, J. (Jason...), 5
Dotseth, J., 172
Dunkelberg, W., 139
Dunley, P., 122
DuPlessis, D., 194, 195, 251
Durand, R., 83
Dyer-Witherford, N., 366

SUBJECT INDEX

390